IRISH PLANNING LAW AND PROCEDURE

AUSTRALIA

The Law Book Company
Brisbane • Sydney • Melbourne • Perth

CANADA

Carswell
Ottowa • Toronto • Calgary • Montreal • Vancouver

Agents

Steimatzky's Agency Ltd, Tel Aviv;
N.M. Tripathi (Private) Ltd, Bombay;
Eastern Law House (Private) Ltd, Calcutta;
M.P.P. House, Bangalore;
Universal Book Traders, Delhi;
Aditya Books, Delhi;
Macmillan Shuppan KK, Tokyo;
Pakistan Law House, Karachi, Lahore.

Irish Planning Law and Procedure

Eamon Galligan

B.A. Mod. (Leg. Sc.), M.R.U.P., Barrister-at-Law

with additional chapter by
Patrick Sweetman, Solicitor

ROUND HALL SWEET & MAXWELL

Published in 1997 by Round Hall Sweet & Maxwell,
Brehon House, 4 Upper Ormond Quay, Dublin 7.
This book was Typeset by Seton Music Graphics,
Bantry, Co. Cork.
Printed by Colourbooks Ltd, Dublin.

ISBN 1-85800-028-9

A catalogue for this book is
available from the British Library.

To Sheelagh, Eoin and my parents

FOREWORD

by

THE HON. MR. JUSTICE HUGH O'FLAHERTY

When I was called to the Bar in 1959 planning law hardly existed in this country. In reading Eamon Galligan's massive new undertaking – *Irish Planning Law and Procedure*, I was struck by the range of persons and places touched by *judicial* – as opposed to administrative – decisions to do with the planning code. There is hardly a town in the country that has not been embroiled in some form of litigation or other to do with planning matters – and many a house, hotel, even a driveway[1] have been encompassed.

The central concept behind the original 1963 Act was that the Minister for Local Government was to be the supreme overlord in relation to all matters of planning. Of course, the idea of regulating development, etc. was a new departure. Therefore, the Minister wanted to keep the reins in his own hands in the first instance. The strange manner in which he came to be dethroned, to some extent at least, is to be found in the Supreme Court decision in *Pine Valley v. Dublin Corporation*.[2] I say "strange" because the Minister's powers were circumscribed in a case in which he was not a party. In a subsequent case where I was briefed on his behalf I was to tell the Court that the Minister would go to his corporate grave not knowing how such an adverse conclusion as regards his powers could have been reached without hearing him!

The first big case in which the whole of the 1963 Act was analysed for the first time was *Central Dublin Development Association Ltd v. Attorney General*.[3] The late Tommy Connolly, S.C., gave a masterly analysis of the Act before Mr Justice Kenny in the High Court without resorting to a single note or, indeed, many authorities.

An Bord Pleanála has now replaced the Minister as the appellate authority – and the Supreme Court has laid out the proper lines of demarcation between the work that it undertakes and the courts' function in reviewing its decisions in *O'Keeffe v. An Bord Pleanála*.[4] Since I was not a member of that Court I can commend the decision without having to abjure any sense of false modesty.

As Mr Justice McCarthy put it, in a typically felicitous phrase, the development plan (at the core of all planning matters) is "an environmental contract between the planning authority, the Council and the community". Look around

---

[1] *Dublin Corporation v. Moore* (1984) I.L.T.R. 339.

[2] (1982) I.L.T.R. 169.

[3] 109 I.L.T.R. 69.

[4] [1993] I.R. 39.

[5] *Attorney General (McGarry) v. Sligo County Council* [1969] I.R. 169.

at any of our cities and towns today and one cannot but be impressed by the scope and pace of development. No doubt the introduction of the "designated areas" scheme has had much to do with all this renewal but surely also it is because of the fact that the planners and developers are able to get reasonably speedy decisions from the local authority. This book also chronicles the new role of local authorities as promoters as well as arbiters of planning development. Frank Feeley, recently retired as Dublin City Manager, could take justifiable pride in the renewal of the area around the Four Courts where we sit which leads me to say that I pen these lines on the occasion of the bicentenary, of the completion of that Gandon masterpiece – which has been an inspiration to judges and advocates over the decades but which also, of course, takes pride of place as the country's chief architectural treasure.

This book will be an essential tool of the trade for anyone having anything to do with the planning process. We have made steady progress over the 33 years since the original 1963 Act to reconcile the rights of what might be called the environmentalist lobby with the need to renew our cities and towns and, of course, to provide much valuable employment.

Eamon Galligan's interest in this speciality was first sparked by my good friend Dr Yvonne Scannell, of The Law School, Trinity College Dublin. He then went on to found *The Irish Planning and Environmental Law Journal* in 1994. *Irish Planning Law and Procedure* is the culmination of a truly prodigious effort on his part. I heartily commend it to all involved with planning.

HUGH O'FLAHERTY
The Supreme Court,
Four Courts,
Dublin 7

6 November 1996

PREFACE

My primary aim in writing this book is to provide a text which is accessible and useful to practitioners. Inevitably, I have concentrated to a greater extent on those areas which recur in practice and have not entered into any academic discussion of the legal complexities surrounding the enforceability of planning agreements, "planning gain" and similar topics which have exercised the minds of some other writers on planning law. Such discussion is of course worthwhile but does not fall within the scope of this book.

There are a number of subjects on which I could usefully have written more and undoubtedly some on which readers would prefer I had written less. In the chapter on compensation, for example, greater emphasis might perhaps have been placed on the purchase notice procedure as in many cases this may be a potentially more profitable avenue than the emasculated compensation provisions under the 1990 Act. There are a number of reforms of the planning code too which are undoubtedly needed but which, unfortunately, I have not had time to address in the first edition of this work.

Valuable comment on individual chapters was received from a number of colleagues and experienced practitioners who generously gave up their time: Berna Grist, Edward Hughes, Andy Johnston, James Macken S.C., Anthony Manahan, Fergal McCabe, Sean Mc Dermott, Bernard McHugh, Terence O'Keefe, Philip O'Sullivan S.C., Tom Phillips, John Reid and Garrett Simons. My colleagues, Tom Flynn and Ciaran Oakes, also provided me with considerable assistance at different stages. I have made many improvements arising out of the advice received but the responsibility for any errors made must remain mine and, as is customary, I would remind readers that this work should not in any way be considered a substitute for first-hand legal advice.

I must also acknowledge a debt to the authors of the many other works published in the area of planning law to which reasonably frequent reference has been made throughout the text. I hope that the present work will be as useful to practitioners as these works have proven to be. More generally, I have benefited considerably during my years of practice and in lecturing, from listening to and arguing with members of other professions associated with property development, with councillors, community representatives and ordinary citizens sharing the same interest. Planning is a curious combination of politics and personalities, preservation and exploitation, rationality and ad hocism. Given the right mix of people it will not fail to provoke excited debate.

One of the most surprising criticisms I received from one of the more direct readers of the initial proofs was of "political correctness". When I considered the charge, I could see clearly its basis and made the necessary changes. My only concern is that political correctness may lie lurking in some of the other chapters, like some kind of computer virus which feeds on this particular species of text. I would be grateful if a dutiful reader would point it out so that I can kill it off. In point of fact, I have tried in the text to stay away from adopting any ideological standpoint which might subtract from the objectivity of any legal analysis.

There is perhaps no other branch of the law which is more immediately visible in its impact on the physical environment than planning law. It is perhaps this which attracted me (if that is not too strong a word) to this relatively new area of the law after I had decided in 1981 to take the novel course on offer in Legal Science in TCD, entitled "Environmental Law".

Some analogy could be drawn between the dynamic in the evolving planning law at that stage with that which had manifested itself in the field of Irish constitutional law during the 1960s and 1970s. Of course, a reasonably sophisticated jurisprudence had by this time been established in interpreting the town and country planning legislation in the U.K. which was to some extent a precursor to the Irish legislation. Much judicial creativity had been expended in an effort to compensate for the under-elaboration of the principle statutory provisions of the U.K. legislation in defining the meaning of "development". Concepts such as "intensification", "primary and ancillary uses" and "abandonment" had already acquired a sanctity of usage despite their non-statutory origin.

The distinctive aspect of the Irish planning code and burgeoning jurisprudence was the primacy given to public participation in both strategic planning and in the development control process. The courts continuously emphasised the doctrine of the trinity in planning law – the developer, the planning authority and the public – and trenchantly upheld the position of the latter in early cases such as the *Torca Cottage* case (*Stanford v. Dun Laoghaire Corporation*), *Finn v. Bray U.D.C.*, the *Alf-a-Bet* cases and others. While drawing on the principles established under the pre-existing case law interpreting the U.K. town and country planning legislation, the Irish courts began to develop a parallel jurisprudence of which the focus was the right of the public to act as watchdogs for their environment. This focus was sharpened by the 1976 Act which for the first time provided a fast and reasonably convenient injunctive type remedy available to any person who wished to enforce the planning laws.

The pendulum has in the 1990s swung in the opposite direction and in favour of the developer's viewpoint. The underlying motivation behind the changing attitudes which can be discerned in more recent planning legislation and in the new "judicial realism" of the courts in dealing with challenges to planning decisions since *O'Keefe v. An Bord Pleanála* has been to remove the brake on economic development caused by delays in the planning process. While the acceleration of the planning appeals process and the short shrift given by the courts to technical procedural arguments on judicial review is welcomed by sensible people there is a sense that the pendulum may have swung too far. The standard of unreasonableness in decision-making which is currently expected by the law before a planning decision can be set aside is in many cases too high.

Chapter 13, which was written by Patrick Sweetman, will probably be that most thumbed by solicitors and, in my view, taken together with the Law Society's Practice Notes which are contained in Appendix A, has achieved the objective of providing a very clear set of guidelines for practitioners in this sometimes troublesome area of conveyancing practice. Patrick wishes to thank the members of the Law Society Conveyancing Committee, in particular, Rory O'Donnell, in addition to John Gore Grimes, his colleagues at Matheson Ormsby Prentice, and his secretary, Esther Fogarty, for their assistance with his chapter.

I would like to thank my publishers at Round Hall Sweet and Maxwell for their patience in dealing with very extensive amendments at the galley stage and, in particular, Ian Harkness and Michael Diviney, who were most immediately concerned with the editing, indexing and tabulation of this book.

Greatest thanks are due to my wife, Sheelagh, for her good humoured tolerance of the time given by me to the book and not to more sociable pursuits.

EAMON GALLIGAN
Law Library Building,
158/9 Church Street,
Dublin 7.

November 11, 1996

TABLE OF CONTENTS

Foreword vii
Preface ix
Table of Cases xxvii
Table of Statutes.. xliii
Table of Statutory Instruments.................................. lvii

1   THE PLANNING AUTHORITY............................... 1
      1.1.1 Definition and functions of the planning authority 1
      1.1.2 The Planning Register 3
      1.1.3 Contents of Planning Register 4
      1.2 **Powers, functions and duties of the planning authority** 5
      1.2.1 The doctrine of *ultra vires* 5
      1.2.2 Executive and reserved functions..................... 7
      1.2.3 Ancillary powers of planning authority 8
      1.2.4 Powers under the Local Government Act 1991 9
      1.2.5 Policy directives and guidelines..................... 10
      1.3 **Development by the planning authority**.................. 10
      1.3.1 Development powers 10
      1.3.2 Cables, wires and pipelines 12
      1.3.3 Application of exempted development provisions to
              local authority development 12
      1.3.4 Local authority development to which notification
              requirements apply 14
      1.3.5 Categories of development to which notification
              requirements do not apply...................... 15
      1.3.6 Notice of proposed development 15
      1.3.7 Report and decision of authority 17
      1.3.8 Environmental impact assessment 18

2   THE DEVELOPMENT PLAN 20
      2.1 **Plan preparation**.................................. 21
      2.1.1 Obligations to make and review development plan...... 21
      2.1.2 Contents of plan 21
      2.1.3 Road Development and the development plan.......... 23
      2.1.4 Notification requirements.......................... 24
      2.1.5 "Material alteration"............................. 26
      2.2 **Adoption and implementation of plan** 27

2.2.1 Adoption of plan 27
2.2.2 "Rezoning" 27
2.2.3 Powers of the Minister in relation to development
      plans and planning policy 28
2.2.4 Constitutionality of development plans and
      "Down-zoning" 29
2.2.5 Interpretation of development plans 30
2.2.6 Extent to which development plans are binding in the
      determination of planning applications 32
2.3 **The plan and Local Authority development** 33
2.3.1 Planning authority cannot effect development in
      material contravention of its own development
      plan 33

3   PRESERVATION OF AMENITY 38
3.1.1 Planning agreements 38
3.1.2 Special amenity area orders 39
3.1.3 Tree preservation orders 41
3.1.4 Planting of trees, shrubs and other plants 43
3.1.5 Notices requiring the removal or alteration of a hedge . . . 43
3.1.6 Conservation orders 44
3.1.7 Public rights of way 45
3.1.8 Repair and tidying of advertisements 46
3.1.9 Licences for petrol pumps, cables, wires, pipelines
      and other structures on public roads 47
3.1.10 Revocation or modification of permission 48
3.1.11 Designation of areas for environmental protection 49
3.1.12 Listed buildings 50
3.1.13 Objects of archaeological, geological or historical
      interest 50
3.1.14 Enforcement of open spaces 51

4   DEVELOPMENT 53
4.1 **Statutory definitions of development** 53
4.1.1 "Works" and "use" 53
4.1.2 Specific situations 55
      4.1.2.1 *Sub-division of dwellings* 56
4.2 **Material change of use** 57
4.2.1 Approach of the courts 57
4.2.2 Difference of approach between U.K. and Irish
      decisions 57
4.2.3 The qualitative approach 58
4.2.4 Material for planning purposes 60

4.2.5 Relevance of development plan 61
4.2.6 "Judicial zoning" 62
4.3 **The planning unit** 62
4.3.1 The planning unit 62
4.3.2 The occupational unit: the first rule of *Burdle* 63
4.3.3 Primary and ancillary uses 65
4.3.4 "Ordinarily incidental" 66
4.3.5 Composite or concurrent uses: the second rule in
       Burdle 67
4.3.6 Seasonal uses 68
4.3.7 Physical and functional separation: the third rule in
       Burdle 68
4.3.8 Ancillary uses where primary use inactive 71
4.3.9 Sub-division of planning unit 72
4.3.10 Intensification of use 73
4.3.11 Resumption of an abandoned use 77
4.3.12 Resumption of an extinguished use 80
4.4 **Development not requiring permission** 82
4.4.1 Resumption of "normal" use of land upon expiration
       of temporary permission for use of land 82
4.4.2 Resumption of use where enforcement notice
       is served 82
4.4.3 Recurrent uses 82
4.4.4 Development required by notices served under
       sections 31, 32, 33, 35 or 36 of the 1963 Act 82
4.4.5 Development required by planning condition 82

5   DEVELOPMENT. EXEMPTED DEVELOPMENT 84
5.1 **Introduction** 84
5.1.1 Section 5 references 85
5.2 **Exempted development under section 4 of the 1963 Act** 86
5.2.1 Section 4 of the 1963 Act 86
5.2.2 Use for agriculture and forestry 87
      5.2.2.1 *The definition of agriculture* 88
      5.2.2.2 *The agricultural planning unit* 89
      5.2.2.3 *Agricultural processes* 90
5.2.3 Development by local authorities 91
5.2.4 Development by statutory undertakers 92
5.2.5 Internal works 92
5.2.6 External works 93
5.2.7 Uses incidental to the enjoyment of a
      dwellinghouse 95

5.2.7.1 *"Curtilage"* 95
5.2.7.2 *"Dwellinghouse"* 96
5.2.8 "... as such" 97
5.2.9 Casual trading areas 100
5.2.10 Land reclamation 100
5.3 **Development by state authorities** 100
5.3.1 Background decisions – Luggala and Mullaghmore 100
5.3.2 Exemptions for certain development by state
        authorities 104
5.3.3 Notification requirements......................... 105
5.3.4 Decision of state authority 106
5.3.5 Development required by reason of an accident or
        emergency 107
5.3.6 Retrospective validation of development commenced
        before the 1993 Act........................... 107
5.4 **Exempted development under the 1994 Regulations, as
    amended** 107
5.4.1 Definitions: article 8............................ 107
5.4.2 Conditions and limitations: article 9 107
5.4.3 Works carried out under a condition of an
        IPC licence.................................. 107
5.4.4 Restrictions on prima facie exemptions under Parts I,
        II and III of the Second Schedule: article 10 108
5.4.5 Use classes: article 11........................... 111
5.4.6 Specific exemptions under article 11 111
5.5 **Second Schedule, Part 1 – General** 112
5.5.1 Development within the curtilage of a dwellinghouse... 113
        5.5.1.1 *Extensions and conversions* 113
        5.5.1.2 *Central heating systems* 113
        5.5.1.3 *Garages, sheds and similar structures*......... 113
        5.5.1.4 *Satellite dishes, wireless and television
                antennae* 114
        5.5.1.5 *Paths, drains, ponds and landscaping works*.... 114
        5.5.1.6 *Gates, walls and fences* 114
        5.5.1.7 *Hard surfacing* 115
        5.5.1.8 *Porches*................................ 115
        5.5.1.9 *Caravans and boats* 115
5.5.2 Gates, walls and fences........................... 116
5.5.3 Painting of structures 117
5.5.4 Private roads, ways, footpaths or paving 116
5.5.5 Changes of use 117
5.5.6 Temporary structures or uses 117
5.5.7 Development for industrial purposes 117

5.5.8 Development by statutory undertakers. 118
5.5.9 Telecommunications. 118
5.5.10 Development for amenity or recreational
     purposes. 119
5.5.11 Other development by public agencies 119
     5.5.11.1 *National flags and emblems*. 119
     5.5.11.2 *Facilities for foreign visits* 119
     5.5.11.3 *Monitoring facilities*. 119
     5.5.11.4 *Works under the Arterial Drainage Acts* 120
     5.5.11.5 *Works within the curtilage of certain public*
             buildings. 120
     5.5.11.6 *Garda Síochána* 120
     5.5.11.7 *Regional Fisheries Boards*. 120
5.5.12 Works necessary to comply with statutory notices,
     licences or certificates 120
5.5.13 Demolition 121
5.5.14 Other miscellaneous development 122
     5.5.14.1 *Local events* 122
     5.5.14.2 *Navigational aids* 122
     5.5.14.3 *Maintenance of community structures or*
             facilities 122
     5.5.14.4 *Archaeological and other excavations*. 122
     5.5.14.5 *Domestic water supply or group water*
             schemes. 123
     5.5.14.6 *Exploratory drilling or excavation* 123
     5.5.14.7 *Connections to premises*. 123
5.6 **Second Schedule, Part II – Advertisements**. 123
5.7 **Second Schedule, Part III – Rural** 123
    5.7.1 Minerals and petroleum prospecting 124
    5.7.2 Agricultural structures 125
       5.7.2.1 *Land reclamation* 125
    5.7.3 Structures for keeping horses, ponies and
       greyhounds 127
5.8 **Second Schedule, Part IV – Use Classes**. 128
    5.8.1 Use classes 127

6   APPLICATION FOR PLANNING PERMISSION. 135
    6.1.1 Obligation to obtain planning permission 135
    6.1.2 Types of application 136
    6.1.3 Compliance with permission regulations. 137
6.2 **Pre-application publicity requirements** 138
    6.2.1 Public participation in the planning process 138
    6.2.2 Who may apply?. 139

6.2.3 Newspaper notice 140
6.2.4 Site notice 142
6.2.5 Name of applicant. 143
6.2.6 Location of land 145
6.2.7 Nature and extent of development 146
6.3 **Particulars to accompany planning application** 148
6.3.1 Plans and particulars to accompany planning
        applications generally 148
6.3.2 Plans and particulars to accompany applications other
        than outline 150
6.3.3 Description of interest 150
6.3.4 Fees for planning applications 151
6.4 **Outline and approval applications** 151
6.4.1 Applications for outline permission 151
6.4.2 When an outline application cannot be made. 151
6.4.3 Effect of outline permission 152
6.4.4 Matters to be dealt with at outline stage. 152
6.4.5 Applications for approval. 153
6.4.6 Parameters of outline permission are binding except
        were change in circumstances. 154
6.4.7 Contents of approval application 155
6.5 **Environmental Impact Statements** 155
6.5.1 Applications to be accompanied by EIS 155
6.5.2 Exemptions from EIS requirement. 156
6.5.3 Outline applications 157
6.5.4 Content of Environmental Impact Statements 157
6.6 **Procedure after receipt of application** 158
6.6.1 Procedure on receipt. 158
6.6.2 Weekly list of applications 158
6.6.3 Persons and bodies to be notified of planning
        applications 159
6.6.4 Requests for further information by planning
        authority. 159
6.6.5 Modifications to proposed development 161
6.6.6 Further notice of application 161
6.6.7 Planning file 162
6.6.8 Submissions or observations on planning
        applications 163
6.6.9 Minimum period for determination of planning
        applications 164
6.6.10 Withdrawal of planning application. 164
6.7 **Notification of decisions** 164
6.7.1 Weekly list of planning decisions. 164

6.7.2 Persons or bodies to be notified of decision on
planning application 165
6.7.3 Form of notification of decision 165

7   ENVIRONMENTAL IMPACT ASSESSMENT 165
7.1.1 Definition of terms 166
7.1.2 The 1985 Directive 167
7.1.3 Projects subject to EIS requirement 169
7.1.4 Exemptions from EIS requirement 172
7.1.5 Significant environmental effects 173
7.1.6 Content of environmental impact statements 174
7.1.7 EPA draft guidelines 176
7.1.8 EIA in the determination of planning applications 177
7.2 **Development by local authorities** 178
7.2.1 Development by state authorities 178
7.2.3 First Schedule: development for the purposes of
these Regulations 179

8   DETERMINATION OF PLANNING APPLICATIONS 186
8.1 **The decision-making power** 186
8.1.1 Relevant considerations 187
8.1.2 Permission for retention of structures and
continuance of use 189
8.1.3 Material contravention of the development plan 190
8.1.4 The interface between planning control and IPC
licensing control 190
8.1.5 Motorway, busway and protected road schemes 193
8.2 **Planning conditions** 193
8.2.1 The power to impose conditions 193
8.2.2 Conditions must be imposed in accordance with their
statutory purpose 194
8.2.2.1 *Conditions must not be imposed for an
ulterior purpose* 194
8.2.2.2 *Conditions restricting the occupation of
buildings* 195
8.2.2.3 *Conditions must not abdicate the jurisdiction
of the planning authority or the Board* 196
8.2.3 Conditions must be fairly and reasonably related to
the development permitted 201
8.2.3.1 *Conditions altering the nature of the
development proposed* 201
8.2.3.2 *Conditions imposing restrictions on existing
use rights may be ultra vires* 203

8.2.4 Conditions must not be unreasonable. 203
 8.2.4.1 *Factors beyond the control of the applicant* 203
 8.2.4.2 *Conditions must not be uncertain* 204
 8.2.4.3 *Conditions must be necessary* 204
 8.2.4.4 *The reason stated for the imposition of the*
     conditions must be sufficient to support the
     imposed condition. 204
8.3 **Specific conditions under section 26(2).** 205
8.4 **Severance of conditions** 211
 8.4.1 Severability of conditions. 211
8.5 **Decision-making procedure** 212
 8.5.1 Material contravention procedure 212
 8.5.2 Time within which planning authority must
    determine planning application 213
 8.5.3 Default decision 214
 8.5.4 Mandamus where default decision 216
 8.5.5 Damages for delayed grant. 216
 8.5.6 Section 4 resolutions. 217
8.6 **Effect of grant of planning permission** 221
 8.6.1 Obligation to make a grant 220
 8.6.2 Reasons for decision. 221
 8.6.3 Planning permission enures for the benefit of
    the land 222
 8.6.4 Interpretation of planning permission 224
 8.6.5 Effect of appeal documents on interpretation of
    permission 228
 8.6.6 Duration of planning permission 229
 8.6.7 Extension of duration of permission 231
 8.6.8 Multiple permissions 234
 8.6.9 Severable permissions 235
 8.6.10 Liability of planning authority arising from grant 235

9 PLANNING APPEALS 237
9.1 **Composition and functions of An Bord Pleanála** 237
 9.1.1 Composition of Board 237
 9.1.2 Functions of the Board 238
9.2 **Procedure for making appeal** 239
 9.2.1 Contents of appeal 239
 9.2.2 Time limit and service 240
 9.2.3 To appeal or not to appeal? 241
 9.2.4 Appeal against conditions only 242
 9.2.5 Availability of documents relating to planning
    applications and appeals 243

9.2.6 Replying submissions by parties to the appeal......... 244
9.2.7 Observations by non-parties........................ 244
9.2.8 Natural justice.................................... 245
9.2.9 Matters other than those raised by the parties 247
9.2.10 Oral hearings.................................... 248
9.2.11 Procedure at oral hearing 249
9.2.12 Powers of inspector at an oral hearing 250
9.2.13 Power to dismiss appeals 251
9.3 **Determination of appeals**............................. 251
9.3.1 Jurisdiction of the Board........................... 251
9.3.2 Relevant considerations 252
9.3.3 Irrelevant considerations: risk of environmental
pollution...................................... 253
9.3.4 Powers of entry on land and ancillary powers......... 254
9.3.5 Modification of applications....................... 254
9.3.6 Costs 254
9.3.7 Notification of decision 255

10   JUDICIAL REVIEW 256
10.1.1 Introduction.................................... 256
10.1.2 Judicial review procedure......................... 257
10.1.3 Procedure for challenge 258
10.1.4 Meaning of "decision" 260
10.1.5 Substantial grounds............................. 260
10.1.6 Appeals to the Supreme Court 262
10.2 **Grounds for judicial review**......................... 262
10.2.1 Unreasonableness 263
10.2.2 Error on the face of the record 264
10.2.3 Failure to observe the rules of natural justice 266
10.2.4 Failure to take into account relevant
considerations and failure to exclude irrelevant
considerations 267
10.2.5 Inadequacy of record of decision 267
10.2.6 Non-compliance with permission regulations 268
10.2.7 Material contravention procedure not followed....... 268
10.2.8 Decision to grant permission in default 270
10.3 **Bars to relief** 270
10.3.1 Time limit..................................... 270
10.3.2 *Locus standi* 272
10.3.3 Adequacy of an appeal to An Bord Pleanála 273
10.3.4 Section 5 procedure more appropriate 275
10.3.5 Other discretionary considerations................. 275

11   ENFORCEMENT OF PLANNING CONTROL 277
        11.1 **The planning injunction** 276
             11.1.1 Scope of remedy 277
             11.1.2 Time limits 280
             11.1.3 Companies as respondents 281
             11.1.4 Onus of proof in section 27 proceedings 282
             11.1.5 *Res Judicata* 253
        11.2 **Principles upon which the Court exercises its
             discretion** 284
             11.2.1 Remedy analogous to an injunction 284
             11.2.2 Delay 285
             11.2.3 Lapse of time 285
             11.2.4 Technicality of the breach 286
             11.2.5 Public convenience 287
             11.2.6 Planning considerations 288
             11.2.7 Other equitable considerations 288
             11.2.8 Section 5 references 290
             11.2.9 Balancing all factors 290
        11.3 **Practice and procedure** 291
             11.3.1 Applications to the High Court: Order 103 of the
                    Rules of the Superior Courts 291
             11.3.2 Applications to the Circuit Court: Order 67A of the
                    Circuit Court Rules 293
             11.3.3 Application by motion 295
             11.3.4 Joinder of parties 295
             11.3.5 Evidence to be heard 296
             11.3.6 Adjournments and liberty to apply 296
        11.4 **Enforcement notices** 297
             11.4.1 The decision by the planning authority to take
                    enforcement action 297
             11.4.2 Service of enforcement notices 298
             11.4.3 Obligation to give information to planning
                    authority 299
             11.4.4 Section 31 notice 300
             11.4.5 Section 32 notice 301
             11.4.6 Section 35 notice 302
             11.4.7 Direct action by the planning authority 302
             11.4.8 Prosecution for non-compliance with enforcement
                    notices 302
             11.4.9 Prosecutions for breach of the obligation to obtain
                    planning permission 304
             11.4.10 Warning notices 305

11.4.10.1 *Warning notices for the preservation of trees and other features* 306
11.4.11 Notices requiring the removal or alteration of structures 307
11.4.12 Notices requiring the discontinuance of a use 308
11.4.13 Enforcement of open spaces 308
11.5 **Summary of enforcement time limits** 308
11.6 **Planning and licensing** 310

12 COMPENSATION 313
12.1 **Introduction** 313
12.2 **Entitlement to compensation for decisions on planning applications** 315
12.2.1 Prohibition against double compensation 316
12.2.2 Determination of claims for compensation 316
12.2.3 Forms of claims 316
12.2.4 Registration of compensation 317
12.2.5 Recovery of compensation by planning authority 317
12.2.6 Notice preventing compensation 318
12.2.7 Power of Minister to order payment of compensation 319
12.2.8 Structures substantially replacing structures demolished or destroyed by fire 320
12.2.9 Prohibition on assignment of compensation 321
12.3 **Development in respect of which a refusal of permission will not attract compensation** 321
12.3.1 Second Schedule to the 1990 Act 321
12.3.2 Road development 322
12.4 **Non-compensatable reasons for refusal for decisions under Part IV of the 1963 Act** 323
12.4.1 Third Schedule: non-compensatable reasons for refusal 323
12.5 **Non-compensatable conditions fourth schedule: conditions which may be imposed without compensation** 329
12.5.1 Non-compensatable conditions under the Roads Act 1993 332
12.6 **Other circumstances in which compensation payable** 332
12.7 **Rules for the determination of the amount of compensation** 334
12.8 **The purchase notice** 337

13   PLANNING AND CONVEYANCING: GUIDELINES FOR
       PRACTITIONERS by *Patrick Sweetman* 340
13.1 **The Law Society of Ireland general conditions of sale** 340
       13.1.1 The planning warranty: general condition 36 340
13.2 **Time limits on enforcement** 345
       13.2.1 Practical considerations 345
       13.2.2 Buildings erected without permission 346
       13.2.3 Alterations without permission to an existing
              authorised building 347
       13.2.4 Works carried out in breach of the conditions or
              terms of a permission 347
       13.2.5 Unauthorised uses. 347
       13.2.6 Licensed premises. 348
13.3 **Contract for sale conditional on planning permission** 348
       13.3.1 Cut-off date. 349
13.4 **Specimen conditions** 350
       13.4.1 Special condition making the contract subject to
              issue of planning permission for a house 350
       13.4.2 Special condition making contract subject to issue of
              retention planning permission 351
       13.4.3 Special condition making the contract subject to
              planning permission 352
13.5 **Purchasing with the benefit of planning permission**. 353
13.6 **Certificates of compliance** 354
       13.6.1 Planning and building control 354
       13.6.2 Check list 355
       13.6.3 Qualifications of persons giving certificates of
              compliance. 356
13.7 **Conditions attaching to planning permission** 357
       13.7.1 Conditions regulating development works. 357
       13.7.2 Conditions precedent 357
       13.7.3 Financial conditions 358
       13.7.4 Conditions restricting future development. 358
       13.7.5 Conditions which incorporate previous
              permissions 359
13.8 **Building control**. 359
       13.8.1 Exemptions. 361
       13.8.2 Commencement notes 361
       13.8.3 A commencement notice is not required in
              respect of: 362
              13.8.3.1 *Definitions* 362
       13.8.4 Fire Safety Certificates. 363
       13.8.5 A fire safety certificate is not required in respect of . . . 364

13.8.6 Alteration or extension of existing buildings 364
13.8.7 Services, fittings and equipment 365
13.8.8 Dispensations/Relaxations 365
13.8.9 Liabillity, penalties and enforcement 365
13.8.10 Building bye-laws 366
13.8.11 Multi-storey buildings 367
13.8.12 Fire Services Act 1981 367
13.9 **Replying to planning requisitions on title** 367
13.10 **Replying to building control requisitions** 375

APPENDIX A: PRACTICE NOTES 378
A.1 **Certificates of compliance with planning permission** 378
A.1.1 From what date must they be obtained? 379
A.2 **Private residential property and Clause 36 of the contract
for sale** 379
A.3 **Compliance with planning conditions when estate in
charge** 380
A.4 **Evidence that roads and services are in charge of the
local authority** 381
A.5 **Who should certify compliance?** 381
A.6 **Architects' certificates** 384
A.7 **Re: Planning/building regulations** 386
A.8 **Laws Society forms of certificate of compliance for
conveyancing purposes** 388
A.9 **RIAI Form of architects opinion on compliance for
conveyancing purposes** 391
A.10 **Joint Committee on Law Society & Building Societies'
Solicitors** 393
A.10.1 House extension – failure to obtain building
bye-laws approval 393
A.11 **Exempted development** 394
A.12 **Building Control Act and Building Regulations** 395
A.13 **Notes extracted from pre-contract requisitions on
the Building Control Act 1990 and the Building
Regulations**
A.14 **The Law Society's Standard General Conditions
of Sale** 399

INDEX 401

TABLE OF CASES

Ireland

Athlone Woollen Mills Co. Ltd v. Athlone U.D.C. [1950] I.R. 1 186
Attorney General (McGarry and Others) v. Sligo County Council
    [1991] 1 I.R. 99 . . . . 34, 36, 37
Avenue Properties Ltd v. Farrell Homes Ltd [1982]
    I.L.R.M. 21 . . . . 284, 286

Barrett (Jack) (Builders) Ltd v. Dublin County Council, unreported,
    Supreme Court, July 28, 1983 226
Bellow v. Cement Ltd [1948] I.R. 62 284
Blainroe Estate Management Co. Ltd v. IGR Blainroe Ltd,
    unreported, High Court, March 18, 1994 287
Blake and Madigan v. Attorney General [1982] I.R. 117 29
Blessington & District Community Council Ltd v. Wicklow County
    Council, unreported, High Court, Kelly J.,
    July 19, 1996 . . . . 144, 148, 265, 271
Boland v. An Bord Pleanála, unreported, High Court, Keane J.,
    December 9, 1994 . . . . 197, 199
Bord na Mona v. An Bord Pleanála and Galway County Council
    [1985] I.R. 205 . . . . 209, 210, 211, 264
Brady v. Donegal County Council [1989] I.L.R.M. 282 . . . . 141, 271
Browne v. An Bord Pleanála [1989] I.L.R.M. 865 . . . . 166, 168, 176
Browne v. Dashel U.D.C., unreported, High Court, March 26, 1993 319
Burke v. Drogheda Corporation [1981] I.L.R.M. 439 . . . . 150, 214

Cairnduff v. O'Connell [1986] I.R. 73 . . . . 93, 94
Calor Teoranta v. Sligo County Council [1991] 2 I.R. 267 . . . . . 148, 215, 269
Carrickhall Holdings Ltd v. Dublin Corporation [1983] I.L.R.M. 268 66
Carroll and Colley v. Brushfield Ltd, unreported, High Court,
    Lynch J., October 9, 1992 . . . . 66, 85, 283
Cavern Systems Dublin Ltd v. Clontarf Residents Association and
    Dublin Corporation [1984] I.L.R.M. 29 257
Central Dublin Development Association v. The Attorney General
    (1975) 109 I.L.T.R. 69 . . . . 29, 313, 321
Chambers v. An Bord Pleanála [1992] 1 I.R. 134 272
Chawke Caravans Ltd v. Limerick County Council, unreported,
    High Court, February 1991 . . . . 32, 33, 187

Child v. Wicklow County Council, unreported, High Court,
    Costello P., January 20, 1995 .... 214, 217, 218
Clarke v. Brady, unreported, High Court, Hamilton P.,
    October 30, 1990 121
Coffey v. Hebron Homes Ltd, Nore Properties and others,
    unreported, High Court, July 27, 1984 227
Comhaltas Ceoiltoirí Éireann, Re, unreported, High Court,
    Finlay P., December 14, 1972 311
Convery v. Dublin County Council [1990] I.L.R.M. 658 235
Cork Corporation v. O'Connell [1978] I.L.R.M. 85 290
Cork County Council v. Ardfert Quarries Ltd, unreported,
    High Court, December 7, 1982 78
Corrigan v. Irish Land Commission [1977] I.R. 317 262
Creedon v. Dublin Corporation [1983] I.L.R.M. 39 .... 214, 216, 274
Crodaun Homes Ltd v. Kidare County Council [1983] I.L.R.M. 1 145
Cullen v. Wicklow County Manager and Wicklow County Council,
    unreported, High Court, June 13, 1996 3
Cunningham v. An Bord Pleanála, unreported, High Court,
    May 3, 1990 .... 148, 264
Cusack and McKenna v. Minister for Local Government,
    unreported, High Court, November 4, 1980 .... 59, 131

DGS Ltd and An Bord Pleanála, Re, unreported, High Court,
    April 10, 1992 190
Dillon v. Irish Cement, unreported, Supreme Court, November 26,
    1986 .... 124, 282
Donegal County Council v. O'Donnell, unreported, High Court,
    June 25, 1982 204
Dooley v. Galway County Council [1992] I.R. 136 146
Dreher v. Irish Land Commission [1994] I.L.R.M. 94 313
Drogheda Corporation v. Gantley and Brothers, unreported,
    High Court, July 28, 1983 .... 279, 280, 296
Dublin Corporation v. Aircold Refrigeration Ltd, unreported,
    High Court, O'Hanlon J., March 8, 1995 75
Dublin Corporation v. Bentham [1993] 2 I.R. 58 .... 57, 60, 94
Dublin Corporation v. Flynn 303
Dublin Corporation v. Kevans, unreported, High Court,
    July 14, 1980 285
Dublin Corporation v. Langan, unreported, High Court,
    May 13, 1982 .... 93, 347
Dublin Corporation v. Maiden Poster Sites [1983] I.L.R.M. 48 ..... 288, 290
Dublin Corporation v. Matra Investments Ltd 114 I.L.T.R. 306 .... 284, 285

Dublin Corporation v. McGinley and Shackelton [1976–77]
   I.L.R.M. 343 335
Dublin Corporation v. McGowan [1993] I.R. 405 289
Dublin Corporation v. McGrath, unreported , High Court,
   McMahon J., November 17, 1978. 6
Dublin Corporation v. Moore [1984] I.L.R.M. 339. .... 61, 62, 98, 282
Dublin Corporation v. Mulligan, unreported, High Court,
   May 6, 1980. 285
Dublin Corporation v. Regan Advertising Ltd
   [1986] I.R. 171 (HC). 63, 66, 68, 72, 283, 290
Dublin Corporation v. Smithwick [1976–77] I.L.R.M. 280 .... 315, 320
Dublin Corporation v. Sullivan, unreported, High Court,
   December 21, 1984 .... 57, 282
Dublin County Council v. Brennan and McGowan Ltd, unreported,
   High Court, February 7, 1983 52
Dublin County Council v. Browne, unreported, High Court,
   October 6, 1987 .... 279, 283
Dublin County Council v. Carty Builders & Co. Ltd [1987]
   I.R. 355 77
Dublin County Council v. Eighty Five Developments Ltd (No. 2)
   [1992] 2 I.R. 392 .... 323, 325
Dublin County Council v. Greally [1990] I.L.R.M. 48 51
Dublin County Council v. Hill [1994] 1 I.R. 86 .... 300, 302
Dublin County Council v. Loughran [1985] I.L.R.M. 166 234
Dublin County Council v. Macken, unreported, High Court,
   May 13, 1994. 280
Dublin County Council v. Morren [1985] I.L.R.M. 593 214
Dublin County Council v. O'Riordan [1986] I.L.R.M. 104 281
Dublin County Council v. Sellwood Quarries Ltd
   [1981] I.L.R.M. 23 .... 54, 287, 288
Dublin County Council v. Shortt [1982] I.L.R.M. 117 335
Dublin County Council v. Tallaght Block Company Ltd
   [1982] I.L.R.M. 534 .... 77, 78, 287, 288
Dun Laoghaire Corporation v. Frescati Estates Ltd [1982]
   I.L.R.M. 469 .... 204, 226
Dun Laoghaire Corporation v. Parkhill Developments Ltd [1989]
   I.R. 447; [1989] I.L.R.M. 469. 281
Dunne (Frank) Ltd v. Dublin County Council
   [1974] I.R. 45 .... 144, 194, 208
Dwyer-Nowlan Developments v. Secretary of State for the
   Environment, unreported, High Court, April 21, 1986. 234

East Wicklow Conservation Community Ltd v. Wicklow County
    Council [1995] 2 I.L.R.M. 16 17
Eighty-Five Developments v. Dublin County Council [1989] I.R.
    296 187
Ellis v. Nolan and others, unreported, High Court, McWilliams J.,
    May 6, 1983 281
ESB v. Gormley [1985] I.R. 129 . . . . 138, 145

Ferris v. Dublin County Council [1993] 3 I.R. 165 35
Finn v. Bray U.D.C. [1969] I.R. 169 . . . . 24, 25
Flanagan v. Galway City and County Manager and Galway County
    Council [1990] 2 I.R. 66 217
Freaney v. Bray U.D.C. [1970] I.R. 253 . . . . 214, 240
Frenchurch Properties Ltd v. Wexford County Council [1992]
    2 I.R. 268 . . . . 231, 232, 280
Frescati Estates Ltd v. Walker (Marie) [1975] I.R. 177 . . . . 139, 141, 144
Furlong v. McConnell [1990] I.L.R.M. 48 . . . . 59, 62

Galway County Council v. Connacht Proteins Ltd, unreported,
    High Court, March 28, 1980 . . . . 66, 80
Galway County Council v. Lackagh Rock
    [1985] I.R. 20 . . . . 55, 60, 66, 74, 76
Garden Village Construction Co. Ltd v. Wicklow County Council
    [1994] 3 I.R. 413 . . . . 232, 233
Geraghty v. Minister of Local Government [1976] I.R. 153 266
Gleason v. Syntex, *Irish Times*, September 29, 1982 284
Glencar Explorations Plc. v. Mayo County Council
    [1993] 2 I.R. 237 . . . . 10, 29, 40, 61, 188, 189
Grange Developments Ltd v. Dublin County Council (No. 1)
    [1986] I.R. 246 . . . . 61, 139, 187, 314
Greendale Building Company v. Dublin County Council
    [1977] I.R. 256 6
Gregory v. Dun Laoghaire Rathdown County Council,
    unreported, Geoghegan J., July 16, 1996 . . . . 196, 260, 263

Haughey, Re [1971] I.R. 217 266
Healy v. Dublin County Council, unreported, High Court,
    April 29, 1993 . . . . 172, 212, 269
Herringdale Developments Ltd v. Naas U.D.C., unreported,
    High Court, Finlay P., November 17, 1977 . . . . 160, 213
Hoburn Homes Ltd v. An Bord Pleanála [1993] I.L.R.M. 368 325
Holiday Motor Homes Ltd v. Dublin County Council, unreported,
    High Court, McWilliam J., December 20, 1977 335

Horne v. Freeny, unreported, High Court, July 7, 1988 93
Houlihan v. An Bord Pleanála, unreported, High Court, Murphy J.,
    October 4, 1993 200
Howard v. The Commissioners of Public Works and Byrne v.
    Commissioners of Public Works
    [1994] I.R. 101 . . . .   13, 100, 101, 102, 104, 221
Hunstsgrove Developments Ltd v. Meath County Council
    [1994] 2 I.L.R.M. 36 27

Inver Resources Ltd v. Limerick Corporation
    [1987] I.R. 159 . . . . 143, 258, 271
Irish Asphalt Ltd v. An Bord Pleanála, unreported,
    Supreme Court, May 22, 1996 . . . . 154, 204, 262, 354
Irish Wildbird Conservancy and the Commissioners of
    Public Works v. Clonakilty Golf and Country Club Ltd,
    unreported, High Court, Costello P.,
    July 23, 1996 . . . . 87, 125, 180, 295

Johnson and Staunton Ltd v. Esso Ireland Ltd [1990] 1 I.R. 289 295

Keane v. An Bord Pleanála and the Commissioners of Irish
    Rights, unreported, Supreme Court,
    July 18, 1996 . . . .   101, 123, 189, 259, 266
Keleghan v. Corby and Dublin Corporation 111 I.L.T.R. 144 . . . . . . 147, 196
Kelly v. Dublin County Council, unreported, High Court,
    O'Hanlon J., February 21, 1986 236
Kenny Homes v. Galway City and County Manager of Galway
    Corporation [1995] I.R. 178 . . . . 7, 219, 220
Keogh v. Galway County Borough Corporation (No. 1)
    [1995] 1 I.L.R.M. 141 . . . . 26, 32, 36
Keogh v. Galway County Borough Corporation (No. 2)
    [1995] 2 I.L.R.M. 312 . . . . 26, 218, 264, 268
Killiney and Ballybrack Development Association Ltd v.
    The Minister for Local Government and Templefinn
    Estates, unreported, Supreme Court,
    April 24, 1978 . . . . 194, 204, 248, 266
Kitterick (Thomas), Application of, 105 I.L.T.R. 105 310
KSK Enterprises v. An Bord Pleanála [1994] 2 I.R. 128 . . . . 257, 259

Law v. Minister for Local Government, unreported,
    High Court, Deale J., May 7, 1974 . . . . 248, 266, 272
Lee and O'Flynn v. O'Riordan, unreported, High Court,
    February 10, 1995 75

Lee and Flynn v. Wicklow County Council, unreported,
    High Court, Flood J., December 1, 1995 234
Leinster Importing Co. Ltd v. Dublin County Council 11

MacPharthalain v. Commissioners of Public Works
    [1992] I.R. 111 50
Maher v. An Bord Pleanála [1993] 1 I.R. 439 . . . . 151, 240
Malahide Community Council Ltd v. Fingal County Council,
    unreported, High Court, December 19, 1994 28
Malloy v. Dublin County Council [1990] 1 I.R. 90. 215
Max Development Ltd v. An Bord Pleanála
    [1994] 2 I.R. 121 . . . . 171, 252, 265
McCabe v. Harding Investments Ltd [1984] I.L.R.M. 105 139
MCD Management Services Ltd v. Kildare County Council
    [1995] 2 I.L.R.M. 532 . . . . 228, 229
McDonagh (Thomas) and Sons Ltd v. Galway Corporation
    [1995] 1 I.R. 191 . . . . 201, 208, 233
McGoldrick v. An Bord Pleanála, unreported, High Court,
    Barron J., May 26, 1995 . . . . 246, 249, 266
McGovern (Kenneth), Application of, unreported, O'Sullivan and
    Shepherd, *Irish Planning Law and Practice*, 5.631 310
McGrath Limestone Works v. Galway County Council,
    unreported, High Court, Egan J., November 17, 1988 . . . . 79, 81
McNally v. Martin [1995] I.L.R.M. 351 249
McNamara v. An Bord Pleanála, unreported, High Court, Barr J.,
    May 10, 1996 . . . . 199, 260
Meath County Council v. Daly (Martin) [1987] I.R. 391 . . . . 79, 283
Meenaghan v. Dublin County Council [1984] I.L.R.M. 616 328
Minister for Justice v. Wang Zhu Jie [1993] 1 I.R. 426 262
Molloy and Walsh v. Dublin County Council [1990] I.R. 90 152
Monaghan County Council v. Brogan [1987] I.R. 333 . . . . 60, 66, 73, 75
Monaghan U.D.C. v. Alf-a-Bet Promotions Ltd
    [1980] I.L.R.M. 64 . . . . 137, 146
Morris v. Garvey [1983] I.R. 319 276
Movie News Ltd v. Galway County Council 11
Mulhall v. An Bord Pleanála, unreported, High Court,
    McCracken J., March 21, 1996 . . . . 240, 247
Murphy v. Bord Telecom [1988] I.L.R.M. 53 . . . . 127, 168
Murphy v. Dublin Corporation [1972] I.R. 215 266
Murray v. Buckley, unreported, High Court, Barron J.,
    December 5, 1990 114
Murray v. Wicklow County Council, unreported, High Court,
    March 12, 1996 214

Nolan v. Minister for the Environment [1991] 2 I.R. 548 193
Nova Colour Graphic Suppplies Ltd v. The Employment Appeals
    Tribunal [1987] I.R. 426 247

O'Connor's Downtown Properties Ltd v. Nenagh U.D.C.
    [1993] 1 I.R. 1 214
O'Connor and Spollen Concrete Group Ltd v. Harrington (Frank)
    Ltd, unreported, High Court, April 26, 1983 288
O'Connor v. Kerry County Council [1988] I.L.R.M. 660 . . . . 275, 298
O'Donoghue v. An Bord Pleanála [1991]
    I.L.R.M. 750 . . . . 145, 148, 221, 268
O'Dwyer Brothers, Re 311
O'Flynn v. O'Riordan, unreported, High Court, February 10, 1995 75
O'Keeffe v. An Bord Pleanála [1993]
    I.R. 39 . . . . 26, 37, 172, 174, 177, 202, 203, 229, 233, 251, 267, 270
O'Leary v. Dublin County Council [1988] I.R. 150 34
O'Neill v. Clare County Council [1983] I.L.R.M. 141 216

Patterson v. Murphy [1978] I.L.R.M. 85 . . . . 55, 73, 74, 75, 85, 290
People (at the suit of the Attorney General) v. Giles (Ronald)
    [1974] I.R. 422 262

Quinn's Supermarkets v. Attorney General [1972] I.R. 1 67

Readymix (Eire) v. Dublin County Council and Minister for Local
    Government, unreported, Supreme Court,
    July 30, 1974 . . . . 225, 226
Rehabilitation Institute v. Dublin Corporation, unreported, High
    Court, January 14, 1988 . . . . 61, 64, 67, 68, 82, 126, 132, 176, 301
RGDATA v. An Bord Pleanála, unreported, High Court,
    April 30, 1996 . . . . 172, 249, 265

Schwestermann v. An Bord Pleanála [1995] I.L.R.M. 269 139
Scott v. An Bord Pleanála and Arcon Mines Ltd, Kilkenny County
    Council and others [1995] 1 I.L.R.M. 424 . . . . 140, 261, 262
Seery v. Gannon, unreported, Blayney J., March 9, 1992 278
Shannon Regional Fisheries Board v. An Bord Pleanála, unreported,
    High Court, Barr J., November 17, 1994 170
Sharpe (P. & F.) Ltd v. Dublin City and County Manager [1989]
    I.R. 710 . . . . 5, 7, 186, 187, 215, 217, 218, 220, 263, 268, 269
Shortt v. Dublin County Council [1983] I.L.R.M. 377 . . . . 324, 328
Simonovich v. An Bord Pleanála, unreported, High Court,
    Lardner J., July 24, 1988 252

Siverhill Development Company Ltd v. An Bord Pleanála,
    unreported, High Court, O'Hanlon J., March 16, 1984 153
South Dublin County Council v. Balfe (Myles) and others,
    unreported, Costello P., November 3, 1995 . . . . 281, 296
State (Abenglen Properties Ltd) v. Dublin Corporation [1984] I.R.
    381 . . . . . 83, 161, 187, 194, 201, 216, 251, 264, 265, 269, 270, 273, 275
State (Alf-a-Bet Promotions Ltd) v. Bundoran U.D.C.
    (1978) 112 I.L.T.R. 9 143
State (Aprile) v. Naas U.D.C. [1985] I.L.R.M. 510 221
State (CIE) v. An Bord Pleanála, unreported, Supreme Court,
    December 12, 1984 253
State (Cogley) v. Dublin Corporation [1970] I.R. 244 49
State (Conlon Construction Ltd) v. Cork County Council,
    unreported, High Court, July 21, 1975 . . . . 214, 216, 274
State (Córas Iompar Éireann) v. An Bord Pleanála, unreported,
    Supreme Court, December 12, 1984 189
State (Finglas Industrial Estates Ltd) v. Dublin County Council,
    unreported, Supreme Court, February 17, 1983 . . . . 143, 210, 260
State (Fitzgerald) v. An Bord Pleanála [1985] I.L.R.M. 117 189
State (FPH Properties SA) v. An Bord Pleanála
    [1987] I.R. 698 . . . . 201, 204, 206, 211
State (Genport) Ltd v. An Bord Pleanála [1983] I.L.R.M. 12 266
State (Haverty) v. An Bord Pleanála [1987] I.R. 485 . . . . 245, 266
State (Keegan) v. Stardust Compensation Tribunal
    [1986] I.R. 642 . . . . 36, 173, 203, 263
State (Kenny and Hussey) v. An Bord Pleanála, unreported,
    Supreme Court, December 20, 1994 . . . . 222, 224, 354
State (Lynch) v. Cooney [1982] I.R. 337 272
State (McCoy) v. Dun Laoghaire Corporation [1985]
    I.L.R.M. 533 . . . . 231, 233
State (Modern Homes Ltd) v. Dublin Corporation
    [1953] I.R. 202 20
State (Murphy) v. Dublin County Council [1970] I.R. 253 . . . . 214, 240
State (N.C.E.) v. Dublin County Council, unreported,
    Supreme Court, May 14, 1980 . . . . 143, 214, 216, 274
State (O'Hara and McGuinness) v. An Bord Pleanála, unreported,
    High Court, May 8, 1986 203
State (Pine Valley Developments Ltd) v. Dublin County Council
    [1982] I.L.R.M. 169 . . . . 154, 212, 215, 271
State (Stanford) v. Dun Laoghaire Corporation [1981]
    I.L.R.M. 87 . . . . 188, 266
State (Sweeney) v. Minister for the Environment and Limerick
    County Council [1979] I.L.R.M. 35 . . . . 204, 221

State (Tern Homes (Brennanstown) Ltd) v. An Bord Pleanála
    [1985] I.R. 725 354
State (Thomas McInerney and Co. Ltd) v. Dublin County Council
    [1985] I.R. 1 338
State (Toft) v. Galway Corporation [1981] I.L.R.M. 439 144
Sunderland v. McGreavey, Rogers and Louth County Council,
    unreported, High Court, October 13, 1995 235

Taisce, An v. Dublin Corporation, unreported, High Court,
    January 31, 1973..36
Teirnan Homes v. Fagan, unreported, Supreme Court,
    July 23, 1981 213
Tennyson v. Dun Loaghaire Corporation
    [1991] 2 I.R. 527 .... 31, 172, 190, 212, 268
Tivoli Cinema, Re, unreported, High Court, January 24, 1994 310
Tralee U.D.C. v. Stack, unreported, High Court, January 13, 1984 ... 99, 125

Viscount Securities Ltd v. Dublin County Council (1976)
    62 I.L.T 17 321
Viscount Securities Ltd, Re 112 I.L.T.R. 17 .... 53, 85

White v. McInerney Construction Ltd, unreported, Supreme Court,
    Hamilton C.J., O'Flaherty and Blayney JJ., *nem. diss.*,
    November 29, 1994 286
Wicklow County Council v. An Bord Pleanála, Bridgefarm
    Company Ltd and Coolattin Woods Action Committeee
    (1990) 8 I.L.T.R. 107 42
Wilkinson v. Dublin County Council [1991] I.L.R.M. 605 .... 31, 35
Wood J., & Co. Ltd v. Wicklow County Council
    [1995] I.L.R.M. 51 .... 326, 327

XJS Investments Ltd v. Dun Loaghaire Corporation
    [1987] I.L.R.M. 659 .... 30, 224, 323, 326, 327

United Kingdom

Adams & Wade Ltd v. Minister for Housing and Local Government
    (1965) 18 P. & C.R. 60 339
Alderson v. Secretary of State for the Environment
    [1984] J.P.L. 429 204
Allen v. Secretary of State for the Environment [1990] J.P.L. 340 90
Associated Provincial Picture Houses v. Wednesbury Corporation
    [1948] 1 K.B. 223 263

Attorney General, Sutcliffe and Others v. Calderdale Borough
  Council (1983) 46 P. & C.R. 399 95

Barling (David W.) v. Secretary of State for the Environment [1980]
  J.P.L. 594. 66
Beddow v. Beddow (1878) 9 Ch.D. 89 284
Belmont Farm Ltd v. Minister for Housing and Local Government
  [1963] J.P.L. 256. . . . . 88, 227
Birmingham Corporation v. Minister of Housing and Local
  Government Habib Ullah [1964] 1 Q.B. 178 . . . . 57, 62
Blackpool Borough Council v. Secretary of State for the
  Environment (1980) 40 P. & C.R. 104 57
Blum (Lilo) v. Secretary of State for the Environment
  [1987] J.P.L. 278. . . . . 61, 71
Borthwick-Norton v. Collier [1950] 2 K.B. 594, (CA) 298
Braddon v. Secretary of State for the Environment
  [1976] J.P.L. 508. 66
Breckland District Council v. Secretary of State for the Environment
  (1992) 65 P. & C.R. 34 203
British Airports Authority v. Secretary of State for Scotland
  (1979) S.L.T. 197 . . . . 201, 203, 206
British Airways Helicopters Ltd v. Secretary of State. 207
British Railways Board v. Secretary of State for the Environment
  [1994] J.P.L. 32. 208
Bromley London Bourough Council v. Hoeltschi (George) & Son
  [1978] J.P.L. 45. 70
Bromsgrove District Council v. Secretary of State for the
  Environment [1977] J.P.L. 797. 64
Brooks and Burton Ltd v. Secretary of State for the Environment
  [1977] 1 W.L.R. 1294 . . . . 74, 111, 128
Burdle v. Secretary of State for the Environment [1972]
  1 W.L.R. 1207. . . . . 63, 64, 67, 68, 69, 126

Calvin v. Carr [1980] A.C. 574; [1979] 2 W.L.R. 755 270
Castell-y-Mynach Estate (Trustee of) v. Secretary of State for Wales
  [1985] J.P.L. 40. 79
Chief Constable of the North Wales Police v. Evans [1982]
  1 W.L.R. 1155. 257
City of London Corporation v. Secretary of State for the
  Environment (1971) 71 L.G.R. 28 203
Clarke v. Minister of Housing and Local Government (1966)
  L.G.R. 346. 57

Copeland Borough Council v. Secretary of State for the
   Environment (1976) 31 P. & C.R. 403 38
Croydon London Borough Council v. Gladden [1994] J.P.L. 723 97
Crystanthou v. Secretary of State for the Environment
   [1976] J.P.L. 371 69
Cynon Valley Borough Council v. Secretary of State for Wales
   (1987) 53 P. & C.R. 68 . . . . 80, 222, 224

Davis (Thomas)(Porthcaw) Ltd v. Penybont R.D.C. [1972]
   1 W.L.R. 1526 55
Duffy v. Secretary of State for the Environment [1972]
   1 W.L.R. 1207 68
Duffy v. Secretary of State for the Environment [1981] J.P.L. 811 89
Dyer v. Dorset County Council [1988] 3 W.L.R. 213 95

Ealing Corporation v. Ryan [1965] 2 Q.B. 486 56
East Barnet U.D.C. v. British Transport Commission
   [1962] 2 Q.B. 484 . . . . 59, 60, 64, 73, 76
Emin v. Secretary of State for the Environment (1989)
   58 P. & C.R. 416 . . . . 65, 97
Emma Hotels v. Secretary of State for the Environment (1980)
   41 P. & C.R. 255 66
Enfield London Borough Council v. Secretary of State for the
   Environment [1975] J.P.L. 155 188

Fawcett Properties Ltd v. Buckingham County Council [1961]
   A.C. 636. . . . . 196, 204
Foster v. British Gas (1988) 2 C.M.L.R. 697 169
Fuller v. Secretary of State for the Environment [1987]
   2 E.G.L.R. 189. 89

Gill v Secretary of State for the Environment [1985] J.P.L. 710 90
Grampian Regional Council v. City of Aberdeen District Council
   (1983) 47 P. & C.R. 633 . . . . 204, 207
Gravesham Borough Council v. Secretary of State for the
   Environment (1947) P. & C.R. 142; [1983] J.P.L. 307 95
Great Portland Estates plc. v. Westminster City Council [1984]
   3 All E.R. 187, 217
Grillo v. Minister for Housing and Local Government (1968)
   208 E.G. 1201 222
Grover's Executors v. Rickmansworth U.D.C. (1959)
   10 P. & C.R. 417 79
Guildford R.D.C. v. Fortesque [1959] 2 Q.B. 112 . . . . 60, 74, 77

Hale (deceased) v. Lichfield District Council [1979] J.P.L. 425 ...... 78, 79
Hammersmith v. Secretary of State for the Environment (1975)
    30 P. & C.R. 19 133
Hartley v. Minister for Housing and Local Government [1970] 1
    Q.B. 413 77
Hawes v. Secretary of State for the Environment (1965)
    17 P. & C.R. 22 68
Hidderley v. Warickshire County Council 14 P. & C.R. 134 90
Hillard v. Secretary of State for the Environment (1978)
    37 P. & C.R. 129
Hooper v. Slater [1978] J.P.L. 252 133
Horne v. Freeney, unreported, High Court, July 7, 1988 92
Horwitz v. Rowson [1960] 2 All E.R. 881 68
Hussain v. Secretary of State for the Environment (1967)
    23 P. & C.R. 330 .... 67, 130

Inner London Educational Authority v. Secretary of State for the
    Environment 132
Irlam Brick Co. v. Warringtoin Borough Council [1982] J.P.L. 209 83

James v. Secretary of State for the Environment and Chichester
    District Council (1990) P. C.R. 234 .... 95, 298
Jennings v. Secretary of State for the Environment [1982] Q.B. 541 81
Jillings v. Secretary of State for the Environment [1984] J.P.L. 32 66
Johnston v. Secretary of State for the Environment (1974)
    28 P. & C.R. 424 .... 63, 64
Jones v. Secretary of State for Wales (1990) 88 L.G.R. 942 207

Kalra v. Secretary of State for the Environment [1995] J.P.L. B14 131
Kent County Council v. Secretary of State for the Environment
    (1976) 33 P. &. C.R. 223 202
Kingston-upon-Thames Royal London Borough Council v.
    Secretary of State for the Environment [1973]
    1 W.L.R. 1549 203
Kwik Save Discount Group v. Secretary of State for Wales
    (1981) P. & C.R. 166 128

Ladbroke (Rentals) Ltd v. Secretary of State for the Environment
    [1981] J.P.L. 427 .... 6, 195
Lambert v. Lewis, unreported, High Court, November 24, 1982 282
Leech v. Reilly, unreported, High Court, May 28, 1987 288
Leighton and Newman Car Sales v. Secretary of State for the
    Environment (1976) 32 P. & C.R 81

Lennon v. Kingdom Plant Hire, unreported, High Court,
December 13, 1991 . . . . 99, 126, 282
Lewis v. Secretary of State for the Environment (1971)
23 P. & C.R. 125 59
London Corporation v. Cusack-Smith [1955] 1 All E.R. 712 298
London Residuary Body v. Secretary of State for the Environment
[1990] 1 W.L.R. 744 131
LTSS Print & Suppply Services v. London Borough of Hackney
[1976] 2 W.L.R. 253 82
Lucas F. & Sons Ltd v. Dorking Borough Council 62 L.G.R. 111 234

Maddern v. Secretary of State for the Environment [1980] J.P.L. 676 63
Manning v. Secretary of State for the Environment [1976] J.P.L. 634 226
Marshall v. Nottingham City Corporation [1960] 1 W.L.R. 707 71
Mary v. Connaughton, unreported, High Court, January 25, 1984 286
McAlpine v. Secretary of State for the Environment [1995]
J.P.L. B43 95
McKellan v. Minister for Housing and Local Government (1966)
E.G. 683 87
Miller-Mead v. Minster for Housing and Local Government [1963]
2 Q.B. 196 225
Mixnam's Properties Ltd v. Chertsey U.D.C. [1964]
2 W.L.R. 1210 204
Monomart (Wharehouses) Ltd v. Secretary of State for the
Environment (1977) 34 P. & C.R. 305 133

Newbury District Council v. Secretary of State for the Environment
[1981] A.C. 578 . . . . 194, 201, 223
Nicholls v. Secretary of State for the Environment [1981]
J.P.L. 890 79
North Warwickshire Borough Council v. Secretary of State for the
Environment (1983) 50 P. & C.R. 47 89
North Wiltshire District Council v. Secretary of State for the
Environment (1992) 65 P. & C.R. 137 222
Northavon District Council v. Secretary of State for the
Environment (1980) 40 P. C.R. 332 . . . . 55, 79

Panayi v. Secretary of State for the Environment [1985] J.P.L. 783 57
Peak Park Joint Planning Board v. Secretary of State for the
Environment [1991] J.P.L. 744 196
Peake v. Secretary of State for Wales (1971) 22 P. & C.R. 889 71
Petticoat Lane Rentals v. Secretary of State for the Environment
[1971] 2 All E.R. 793 80

Philglow Ltd v. Secretary of State for the Environment [1985]
J.P.L. 318. 68
Pilkington Secretary of State for the Environment [1973]
1 W.L.R. 1527. . . . . 81, 154
Pioneer Aggregates (U.K.) Ltd v. Secretary of State for the
Environment [1985] A.C. 132. . . . . 79, 223
Pittman v. Secretary of State for the Environment [1988] J.P.L. 391. 88
Prossar v. Minister for Housing and Local Government
(1968) 76 L.G.R. 109 81
Pyx Granite Co. Ltd v. Minister for Housing and Local Government
[1958] 1 Q.B. 554 . . . . 194, 206

R. v. Derbyshire Borough Council [1980] J.P.L. 398 83
R. v. Hendon U.D.C., *ex p.*, Chorley [1933] 2 K.B. 249, 266
R. v. Hillingdon Borough Council., *ex p.*, Royco Homes Ltd
[1974] Q.B.720 . . . . 6, 195, 256
R. v. St Edmundsbury Borough Council [1985] 1 W.L.R. 1168 202
R. v. Swale Borough Council, *ex p.*, Royal Society for the Proection
of Birds [1991] J.P.L. 39. 173
R. v. Secretary of State for the Environment [1995] J.P.L. 135;
[1995] EGCS 95, (CA) 225
R. v. Thurrock Borough Council, *ex p.*, Tesco Stores Ltd [1994]
J.P.L.328 . . . . 129, 131
Rael-Brook B. Limited v. Minister for Housing and Local
Government [1987] 2 Q.B. 65 132
Rolls v. Miller (1884) 27 Ch.D. 71 132
Royal Borough of Kensington and Chelsea v. Secretary of State for
the Environment [1981] J.P.L. 50. 73
Royal Borough of Kensington v. Mia Carla [1981] J.P.L. 50. 129

Sampson's Executors v. Nottinghamshire County Council
[1949] 2 K.B. 439 95
Scrivener v. Minister of Housing and Local Government (1966)
18 P. & C.R. 357. 67
Scurlock v. Secretary of State for Wales (1976) 33 P. & C.R. 202. 96
Shephard v. Buckinghamshire County Council (1966)
18 P. & C.R. 419 131
Simmonds v. Secretary of State for the Environment [1981]
J.P.L. 509. 121
Sinclair Lockhart's Trustees v. Central Land Board 1951 S.C. 258;
1951 S.L.T. 121. 95
SJD Properties Ltd v. Secretary of State for the Environment
[1981] J.P.L. 673. 130

Slough Estates Ltd v. Slough Borough Council (No. 2) [1969]
2 Ch. 305 . . . . 223, 226
Smith v. East Elloe Rural District Council [1956] A.C. 736. 5
South Staffordshire District Council v. Secretary of State for the
Environment (1987) 55 P. & C.R. 258 81
Southend-on-Sea Corporation v. Hodgson (Wickford) Ltd [1961]
2 All E.R. 46 7
Stafford v. Roadstone Ltd, unreported, January 17, 1980 . . . . 287, 288
State of West Bengal v. The Corporation of Calcutta 102
Stephens v. Cuckfield R.D.C. [1960]
Stringer v. Minister for Housing and Local Government [1971] 1
All E.R. 65 . . . . 217, 263
Sutton London Borough Council v. Secretary of State for the
Environment (1975) 119 S.J. 321 227
Sykes v. Secretary of State for the Environment and South Oxford
District Council [1981] 1 W.L.R. 1092 . . . . 89, 124

Tessier v. Secretary of State for the Environment (1975) 31 P. &
C.R. 161 132
Trentham (G. Percy) Ltd v. Gloucestershoire County Council
[1966] 1 W.L.R. 506 . . . . 64, 72, 89

Uttlesford District Council v. Secretary of State for the Environment
[1992] J.P.L. 171 99

Vickers-Armstrong v. Central Land Board (1957) 9 P. & C.R. 33 64

W.T. Lamb Properties Ltd v. Secretary of State for the
Environment, unreported, *The Times*, November 11, 1982 132
Wain v. Secretary of State for the Environment (1981)
44 P. & C.R. 289 338
Wakelin v. Secretary of State for the Environment (1983)
46 P. & C.R. 214 72
Wallington v. Secretary of State Wales (1990) 62 P. & C.R. 150;
[1990] J.P.L. 942 . . . . 65, 66, 90, 97
Warnock v. Secretary of State for the Environment [1980]
J.P.L. 590 90
Webber v. Minister of Housing and Local Government [1968]
1 W.L.R. 29 . . . . 68, 82
Wessex Regional health Authority v. Salisbury District Council
[1984] J.P.L. 344 . . . . 202, 203
West Bowers Farm Products v. Essex County Council
[1985] J.P.L. 857 55

Westminster Bank Ltd v. Minister for Housing and Local
  Government [1971] A.C 508 203
Wheatcroft (Bernard) v. Secretary of State for the Environment
  (1982) 42 P. & C.R. 233 202
Whitehead v. Secretary of State for the Environment and Mole
  Valley District Council [1992] J.P.L. 561 99
Williams v. Minister for Housing and Local Government
  (1967) 65 L.G.R. 495; (1967) 18 P. & C.R. 514 .... 60, 89, 131
Wilson v. West Sussex County Council [1963] 2 Q.B. 764 227
Wimpey (George) & Co. Ltd v. New Forest District Council
  [1979] J.P.L. 314 206
Winton v. Secretary of State for the Environment (1982)
  46 P. & C.R. 205 .... 64, 69, 72
Wipperman v. Barking London Borough Council (1965)
  17 P. & C.R. 225 68
Wivenhoe Port Ltd v. Colchester Borough Council [1985]
  J.P.L. 396 225
Wood v. Secretary of State for the Environment [1973]
  1 W.L.R. 707 .... 70, 89, 96
Wycombe District Council v. Secretary of State for the Environment
  [1995] J.P.L. 223 115
Young v. Secretary of State for the Environment
  [1983] 2 A.C. 662 .... 79, 82, 301

United States

Hanly v. Kliendrenst 417F. to d.283 (2nd Cir. 1972) 173

TABLE OF STATUTES

Ireland

Air Pollution Act 1987 (No. 6) 191, 192
    s.26 121
    s.56 191
Acquisition of Land (Assessment of Compensation) Act 1919
    (9 & 10 Geo. 5, c.57)....................................... 316
Arterial Drainage Act 1945 (No. 3)............................. 120
    Pt. II 104
Building Control Act 1990 (No. 3) 120, 195, 341, 343, 345, 346, 348,
                                        359, 360, 366, 371, 373, 375,
                                        389, 395, 396, 397, 399
    s.8 377
    s.9 377
    s.12 377
    s.22 374
       (7) 342, 343, 366, 368, 391, 399
Casual Trading Act 1980 (No. 43)............................... 86
    s.7(3)... 99
City and County Management (Amendment) Act 1955 (No. 12)
    s.2(7)... 18
    s.3 16
    s.4 .... 7, 21, 217, 218, 220
       (1)... 7
Companies Acts 1908 to 1959 8
Companies Act 1963 (No. 33) 337
County Management Act 1940 (No. 12)
    s.2 7
    s.17 7
    s.27 3
Courts (No. 2) Act 1986 (No. 26)
    s.4(7).. 310
Derelict Sites Act 1990 (No. 14) 120
Dublin Corporation Act 1890 (53 & 54 Vict., c. 246)
    s.33 366
Environmental Protection Agency Act 1992
    (No. 7) 85, 117, 120, 155, 165, 169, 177, 190, 191, 193
    s. 4(2) 191
       (b) 192

Environmental Protection Agency Act 1992 (No. 7)—*contd.*
          s. 72.. 176
              (2) 188
          s.75 .... 177, 188, 252
          s. 98................................ 177, 188, 191, 327
              (1) 191, 253
              Pt. IV...................................... 111
          s.106(3)...................................... 22, 107
Fire Services Act 1981 (No. 30) 215, 348, 367
          s.20 364
Gas Act 1976 (No. 30)
          s.42 47
              (2) 47
Harbours Act 1946 (No. 9)................................ 337
          s.2 253
Health Act 1970 (No. 1)................................ 337
Housing Act 1966 (No. 21)
          s.86 11
Housing (Private Rented Dwellings) Act 1982 (No. 6)................. 11
Intoxicating Liquor Act 1960 (No. 18) 310, 311
Interpretation Act 1937 (No. 38) 125, 241
          s.11(h)................................... 213,240
          s.18(a)................................... 129
              (h)................................... 213
          Sched 213
Land Reclamation 1949 (No. 25)............................ 86
Landlord and Tenant (Amendment) Act 1980 (No. 10) 11
Licensing (Ireland) Act 1833(3 & 4 Wm. 4, c. 68)
          s.4 311
Local Government (Ireland) Act 1898 (61 & 62 Vict., c.37)
          s.10 11
Local Government Act 1941 (No. 23)........................... 337
Local Government Act 1946 (No. 24)........................... 23
          s.84(4)...................................... 46
Local Government (No. 2) Act 1960 (No. 40)
          s.10 11
Local Government Act 1925 (No. 5)
          s.34 42
Local Government Act 1991 (No. 11)............................ 9
          ss.6–8 5
          s.6 9
              (1) 9
              (2) 9

Local Government Act 1991 (No. 11)—*contd.*
   s.7 . . . . 9, 28, 189
     (1) 188
   s.8 10
     (1) 10
   s.43 25
   s.45 . . . . 39, 212
Local Government (Dublin) Act 1993 (No. 31) 2, 13
   s.11 . . . . 15, 91
Local Government (Multi-Storey) Act 1988 (No. 29). 367
Local Government (Planning and Development) Act 1963
 (No. 28) 1, 20, 24, 75, 102, 144, 246, 273, 313, 342, 364, 394
   Preamble. 38, 61
   Pt. II 7
   Pt. IV. 41, 42, 111, 113, 122, 189, 191, 258, 277,
         321, 322, 323, 323, 329, 334, 336, 337
   Pt. VI. 313, 323, 337
   s.2 . . . . 21, 29, 47, 54, 85, 89, 123, 133, 232, 283, 321
     (1) 92, 136
     (2) 1
     (7) 32, 33, 41, 187
   s.3 . . . . 62, 116, 233
     (1) 53, 54, 278
     (2) 55–56, 57
     (3) 56
   s.4 . . . . 12, 33, 65, 84, 86, 87, 94, 96, 102
     (1) 13, 87
     (a). 50
     (e). 13, 15, 91
     (f). 12, 13, 91
     (g) 50, 92, 93, 94, 118, 125, 246
     (h) 95, 98, 282
     (i). 98, 126
     (1A). 92, 93
     (2) 84
   s.5 . . . . 6, 62, 85, 238, 246, 275, 290, 298
     (1) 290
   s.6 8
   s.7 . . . . 8, 240
     (1) 298–299
     (2) 298, 299
     (3) 299
     (4) 87

Local Government Act 1991 (No. 11), s.7—*contd.*

(5) 8
(6) 8
s.8 .... 3, 140, 343
s.9 .... 8, 299
s.14(2)...................................... 38
s.18 255
s.19 .... 21, 22, 29, 335
(2) 9, 21, 336
(a). 21–22
(6) 21
s.20 29
(1A). 21, 25
s.21 .... 29, 45, 329
(1)(c) 24
(d) 24
(2) 24
(3) 24
(6) 27
s.21(A) 329
s.22 .... 32, 36, 188, 319
(1) 32, 33
(2) 28
(3) 28
(5) 28
s.23 28
s.24 .... 103, 304, 305, 308
(1) 135
(2) 135, 307
(3) 348
(4) 304
s.25(3). 156, 172
s.26 .... 4, 32, 136, 138, 169, 176, 186, 187,
191, 194, 197, 201, 202, 220, 253
(1) 6, 39, 137, 172, 186–187,
193, 194, 201, 205, 217
(1)(A) 177, 188
(b) 177
(2) 187, 193, 194, 201, 205, 208, 252, 321, 357
(a). 201, 205, 206, 233
(bb) 190, 195
(d) 43
(e). 222, 329

Local Government Act 1991 (No. 11), s.26(2)—*contd.*

(f)	163, 209
(g)	209, 222, 329
(h)	209, 210, 222, 330
(j)	163, 330
(3)	33, 39, 190, 212, 213, 268
(c)	217
(4)	146, 193, 214, 270, 274, 283, 322
(b)	146
(4)(A)	213
(5)	177, 241, 247
(b)	229, 251
(d)	252
(f)	240
(7)	159, 208
(8)	204, 267
(9)	221
(10)(b)	222
(11)	221
s.27	76, 136, 189
s.28	136
(1)	189
(2)	136, 190
(4)	190
(5)	80, 222, 224
(6)	71, 80, 195, 196, 221, 226
s.29	239, 307, 308
s.30	5, 48, 49, 239
(5)	49
(2A)	49
(2B)	49
s.31	4, 5, 82, 297–298, 300, 301, 302, 303, 305, 306, 308
(c)(i)	300
(ii)	300
(1)	310
(4)	300
(5)	302
(6)	300
(7)	305
(8)	300–301, 303
(9)	82, 301
s.32	4, 5, 82, 297–298, 301, 306, 309

Local Government Act 1991 (No. 11), s.32—*contd.*
                    (1)(c) 301
            s.33 . . . . 82, 301
            s.34 . . . . 301, 302, 303
                    (1) 303
                    (5) 303
            s.35 . . . .   4, 5, 82, 276, 297–298, 301, 302, 306, 309
                    (1) 302
                    (2) 302
            s.36 . . . . 5, 82, 301, 307, 308, 333, 346
                    (9) 307, 333
            s.37 . . . . 4, 5, 239, 308, 333, 346
                    (8) 333
                    (9) 308
            s.38 . . . . 4, 38, 39, 38, 373
                    (2) 39
            s.39 . . . . 13, 33
                    (2) 36
            s.40(a) 82
                    (b) 68
                    (c) 82, 301
            s.41 4
            s.42(5) 41
            s.43 . . . .
                    (1) 41
                    (2) 8
                    (3) 41
            s.44 . . . . 4, 5, 43, 239, 332
                    (2) 44
            s.45 . . . . 4, 41, 239, 332, 333
                    (5) 42
                    (7) 42
            s.46 . . . . 5, 44, 239
                    (6) 44
                    (8) 44
            s.47 5
            s.48 . . . . 5, 45, 239, 332
            s.49 . . . .
                    (2) 45
                    (4) 46
            s.50 . . . . 5, 43
            s.54 46
            s.55 322

Local Government Act 1991 (No. 11)—*contd.*

s.56(1)(a) 54, 321

(e)...................................... 325

(g) 326

(i)

(iii) 327

s. 57... 314

s.75(2)....................................... 11

s.76 46

s.77 46

(1) 10, 11

(2) 11

s.78 .... 13, 14

s. 82(3) 189, 250, 252

(3)(A) 257, 260, 271

(3)(B)................ 257–258, 258, 259, 261, 270

(5)(a) 250

(6) 250

(7) 250

(8)(a) 260

s.83 .... 250, 254, 332

(4) 254

s.84 .... 13, 100, 101, 102, 106

s.85 .... 239, 332

s.86 195

s.89 .... 46, 48, 239

(2) 48

(6) 48

(10) 48

s.90 51

Sched. 1 .... 21, 107, 123

Sched. 2 40

Sched. 3 .... 21, 38, 50, 87

Sched. 4 335

Local Government (Planning and Development) Acts
1963–1991.. 191, 371

Local Government (Planning and Development) Act 1976
(No. 20) 103, 237, 273, 276, 291, 293, 366

s.2 237

(7)(b) 39

s.5 .... 189, 253

s.6 28

s.13 250

Local Government (Planning and Development) Act 1976
   (No. 20)—*contd.*
   s.14 . . . . 42, 44, 45
       (4) 197, 199, 210, 238
       (8) 33, 190, 252
   s.19 255
       (1)(a) 300
       (2) 255
   s.22 240
   s.23 250
   s.25 . . . . 5, 239, 308
       (10) 51
   s.26 . . . . 43, 305, 307, 309
       (1) 305
       (3) 39, 306
       (4) 306, 306
       (5)(A) 177
       (6) 300, 301, 302
       (7)(a) 306
           (b) 306
       (8) 306
       (9) 307
   s.27 . . . . 58, 69, 73, 93, 100, 138,
                           276 *et seq.*, 309, 309, 366, 377
       (1) 277, 280
           (a). 283
           (b) 278
       (2) 277, 279, 284
       (3) 277–278, 284, 295
       (4) 280, 291
       (6) 280
           (b)(i) 281
               (I) 280
               (II) 280
               (III). 281
           (a)(i). 280
   s.28 . . . . 44, 298
       (2) 5
   s. 30. 309
       (1) 304
       (2) 304
       (5) 307
   s.36 . . . . 305, 306

Local Government (Planning and Development) Act 1976
(No. 20)—*contd.*
s.39(c) 190, 195
　　(d) 39
　　(f) 213
　　(i) 49
s.42(a) 257, 271
　　(b) 40
s.43 87
　　(1) 22, 50
　　(c) 50, 92, 93
　　(e) 21
　　(h) 28
s.46(1) 40
Local Government (Planning and Development) Act 1982 (No. 21)
ss.2–4 234
s.2 . . . . 210, 224, 229, 302, 354, 371
　　(2) 230
s.3 . . . . 253, 300, 310
s.4 . . . . 270, 300, 310, 354, 370
　　(1) 231
　　(c) 231
　　　(ii) 232, 233
s.4(2) 234
　　(3) 234
s.5 189
s.7 . . . . 10, 28, 252, 370
s.9(1) 304, 306
s.10 240
　　(2)(a) 151
　　　(b) 151
s.15(2) (a) 28
Local Government (Planning and Development) Act 1983 (No. 28)
s.3 237
s.5(2) 238
　　(11) 238
　　(12) 238
s.7(1) 238
　　(2)(e) 238
s.14 238
Local Government (Planning and Development) Act 1990
(No. 11) . . . . . . 30, 50–51, 190, 241, 308, 313 *et seq.*, 332, 338, 343, 373
Pt. III 340

Local Government (Planning and Development) Act 1990
(No. 11)—*contd.*
s.6 332
s.7 316
s.9 . . . . 5, 317, 374
   (2)(b) 317
s.10 . . . . 317, 337, 374
   (6) 318
Local Government (Planning and Development) Act 1990
(No. 11)—*contd.*
s.11 . . . . 30, 315, 321, 322
s.12 . . . . 42, 51, 315, 319, 323, 323, 329–331
   (1) 40, 323–324
s.13 . . . . 318–319, 320, 324, 374
   (2) 319, 337
s.14 319
s.15 . . . . 239, 320
s.16 321
s.17 . . . . 332, 333
s.18 . . . . 332, 333, 347
s.19 . . . . 332, 333, 347
s.20 332
s.21 . . . . 42, 332, 333
s.22 332
s.23 332
s.24 332
s.25 324
s.26 324
Sched. 1. . . . . 316, 334 *et seq.*
Sched. 2. . . . . 40, 315, 321
Sched. 3. . . . . 190, 241, 315, 323 *et seq.*, 327
Sched. 4. . . . . . . 42, 190, 241, 315, 319, 320, 322, 329 *et seq.*
Local Government (Planning and Development) Act 1992
(No. 14) 237, 257, 276, 278, 293, 307, 346, 347, 366, 377
s.3 . . . . 229, 241, 251
   (a). 240, 247
s.4(1). 239–240
s.4(3). 246, 247
s.4(5). 241
s.5 . . . . 243, 244
s.7 240
   (1) 244
s.9 . . . . 240, 245, 246, 247
   (a). 177

Local Government (Planning and Development) Act 1992
(No. 14)—*contd.*

s.10 245
s.12 248
s.14 251
s.15(1)................................... 229, 243
(2)................................... 243, 253
s. 16.............................. 160, 242, 251
s.17(1)(a) 240, 241
(b) 241
s.19 .... 58, 399
(1)(a) 300
(b)................................... 301
(3) 257, 260, 261, 270
(4) 305, 306
(e)................................... 305
(g) 277, 280, 293, 295
s.20(1)................................ 43, 44, 303
(3)................................... 306
(4)................................... 306
(5)(a) 303
(7)................................ 304, 306
s.22 .... 43, 177, 240
s.39(a)....................................... 252

Local Government (Planning and Development) Act 1993
(No. 12)................................... 51, 103

s.2(1)(b) 106, 179
(2)................................... 106
s.4 106
(2)................................... 106
s.3 14
s.5 .... 100, 101
s. 16.. 164
s.73 46
(4)(a) 46
(12) 46
(14) 46
s.85 12
s.89 12

Local Government (Reorganisation) Act 1985 (No.7)
s.9 123

Local Government (Sanitary Services) Act 1948 (No. 3)
s.34 121

Local Government (Water Pollution) Act 1977 (No. 1) 121, 192
                           s.1 192
                           s.12 121
Local Government (Water Pollution) (Amendment) Act 1990 (No. 21)
                           s.8 278
Minerals Development Acts 1940–1979 . . . . 124, 181
Minerals Development Act 1979 (No. 12)
                           s.12 140
National Monuments Act 1930 (No. 2) 122
National Monuments (Amendment) Act 1987 (No. 17)
                           s.5 327
Petroleum and Other Minerals Development Act 1960 (No. 24) 124
Postal and Telecommunications Services Act 1983 (No. 24) 142
Public Dance Halls (Ireland) Act 1935 (No. 2) . . . .
                           s.2 . . . . 311, 311
                             (2) 310
Public Health (Ireland) Act 1878 (41 & 42 Vict., c. 52)
                           s.23 324
                           s.41 366
                           s.55 16
                           s.63 15
Public Health (Ireland) (Amendment) Act 1890
    (53 & 54 Vict., c. 59) 366
Public Health Acts 1878–1885 348
Rent Restrictions Act 1946 (No. 4) 29
Roads Act 1993 (No. 14) 178, 332
                           s.4 . . . . 42, 46
                           s.6 48
                           s.18 23
                           19(6) 91
                           s.20 . . . . 23, 39
                             (1) 23
                             (2) 23
                           s.22(2) 23, 40
                                (c) 40, 43
                           s.43(2) 322
                           s. 46(1) 193, 322
                             (3) 322, 332
                           s.47 49
                             (4) 49
                                (c) 49
                           s.49 46
                           s.51 175

Roads Act 1993 (No. 14)—*contd.*
s.52(6) 49
s.70 .... 42, 43
s.73 ....
(1) 46
(2) 46
(3) 46
(5) 46
(8) 46
(15) 46
Road Traffic Act 1961(No. 24) 47
Safety Health and Welfare at Work Act 1989 (No. 7) 348
State Authorities (Development and Management) Act 1993 (No. 1)
s.2 101
(3) 101
Statutory Declarations Act 1938 (No. 37) 394
Town and Regional Planning Acts 1934 to 1939 .... 20, 367
Town and Regional Planning Act 1934 (No. 22) 371
s.15 136
s.26 135
Vocational Education Act 1930 (No. 29) 337
Waterworks Clauses Act 1847 (26 & 27 Vict., c. 93)
s.23 324
Wildlife Act 1976 (No. 39)
s.15 119

United Kingdom

Town and Country Planning Act 1990 (c. 8) 223
Town and Country Planning Act 1962 (c. 38)
s.12(3) 56
Town and County Planning Act 1971 (c. 78) 223, 225
s.52(2)(d) 96, 339

United States

National Environmental Protection Act 1969 173

TABLE OF STATUTORY INSTRUMENTS, RULES AND ORDERS

Ireland

Access to Information on the Environment Regulations 1996
(S.I. No. 185 of 1996) 3
Building Control Regulations 1991
(S.I. No. 305 of 1991) 121, 359, 377, 390
Building Control (Amendment) Regulations 1994
(S.I. No. 153 of 1994) 359
Building Regulations 1991 (S.I. No. 306
of 1991) 107, 120, 359, 389, 390, 392, 393, 395, 396, 397
Sched. 1, Pt. B 363
Building Regulations (Amendment) Regulations 1994
(S.I. No. 154 of 1994) 359
Dublin County Council (Lucan Bridge to Palmerston) Special
Amenity Area Order (Confirmation) Order 1990
(S.I. No. 59 of 1990) 39
European Communities (Environmental Impact Assessment)
Regulations 1989 (S.I. No. 349 of 1989) 87, 135, 169
art. 5 167
art. 6 87
art. 7 . . . . 156, 172
art. 8 177
art. 10(1)(c). 177
art. 23 179
(2). 179
art. 24 . . . . 18, 151, 155, 157, 169, 170, 171, 177
(1). 156, 169
art. 25 . . . . 157, 174, 175
(1). 158
(2). 173
Sched. 1 . . . . 18, 85, 87, 108, 156, 167, 169,
170, 171, 177, 261, 265
Pt. I. . . . . 179 *et seq.*
Pt. II. 180–185
Sched. 2 . . . . 157, 174–175
European Communities (Environmental Impact Assessment)
(Amendment) Regulations 1996 (S.I. No. 101 of 1996) 87, 180

European Communities (Environmental Impact Assessment)
(Motorways) Regulations 1988 (S.I. No. 221 of 1988) 184
European Communities (Major Accident Hazards of Certain
Industrial Activities) Regulations 1986
(S.I. No. 292 of 1986) 111, 149, 183
European Communities (Major Accident Hazards of Certain
Industrial Activities) (Amendment) Regulations 1989
(S.I. No. 194 of 1989) 111, 149
Sched. 1 155
European Communities (Major Accident Hazards of Certain
Industrial Activities)(Amended) Regulations 1992
(S.I. No. 21 of 1992) 111, 149
Local Government Act 1991 (Removal of Control) Regulations
1993 (S.I. No. 172 of 1993) 11
Local Government (Dublin) Act 1993 Commencement Order 1993
(S.I. No. 400 of 1993) 2, 13, 91
Local Government (Planning and Development) General Policy
Directive 1982 (S.I. No. 264 of 1982) 10, 28
Local Government (Planning and Development) General Policy
Directive 1988 (S.I. No. 317 of 1988) 10, 28
Local Government (Planning and Development) Regulations 1964
(S.I. No. 216 of 1964) 150, 272
Local Government (Planning and Development) Regulations
1977–1993 135
Local Government (Planning and Development) Regulations 1977
(S.I. No. 65 of 1977) 66, 107, 111, 113, 118, 123,
128, 131, 133, 142, 282, 394
art. 11 108
(1)(a)(iv). 343
(x) 94
art. 15 . . . . 141, 146
Sched. 3 . . . . 119, 128
Local Government (Planning and Development) (Amendment)
Regulations 1981 (S.I. No. 154 of 1981) 394
Local Government (Planning and Development) (Exempted
Development and Amendment) Regulations 1984
(S.I. No. 348 of 1984)
art. 6 282
Local Government (Planning and Development) Regulations 1990
(S.I. No. 25 of 1990) 135, 274
Sched. 1 135
Local Government (Planning and Development) (Compensation)
Regulations 1990 (S.I. No. 144 of 1990) 316

Local Government (Planning and Development) Act 1992
    Commencement Order 1992 (S.I. No. 221 of 1992) 277, 280, 309
        art. 3(3) 278
Local Government (Planning and Development) Regulations 1994
    (S.I. No. 86 of 1994) 13, 66, 84, 106, 114, 131, 133, 135, 136,
                             142, 146, 148, 155, 163, 169,
                      188, 310, 316, 343, 346, 359, 369
          Pt. I 112–113, 129
             Class 39 51
          Pt. II 123
          Pt. III 107, 123–127
          Pt. IV 117, 127–134, 135, 186, 203, 370
          Pt. VII 151
          Pt. VIII 316
          Pt. IX 18, 177, 178
          Pt. X 3, 13, 15, 17
          art. 3 . . . . 136, 148, 151, 153, 243
          art. 5 25
          art. 6 188
          arts. 8–13 . . . . 84, 107
          art. 8 . . . . 96, 107, 128, 321
          art. 9 . . . . 50, 85, 107, 108, 112, 169, 177
             (1)(b) 107
             (2)(b) 123
             (4) 107, 120
             (5) 2, 13, 91
          art. 9A 107, 120, 193
          art. 10 . . . . 107, 108–111, 126, 128, 370
             (1)(a)(i) 358
                 (ii) 116
                 (vi) 111
                 (vii) 50
                 (viii) 96, 346, 347
                 (ix) 50, 94, 116
                 (xi) 50
             (b)(iii) 40
             (c) 155
                 (i) 85, 108
             (2) 108
          art. 11 111
             (b) 129
             (1) 127, 203
             (2) 112

Local Government (Planning and Development) Regulations 1994,
art. 11—*contd.*

(3).	103, 112, 128
(4)	65, 67
(b).	127
art. 12	84
art. 13	87
art. 14	140, 142
(2).	142
art. 15	141
art. 16	142, 143
(5).	142
art. 17(1).	141
(2).	142, 143, 161
(c)	143
art. 18	149
art. 19	149, 155
art. 20	136, 149, 151
(2).	157
(b)(i)	151
(ii).	152
(3).	152, 157
art. 21	152, 153
art. 22(1)(a).	155
(b)	153
(2).	155
art. 23	150
art. 24	152, 155
(3)(b)	156
(10)(b)	155, 169
art. 25(1).	141, 156
(2)(b)	156
(3).	156
(a).	156
(20)(a).	156
art. 26(1).	141
art. 27(1).	156, 169
art. 28(2)(a).	157
(b)	157
art. 29	158
art. 30	158
art. 31	159

Local Government (Planning and Development) Regulations
 1994—*contd.*

art. 32 165
    (1).. 159
    (4).. 159
art. 33 160
    (1)............................... 150, 159–160
    (2)................................. 160, 213
    (2)(A) 160
art. 34 .... 138, 164, 188, 202
    (2)....................................... 188
art. 35 .... 161, 201, 254
art. 36 .... 4, 162
art. 36 (2)(a) 163
art. 39 .... 164, 213
art. 40 164
art. 41 165
art. 42 164
art. 43 165
art. 45–48 238
art. 49(6)(ii) 241
art. 56(1) 171, 172
art. 59 243
    (1)....................................... 244
    (2)....................................... 244
art. 64 244
art. 65 255
art. 72A 244
art. 74 249
    (2)....................................... 248
    (5)....................................... 249
art. 76 250
art. 77 250
art. 80 231
art. 81 231
art. 82 234
art. 88 151
art. 107 151
art. 109(1) 316
art. 110 317
art. 111 317
art. 112 320
art. 113 319

Local Government (Planning and Development) Regulations
1994—*contd.*
        art. 117 . . . . 18, 178
        art. 120 . . . . 18, 178
        art. 124 . . . . 19, 178
        art. 125 . . . . 19, 178
        art. 126 . . . . 19, 178
        art. 130 14
              (1)(a). 15
                (b). 15
              (2)(a). 15
                (b). 15
                (3). 15
        art. 131 15
        art. 133 16
        art. 132 18
              (d) 16
        art. 134 16
        art. 136 18
        art. 151 47–48
        art. 152–155 47
        art. 156 103–104
              (1)(a) 120
                (c)(ii). 120
              (2) 104
        art. 157 104
        art. 158 105
              (3) 105
              (4) 105
        art. 162 106
        art. 163 44
        art. 164 253
        Sched. 2 . . . . 24, 87, 92, 99, 107, 108,
                               109, 110, 111, 112–134
Local Government (Planning and Development) Regulations 1995
  (S.I. No. 69 of 1995) 84, 107, 135, 369
        art. 6 160
                (b). 160
        art. 7(a) 14
                (b). 15
        art. 9 112
              (2) 117
              (3) 117

Local Government (Planning and Development) Regulations 1996
  (S.I. No. 100 of 1996) 84, 87
North Bull Island Special Amenity Area Order 1994 (Confirmation)
  Order 1995 (S.I. No. 70 of 1995) 39
Wireless Telegraphy (Wired Broadcast Relay Licence) Regulation
  1974 (S.I. No. 67 of 1974) 47

Rules of Court

Circuit Court Rules 1950 (S.I. No. 179 of 1950)
              Ord. 67 . . . . A293 *et seq.*
Circuit Court Rules (No. 1) 1995 (S.I. No. 215 of 1995) 280, 293
Rules of the Superior Courts 1986 (S.I. No. 15 of 1986)
              Ord. 84 . . . . 257, 258, 262
                    r. 20(4) 272
              r. 22 258
              App. O 258
              Ord. 103 . . . . 291 *et seq.*
                    r. 7 296
                    r. 8 291
Rules of the Superior Courts (No. 1) 1996 (S.I. No. 5 of 1996) 291

United Kingdom

Town and Country Planning General Development Order 1973 96
Town and Country Planning (Use Classes) Order 1987
  (S.I. No. 764 of 1987) 67, 129, 131

Chapter 1

THE PLANNING AUTHORITY

The planning authority is the fulcrum of the system of development planning and control and the quality of its decision-making has an enormous impact on the built environment. There are two primary aspects to its functions – the promotion of development and development control. The marriage of these two functions contains its own inherent tensions. Although the emphasis at the time of the introduction of the Local Government (Planning and Development) Act 1963 by the then Minister for Local Government, Mr Neil Blayney, was on the promotion of development, planning authorities were subsequently criticised for failing to exercise their developmental functions under the new legislation to the full.[1]

In its long title, the 1963 Act is described as:

> "An Act to make provision, in the interest of the common good for the proper planning and development of cities, towns and other areas, whether urban or rural (including the preservation and improvement of the amenities thereof), to make certain provisions with respect to acquisition of land, to appeal the town and regional planning acts, 1934 and 1939, and certain other enactments and to make provisions for other matters connected with the matters aforesaid."

The 1963 Act came into operation on October 1, 1964, and as one commentator put it, "overnight local authorities became planning authorities" with all of the attendant shock to the system that this image suggests.[2] The planning legislation was initially perceived merely as a licensing code under which development which was considered to be contrary to proper planning and development was prevented or permitted subject to restrictions. In more recent times, planning authorities have, assisted by the operation of fiscal incentives, assumed a greater developmental role.

1.1.1 Definition and functions of the planning authority

"Planning authority" is defined under section 2(2) of the 1963 Act as:

> "(a) in the case of a county exclusive of any borough or urban district therein, the council of the county,
> (b) in the case of a county or other borough, the corporation of the borough, and
> (c) in the case of an urban district, the council of the district."

---

[1]   See Bannon, *Planning – The Irish Experience* (1989), pp.127–138.
[2]   O'Sullivan, Society of Young Solicitor's Lecture No. 145.

The Local Government (Dublin) Act 1993 provided for the creation of three new administrative counties to replace the administrative county of Dublin. It simultaneously provided for the establishment of a council for each of these counties, to be described as Fingal, Dun Laoghaire–Rathdown and South Dublin.[3] Article 9(5) of the 1994 Regulations provides that development which any of these county councils commences within the functional area of another of these councils before December 31, 1995 is exempted development.

The main functions of the planning authority are as follows:

Strategic planning and development: Planning authorities are responsible for the strategic planning of development in their administrative areas, which they achieve by the adoption and implementation of a development plan or plans for their area. Strategic planning under the development plan involves the allocation of particular areas of land for future development in accordance with zoning objectives and the adoption of short-term and long-term proposals for infra-structural services intended to facilitate such development. Special amenity area orders are another strategic planning tool used to protect high amenity areas and to introduce tighter controls on development.

Development control: To ensure that development, including changes in the type of activity which take place on land, or in a particular structure, are carried out in conformity with the provisions of the development plan or any special amenity area order for the relevant area, individual development proposals are subject to a permit procedure. On an application for permission being made, the planning authority may refuse or grant planning permission, usually subject to conditions which seek to remove or reduce the negative aspects of the development in planning terms.

Appeals: Planning authorities have an important role in the appeals process. They are automatically parties in any appeal against their decision to grant or refuse permission.

Enforcement: The powers of the planning authority to enforce breaches of the planning code are exercised principally to ensure compliance with the obligation to obtain planning permission or with the terms and conditions of any permission in existence.

Provision of Access to Information: Planning authorities are required to maintain a public register containing the planning history for all land within their functional area and, in particular, must make available documentation concerning current planning applications. Information must also be made available concerning certain types of development intended to be carried out by the planning authority itself

---

[3]   See Local Government (Dublin) Act, 1993 Commencement Order, 1993 (S.I. No. 400 of 1993).

within its own functional area as the planning authority is exempt from the obligation to obtain planning permission for such development.[4]

Environmental Assessment: Planning authorities are responsible for the implementation of the E.U. principle of the "prevention of pollution at source" by assessing environmental impact statements submitted with planning applications for certain categories of large-scale development. Such an assessment must not involve a consideration of the control of the risk of pollution from the proposed development where an integrated pollution control licence (IPC) must be obtained from the Environmental Protection Agency.

Payment of Compensation: Planning authorities are required to pay compensation in certain limited circumstances where planning permission is refused or where conditions are attached to a planning permission which restrict the development of property.

Development: Planning authorities are expressly empowered to acquire and dispose of land, to provide sites for development and to develop land themselves. They are, however, precluded from carrying out development in material contravention of their own development plans.

1.1.2 The planning register

Planning authorities must maintain a register for all land within their functional area and must make such entries and corrections as are required by the Act or Regulations.[5] The register, which incorporates a map, must be made available for inspection at the offices of the planning authority during office hours. A certified copy of an entry in the register is regarded as prima facie evidence of the entry without proof of signature or producing the register itself. It is possible to obtain a copy of an entry on payment to the planning authority of the prescribed fee.

Any person may inspect the planning file for a particular application at the office of the planning authority during office hours. Each application has an individual file which is cross-referenced according to its planning register reference number to location maps in the planning office. A number of different reference numbers may exist for the same site, depending on the number of applications which have been made, and often the planning authority will maintain separate maps for different periods of years.

---

[4] 1994 Regulations, Pt. X. See generally, Access to Information on the Environment Regulations 1996 (S.I. No. 185 of 1996). See recently, *Cullen v. Wicklow County Manager and Wicklow County Council*, unreported, High Court, June 13, 1996, in which McCracken J. held that the chairman of Wicklow County Council was entitled under s.27 of the County Management Act 1940, to have access to documents on the Law Agent's file relating to a site which was the subject of enforcement proceedings and which it was proposed to re-zone under the second draft development plan for Blessington. McCracken J. also held that there was no requirement that the request for information be in writing.

[5] 1963 Act, s.8.

1.1.3 Contents of planning register

The planning authority is obliged to enter particulars of the following matters in the register[6]:

(a) Applications for full or outline permission, for an approval or for the retention of an unauthorised structure or unauthorised use relating to or for development within their area.[7] Particulars must be entered within a period of seven days of receipt of the application. A copy of any drawings, maps, particulars, evidence, environmental impact statement, other written study or further information received or obtained by the planning authority from the applicant in accordance with the regulations must also be available for inspection.

(b) Any submissions or observations in writing on the planning application which are received by the planning authority.[8]

(c) A copy of any report prepared by or on behalf of the planning authority on the planning application, *e.g.* the reports of the planning officer and traffic engineer.[9]

(d) The decision of the planning authority and a copy of the notification of the decision given to the applicant on any planning applications referred to under (a) above and the date of the decision. Particulars must be entered within seven days of the decision.[10]

(e) The date and effect of any decision on appeal of the Board in respect of any of the applications referred to under (a) above. The entry must be made within seven days of the date of the decision.[11]

(f) Notices of revocation or modification of planning permission, stating the reasons for which they are given.

(g) Enforcement notices under sections 31, 32, 35 of the 1963 Act.

(h) Notices requiring removal or alteration of a structure under section 26 of the 1963 Act.

(i) Notices requiring discontinuance of use under section 37 of the 1963 Act.

(j) Agreements under section 38 of the 1963 Act regulating the development or use of land.

(k) Notices under section 44 of the 1963 Act requiring the removal or alteration of a hedge.

(l) Tree preservation orders under section 45 of the 1963 Act.

---

[6] The author wishes to acknowledge that the list which follows is merely an updating of the list which appears in Walsh, *Planning and Development Law* (2nd ed., Keane R. ed.).

[7] 1963 Act, s.41 and 1994 Regulations, art. 36.

[8] 1994 Regulations, art. 36.

[9] *ibid.*

[10] 1963 Act, s.41.

[11] *ibid.*

(m) Conservation orders under section 46 of the 1963 Act.

(n) Right of way agreements over public land under section 47 of the 1963 Act.

(o) Rights of way created by order of the planning authority under section 48 of the 1963 Act.

(p) Agreements for the planting of trees, shrubs and other plants under section 50 of the 1963 Act.

(q) Statements in relation to the payment of compensation made under section 9 of the Local Government (Planning and Development) Act 1990.

(r) Acquisition notices under section 25 of the Local Government (Planning and Development) Act 1976, the date and effect of any decision on appeal against a notice, and the particulars of any order made.

(s) Where any notice under sections 30, 31, 32, 35, 36, 37 or 44 of the 1963 Act is withdrawn, particulars of the fact that it was withdrawn.[12]

(t) A copy of any environmental impact statement submitted with the application.

The documents must be available for public inspection from the time of their receipt until the application or any appeal relating to it has been determined. Where permission or approval is granted, the period for inspection is extended until the life of the planning permission has expired.[13]

1.2 POWERS, FUNCTIONS AND DUTIES OF THE PLANNING AUTHORITY

1.2.1 The doctrine of *ultra vires*

Planning authorities are bound by the doctrine of *ultra vires* although recent local government legislation has attempted to put the exercise of their powers on a broader footing.[14] The doctrine of *ultra vires* might "fitly be described as the central principle of administrative law",[15] and means essentially that a planning authority or other administrative body cannot act in excess of the authority conferred on it by law. A classic summary statement of the principle is contained in the judgment of Lord Radcliffe in *Smith v. East Elloe Rural District Council*,[16] where he stated:

> "Of course, it is well known that courts of law have always exercised certain authority to restrain the abuse of statutory powers. Such powers are not conferred

---

[12] See 1976 Act, s.28(2).
[13] The availability of the planning file on a particular application where an appeal has been made is considered below at para. 9.2.5.
[14] See Local Government Act 1991, ss.6 to 8, considered below at para. 1.2.4.
[15] Wade, *Administrative Law* (7th ed., 1994), p.41.
[16] [1956] A.C. 736; quoted with approval by O'Hanlon J. in *Sharpe (P. & F.) Ltd v. Dublin City and County Manager* [1989] I.R. 701.

for the private advantage of their holders. they are given for certain limited purposes, which the holders are not entitled to depart from; and if the authority that confers them prescribes, explicitly or by implication, certain conditions as to their exercise, those conditions ought to be adhered to. It is, or may be, an abuse of power not to observe the conditions. It is certainly an abuse of power to seek to exercise it when the statute relied upon does not truly confer it, and the invalidity of the act does not depend in any way upon the question whether the person concerned knows or does not know that he is acting *ultra vires*. It is an abuse of power to exercise it for a purpose different from that for which it is entrusted to the holder, not the less because he may be acting ostensibly for the authorised purpose. Probably most of the recognised grounds of invalidity could be brought under this head: the introduction of illegitimate considerations, the rejection of legitimate ones, manifest unreasonableness, arbitrary or capricious conduct, the motive of personal advantage or the gratification of personal ill-will."

The powers vested in the planning authority under the provisions of the planning code must, as a general rule, be exercised for planning purposes and must not be deployed to achieve objectives of the local authority relating to other codes although, in practice, some local authority functions may overlap different codes.[17]

A planning authority must not fetter its discretion to exercise its statutory powers. In *Greendale Building Company v. Dublin County Council*,[18] Henchy J. stated:

"The general rule is that a plea of estoppel of any kind cannot prevail as an answer to a well-founded claim that something done by a public body in breach of a statutory duty or limitation of function is *ultra vires*."

There are a number of specific applications of this rule to the exercise of the powers of the planning authority. A representation by an official of a planning authority to a developer that a building which he is erecting amounts to an exempted development cannot bind the planning authority as no power is given to planning authorities to decide whether a particular development is or is not an exempted development.[19] Similarly, a representation by an inspector or other official of a planning authority that planning permission will be granted for a proposed development cannot fetter the discretion of the authority to grant or refuse permission. The planning authority is restricted to considering the proper planning and development of its area in adjudicating on planning applications.[20] If a planning authority was bound by a

---

[17] See for example, *R. v. Hillingdon B.C., ex p. Royco Homes Ltd* [1974] 1 Q.B. 720 (imposition of a condition on planning permission which restricted the occupants of houses to those persons on the local authority waiting list held to be *ultra vires* the authority's powers *qua* planning authority; as an example of the duplication of controls, see *Ladbroke (Rentals) Ltd v. Secretary of State for the Environment* [1981] J.P.L. 427 (which concerned the overlap of powers for the restriction of opening hours under planning and gaming legislation).

[18] [1977] I.R. 256.

[19] *Dublin Corporation v. McGrath*, unreported, High Court, McMahon J., November 17, 1978. Such a power is vested in An Bord Pleanála under the 1963 Act, s.5.

[20] 1963 Act, s.26(1). As to the liability of planning authorities arising from the grant of planning permission, see para. 8.6.9. below.

representation that it would grant permission for a particular development, third parties would effectively be deprived of their statutory entitlement to object to the granting of permission. Nor can estoppel operate to prevent or hinder the discretion to serve an enforcement notice.[21]

1.2.2 Executive and reserved functions

The functions of the planning authority may be divided into those exercisable by the manager of the planning authority, described as "executive" functions, and those which may be implemented only by a resolution of the elected members of the planning authority, known as "reserved" functions.[22] Certain functions of the planning authority are expressly stated to be "reserved functions". Any function of the planning authority which is not specified as being a reserved function is an executive function.[23]

Section 4 of the City and County Management (Amendment) Act 1955 allows the elected members of a local authority to exercise a degree of control over their officials in the performance of their executive functions. Section 4(1) provides as follows:

> "Subject to the provisions of this section, a local authority may by resolution require any particular act, matter or thing specifically mentioned in the resolution and which the local authority or the manager can lawfully do or effect to be done or effected in the performance of the executive functions of the local authority."

While the intention of the legislature to apply section 4 of the City and County Management (Amendment) Act 1955 to decisions on planning applications was confirmed by the Supreme Court in *Sharpe (P. & F.) Ltd v. Dublin City and County Manager*,[24] it seems that in practice the provision may be inoperable, because of the impossibility of obtaining a decision from the elected members of the planning authority which may be said to have been reached in a judicial manner. Although section 4 has in the past frequently been used by councillors to compel the manager of the planning authority to grant permission for particular development proposals, in *Kenny Homes v. Galway City and County Manager and Galway Corporation*,[25] Blayney J. expressed the view that the form of such resolutions does not enable the councillors to take into account all of the options available as to any conditions which might be attached to a grant of permission. He suggested that section 4 can only be resorted to by the elected members to compel the performance of executive functions which do not have to be exercised in a judicial manner.

---

21   *Southend-on-Sea Corporation v. Hodgson (Wickford) Ltd* [1961] 2 All E.R. 46 (borough engineer incorrectly represented that a site enjoyed existing-use rights as a builder's yard).

22   Financial provisions affecting planning authorities are contained in Pt. II of the 1963 Act.

23   See the definition of "reserved functions" under s.2 and s.17 of the County Management Act 1940. See further Keane, *The Law of Local Government in the Republic of Ireland*, pp.18–31.

24   [1989] I.R. 701.

25   [1995] I.R. 178.

1.2.3 Ancillary powers of planning authority

Section 6 of the 1963 Act enables the planning authority to exercise such powers of examination, investigation and survey as may be necessary for the performance of any of their planning functions or of any of their other functions which are affected by the performance of their planning function. In particular, the planning authority is empowered to carry out examinations of tourist potential, land use, traffic, sociological and demographic surveys.

Section 7 of the 1963 Act describes the methods of service of notices or copy orders under the planning code. A person may be served in the following ways:

- where it is addressed to him by name, by delivering it to him,
- by leaving it at the address at which he ordinarily resides,[26] or in a case in which an address for service has been furnished, at that address,
- by sending it by post in a prepaid registered letter addressed to him at the address at which he ordinarily resides, or, in a case in which an address for service has been furnished, at that address,
- where the address at which he ordinarily resides cannot be ascertained by reasonable enquiry and the notice or copy is so required or authorised to be given or served in respect of any land or premises, by delivering it to some person over 16 years of age resident or employed on such land or premises or by affixing it in a conspicuous position on or near such land or premises.

Where the owner or occupier cannot be ascertained by reasonable enquiry, the notice may be addressed to "the owner" or "the occupier", without naming him. Where a notice or copy of an order is served on or given to a person by affixing it in a conspicuous position on or near the land or premises to which it relates, a copy of the notice or order must be published within the following two weeks in at least one newspaper circulating in the area in which the person is last known to have resided.[27] There is provision also for the Minister or An Bord Pleanála to dispense with service of a notice or a copy order.[28]

A planning authority may serve a notice on the occupier of any land or on any person receiving rent from the land, either on his own behalf or for some other person, requiring him to give details of his interest in the land and the name and address of every person who has an interest in the lands.[29] The information must

---

[26] A company registered under the Companies Acts 1908 to 1959, is deemed to be ordinarily resident at its registered office. Every other body corporate and every unincorporated body is seen to be ordinarily resident at its principal office or place of business.

[27] It is an offence for any person to remove, damage or deface such a notice without lawful authority during the period of three months after it has been affixed: 1963 Act, s.7(5).

[28] 1963 Act, s.7(6) as amended by 1976 Act, s.43(2).

[29] 1963 Act, s.9.

be furnished to the planning authority within the period specified in the notice which should not allow less than 14 days.[30]

1.2.4 Powers under the Local Government Act 1991

Concerns about the *vires* of local authorities to do certain things for which no express statutory authority was conferred was one of the principle factors which led to the enactment of the Local Government Act 1991.

Section 6 confers a general competence on local authorities to:

> "engage in such activities or do such things . . . as it considers necessary or desirable to promote the interests of the local community."

A decision by a local authority under section 6 to exercise any of its functions (other than the provision of services of the local authority) is a reserved function. A planning authority is not entitled to perform any function under section 6 which is conferred on the authority by any other provision of the 1991 Act, the planning code or under any other enactment. More specific powers are conferred by section 6(2), "without prejudice to the generality" of subsection (1). These include powers to:

- carry out and maintain works of any kind,
- provide, maintain, preserve or restore land, structures of any kind or facilities
- fit out, furnish or equip any building, structure or facility for particular purposes,
- provide utilities, equipment or materials for particular purposes,
- provide any service or other thing or engage in any activity likely to be of benefit to the local community.

Section 7 of the 1991 Act provides that a local authority must have regard to a number of considerations in performing its statutory functions[31]:

- the resources available to it and the need to secure the most beneficial, effective and efficient use of those resources.
- the need to maintain adequately its essential services and to ensure that a reasonable balance is achieved between its functional programmes.
- the need for co-operation with and the co-ordination of its activities with related activities of other local authorities and public authorities so as to ensure efficiency and economy.
- the need for consultation with other local authorities and public authorities in appropriate cases.

---

[30] Failure to comply with the notice or the making of a statement in writing which is false or misleading in a material respect to the knowledge of the person served constitutes an offence: 1963 Act, s.9(2).

[31] Local Government Act 1991, s.7.

— policies and objectives of the government or any government minister which affect or relate to its functions.[32]

Section 8 of the 1991 Act endeavours to remove any doubts as to the *vires* or validity of any action taken by a local authority which is ancillary to the performance of the functions conferred on it by the 1991 Act or any other enactment. Section 8(1) provides:

> "A local authority may do anything which is ancillary, supplementary or incidental to or consequential on or necessary to give full effect to, or which will facilitate or is conducive to the performance of, a function conferred on it by this or any other enactment or which can advantageously be performed by the authority in conjunction with the performance of such a function."

1.2.5 Policy directives and guidelines

The Minister is obliged to issue general policy directives to which planning authorities and An Bord Pleanála are obliged to have regard.[33] Policy directives have been issued in relation to large scale retail shopping development and the air quality standard for suspended particulates.[34] The Department of the Environment also issued important guidelines for planning authorities in 1980 on the exercise of their functions. More recently, draft guidelines have been issued by the Department on development plan and development control policies in relation to telecommunications.[35]

1.3 DEVELOPMENT BY THE PLANNING AUTHORITY

1.3.1 Development powers

Planning authorities have general powers to develop or secure the development of land. They also enjoy specific powers under section 77(1) of the 1963 Act to:

---

[32] The consideration of these matters does not affect or diminish the obligation of the planning authority to perform any of its statutory functions.

The extent of the obligation to "have regard to" government policy was considered by the High Court in *Glencar Explorations Plc. v. Mayo County Council* [1993] 2 I.R. 237, in which Blayney J. stated that the County Council could not be said to have had regard to government mining policy where it adopted as part of its Development Plan a policy which was diametrically opposed to that policy.

[33] Local Government (Planning and Development) Act 1982 Act, s.7.

[34] Local Government (Planning and Development) General Policy Directives (S.I. No. 264 of 1982 and S.I. No. 317 of 1988).

[35] The draft guidelines place strong emphasis on the planning authority's obligation to have regard to national policy – "The government's telecommunications policy aims to place ireland in the top quartile of OECD economies as regards the availability, price and quality of telecommunications services in order to promote industrial and commercial development and for the enhancement of social exchange and mobility." See further, Casey, "Planning and Telecommunication Masts: Some Recent Issues" (1996) IPELJ 3.

(a) Secure, facilitate and control the improvement of the frontage of any public road by widening, opening, enlarging or otherwise improving;
(b) develop any land in the vicinity of any road or bridge which it is proposed to improve or construct;
(c) provide areas with roads and such services and works as may be needed for development;
(d) provide areas of convenient shape for development;
(e) secure or carry out, as respects obsolete areas, the development or renewal thereof and the provision therein of open spaces;
(f) secure the preservation of any view or prospect, any structure or natural physical feature, any trees subject to a tree preservation order, any site of geological, ecological or archaeological interest or any flora or fauna subject to a conservation order.

The powers of compulsory acquisition vested in local authorities may be exercised by planning authorities in connection with any "land" referred to under section 77(1).[36] Planning authorities no longer require Ministerial consent to appropriate for planning purposes, land which had previously been acquired for other purposes under local government legislation.[37] Land which has been acquired or appropriated for planning purposes may be sold, leased or exchanged subject to such conditions as may be necessary to secure its best use, or to ensure that any structures which have been built or intended to be built on the land.

The consent of the Minister is only required for any sale, lease or exchange where the price or rent, or what is obtained by the planning authority on the exchange, is not the best reasonably obtainable, or where the development proposed for the land would be in material contravention of the development plan.[38] If a planning authority does not require any land which has been acquired or appropriated for planning purposes, for immediate use, they may lease the land temporarily. Neither the provisions of the Landlord and Tenant (Amendment) Act 1980, or of the Housing (Private Rented Dwellings) Act 1982, apply to such temporary leases. This protects planning authorities from claims from tenants for loss of entitlements to a new lease.[39]

Section 77(2) of the 1963 Act enables planning authorities to play a very active role in development. They may provide sites for the establishment or relocation of industries, businesses (including hotels, motels and guest-houses), dwellings, offices, shops, schools, churches and other community facilities. In

---

[36] Compulsory acquisition powers are vested in local authority under The Local Government Act (Ireland) 1898, s.10 as amended by the Local Government (No. 2) Act 1960, s.11, s.86: see *Leinster Importing Co. Ltd v. Dublin Co. Council*; *Movie News Ltd v. Galway County Council*.
[37] See Local Government Act 1991 (Removal of Control) Regulations 1993 (S.I. No. 172 of 1993).
[38] 1963 Act, s.75(2)
[39] See Nowlan, *A Guide to Planning Legislation*, (1988), p.103, n.3.

addition, they may provide the buildings themselves.[40] The planning authority is also entitled to provide any services which they consider ancillary to any site or structure provided. It may enter into an arrangement with any person or body for the development or management of land in connection with any of their functions under the 1963 Act.

1.3.2 Cables, wires and pipelines

Planning authorities are authorised, with the consent of the owner and occupier of the land in question to place, erect or construct cables, wires and pipelines (other than water pipes, sewers and drains), and any apparatus incidental to such cables, wires and pipelines, on, under or over the land.[41] No consent is required where the land forms part of the public road. They may also inspect, repair, alter or renew, any cables, wires or pipelines which have been installed by them, from time to time, and may also remove them at any time.[42]

The purpose of these authorisations is to facilitate the construction or erection of commercial pipelines and cables. The planning authority is entitled to permit the use of any cables, wires or pipelines installed by them subject to such conditions and changes as they consider appropriate.[43] These are licensable under section 89 of the 1993 Act where they run on, under, over or along a public road.

1.3.3 Application of exempted development provisions to local authority development

Development undertaken by local authorities within their own areas is exempt from the obligation to obtain planning permission.[44] Where development is carried out within the area of another local authority, permission is generally required. However, no permission is required for the construction of a new road

---

[40] Those buildings which may be provided are listed: factory buildings, office premises, shop premises, dwellings, amusement parks and structures for the purpose of entertainment, caravan parks, buildings for the purpose of providing accommodation, meals and refreshments, buildings for providing trade and professional services and advertisement structures, buildings or other structures for the purposes of providing homes or shelters for stray or unwanted dogs and cats. Sites for these types of buildings may also be provided by the planning authority.

[41] 1993 Act, s.85. Planning authorities are also authorised, again with the consent of the owner and of the occupier of the structure affected, to attach to a structure any bracket or other fixture required for the carrying or support of any cable, wire or pipeline placed, erected or constructed by the authority. They may also erect and maintain notices which indicate the position of cables, wires or pipelines which have been installed by them, and may affix such notices to a structure with the consent of the owner and occupier.

In each of the cases referred to where the consent of an owner or occupier is required, the refusal of consent may be appealed by the planning authority to An Bord Pleanála which may determine that the consent has been unreasonably witheld, in which case it will be treated as having been given.

[42] Any works necessary for the purposes are exempted under the 1963 Act, s.4(1)(f).

[43] See Nowlan, *op. cit.*, pp.114–115.

[44] 1963 Act, s.4.

or for the maintenance or improvement of an existing road which is outside the administrative boundary of the authority effecting the development.[45] A local authority is also entitled to carry out development outside its own area without applying for planning permission where the development comprises "works for the purpose of inspecting, repairing, renewing, altering or removing any sewers, mains, pipes, cables, overhead wires, or other apparatus, including the breaking open of any street or other land for that purpose".[46] The wording of section 4(1)(f) does not authorise the carrying out of development for the first time.

The Local Government (Dublin) Act 1993 provided for the creation of three new administrative counties to replace the administrative county of Dublin.[47] It simultaneously provided for the establishment of a council for each of these counties, to be described as Fingal, Dun Laoghaire-Rathdown and South Dublin. Article 9(5) of the 1994 Regulations provided that development which any of these county councils commenced within the functional area of another of these councils before December 31, 1995 was exempted development.

While the scope of the exemptions granted to local authorities under section 4(1) of the 1963 Act for development within their own functional areas is very wide indeed, local authorities are nonetheless restricted by the obligation imposed by section 39 of the 1963 Act not to effect any development in their area which would contravene materially the development plans. It is perhaps curious that a local authority is not prevented from carrying out exempted development in the area of another authority which is in material contravention of the development plan for that area. In a number of cases, injunctions have been granted to restrain local authorities from effecting development in material contravention of their own development plan.[48]

Further democratisation of public sector development was brought about by judicial decisions on a number of controversial interpretative centres the development of which had been commenced by the Commissioners of Public Works.[49] Section 78 of the 1963 Act had given the Minister power to make regulations which would require public notification of certain specified classes of development to be carried out by local authorities so that interested members of the public could lodge objections, but no such regulations were made until the Local Government (Planning and Development) Regulations 1994.[50] As originally envisaged, these Regulations would have required the consent of the Minister

---

[45]   1963 Act, s.4(1)(e).

[46]   This type of development is also exempted when carried out by statutory undertakers.

[47]   The remaining provision of this Act came into force on January 1, 1994: see S.I. No. 400 of 1993.

[48]   See para. 2.3.1, below.

[49]   Until the decision of the Supreme Court in *Howard v. The Commissioners of Public Works* [1994] 1 I.R. 101, it was believed that State authorities enjoyed the benefit of an exemption from the obligation to obtain planning permission by implication from s.84 of the 1963 Act, which has since been repealed.

[50]   Pt. X of the 1994 Regulations deals with notification requirements.

before the local authority could proceed with any development in relation to which an objection was made. This requirement for the consent of the Minister was subsequently dropped by section 3 of the Local Government (Planning and Development) Act 1993 which substituted a new enabling provision which required the preparation of a report by the local authority to be submitted to its elected members.[51]

1.3.4 Local authority development to which notification requirements apply

Article 130 of the 1994 Regulations provides that the requirement of notification applies to the following classes of development to be carried out by or on behalf of local authorities within their own functional areas:

(a) the construction or erection of a house or other dwelling;

(b) the construction of a new road or the widening or realignment of an existing road, where the length of the new road or of the widened or realigned portion of the existing road, as the case may be, would be:
    (i)   in the case of a road in an urban area, 100 metres or more, or
    (ii) in the case of a road in any other area, 1 kilometre or more;

(c) the construction of a bridge or tunnel;

(d) the construction or erection of pumping stations, treatment works, holding tanks or outfall facilities for waste water or storm water;

(e) the construction or erection of water intake or treatment works, overground aquaducts, or dams or other installations designed to hold water or to store it on a long-term basis;

(f) drilling for water supplies;

(g) the construction of a swimming pool;

(h) the use of land, or the construction or erection of any installation or facility, for the disposal of waste;

(i) the use of land as a burial ground;

(j) the construction or erection of a fire station, a library or a public toilet; and

(k) any other development, the estimated cost of which exceeds £50,000, not being–
    (i)   development of a class specified in the foregoing paragraphs, or
    (ii) development consisting of the provision of sites pursuant to section 13 of the Housing Act 1988, or
    (iii) development consisting of the laying underground of sewers, mains, pipes or other apparatus.[52]

---

[51]   See 1963 Act, s.78 as amended.
[52]   This paragraph was substituted by the 1995 Regulations (S.I. No. 69 of 1995), art. 7(a).

1.3.5 Categories of development to which notification requirements do not apply

The requirements of Part X of the Regulations do not apply to proposed development by a local authority outside its own area with three exceptions:

- Development proposed to have been carried out by one of the new county councils established by section 11 of the Local Government (Dublin) Act 1993 within the functional area[53] of another county council established by that section where such development was proposed to have been carried out before December 31, 1995.
- Road development specified under art. 130(1)(b) (referred to above).[54]
- The construction of a bridge or tunnel.[55]

Article 130(3) provides that the notification requirements under Part X do not apply to the following categories of proposed development whether within or outside the area of the authority:

- development consisting of works of maintenance or repair,
- development necessary for dealing in a prompt manner with any situation which the manager considers to be an emergency situation,
- any variation or modification of proposed development required by the Minister for which an Environmental Impact Statement has been submitted and which the Minister has certified,
- any development required by any other statutory provision to comply with procedures for the purpose of giving effect to the 1985 Directive on Environmental Assessment,
- works which the local authority are required by or under statute or by order of a court to undertake,
- the construction of a reservoir to which the requirements of section 63 of the Public Health (Ireland) Act 1878 apply.

1.3.6 Notice of proposed development

A local authority must publish notice of a proposed development to which Article 130 applies in a newspaper circulating in the area in which the proposed development would be located.[56] The notice must indicate the location, nature and extent of the proposed development. It should state that plans and particulars

---

[53] The "functional area" of a county council is treated as the area of the county exclusive of any borough or urban district contained within that area.
[54] 1994 Regulations, art. 130(2)(a) as inserted by the 1995 Regulations, art. 7(b). It is appropriate that the notification requirements should apply in this case as road development carried out by a road authority outside its own functional area is exempted under the 1963 Act, s.4(1)(e).
[55] *ibid.*
[56] 1994 Regulations, art. 131.

of the proposed development will be available for inspection at the offices of the local authority at specified times for a period of not less than one month from the date of publication of the notice. It should also indicate that submissions or observations of a planning nature on the proposed development may be made in writing to the local authority before a specified date (not less than two weeks after the expiration of the period during which the plans and particulars were on display).

The local authority must notify certain specified bodies, depending on the interests affected, of the proposed development. Plans and particulars of the proposed development should accompany any such notice. The relevant bodies are:

- The Arts Council, Bord Failte Éireann and An Taisce, where it appears to the local authority that the proposed development would be located in an area of special amenity, whether or not a special amenity order has been made,
- Bord Failte Éireann, where it appears to the local authority that the proposed development would affect the value of any tourist amenity or tourist amenity works,
- The Arts Council, Bord Failte Éireann, The Commissioners of Public Works in Ireland, The National Monuments Advisory Council and An Taisce, where it appears to the local authority that the proposed development would affect any cave, site, feature or other object of archeological, geological, scientific or historical interest or any building of artistic, architectural or historical interest,
- any local authority which would appear to be affected by the proposed development,
- The Irish Aviation Authority, where it appears to the local authority that the proposed development might endanger or interfere with the safety of aircraft or the safe and efficient navigation of aircraft,
- the appropriate regional fisheries board, where it appears to the local authority that the proposed development might give rise to appreciable discharges of polluting matters to waters,
- the appropriate health board, where it appears to the local authority that the proposed development might have significant effects on public health,
- The Commissioners of Public Works in Ireland, where it appears to the local authority that the proposed development might have significant effects on nature conservation,
- The Shannon Free Airport Development Company Limited, in the case of a proposed development which would be located in its functional area where the obligation to notify Bord Failte Éireann also arises.

Article 133 of the 1994 Regulations provides that the local authority shall make the following plans and particulars available for inspection by members of the public for a period of at least one month from the date of publication of the newspaper notice relating to the proposed development:

- a document describing the nature and extent of the proposed development and its principal features,
- a location map, drawn to a scale of not less than 1:10,560 and marked or coloured so as to identify clearly the land on which it is proposed to carry out the proposed development,
- a site layout plan, drawn to a scale of not less than 1:500, showing the boundary of the site on which it is proposed to carry out the proposed development and buildings or other structures, and roads or other features, in the vicinity of the site, and
- such other plans and drawings, drawn to a scale of not less than 1:100, as are necessary to describe the proposed development.

A scale of 1:2500 is sufficient for plans and drawings submitted in connection with road development to which the notification requirements apply and a scale of 1:200 is required for the construction of bridges and tunnels.[57]

1.3.7 Report and decision of authority

After the expiration of the period for the making of submissions, the local authority is obliged to prepare a report on the proposed development.[58] The report describes the nature and extent of the proposed development and its principal features. It evaluates the likely implications, if any, of the proposed development on the proper planning and development of the area in which the development would be located. The report is also intended to summarise the planning issues raised by the various submissions made by interested persons and bodies, as well as the response of the local authority to those submissions. Finally, the report should indicate whether it is proposed to proceed with the proposed development, either with or without variations or modifications, or not to proceed. The report is then submitted to the members of the local authority who may direct the local authority not to proceed with the proposed development, if they see fit, provided that the development concerned does not constitute "works which the local authority are required by or under statute or by order of a court to undertake".[59] Notice of the local authority's

---

[57] 1994 Regulations, art. 133(d) as inserted by art. 8 of the 1995 Regulations.

[58] 1994 Regulations, art. 134.

[59] See City and County Management (Amendment Act) 1955, s.3. In *East Wicklow Conservation Community Ltd v. Wicklow County Council* [1995] 2 I.L.R.M. 16 (appeal pending) Costello J. held that as the local authority were under a statutory obligation under s.55 of the Public Health (Ireland) Act 1878 to provide fit places for the deposit of domestic refuse, the Manager's decision to proceed with plans for a landfill site at Ballynagran, County Wicklow, could not validly be made the subject of a direction by the elected members under s.3 of the 1995 Act. Section 3 excludes from its ambit "works which the local authority are required by or under statute or by order of a court to undertake".

decision to proceed or not to proceed with the proposed development must be sent to each of the bodies notified pursuant to Article 132 of the 1994 Regulations and to any other persons or bodies who have made submissions or observations.

Article 136 provides that the notification requirements under Part X do not apply to proposed developments where the members of the local authority were informed of the works involved pursuant to section 2(7) of the City and County Management (Amendment) Act 1955 before June 15, 1994, *i.e.* the date on which Part X came into operation. Nor does Part X apply to a proposed development which was commenced before December 31, 1994 or, in the case of a proposed development which was to be carried out by an agent of the local authority, where a contract for the carrying out of the development was signed before December 31, 1994.

1.3.8 Environmental Impact Assessment

An environmental impact statement must be prepared by or on behalf of a local authority for any development to which Part IX of the Local Government (Planning and Development) Regulations 1994 applies and which is "specified development" under article 24 of the E.C. (Environmental Impact Assessment) Regulations 1989.[60] A project which amounts to specified development loses its exempted development status under the planning code. In addition, the Minister must request an EIS to be submitted where the development proposed would have been specified development were it not for the fact that it falls short of the threshold laid down for that type of development under the First Schedule to the 1989 Regulations, if the Minister is of the opinion that the development would be likely to have significant effects on the environment".[61]

The EIS must be made available for inspection and for purchase for a period of at least one month from the date of publication of a newspaper notice of the application.[62] The local authority must apply to the Minister for certification, enclosing three copies of the EIS prepared, "as soon as may be" after it has published the newspaper notice of the application and notified certain specified bodies.[63] Further information may be sought by the Minister as to the effects on the environment of the proposed development. The additional information received may necessitate the publication by the local authority of a fresh newspaper notice and further notification of the relevant bodies to which notice

---

[60] (S.I. No. 349 of 1989). Article 24 provides that all types of development listed under Pts. I and II of Sched. 1 are specified for the purposes of the Regulations. See further Chap. 7, below.

[61] 1994 Regulations, art. 117.

[62] *ibid.*, art. 120.

[63] A notice must be sent to the following bodies where certain of their interests are affected: the Arts Council, Bord Failte, An Taisce, the Commissioners of Public Works, the National Monuments Advisory Council, other local authorities whose areas would be affected, the Irish Aviation Authority, the appropriate Regional Fisheries Board or Health Board, or Shannon Free Airport Development Company Limited.

was given, where the minister so requires.[64] There is provision for consultation with another E.U. Member State where the Minister considers that the proposed development would have significant effects on its environment or where that State is likely to be so affected and so requests.[65] The Minister is obliged to have regard to the EIS prepared by the local authority (including any additional information furnished at his request) and to any submissions made to him by interested persons or bodies, or member states which have been consulted.[66]

Development for which an EIS is required may not be undertaken unless the Minister has certified:

(i) that the proposed development (or the proposed development as varied or modified by him) will not, in his opinion have significant and adverse effects on the environment; or

(ii) that it will embody the best practicable means to prevent or limit such effects.

---

[64] 1994 Regulations, art. 124.
[65] *ibid.*, art. 125.
[66] *ibid.*, art. 126.

Chapter 2

THE DEVELOPMENT PLAN

The main instrument of planning control is land-use zoning under the development plan whereby future land uses are allocated to particular areas of land within the functional area of the planning authority. Planning in this context may be seen as intervention in market forces for the development of cities and towns as well as the surrounding countryside. It predicts physical change and attempts to accommodate it in a rational and ordered way. A development plan is essentially a strategic document in which long term and short term goals are identified for the period of the plan so that development will take place on a planned basis. Ideally, spatial planning should be dynamic and have regard to the inter-relationship between the different sub-systems which make up the planning system as a whole: transport, housing, sanitary services, commerce and so on.

The predecessors to the current planning and development legislation, *i.e.* the Town and Regional Planning Acts of 1934–39, were passed "to make provision for the orderly and progressive development of cities, towns and other areas whether urban or rural and to preserve and improve the amenities thereof. . ." The 1934 Act provided for the making of planning schemes. It placed an obligation on local authorities to implement these schemes "with all convenient speed", but in fact no local authority did so, with the exception of one, and in that case only after legal action had compelled it.[1] The Act provided, however, that if a planning scheme was brought into operation, it became legally binding. Powers were vested in the local authority to take enforcement measures against development which did not conform with the provisions of the plan. This element was not carried through to the new legislation.[2]

The Local Government (Planning and Development) Act 1963 enabled local authorities to adopt development plans for their areas on the basis of which applications for planning permission could be assessed. It was envisaged that plans would be reviewed every five years but this did not occur in practice. Initially, plans were very basic documents but have since become increasingly sophisticated and influential in the area of public and private sector development.[3]

---

[1] *State (Modern Homes (Ireland) Ltd) v. Dublin Corporation* [1953] I.R. 202.
[2] See Miley and King, *Town and Regional Planning in Ireland* (1951).
[3] See Grist, *Twenty Years of Planning – A Review of the System Since 1963* (1983); Convery and Schmid, *Policy Aspect of Land Use Planning in Ireland* (1983).

2.1 PLAN PREPARATION

2.1.1 Obligation to make and review development plan

Section 19 of the 1963 Act required planning authorities to make a plan, consisting of a written statement and a plan or map indicating development objectives for their areas within a period of three years of the appointed day.[4] A planning authority may make two or more development plans for either the whole or part of its functional area.

The making of a development plan or variation to a development plan is a reserved function.[5] The planning authority are required to review the plan at least once in every five year period, and to make any variations (whether by way of alteration, addition or deletion) which they consider proper.[6] Alternatively, they can make a new development plan. The Minister may extend the period for the review of a development plan.[7] Where a planning authority have made two or more development plans, the five year period runs from the date of making the last plan.

2.1.2 Contents of plan

A development plan must include certain mandatory objectives.[8] These objectives vary according to the area to which the development plan relates. Objectives which are mandatory for county boroughs, boroughs, urban districts and scheduled towns[9] are set out at paragraph (a) of section 19(2) of the 1963 Act , namely, objectives:

> "(I) for the use solely or primarily (as may be indicated in the development plan) of particular areas for particular purposes (whether residential, commercial, industrial, agricultural or otherwise),

---

4   For an insight into the rather limited development plans within the first 10 years of the implementation of the 1963 Act, See Bannon, *Planning – The Irish Experience 1920–1988*, pp.131–136.

5   1963 Act, s.19(7).

6   In practice, planning authorities have not reviewed their plans every five years, a fact which has provided justification for the proponents of resolutions under s.4 of the City and County Management (Amendment) Act 1955 to compel managers to grant planning permission in material contravention of the development plan. The use of the s.4 procedure in this context has become fraught with legal difficulties. See para. 8.5.6, below.

7   1963 Act, s.20(1A), inserted by s.43(1)(e) of 1976 Act. The minimum five-year period may be extended by the Minister, either in relation to planning authorities in general, or in a particular case. The making of an application to the Minister to extend the five year peiod is a reserved function: 1963 Act, s.19(6). Notice of the application must be published in one or more newspapers circulating in the area of the authority and in *Iris Oifigiúil*.

8   1963 Act, s.19(2).

9   "Scheduled town" is defined under the 1963 Act, s.2 as (a) any town specified in Pt. I of Sched. 1 or (b) any non-municipal town specified in Pt. II of that Schedule. The area of a town specified under Pt. II of Sched. 1 is determined by a declaration of the members of the council of the county in which the town is located. The area of the town can similarly be amended by declaration of the councillors.

(II) for securing the greater convenience and safety of road users and pedestrians by the provision of parking places or road improvements or otherwise,

(III) for development and renewal of obsolete areas,

(IV) for preserving, improving and extending amenities."

Mandatory objectives for other areas[10] do not include land use zoning objectives as most land in rural areas is in agricultural use. In contrast, issues such as the availability of a water supply and foul drainage provision gain greater significance, a fact which is reflected in the mandatory objectives which must be included in development plans for rural areas. Such plans must include objectives:

"(I) for development and renewal of obsolete areas,

(II) for preserving, improving and extending amenities,

(III) for the provision of new water supplies and sewerage services and the extension of such existing supplies and services."

Discretionary objectives, *i.e.* objectives which all planning authorities may indicate in the development plan, are listed in the Third Schedule to the 1963 Act.[11] Those objectives which are mandatory for development in county boroughs, boroughs, urban districts and scheduled towns may also be included in development plans for rural areas. Where a planning authority proposes to include in a development plan an objective which would have to be implemented by another planning authority, prior consultation with the planning authority concerned is required. Section 19 also envisages a planning authority making two or more development plans for either the whole or part of its functional area. A plan for part of the area of the planning authority must include all of the mandatory objectives relating to that area.

A development plan consists of a written statement of objectives together with maps illustrating the physical impact of these objectives. The written statement is generally divided into three sections, dealing with policy, specific development objectives and development control.

(1) The first section sets out the policy objectives to be achieved over a twenty year period following the making of the plan "concentrating on broad goals and avoiding details". Policy is formulated on the basis of surveys and studies carried out in the area of the authority and is also influenced by the experience of working the previous plan.

(2) The development control section outs out the standards and design criteria which will be applied to development proposals. It indicates

---

[10] For ease of reference, these are referred to as "rural areas".

[11] Additional objectives were added to Sched. 3 by the 1976 Act, s.43(1) (preservation of fixtures and features) and by the Environmental Protection Agency Act 1992, s.106(3) (securing the reduction or prevention of noise).

objectives relating to land use zoning, densities, site development standards, height of buildings, building lines and other design considerations.

(3) The third section deals with specific development objectives relating to particular sites or projects which it is the intention of the planning authority to implement within the five year period of the plan.

The maps are visual representations of the policies and objectives of the planning authority in its areas. Land use zonings and maximum densities permissible, together with specific objectives and proposals, are illustrated and cross-referenced to the written statement.

2.1.3 Road development and the development plan

Planning authorities are obliged to consider recommendations made to them by the National Roads Authority concerning the content of their development plan.[12] The National Roads Authority is obliged to prepare a draft plan for the construction and maintenance of national roads every five years, having obtained the views of local authorities.[13] When preparing a development plan, the authority must take planning considerations into account and have regard to the provisions of the development plan and any special amenity area plan for the area in question. The environmental effects of the authority's proposed plan must also be considered.[14]

The National Roads Authority may also issue directions under section 20 of the Roads Act 1993 to a road authority to, *inter alia*:

(a) make a motorway scheme and submit it to the Minister for his appproval,

(b) make an application to the Minister for a bridge order under the Local Government Act 1946,

(c) make a protected road scheme and submit it to the Minister for approval,

The road authority is obliged to comply with such a direction within the time specified, but any direction which would necessitate a material contravention of a development plan must be preceded by a newspaper notice circulating in the area in which the proposed works are to be carried out and by a notice to the road authority to enable representations to be made and considered.[15] A minimum period of one month from the date specified in either notice must be allowed for representations.

---

12 Roads Act 1993, s.22(1).
13 *ibid.*, s.18.
14 *ibid.*, s.22(2).
15 *ibid.*, s.20(2).

2.1.4 Notification requirements

Although the 1963 Act places no express obligation on the planning authority to prepare a draft or a proposed plan, the only interpretation of the Act which is consonant with the protection of property rights under the Constitution suggests that owners and occupiers of properties should be given an opportunity to object to a proposed development plan before it is brought into operation. In *Finn v. Bray U.D.C.*,[16] Butler J. held that the planning authority had an obligation to prepare a draft development plan, to give notice of having done so, to make it available for inspection and to receive and consider objections.

A notice of the preparation of the draft must be published in *Iris Oifigiúil* and in at least one newspaper circulating in the area of the planning authority.[17] A copy of the draft plan or any proposed variation must be displayed for a period of at least three months at a location to be specified by the planning authority. Members of the public are entitled to make submissions which are to be taken into consideration by the planning authority. Any objector who is a ratepayer may request to be afforded an opportunity to state his case before officers appointed by the planning authority.[18]

It is reasonable that an owner or occupier of land who is particularly affected by a provision of a draft development plan should be notified of that provision.[19] Where the draft development plan provides for the preservation of any structure or internal feature because of its artistic, historic or architectural interest, the planning authority must serve a notice, incorporating particulars of the relevant provision and of the preparation of the draft, on the owner and on the occupier of the structure affected.[20] The exemptions described at Parts I–III of the Second Schedule to the 1994 Regulations apply to structures which are indicated for preservation in this manner. Similarly, where a draft development plan includes a provision for the preservation of a public right of way, a notice must be served on the owner and occupier of the land affected.[21] Any person may appeal to the Circuit Court against the inclusion in a draft plan or variation to the plan of any provision relating to the creation of a public right of way. If the court is satisfied that no public right of way subsists, it will make a declaration to this effect.[22]

---

[16] [1969] I.R. 169.
[17] A copy of this notice is also sent to the prescribed authorities.
[18] See 1963 Act, s.21(2).
[19] It has been observed that planning authorities are in some cases somewhat reluctant to make amendments to the plan following the consideration of objections because of the danger that the process of amendments and display described above could continue indefinitely. In practice, submissions from private individuals will probably receive a more attentive ear if they are made to the planning authority during the plan preparation period.
[20] 1963 Act, s.21(1)(c).
[21] *ibid.*, s.21(1)(d).
[22] *ibid.*, s.21(3). The appeal must be taken either during the period within which the plan is on display or within 21 days of the end of that period.

Planning authorities are required to send a draft copy of the written statement, or a copy of proposed variations of the development plan, as the case may be, to certain prescribed authorities. These authorities are set out under article 5 of the 1994 Regulations:

- Bord Failte Éireann,
- the Central Fisheries Board,
- An Chomhairle Ealaíon,
- the Commissioners of Public Works in Ireland,
- the Electricity Supply Board,
- Forfas,
- the Minister for Agriculture, Food and Forestry,
- the Minister for Arts, Culture and the Gaeltacht,
- the Minister for Defence,
- the Minister for Transport, Energy and Communications,
- the National Authority for Occupational Safety and Health,
- the National Monuments Advisory Council,
- the appropriate Regional Fisheries Board,
- in the case of a planning authority any part of whose functional area is situate within the functional area of the Shannon Free Airport Development Company Limited, that Company,
- An Taisce – the National Trust for Ireland,
- the Minister for the Environment,
- An Bord Pleanála,
- the National Roads Authority,
- every planning authority whose area is contiguous to the area of the planning authority which prepared the draft,
- every local authority in the area to which the draft relates, and
- the regional authority established by order under section 43 of the Local Government Act 1991 within whose region the functional area of the planning authority is situate, and any regional authority whose region is contiguous to the region of the first-mentioned regional authority.

In *Finn v. Bray U.D.C.*,[23] it was held that the planning authority must give further notice of any amendments to the draft plan which amount to a "material alteration" of the earlier draft and must allow the public to make submissions on the amended draft. The decision necessitated the insertion of section 21(A) in the 1963 Act which provides that any "material alteration" to a draft variation must also be put on display for a period of one month. A notice of the proposed amendment must be placed in *Iris Oifigiúil* and in one newspaper circulating in the functional area of the authority so as to enable members of the public to make representations.[24]

---

[23] See above, n.15.
[24] Similar provisions as to notice in relation to structures to be preserved and rights of way to be created apply as under the procedure for the draft plan. However, there is no provision for an oral hearing of an objection to the proposed amendment.

2.1.5 "Material alteration"

In *Keogh v. Galway County Borough Corporation (No. 2)*,[25] judicial review proceedings were brought to challenge a decision of Galway Corporation to adopt a
variation to the provisions of the Galway County Borough Development Plan 1991
relating to the provision of halting sites for travellers on the grounds that an amendment to the variation originally proposed had not in fact been put on display.[26]

The site was the subject of an earlier decision[27] in which a decision of the
corporation to develop the lands for use as a halting site was set aside because it
was not one of the four sites for which such an objective was indicated in the
Development Plan. The effect of the original proposed variation put on public
display in the later case was to delete the specific objective for these four sites,
substituting a general objective for the accommodation of travellers, and to add
the "use for the accomodation of travellers" as a land use objective for each of
the 10 zoning designations under the development plan. However, when the
period of display ended the councillors adopted by resolution a variation which
removed the halting site objective from three of the zones.

The corporation contended, relying on *O'Keeffe v. An Bord Pleanála*,[28] that
their decision that the amendment to the proposed variation did not constitute a
"material variation" was not so unreasonable as to be reviewable by the court.
The corporation also argued that the applicants had been given an opportunity to
make a comprehensive objection to the original variation involving the addition
of the halting site objective to each of the zones in question. However, the
applicants contended that the amendment could result in a greater concentration
of halting sites in the remaining seven sites and that they should have been given
an opportunity to address this point.

Morris J. found that there was no evidence in the minutes of the corporation
that the question of "material alteration" had been considered, and that, consequently, he was entitled to consider the matter *de novo*. He held that there had
been a "material alteration" in relation to which the applicants were entitled to
make submissions but had not been given such an opportunity, and he granted
the relief sought.

Keogh (No. 2) raises interesting questions as to the practice of many planning
authorities of using "broad brush strokes" to indicate the location of road proposals as specific objectives under their development plans without committing
themselves to a particular location or to the compulsory acquisition of particular
properties. This practice would appear to avoid the "material alteration" problem
when a defined route is eventually chosen but at the same time has the effect of
excluding members of the public and, in particular, the owners of land whose

---

[25] [1995] 2 I.L.R.M. 312.

[26] An injunction was also sought by the applicants to restrain the Corporation from proceeding
with the erection of a hard stand or halting site at "the Bishop's Field", Galway.

[27] Above, n.25.

[28] [1993] I.R. 39.

property may be compulsorily acquired, from making representations on the road design ultimately implemented by the planning authority.

The decision also serves as a pointer to a route to circumvent the effects of the *O'Keeffe* standard of unreasonableness. Where the decision to alter the plan could only have been properly based on a particular finding and there is no record of such finding having been made, the court is entitled to form its own view as to the nature of the decision reached without the need to review its reasonableness.

2.2 ADOPTION AND IMPLEMENTATION OF PLAN

2.2.1 Adoption of Plan

When the plan or variation of the plan, in its final form, including any amendments made, is adopted by resolution of the elected members of the planning authority, a notice of the making of the plan or variation must be published in *Iris Oifigiúil* and in at least one newspaper circulating in the area of the authority. The plan must be made available for inspection by the public at the times and place specified in the notice. The planning authority is required, on application by a member of the public, to issue a copy of the development plan or an excerpt, certified by an officer of a planning authority as a correct copy, for a fee not exceeding the reasonable cost of making the copy. Such a copy is prima facie evidence of the plan or plan excerpt. It is not necessary to produce the plan itself.[29]

2.2.2 "Rezoning"

This is a term which is applied to a change in the zoning or land use obective which attaches to a particular area or parcel of land arising from the adoption of a new plan or variation to the existing plan. It is also sometimes confusingly applied to a situation where planning permission is granted for a development which materially contravenes the provisions of the plan following a resolution of the elected members of the authority. In this situation the "zoning" of the area does not alter – the decision merely results in the establishment of a non-conforming use to which more stringent conditions for further development usually apply under the provisions of the development plan.

A re-zoning measure may appear to benefit some persons more than others, but this is not of itself sufficient to make it bad. In *Huntsgrove Developments Limited v. Meath County Council*,[30] not only did the re-zoning decision appear to favour one particular developer but it occurred in the unusual circumstances of the same developer having made a contribution of £20,000 towards the cost of the review of the development plan for the area, which would not otherwise have taken place. Lardner J. pointed out that if the applicants had established "a real

---

[29]   1963 Act, s.21(6).
[30]   [1994] 2 I.L.R.M. 36

likelihood of actual bias" they would have been entitled to have the measure set aside, but they had not.

The decision to re-zone lands can only be taken after the elected members have taken into account the proper planning and development of the area to be re-zoned. They must exclude from their consideration non-planning considerations. In *Malahide Community Council Ltd v. Fingal County Council.*[31] Kinlen J. quashed a decision of Fingal County Council to refuse to rescind its earlier decision to re-zone 36 acres of land located between Malahide and Portmarnock from "Green Belt" to "Residential" on the grounds that the planning authority had failed to consider relevant planning considerations, such as the provision of services and the suitability of the lands for residential or green-belt zoning. The debate on the motion had been restricted almost exclusively to the consideration of a private agreement which had been entered into by the intending developers and certain sports clubs for the area to which considerable financial and other benefits were to accrue in the event that the lands were re-zoned for housing.

2.2.3 Powers of the Minister in relation to development plans and planning policy

The Minister may require a planning authority to vary a development plan.[32] The planning authority must comply with such a requisition, although the proposed variation must be put on display in the usual manner. Once the requisition is made, the planning authority must have regard to it in the performance of their functions under the 1963 Act, pending the adoption of the variation.[33] Following the consideration of any objections or representations on the draft variation, the planning authority may decide, with the consent of the Minister, to alter the proposed variation and to adopt it so altered.

The Minister may require the co-ordination of the development plans of two or more authorities.[34] He may also prepare and publish general instructions and model forms for the preparation of developments plans for guidance of planning authorities.[35]

The Minister is obliged to issue general directives from time to time concerning planning and development policy.[36] Both planning authorities and An Bord Pleanála must have regard to any ministerial directive in existence which is relevant to the exercise of its planning function.[37] However, section 7 of the 1982 Act

---

[31] Unreported, High Court, December 19, 1994.
[32] 1963 Act, s.22(3).
[33] *ibid.*, s.22(5), as inserted by 1976 Act, s.43(1)(h).
[34] *ibid.*, s.22(2).
[35] *ibid.*, s.23.
[36] 1982 Act, s.7. Only two such directives have in fact been issued: Local Government (Planning and Development) General Policy Directive 1982 (S.I. No. 264 of 1982) (concerning large-scale shopping development) and Local Government (Planning and Development) General Policy Directive 1988 (S.I. No. 317 of 1988) (concerning the limitation of emissions of suspended particulates).
[37] 1982 Act, s.15(2)(a) repealed 1976 Act, s.6 under which the Board, but not planning authorities, were required to have regard to ministerial directives.

is careful to point out that ministerial directives may not be used "to exercise any power or control in relation to any particular case with which a planning authority or the Board is or may be concerned".

The extent of the obligation to "have regard to" government policy, in a more general sense, under section 7 of the Local Government Act 1991, was considered by the High Court in *Glencar Explorations Plc. v. Mayo County Council*,[38] in which Blayney J. stated that the County Council could not be said to have had regard to government mining policy where it adopted as part of its Development Plan a policy which was diametrically opposed to that policy.

2.2.4 Constitutionality of development plans and "Down-zoning"

The constitutionality of development plans and, in particular, the power of planning authorities to designate certain areas as "obsolete areas" under the development plan was considered by Kenny J. in *Central Dublin Development Association Ltd v. The Attorney General*.[39] The plaintiffs were property owners in the Capel Street area of Dublin. They claimed, *inter alia*, that their property rights would be adversely affected by certain proposals of the planning authority for the development and renewal of property in the Central Dublin Development Area which was designated as an "obsolete area". These proposals would have involved the acquisition of property and businesses owned by the plaintiffs. Kenny J. said:

> "In paragraph nine (of the plaintiffs' Statement of Claim) it is said that as sections 19, 20 and 21 make it obligatory on the planning authority to make a development plan and to review it, that this is left to the arbitrary discretion of the authority and there is no right of appeal to any court against a plan. The result of this, it is pleaded, is that some private property within the areas to which the plan relates will be substantially reduced in value. I do not think that the giving of power to a planning authority to make a development plan after they have considered and heard objections to the draft is an unjust attack on property rights. A plan of development for each city and town is necessary for the common good. Someone must prepare it and the planning authority who have staff trained in this work seem to me to be the best persons to do it. . . . The making of a plan will necessarily decrease the value of some property but I do not think that the Constitution requires that compensation should be paid for this as it is not an unjust attack on property rights. If this argument were correct, many owners of houses would have been entitled to be paid compensation when the Rent Restrictions Act 1946 was passed."[40]

The plaintiffs had claimed, *inter alia*, that the definition of "obsolete area" under section 2 of the 1963 Act did not prescribe any standard by which the authority should determine whether "the principle land" was badly laid out or whether its development had become obsolete. They argued that the concept of an obsolete

---

[38]   [1993] 2 I.R. 237.
[39]   109 I.L.T.R. 69.
[40]   *ibid*. at 90. Ironically, the Rent Restrictions Acts were subsequently held to be unconstitutional in *Blake and Madigan v. Attorney General* [1982] I.R. 117.

area was so vague and uncertain as to render it likely that property rights would be infringed by such designation. In response to this argument, Kenny J. said:

> "In my opinion the standards prescribed are sufficiently precise to be interpreted and applied in a Court of Law."[41]

There is no entitlement to compensation under planning legislation or the "down-zoning" of land *per se*. An entitlement to compensation may only be triggered by a refusal of planning permission or by the imposition of onerous conditions on a grant of permission.[42]

While the planning code recognises the right to compensation of property owners due to the refusal of planning permission or the attachment of onerous conditions, no entitlement to compensation is conferred on a person the value of whose property is substantially eroded by the grant of permission for an inimical use. The Local Government (Planning and Development) Act 1990, which contains the principal compensation provisions of the planning code, recognises the interest of such a person by providing that where injury to the amenities or depreciation in the value of property in the vicinity of the proposed development would result from a grant, permission can be refused without any requirement to pay compensation to the applicant. If the planning authorities were to operate the provisions of the Act so as to protect individual property rights from unjust attack, no constitutional difficulties could arise. The reality of planning decisions is that individual property rights are frequently sacrificed because of other planning needs.

2.2.5 Interpretation of development plans

A development plan must be objectively construed as:

> "there is a right in any citizen who may be affected by it to read the development plan of any planning authority area, and he must be entitled to see that as the actual plan and not to be told afterwards of some other and earlier document altering it."[43]

In *XJS Investments Ltd v. Dun Laoghaire Corporation*,[44] McCarthy J. stated that in the Supreme Court:

> "Certain principles may be stated in relation to the true construction of planning documents:
> (a) To state the obvious, they are not Acts of the Oireachtas or subordinate legislation emanating from skilled draftsmen and inviting the accepted canonms of construction applicable to such material.

---

[41] See Chap 12, below.
[42] s.11 of the 1990 Act confers an entitlement to compensation in certain circumstances on any person whose interest in land has reduced in value as a consequence of the refusal of planning permission or the attachment of onerous conditions.
[43] *Ferris v. Dublin County Council* [1993] 3 I.R. 65.
[44] [1987] I.L.R.M. 659.

(b) They are to be construed in their ordinary meaning as it would be understood by members of the public without legal training as well as by developers and their agents, unless such documents, read as a whole, necessarily indicates some other meaning . . .".[45]

In *Ferris*, it was argued that the term "halting site" as used in an amendment in 1989 to the Dublin County Development Plan 1983 should be interpreted by reference to the 1986 Programme for the Settlement of Travelling People which had been adopted under the terms of a 1986 resolution of the council. The programme was based on the provision of 30 halting sites for not more than five families each. At a meeting of the council in 1989 which considered the resolution to vary the plan so as to introduce halting sites at different locations throughout the county, a report had been read to the council by the Dublin planning officer which made a number of specific references to the programme.[46] Notwithstanding this, the Supreme Court held that no recourse could be had to the programme as a guide to the interpretation of the development plan.

One feature of many development plans which is of particular assistance to developers or owners who wish to change the use of their properties is the inclusion of matrix tables, indicating the accessibility of various uses within specific land use zones. Uses are categorised as "permitted", "may be permitted" or "not usually permitted", or according to some other similar categorisation.

Most of the technical terms used in the development plan are defined in the text and should be noted carefully. For example, in the Dun Laoghaire development plan 1991, plot ratio is defined as "the gross floor area of buildings on a site divided by the gross site area". If the definition of "gross floor area" is consulted, it can be seen that it excludes floor space taken up by plant, tank rooms and car parking areas. Consequently the site of a proposal which includes a sizeable element of car parking can be more intensively developed than a site on which there is no element of car parking. Site details are generally not shown in development plan maps so that, for example, it may be difficult to gauge from an examination of the map the exact effect of road proposals on individual properties.

The real weakness of development plans from the point of view of enforceability is that they are usually amenable to widely diverging interpretations. They are not presented as, nor are they intended to be, legal documents. Although this has the advantage of permitting greater accessibility for the layman, it is difficult to

---

[45] This excerpt was adopted by Barr J. in the context of the interpretation of the residential density Standards under the 1984 Dun Laoghaire Development Plan in *Tennyson v. Dun Laoghaire Corporation* [1991] 2 I.R. 527.

[46] It had been indicated by Costello J. (as he then was) in *Wilkinson v. Dublin County Council* [1991] I.L.R.M. 605, that there were "plausible arguments" in favour of interpreting the words "halting site" in the 1989 amendment by reference to the Programme, so that each halting site would only contain a small number of families although not necessarily less than five as the Programme stipulated. The learned judge did not, however, find it necessary to decide the case on this point as he held that the decision of the council to settle 84 families at Tyrellstown Cross, Mulhuddart was in material contravention of the development plan for other reasons.

judge which objectives of the plan will have precedence in areas of apparent conflict. On the other hand, it may be argued that it is difficult to remove this interpretative freedom from the decision framework without also removing the flexibility generally considered to be an essential requisite for a planning system. In *Tom Chawke Caravans Ltd v. Limerick County Council*,[47] Flood J. stated:

> "It is obvious that there must be a degree of flexibility in the interpretation of zoning by the planning authority but the decision of the planning authority must be in broad agreement with the parameters set down for the particular area in the County Development Plan."

2.2.6 Extent to which development plans are binding in the determination of planning applications

Section 26 of the 1963 Act requires the planning authority to have regard to the provisions of the development plan. The phrase "have regard to" has also been used under the equivalent provisions of English and Scottish legislation.[48] In those jurisdictions the phrase has been interpreted not as meaning "slavish adherence" to the provisions of the development plan, but merely that the development plan should be taken into account by the planning authority in reaching a decision. Section 26 of the 1963 Act is, however, set against a back-drop of substantially different legislative provisions. In the first place section 22(1) of the 1963 Act provides that:

> "It shall be the duty of a planning authority to take such steps as may be necessary for securing the objectives which are contained in the provisions of the development plan."

This means that the planning authority in exercising its discretionary power to grant or refuse an application under section 26 is obliged not only to consider the development plan but to give effect to its objectives.

Section 2(7) provides that where reference is made to the development plan under certain provisions of the Act, these are to be construed as "references to the provisions which the planning authority consider will be included in that plan". In *Tom Chawke Caravans Ltd v. Limerick County Council*[49] Flood J. held that the planning authority was obliged to have regard to the provisions of the current development plan and not the draft development plan in deciding whether to carry out development itself.[50] It was held that the provision of a

---

47 Unreported, High Court, February 1991.
48 See Nowlan, *A Guide to the Planning Legislation* (1988), p.42.
49 Above, n.46.
50 It would appear that s.2(7) was intended as a transitional provision to enable a planning authority to have regard to its draft development plan prior to the adoption of its first plan although a contrary view is suggested by Nowlan, above n.48, *op. cit.*, p.13. A duty to have regard to provisions of the draft plan would appear to be inconsistent with the planning authority's obligation under 1963 Act, s.22 to implement the provision of the development plan, as there may be circumstances where the provisions of each are in conflict, whether expressly or *sub silentio*: see *Keogh*, above n.25. See, *contra*, Scannell, *Environmental and Planning Law* (1995), p.195.

temporary halting site for members of the travelling community in an area zoned for commercial and business use at Castletroy, County Limerick, amounted to a material contravention of the 1983 Development Plan for Limerick County.

The planning authority may not grant a planning permission in material contravention of the plan unless the prescribed statutory procedure for such decisions is followed.[51] This involves the publication of a notice of intention to grant planning permission in a newspaper circulating in the area of the proposed development and the passing of a resolution by the elected representatives of the planning authority that a decision to grant permission be made. Where a planning authority grants permission in material contravention of the development plan without following this procedure the decision is invalid. An order quashing the decision may be obtained in reliance on this ground only where it can be established that the opinion of the planning authority that the decision did not involve a material contravention of the plan was totally unreasonable. On the other hand, An Bord Pleanála may, at its discretion, grant planning permission for a development which would materially contravene the provisions of the development plan.[52] While the Board is obliged to have regard to the provisions of the development plan, it is not under any statutory duty to give effect to its objectives.

2.3 THE PLAN AND LOCAL AUTHORITY DEVELOPMENT

2.3.1 Planning authority cannot effect development in material contravention of its own development plan

Development carried out by a planning authority within its own functional area is exempted under section 4 of the 1963 Act. However, the planning authority has a duty to give effect to the objectives of, and cannot effect development in material contravention of its own development plan.[53] Section 2(7) provides that where reference is made to the development plan under certain provisions of the Act, these are to be construed as "references to the provisions which the planning authority consider will be included in that plan". In *Tom Chawke Caravans Ltd v. Limerick County Council*,[54] Flood J. held that the planning authority was obliged to have regard to the provisions of the current development plan and not the draft development plan in deciding whether to carry out development itself. It seems likely that section 2(7) was intended as a transitional provision to enable a planning authority to have regard to its draft development plan prior to the adoption of its

---

[51] 1963 Act, s.26(3).
[52] 1976 Act, s.14(8).
[53] 1963 Act, ss.22(1) and 39.
[54] Above n.47, in which Flood J. held that the provision of a temporary halting site for members of the travelling community in an area zoned for commercial and business use at Castletroy, County Limerick, amounted to a material contravention of the 1983 Development Plan for the County of Limerick.

first plan. The appropriate remedy where a planning authority is carrying out development in material contravention of its own development plan is an injunction to restrain the breach of statutory duty involved. In *Attorney General (McGarry and Others) v. Sligo County Council*,[55] an injunction was obtained restraining the county council from using as a dump a quarry pit situated in close proximity to Carrowmore Passage Grave Cemetery, which it was an objective of the planning authority to preserve as an amenity. McCarthy J. stated that the development plan:

> "forms an environmental contract between the planning authority, the council and the community, embodying a promise by the council that it will regulate private development in a manner consistent with the objective stated in the plan, and further, that the council itself shall not effect a development which contravenes the plan materially."[56]

A plethora of cases dealing with the implementation of Dublin County Council's "Programme for the Settlement of Travelling Peoples", which was adopted by the council in 1986, concern the local authority's obligation not to carry out development in material contravention of their own plan. In the first of these cases, *O'Leary v. Dublin County Council*,[57] O'Hanlon J. emphasised that the same standards under the development plan are to be applied to local authority developments as are applied to proposals by private developers; a development which would, if carried out by the private sector, amount to a material contravention of the plan, will likewise be so if carried out by a local authority.

Residents in the Templeogue area had applied for an order restraining the county council from proceeding further with the development of a proposed halting site at Cherry Field Linear Park. The county council conceded that the project could not be implemented if it involved a material contravention of the county development plan, but it argued that any contravention of the "High Amenity" zoning under the development plan was not "material" as the proposed development only involved the use of a small site of five families in an area of several hundred acres of high amenity. O'Hanlon J. refused to accept this contention. Residential caravan parks were indicated as "not permitted" under the development plan in areas zoned "High Amenity". If a private developer applied for permission for a residential development of a comparable size in the same area, the county council would undoubtedly refuse planning permission on the grounds that the proposed development, if permitted, would be in material contravention of the plan. He concluded that:

> ". . . the requirements of the planning law have to be applied with the same stringency against the local authority in this case as would be the case if the proposal came from a private developer."

---

55 [1991] 1 I.R. 99.
56 McCarthy J. also observed that where a development plan identifies a particular area as an area for conservation for amenity reasons, development which is inimical to the amenity zoning should not be permitted up to the boundary of that area: a "fallow area" should be interposed.
57 [1988] I.R. 150.

Some planning authorities have sought to avoid the restrictions which such a philosophy might impose simply by omitting to refer to specific local authority proposals or by inserting provisions in the development plan which would appear to allow contentious development such as halting sites or landfill sites in areas zoned for high amenity use. However, in *Wilkinson v. Dublin County Council*,[58] Costello J. held that development may be in material contravention of the development plan even if it is in accordance with zoning provisions, if it is inconsistent with the proper planning and development of the area. But the courts will be slow to set aside a decision by the manager to carry out development on such grounds unless it can be shown that "no reasonable planning authority" would conclude that such a development would be consistent with the proper planning and development of an area".

In *Wilkinson*, the council decided to develop a halting site at Tyrellstown Cross, Mulhuddart, which was to accommodate 84 caravans. The proposal was in accordance with the relevant zoning provisions for the area concerned as "halting sites" were listed as permitted uses as a result of a 1989 amendment to the 1983 County Development Plan. Costello J. held, however, that the development was in material contravention of the plan as it was not consistent with the proper planning and development of the area, and he was prepared to set aside the decision of the manager for this reason. He stated:

> "A development may still amount to a material contravention of the plan if it is one which was not consistent with the proper planning and development of the area. Accordingly, the question can be posed, as it was in O'Leary's case, suppose a private individual had applied for permission to erect a residential caravan park on this site catering for 84 caravans and about 400 persons in accordance with the exiguous plans now proposed, would planning permission have been given? I have no hesitation in concluding that no reasonable planning authority could conclude that such a development could be consistent with the proper planning and development of the area. Let me suppose that a concerned voluntary organisation applied to erect a halting site for members of the travelling community, as now proposed, would planning permission be granted? It is perfectly clear that it is the policy of the council that halting sites should only be small in size but I conclude that apart from this consideration no planning authority could regard a development of this magnitude, catering for so many persons in such barely adequate conditions, as being consistent with the proper planning and development of the area."

Costello J. went on to indicate that the legal standing of a halting site of this size *vis-à-vis* the development plan might be different if it was intended to be temporary rather than permanent.

Subsequently, the Supreme Court in *Ferris v. Dublin County Council*[59] were required to adjudicate on a scheme of the County Manager to accommodate 30 families on a temporary halting site. Sixty-five travelling families had been evicted from an area of Blanchardstown and were living along the side of the road.

58 [1991] I.L.R.M. 605.
59 Above, n.43.

Applying the standard of reasonableness which had been established by *State (Keegan) v. Stardust Compensation Tribunal*[60] to the manager's decision, Finlay C.J., giving the judgment of the court, found that "it could not be said . . . that the County Manager in deciding to make this temporary provision for this particularly urgent problem was acting in the face of fundamental common sense". A court will not usually be prepared to embark on a resolution of a conflict between the evidence of the planning authority and professional experts, acting on behalf of a person seeking to impugn a planning decision.[61]

Section 22 of the 1963 Act imposes a duty on the planning authority to give effect to the objectives of the plan. It can be argued that the planning authority have a corollary duty not to effect development which is excluded from a list of similar development proposals listed as objectives under the development plan. It follows, for example, that the power to make road reservations or road proposals which are not specified as specific objectives in the development plan must be in some doubt.

In *Keogh and Others v. Galway County Borough Corporation (No. 1)*,[62] the applicants, who were officers of the Lower Salthill Residents' Association, sought to challenge by way of judicial review the decision of the respondent corporation to develop a halting site for travellers on lands known as the "Bishop's Field" at Lower Salthill in Galway. The Galway County Borough Development Plan 1991 specified four locations for which the provision of a halting site was an objective, but the "Bishop's Field" was not one of them.

The applicants contended that they had been deprived of an opportunity to make representations about the proposed development in the context of the development plan because the draft development plan did not refer to it. They argued that they were entitled to assume that the list of locations for halting sites, which it was a specific objective of the development plan to provide, was exhaustive, and that, consequently, the "Bishop's Field" development amounted to a material contravention of the development plan which was prohibited by section 39(2) of the 1963 Act.

The corporation argued that the development could be carried out under certain other provisions of the development plan which appeared to allow greater flexibility. In particular, they relied upon paragraph 18.2 of the development plan which included the following passage:

> "Particular objectives may be modified or deleted, and new works which become necessary and are not included as specific objectives, may be initiated depending on the availability of finance and the sanctioning of schemes or works by central government."

The corporation also argued that the decision of the corporation to carry out the development at the proposed halting site could not be successfully challenged

60   [1986] I.R. 642.
61   *An Taisce v. Dublin Corporation,* and *Attorney General (McGarry)*, above, n.55.
62   [1995] 1 I.L.R.M. 141.

because the necessary degree of unreasonableness referred to in *O'Keeffe v. An Bord Pleanála* had not been established. This argument was rejected by Carney J. as it was not applicable to the issues in the case.

Following *Finn v. Bray U.D.C.*,[63] he held that, in their proposal, the corporation was seeking to by-pass the mandatory consultation process which preceded the adoption of a development plan under the provisions of the 1963 Act, and was seeking to materially contravene their own development plan. The applicants were entitled to assume that the four locations specified in the plan were the only locations where the corporation intended to develop halting sites. Carney J. referred also to McCarthy J.'s description of the development plan in *Attorney General (McGarry) v. Sligo County Council*[64] as "an environmental contract between the planning authority, the Council and the community".

The exact boundaries of this decision as it affects the interpretation of the plan are not certain. In granting the relief sought by the applicants, Carney J. left open the question as to whether the position would have been different if the development plan did not contain a specific objective for halting sites. The *ratio* of the decision would appear to extend to other areas of the plan for which there are specific objectives, *e.g.* road proposals, so that if a number of road proposals are specified in a development plan, the development of any other road would amount to a material contravention of the plan.

---

[63]   [1969] I.R. 169.
[64]   Above, n.55.

Chapter 3

PRESERVATION OF AMENITY

The preservation of amenity is one of the principle objectives of planning legislation as expressed in the preamble to the 1963 Act.

> "The purpose of all town and country planning is to preserve amenities and the sensible and attractive lay-out of properties".[1]

Specific mechanisms are provided under the planning code for the conservation of areas and structures of recognised beauty, archaeological, historical or scientific interest. Policies of preservation and conservation are also pursued by planning authorities under their development plans.[2] Many of these policies and objectives are inspired by the need to comply with European Union directives on environmental protection. In addition, planning authorities possess enforcement and other ancillary powers to enable them to secure preservation objectives.[3] They may also provide financial and other assistance to persons or bodies concerned with the preservation, development or maintenance of amenities.[4]

3.1.1 Planning agreements

Planning authorities can enter into an agreement under section 38 of the 1963 Act with any person having an interest in land for the purpose of restricting or regulating the development or use of the land. For example, applicants for planning permission are sometimes required by a planning condition to enter into agreements sterilising land which is outside the application site but is owned by them. Similarly, planning permission may be granted subject to a condition specifying that the use as a dwelling shall be restricted to use by persons of a particular class or description and that provision to that effect should be embodied in a section 38 agreement.[5]

Section 38 enables planning authorities to regulate the development or use of land where it would be unable to do so by way of planning condition.[6] They provide

---

[1] *Copeland Borough Council v. Secretary of State for Environment* (1976) 31 P. & C.R. 403.
[2] See 1963 Act, Sched. 3, Pt. IV, where the full range of objectives are set out.
[3] Unfortunately the special conservation powers enjoyed by planning authorities have been little used with the exception of tree preservation orders. See Mawhinney, "Environmental Conservation and Action, 1920–1970" in Bannon, *Planning – The Irish Experience 1920–1988*.
[4] 1963 Act, s.14(2).
[5] The validity of such conditions is extremely doubtful where the occupation is restricted to persons related to the applicant.
[6] *Good v. Epping Forest District Council* [1994] 1 W.L.R. 376.

an alternative enforcement mechanism. Section 38(2) provides that the planning agreement may be:

> "enforced by the planning authority or any body[7] joined with them against the persons deriving title under that person in respect of that land as if the planning authority or such body, as may be appropriate, were possessed of adjacent land and as if the agreement had been expressed to be made for the benefit of that land."

Notwithstanding the clear intention that the agreement should run with the land, there are a number of legal difficulties associated with the enforceability of section 38 agreements including lack of consideration, the fettering of the discretion of the planning authority to determine applications and the unenforceability of positive covenants.[8] But despite the doubts about the enforceability of these agreements, the property affected will in most cases be regarded as lacking good marketable title.[9]

3.1.2 Special amenity area orders

A special amenity area order (SAAO) is a potentially highly effective instrument for the control of development in areas of outstanding beauty or scientific interest, although only two such orders have been confirmed at the time of writing.[10] In determining planning applications, both the planning authority and An Bord Pleanála are obliged to have regard to the provisions of an SAAO or a draft SAAO relating to an area in which the proposed development is located.[11] A planning authority may not grant permission in material contravention of an SAAO unless the material contravention procedure prescribed under section 26(3) of the 1963 Act is followed.[12] This entails the publication of a newspaper notice indicating the authority's intention to make an SAAO and the passing of a resolution of three quarters of the elected members.[13]

The National Roads Authority (NRA) must publish a newspaper notice of any proposed direction to a road authority under section 20 of the Roads Act 1993 in relation to any works which would, in the opinion of the authority, if carried out,

---

[7] It is not uncommon for prescribed bodies such as An Taisce to be joined as parties to s.38 agreements.

[8] These complex and convoluted problems have been discussed elsewhere. See Stevenson, "Negotiated Planning: Circumventing the Planning System" (1984) Ir. Jur. 14 and 226; Hawke, "Planning Agreements in Practice" (1981) J.P.L. 5 and 86; Purdue, Young, Rowan-Robinson, *Planning Law and Procedure*, pp.278–295.

[9] In the past, it would appear that some planning authorities have been prepared to assuage the concerns of building societies by giving a commitment that in the event of the purchaser getting into financial difficulties they would terminate the agreement: see Stevenson, *Negotiated Planning*, (1984) Ir Jur. 15. See generally, Ward, "Planning Bargaining – where do we stand?" (1982) J.P.L. 74.

[10] See SAAOs for the Liffey Valley and Bull Island. Dublin County Council (Lucan Bridge to Palmerston) Special Amenity Area Order (Confirmation) Order 1990, (S.I. No. 59 of 1990); North Bull Island Special Amenity Area Order 1994 (Confirmation) Order 1995. See also Gough in (1984) 1 *Pleanáil* 46, which refers to the reasons for the refusal in November 1981 by the Minister for the Environment, Mr Peter Barry, to confirm the Dublin Bay Special Amenity Area Order.

[11] 1963 Act, s.26(1). The reference to a draft SAAO is imported into s.26(1) by s.2(7)(b) of the 1976 Act.

[12] See 1976 Act, s.39(d) which substituted a new s.26(3).

[13] Local Government Act 1991, s.45 altered voting requirements.

require the road authority to materially contravene an SAAO.[14] Notice of the proposed direction must also be served on the road authority and on the planning authority for the area, where the road authority is not also a planning authority. Any written representations made before the date specified in the notice in each case must be considered by the authority.[15] In preparing its development plan for national roads and in performing any function in relation to the construction or improvement of a national road, the NRA must have regard to any special amenity area plan for the area in question.[16]

In addition to providing a policy framework for decision making, the scope of development control is enlarged by the removal of certain classes of exemptions within the area delineated by the order.[17] In *Glencar Exploration Plc v. Mayo County Council*,[18] Blayney J. observed that the only manner in which a planning authority could remove the statutory exemption for mining in a rural area would be by making an SAAO for that area.[19] The planning authority have no other power to prohibit the carrying out of exempted development under its development plan.

Planning authorities can also determine planning applications free from the oppressive influence of ensuing compensation claims: no compensation is payable for the refusal of permission for development in an area to which a special amenity area order relates.[20] Confirmation of a special amenity area order permits a planning authority to make a conservation order for the protection of the flora and fauna of any area within a special amenity area.[21]

A special amenity area order may be made by the planning authority, either of its own volition, or at the direction of the Minister. The making of an order is a reserved function.[22] A planning authority may make an order for an area located within or partly within a functional area of another authority which is contiguous with its own, provided it has obtained the consent of that authority. The factors which may influence a planning authority decision to declare an area to be an area of special amenity are:

    (a) its outstanding natural beauty;
    (b) its special recreational value; or
    (c) a need for nature conservation.

---

[14] Roads Act 1993, s.22(2).
[15] The specified date must be not less than one month after the date on which the notice in each case was published or served.
[16] Roads Act 1993, s.22(2)(c).
[17] 1994 Regulations, art. 10(1)(b).
[18] [1993] 2 I.R. 237.
[19] Art. 10(1)(b)(iii) provides, *inter alia*, that development of a type described in Class 5 of Pt. III of Sched. 2 (which relates to minerals and petroleum prospecting) will not be exempted development in an area to which an SAAO relates.
[20] 1990 Act, s.12(1) and Sched. 2, para. 6.
[21] See 1963 Act, s.46(1).
[22] 1963 Act, s.42(6).

When a planning authority makes an order they must publish notice of the fact in at least one newspaper circulating in the area to which the order relates.[23] The notice should describe the area delimited by the order and should indicate where a copy of the order and any map referred to may be inspected during office hours. It should specify the duration of the inspection period (which should not be less than one month) and the manner in which objections to the order may be made to the planning authority. The notice should also state that the order requires confirmation by the Minister before it becomes effective and that if any objections are made which are not withdrawn, a public local enquiry will be held and the objections considered before the order is confirmed.

The planning authority should enclose any objections to the order which have been duly made and not withdrawn when they are submitting the order for confirmation by the Minister. If there are no objections to be considered, the Minister may confirm the order with or without modifications or, alternatively, refuse to confirm it. Assuming the existence of live objections, the Minister is obliged to cause a public local enquiry to be held.[24] Having considered any objections still subsisting and the report of the inspector who held the enquiry, he may confirm the order with or without modifications or, alternatively, refuse to confirm it.[25]

A planning authority must have regard to any provisions which the planning authority consider will be included in a special amenity order relating to their area.[26] A special amenity area order enjoys a higher status on the democratic scale than the development plan because a public inquiry is mandatory where objections exist. It must be reviewed every five years for the purpose of deciding whether it should be revoked or amended.[27]

3.1.3 Tree preservation orders

Planning authorities may make orders, known as tree preservation orders (TPOs), under section 45 of the 1963 Act for the preservation of any tree, trees, group of trees or woodlands.[28] The order may prohibit the cutting down, topping, lopping or wilful destruction of trees except with the consent of the planning authority which may be granted subject to conditions. It may also provide that the provisions of Part IV of the 1963 Act concerning planning applications and

---

[23] 1963 Act, s.43(1).

[24] *ibid.*, s.43(3).

[25] An order which is confirmed by the Minister must be laid before both Houses of the Oireachtas "as soon as may be" after it is made. Either House may annul the order by passing a resolution within the following 21 days on which that House sits after the order is laid before it.

[26] 1963 Act, s.2(7).

[27] *ibid.*, s.42(5).

[28] See *Tree Preservation – Guidelines for Planning Authorities*, Department of the Environment, 1994. The making of a TPO is an executive function which means that one can be made in a matter of hours where there is an imminent threat to important trees: see Goodbody, "Tree Preservation Orders" in (1984) 1 *Pleanáil* 46–50.

planning permission are to be applied to any application for a consent under the order and its determination by the planning authority.[29] A person whose interest in land has been reduced or who has suffered damage by being disturbed in his enjoyment of the land as a result of the decision of the planning authority to refuse a felling consent, has a prima facie entitlement to be paid compensation by the planning authority.[30]

A TPO may be revoked or varied by a subsequent order of the planning authority. Notice of the making of an order and a copy of the order must be served by the planning authority on every person who is the owner or occupier of any land affected by the order, and on any other person at that time known to them to be entitled to fell any tree, trees, group of trees or woodlands to which the order relates.

The order may be appealed to An Bord Pleanála before the appeal date specified in the notice (which may not be earlier than one month after the service of the notice) by any person who has been served by a notice and copy of the order.[31] An Bord Pleanála may annul the order or confirm it with or without modifications. The appeal lies from the making of the tree preservation order but not from a decision on an application for a consent to fell trees on the land to which the order relates, unless the order expressly applies the provisions of Part IV of the 1963 Act, or at least those provisions which allow an appeal to be made. In *Wicklow County Council v. An Bord Pleanála, Bridgefarm Company Limited and Coolattin Woods Action Committee*,[32] Barrington J. did not consider the failure of a tree preservation order to provide a right of appeal against a refusal to grant a felling consent amounted to a breach of the constitutional right to fair procedures.

Tree preservation orders do not apply to the cutting down, topping or lopping of trees which are dying or dead or have become dangerous, or where such action is necessary to comply with any statutory obligation or to prevent or abate a nuisance.[33] It is an offence to contravene the provisions of any order under the

---

[29] See *Wicklow County Council v. An Bord Pleanála, Bridgefarm Company Limited and Coolattin Woods Action Committee* (1990) 8 I.L.T.R. 107.

[30] See 1990 Act, s.21, considered further at 12.2, below. But note that a condition relating to the preservation and protection of trees, shrubs, plants and flowers does not give rise to an entitlement to compensation: 1990 Act, s.12 and Sched. 4, para. 19.

[31] 1963 Act, s.45(5) as amended by 1976 Act, s.14 which substituted An Bord Pleanála as the appellate body instead of the Minister.

[32] (1990) 8 I.L.T.R. 107.

[33] 1963 Act, s.45(7). Section 70 of the Roads Act 1993 enables a road authority to serve a notice on the owner or occupier of land requiring him to trim or cut hedges or trees which interfere with the safety of the road or make its maintenance more difficult, or to preserve them. A road authority may prosecute for failure to comply with the terms of such a notice. It may also take the necessary steps itself in the event of such failure to comply with the notice and may subsequently recover the costs incurred by this action from the owner or occupier served. Section 34 of the Local Government Act 1925, under which a similar power was exercised, was repealed by s.4 of the Roads Act 1993.

section punishable on summary conviction by a fine not exceeding £1000.[34] Particulars of tree preservation orders are entered in the planning register.

Planning authorities are also empowered to serve a warning notice on the owner of land where any tree the preservation of which is required by a condition subject to which a permission for the development of any land was granted, may be removed or damaged.[35] The warning notice may require the owner of the land to take any reasonable steps necessary for the preservation of any trees specified in the notice.[36]

When preparing its development plan for national roads or when exercising any other function in relation to the construction or improvement of a national road, the National Roads Authority must have regard to the provisions of any TPO in an area affected.[37]

3.1.4 Planting of trees, shrubs and other plants

Planning authorities can plant trees, shrubs or other plants on land owned by them, and on other land, where they have obtained the consent of every person having an interest in the land, in order to preserve or enhance its amenities or natural beauty.[38] They may also provide assistance to any person or body proposing to carry out planting, either by way of a grant or by providing the trees, shrubs or other plants to be used. The planting or management of land not in the ownership of the planning authority may be undertaken either by the authority itself or by a person interested in the land on such terms as may be agreed with the authority.[39]

3.1.5 Notices requiring the removal or alteration of a hedge

If a planning authority considers it "expedient in the interests of amenity" that any hedge should be removed or altered, they may serve on the owner and on the occupier of the land on which the hedge is situated a notice requiring it to be removed or altered.[40] If removal of the hedge is required, the notice may specify

---

[34] Local Government (Planning and Development) Act 1992, s.20(1). Section 8 of the 1976 Act was repealed by the 1992 Act, s.22.

[35] 1976 Act, s.26. See para. 11.4.10, below.

[36] See further para. 11.3.10.1, below.

[37] Roads Act 1993, s.22(2)(c).

[38] 1963 Act, s.50. Note also that conditions requiring the planting of trees, shrubs or the landscaping of structures or other land may be attached to the grant of planning permission. See 1963 Act, s.26(2)(d).

[39] Any management agreement must be entered in the planning register. The provision of a grant for planting is a reserved function.

[40] 1963 Act, s.44. Particulars of these notices must be entered in the planning register. See also the powers of the road authority under s.70 of the Roads Act 1993 to serve notices in relation to trees, shrubs and hedges which may constitute a road hazard. See n.33, above.

a suitable replacement to be put in its place. An appeal may be brought before the appeal date specified in the notice to An Bord Pleanála.[41]

On appeal, the notice may be annulled or confirmed with or without modifications on appeal. If the hedge is not removed or altered as required by the notice within the time specified, or within such extended period as the planning authority may allow, the authority may enter on the land and remove or alter the hedge themselves and make any replacement which has been required by the notice.

A person complying with a notice served upon him is entitled to recover any reasonable expenses incurred by him in so doing. Any person who has an interest in the land at the time of the notice may also be entitled to be paid compensation by the planning authority for the reduction in value of his interest or for any damage which he has suffered as a result of being disturbed in his enjoyment of his land.[42] A notice under section 44 may be withdrawn by the planning authority.[43]

3.1.6 Conservation Orders

The confirmation of an SAAO enables the planning authority to impose an even more specialised and localised form of control in the interests of amenities. A "conservation order" may be made by the planning authority under section 46 of the 1963 Act, after consultation with the prescribed authorities, for the preservation and protection of flora or fauna of special amenity value or special interest which are to be found in an area included in a special amenity area order.[44] The "prescribed authorities" are the Commissioners of Public Works, the Royal Irish Academy, Bord Failte and An Taisce.[45] The order may prohibit the taking, killing or destroying of flora or fauna, although there is provision for exemptions to be prescribed for certain types. A conservation order may be revoked or varied by subsequent order.

Notice of the making of an order and of the right of appeal against such order, must be placed by the planning authority in at least one newspaper circulating in the area affected by the order. Any person may appeal to An Bord Pleanála against the order within a period of one month after the publication of the notice.[46] An Bord Pleanála may confirm the order with or without modifications or annul it. An offence is committed where any person contravenes the provisions of a conservation order, unless the order has been annulled.[47]

---

[41] 1963 Act, s.44(2) as amended by s.14 of the 1976 Act, which substituted An Bord Pleanála as the appellate body in place of the Minister. The appeal date must be at least one month after the date of service of the notice.

[42] See para. 12.6, below.

[43] 1976 Act, s.28.

[44] Particulars of a conservation order must be entered in the planning register.

[45] 1994 Regulations, art. 163.

[46] 1963 Act, s.46(6) as amended by s.14 of the 1976 Act under which the Board replaced the Minister as the appellate body.

[47] 1963 Act, s.46(8). The maximum fine is increased to £1,000 by 1992 Act, s.20(1).

3.1.7 Public rights of way

Planning authorities may adopt objectives in their development plan for the preservation of any existing public right of way giving access to the seashore, mountain, lakeshore, riverbank or other places of natural beauty or recreational utilities. Both the owner and occupier of land over which such a right of way exists must be notified when an objective for its preservation is included in draft plan, or amendment or variation of a draft plan.[48] He or she may, as a ratepayer, make representations to the planning authority and is entitled to an oral hearing of his or her objection. Additionally, an appeal lies to the Circuit Court against the inclusion of an objective relating to the right of way in question.

Planning authorities can also enter into agreements for the preservation of a public right of way over land with any person having the necessary power of dedication.[49] Such an agreement may involve payment to the person dedicating the public right of way and may also limit or impose conditions affecting it. The planning authority have a duty to take any necessary steps to ensure that the public right of way is created in the manner intended by the agreement. Particulars of any agreement for the creation of a public right of way must be entered in the planning register.

Planning authorities may also use compulsory powers to create a public right of way by making an order under section 48 of the 1963 Act.[50] Notice of the making of an order and a copy of the order must be served on every person who is the owner or occupier of any land over which the order creates a public right of way, and on any other person who in the opinion of the planning authority will be affected by the creation of the public right of way. Any person who is so served may appeal to An Bord Pleanála against the order at any time before the appeal date specified in the notice.[51] An Bord Pleanála may annul the order or confirm it, with or without modifications. The planning authority are obliged to maintain any public right of way created by agreement under the Act or in exercise of their compulsory powers or where a provision is included in the development plan for its preservation. Any person who damages or obstructs the way, or hinders or interferes with the exercise of a right of way which is to be maintained by the planning authority, commits an offence.[52] If the way is damaged or obstructed by a person, the planning authority maintaining the right of way may repair the damage or remove the obstruction and may recover the expenses incurred by them in so doing from the person causing the damage or obstruction. Ancillary powers of entry are granted to the planning

---

[48] 1963 Act, s.21.

[49] *Ibid.*

[50] Particulars of any right of way created by order of the planning authority must be entered in the planning register. Section 48 was amended by s.14 of the 1976 Act so that An Bord Pleanála is now the appellate tribunal instead of the minister.

[51] The appeal date must be at least one month after the date of service of the notice.

[52] 1963 Act, s.49(2).

authority for the maintenance of rights of way and for the repair of any damage or the removal of any obstruction caused to the right of way.[53]

The power to extinguish public rights of way is now exercised by the local authority *qua* road authority under section 73 of the 1993 Act rather than in exercise of its powers under the planning code as was formerly the case.[54] Where the council proposes to extinguish a public right of way the requirements for newspaper notices and for a notice to be affixed at each end of the public right of way are the same as for the abandonment of a public road. There are similar requirements also for the consideration of objections, oral hearings and the necessity for the Minister for the Environment to approve the making of an extinguishment order relating to a national or regional road before it takes effect. The Minister must also consult with the National Roads Authority before making an order in relation to a national road.[55] The making of the order is once again a function of the elected members who must also consider any representations made together with the report and recommendations of the person appointed to conduct any oral hearing which was held.[56]

The order may specify a date on which the extinguishment will come into effect but if no date is specified it will come into effect on the date on which the order is made by the council or, in the case of a national or regional road, approved by the Minister.[57] The order may also specify conditions to be complied with before the extinguishment comes into effect. These may include conditions relating to the recovery of all or a reasonable portion of the cost of extinguishing a public right of way where this was done solely or partly for the purpose of facilitating the development of land.[58] Any such costs may be recovered from the person developing or proposing to develop the land in question.

3.1.8 Repair and tidying of advertisements

Planning authorities also enjoy power under section 54 of the 1963 Act to control advertisements in the interest of public safety or to protect amenities.[59] If it appears

---

[53] 1963 Act, s.49(4).

[54] See Local Government (Planning and Development) Act, 1963, s.76 which now stands repealed by the Roads Act 1993, s.4. The procedure under s.84(4) of the Local Government Act 1946 under which public rights of way attached to land within the ownership of the council were extinguished has also been replaced by this provision. See Roads Act 1993, s.4 and also s.73(15).
    The procedure for the extinguishment of public rights of way does not have to be followed where a right of way is extinguished under the terms of a compulsory purchase order or where the Minister approves a scheme under s.49 of the Roads Act 1993. See s.73(14) of the 1993 Act.

[55] Roads Act 1993, s.73(1), (2) and (3).

[56] *ibid.*, s.73(8).

[57] Note that the extinguishment order discharges the council from any obligation it previously had to maintain the road or whatever part of the road as is affected by the order: Roads Act 1993, s.73(5). Note also that an order by the Minister under s.12 of the Roads Act 1993 declaring that a road is to be abandoned does not affect the right of way of the public over the surface of such a road.

[58] *ibid.*, s.73(4)(a) and 73(12).

[59] Advertisements and advertisements on public roads are also regulated under s.89. See para. 3.1.9, below.

to the planning authority, that an advertisement structure or advertisement in their area should be repaired or tidied, they may serve on the person having control of the advertisement structure or advertisement, a notice requiring that person to repair or tidy the advertisement structure or advertisement within a specified period.[60] In the event of non-compliance with the terms of the notice within the period specified, the planning authority may enter on the land concerned, and carry out the work required themselves. The planning authority are entitled to recover any reasonable costs incurred by them as a result of such action.

3.1.9 Licences for petrol pumps, cables, wires, pipelines and other structures on public roads

Section 89 of the 1963 Act empowers planning authorities to grant to any person a licence to erect, construct, place and maintain petrol pumps, vending machines, touristic maps, hoardings, fences, scaffolds, advertisement structures, cables, wires, pipelines[61] and other prescribed appliances on, under, over or along a public road.[62] Article 151 of the 1994 Regulations prescribes the following appliances and structures:

(a) a petrol, oil or other storage tank (together with any associated manhole, inlet, outlet, or pipe for connection with a pump),

(b) a delivery pipe or hose attached to a petrol pump or oil pump, which is erected in a permanent position and which is not on a public road,

(c) a moveable pump or other appliance for dispensing any oil or any oil derivative or mixture thereof,

(d) a case, rack, shelf or other appliance or structure for displaying articles for the purposes of advertisement or of sale in or in connection with any adjacent business premises,

(e) tables and chairs outside a hotel, restaurant or public house,

(f) a cabinet used as part of a wired broadcast relay service by a person licensed under the Wireless Telegraphy (Wired Broadcast Relay Licence) Regulations, 1974 (S.I. No. 67 of 1974),

(g) a lamp post,

(h) a bridge, arch, tunnel, passage or other similar structure which is used or is intended to be used other than by the public and was constructed on or after October 1, 1964,

(i) a cellar or other underground structure constructed on or after October 1, 1964,

---

[60] For the definition of "advertisement" and "advertisement structure", see 1963 Act, s.2.

[61] Pipelines provided by An Bord Gais or required by the Minister under s.42(2) of the Gas Act 1976 are not subject to the licensing procedure under s.89: see Gas Act, 1976, s.42.

[62] Provisions as to fees for licences are to be found in the 1994 Regulations, arts. 152–155. For definition of "public road", see 1963 Act, s.2 which in turn refers to the definition under the Road Traffic Act 1961.

(j) a coin operated machine other than a vending machine, and

(k) an advertisement consisting of any symbol, emblem, model, device or logo.

A person applying for such a licence is obliged to furnish the planning authority with such plans and other information concerning the position, design and capacity of the appliance or structure as the authority may require.[63] The licence may be withdrawn and the licensee required to remove the appliance or structure at his own expense where, in the opinion of the planning authority, it is causing an obstruction or has become dangerous as a result of an increase or alteration of traffic on the road or because of the widening of or any improvement to the road. Any person may appeal to An Bord Pleanála against the grant, refusal, withdrawal or continuation of a licence, or against any condition attached to it.

The granting of licence under section 89 does not prevent the licensee from being amenable to proceedings under other legislation or at common law.[64] An offence is committed where any person who is obliged to obtain a licence fails to do so or acts in breach of the licence or a condition attached to it.

Planning authorities are themselves entitled to erect on public roads any appliance or structure referred to in the section without obtaining a licence. A planning authority may not grant a licence in respect of a national or regional road for which they are not the road authority, unless they have first consulted with the appropriate road authority.[65]

3.1.10 Revocation or modification of permission

If a planning authority decide that it is expedient that any planning permission should be revoked or modified, they may, by serving a notice under section 30 of the 1963 Act on the owner and the occupier of the land, revoke or modify the permission. The making of an order under the section is a reserved function. The authority are restricted to considering the proper planning and development of their area (including the preservation and the improvement of the amenities thereof) in deciding whether it is expedient to serve such a notice. They are also obliged to have regard to the provision of the development plan and any special amenity area order relating to the area.

The power to revoke or modify a permission may be exercised:

(a) where the permission relates to the carrying out of works, at any time before those works have commenced,

---

[63] 1963 Act, s.89(2).
[64] *ibid.*, s.89(6).
[65] "National or regional road" was substituted for "main road" under s.89(10) by the Roads Act 1993, s.6.

(b) in the case of works which have been commenced and which, consequent on the making of a variation in the development plan, will contravene such a plan, at anytime before those works have been completed[66];

(c) where the permission relates to a change of the use of land, at any time before the change has taken place.

A planning authority is only entitled to revoke or modify a permission where there has been a change in circumstances relating to the proper planning and development of the area concerned since the annulment of any previous enforcement notice, or, where no notice has been served, since the granting of permission.[67] They are obliged to specify in their decision the change in circumstances which warranted the revocation or modification.[68] A planning authority cannot revoke or modify an approval but may render it nugatory by revoking the underlying outline permission.[69]

A planning permission may be revoked by a road authority under a motorway scheme, busway scheme or protected road scheme under section 47 of the Roads Act 1993, which is approved by the Minister.[70] Where the scheme specifies a planning permission to be revoked, the permission stands suspended until the Minister approves or refuses to approve the scheme. Any modification of a planning permission becomes operational on the making of the scheme and continues to have effect during the period between the making of the scheme and the Minister's decision on the application for approval. A claim for compensation may be made where the Minister has approved the scheme as if the revocation or modification had been made by order of the planning authority under section 30 of the 1963 Act.[71] Particulars of planning permissions proposed to be revoked or modified under the scheme and the decisions of the minister to the extent that it affects such permissions must be entered on the planning register.[72]

3.1.11 Designation of areas for environmental protection

The designation of areas for special environmental protection arising out of Ireland's obligations under E.U. directives or regulations, or otherwise, may influence a planning authority in adjudicating on a particular application.[73] Where such a designation amounts to a determination affecting the rights and liabilities of individuals, proper notification procedures must be observed to ensure that those affected have a reasonable opportunity to object to or make

---

66 The revocation or modification of permission for the carrying out of works cannot affect so much of the works as has been previously carried out. See s.30(5) of the 1963 Act.

67 1963 Act, s.30(2A), inserted by 1976 Act, s.39(i). Costello P., July 28, 1995.

68 1963 Act, s.30(2B) inserted by 1976 Act, s.39(i).

69 *State (Cogley) v. Dublin Corporation* [1970] I.R. 244.

70 Roads Act 1993, s.47(4).

71 *ibid.*, s.52(6).

72 *ibid.*, s.47(4)(c).

73 See further, Scannell, *Environmental and Planning Law* (1995), pp. 118–123.

representations on the proposed designation; otherwise the courts may declare such a designation to be invalid. In *MacPharthalain v. Commissioners of Public Works*,[74] the Supreme Court held that the extension of an area originally designated by the Wildlife Service as an area of international scientific importance (A.S.I.), amounted to a decision which affected the rights of landowners within that area as it removed their entitlement to afforestation grants. The decision by Blayney J. to grant an order of certiorari quashing the designation was upheld.

3.1.12 Listed buildings

Planning authorities may include objectives in their development plans for:

- the preservation of buildings of artistic, architectural or historical interest[75]
- the preservation of plasterwork, staircases, woodwork, or other fixtures or features of artistic, historic or architectural interest and forming part of the interior of structures.[76]

Buildings and interiors listed for preservation are in practice normally scheduled to the development plan. The exemptions conferred under article 9 of the 1994 Regulations do not apply to buildings or interiors which are listed in a development plan or draft development plan.[77] Similarly the exemptions for certain internal works conferred by section 4(1)(g) of the 1963 Act do not apply to listed buildings under the development plan, but not under a draft plan.[78] The same effect would appear to be achieved by the wording of section 4(1)(g) of the 1963 Act in relation to the exemption for certain external works.[79] Compensation provisions concerning listed buildings and interiors are considered elsewhere.[80]

3.1.13 Objects of archaeological, geological or historical interest

Planning authorities may include objectives in their development plan relating to the "preservation of caves, sites, features and other objects of archaeological, geological or historical interest. Such objects are to some extent protected from despoilation by development by the introduction of a new provision under Article 10(i)(a)(vii) of the 1994 Regulations which "de-exempts" the exemptions created under article 9. The protection of such features and objects of interest is also assisted by the compensation provisions under the Local Government (Planning

---

74 [1994] 3 I.R. 353.
75 1963 Act, Sched. 3, Pt. IV, para. 5.
76 *ibid.*, para. 5A, inserted by 1976 Act, s.43(1).
77 Art. 10(1)(ix). See also the restriction on the use of listed buildings under art. 10(1)(xi) in certain cases. A more detailed treatment of this particular topic is contained in Scannell, above n.73, *op. cit.*, pp. 260–264. See also *Blessington.*
78 1963 Act, s.4(1)(A), inserted by the 1976 Act, s.43(1)(c).
79 See further below at para. 5.2.6.
80 See paras. 12.4 and 12.5, below.

and Development) Act 1990.[81] This of course represents a very limited form of protection unless strong development control policies are pursued by the planning authorities and An Bord Pleanála.[82] Any archaeological programme stipulated under a planning condition together with accompanying time delays may be a significant cost burden for the developer but "in general, the expectation is that the site owner/developer will have to pay for excavation that may be necessary where a site is of particular importance or where the structures will unavoidably penetrate archaeological strata".[83]

Class 39 of Schedule 2, Part I of the 1994 Regulations provide an exemption for:

> "The excavation for the purposes of research or discovery–
> (a) pursuant to and in accordance with a licence under section 26 of the National Monuments Act, 1930 (No. 2 of 1930), of a site, feature or other object of archaeological or historic interest;
> (b) of a site, feature or other object of geological interest."

3.1.14 Enforcement of open spaces

Section 25 of the 1976 Act was introduced to tackle the problem of unfinished housing estates. It gives planning authorities powers of compulsory acquisition where a developer is not complying with the terms and conditions of a planning permission which require certain provision for open space.[84] The planning authority may request the owner of the land to provide, level, plant or otherwise maintain the open spaces referred to within a specified period of not less than two months from the date of the request. If the owner fails to comply, the planning authority may then publish an acquisition notice in a newspaper circulating in the district stating that the authority intends to acquire the land and specifying a period during which an appeal may be made.[85] A copy of the notice must be served on the owner of the land. In the event that no appeal is lodged or any appeal submitted has been withdrawn the planning authority may make an

---

81 See 1990 Act, s.12 and Sched. 2, class 3; Sched. 3, class 10; Sched. 4, classes 15, 17, 18. See paras. 12.4 and 12.5, below. See also notification requirements for planning applications and decisions which impinge on such objects.

82 Note that any work carried out by the Commissioners of Public Works under the National Monuments Acts is unaffected by planning controls: 1963 Act, s.90. See also Local Government (Planning and Development) Act 1993, discussed below at para. 5.3.

83 McCarron, "The Developer and the Archaeologist", *Insite, Irish Branch, Southern Section, Royal Town Planning Institute Newsletter* (August, 1989) Dublin; quoted in Hyde, *Building on the Past – Urban Change and Archaeology*, Environmental Institute, University College Dublin, which contains some case studies of developments at Rathdown Upper, Greystones, Christchurch Place (the Jury's Hotel site) and Nos. 16 and 17 Cook Street, Dublin.

84 The power under this section may not be used to acquire land which is described as private open space in the application: 1976 Act, s.25(10). See also *Dublin County Council v. Greally* [1990] I.L.R.M. 48.

85 The period within which an appeal can be made should not be less than two months from the date of publication of the notice.

acquisition order which operates to vest the land in the authority. If the matter goes to appeal the An Bord Pleanála may annul the acquisition notice or confirm it with or without modification.[86]

In *Dublin County Council v. Brennan and McGowan Ltd*,[87] an area of land which was described in a site layout plan accompanying a planning application as an "open green area" was held to be public open space to which an acquisition notice could apply, although a condition requiring the provision of public open space referred only to areas specifically described as such.[88] Barron J. stated that "it is explicit in the application for permission that the land would be provided as open space and at least implicit that it would be maintained as such."

---

[86] A very limited entitlement to compensation exists: see Nowlan, *op. cit.*, p. 60, n.4: comments on the constitutionality of the provision.

[87] Unreported, High Court, February 7, 1983.

[88] The application variously described the area in question as a "reserved area", a "public open area" and as "an amenity area".

Chapter 4

DEVELOPMENT

Development control is a function of planning involving the assessment of applications for permission to carry out physical alterations to or changes in the use of land or other structures which have implications for the planning system. The definition of development determines what physical alterations or changes of use are to be brought within the control net. An obligation to obtain planning permission arises where development has occurred since October 1, 1964 unless it is exempted under the planning code. In conveyancing, the definition of development assumes an additional significance in the light of Article 36(a)(1) of the Law Society General Conditions of Sale (1996) which provides:

> "36. (a) Unless the Special Conditions contain a provision to the contrary, the Vendor warrants:
>
> (1) either
>
> > (i) that there has been no development (which term includes material change of use) of, or execution of works on or to, the subject property since the 1st day of October, 1964, for which Planning Permission or Building Bye-Law Approval was required by law; or
> > (ii) that all Planning Permissions and Building Bye-Law Approvals required by law for the development of, or the execution of works on or to, the subject property as at the date of sale, or for any change in the use thereof to that ruling at the date of sale, were obtained (save in respect of matters of trifling materiality), and that, where implemented, the conditions thereof and the conditions expressly notified with said Permissions by any Competent Authority in relation to and specifically addressed to such development or works were complied with substantially . . ."

The effect of this condition is that the vendor warrants that there has been no unauthorised development requiring planning permission since October 1, 1964 (the date of the commencement of the Act).

4.1 STATUTORY DEFINITIONS OF DEVELOPMENT

4.1.1 "Works" and "use"

Development is defined under section 3(1) of 1963 Act as follows:

> "Development" in this Act means, save where the context otherwise requires, the carrying out of any works on, in, or under land or the making of any material change in the use of any structures or other lands.

Irish Planning Law and Procedure

The definition refers to (1) the carrying out of "works" and, (2) the making of any "material change of use". Section 2 of the 1963 Act contains a number of definitions relevant to the meaning of "development'. "Works" are defined as "including any act or operation of construction, excavation, demolition, extension, alteration, repair or renewal". "Alterations" include "any plastering or painting which materially alters the external appearance of the structure so as to render such appearance inconsistent with the character of the structure or of neighbouring structures". "Use . . . does not include the use of land by the carrying out of works thereon." It is essentially a description of a factual state of affairs, *i.e.* the activities defined from a planning point of view which at any given time are being carried out on that land.[1] The definition of "land" in this context "includes any structure and any land covered with water (whether inland or coastal). . .".

The exclusionary nature of the definition of "use" was examined in the context of the compensation provisions of the planning code in *Re Viscount Securities Ltd*.[2] The claimant had been refused planning permission by Dublin County Council for the erection of 288 four bedroomed houses on 47 acres of agricultural land. Under section 56(1)(a) of the 1963 Act, no compensation was payable where the development included the making of any material change in the use of land. The County Council contended that the development necessarily consisted of, or at least included the making of a material change in the use of the agricultural land, so that no compensation was payable. The claimants, relying on the artificial definition of "use" under section 2 of the 1963 Act, argued that since the erection of the houses would necessarily consist of works, the proposed development did not amount to the making of any material change in the use of the land, so that the right to compensation was not excluded. On a case stated by the property arbitrator to the High Court, Finlay P. gave a strict interpretation to the provision having regard to its purpose which was to restrict property rights:

> "The provisions in general contained in the Act of 1963 entitling a planning authority to refuse permission and the Minister on appeal to confirm such refusal or issue in effect a new refusal for the development of land is an invasion or restriction of the full property rights of an owner of land. If, therefore, the legislature intended that such invasion, restriction or reduction of property rights should be enacted without providing compensation in the event of a reduction in value for damage suffered, it is a necessary principle of the construction statutes in accordance with the constitution that they should have expressly and unambiguously so provided".

Finlay P. held that the development being "works" could not be a "material change of use" so that it did not fall within the scope of section 56(1)(a).

---

[1] Alder, "The Loss of Existing Use Rights – What Difference does Planning Permission Make" (1989) J.P.L. 816.

[2] 112 I.L.R.M 17. Note that in *Dublin County Council v. Sellwood Quarries Ltd* [1981] I.L.R.M. 23, Gannon J. said that the reference to "use" under s.2 of the 1963 Act was "not a definition but a distinction necessarily made to relate to the word "development" as defined in s.3(1) of that Act.

This separation of the two limbs of the definition of development is of importance in determining the scope of exempted development provisions; some exemptions apply only to works, others only to changes of use. Similarly, enforcement action may be directed solely against the use of land, leaving intact physical structures in which the unauthorised activity is being carried out. The two broad divisions of development are not necessarily always exclusive and may sometimes overlap. The same activity might constitute both works and a change of use.[3]

A case in point is mining activity, which has been variously found to constitute "works" and "use" respectively. In *Patterson v. Murphy*,[4] Costello J. held that quarrying activities involving the blasting of rock, the crushing and screening of stones and their transport from the site constituted "operations" rather than a change in the use of land because the statutory definition of "works" included "any act or operation of excavation", and the definition of "use" expressly excluded works.

In the subsequent decision in *Galway County Council v. Lackagh Rock*,[5] Barron J. treated similar quarrying activity as involving the use of land rather than works. More confusingly still, in *Dublin County Council v. Sellwood Quarries Ltd*,[6] Gannon J. said that the quarrying activity constituted "the carrying out of works on the land, and in relation to the land involves a material change of use. . .". The leading U.K. decision on this point is *Thomas Davis (Porthcawl) Ltd v. Penybont R.D.C.*,[7] in which it was held that "each bite of the shovel" was a fresh mining operation and constituted a separate act of development.[8] However, activities ancillary to mining excavation to the land and physical alteration to the land can be referred to in terms of the use of land.

4.1.2 Specific situations

Section 3(2) specifies a number of situations which are to be treated as a material change of use. It provides:

> "(2) for the purposes of sub-section (1) of this section and without prejudice to the generality thereof—
> (a) where any structure on the land or any tree or other object on land becomes use for the exhibition of advertisements; or

---

[3]   *West Bowers Farm Products v. Essex County Council* [1985] J.P.L. 857: see also *Northavon District Council v. Secretary of State for the Environment* (1980) 40 P & C.R. 332.

[4]   [1978] I.L.R.M. 85.

[5]   [1985] I.R. 20.

[6]   Above, n.2.

[7]   [1972] 1 W.L.R. 1526.

[8]   This has consequences for the operation of the time limits for the enforcement of breaches of planning control under the Local Government (Planning and Development) Act 1992, s.19, as it brings forward the date of any unauthorised development.

(b) where land becomes used for any of the following purposes:
    (i) the placing or keeping of any vans, tents or other objects, whether
        or not moveable and whether or not collapsible, for the purpose
        of caravaning or camping or the sale of goods;
    (ii) the storage of caravans or tents;
    (iii) the deposit of bodies or other parts of vehicles, old metal, mining
        or industrial waste, builders' waste, rubble or debris, the use of
        the land shall be taken as having materially changed."

4.1.2.1 *Sub-division of dwellings*

Section 3(3) provides that a material change of use may occur where a single
dwelling is sub-divided:

> "For the avoidance of doubt it is hereby declared that for the purposes of this
> section the use as two or more dwellings of any structure previously used as a
> single dwelling involves a material change in the use of the structure and of each
> part thereof which is so used".

Notwithstanding the intent of this provision, there is still a substantial area of
"doubt" as to when the sub-division of a single dwelling into separate dwellings
occurs. In *Ealing Corporation v. Ryan,*[9] an enforcement notice was served on the
respondents requiring the use of their property as two or more separate dwellings
to be discontinued. The house was occupied by three families and one individual
who inhabited different parts of the house. All of the occupants shared kitchen
facilities which were on the ground floor, and it appeared that lavatory facilities
were also shared. The court had to decide whether the property was being used
for two or more separate dwelling-houses within the ambit of the equivalent provision of section 12 of the Town and Country Planning Act 1962. Ashworth J.,
who read the judgment of the court said:

> "In my judgement, a house may well be occupied by two or more persons, who
> are to all intents and purposes living separately, without that house being thereby
> used as separate dwellings. In other words, persons may live separately under one
> roof without occupying separate dwellings . . .
>
> The important words in sub-section 3 are 'separate dwelling' houses: multiple
> occupation, as it is sometimes called, is not enough by itself, and to bring the
> sub-section into play the dwelling house and houses formed out of the building
> previously used as a single dwelling house must in truth be separate. In many cases, of
> which the present case is an example, the question whether there has been a change of
> use within the ambit of sub-section 3 is one of fact and degree. The existence or
> absence of any form of physical reconstruction is a relevant fact; another is the extent
> to which the alleged separate dwellings can be regarded as separate in the sense of
> being self-contained and independent of other parts of the same property. There are, no
> doubt, other matters which it is necessary to set out, and indeed it would be unwise to
> attempt an exhaustive list of the factors which may prove to be relevant."

---

[9]   [1965] 2 Q.B. 486

Even where the statutory provision does not apply, an increase in the number of occupants may result in an intensification of use amounting to a material change of use. A change in the type of occupancy may also be material, as for example, where a private dwelling is let commercially[10] or where a dwelling house becomes used as a hostel for the homeless.[11] But in *Dublin Corporation v. Sullivan*,[12] Finlay P. (as he then was) held that the applicants had not established an intensification of use amounting to a material change of use arising out of the conversion of premises containing two separate flats which "could well have contained a family of four or even five people each" into five flat units providing accomodation for seven students. He said:

> "In particular, I am satisfied that as a matter of common sense, intensification of user cannot merely be established by proving the existence of separate tenancies."[13]

4.2 MATERIAL CHANGE OF USE

4.2.1 Approach of the courts

The expression "material change of use" has not been defined in the planning code and it has consequently proved a fertile ground for judicial reasoning. The courts have evolved a number of concepts in order to describe the many and varied situations in which it becomes necessary to submit alterations in the use of land t planning control. A number of recent decisions have illustrated the dangers in straying too far from the statutory wording and its implications.

The determination of "materiality" firstly involves the identification of two uses which are capable of being separately defined, and secondly, a comparison of these uses to decide whether the change is material.

4.2.2 Difference of approach between U.K. and Irish decisions

English and Scottish jurisprudence on the meaning of "material change of use" has developed in a different manner to the Irish case law, partly due to an early U.K. ministerial circular[14] which advised planning authorities to ignore the

---

[10] See *Blackpool Borough Council v. Secretary of State for the Environment* (1980) 40 P. & C.R. 104; *Birmingham Corporation v. Minister of Housing and Local Government Habib Ullah* [1964] 1 Q.B. 178. See also An Bord Pleanála section 5 reference determination no. 69. R.F. 0749.

[11] See also *Panayi v. Secretary of State for the Environment* [1985] J.P.L. 783 (change from use as four self-contained flats to use as a hostel); *Clarke v. Minister of Housing and Local Government* (use as a single family residence of a house used by the gardener attached to the main house to use as a hostel by waiters employed in the main house which had become a hotel was held to be capable in law of being a material change of use). See also *Dublin Corporation v. Bentham* [1993] 2 I.R. 58 (change from bedsitters to a guest house held to be a material change of use).

[12] Unreported, High Court, December 21, 1984.

[13] Presumably, if the Corporation had shown that each of the flats had its own kitchen and bathroom facilities, the change of use could have been brought within s.3(2).

[14] Circular 67/49.

planning implications of a change of use in determining its materiality. Most of the English and Scottish cases dealing with the definition of "development" concern appeals from, ministerial decisions on enforcement notices or appeals against refusals of permission by the planning authorities. These decisions consequently reflect the reluctance of the courts to interfere with the findings of fact of the Secretary of State and consistently emphasise that the question as to whether a material change of use has occurred is a question of fact and degree in every case. The findings of fact of the minister will only be set aside if he has misdirected himself on the law or in circumstances where he could not reasonably have come to the conclusion he did on the basis of the facts agreed as found by him. In other words, the U.K. decisions in many instances establish that a particular change of use is capable of being a material change of use but not that it actually constitutes a material change of use.

Ministerial decisions which depend on their individual facts are not regarded as persuasive authority in this jurisdiction. Case law authorities are, however, important in establishing the relevant criteria in deciding whether development has occurred.

By contrast, the Irish courts regularly have to consider *ab initio* the question as to whether development has taken place on the facts of a particular case in exercising their jurisdiction to grant or refuse orders under section 27 of the Local Government (Planning and Development) Act 1976.[15] It is suggested that the Irish courts are justified in taking a less conceptual approach to the definition of development than their English counterparts and should rely to a greater extent on the wording of the statutory definition and on a consideration of the planning effects of the change of use under consideration in the context of the development plan and general principles of proper planning and development.

4.2.3 The qualitative approach

The early English decisions were based on the principle that a change in the kind of use was always material, while a change in the degree of use was not usually so, unless it was very marked. They focused on the *terminus a quo* and the *terminus a quem*. This approach, stemming from the ministerial circular referred to concentrated on the verbal description of the uses concerned so that the consequences of the change of use were largely ignored. The determination as to whether the use was material or not consequently depended on the level of generality of the use description. For example, a change of use from use as an ordinary dwelling house to use as a house let in lodgings or for short term holiday periods would not be material if both were classified as "residential". A further difficulty was that the test failed to take full account of the fact that the intensification of

---

15   As amended by 1992 Act, s.19.

activity on a site might present fresh planning problems although no change in the type of use had occurred.[16]

This qualitative approach adopted in the earlier English and Scottish decisions, has often been expressed in the requirement that there should be a change in the "character" of the use or that the change of use should "affect a definable character of the use". So, a change in the subjective purpose of an occupier for a particular activity is not regarded as affecting the character of the use: It is the character of the use of the land, not the particular purpose of a particular occupier which is to be considered.[17] A change in the identity of the person carrying out an activity or a change in the ownership or supply of goods used in the course of that activity do not of themselves bring about a material change of use. In *East Barnet U.D.C. v. British Transport Commission*,[18] two parcels of land adjacent to a railway which had been used for the storage of coal transported by rail by BTC became used for the handling and storage of crated vehicles by Vauxhall. Lord Parker C.J. said:

> "The mere fact that the commodity changes does not necessarily mean that the land is being used for a different purpose nor is there any relevance in the fact that the purpose for which the land is used is effected by other hands. Again, it can make no difference that the new commodity is not owned by the British Transport Commission."

In *Lewis v. Secretary of State for the Environment*,[19] a garage had been used for the repair and maintenance of a fleet of 25 to 32 vehicles owned by a company engaged in the wholesale and retail business at a completely different location. There was no question of the repair use being "ancillary" to the wholesale and retail business because of its geographical separation. Subsequently, the garage ceased to be used by the company and a motor repair business commenced as an independent use. On an appeal against an enforcement notice, the Secretary of State found that the later use as a commercial garage for the benefit of the public at large was different in character from the previous use, and that the resultant change was one which, as a matter of fact and degree, was material. A Divisional Court allowed an appeal against the decision of the Secretary of State, Lord Widgery C.J. stating as follows:

---

[16]   See further, Alder, *Development Control* (2nd ed., 1989), pp.74–77, on the dangers associated with the *genus et speciem* approach.

[17]   See also *Furlong v. McConnell* [1990] I.L.R.M. 48. An unusual Irish decision is *Cusack & Mc Kenna v. Minister for Local Government*, unreported, High Court, November 4, 1980, in which McWilliam J. concluded, *obiter*, that a change from use as a dentist's practice to use as a solicitor's office was material. The learned judge did not analyse the uses in terms of their land use implications but in the context of the nature of the professions concerned:

> "The two professions have nothing in common other than the attributes common to all professions and to hold that there is not a material change in use would, to my mind, be perverse. The professions are completely different in their training, in their skills and their nature."

[18]   [1962] 2 Q.B. 484.

[19]   (1971) 23 P. & C.R. 125.

"It is not my understanding of the law that, if the activities remain exactly the same throughout the relevant period, a material change of use can occur merely because of a change in the identity of the person carrying out that activity.

Similarly, I am not prepared to accept that, if the use throughout the relevant period is the repair of motor vehicles, a material change of use can occur, merely because the ownership or source of supply of those motor vehicles has changed."

In some cases, the characteristics of particular uses have been identified. The change of use of premises from user as bed-sitters or flats into a guest-house has been held in *Dublin Corporation v. Bentham*[20] to amount to a material change of use. Morris J. stated:

"While I accept that in many instances the distinction may be unclear (for instance the distinction between hostel and a guest-house), in this particular case I have no doubt whatever that there is a clear distinction between on the one hand a bed-sitter or a flat and on the other hand a guest-house. I accept Mr. Pascal Dunne's evidence in which he drew factual distinctions between bed-sitters, flats, hotels and guest-houses. A large number of the features which are to be found in a guest-house or hotel are not to be found in a flat or bed-sitter."

Changes of use which are *de minimis* can be ignored, as they do not affect the character of the use.

4.2.4 Material for planning purposes

"Material" in this context means "material for planning purposes".[21] The considerations to be taken into account in determining materiality must at least be relevant to "proper planning and development and the preservation of amenities" which are the twin objectives of the preamble to legislation. The question is whether there are sufficient planning considerations raised by the change in activity to justify its submission to development control.[22] It is not necessary to establish that the planning consequences of the change of use would merit a refusal of planning permission, or that they would meet with objections from local residents or members of the public in general.[23] These questions only become relevant when an application has been submitted.

A systems approach to planning divides the planning system as a whole into a number of different sub-systems – transport, housing, education and so on –

---

20   Above, n.11.

21   See *Monaghan County Council v. Brogan* [1987] I.R. 333, in which Keane J. endorsed Lord Parker C.J.'s statement to this effect in *East Barnet U.D.C. v. British Transport Commission*, above n.18. In *Williams v. Minister for Housing and Local Government*, local economic considerations were taken into account as an element of the planning impact of the change of use from the ancillary sale of home grown produce to the additional sale of imported produce.

22   See Barron J.'s test in *Galway County Council v. Lackagh Rock*, but note the more qualitative approach taken by Keane J. in *Brogan* discussed below at para. 4.3.10. Alder, above, n.16, *op. cit.*, pp.71–72 has also suggested that the change must be physical as distinct from mental and substantial rather than merely trivial.

23   See *Monaghan County Council*, above, n.21, *per* Keane J.

with interrelationships between each of these sub-systems. Any significant increase in pressure on the supply side of any one of these systems produced by new development would be regarded as "material" from a planner's point of view.[24] But the claims of modern town planning philosophy on the city in the economic, social and spatial fields have become so extensive and, as a corollary, so potentially invasive of property rights, that a more restrictive view of what constitutes "planning matters" is needed.[25] In *Dublin Corporation v. Moore*,[26] McCarthy J. said:

> "It is important to recognise that the consequences of breaches of the planning code are penal in nature and, therefore, the statutes enforcing them must be strictly construed".

This suggests that planning considerations are confined to the matters expressly referred to in the planning code itself – the purposes for which objectives may be indicated in development plans, the types of conditions which may be imposed on planning permission, the reasons for refusal, and for the imposition of conditions, for which the right to compensation is excluded.[27] In practice, most of the planning considerations applicable to a particular proposal may be found in the development plan.[28]

4.2.5 Relevance of development plan

A change of use must be established to be material on the facts of the particular case under consideration, and not merely in the abstract, based on an application of the development plan to the type of use involved. In other words, the approach is to look at the actual uses involved and their actual consequences, as distinct from the notional uses and their normal consequences.[29] This approach appears to have been followed by Barron J. in *Rehabilitation Institute v. Dublin Corporation*.[30] A four storey building had been used by the Institute, largely for administrative purposes, but one of the floors was devoted to the training of the handicapped. When the Institute decided to sell the premises, it submitted a reference to An Bord

---

[24] See B. McLoughlin, *A Systems Approach to Planning*. This sort of approach is evident in Barron J.'s judgment in *Galway County Council*, above, n.5. See also *Guildford R.D.C. v. Fortescue* [1959] 2 Q.B. 112 at 125.

[25] See the preamble to the 1963 Act.

[26] [1984] I.L.R.M. 339.

[27] See *Development Control – Advice and Guidelines* (Department of the Environment, 1982), para. 10.201.

[28] However, a matter referred to in the development plan may not always be a valid planning consideration: see *Grange Developments v. Dublin County Council* [1986] I.R. 246 (liability of planning authority to pay compensation arising out of a decision on a planning application); *Glencar Explorations plc v. Mayo County Council* [1993] 2 I.R. 237.

[29] See *Blum (Lilo) v. Secretary of State for the Environment* (1987) J.P.L. 278.

[30] Unreported, High Court, January 14, 1988. But note that Grant refers to similar views expressed by Diplock L.J. in *Wilson v. West Sussex County Council* [1963] 2 Q.B. 764 at 785, as an "extreme approach [which] has not found subsequent endorsement": See *Urban Planning Law* (1982), p.164.

Pleanála under section 5 of the 1963 Act to determine whether the change from the existing use of the building to a use solely to office purposes would consitute a material change of use. The Board determined that the change of use of the first floor to offices would constitute development which was not exempted, but this decision was appealed to the High Court. Barron J. held that the planning authority had failed to establish that a material change of use would occur, stating as follows:

> "Evidence was given that greater consideration would be given to the question of car parking in relation to premises used for offices as opposed to premises used for educational purposes. But no evidence was given to indicate whether this consideration would have been material in considering the actual alleged change of use in the present case, *i.e.* the change of use from either general administrative purposes or educational purposes to office purposes. On balance, it seems to me that the defendant has been unable to show that the alleged change of use on the first floor amounts to a material change of use."

4.2.6 "Judicial zoning"

The courts may be reluctant to treat as relevant to planning, certain types of reduction in "neighbourhood amenity" resulting from a change of use, as this could lay the Court open to charges of "judicial zoning".[31] In *Dublin Corporation v. Moore*,[32] where the Supreme Court had to determine in the context of enforcement proceedings whether the parking of an ice-cream van in the driveway of an ordinary dwelling house constituted a material change of use, McCarthy J. said:

> "The driveway of a house is always intended for the parking of vehicles; it would be difficult to find a driveway to a house in the City or County of Dublin where it was not so used . . . the residents of a quiet suburb naturally resented the presence of what may well be out of keeping with what they conceived to be the standards appropriate to the neighbourhood. There cannot, however be one law for Cabra and another for Clondalkin, yet others for Finglas and Foxrock. Considerations of this kind are not appropriate to planning law – if they were they might well offend against rights of equality. The ordinary law of nuisance remains if nuisance there be. . ."

4.3 THE PLANNING UNIT

4.3.1 The planning unit

Section 3 of the 1963 Act, which defines development, is silent as to the unit of land which is to be selected in order to determine whether a material change of

---

[31] See the comments of Gannon J. in *Furlong v. McConnell* [1990] I.L.R.M. 48. See *Birmingham Corporation v. Hibib Ullah* [1964] 1 Q.B. 178 at 188, *per* Parker L.C.J. On the other hand, Alder has remarked that the planning impact approach to "materiality", while preferable to the *genus et speciem* aproach, "invites local planning authorities to make value judgments about the social quality of a neighbourhood."

[32] [1984] I.L.R.M. 339.

use has occurred, referring merely to the "making of any material change in the use of any structure or other land". As Lord Widgery C.J. remarked in *Johnston v. Secretary of State for the Environment*:

> "It is quite obvious that a single activity may be a material change in the use of a relatively small area in which it takes place without being a material change of use of a much larger area of which that area is a part, and so one must begin by deciding what is the planning unit."[33]

The *locus classicus* is *Burdle v. Secretary of State for the Environment*,[34] in which Bridge J. formulated three principles for the determination of the appropriate planning unit:

> "First, that whenever it is possible to recognise a single main purpose of the occupier's use of his land to which secondary activities are incidental or ancillary, the whole unit of occupation should be considered . . . but, secondly, it may equally be apt to consider the entire unit of occupation even though the occupier carries on a variety of activities and it is not possible to say that one is incidental or ancillary to another. This is well settled in a case of a composite use where the component activities fluctuate in their intensity from time to time but the different activities are not confined within separate and physically distinct areas of land.
>
> Thirdly, however, it may frequently occur that within a single unit of occupation two or more physically separate and distinct areas are occupied for substantially different and unrelated purposes. In such a case, each area used for a different main purpose (together with its incidental and ancillary activities), ought to be considered as a separate planning unit."

These principles are a useful vehicle for analysis of the process of determining the appropriate planning unit, and are considered in turn below.

4.3.2 The occupational unit: the first principle of *Burdle*

The unit of occupation is the normal unit of independent economic and social activity and in *Burdle*, Bridge L.J. suggested that "as a useful working rule" it should be taken as the appropriate planning unit.[35] Its selection as the planning unit may also be justified in order to prevent the unfair operation of enforcement powers. As Lord Widgery C.J. pointed out in *Johnston v. Secretary of State*[36]:

> "It is not to be overlooked in these cases that it may be in the interest of the occupier himself to have the planning unit confined to the land in his own occupation. If it is so confined, he is at least in control of everything which happens in the planning sphere which may adversely affect him, whereas if he

---

33   (1974) 28 P. & C.R. 424 at 426.
34   [1972] 1 W.L.R. 1207.
35   Approved by Blayney J. in *Dublin Corporation v. Regan Advertising Ltd* [1986] I.R. 171, (HC). In *Johnston*, above, n.33 at 427 Lord Widgery C.J. remarked that — "Mr Harris has not been able to show us any reported case in which the planning unit has been settled as being an area of land comprised in two different holdings or occupations".
36   (1974) 28 P. & C.R. 424 at 428. See also *Maddern v. Secretary of State for the Environment* [1980] J.P.L. 676.

was compelled to share a planning unit with another or others he might find enforcement action being taken against himself when the true fault lay with one of the other occupiers of the unit."

On the facts of *Johnston*, 44 garages were purpose built to house a fleet of taxis but were subsequently occupied by individual owners. The finding of the Secretary of State that each separately occupied garage constituted a planning unit was upheld by the court.[37]

The first principle in *Burdle* invites the identification of the primary use of the occupational unit and those activities which are "ancillary" or incidental to it. The character of the use of land is determined by its primary use and not by parts of its use.[38] For example a large retail store will normally have ancillary office and storage uses without which the functioning of the primary use would not be possible. Buildings and other physically separate areas which are contiguous to one another but are used for different purposes may all form one planning unit if there is one primary use to which the other uses are ancillary.[39] Similarily, an unused portion of a site may partake of the character of the site as a whole where it forms one planning unit.[40]

The first principle in *Burdle* echoes the earlier judgment of Diplock C.J. in *Trentham (G. Percy) Ltd v. Gloucestershire County Council*[41] in which a farmhouse and outbuildings which had been used for the storage of livestock and agricultural machinery were sold to a firm of civil engineering contractors who then used the outbuildings, *inter alia*, for the storage of building materials for use in their business. The Court of Appeal held that the prior use of the outbuildings by the farmer was merely ancillary to the use of the farm, and that they had not been used as a "repository" within the ordinary meaning of the word. Lord Diplock L.J. said that the local authority were entitled to look at:

"the whole of the area which was used for a particular purpose, including any part of that area whose use was incidental to or ancillary to the achievement of that purpose."

The Court of Appeal decided that the proper planning unit to be considered in determining the use of the outbuildings was not the outbuildings themselves, in

---

[37] In the context of a purpose built block of apartments, each individual apartment would appear to be a separate planning unit: *per* Lord Widgery C.J. in *Johnston*, above, n.33. Mere subdivision of the planning unit does not necessarily result in a material change of use. See *Winton v. Secretary of State for Environment* (1982) 46 P. & C.R. 205, discussed below at para. 4.3.9.

[38] *Pollock v. Secretary of State for the Environment* (1979) 40 P. & C.R. 94.

[39] *Vickers-Armstrong v. Central Land Board* (1957) 9 P. & C.R. 33. See also *Bromsgrove District Council v. Secretary of State for the Environment* [1977] J.P.L. 797. (use for the repairing of cars and farm machinery shifting from one building to another on a site containing three buildings; held that Secretary of State could properly have come to the conclusion that the planning unit was the appeal site as a whole).

[40] *East Barnet U.D.C. v. British Transport Commission* [1962] Q.B. 484.

[41] [1966] 1 W.L.R. 506; approved by Barron J. in *Rehabilitation Institute*, above, n.30.

isolation from the rest of the farm, but the farm as a whole, as the outbuildings had been used for ancillary agricultural purposes. Consequently, the change of use to be considered was a change from agricultural use to storage use, not from one type of storage use to another. On the facts of the case, it was "as plain as a pikestaff that there was a change of use from an agricultural use as farm buildings to a storehouse for other purposes".

4.3.3 Primary and ancillary uses

The ancillary use has its statutory basis in section 4 of the 1963 Act and in Article 11(4) of the 1994 Regulations which both refer to an "incidental" use. Section 4 refers to developments:

> "consisting of the use of any structure or other land within the curtilage of a dwelling-house for any purpose incidental to the enjoyment of the dwellinghouse as such"

– as being exempted from the obligation to obtain planning permission. In *Emin v. Secretary of State for the Environment*,[42] Sir Graham Eyre Q.C. (sitting as a deputy High Court Judge) said that the word incidental "connoted an element of subordination in land use terms".[43]

Article 11(4) provides:

> "A use which is ordinarily incidental to any use specified in Part IV of the Third Schedule is not excluded from that use as an incident thereto merely by reason of its being specified in the said part of the said Schedule as a separate use".

The concept of an ancillary activity or use has been judicially developed to describe a situation where one or more uses are subordinate or incidental to a main use. It recognises that a certain amount of economic activity is symbiotic. Planning law should not hinder normal economic activity by preventing the introduction of new ancillary uses or the re-arrangement of different functions within the occupational unit as a whole in the absence of any cogent planning reasons. The land on which or the structure within which an ancillary activity takes place is deemed to have the same use as the primary use of the land as a whole. The ancillary uses are not recognised as uses in their own right but in law partake of the character of their parent use.[44] For example, in a large department store, the use of storage and office areas may be treated as a shop use. This facilitates the introduction of new ancillary uses, changes from one type of ancillary use to another, and the displacement of an ancillary use by the primary use, without the necessity of applying for planning permission. Thus storage areas may be reclaimed for sales and an office area may become a restaurant for customers. But in certain circumstances the introduction of an ancillary use may lead to arguments

---

[42] (1989) 58 P. & C.R. 416.
[43] See para. 5.2.7, below. This view was subsequently endorsed by Slade C.J. and Farquharson J. in *Wallington v. Secretary of State for Wales* (1990) 62 P. & C.R. 150; [1991] J.P.L. 942.
[44] See Alder, above n.16, *op. cit.*, p.81.

that the use of the planning unit has been intensified where the increased level of activity is material in planning terms.[45]

In *Carroll and Colley v. Brushfield Limited* ("The Clarence Hotel" case),[46] it was contended that the change of use of the garage portion of a hotel to bar use did not amount to a material change of use as the planning unit was the hotel taken as a whole. Lynch J. stated:

> "*Prima facie*, I am of the view that the planning unit to be considered is the whole hotel complex, including bars, restaurants, bedrooms, lounge, television rooms, storerooms and the garage. *Prima facie* the swapping around or substitution of the use of part of the hotel does not alter the use of the planning unit as a hotel. The onus is on the applicants to show that in the circumstances of this particular case that *prima facie* state of affairs is ousted."

There are three situations in which an ancillary use may undergo a transformation so that a change of use may occur:

(a) When the link connecting the ancillary use and primary use is broken so that the ancillary use becomes a use in its own right[47];

(b) When the primary use ceases – once again, the ancillary use becomes an independent use[48];

(c) When the ancillary use is intensified to such an extent as to amount to a material change of use.[49]

It is submitted that in each of these three situations it remains necessary to establish that the change from one use to another is material in planning terms.[50]

4.3.4 "Ordinarily incidental"

Although there are no decided cases as to whether a use must be "ordinarily incidental" to a primary use which does not belong to any of the use classes that

---

[45]   See para. 4.3.10, below.

[46]   Unreported, High Court, Lynch J., October 9, 1992, for a similar decision in the U.K., see *Emma Hotels v. Secretary of State for the Environment* (1980) 41 P. & C.R. 255. Contrast *Carrickhall Holdings Ltd v. Dublin Corporation* [1983] I.L.R.M. 268. Note also that use as a hotel providing sleeping accommodation formerly fell within Sched. 3, Pt. IV, Class X to the 1977 Regulations so that intensification of the hotel use would have been exempted. This use class was dropped under the 1994 Regulations.

[47]   See *e.g.*, *Dublin Corporation v. Regan Advertising Ltd*, above, n.35. See also *Barling (David W.) v. Secretary of State for the Environment* [1980] J.P.L. 594; *Jillings v. Secretary of State for the Environment* [1984] J.P.L. 32.

[48]   See *e.g.*, *Galway County Council v. Connacht Proteins Ltd*, unreported, High Court, March 28, 1980; *Braddon v. Secretary of State for the Environment* [1976] J.P.L. 508.

[49]   *Hilliard v. Secretary of State for the Environment* (1978) 37 P. & C.R. 129. The principle would appear to be that an ancillary use may not intensify beyond the point where it ceases to be subordinate in land use terms to the primary use. See *Wallington v. Secretary of State for the Environment* [1991] J.P.L. 942. See also *Encyclopaedia of Planning Law and Practice*, P55.29.

[50]   See *Monaghan County Council v. Brogan* and *Galway County Council v. Lackagh Rock*, referred to above at nn.21, 22.

in order to partake of its legal character, there is an argument that *a fortiori* this must be so.[51] However, the question as to when a use may be regarded as "ordinarily incidental" inevitably involves a subjective assessment. Grant says:

> "Much decision making in this area necessarily involves the forming of value judgements as to the type and scope of ancillary activities ordinarily regarded as incidental to particular use descriptions. It involves the making of two determinations, first as to the level of abstraction at which the primary use is to be defined, and second as to the types of ancillary uses normally found in such cases."[52]

Hussain v. Secretary of State for the Environment concerned a decision of the Minister that the killing of live chickens at the back of a shop serving a predominantly Moslem neighbourhood in Birmingham was not ancillary to the retail use.[53] Evidence had been given that it was one of the tenets of the Moslem faith that chickens intended for human consumption should be slaughtered in a particular way and that "a really strict Moslem will see the chicken killed with his own eyes in order to be sure that proper formalities are observed". Lord Widgery C.J. said:

> "In deciding whether it is ordinarily incidental to retail trade generally one has not to consider the special requirements of particular localities, particular areas and particular customers; the question has to be judged by looking at the shop as an activity as a whole and asking whether this new activity is one which is ordinarily incidental to the operation of keeping a retail shop."

4.3.5 Composite or concurrent uses: the second rule in *Burdle*

The second rule in *Burdle* states that:

> "it may equally be apt to consider the entire unit of occupation even though the occupier carries on a variety of activities and it is not possible to say that one is incidental or ancillary to another. This is well settled in a case of a composite use where the component activities fluctuate in their intensity from time to time but the different activities are not confined within separate and physically distinct areas of land."

Where two or more uses are carried out without any clear physical separation, some fluctuation in the level of user is possible without a material change of use taking place.[54] The cessation of one of these uses does not of itself produce a

---

[51] The cases interpreting the provision under the Town and Country Planning Use Classes Order 1987 (U.K.) which corresponds with art. 11(4) of the 1994 Regulations have decided that a use which falls outside a particular use class may only be subsumed within that use class if it is ordinarily incidental to the use class *as a whole*. It was held in *Scrivener v. Minister of Housing and Local Government* that "ordinarily incidental" means incidental to the use class generally, and not to a particular process or use within that use class. See also *Rehabilitation Institute v. Dublin Corporation*, discussed at para. 4.2.5.

[52] See Grant, *Urban Planning Law* (1982), p.169.

[53] The scale of the activity was considered to be an important factor — up to 300 birds were slaughtered and sold each week. There are possible constitutional implications of the *Hussain* decision in the Irish context: see *Quinn's Supermarkets v. Attorney General* [1972] I.R. 1.

[54] See Grant, above, n.52, *op. cit.*, p.171.

material change of use. However, if the remaining use is extended to cover the area of the previous use, a material change of use will normally takes place by virtue of the displacement.[55] This will likewise occur where one of the use is intensified so as to give rise to fresh planning considerations.[56]

4.3.6 Seasonal uses

Section 40(b) of the 1963 Act shielded recurrent uses which were in place prior to the commencement of the Act by providing that permission would not be required:

> "in the case of land which, on the appointed day, is normally used for one purpose and is also used on occasions, whether at regular intervals or not, for any other purpose, in respect of the use of the land for that other purpose on similar occasions after the appointed day . . ."

This provision leaves a number of questions unanswered and there is no other guidance under the planning code as to whether seasonal uses require permission.[57]

4.3.7 Physical and functional separation: the third rule of *Burdle*

The third rule in *Burdle* refers to a situation where a number of different uses which are physically and functionally separate are taking place within the one occupational unit. If parts of land under the same occupation are physically separated to a significant extent, this may lead to a finding that they do not form a single planning unit. In *Duffy v. Secretary of State for the Environment*,[58] it was held that a staff hostel, which was situated 150 yards on the other side of a main road from the hotel where the staff worked, was capable of forming a separate planning unit.[59]

In other cases, functional separation has proven the dominant factor. In *Dublin Corporation v. Regan Advertising Ltd*, the two storey facade of industrial premises had been used over a period of 30 years to display the name of the company who owned the building and to advertise their business as "Commercial Body Builders and Engineers". The words were painted in large scripted letters across almost the entire 70 feet of the facade. In 1984, the first named respondents, who had entered a

---

[55]   See *Wipperman v. Barking London Borough Council* (1965) 17 P. & C.R. 225. But see Barron J.'s analysis of the facts in *Rehabilitation Institute*, above, n.30.

[56]   See *Philglow Limited v. Secretary of State for the Environment* [1985] J.P.L. 318; see also *Wipperman*, above.

[57]   In the context of U.K. legislation, it was held by the Court of Appeal in *Webber v. Minister of Housing and Local Government* [1968] 1 W.L.R. 29, that no material change of use occurred on each occasion that a seasonal use of land alternated. But see Grant, above n.52, *op. cit.*, p.172, who notes that Widgery L.J. while believing such an approach to be just and sensible, felt unable to adopt it on his interpretation of the legislation. See *Hawes v. Secretary of State for the Environment* (1965) 17 P. & C.R. 22.

[58]   [1972] 1 W.L.R. 1207.

[59]   See also *Fuller v. Secretary of State for the Environment* (1988) 56 P. & C.R. 84 and *Horwitz v. Rowson* [1960] 2 All E.R. 881.

licensing agreement with the new owners of the building, began to use the facade for the display of advertisements. Initially, free advertising structures were erected, but subsequently these were removed and instead, advertisements were affixed directly to the wall of the premises. These advertisements had no connection with the business being carried on within the premises or with the identity of the new owners. Dublin Corporation brought enforcement proceedings under section 27 of the 1976 Act to prohibit the continuance of an alleged unauthorised use of the building.

Blayney J. held that there had been a change of use of the facade as it was being used for the business of displaying advertisements, the purpose of which was different from that of the previous use. In considering whether this change of use was material, Blayney J. placed considerable reliance on the creation of a new planning unit, as is evident from his judgment:

> "Is this change a material one? In my opinion it is, since it involves a portion of the premises being used for a new and separate business. In this connection, it seems to me that the facade of the premises must be looked upon as a separate planning unit. In *Burdle and Another v. Secretary of State for the Environment*, [1972] 1 W.L.R. 1207 a decision of the Court of Appeal in England, Bridge J. said in the course of his judgment at p. 213:
>
>> It may be a useful working rule to assume that the unit of occupation is the appropriate planning unit unless and until some smaller unit can be recognised as the site of activities which amount in substance to a separate use both physically and functionally.
>
> In my opinion, the facade has become the site of activities, namely, the display of commercial advertisements, which amount to a separate use both physically and functionally from the remainder of the premises. And if one regards the facade as the planning unit, I think there is no doubt as to the change in its use being a material one."[60]

The degree of functional dependence or symbiosis necessary for a use to be treated as ancillary has been examined in a number of cases involving the sale of imported produce on agricultural land. An ancillary use may become a use in its own right even though the ancillary link with its parent use is not fully broken.

In *Chrysanthou v. Secretary of State for the Environment*,[61] premises were used as a retail baker's and confectioner's shop. All the bread sold in the shop was baked on the premises. The premises were then sold and a new oven was installed together with other more modern machinery than was previously employed in the business. The new owner began to sell his bread partly through the shop but partly also for wholesale to other businesses. Additional traffic was generated in the area which was a residential one. Lord Widgery C.J. upheld the

---

[60] [1986] I.R. 171 at 176. The conclusion could be reached from this passage from Blayney J.'s judgment that the mere subdivision of the planning unit without any attendant planning consequences amounts to a material change of use. In *Winton v. Secretary of State for the Environment* (1982) 46 P. & C.R. 205, Woolf J. held that such a conclusion was not justified. See para. 4.3.9, below.

[61] [1976] J.P.L. 371.

conclusion of the Secretary of State on an appeal from an enforcement notice that the bakery use had ceased to be ancillary and that the introduction of the wholesale trade had created a new and separate industrial use for the baking of bread, which was, as a matter of fact and degree, a material change of use.

In *Williams v. Minister of Housing and Local Government*,[62] the owner of a nursery garden commenced selling "imported fruits", in a structure in the nursery area which had previously been used for the retail sale of vegetables, flowers and fruit grown in the nursery garden. It was found that the primary use of the whole of the premises before the activity complained of began was used for agricultural purposes which carried with it incidental use rights for the sale of the produce of the land. Widgery C.J. held that the introduction of imported oranges, lemons and bananas which amounted to about 10 per cent of sales was capable of being material in planning terms:

> ". . . There is clearly, from a planning point of view, a significant difference in character between a use which involves selling the produce of the land itself, and a use which involved importing goods from elsewhere for sale. All sorts of planning considerations may arise which render one activity appropriate and desirable in a neighbourhood and the other activity quite unsuitable. Since there was that change in character of the use, and since the Minister has held, and again I think rightly, that the change could not be dismissed as *de minimis*, then in my judgement there was here material upon which the Minister could find that a material change of use has occurred."[63]

It has been held that there is a presumption that a dwelling-house constituted a single planning unit. In *Wood v. Secretary of State for the Environment*,[64] a farmer enjoyed existing use rights to sell both imported produce as well as home grown produce from the farmhouse and other buildings on the farm. A conservatory was then built onto the farmhouse, from which the sale of produce was carried on at a higher intensity than in other parts of the farmhouse. On appeal from a decision of the Secretary of State, the issue was as to whether the conservatory could be treated in isolation as a separate planning unit, against which the materiality of the change of use could be judged. Lord Widgery C.J. said:

> "In no case known to me, however, has it been said that, unless the circumstances are highly special, it is permissible to dissect a single dwellinghouse into different parts and treat them as different planning units for this purpose. Indeed, so far as authority goes it all seems to me to go the other way."

It followed that the permitted uses in the conservatory were the same as the permitted uses in the house. Lord Widgery C.J. upheld the Secretary of State's conclusion that, although the sale of imported produce had increased, it was not

---

[62] (1967) 18 P. & C.R. 514.
[63] *ibid.* at 518. See also *Bromley London Borough Council v. Hoeltschi (George) & Son* [1978] J.P.L. 45.
[64] [1973] 1 W.L.R. 707.

sufficient to amount to a material change of use. He indicated, however, that the level of sales of imported produce might increase to the extent that a change in the use of the holding as a whole would take place.[65]

4.3.8 Ancillary use where primary use inactive

Strangely, a use may be incidental to a primary use which is the subject of a planning permission, although the primary use has never actually begun. This is because section 28(6) of the 1963 Act provides as follows:

> "Where permission is granted under this Part of this Act for the construction, erection or making of a structure, the grant of permission may specify the purposes for which the structure may or may not be used . . . and if no purpose is so specified, the permission shall be construed as including permission to use the structure for the purpose for which it is designed."

In *Peake v. Secretary of State for Wales*,[66] planning permission was granted for an ordinary private garage, but the owner had never used it for that purpose. Instead he had used it for the repair and maintenance of motor vehicles for payment. Originally, this activity was carried out on a part-time basis but subsequently became full-time. A Division Court held that the Secretary of State had been entitled to conclude as a matter of fact and degree that the original use of the garage had been incidental to its designed use as a private garage, but that subsequently this use had intensified to such an extent as to amount to a material change of use.

On the other hand, where there is change from use A to use B, no regard is to be had to any ancillary use rights which attach to use A in determining whether a material change of use has occurred, unless those rights are in fact being exercised. In *Blum (Lilo) v. Secretary of State for the Environment*,[67] Simon Browne J. had to consider whether a change of use from livery stables to a riding school constituted a material change of use. Reference was made to the definition of "livery stable" contained in the *Oxford English Dictionary*, as "a stable where horses are kept at livery or are let out for hire". The livery stables in *Lilo Blum* had never actually been used for hiring purposes over a period of 30 years since the use had begun, although the owner would have been entitled to have used them for such purposes. Simon Browne J. held that although the stables could have been used for the ancillary purposes of letting horses for hire, this possible ancillary use was not to be considered in determining whether a material change of use had occurred; what mattered was what had actually been done. On the facts of the case, the change of use from livery stables to a riding school was capable of being material.

---

65   The mere fact that a manufacturer who sells goods made on his own land begins to sell goods on the land which are manufactured elsewhere does not necessarily mean that a material change of use must be taken to have ocurred if the main use of the land as a whole remains retail: see *Marshall v. Nottingham City Corporation* [1960] 1 W.L.R. 707.

66   (1971) 22 P. & C.R. 889.

67   Above, n.29.

4.3.9 Subdivision of planning unit

There does not appear to be any reason why the subdivision of a planning unit should necessarily give rise to a material change of use if no significant planning consequences result. The generally accepted view is that it does not, although there is a suggestion in at least one of the cases to the contrary.[68]

In *Winton v. Secretary of State for the Environment*, Woolf J. said:

> "It is only material changes of use – and I emphasise the word "material" – that amount to development that requires planning permission. If the division of a single planning unit into two separate planning units has no planning consequences, then it would be surprising if that amounted to development that required planning permission."

In *Winton*, a building which had previously been used by the occupier for the making of breeze blocks, was sub-divided, part of the building being used for sheet and solid metal working, and part for the conversion of motor-vehicles from left-hand drive to right-hand drive, each part being occupied separately. Enforcement notices were served on the occupiers, alleging a material change of use of each part of the building. The notices were upheld on appeal to the Secretary of State, but the appellants argued before Woolf J. that he had erred in his decision by concluding that a material change of use had occurred on the basis of the sub-division of the planning unit alone. Woolf J. found, upon examining the decision letter of the Secretary of State, that he had in fact addressed himself to the question as to whether a material change of use had occurred as a question of fact and degree, but agreed, *obiter*, that the sub-division alone did not constitute a material change of use.

A material change of use may occur where the sub-division of the planning unit results in the ancillary link between a primary and ancillary use being severed. In such circumstances the ancillary use becomes an independent use in its own right.[69] The change to this use from the former "parasitic" use may be material in planning terms.

---

[68]   There had been a suggestion to the contrary in the judgment of Lord Denning M.R. in *Wakelin v. Secretary of State for the Environment* (1983) 46 P. & C.R. 214. Browne L.J. in the same case, while holding that in the particular circumstances the creation of a new planning unit did involve a change of use, left open the question as to whether it would always amount to a material change of use. In *Winton*, Woolf J. considered that Lord Denning M.R. had addressed the question of materiality, and expressed the view that *Wakelin* should be confined to its own peculiar facts. See also *Dublin Corporation v. Regan Advertising*, above, n.35, and in particular the passage quoted at para. 4.3.7, above.

[69]   *Trentham (G. Percy) v. Gloucestershire County Council* [1966] 1 W.L.R. 506. See also *Dublin Corporation v. Regan Advertising*, above, n.35, although Blayney J. did not expressly refer to the concept of an ancillary use, (facade of premises originally used to display the name of the occupants and the business conducted within became used to advertise goods and services not related to the occupant's business).

4.3.10 Intensification of use

The expression "intensification of use" has no statutory origin, but has been employed by the courts to describe a situation where the activity on land increases in intensity, although the primary purpose for which the land is being used remains the same. As a doctrine, it has been described as "somewhat artificial or semantic", which has tended to obscure the requirement that there must be a change of use which is "material in planning terms".[70] In *Royal Borough of Kensington and Chelsea v. Secretary of State for the Environment*,[71] Donaldson L.J. commented critically that:

> ". . . Half the trouble in this case (and perhaps in other cases) was that the word 'intensification' had a perfectly clear meaning in ordinary language. It had a wholly different meaning in the mouths of planners. In ordinary language, intensification meant more of the same thing or possibly a denser composition of the same thing. In planning language, intensification meant a change to something different. It was much too late to suggest that the word 'intensification' should be deleted from the language of planners, but it had to be used with very considerable circumspection, and it had to be clearly understood by all concerned that intensification did not amount to a material change of use, was merely intensification and not a breach of planning controls.
>
> He (Donaldson L.J.) hoped that, where possible, those concerned with planning would get away from the term and try to define what was a material change of use by reference to the *terminus a quo* and the *terminus a quem*. Indeed, if the planners were incapable of formulating what was the use before 'intensification' and what was the use after 'intensification', then there had been no material change of use."

Curiously, the doctrine first arose for consideration in the Irish courts in the context of the intensification of "works" rather than "use". In *Patterson v. Murphy and Trading Services Ltd*,[72] the applicants, a well known tenor and his wife, took up residence close to a quarry in County Wicklow which was at the time unused, although it had been used sporadically, prior to the commencement of the Act, for the extraction of shale. Subsequently, blasting took place at the quarry for the first time and a large crushing and screening plant was installed. The owner and operator of the quarry, as respondents to an application for orders under section 27 of the 1976 Act to restrain the alleged unauthorised use of the quarry, contended that the activities taking place were immune from enforcement as they had commenced prior to October 1, 1964, *i.e.* the commencement date of the Act.

Costello J. found that the activities constituted "works" rather than a change in the use of the land since the statutory definition of "use" expressly excluded "works", and quarrying fell within that part of the definition of "works" which referred to "any act or operation of excavation". He also found as a fact that the

---

[70] *Monaghan County Council v. Brogan* [1987] I.R. 33, approving Parker L.C.J's *dictum* to this effect in *East Barnet U.D.C. v. British Transport Commission*, above, n.40.

[71] [1981] J.P.L. 50.

[72] [1978] I.L.R.M. 85.

operations being carried out were materially different in character to the operations in existence prior to the appointed day, so that it could not be said that the activities which the applicants sought to restrain were lawful for that reason. He analysed the change in the nature of the operations in the following passage:

> "The present operations differ materially from those carried on prior to the 1st. October, 1964. I have reached this conclusion bearing in mind the following considerations. The object of the present operations is to produce a different product to that being produced in 1964. As stated in the parties agreement, the operations are designed to manufacture stone. The 4 inch stone now being produced is different to shale; it is used for a different purpose in the building industry, and it fetches a different price. The method of production is different to that obtaining in and before 1964. The raw materials (rock) for the end product is now obtained by means of blasting and this is done on a regular basis. A large crushing and screening plant is used to produce stones of the correct dimensions. Considerable ancillary equipment is used and a considerable labour force employed. Finally, the scale of operations is now a substantial one, and bears no relationship to the scale of operations carried on prior to the appointed day. In England it has been held that an intensification of use may amount to a material change of use (see *Guildford Rural District Council v. Fortescue* [1959] 2 Q.B. 112, 115 and *Brooks and Burton Limited v. Secretary of State for the Environment* [1977] 1 W.L.R. 1294, 1306. It seems to me that this concept is a correct one and that it applied whether the Court is considering "development" under the second limb of the definition (i.e. material change of use) or under the first limb (i.e. the carrying out of works on land), which was commenced prior to the appointed day. So, if it appears that the scale of operations has so intensified as to render contemporary operations materially different from those carried on before the appointed day, this fact can be taken into account in considering whether what is at present being done commenced prior to the 1st. October, 1964."

In the later case of *Galway County Council v. Lackagh Rock*, the applicant County Council relied on Costello J.'s analysis in *Patterson* in an attempt to establish that the modernisation and stepping up of quarrying activity, amounted to a material change of use.[73] The council pointed to the fact that the scale of the operations had increased very considerably; that the plant and machinery had also changed; and that the respondents were manufacturing a totally different product *viz.* ground limestone. Barron J. held that it was not sufficient for the council to establish that an intensification of use had taken place. It had to prove that the intensification of activity amounted to a change of use which was material *i.e.* had given rise to fresh planning considerations.

> "The importance of this principle lies not so much in the intensification of use of itself, but in the fact that such use may impose burdens on the local authority or otherwise infringe in a materially different manner upon the proper planning for the area. In the present case, there is little doubt but that the site is being used quite differently from the manner on which it was used on the appointed day."

---

[73] It is significant that in this case the quarrying activity was treated as involving an intensification of the use of land rather than "works", as Costello J. (as he then was) treated the quarrying operations in *Patterson*, above. See discussion at para. 4.1.1, above,

He then went on to lay down a test to be applied:

> "To test whether or not the use are materially different it seems to me that what should be looked at are the matters which the planning authority would take into account in the event of a planning application being made either for the use on the appointed day or for the present use. If these matters are materially different, then the nature of the use must equally be materially different."

In the result, Barron J. held that the council had not shown that it would have taken any such different matters into account. He upheld the respondent's contention that there was no material change of use.[74]

In the subsequent case of *Monaghan County Council v. Brogan*,[75] Keane J. at first sight appeared to disagree with Barron J.'s "test" on the grounds that it relegated the role of the judge and elevated the planning authority so as to make it the arbiter as to what constituted development. The case concerned slaughtering activities which had taken place on a small scale during the 1940s and 1950s on one of the respondents farm, to provide animal food for greyhounds owned by the respondent's brother. The activity was carried on at a similar level until 1983, when an advertisement was placed by the respondent in the "Northern Standard", in the following terms:

> "Casualty Cattle Wanted, Highest prices paid. Telephone Clones 126".

The scale of the slaughtering activity was stepped up and an application was brought by the County Council to restrain the unauthorised use of the farm. At the close of the hearing, the respondents, relying on Barron J.'s "test", submitted that the applicant County Council had not adduced any evidence to indicate that it would have taken into account any matters other than those which it would have considered had an application been made in respect of the earlier and more modest operation. Keane J. did not regard this submission as relevant, holding that the question of materiality was one to be determined by the court. He said:

> "It is true that neither of the Planning Officers in the present case referred in their evidence to any different matters that they would have taken into consideration had an application for planning permission been made now rather than on the appointed day. It is however, in my view, for the Court to determine whether or not there has been a material change in the use of land when an application is made under section 27. No

---

[74] Barron J.'s test may be applied generally to cases where there is a change of use, though not necessarily because of intensification. It was applied by O'Hanlon J. in *Dublin Corporation v. Aircold Refrigeration Limited and others*, unreported, High Court O'Hanlon J., March 8, 1995, to a change of use from use as a haulier's yard which had started prior to October 1, 1964 (the commencement date of the Act) to use for the storage, manufacture or maintenance of freezer units or plant. Having regard to the points of difference between the two operations, he held that a material change of use had occurred and granted the restraining order sought. More recently, in *Lee and O'Flynn v. O'Riordan*, unreported, High Court, February 10, 1995 O'Hanlon J. declined to apply Barron J.'s test to the particular facts of the case which involved the intensification of quarring activity, preferring to rely on the analysis used in *Patterson v. Murphy*, above n.72.

[75] Above, n.70.

doubt, as Lord Parker C.J. pointed out in *East Barnet UDC v. British Transport Commission*[76] "material" in this context means "material for planning purposes". Whether or not it is so material must be determined by the Court as a matter of fact and the absence of any evidence as to the views of the planning authority on the matter is not crucial. It would be strange if it were otherwise, since a person other than the planning authority can set in motion the machinery under section 27 and there is nothing in the wording of the section to suggest that his right to do so may be stultified simply because the planning authority have taken a view, which may or may not be in law correct, that no material change of use is involved."

It is submitted that this statement does not necessarily conflict with Barron J.'s "test" in *Lackagh Rock*. The purpose of that test was to establish two principles. First, that where an applicant in section 27 proceedings wishes to establish a material change of use in relation to an activity which preceded the commencement date of the Act, a comparison must be made between the intensity of use as it existed at that date and the current level of activity. The respondent would usually be entitled to claim existing use rights in the level of activity taking place before October 1, 1964. Secondly, the applicant must establish that there is objective planning evidence to suggest that the change in the intensity of use is material. It was clearly not Barron J.'s intention to require an applicant planning authority to present such objective evidence in a hypothetical form. It would be unfair of the court to impose a different onus of proof on the planning authority than on an ordinary applicant who would have no particular knowledge as to what a planning authority might have considered to be a relevant planning matter at a particular point in time.

On the face of the judgment, Keane J. appears to favour the qualitative approach, discussed earlier, which has been adopted in many of the U.K. decisions, rather than an approach based on an assessment of the planning implications or off-site effects of the change of use involved:

> "The extensive scale on which the slaughtering is being carried on, the appearance of the newspaper advertisements and the violent methods employed by the respondents to prevent any access to their premises satisfies me beyond any doubt that, not merely has there been a significant increase in the amount of slaughtering going on, but that the object of the operation, now, is the supply of food for human consumption. It is also clear that the activity now being carried on is essentially a commercial operation in contrast to the relatively modest and intermittent slaughtering which went on prior to 1983."
> . . . The question accordingly resolves itself into one as to whether a change in use which involves the slaughtering of animals on a scale significantly greater than before, forming part of a commercial operation established for the first time on a particular farm, is material 'in the context of planning'. Were such an operation to be established in an urban environment, there could not be the slightest doubt that it would be a material change in the use of the land. It is true that, in the present case, it has been established in a rural area but I am satisfied that it is nonetheless a material change in the use of the land in the context of the proper planning and development of the area."

---

[76] Above, n.40.

It is unlikely that the courts will allow the doctrine of intensification to act as an inhibiting factor on the growth of economic activity unless the character of the use has changed. The late Judge Walsh wrote:

> "Many businesses expand and grow with the passage of time but, of course, it could not be seriously contended that a material change of use had taken place when some additional machines are installed in a premises to cope with increasing demands. In such a case the use remains the same but it becomes intensified".[77]

This passage was quoted by Murphy J. in *Dublin County Council v. Carty Builders & Co. Ltd*,[78] who held that an increase in the number of caravans on a field of 2.9 statute acres from 10 to 17 did not constitute a material change of use. It is not clear from the judgment whether Murphy J. admitted of any circumstances in which the intensification of a caravan use could amount to to a material change of use. It is likely that an increase in the number of caravans which places a considerable additional burden on services would be regarded as a material change of use.[79]

4.3.11 Resumption of an abandoned use

It has already been established that it is the change of use which has planning consequences, as distinct from the use of land itself, which is the subject of development control. The notion that a change of use may occur where a site which has no use, or a "nil" use, is put to some use either through the introduction of a new use or the resumption of a use which has been discontinued may be justified on the basis that what happens will normally have planning consequences.[80] The concept of abandonment has been imported into planning law to describe a situation where land may be deemed to have acquired a "nil" use. But it would be unjust to require an occupier in every case to re-apply for planning permission for the resumption of a business where it had ceased to operate for a time due to lack of demand for a product. The test as to whether a use has been abandoned must therefore respect the property rights of the owner or occupier of the land.

The doctrine of abandonment, was adopted by Costello J. in *Dublin County Council v. Tallaght Block Company Limited*,[81] following the decision of the Court of Appeal in *Hartley v. Minister for Housing and Local Government*.[82] In *Hartley*, a

---

77 *Planning and Development Law* (1st ed.) p.17.
78 [1987] I.R. 355.
79 See the excerpt from Lord Evershed M.R.'s judgment in *Guildford Rural District Council v. Fortescue* [1959] 2 Q.B. 112, at 125, quoted with approval by Barron J. in *Lackagh Rock*, whose judgement suggests that "more of the same" can result in a material change of use.
80 The artificiality of the idea of a "nil" use is highlighted by Sharman, F., in [1980] J.P.L. 807, where he says:
    "No-one would say that someone had *changed* is car if he had just bought one for the first time never having owned one before; nor would he say that he had *changed* his clothes if he had just got dressed for the first time after two weks in a nudist camp."
81 [1982] I.L.R.M. 534.
82 [1970] 1 Q.B. 413.

site had originally been used for two uses – as a petrol filling station and for car sales – but subsequently the use for car sales was discontinued. The Court of Appeal held that the Minister was entitled to conclude that the resumption of the car sales use four years later was a material change of use. Lord Denning M.R. stated:

> "The question in all such cases is simply this: has the cessation of use (followed by non-use) been merely temporary, or did it amount to an abandonment? If it was merely temporary, the previous use can be resumed without planning permission being obtained. If it amounted to abandonment, it cannot be resumed unless planning permision is obtained. . . . Abandonment depends on the circumstances. If the land has remained unused for a considerable time, in such circumstances that a reasonable man might conclude that the previous use had been abandoned, then the tribunal may hold it to have been abandoned."

The abandonment of a use, as with abandonment at private law, involves an *actus* and an *animus*. A use which has been discontinued is regarded as having been abandoned if there is:

(i) a factual cessation of activity;
(ii) an intention not to resume the said activity.

The property or site involved is then deemed to have "no use". The change from "a nil use" back to the "abandoned use" is regarded as a material change of use.

The *animus* or intention to abandon the use of the property may be determined from circumstantial evidence of intention. In particular, where a use had been discontinued a presumption of abandonment exists which increases with the passage of time.[83] Thus, in *Dublin County Council v. Tallaght Block Co. Ltd*,[84] where the use of a site for the manufacture of concrete blocks had ceased for a period of eight years and then re-commenced, a material change of use was taken to have occurred. A similar finding was made by Murphy J. in *Cork County Council v. Ardfert Quarries Limited*[85] where the use of a premises as a general industrial building was discontinued for a period of four years, no reasonable explanation for the discontinuance having been tendered.

While Lord Denning M.R.'s judgment in *Hartley* emphasises the importance of the period of time during which the use is discontinued, Lord Widgery C.J. pointed out in the same case that the intention of the occupier not to resume the use should not be ignored and this has been considered to be an important factor in a number of subsequent decisions. In *Hale (deceased) v. Lichfield District Council*[86] a declaration was granted to the effect that a residential use of premises had not been abandoned although they were in a state of dilapidation and the last occupant had entered hospital in 1961 and remained there until her death in

---

[83]   *per* Lord Denning M.R. in *Hartley*.
[84]   Above, n.81.
[85]   Unreported, High Court, December 7, 1982
[86]   [1979] J.P.L. 425.

1974. It was established in evidence that she always intended to return to live in the house.[87]

At the same time, where the intention expressed by the owner or occupier as to the use to which the land was to be put conflicts with objective evidence as to his intention, the latter evidence is more likely to prevail. In *Nicholls v. Secretary of State for the Environment*,[88] McNeill J. stated:

> "Indeed in any particular case it may be that whatever the owner or occupier has said at the material time may be contradicted by facts and circumstances so that his intention may be rejected."

In *Castell-y-Mynach Estate (Trustees of) v. Secretary of State for Wales*[89] a Divisional Court of the Queen's Bench held that in determining whether a use as a dwelling-house had been abandoned, an important factor is the state of repair of the building and whether it is habitable.[90] But the fact that the use of land is discontinued and the land is sold with vacant possession does not necessarily indicate an intention to abandon the use as it may simply mean that the owner wishes to obtain a better price for the land.[91] It has also been held in *McGrath Limestone Works Ltd v. Galway County Council*,[92] that the implementation of a planning permission for a mushroom growing development on less than five per cent of a site on which quarrying had been discontinued for a short time could not be relied on to demonstrate the abandonment of the quarrying use.

It is preferable that the concept of abandonment should only be applied to circumstances where a use has been discontinued, rather than where one use replaces another use.[93] A more flexible use of the term was adopted by Egan J. in *Meath County Council v. Daly*.[94] The facts were that there was a pre-October 1, 1964 use of a site for a motor car garage business, which had continued at intermittent periods up to the date of enforcement by the planning authority. At times the site became disused and at times it had been put to other uses. Egan J. concluded that the original "use right" had been abandoned on a few occasions.

The cases discussed above concern "existing use rights" which were not the subject of planning permission. In *Pioneer Aggregates (U.K.) Ltd v. Secretary of State for the Environment*[95] the House of Lords held that the doctrine of

---

87 In *Northavon District Council v. Secretary of State for the Environment* [1990] J.P.L. 579 the court upheld the Minister's conclusion that the use of the land for the purpose of siting a residential caravan had not been abandoned despite the fact that it remained inactive for about 15 years. The caravan had remained on site throughout most of the period in the expectation of the owner's return from hospital. As to the significance of intention as a factor, see also *Castell-y-Mynach Estate (Trustees of) v. Secretary of State for Wales* [1985] J.P.L. 40.

88 [1981] J.P.L. 890.

89 Above, n.87.

90 But see *Hale (deceased)*, above, n.86.

91 See *Grover's Executors v. Rickmansworth U.D.C.* (1959) 10 P. & C.R. 417.

92 Unreported, High Court, Egan J., November 17, 1988.

93 *Young v. Secretary of State for the Environment* [1983] 2 A.C. 662.

94 [1987] I.R. 391.

95 [1985] A.C. 132.

abandonment did not apply to use rights derived from a planning permission because of an express statutory provision that planning permission enures for the benefit of the land. The equivalent Irish provision is section 28(5) of the 1963 act which provides:

> "Where permission to develop land or for the retention of a structure is granted under the Act, then, except as may be otherwise provided by the permission, the grant of permission shall enure for the benefit of the land or structure and of all persons for the time being interested therein, but without prejudice to the provisions of this Part of this Act with respect to the revocation and modification of permissions granted thereunder."

This decision has been doubted and appears to be inconsistent with the arguments accepted by the Court of Appeal in the later case of *Cynon Valley Borough Council v. Secretary of State for Wales.*[96]

4.3.12 Resumption of an extinguished use

Existing use rights which attach to land may be extinguished as the result of the implementation of a permission or the erection of a new building. A use may also be extinguished if a structure or land perishes.[97] The concept of extinguishment has been described as "similar to that of abandonment with the difference that the intention is of much less importance."[98] A material change of use occurs where the extinguished use is resumed.

In certain circumstances the erection of a new building has the effect of displacing the existing use of the land on which it is built even where the permission does not refer to the purpose for which the building may be used or none may be discerned.[99] The initial view, expressed by Lord Widgery C.J. in *Petticoat Lane Rentals Limited v. Secretary of State for the Environment* was that:

> "One gets in my judgement an entirely new planning unit created by the new building. The land as such is merged in that new building and a new planning unit with no planning history is achieved. the new planning unit, the new building starts with a nil use . . ."[100]

It is a question of fact and degree as to whether the erection of a building on part of a site, amounts to a change in the planning unit so as to extinguish the existing use of land covered by the building.[101] In *Jennings v. Secretary of State for the*

---

96 (1987) 53 P. & C.R. 68.

97 *Galway County Council v. Connacht Proteins Limited*, above, n.48.

98 Purdue, Young, Rowan-Robinson, *Planning Law and Procedure* (1989), p.113.

99 But see 1963 Act, s.28(6), discussed below at para. 8.6.4.

100 [1971] 2 All E.R. 793 at 796. In this case it was held that the erection of an office block on stilts on a site previously used as a market extinguished that use, and that the continued use of the ground floor of the building by market traders constituted an unauthorised use.

101 Bridge J. and Lord Parker C.J. in *Petticoat Lane Rentals* reserved the question as to what the position would be where the building was situated on part only of a site having a prior existing use.

Environment,[102] a half acre site had a mixed use for the repair and maintenance of vehicles and the sale and hire of cars. A garage workshop was demolished and a new building erected, without planning permission, in its place, covering approximately six per cent of the site. The local authority took enforcement proceedings to secure the discontinuance of the use of the building but not the removal or alteration of the building because it was considered to be more suitable in terms of apearance. The court held that the erection of the new building had not resulted in the creation of a new planning unit and that the appellants were entitled to continue the existing use.[103] Lord Denning M.R. nonetheless said that in certain circumstances, the construction of a new building on a site could result in the creation of a new planning unit or a "new chapter in the planning history of the site" so that it would be no longer possible to rely on existing use rights. Referring to the earlier decision in *Petticoat Lane Rentals*, Lord Denning M.R. pointed out that the extinguishment of the existing use was brought about by the erection of the building not by the acceptance of the planning permission, so that the concept could equally apply where a building was erected without permission as in *Jennings*.[104]

An existing use may be extinguished by the implementation of a planning permission which is inconsistent with the continuance of that use.[105] But in *South Staffordshire District Council v. Secretary of State for the Environment*,[106] Glidewell L.J. stated:

> "In our opinion, if land forming part of a larger area in one ocupation has an established use, and if planning permission for the erection or enlargement of a building on another part of the same area is granted and the development takes place, this does not necessarily terminate or remove the established use. It only does so if in some way the development which takes place is inconsistent with the established use."

---

[102] [1982] Q.B. 541.

[103] See also *McGrath Limestone Works Ltd v. Galway County Council*, unreported, High Court, Egan J., November 17, 1988.

[104] This theory of the formation of a new planning unit in these circumstances may be regarded as supported by the requirements of the permission regulations to state the nature and extent of development in notices of planning applications.

[105] See *Pilkington v. Secretary of State for the Environment* [1973] 1 W.L.R. 1527, *Prossor v. Minister for Housing and Local Government* (1968) 67 LGR 109; *Leighton and Newman Car Sales v. Secretary of State for the Environment* (1976) 32 P. & C.R. It may be advisable when applying for permission to avoid any uncertainty at the outset by including existing uses within the application site, and by indicating in plans or other documentation accompanying the planning application that certain existing uses are intended to be retained.

[106] (1987) 55 P. & C.R. 258.

4.4 DEVELOPMENT NOT REQUIRING PERMISSION

4.4.1 Resumption of "normal" use of land upon expiration of temporary permission for use of land

When permission is granted for a limited period only and this period has expired, no permission is required for the last lawful use preceding the use which is the subject of the permission.[107]

4.4.2 Resumption of use where enforcement notice is served

Section 31(9) provides:

> "Nothing in this Part of this Act shall be construed as requiring permission to be obtained thereunder for the use for any land for the purpose for which it could lawfully have been used under this Part of this Act if the development in respect of which an enforcement notice is served had not been carried out."

The section permits reverter to the use immediately preceding the one which is the subject of an enforcement notice, provided that the preceding use is a lawful one.[108]

4.4.3 Recurrent uses

Section 40(a) of the 1963 Act provides that planning permission is not required for the interchange of recurring uses on the same land which commenced prior to October 1, 1963.[109]

4.4.4 Development required by notices served under sections 31, 32, 33, 35 or 36 of the 1963 Act

No permission is required for development necessitated by compliance with such notices.[110]

4.4.5 Development required by planning condition

There is a certain amount of English authority for the proposition that planning permission may be implied for development which is stipulated by a condition

---

[107] See *Young* above, n.93; *LTSS Print & Supply Services v. London Borough of Hackney* [1976] 2 W.L.R. 253.

[108] See *Young* above, n.93, which was cited with apparent approval in *Rehabilitation Institute* above, n.30.

[109] This might be taken to suggest *sub silentio* that planning permission is needed for seasonal changes of use which did not take place before the commencement of the 1963 Act. See *Webber v. Minister of Housing and Local Government* [1967] 3 All E.R. 981. See para. 4.3.6, above.

[110] 1963 Act, s.40(c).

attached to a planing permission.[111] These cases must be approached with caution because of the more stringent notification requirements under the planning code in this jurisdiction.[112] It is unlikely that a planning authority would be taken to have granted planning permission for ancillary works required by a condition if the result would be to authorise a development which was substantially different from that for which permission was applied.[113]

---

[111] See *Irlam Brick Co. v. Warrington Borough Council* [1982] J.P.L. 209; *R. v. Derbyshire Borough Council* [1980] J.P.L. 398 (condition requiring opencast site to be backfilled).

[112] See in particular, the regulations requiring the nature and extent of the development to be described in the newspaper notices and site notices concerning planning applications, discussed at Chap. 6.

[113] See *State (Abenglen Properties Ltd) v. Dublin Corporation* [1984] I.R. 381, discussed at para. 8.2.3.1, below.

Chapter 5

EXEMPTED DEVELOPMENT

5.1 INTRODUCTION

The exemption of certain kinds of development from the obligation to obtain planning permission may be justified on the basis of the reduction in administrative costs for minimal environmental harm.[1] Two main categories of exempted development may be recognised: those developments which by their nature and limitations have no significant impact on the planning system, and those developments which, by virtue of the identity of the person or body carrying out the development, are presumed to be in the interests of the common good. The former category includes such typical exemptions as garage conversions and porch extensions, as well as changes of use within certain use groupings. The latter category largely comprises public sector development. The proposition that public sector development is carried out in the interests of the common good, while literally true in the subjective sense, is not necessarily borne out by an objective assessment of the planning consequences and environmental impact of such development. In certain instances, more specific reasons, such as security or defence interests, may be advanced for particular exemptions under the heading of public interest.

The principle provisions on this topic are contained in section 4 of the Local Government (Planning and Development) Act 1963 and in articles 8–13 of the Local Government (Planning and Development) Regulations 1994.[2] The earlier regulations made under section 4(2) of the Act which have been revoked by the 1994 Regulations will continue to be of importance in property transaction where the planning history of a site must necessarily be considered. Article 12 expressly provides that any development commenced prior to the coming into operation of the regulations and which was exempted development under the previous regulations will continue to be exempted development. Consequently, in order to ascertain the current planning status of property, it may be necessary to consult the provisions of the previous regulations in some detail.[3]

---

[1]   An extension of this type of analysis to the planning system as a whole may be found in Ellickson, "Alternatives to Zoning: Covenants, Nuisance Rules and Fines as Land Use Controls" (1973) 40 U.C.L.R. 688.

[2]   See also Local Government (Planning & Development) Regulations 1995 (S.I. No. 69 of 1995) and Local Government (Planning & Development) Regulations 1996 (S.I. No. 100 of 1996).

[3]   Consideration is given in this chapter to some of the exemptions which applied prior to May 16, 1994, the date on which the 1994 Regulations came into operation.

Where certain types of large-scale development are concerned, it is also necessary to consider the categories of "specified development" under the First Schedule to the European Communities (Environmental Impact) Assessment Regulations 1989, as such development for which an environmental impact statement (EIS) prepared is not exempted development.[4] A proposed development which is of the same nature as a class of specified development but which falls short of the threshold indicated in the First Schedule will likewise be deprived of its exempted development status if it relates to an activity for which an integrated pollution control (IPC) licence under the Environmental Protection Agency Act 1992 will be required. Development for which an exemption from the requirement of an EIS is granted will, on the other hand, retain its status as exempted development.

In reading the exempted development regulations, it is important to bear in mind the distinction between the use/works components of development. "Use" is given an exclusionary definition under section 2 of the 1963 Act: it "does not include the use of the land by the carrying out of any works thereon".[5] Many of the exemptions created under the regulations apply to works only, so that permission may still have to be obtained for any change of use intended when the exempted works have been completed.

5.1.1 Section 5 references

Where a dispute exists, any person can refer a particular case to An Bord Pleanála to determine whether what is involved constitutes development or exempted development.[6] There is also provision for appeal to the High Court within a period of three months of the Board's decision or such longer period as the High Court may allow. The determination by the Board or the court on a reference is only applicable to the facts of the particular case, although in some instances, the Board has indicated that their determination is of more general application.

It would appear that section 5 does not apply to disputes of a private nature as to what constitutes development requiring planning permission, but to questions arising between a planning authority and another person in the course of the procedures established by the 1963 Act.[7]

---

4   See 1994 Regulations, art. 10(c)(i). Note that this provision "de-exempts" only the categories of development to which art. 9 relates.

5   *Re Viscount Securities Ltd*, 112 I.L.T.R. 17.

6   1963 Act, s.5. See further paras. 10.3.4 and 11.2.8, below.

7   *per* Costello J. in *Patterson v. Murphy* [1978] I.L.R.M. 85 approved in *Carroll and Colley v. Brushfield Limited*, unreported, High Court, Lynch J., October 9, 1992.

5.2 EXEMPTED DEVELOPMENT UNDER SECTION 4 OF THE 1963 ACT

5.2.1 Section 4 of the 1963 Act

Section 4 of the 1963 Act provides for a number of exemptions from the obligation to obtain planning permission which are very important in practical terms:

(a) Development consisting of the use of any land for the purposes of agriculture or forestry (including afforestation), and development consisting of the use of any for those purposes of any building occupied together with land so used;

(b) Development by the council of a county in the county health district;

(c) Development by the corporation of a county or other borough in such borough;

(d) Development by the council of an urban district in such district.

(e) Development consisting of the carrying out by the corporation of a county or other borough or the council of a county or an urban district of any works required for the construction of a new road or the maintenance or improvement of a road;

(f) Development consisting of the carrying out by any local authority or statutory undertaker of any works for the purpose of inspecting, repairing, renewing, altering or removing any sewers, mains, pipes, cables, overhead wires, or other apparatus, including the breaking open of any street or other land for that purpose;

(g) Development consisting of the carrying out of works for the maintenance, improvement or other alteration of any structure, being works which affect only the interior of the structure or which do not materially affect the external appearance of the structure so as to render such appearance inconsistent with the character of the structure or of neighbouring structures;

(h) Development consisting of the use of any structure or other land within the curtilage of a dwellinghouse for any purpose incidental to the enjoyment of the dwellinghouse as such;

(i) Development consisting of the use of land for the purposes of a casual trading area (within the meaning of the Casual Trading Act, 1980);

(j) Development consisting of the carrying out of any of the works referred to in the Land Reclamation Act, 1949, (not being works comprised in the fencing or enclosure of land which has been open to or used by the public within the 10 years preceding the date on which the works are commenced.

A planning authority may include in its development plan objectives to preserve plasterwork, staircases, woodwork, or other features of artistic, historic or architectural interest which form part of the interior of certain structures listed in the plan.[8] Any works which involve the alteration or removal of, or which may cause injury to, any such fixture or feature are not exempted under section 4. The scope of the exemptions contained in section 4(1) is further reduced as the Minister can prescribe certain categories of developments the effect of which is to remove their exempted status.[9] Four categories of development have been prescribed under article 13 of the 1994 Regulations.[10]

> " (a) The use of uncultivated land or semi-natural areas for intensive agricultural purposes, where the area involved would be greater than 100 hectares;
>
> (b) Initial afforestation where the area involved, either on its own or taken together with any adjacent area planted by or on behalf of the applicant within the previous three years, would result in a total area planted exceeding 70 hectares and for the purposes of this subparagraph an area, other than an area planted before the 1st day of October, 1996, shall be deemed to be adjacent if its nearest point lies within 500 metres of any part of the area involved.
>
> (bb) Replacement of broadleaf high forest by conifer species, where the area involved would exceed 10 hectares.
>
> (c) Peat extraction which would involve a new or extended area of 50 hectares or more."

5.2.2 Use for agriculture and forestry

The privileged position which agriculture and forestry enjoys under the system of development control can be traced back to post-war planning policies in Britain for the preservation of agriculture. The exemption applies to changes of use within the category of agricultural use, as well as changes from other types of use to agricultural use.[11] Illogically, the wording refers to the *use* of land for agricultural or afforestation purposes although the obligation to obtain planning permission arises where a material *change* of use occurs.

The extent of the exemption has been dramatically reduced by the European Communities (Environmental Impact Assessment) Regulations 1989 to reflect European concern about the environmental effects of intensive agriculture. Section 4(4) of the 1963 Act, as inserted by article 6 of the 1989 Regulations, enables the Minister to prescribe certain categories of development so that they no longer amount to exempted development. Article 13 of the 1994 Regulations prescribes three categories of development.

---

[8] 1963 Act, Sched. 3, Pt. IV, para. 5A, as inserted by 1976 Act, s. 43.

[9] 1963 Act, s.4(4), as inserted by the 1989 Regulations, art. 6.

[10] Paragraph (b) substituted para. (bb) inserted by the Local Government (Planning and Development) Regulations, 1996. See also the European Communities (Environmental Impact Assessment) (Amendment) Regulations, 1996 (S.I. No. 101 of 1996) which introduce parallel changes to Pt. 11 of Sched. 1 to the European Communities (Environmental Impact Assessment) Regulations, 1989 (S.I. No. 349 of 1989).

[11] *McKellan v. Minister of Housing and Local Government* (1966) E.G. 683. It does not apply to drainage or land reclamation works although specific exemptions for these are provided by art. 9 and Sched. 2, Pt. III, Classes 3 and 9 of the 1994 regulations. See *Irish Wildbird Conservancy and the Commissioners of Public Works v. Clonakilty Golf and Country Club Limited*, unreported, High Court, Costello P., July 23, 1996 (under appeal).

5.2.2.1 *The definition of agriculture*

"Agriculture":

> "includes horticulture, fruit growing, seed growing, dairy farming, the breeding and keeping of livestock (including any creature kept for the production of food, wood, skins or fur, or for the purpose of its use in the farming of land), the use of land as grazing land, meadow land, osier land, market gardens and nursery grounds, the use of land for turbary, and the use of land for woodlands where that use is ancillary to farming of land for other agricultural purposes, and 'agricultural' shall be construed accordingly."

It would appear that this is not intended to be an exhaustive list of the activities embraced by "agriculture", and that the word "includes" is used in its extensive sense. The exclusion of crop-growing, which is not mentioned in the definition, would not otherwise make sense.[12]

By contrast, it has been held that the phrase, "the keeping of livestock", is limited by the words in parentheses which follow. For example, fish-farming falls within the definition of agriculture where fish are kept for the production of food.[13] But fish-farming which is carried out to supply fish for ornamental tanks or ponds, or to fishing clubs to stock lakes or rivers, lies outside the definition of "agriculture". This distinction may be criticised because it is not based on land use considerations but on the destination of the end product. As one commentator has observed, there are "difficulties involved in making plannning considerations depend on a definition of agriculture which is concerned with the *purpose* rather than the *nature* of the activity involved".[14]

Many of the problems of definition occur at "the frontier between farming and leisure".[15] In *Belmont Farm Limited v. Minister for Housing and Local Government*,[16] Lord Parker C.J. held that the breeding of horses and their training for show-jumping fell outside the scope of the exemption for agricultural use because the horses were not being kept either for the production of food for their use in the farming of land.[17] But the keeping of livestock for grazing

---

12 *Belmont Farm Limited*, below, n.16, *per* Lord Parker C.J.

13 There is no qualification placed on the type of "food" involved, so that it need not be food for human consumption but could be animal food such as fishmeal. In this context; see An Bord Pleanála section 5 determination, ref. no. 07/RF/674, reported at (1994) IPELJ 155.

14 See Howarth, "The Legal Status of Fish Farming" (1987) J.P.L. 484, who asks at 492 — "...what is the position of a carp farmer who proposes to sell his fish to whoever wishes to but without enquiring as to the purchaser's purposes? Is he to lose the benefit of the planning exemption merely because some person may choose to buy one of his fish to keep as a domestic pet?"

15 See Scrase, "Agriculture – 1980's Industry and 1947 Definition" (1988) J.P.L. 447 at 459. He instances the recent phenomenon of the "dude ranch", "offering such delights as driving a horse and cart and joining in with traditional haymaking". See also *Pittman v. Secretary of State for the Environment* [1988] J.P.L. 391.

16 [1963] J.P.L. 256.

17 Scrase remarks, *op. cit.*, p.457, that at the time of the *Belmont Farm* case in 1962 "the prevailing British taboo meant that nobody even considered the possibility that horses might be used as food. Now that we are EEC members and there is a considerable export trade to other countries who lack our scruples, the matter may have to be addressed at some time."

purposes falls within the exemption as the definition also refers to "the use of land as grazing land". Where animals graze the land but are also used for recreational purposes, it is the primary purpose for which the land is used that will determine the use of the land. This is a question of fact and degree.

In *Sykes v. Secretary of State for the Environment and South Oxford District Council*,[18] Donaldson L.J. felt that the respondents were rather fortunate that the Secretary of State had found that three horses, two point to point horses, a driving pony, two family ponies and one retired mare were using the land for grazing purposes so as to fall within this part of the definition. The learned judge illustrated the circumstances in which a contrary finding might have been reached:

> "If horses were simply turned out onto the land with a view to feeding them from the land, clearly the land was being used for grazing. But if horses were being kept on the land and were being fed wholly or primarily by other means so that such grazing as they did was completely incidental and perhaps achieved merely because there were no convenient ways of stopping them doing it, then plainly the land was not being used for grazing but was merely being used for keeping the animals."

5.2.2.2 *The agricultural planning unit*

The appropriate planning unit to consider in order to determine the extent of agricultural use is the entire area which is used for agricultural purposes including any area of which use is incidental to or ancillary to the achievement of those purposes. A building which is "occupied together with land" in agricultural use but is located at some distance from the main farm, may be regarded as part of the same planning unit so that it shares the same agricultural use.[19] Any building which is not occupied together with land but is used for agricultural purposes is exempted, as the definition of "land" includes "any structure".[20]

It has been held that the storage of farm machinery and equipment,[21] and the use of a caravan in connection with the storage and preparation of animal feed and sheltering for livestock[22] amount to ancillary agricultural uses. The sale of home-grown produce from a farmhouse and the sale of produce of a nursery garden are also capable of being regarded as ancillary to agricultural use although the introduction of imported produce may bring such "farm gate sales" outside the category of an ancillary use.[23] A greater sophistication in the methods engaged in by those carrying out ancillary activities may lead to the conclusion that a

---

[18] [1981] 1 W.L.R. 1092.
[19] *Williams v. Ministry of Housing and Local Government* (1967) 65 L.G.R. 495. See also *Fuller v. Secretary of State for the Environment* [1987] 2 E.G.L.R. 189; *Duffy v. Secretary of State for the Environment* [1981] J.P.L. 811.
[20] See 1963 Act, s.2 and *North Warwickshire Borough Council v. Secretary of State for the Environment* (1983) 50 P. & C.R. 47.
[21] *Trentham (G Percy) Ltd v. Gloucestershire County Council* [1966] All E.R. 701.
[22] [1988] J.P.L. 268.
[23] See *Williams*, above, n.19. See also *Wood v. Secretary of State for the Environment* [1973] 1 W.L.R. 707.

separate retail use has been established, depending on the kind and degree of the change. In *Hidderley v. Warwickshire County Council*[24] where sale of eggs produced on a farm was transferred from the farmhouse to a vending machine on the main road beside the farm with advertisements drawing attention to it, it was held that this was capable of amounting to a material change of use, Lord Parker C.J. stating:

> "It seems to me here that the expressing using land "for the purposes of agriculture" is clearly referring to those productive processes (referred to in the definition of agriculture); it is nothing to do with agriculture for gain or the business of agriculture."

5.2.2.3 *Agricultural processes*

To what extent can agricultural goods be processed so that they can be sold on the farm, without introducing an independent use. In *Gill v. Secretary of State for the Environment*[25] which concerned a fairly extensive fox farm, Glidewell J. said:

> "It might be that the occasional killing of animals kept on a farm was *de minimis* or could reasonably be considered to be ancillary to normal agricultural activities. He was certainly not to be understood as saying that a farmer who had pigs, sheep, poultry or whatever which he reared and bred and who killed some of them, was not behaving within the normal use of the land . . .".[26]

In another case, it was held that the conclusion of the Secretary of State that the institution of a cheese-making process on a farm brought about a change of use to mixed farming and manufacture was not unreasonable.[27]

The implications of these decisions, *i.e.* that there is a level beyond which the processing of farm produce is no longer ancillary to an agricultural use, sits uneasily in the company of the decision in *Allen v. Secretary of State for the Environment*.[28] Here Mr Vandermeer, Q.C., sitting as a deputy judge, having examined some of the authorities on the sale of agricultural produce, held that the sale of homegrown produce on a farm was ancillary even if carried out on a large scale.

Such a conclusion can lead to serious planning problems. Perhaps a solution may be found in the application of the requirement that ancillary uses must be "ordinarily incidental" to take on the legal character of the primary use. It is clear that this requirement applies to development within the use classes, but there is authority also to suggest that it should equally apply to other primary uses.[29]

---

[24]   14 P. & C.R. 134.
[25]   [1985] J.P.L. 710.
[26]   See also *Warnock v. Secretary of State for the Environment* [1980] J.P.L. 590.
[27]   *Cumbo v. Secretary of State for the Environment*.
[28]   [1990] J.P.L. 340.
[29]   See *Wealden District Council v. Secretary of State for the Environment* [1988] J.P.L. 268; and *Wallington v. Secretary of State for the Environment* [1991] J.P.L. 942; and commentary to *Allen* above.

5.2.3 Development by local authorities

Development carried out by local authorities within their own areas is exempted from the obligation to obtain planning permission. This exemption may be justified on the grounds that a local authority cannot apply for permission to itself and that local authority development, by definition, is carried out in the interests of the common good.[30] Where development is carried out within the area of another local authority, permission is generally required. However, no permission is required for the construction of a new road or the maintenance or improvement of an existing road which is outside the administrative boundary of the authority effecting the development.[31] A local authority is also entitled under section 4(1)(f) of the 1963 Act to carry out development outside its own area without recourse to the planning process where the development comprises "works for the purpose of inspecting, repairing, renewing, altering or removing any sewers, mains, pipes, cables, overhead wires, or other apparatus, including the breaking open of any street or other land for that purpose".[32] The wording of this paragraph does not authorise the carrying out of development for the first time.

The Local Government (Dublin) Act 1993 provided for the creation of three new administrative counties to replace the administrative county of Dublin. It simultaneously provided for the establishment of a council for each of these counties, to be described as Fingal, Dun Laoghaire–Rathdown and South Dublin.[33] Article 9(5) of the 1994 Regulations provided that development which any of these county councils commenced within the functional area of another of these councils before December 31, 1995 was exempted development.[34]

5.2.4 Development by statutory undertakers

Section 4(1)(f) of the 1963 Act also exempts any works carried out by a statutory undertaker for the purpose of:

---

[30]   In an article entitled, "Public Development and the Irish Planning System", (1986) pp.33–51, Colin Stevenson concludes, at pp.47–8: "It is difficult to understand why Irish public bodies should enjoy as extensive a privileged position as they do as regards exemption from the strict requirements of the planning system . . . Most commentators would certainly accept that some exceptions are appropriate for certain categories of public development. The real question is the scope of these exemptions. It would appear that at present the Irish exemptions are drafted illogically and unduly broadly. More precise exemptions should be introduced specifying the particular development to be excluded from the planning system."

[31]   1963 Act, s.4(1)(e). Note also that the carrying out of works by or at the direction of, or on behalf of, the National Roads Authority, in relation to the construction or maintenance of a national road, is exempted development: Roads Act 1993, s.19(6).

[32]   This type of development is also exempted when carried out by statutory undertakers.

[33]   The remaining provisions of this Act came into force on January 1, 1994: See Local Government (Dublin) Act 1993, Commencement Order 1993 (S.I. No. 400 of 1993).

[34]   Exemptions for local authority development are discussed in greater length at para. 1.3.3, above.

"inspecting, repairing, renewing, altering or removing any sewers, mains, pipes, cables, overhead wires, or other apparatus, including the breaking open of any street or the land for that purpose."[35]

It does not authorise the carrying out of development for the first time. A "statutory undertaker" is defined as:

"a person authorised by a British or Saorstát Eireann Statute or an Act of the Oireachtas or an order having statutory force to construct, work, or carry on a railway, canal or inland navigation, dock, harbour, gas, electricity, or other public undertaking."[36]

Bodies such as CIE, Bord Gais, the ESB and Bord Telecom are "statutory undertakers" for the purpose of this exemption.

5.2.5 Internal works

Works which affect only the interior of a structure are exempted except where they would involve the alteration or removal of, or might cause injury to, any feature or fixture which forms part of the interior of a structure listed for preservation under the development plan which is stated to be of artistic, historic or architectural interest.[37]

A developer may not rely on this exemption to carry out alterations to the interior of a structure for which he has obtained planning permission if the alterations have not been indicated in the plans accompanying the application; the planning permission must be implemented in its entirety or not at all. In *Horne v. Freeney*,[38] the respondent was granted planning permission for the construction of an amusement arcade. It was to have a concrete slab roof; an open area for dodgem cars on the ground floor; toilets and other facilities on the first floor. Instead a steel roof was built, two rows of 15 pillars with rooms behind were constructed on the ground floor and the open area for dodgem cars was moved to the first floor. The court held that the planning permission should have been implemented in its entirety and that it was not possible to deviate from the terms of the permission in reliance on the exemption for internal works. Murphy J. said:

"planning permission is indivisible: it authorises the carrying out of the totality of the works for which approval has been granted and not some of them only. A developer cannot, at his election, implement a part only of the approved plans as no approval is given for the part as distinct from the whole".

A developer may not take the benefit of this exemption where other unauthorised development has been carried out on the same structure. In *Dublin Corporation v.*

---

[35] See also the exemptions for development by statutory undertakers contained in Sched. 2, Pt. 1, Classes 21–29 to the 1994 Regulations.
[36] 1963 Act, s.2 (1).
[37] *ibid.*, s.4(1)(g) and s.4(1A). The latter subsection was inserted by the 1976 Act, s.43(1)(c).
[38] Unreported, High Court, July 7, 1988.

Langan,[39] the respondent demolished a portion of his shop premises which projected beyond the building line, replacing it with a new shop front of similar proportions. He also carried out works on the interior of the premises which extended for a considerable distance back from the building line. The respondent conceded that the replacement shop front constituted development but argued that the internal works were exempted. Gannon J. held that the front and back portions of the shop had to be considered as one structure so that the entire structure became unauthorised as a result of the demolition and replacement of the front portion of the shop.

5.2.6 External works

External works are also exempted provided they do not "materially affect the external appearance of the structure so as to render such appearance inconsistent with the character of the structure or of neighbouring structures".[40] This exemption is also subject to the restriction that the works must not involve the alteration or removal of or any likelihood of injury to any feature or fixture which forms part of the interior of a structure listed for preservation under the development plan which is stated to be of artistic, historic or architectural interest.[41]

The meaning of "character" in this context was examined in *Cairnduff v. O'Connell*[42] which concerned the replacement of an exterior balcony and staircase to the rear of one of the Victorian terraced houses on Waterloo Road. The new balcony was different in size and appearance from that which had existed 15 years previously. In proceeding taken under section 27 of the 1976 Act, the applicant argued that the respondent could not rely on the exemption for external works because the appearance of the house had been affected materially by reference to its condition at the time of the replacement of the stairs and balcony. The applicant also contended that the new stairs and balcony would render the appearance of the respondent's house inconsistent with the character of the applicant's house, as it would result in substantial overlooking of his property.

While it was accepted by the Supreme Court that the appearance of the house had been materially affected because of the interval of 15 years before its replacement, it was held that its appearance had not been rendered inconsistent with its own character or that of the applicant's house because the type of balcony and staircase in question was a feature of all the houses on the terrace. It was also relevant that the alterations were to the rear of the premises rather than to the appearance which the building presented to the street. Furthermore, the invasion of privacy of the applicant's patio was not a consideration relating to the "character" of the structure. Finlay C.J. said:

---

[39] Unreported, High Court, May 13, 1982
[40] 1963 Act, s.4(1)(g).
[41] *ibid.*, s.4(1A) as, inserted by the 1976 Act, s.43(1)(c).
[42] [1986] I.R. 73.

"On the question as to whether these works affected the external appearance of the structure so as to be inconsistent either with its character or the character of neighbouring structures, it seems to me the following considerations must apply. Firstly, in relation to a terraced house, at least, its character would, it seems to me, be much more dominantly affected by its street appearance than by its rear appearance. Secondly, I am satisfied that the character of the structure provided for in the sub-section must relate, having regard to the provisions of the Act in general, to the shape, colour, design, ornamental features and layout of the structure concerned. I do not consider that the meaning of this sub-section can depend on its particular use at any time in such a way as to make, as the appellants contend, an invasion of the privacy of a patio at the rear of a Victorian terraced house something inconsistent with the character of the structure of that house."

Finlay C.J. also expressed the view, *obiter*, that the replacement of part of the exterior of a premises with a similar part of the same size and appearance would not materially affect the exterior of the premises where the interval between demolition or removal of the part and its replacement was relatively short.

It is clear from *Cairnduff* that the effect of the works on both the character of the building itself as well as on neighbouring buildings or structures must be taken into account. In *Dublin Corporation v. Bentham*,[43] it was held that the replacement of Georgian double sash windows with aluminium outward opening sash windows was not exempted development under section 4(1)(g) because it rendered the external appearance of the structure inconsistent with the character of the premises itself, although the replacement windows were not inconsistent with the character of neighbouring structures, the windows of which had already been altered to the detriment of their character.[44]

5.2.7 Uses incidental to the enjoyment of a dwellinghouse

Section 4 also provides that "developments consisting of the use of any structure of other land within the curtilage of a dwellinghouse for any purpose incidental to the enjoyment of the dwellinghouse as such" are exempted development.

5.2.7.1 *"Curtilage"*

The definition of "curtilage" most commonly quoted is that given in *Sinclair Lockhart's Trustees v. Central Land Board* where it was stated that:

---

[43] Unreported, High Court, July 22, 1992.

[44] There are a number of reference determinations by An Bord Pleanála under s.5 of the 1963 Act which deal with the application of s.4(1)(g) to particular circumstances. PL 6/8/531 related to the installation of three velux roof lights at Stillorgan Road, Stillorgan, County Dublin. The Board determined that this fell within the scope of s.4(1)(g). Reference no. 29/RF/561 appears to have related to a building with preservation listing. The Board determined that the replacement of traditional timber sash windows with aluminimum windows (at Elgin Road, Ballsbridge, Dublin 4), did not amount to exempted development having regard to s.4(1)(g) and to art. 11(1)(a)(x) of the 1977 Regulations (now to be found under the 1994 Regulations, art. 10(1)(a)(ix)). See also PL 295/RF/681.

"the ground which is used for the comfortable enjoyment of a house or other building may be regarded as being within the curtilage of a house or building although it has not been marked off or enclosed in any way. It is enough that it serves the purpose of the house or building in some necessary or reasonably useful way".[45]

In the more recent decision of *McAlpine v. Secretary of State for the Environment*[46] it was stated that the curtilage was constrained to a small area about a building but that it was "not necessary for there to be any physical enclosure with the house and overall the term has a restrictive meaning."[47] In *Attorney General ex. rel., Sutcliffe and Others v. Calderdale Borough Council*,[48] Stephenson L.J. based his determination as to whether a structure was within the curtilage of a listed building on three criteria:

    (1)   the physical "layout of the listed building and the structure,

    (2)   their ownership, past and present,

    (3)   their use and function, past and present".

It is not absolutely clear whether land may be appropriated for uses incidental to the enjoyment of the dwellinghouse by extending its curtilage, *e.g.* by landscaping agricultural land or an area of waste land, but it is submitted that the better view is that the exemption contained in section 4(1)(h) applies only to the incidental use of land which is already within the curtilage of the dwellinghouse.[49]

5.2.7.2 *"Dwellinghouse"*

There is no definition of "dwellinghouse" in the planning code, and presumably its meaning must be distinguished from that of "habitable dwelling". The distinctive characteristic of a dwellinghouse is its "ability to afford to those who use it the facilities required for day to day private domestic existence".[50] In *Gravesham Borough Council v. Secretary of State for the Environment* it was held that a chalet which could not be lived in for four months of the year under a condition attached to its planning permission was nonetheless capable of being a "dwellinghouse". It is its actual rather than potential use as a dwelling that determines its status so that a

---

[45]   In *Dyer v. Doreset County Council* [1988] 3 W.L.R. 213, Nourse L.J. relied on the definition contained in the *Oxford English Dictionary* which is as follows:

     "A small court, yard, garth, or piece of ground attached to a dwellinghouse, and forming one enclosure with it, or so regarded by the law; the area attached to and containing a dwelling-house and its outbuildings."

[46]   [1995] J.P.L. B43.

[47]   See also the decision in *James v. Secretary of State for the Environment and Chichester District Council* (1990) P. & C.R. which involved the consideration of whether a tennis court situated in a field 'adjacent to a dwellinghouse was within its curtilage.

[48]   (1983) 46 P. & C.R. 399.

[49]   Support for this view may be found in the *Encyclopaedia of Planning Law and Practice*, 3B–1094; see further *Sampson's Executors v. Nottinghamshire County Council* [1949] 2 K.B. 439; *Stephens v. Cuckfield Rural District Council* [1960] 2 Q.B. 373.

[50]   *per* McCullough J. in *Gravesham Borough Council v. Secretary of State for the Environment* (1982) 47 P. & C.R. 142.

building which was originally designed for use as a dwellinghouse may lose that status if a substantial part of it is put to another use. This is demonstrated in *Scurlock v. Secretary of State for Wales*, where the appellant against an enforcement notice lived in the upper part of a three storey georgian style property but was in practice as an estate agent in two rooms on the ground floor.[51] A Divisional Court of the Queen's Bench decided that the building could not be termed a dwellinghouse.[52]

It would appear likely that the term "dwellinghouse" under section 4 of the 1963 Act does not include individual apartments or apartment blocks, although there is no express exclusion as exists under the definition of "dwellinghouse" under article 8 of the 1994 Regulations. A dwelling which is unauthorised may nonetheless constitute a dwellinghouse for the purpose of section 4 as there is no express requirement that the dwelling be authorised.[53]

5.2.8 ". . . as such"

The significance of the words "incidental" and "as such" were examined in *Wallington v. Secretary of State for Wales*.[54] Mrs Wallington resided with her 44 dogs which were not kept for commercial purposes in an ordinary house. The planning authority served an enforcement notice on her, alleging that a material change of use had occurred. In the Court of Appeal, Mrs Wallington did not deny that the keeping of 44 dogs constituted in the particular circumstances a material change of use. Instead she relied upon section 52(2)(d) of the Town and Country Planning Act 1971 which uses the same wording as section 4 of the 1963 Act.

The judgments of Slade L.J. and Farquharson J. differ in regard to whether an objective or subjective test should be applied in determining whether the use was incidental or not. Slade L.J. expressed the view that only uses which could be described as reasonably incidental to the enjoyment of the dwellinghouse fell within the scope of the exemptions.[55] He endorsed the opinion of Sir Graham

---

[51] (1976) 3 P. & C.R. 202. The decision concerned "permitted development" under Sched. 1, Class 1 of the Town and Country Planning General Development Order 1973.

[52] The decision in *Scurlock* may be contrasted with that in *Wood v. Secretary of State for the Environment* [1973] 2 All E.R. 404.

[53] However, the exemptions under Sched. 2, Pt. I for development within the curtilage of a dwellinghouse will not apply where the structure is unauthorised or where the use of the structure is unauthorised because of the effect of the restriction under art. 10(1)(a)(viii) of the 1994 Regulations. See *Encyclopaedia of Planning Law and Practice*, 3B–1092.

[54] *i.e.* in the context of the equivalent provision of s.52(2)(d) of the Town and Country Planning Act 1971.

[55] The effect of the phrase "as such" was, according to Slade L.J., that the provision should be read as "incidental to the enjoyment of the dwellinghouse, as a dwellinghouse", although it may be doubted whether this creates any major additional insight into the interpretation of the provision. The libertarian implications of Slade L.J.'s approach has been examined by Barry Hough in [1992] J.P.L. 906, "Planning Law and Domestic Privacy": "The avid model train enthusiast may find that if his model railway layouts spread through the greater part of his dwelling-house, he would fall foul of Farquharson LJ's ruling that the enjoyment of the dwelling house 'as such' has become subordinate to the pursuit of the hobby".

Eyre Q.C. (sitting as a deputy High Court Judge) in *Emin v. Secretary of State for the Environment*,[56] where he stated:

> "The fact that such a building had to be required for a purpose associated with the enjoyment of a dwellinghouse could not rest solely on the unrestrained whim of him who dwelt there but connoted some sense of reasonableness in all the circumstances of the particular case. That was not to say that the arbiter could impose some hard objective test so as to frustrate the reasonable aspirations of a particular owner of occupier so long as they were sensibly related to his enjoyment of the dwelling. The word 'incidental' connoted an element of subordination in land use terms in relation to the enjoyment of the dwellinghouse."

Farquharson L.J., on the other hand, was slightly more libertarian in his approach, saying that it was "sensible to consider what would be a normal use of a dwellinghouse although it was not of course determinative of the question". He agreed that the word "incidental" meant subordinate in land use terms to the enjoyment of a dwellinghouse as a dwellinghouse. He set out a number of matters to which it was appropriate to have regard in deciding a use rather than the exemption:

> "(1) Where was the dwellinghouse situated? Different considerations might apply depending on whether it was in the country on the one hand or in the centre of a town on the other . . . ;
>
> (2) What was the site of the dwellinghouse in the context of the user which was said to be incidental to its enjoyment. How much ground was included in its curtilage?
>
> (3) What was the nature and scale of the activity which was said to be incidental to the enjoyment of the dwellinghouse as such? The more dominant the activity the less likely it was to be described as incidental. The indulgence of a hobby was more likely to qualify than some commercial activity.
>
> (4) What was the disposition and character of the occupier? While, as already stated, his or her view of whether the activity was incidental was not in any sense conclusive, it was nevertheless something to which regard should be paid. One person might consider a particular hobby was incidental to his or her enjoyment of the dwellinghouse, where another would say that such an activity was unthinkable in or near a dwellinghouse."[57]

In the result, all three judges held that the decision of the Inspector was not unreasonable.

The necessity for reasonableness in the use of the curtilage was highlighted in *Croydon London Borough Council v. Gladden*[58] where it was held that the storage

---

[56] [1989] J.P.L. 909.
[57] Indoor archery was considered to be capable of being incidental to the enjoyment of the dwellinghouse in *Emin*, above.
[58] [1994] J.P.L. 723.

of a replica Spitfire aeroplane in the garden of a dwellinghouse was not incidental to the enjoyment of the dwellinghouse as such.[59]

In *Dublin Corporation v. Moore*[60] it was accepted by both parties in the Supreme Court that the trial judge was correct in holding that the keeping of an ice-cream van in the driveway of a dwellinghouse did not constitute exempted development under section 4(1)(h) of the 1963 Act. However, the corporation sought to establish that it amounted to material change of use of the driveway. McCarthy J. dismissed this contention. He said:

> "The driveway of a home was always intended for parking of vehicles; it would be difficult to find a driveway to a home in the city of county of Dublin where it was not so used; section 3, sub-section 2 is clearly intended to prevent an alteration of that particular type of use to one where it is supplemented by a use "in situ". It may well be that a driveway is not the ordinary parking place for a caravan or a boat – ergo, the exemption by Class 16. If one were to extend the ban contended for by the Corporation, one would have to contemplate that the taxi-driver, the small grocer who has a van, the small building contractor, the artisan, the discotheque provider, the children's entertainer, indeed the gas, electrical or light special employees of Dublin Corporation, may not, lawfully keep the vehicle attached to such trade or profession parked at home. In my view, it is a complete shutting out of reality not to recognise the people of the kind I have mentioned and, no doubt, a great variety of others, keep the vehicles of their trade at home. To avail of the electricity supply does not, in my view, affect the situation any more than the overnight charging of the battery of the car".

This statement appears to suggest that the ordinary user of dwellinghouses in general does not require planning permission. McCarthy J. went on to make observations to the effect that the planning position could not be affected by the quality of or standards applied in a particular residential neighbourhood:

> "There cannot, however, be one law for Cabra and another for Clondalkin – yet others for Finglas and Foxrock. Considerations of this kind are not appropriate to planning law – if they were, they might well offend against rights of equality. The ordinary law of nuisance remains, if nuisance there be. . .".

The use of garages or other structures within the curtilage of a dwellinghouse for living purposes has been given some consideration but these cases tend to

---

[59] Dillon L.J. observed that although the occupant would no doubt derive great enjoyment from keeping the replica spitfire on the land at 42 St Ormond's Road, because "that would be one in the eye for the council, . . . that sort of personal pleasure however exquisite was not "enjoyment of the dwelling house as such". Mr Gladden's efforts to annoy the council were indeed determined: he had, *inter alia*, previously fixed a 14 foot long fibreglass replica of a fish to the roof of an extension and at one stage placed a large inflatable figure of Winston Churchill in the front garden. On the day of the court hearing the Spitfire, fibreglass marlin and the inflatable model of Winston Churchill with his customary victory salute reversed "in an irreverent gesture aimed at the Plannery of Croydon" were to be seen in attendance in a truck parked outside the courthouse. See [1994] J.P.L. 734 and Martin and Edwards, "Examining Injunctive Provisions" (1994) E.G. 149.

[60] [1984] I.L.R.M. 339. See also An Bord Pleanála, section 5 reference determination no. 78/RF/0735, reported at (1996) IPELJ 32, in which it was decided that the parking of a mechanical digger within the curtilage of a dwellinghouse was *not* exempted development.

depend very much on their peculiar facts. In *Uttlesford District Council v. Secretary of State for the Environment*[61] it was held that the existence of separate living facilities in a garage or other structure used as a "granny flat" may not necessarily mean that planning permission will be required. In *Whitehead v. Secretary of State for the Environment and Mole Valley District Council.*[62] Mr Malcolm Spence Q.C., sitting as a Deputy Judge, upheld the finding of the Secretary of State that the use of a converted barn within the curtilage of a dwelling for the accommodation of a housekeeper was a use "incidental to the enjoyment of the dwelling as such". He stressed that "it mattered not, whether this building, as converted, happened to include its own kitchen or bathroom". What mattered was that it "would form an integral part of the main use of the planning unit as a single dwellinghouse . . . the whole purpose of it was to provide somewhere to live for the housekeeper, who would doubtless be looking after the house to cook meals in it and so on."

It is by no means certain that these decisions would be followed in this jurisdiction. From a planning enforcement point of view such "incidental" uses would be difficult to monitor and could be used to disguise sub-division or a use for holiday lettings.

5.2.9 Casual trading areas

Development consisting of the use of land for the purpose of casual trading is exempted development.[63]

5.2.10 Land reclamation

Only land reclamation carried out by the Minister for Agriculture either at the request of the occupier of the land or on the Minister's own initiative is exempted under section 4(1)(i).[64] Land reclamation by a private individual is not exempted under this provision.[65] In determining whether works constitute land reclamation so as to gain the benefit of the exemption the "primary object" of the works should be examined. In *Lennon v. Kingdom Plant Hire*,[66] Morris J. held that exemption did not apply where the primary object of the extensive excavation being carried out by the rock was not to improve the land but to gather boulders to enable them to fulfil their contract to provide boulders for the County Council's coastal protection scheme.

---

[61]   [1992] J.P.L. 171.
[62]   [1992] J.P.L. 561.
[63]   Inserted by the Casual Trading Act 1980, s.7(3).
[64]   *Tralee Urban District Council v. Stack*, unreported, High Court, January 13, 1984.
[65]   However, see exemptions for land reclamation under Sched. 2, Pt. III, Class 9, to the 1994 Regulations. See also Class 3 of Pt. III.
[66]   Unreported, High Court, December 13, 1991.

5.3 DEVELOPMENT BY STATE AUTHORITIES

5.3.1 Background decisions – Luggala and Mullaghmore

Until the ground-making decisions in the cases of *Howard v. The Commissioners of Public Works* and *Byrne v. The Commissioners of Public Works*,[67] it was generally believed that development by state authorities was exempted from the requirement of obtaining planning permission. Section 84 of the 1963 Act prescribed a procedure whereby state authorities were obliged to consult with the planning authority in relation to the construction or extension of any building, and if any objections raised by the planning authority remained unresolved, they were obliged, to consult with the Minister.[68] It was argued that the necessity to consult with the planning authority would not arise if state authorities were not otherwise relieved of the obligation to apply for planning permission. At that time, a "State authority" was defined as either (a) a member of the Government or (b) The Commissioners of Public Works in Ireland or (c) The Irish Land Commission. The fact that the limited control imposed by the reqirement of consultation did not exist where demolition or a change in the use of a building was proposed caused one learned judicial author to remark[69]:

> "If such an exemption exists, it would mean that buildings of such unique importance as The Royal Hospital, Kilmainham, The Four Courts or The Custom House could be demolished or materially altered by the body now entrusted with their custody without any permission being sought or even without any consultation being held with any other State or local authority."

The status of exempted development accorded to developments carried out by state authorities was challenged in two cases involving interpretative centres to be carried out by The Commissioners of Public Works, one at Luggala in County Wicklow and the other at the Burren National Park, near Mullaghmore in County Clare. In the *Luggala* case, or *Byrne v. The Commissioners of Public Works*, the question as to whether the visitors' centre, then under construction, was exempted development arose in the context of proceedings to restrain further development under section 27 of the Local Government (Planning and Development) Act 1976. Lynch J. came to the conclusion that no rational effect could be ascribed to section 84 unless one construed it as excluding state authorities by implication from the obligation to apply for planning permission.[70] He said that the contrary conclusion would result in a "convoluted course of futile consultations" with the planning authority and, in the event of an objection, with the Minister for Local Government, both of whom could subsequently be asked to adjudicate on a planning application for the proposed development. He said:

---

67 [1994] 1 I.R. 101.
68 Section 84 was repealed by the Local Government (Planning and Development) Act 1993, s.5.
69 *per* Mr Justice Keane in Walsh, *Planning and Development Law* (2nd ed.), p. 26.
70 In *Howard*, above n.67. Costello J. (as he then was) reached a contrary conclusion.

"The philosophy behind section 84 would appear to me to be that development by a State authority will not involve any element of private profit or gain. On the contrary, development by a State authority may be presumed to be for public purposes and for the common good. As the main object of requiring planning permission by other persons is to ensure that the proposed development does not conflict with the common good, it is logically unnecessary to require planning permission for development by a State authority."

An argument with even more far-reaching consequences was introduced by the applicants in judicial review proceedings in *Howard and Others v. The Commissioners of Public Works in Ireland*[71] where it was claimed on an application for judicial review that the Commissioners had no statutory power to build or maintain the proposed centre at Mullaghmore. He held that no general power could be derived from the statutory provisions governing the functions and duties of the Commissioners which would enable them to carry out the very specific public works intended.

"this early 19 century administrative machine is being asked to perform functions it was never designed to perform – to meet 20 century demands it needs to be supplied with new parts, as was done in the case of the Blasket Islands; perhaps, even, it requires to be replaced altogether."

The outcome of this ruling by Costello J. in *Howard* was the repeal of section 84 of the 1963 Act by section 5 of the Local Government (Planning and Development) Act 1993 and the enactment of the State Authorities (Development and Management) Act 1993, which retrospectively conferred on state authorities the power, *inter alia*, to carry out development. Section 2(3) of the latter Act provided a saver to protect the constitutionality of this provision. In *Howard and Others v. The Commissioners of Public Works in Ireland and The Attorney General (No. 2)*,[72] the plaintiffs sought clarification from the High Court as to the effect of section 2 on the future development of the controversial visitors' centre and on the orders which had been made by the High Court in the earlier proceedings relating to the centre.

The plaintiffs argued that section 2(3) of the 1993 Act precluded the application of the 1993 Act to the proposed visitors' centre as otherwise the plaintiffs' constitutional rights would be unconstitutionally affected by depriving them of the fruits of the earlier judgment in this case. The plaintiffs also advanced the argument that if the 1993 Act were construed so as to apply to the judgment and order of Costello J., it would involve an invasion of the exclusive domain of the courts in the administration of justice.

---

[71] Above n.67. See also *Keane v. An Bord Pleanála and the Commissioners of Irish Rights*, unreported, Supreme Court, July 18 1996, in which the *vires* of the Commissioners to erect a Loran-C radio mast at Loophead, County Clare was successfully challenged. The appeal by the Commissioners was disallowed by a 3:2 majority.

[72] Unreported, High Court, Lynch J., June 8, 1994. (On February 12, 1993, Costello J. had granted a declaration in those proceedings, that the development by the Commissioners was *ultra vires* their powers and a further declaration that the development was illegal as there was no planning permission for the development. Accordingly, Costello J. had ordered that the Commissioners be restrained from proceeding with the development of the centre and related works.)

Lynch J. concluded that the effect of the 1993 Act was not to reverse Costello J.'s finding or declaration that the Commissioners of Public Works did not have statutory power to carry out the development proposal at Mullaghmore at the time of the making of his order. To this extent, it did not contravene the doctrine of the separation of powers by permitting a trespass into the judicial domain by the legislature. In his view, there was no reason why the Oireachtas could not now confer retrospective powers on the commissioners when such powers could have been conferred in the past. Lynch J. refused the leave sought by the plaintiffs but declined also to vacate or amend the earlier injunction granted by Costello J. as that order had been made in completely separate judicial review proceedings.

Both *Byrne and Howard* were appealed to the Supreme Court, which restricted itself to addressing the arguments on the exempted development issue. In the result, it was unnecessary to consider the *vires* argument. The applicants argued in effect that the purpose of the obligation to consult under section 84 of the 1963 Act was to avoid both the cost and expense involved in an unsuccessful planning application. It was also undesirable for state agencies to be seen proposing developments which were inconsistent with the planning policies created by other state agencies, namely the planning authorities. The applicants also argued that section 4 of the 1963 Act, was such an obvious vehicle for the exemption of state agencies, that if the legislature intended to exempt State authorities they would undoubtedly have done it under that section.

The OPW reiterated the arguments in favour of the continuance of the prerogative of the crown as a constitutional principle which prevented the state from being bound by statute. In holding that "the presumption of exemption in the absence of express inclusion, or inclusion by necessary implication, is not part of a judicial precedent binding upon this court . . .". Finlay C.J. placed reliance on the constitutional principle of equality, quoting with approval from the judgment of Subba Rao C.J. in *The State of West Bengal v. The Corporation of Calcutta*. Denham J. emphasised that the court was bound to give effect to the clear language of section 84, even if it was satisfied that the legislature did not contemplate the consequences of the provision.[73] She said that while section 84 expressly required a consultation by state authorities, to read any further meaning into it would be "a misconstruction to repair a perceived defect in the Act".

O'Flaherty J., although initially putting forward the proposition that "a mistake in the view of the law cannot be invoked as a key to unlock a statutory provision", proceeded to uphold the existence of a presumption that the state is not bound by legislation, unless a statute expressly so requires, or does so by necessary implication. Egan J. also gave a minority dissenting judgment in which he emphasised

---

[73] The intention of the legislature to have exempted State authorities from the obligation to obtain planning permission would appear to have been confirmed by the Dáil debates at the time of the enactment of the 1963 Act: see Vol. 201 *Dáil Debates*, Col. 199–230, and various Government circulars including P.L. 202/6/6 on September 24, 1964 and P.D. 67/5 on December 23, 1983.

the incongruity of an appeal to the Minister for Local Government where he had already been consulted, and of such an appeal where he himself was the developer applicant.[74] While disallowing the existence of any presumption in favour of state exemption, he held that the intention of the legislature as expressed in the wording of the statute as a whole indicated that the exemption applied to state authorities.

The final judgment of the court from Blayney J. "unlocked" the result of the decision. In holding that the court was obliged to give effect to the clear words of the statute, he held that the State did not enjoy any exemption from the general obligation to obtain planning permission under section 24 of the 1963 Act. In doing so, Blayney J. also pointed out that interpretative centres involved the construction of a number of structures which were not "buildings", such as a waste water treatment plant, storage tanks and a 6,500 sq.m car park, so that permission would at any rate have been required for the erection of these structures.

5.3.2 Exemptions for certain development by state authorities

In the aftermath of the decision of the Supreme Court in *Howard*, the Local Government (Planning and Development) Act 1993 was passed to validate all development previously carried out by state authorities without planning permission. A further object of the new legislation was to enable the Minister to exclude certain specified classes of development from the obligation to obtain planning permission. In accordance with the doctrine of the separation of powers, the Act made it clear that its provisions did not affect in any way any of the particular developments which had been made the subject of litigation prior to May 26, 1993, when it had been determined that permission was required. A "State authority" is defined under the 1993 Act as either (a) a Minister of the Government or (b) The Commissioners of Public Works in Ireland.

Section 2(1)(a) of the 1993 Act enables the Minister to make regulations excluding specified classes of development by or on behalf of a state authority from the application of the planning code, where the development is, in the opinion of the Minister, related to public safety or order, the administration of justice or national security or defence; or where the carrying out of such development must be authorised by statute.[75] Article 156 of the 1994 Regulations specifies the following classes of development as excluded from the application of the Acts:

    (a) Development consisting of the provision of:
        (i) Garda stations or other buildings, or other premises or installations, or other structures or facilities, used for the purposes of or in connection with the operations of An Garda Siochana,

---

[74] Planning appeals were determined by the Minister for Local Government prior to the establishment of An Bord Pleanála under the 1976 Act.

[75] See exemption under 1994 Regulations, art. 11(3) and para. 5.4.6, below. See also exemptions under Classes 34, 35, 42 and 46; see para. 5.5.11, below.

    (ii) prisons or other places of detention,

    (iii) courthouses,

    (iv) barracks or other buildings, or other premises or installations (including airfields and naval yards), or other structures or facilities, used for the purposes of or in connection with the operations of the Defence Forces,

    (v) office buildings or other premises used for the purposes of or in connection with the business of Úachtarán na h-Éireann, Dáil Éireann, Seanad Éireann, the Department of the Taoiseach, the Office of the Tánaiste, the Department of Defence, the Department of Foreign Affairs, the Department of Justice, the Office of the Attorney General, the Chief State Solicitor's Office and the Office of the Director of Public Prosecutions;

(b) (i) development consisting of the provision of an extension of any building referred to in paragraph (a) where such extension will be situate, in whole or in part, outside the curtilage of the existing building or, where the building is situate within a premises or other installation referred to in the said paragraph, outside the curtilage of the premises or other installation;

    (ii) development consisting of the provision of an extension of a premises or other installation, other than a building, referred to in paragraph (a) which will extend the premises or other installation beyond the curtilage of the existing premises or other installation;

(c) (i) development consisting of the carrying out of any works, for reasons of national security, within, or bounding, the curtilage of any building, premises or other installation occupied by, or under the control of, a state authority, other than a building, premises or other installation referred to in paragraph (a),

    (ii) development consisting of the carrying out, by or on behalf of a state authority, for reasons of national security, of any works within, or bounding, the curtilage of the residence of a holder, or former holder, of a public office or any other public servant or former public servant.

Article 156(2) provides that a building, premises, installation, structure or facility may be "provided" by the carrying out of works or by the making of a material change in its use. Article 157 further excludes from the application of the Acts the carrying out of works by the Commissioners of Public Works specified in a drainage scheme confirmed by the Minister for Finance under Part II of the Arterial Drainage Act 1945.[76]

---

[76] Any additions, omissions, variations and deviations as may be found necessary in the course of such arterial drainage works are likewise excluded.

5.3.3 Notification requirements

Section 2(1)(b) of the 1993 Act enables the Minister to make regulations concerning certain procedures to be followed by state authorities prior to carrying out development of a type specified under the regulations as being excluded from the application of the planning code. Article 158 of the 1994 Regulations requires a state authority to publish a newspaper notice and to erect a site notice of the proposed development, but these requirements do not apply to development by a state authority which is subject to the normal planning process or to development consisting of the construction or erection of temporary structures in connection with the operations of the defence forces which are urgently required for the reasons of national security. Article 158(3) provides that the newspaper notice:

> ". . . shall contain as a heading the name of the State authority by which the development is proposed to be carried out and shall state –
> (a) the location, nature and extent of the proposed development,
> (b) that plans and particulars of the proposed development will be available for inspection, at the offices of the State authority in Dublin and at a specified location in the area in which the development will be situate, at specified times during a period of one month beginning on the day of the publication of the notice,
> (c) that submissions or observations with respect to the proposed development, dealing with the proper planning and development of the area in which the development would be situate, may be made in writing to the State authority within a period of six weeks beginning on the day of publication of the notice."

Similar requirements are applied to site notices to be erected.[77]

State authorities are also obliged to send notice of proposed developments to the planning authority for the area in which the proposed development will be located who may make submissions on the planning considerations affecting the proposed development.

The following documents must be made available for inspection by members of the public for a period of one month from the date of publication of the newspaper notice:

– a document describing, in general terms, the nature and extent of the proposed development,
– a location map, drawn to a scale of not less than 1:10, 560 and marked or coloured so as to identify clearly the land on which it is proposed to carry out the proposed development, and
– plans or drawings describing, in outline, the external appearance of the building or other premises or installation, or other structure or facility, to be provided or extended (as the case may be).

---

[77] The provisions regulating site notices are the same as those under the ordinary planning application procedure: see 1994 Regulations, art. 158(4).

The Minister has power to make regulation requiring the preparation of an environmental impact statement for development by state authorities which is exempted, but no such regulations have as yet been made.[78]

5.3.4 Decision of state authority

Each state authority is obliged to have regard to any submissions or observations made by a planning authority or by any other person or body during the period of inspection. Having considered such submissions as have been made, the state authority can decide whether or not to carry out the proposed development with or without variations or modifications, as it considers appropriate.[79]

5.3.5 Development required by reason of an accident or emergency

Section 2(2) of the 1993 Act provides that a Minister or, in the case of the Commissioners, the Minister for Finance may make an order providing that some or all of the requirements of the notification procedure prescribed by Part XIII of the 1994 Regulations will not be applicable to certain development proposed to be carried out by that Minister or the Commissioners. Such an order may be made where the minister concerned or the Minister for Finance, as the case may be, is satisfied that the carrying out of the development is required by reason of an accident or emergency.

5.3.6 Retrospective validation of development commenced before the 1993 Act

Section 4 of the 1993 Act validates all development carried out or commenced by or on behalf of a state authority before the date of commencement of the section, *i.e.* June 15, 1993, by providing that permission will be deemed never to have been required, or never will be required, for such development.[80]

5.4 EXEMPTED DEVELOPMENT UNDER THE 1994 REGULATIONS, AS AMENDED

The Local Government (Planning and Development) Regulations 1994 came into operation on May 16, 1994. They revoked all previous planning regulations and

---

[78] See Local Government (Planning and Development) Act 1993, s.2(1)(b).

[79] Notice of its decision must be sent within three working days to the planning authority for the area in which the proposed development will be located. Similar notice must be given to any person or body which has made submissions concerning the proposed development unless the state authority has published notice of its decision in a newspaper circulating in the area of the proposed development within seven days of the making of the decision. See art. 162.

[80] In accordance with the doctrine of the separation of powers; the section did not affect cases where a court had made such a finding after the commencement of the section provided that the proceedings concerned were initiated before May 26, 1993. Section 4(2) also provides that permission would not be required for any development commenced by or on behalf of a state authority on or before June 14, 1994, or for any such development commenced after that date for which the consultation procedure under s.84 of the 1963 Act had been completed before that date.

the new regulations relating to exempted development are set out at Part III, articles 8 to 13. In some cases, the changes introduced had the effect of validating development which, at the time it occurred, was unauthorised. Conversely, the removal of exemptions which existed under the 1977 Regulations did not render development unauthorised where it was carried out in reliance on those provisions prior to the coming into operation on May 16, 1994. Article 12 of the 1994 Regulations provides that such development will continue to be regarded as exempted.

5.4.1 Definitions: article 8

In ascertaining whether a particular development is exempted, articles 8 to 13 are to be read in conjunction with the Second Schedule to the Regulations. Article 8 supplies definitions for words used in these articles and in the Second Schedule. For example, "dwellinghouse", "habitable house", "light industrial building", "repository", "shop", and "wholesale warehouse" are all defined and, in turn, define the scope of the exemptions.

5.4.2 Conditions and limitations: article 9

Article 9 indicates the method by which Parts I to III of the Second Schedule are to be read.[81] Part I lists different categories of exempted development under the heading "General"; Part II lists those exemptions applying to advertisements; and Part III deals with exempted development under the heading "Rural". These latter categories of rural exempted development do not apply in county boroughs, boroughs, urban districts, towns specified in the First Schedule to the 1963 Act or to the excluded areas as defined in section 9 of the Local Government (Reorganisation) Act 1985, but apply to all other areas. Parts I to III are set out in tabular form, the left hand column describing the class of development to which the exemption relates, the right hand column specifying the conditions and limitations which must attach or exist before the exemption will apply.

Article 9(4) also exempts the carrying out of such works as are necessary to secure compliance with the Building Regulations 1991 (S.I. 306 of 1991) where it relates to the construction of a dwelling or dwellings for which planning permission was granted before the June 1, 1992. This exemption does not apply to apartment blocks or any buildings designed for two or more dwellings.

5.4.3 Works carried out under a condition of an IPC licence

Article 9A exempts works which are required to be carried out under a condition attached to an integrated pollution control (IPC) licence under the Environmental Protection Agency Act 1992.[82]

---

[81] 1994 Regulations, art. 9(1)(b) also provided that certain exemptions for telecommunications masts would only be available for six months from the commencement of the Regulations, *i.e.* May 16, 1994.

[82] Inserted by the 1995 Regulations. It appears that art. 9A of the 1994 Regulations may be regarded as a separate article to art. 9 with the effect that the restrictions enumerated under art. 10 do not apply to development under art. 9A.

5.4.4 Restrictions on prima facie exemptions under Parts I, II and III of the second Schedule: article 10

Article 10 further cuts down the scope of the exemptions by imposing further restrictions on the categories of qualifying development specified under Parts I to III. It broadly reiterates the restrictions on exemptions formerly set out in article 11 of the 1977 Regulations, but there are some important changes. It is no longer necessary for a developer to comply with bye-laws or building regulations in order to avail of an exemption. A new restriction has been added which de-exempts any development involving the excavation, alteration or demolition of caves, sites, features or other objects of archeological, geological or historical interest, the preservation of which is an objective of a development plan or draft development plan.

Many of the restrictions contained in article 10 of the 1994 Regulations are intended to ensure the implementation of specific objectives of the development plan or of objectives which are in the process of being incorporated into the development plan for a particular area. Other restrictions seek to ensure the protection of certain accepted development control standards relating to road access, traffic hazard, and the building line. Special protection is afforded also to areas to which a special amenity area order applies by removing the application of certain exemptions to such areas. Development which is specified under the First Schedule to the European Communities (Environmental Impact Assessment) Regulations 1989 are not exempted as such development is subject to development control and requires an Environmental Impact Statement to be submitted with any planning application.[83] A proposed development which is of the same nature as class of specified development but which falls short of the threshold indicated for that development will likewise be deprived of its exempted status if it relates to an activity for which an integrated pollution control (IPC) licence will be required. Development for which an exemption from the requirement of an EIS is granted will continue to be exempted development.

Although article 10(1)(a)(vi) seeks to protect views under the development plan, article 10(2) provides that this restriction will not apply to development consisting of the construction by any electricity undertaking of an overhead line or cable not exceeding 100 metres in length for the purpose of conducting electricity from a distribution or transmission line to any premises.

The restrictions in article 10 are of considerable practical importance and are as follows:

"10.　(1)　Development to which article 9 relates shall not be exempted development for the purposes of the Acts –
　　　　(a) if the carrying out of such development would:
　　　　　　(i)　contravene a condition attached to a permission under the Acts or be inconsistent with any use specified in a permission under the Acts,

---

[83]　1994 Regulations, art. 10(c)(i).

(ii) consist of or comprise the formation, laying out or material widening of a means of access to a public road the surfaced carriageway of which exceeds 4 metres in width,

(iii) endanger public safety by reason of traffic hazard or obstruction of road users,

(iv) except in the case of a porch to which class 7 specified in column 1 of Part I of the Second Schedule applies and which complies with the conditions and limitations specified in column 2 of the said Part I opposite the mention of that class in the said column 1, comprise the construction, erection, extension or renewal of a building on any street to as to bring forward the building, or any part of the building, beyond the front wall of the building on either side thereof or beyond a line determined as the building line in a development plan for the area or, pending the variation of a development plan or the making of a new development plan, in the draft variation of the development plan or the draft new development plan,

(v) consist of or comprise the carrying out under a public road of works other than a connection to a wired broadcast relay service, sewer, water main, gas main or electricity supply line or cable, or any works to which class 23, 24 or 29(a) specified in column 1 of Part I of the Second Schedule applies,

(vi) interfere with a view or prospect of special amenity value or special interest the preservation of which is an objective of a development plan for the area in which the development is proposed or, pending the variation of a development plan or the making of a new development plan, in the draft variation of the development plan or the draft new development plan,

(vii) consist of or comprise the excavation, alteration or demolition of caves, sites, features or other objects of archaeological, geological or historical interest the preservation of which is an objective of a development plan for the area in which the development is proposed or, pending the variation of a development plan or the making of a new development plan, in the draft variation of the development plan or the draft new development plan,

(viii) consist of or comprise the extension, alteration, repair or renewal of an unauthorised structure or a structure the use of which is an unauthorised use,

(ix) consist of or comprise the alteration, extension or demolition of a building or other structure, other than an alteration consisting of the painting of any previously painted part of such building or structure, where such building or structure is specified in a development plan for the area or, pending the variation of a development plan or the making of a new development plan, in the draft variation of the development plan or the draft new development plan, as a building or other structure, or one of a group of buildings or other structures, of artistic, architectural or historical interest:

(I) the preservation of which is an objective of the planning authority to secure, or

(II) the preservation of which it is the intention of the planning authority to consider in the event of an application being made for permission to alter, extend or demolish the building or structure,

(x) consist of –

(I) the use for the exhibition of advertisements, other than advertisements of class 5, 9 or 15 specified in column 1 of Part II of the Second Schedule, of a building or other structure, where such building or structure is specified in a development plan for the area, or pending the variation of a development plan or the making of a new development plan, in the draft variation of the development plan or the draft new development plan, as a building or other structure, or one of a group of buildings or other structures, of artistic, architectural or historical interest the preservation of which it is an objective of the planning authority to secure,

(II) the erection of an advertisement structure, other than a structure for the exhibition of an advertisement of class 5, 9 or 15 as aforesaid, on, or within the curtilage of, a building or other structure as aforesaid,

(III) the erection on a building or other structure as aforesaid of a satellite television signal receiving antenna,

(xi) consist of the demolition or such alteration of a building or other structure as would preclude or restrict the continuance of an existing use of a building or other structure where it is an objective of the planning authority to ensure that the building or other structure would remain available for such use and such objective has been specified in a development plan for the area or, pending the variation of a development plan or the making of a new development plan, in the draft variation of the development plan or the draft new development plan,

(xii) consist of the fencing or enclosure of any land habitually open to or used by the public during the 10 years preceding such fencing or enclosure for recreational purposes or as means of access to any seashore, mountain, lakeshore, riverbank or other place of natural beauty or recreational utility,

(xiii) obstruct any public right of way, or

(b) in an area to which a special amenity area order relates, if such development would be development:

(i) of class 1, 3, 15, 19, 20, 25, 26, 27 or 29 (other than paragraph (a) thereof) specified in column 1 of Part I of the Second Schedule,

(ii) consisting of the use of a structure or other land for the exhibition of advertisements of class 1, 4, 6, 11, 16 or 17 specified in column 1 of Part II of the said Schedule or the erection of an advertisement structure for the exhibition of any advertisement of any of the said classes, or

(iii) of class 3, 5, 6, 7, 8, 9, 10, 11 or 12 specified in column 1 of Part III of the said Schedule, or

(c) if it is development:

(i) which is of a class for the time being specified under Article 24 of the Environmental Impact Assessment Regulations, or under any provision amending or replacing the said Article 24, or

(ii) which work would be of a class referred to in subparagraph (i) but for not exceeding a quantity, area or other limit for the time being specified in relation to that class and which comprises or is for the purposes of an activity in relation to which a licence under Part IV of the Environmental Protection Agency Act 1992 (No 7 of 1992) is required, unless that development is required by the Environmental Impact Assessment Regulations or any other statutory provision to comply with procedures (not being procedures relating to applications for permission under Part IV of the Act of 1963 or to applications for licences under Part IV of the Environmental Protection Agency Act 1992) for the purpose of giving effect to the Council Directive of 27 June 1985 (No 85/337EEC, O.J. No L175/40, 5 July 1985), or

(d) if it consists of or comprises an industrial activity or isolated storage to which Regulations 12 to 18 of the European Communities (Major Accident Hazards of Certain Industrial Activities) Regulations 1986 (S.I. No 292 of 1986), as amended by the European Communities (Major Accident Hazards of Certain Industrial Activities) (Amended) Regulations 1989 (S.I. No 194 of 1989), as amended by the European Communities (Major Accident Hazards of Certain Industrial Activities) (Amended) Regulations 1992 (S.I. No 21 of 1992), apply.

(2) Sub-article (1)(a)(vi) shall not apply where the development consists of the construction by any electricity undertaking of an overhead line or cable not exceeding one hundred metres in length for the purposes of conducting electricity from a distribution or transmission line to any premises."

5.4.5 Use classes: article 11

Part IV of the Second Schedule describes 11 use classes, reduced from 16 under the 1977 Regulations. Article 11 provides that a change of use within any one of these classes constitutes exempted development unless the change involved would contravene a condition of a planning permission or would be inconsistent with any use specified or included in such a permission. Any intensification of a particular use within one of these classes also amounts to exempted development.[84]

5.4.6 Specific exemptions under article 11

Article 11 also provides for two specific exemptions for changes of use. The conversion of private houses into bed and breakfast accommodation is exempted where it involves "the use of not more than four bedrooms in a dwelling house as overnight guest accommodation", provided that such development is not pre-

---

[84] *Brooks & Burton Ltd v. Secretary of State for the Environment* [1977] 1 W.L.R. 1294.

cluded by a pre-existing planning permission.[85] Some of the problems to which this exemption may give rise in residential areas have been highlighted.[86]

The growth in the number of interpretative centres is reflected in the exemption accorded to "the provision within a building occupied by, or under the control of, a State authority of a shop or restaurant for visiting members of the public".[87]

5.5 SECOND SCHEDULE, PART I – GENERAL

5.5.1 Development within the curtilage of a dwellinghouse

These exemptions are grouped under Classes 1–7 of Part I but there are a number of other exemptions which may be applicable to the domestic situation scattered throughout Part I.[88] Article 9 provides that "dwellinghouse" does not apply to a "building designed for use and (sic)[89] used as two or more separate flats or apartments, or a flat or apartment contained in such building", where development of the type described under classes 1, 2, 4, 6(b)(ii) or 7 is concerned.

5.5.1.1 Extensions and conversions

Class 1 relates to (a) extensions to the rear of a dwellinghouse (including the erection of a conservatory) and (b) the conversion of a garage, store, shed or other similar structure attached to the rear or to the side of a dwellinghouse. It should be noted that both of these types of development are described as an "extension" so that the conditions referred to in the right hand column apply to both.

The first condition only permits an extension to the extent of the threshold floor area of 23 square metres where there has been no previous extension to the dwelling. If the dwellinghouse has previously been extended, the exempted threshold is reduced by the cumulative area of any previous extension.

The height of the extension was initially restricted to eaves or parapet level but this unsatisfactory requirement has since been removed.[90] The extension must not reduce the size of the open space to the rear of the dwellinghouse to less than 25 square metres. The insistence on a reasonable area of private open space to the rear of the dwelling house is a welcome environmental improvement.

---

85   1994 Regulations, art. 11(2).
86   See Grist, (1994) IPELJ 51. For example, there is no requirement that the operator of the bed and breakfast live on the premises, a factor which normally inhibits bad neighbour development. Grist also comments that the number of bedrooms is a very crude measurement of land use demands: the number of bed spaces would more closely approximate to the number of guests. Further problems may also be caused by the proliferation of signs in residential areas as Class 6 of Pt. II exempts "advertisements relating to . . . any guesthouse or other premises (other than a hotel) providing overnight guest accommodation", subject to certain restrictions.
87   1994 Regulations, art. 11(3).
88   The meaning of "dwellinghouse" is discussed at para. 5.2.7.2, above.
89   It may be that "or" was intended here instead of "and".
90   1995 Regulations, art. 9.

In practice, planning permission was not normally sought for minor demolition works associated with an extension to the rear or side of a dwellinghouse which fell within the scope of Class 1. From a legal perspective, however, such demolition works nonetheless related to "part of a building" which fell within the definition of "habitable house", and were therefore excluded from the exemption for demolition.[91] Class 45(b) removes any legal uncertainty attaching to this practice by providing an exemption for:

> "the demolition of part of a habitable house in connection with the provision of an extension or porch in accordance with Class 1 or 7, respectively, of this Part of this Schedule or in accordance with the permission for an extension or porch granted under Part IV of the Act of 1963."

5.5.1.2 Central heating systems

The provision, as part of a central heating system of a dwellinghouse, of a chimney, boiler house or oil storage tank is exempted, but the capacity of any oil storage tank should not exceed 3,500 litres.[92]

5.5.1.3 Garages, sheds and similar structures

Class 3 exempts (subject to certain conditions):

> "the construction, erection or placing within the curtilage of a dwellinghouse of any tent, awning, shade or other object, greenhouse, garage, store, shed or other similar structure."

While previously such structures could be constructed anywhere within the curtilage of a dwellinghouse, if they are to be positioned forward of the front wall of the dwellinghouse, planning permission will be required. The new structure should not reduce the size of the open space to the rear of the dwellinghouse to less than 25 square metres. A cumulative area restriction on the structure itself has also been introduced to redress the situation where garages of up to 1,500 square feet had been constructed in reliance on the former Class 3.[93] Tighter design control is also introduced by the stipulation that the external finishes and the roof of any garage or other structure constructed to the side of a dwellinghouse must conform with those of the dwellinghouse. Height and use restrictions apply as under the former regulations. The exclusion of animals from such structures has been extended to horses, ponies and pigeons.

---

[91] See 1977 Regulations, Class 36.

[92] Class 2.

[93] In *Murray v. Buckley*, unreported, High Court, Barron J., December 5, 1990, held that a building having a floor area approaching 1,500 square feet was not so large that it could not properly be called a garage, or that it should be inferred that other uses were intended other than those indicated. This decision was upheld in an *ex-tempore* judgment of the Supreme Court on the October 14, 1991: see O'Sullivan and Shepherd, para. 2.655.

5.5.1.4 *Satellite dishes, wireless and television antennae*

Class 4 of Part I caters for a new feature of modern life – the satellite dish or satellite television signal receiving antenna. Prior to the introduction of the 1994 Regulations, An Bord Pleanála would appear to have been of the view that the erection of a satellite dish did not fall within the scope of the exemption for the erection of a wireless or television aerial which has also been retained under Class 4.[94] Satellite dishes have tended to interfere with visual amenities in residential areas because of the necessity for those receiving the Astra satellite to have a southeast orientation in order to receive its signals. The orientation of the house itself may determine that the dish has to be located on the side or front of a roof where such dishes may be more visually obtrusive.[95]

The conditions attaching to the exemption under Class 4(b) stipulate that not more than one satellite dish be erected on or within the curtilage of a dwelling-house, and the diameter of the antenna cannot exceed one metre. In order to avail of the exemption, dishes cannot be erected on, or forward of, the front wall of the dwellinghouse. Nor can the antenna be erected on the front roof slope of the dwellinghouse or higher than the highest part of the roof of the dwellinghouse. Unfortunately, these conditions do not preclude the placement of the dish on the gable wall of the house towards the apex of the roof or, indeed, if the house has a hipped rather than a gable roof, it may be possible to place the dish on the portion of the roof which slants to the side of the house.[96] The problem of orientation may be solved by placing the dish on a shed or garage in the rear garden.

5.5.1.5 *Paths, drains, ponds and landscaping works*

The construction of any path drain or pond or the carrying out of any landscaping works within the curtilage of a dwellinghouse is exempted, provided that the level of the ground is not altered by more than 1 metre above or below the adjoining ground.[97]

5.5.1.6 *Gates, walls and fences*

The construction, erection or alteration, within the curtilage of a dwellinghouse, of a gate, gateway, railing or wooden fence or a wall, is exempted under class 5. Gates, gateways and railings must not exceed a height of 2 metres.[98] Walls and fences must not exceed a height of 1.2 metres. Walls must be constructed of brick, stone, blocks with decorative finish, other concrete blocks or mass concrete.

---

[94]   See An Bord Pleanála section 5 Ref. No. PL 57/8/508.
[95]   See further, Grist, above, n.86, *op. cit.*, p.55.
[96]   *ibid.*
[97]   Class 6(a).
[98]   A similar exemption exists for gates and gateways outside the context of a dwellinghouse under Class 8.

5.5.1.7 *Hard surfacing*

Class 6(b) has added new exemptions for:

(i) the provision to the rear of the dwellinghouse (but within its curtilage) of a hard surface for use for any purpose incidental to the enjoyment of the dwellinghouse as such, and

(ii) the provision to the front or the side of the dwellinghouse (but within its curtilage) of a hard surface for the parking of not more than two motor vehicles used for a purpose incidental to the enjoyment of the dwellinghouse as such.

The only condition attached to these exemptions is that the level of the ground cannot be altered by more than one metre above or below the level of the adjoining ground.[99] There is no limitation on the area which may be hard surfaced. Sub-paragraph (i) allows for the construction of patio areas or possibly even a heli-pad, but fencing of sufficient height for a tennis court would require permission.

While the purpose of availing of this exemption may be to facilitate the parking of cars, the creation of an access to this parking area will normally require permission. Although the demolition of a wall or gate is prima facie exempted by virtue of class 45 of Part I, the scope of the exemption is significantly reduced by article 10(1)(a)(ii) which precludes all Part I works which involve the formation or material widening of an access to a public road, the surface carriageway of which exceeds four metres in width.

5.5.1.8 *Porches*

The construction or erection of a porch outside any external door of a dwelling-house is exempted development subject to certain specific conditions. It must be situate not less than two metres from any road and its floor area should not exceed two square metres. Where the porch has a tiled or slated pitched roof, it should not exceed four metres in height, and in any other case should be not more than three metres in height.[100] The demolition of part of a habitable house in connection with the provision of an extension or porch within Class 7 is exempted.[101]

5.5.1.9 *Caravans and boats*

Class 18 provides an exemption for the keeping or storing of a caravan or boat within the curtilage of a dwellinghouse, but not more than one of each can be stored. The caravan or boat cannot be used for the storage, display, advertisement or sale of goods, or for the purposes of any business. It can be stored for a maximum of nine months in any year and cannot be occupied as a dwelling. Some size restriction would have been in the interests of residential amenities.

---

[99]   See *Wycombe District Council v. Secretary of State for the Environment* [1995] J.P.L. 223.
[100] Class 7.
[101] Class 45(b).

5.5.2 Gates, walls and fences

The construction, erection, renewal or replacement, other than within or bounding the curtilage of a dwellinghouse, of any gate or gateway is exempted under Class 8, subject to a height restriction of two metres.[102]

Exemptions are also granted for the construction, erection, lowering, repair or replacement, outside the context of the dwellinghouse, of fences and walls. Hoardings or sheet metal fences are excluded. The height of any new wall or fence should not exceed 1.2 metres or the height of the structure being replaced, whichever is the greater, subject ot an overall height restriction of two metres. The exemption applies to walls constructed of brick, stone, blocks with decorative finish, other concrete blocks or mass concrete. Walls (other than dry stone walls) which bound a road must be capped and plastered, although the latter is not necessary to avail of the exemption in the case of blocks with a decorative finish.[103] The plastering or capping of any wall of concrete blocks or mass concrete is exempted under Class 9.

5.5.3 Painting of structures

Class 11 retains the exemption which previously applied to "any alteration consisting of the painting of any external part of any building or other structure" but attaches a condition which may have been introduced to temper the exuberance of Irish World Cup supporters. The effect of the condition is to prohibit the creation of murals on buildings or structures, with the exception of hoardings or a site on which authorised works are or will be carried out.

The painting of a building or structure of artistic, architectural or historical interest will not be exempted where it is listed for preservation under a development plan or draft development plan.[104] If any such painting "materially alters the external appearance of a structure so as to render such appearance inconsistent with the character of the structure of neighbouring structures", it amounts to an "alteration" which in turn constitutes "works" for the purposes of section 3 of the 1963 Act and, therefore, requires permission.

5.5.4 Private roads, ways, footpaths or paving

Class 12 exempts the repair of any private street, road or way where the works are carried out on land within the boundary of the street, road or way. The construction of any private footpath or paving is also exempted subject to a width restriction of three metres.

---

[102] A similar exemption is conferred on gates and gateways in the context of a dwellinghouse under Class 5.
[103] Class 10.
[104] See 1994 Regulations, art. 10(1)(a)(ix).

5.5.5 Changes of use

Class 13 exempts certain changes of use presumably because they represent an improvement in amenity terms. Uses for the sale of hot food off the premises (take-aways), public houses, funeral directors, funeral homes, amusement arcades and restaurants are all excluded from Class I of Part IV – use as a shop. Changes from any of these uses to use as a shop are exempted.[105]

Similarly changes of use from the service uses listed under, Class 2 of Part IV and from office use under Class 3 of the same part to shop use are exempted. The former uses present 'dead frontages' to the street and tend to subtract from the vitality of shopping areas.

The reconversion to single occupation of a dwellinghouse which had been used as two or more dwellings is also covered by this exemption. Finally, Class 13(f) exempts a change "from use as a dwellinghouse to use as a residence for persons with an intellectual or physical disability or a mental illness and persons providing care for such persons."[106] This is subject to the condition that "the number of persons with an intellectual or physical disability or a mental illness in any such residence shall not exceed 6 and the number of resident carers shall not exceed 2."

5.5.6 Temporary structures or uses

Certain temporary stuctures and uses are exempted under classes 14–18. The most significant of these is the exemption given for structures, works, plant or machinery needed temporarily in relation to development works or the preparatory works for mining development.[107] In the case of ordinary development these must be removed at the end of the period during which the works are carried out and the land must be reinstated immediately. In the context of mining they must be removed prior to the commencement of the mining.

5.5.7 Development for industrial purposes

The category of development which is exempted within the curtilage of an industrial building or on land used as a dock, harbour or quay for the purposes of any industrial undertaking, has been expanded to include, *inter alia*, the provision of a hard surface to be used in connection with the industrial process carried on in the building.[108] Class 19 also includes the following types of development

---

[105] Pt. I, Class 13.
[106] The words "or a mental illness" were added by the 1995 Regulations, art. 9(2).
[107] See Classes 15 and 15A (the latter added by the 1995 Regulations) art. 9(3). Note that these works do not appear to be within the ambit of integrated polution control licensing under the Environmental Protection Agency Act 1992 either, despite the fact that they can have potentially serious consequences for environmental amenity.
[108] Class 19(b).

subject to the condition that they do not materially alter the external appearance of the premises of the undertaking:

- the provision, rearrangement, replacement or maintenance of private ways or railways, sidings or conveyors,
- the provision, rearrangement, replacement or maintenance of sewers, mains, pipes, cables, or other apparatus,
- the installation or erection by way of addition or replacement of plant or machinery, or structures of the nature of plant or machinery.[109]

The exemption for storage within the curtilage of a building is continued under Class 20 but an attempt is made to reduce any visual disamenities which might arise by the attachment of a condition which stipulates that the raw materials, products, packing materials, fuel or waste stored must not be visible from any public road contiguous or adjacent to the curtilage of the industrial building.

The exemptions for changes of use from the use of "general industrial buildings", as defined by the 1977 Regulations, and from the use of certain special industrial buildings to "light industrial buildings" have been removed.

5.5.8 Development by statutory undertakers

Certain development by statutory undertakers is exempted under Classes 21–29 and Class 31. These include certain development carried out by railway undertakings, harbour authorities, An Bord Gais, other gas undertakings, electricity undertakings, An Post, An Bord Telecom, and certain developments carried out by or on behalf of a statutory undertaker in connection with inland waterways.[110]

5.5.9 Telecommunications

Class 29 exempts a number of developments carried out for the purposes of telecommunications. Article 9(1)(b) provided that the exemption under Class 29(f) which relates to antenna support structures would be available for a period of six months after the date on which paragraph (b) came into operation.[111] Curiously, the class does not include any exemption for the antennae themselves but it can be argued that these may be within the scope of the exemption for external works under section 4(1)(g) of the 1963 Act.[112]

---

[109] The height of any such structures should not exceed 15 metres or the height of the structures replaced whichever is the greater: Class 19(a).

[110] These latter developments are referred to under the heading of "Development for amenity or recreational purposes" under Pt I. See also exemptions for connections to premises under Class 44.

[111] *i.e.* May 16, 1994.

[112] See further, Casey, "Planning and Telecommunications Masts: Some Recent Issues" (1996) IPELJ 3. See also the Department of the Environment draft Guidelines for Planning Authorities entitled, "Telecommunications Antennae and Support Structures" (December 1995).

5.5.10 Development for amenity or recreational purposes

The exemption for golf courses and pitch and putt courses contained in the former Class 26 has been expressly removed from the exemption attaching to the laying out and use of lands for athletics or sports under Class 30(c). Sports involving the use of motor vehicles, aircraft or firearms have likewise been excluded. Class 30 continues the former exemptions which existed for the laying out and use of land as a park, private open space, or ornamental garden, and for roadside shrines.[113] Class 31 refers to certain developments carried out by or on behalf of a statutory undertaker in connection with inland waterways.[114] Class 32 contains exemptions for the provision by a state authority or other public body of structures incidental to the use of a public work, and for the provision by the Comissioners of Public Works of structures to be used in connection with a nature reserve.[115]

The exemption for the construction of an outdoor swimming pool, the plans for which had been approved by a sanitary authority, has been removed.[116]

5.5.11 Other development by public agencies

5.5.11.1 *National flags and emblems*

Class 34 exempts the placing or erection on, or within the curtilage of, a building, or on any other land, occupied by, or under the control of, a State authority, of flags, banners of national emblems and any structures for the display of flags, banners or national emblems.

5.5.11.2 *Facilities for foreign visits*

Class 35 exempts the provision, construction or erection by or on behalf of a State authority of temporary structures or other temporary facilities required in connection with a visit of a foreign dignitary or delegation, subject to the condition that:

> "the temporary structure and facilities shall be removed after the conclusion of the visit and the land concerned shall be forthwith reinstated."

5.5.11.3 *Monitoring facilities*

The importance of pollution control is emphasised in Class 42 which exempts the provision, construction or erection by the Commissioners of Public Works in Ireland or the Environmental Protection Agency, or by a local authority outside

---

[113] The new restrictions are that the area of any such shrine shall not exceed two square metres, the height shall not exceed two metres above the centre of the road opposite the structure and it shall not be illuminated. There is no limitation on moving statues!

[114] See para. 5.5.8, above.

[115] See Wildlife Act 1976, s. 15.

[116] Class 27, Pt. I of Sched. 3 to the 1977 Regulations contained the former exemption.

the functional area of the authority, of any equipment or structure for or in connection with levels, volumes and flows of water in rivers or other watercourses, lakes or groundwaters, and any development incidental thereto. The floor area of any such building or other structure must not exceed eight square metres and its height must not exceed four metres.

5.5.11.4 *Works under the Arterial Drainage Acts*

Class 46 exempts the carrying out by the Commissioners of Public Works in Ireland of any works for the maintenance of works and structures for which the Commissioners are responsible under the provisions of the Arterial Drainage Act 1945 or any order made thereunder, and any development incidental to such works.

5.5.11.5 *Works within the curtilage of certain public buildings*

Class 47 applies to works carried out by, or, on behalf of, a state authority within the curtilage of a building, premises or installation specified under article 156(1)(a) which includes Garda stations, prisons, courthouses, army barracks, airfields, naval yards and certain government buildings.

5.5.11.6 *Garda Síochána*

Class 48 exempts any works carried out by or on behalf of an Garda Síochána for security reasons within or bounding the curtilage of the residence of a person in receipt of protection from An Garda Síochána, other than a person referred to in article 156(1)(c)(ii).

5.5.11.7 *Regional Fisheries Boards*

Class 49 exempts the construction or erection by a Regional Fisheries Board of –
- a footbridge not exceeding 1.2 metres in width or eight metres in length,
- a fish pass,
- a fish screen or barrier,
- a walkway not exceeding 1.2 metres in width or a fishing stand not exceeding 10 square metres in area.[117]

5.5.12 Works necessary to comply with statutory notices, licences or certificates

Class 38 exempts works necessitated by the obligation to comply with certain statutory provisions.[118] These include:

---

[117] Class 49.

[118] Note that art. 9(4) also exempts the carrying out of such works as are necessary to secure compliance with the Building Regulations 1991 where it relates to the construction of a dwelling or dwellings for which planning permission was granted before the commencement date of the Building Control Act, *i.e.* June 1, 1992. This exemption does not apply to apartment blocks or any buildings designed for two or more dwellings. Similarly, art. 9A (inserted by S.I. No. 69 of 1995) exempts works which are required to be carried out under a condition attached to an integrated pollution control (IPC) licence under the Environmental Protection Agency Act 1992. Note also that s.11(6) of the Derelict Sites Act 1990 exempts the carrying out of works in compliance with a derelict sites notice.

    – works necessary to ensure compliance with the terms of any licence granted under section 34 of the Local Government (Sanitary Services) Act 1948, but not including the erection of any building, hut or chalet or the construction of any road or hard standing,

    – the removal of any structure or object or the carrying out of any works required by a planning authority under statute,

    – development required to ensure compliance with a notice under section 12 of the Local Government (Water Pollution) Act 1977,

    – works necessary to comply with a notice under section 26 of the Air Pollution Act 1987,

    – works necessary to ensure compliance with a condition or conditions attached to a fire safety certificate granted under the Building Control Regulations 1991[119] other than the construction or erection of an external fire escape or water tank.

Class 38 only authorises works which are *necessary* to ensure compliance with the notices referred to under (d) and (e) above, even where additional works not referred to in the notice may be desirable. In *Clarke v. Brady*,[120] it was held that a letter from Meath County Council which gave their approval for certain works proposed to be carried out by the respondent, on whom a notice under section 12 of the Local Government (Water Pollution) Act 1977 had been served, did not constitute an amendment to the provisions of the notice as the planning authority's letter had specifically advised that planning permission would be required for the works intended.

5.5.13 Demolition

Class 45(a) exempts the demolition of a building or other structure, other than:

    (i) a habitable house, or
    (ii) a building which forms part of a terrace of buildings, or
    (iii) a building which abuts[121] on another building in separate ownership.

The definition of "habitable house" remains unchanged and means:

"A building or part of a building which –

(a) is used as a dwelling;
(b) is not in use but when last used was last used, disregarding any unauthorised use, as a dwelling; or
(c) was provided for use as a dwelling but has not been occupied."

As referred to earlier, Class 45(b) removes any legal uncertainty which formerly existed as to whether demolition ancillary to an exempted extension or conversion required permission, by providing an exemption for –

---

119 S.I. No. 305 of 1991.
120 Unreported, High Court, Hamilton P., October 30, 1990.
121 As to the meaning of "abuts", see *Simmonds v. Secretary of State for the Environment* [1981] J.P.L. 509.

"the demolition of part of a habitable house in connection with the provision of an extension or porch in accordance with Class 1 or 7, respectively, of this Part of this Schedule or in accordance with the permission for an extension or porch granted under Part IV of the Act of 1963."[122]

5.5.14 Other miscellaneous development

5.5.14.1 Local events

The use of land for any fair, funfair, bazaar or circus or any local event of a religious, cultural, educational, political, social, recreational or sporting character and the placing or maintenance of tents, vans of other temporary or movable strucures or objects on the land in connection with such activities, subject ot the following conditions:

"the land shall not be used for any such purpose either continuously for a period exceeding 15 days or occasionally for periods exceeding in aggregate 30 days in any year.

. . . on the use for such purposes being discontinued, the land shall be fortwith reinstated save to such extent as may be authorised or required by a permission granted under Part IV of the Act of 1963."[123]

5.5.14.2 Navigational aids

The erection, placing or keeping, on water or in the air, of any lighthouse, beacon, buoy or other aid to navigation not exceeding 40 metres in height.[124]

5.5.14.3 Maintenance of community structures or facilities

Works incidental to the use or maintenance of any burial ground, churchyard, monument, fairground, market, schoolyard, or showground except:

- the erection or construction of any wall, fence or gate bounding or abutting on a public road,
- the erection or construction of any building other than a stall or store which is wholly enclosed within a market building, or
- the reconstruction or alteration of any building other than a stall or store which is wholly enclosed within a market building.[125]

5.5.14.4 Archaeological and other excavations

The excavation for the purposes of discovery:

(a) pursuant to and in accordance with alicence under section 26 of the National Monuments Act, 1930, of a site, feature or other object of archaeological or historical interest,

(b) of a site, feature or other object of geological interest.[126]

---

[122] See Class 1 above.
[123] Class 33.
[124] Class 36. As to the meaning of "beacon", see *Keane*, above, n.71.
[125] Class 37.
[126] Class 39.

5.5.14.5 *Domestic water supply or group water schemes*

Class 40 exempts the sinking of a well, drilling of a borehole, erection of a pump, or construction of a pumphouse, or other works necessary for the purposes of providing a domestic water supply, or a group water scheme in accordance with a plan or proposal approved by the Minister or a local authority for the purpose of making a grant towards the cost of such works.

5.5.14.6 *Exploratory drilling or excavation*

Class 41 exempts any drilling or excavation for the purpose of surveying land or examining the depth and nature of the subsoil. Drilling for minerals prospecting is excluded. In *Dillon v. Irish Cement*[127] it was held that the excavation of 10,500 tons of shale by the respondent cement company in order to ascertain its quality for building purposes did not fall within the equivalent class under the 1977 Regulations.[128]

5.5.14.7 *Connections to premises*

Class 44 exempts the connection of any premises to a wired broadcast relay service, sewer, watermain, gas main or electricity supply line or cable, including the breaking open of any street or other land for that purpose.

5.6 SECOND SCHEDULE, PART II – ADVERTISEMENTS

Part II of the Second Schedule lists 19 classes of exempted advertisements which are subject to conditions and limitations relating to number, area, height of affixation, diameter and so on. Article 9(2)(b) makes it clear that it is the erection of the advertisements structure for the exhibition of an advertisement which is exempted. "Advertisement" is defined under section 2 of the 1963 Act as "any word, letter, model, balloon, kite, poster, notice, device or representation employed for the purpose of advertisement, announcement or direction". "Advertisement structure" means "any structure which is a hoarding, scaffold, framework, pole, standard, device or sign (whether illuminated or not) and which is used or intended for use for exhibiting advertisements".

5.7 SECOND SCHEDULE, PART III – RURAL

Exempted categories of development in areas outside the boundaries of county boroughs, boroughs, urban districts, towns specified in the First Schedule to the 1963 Act and the excluded areas as defined in section 9 of the Local Government (Reorganisation) Act 1985, are listed in Part III of the Second Schedule.

---

[127] Unreported, Supreme Court, November 26, 1986.
[128] Class 34 of the 1977 Regulations referred to: "Any building or excavation for the purpose of surveying land or examining the depth and nature of the sub-soil".

5.7.1 Minerals and petroleum prospecting

Class 5 exempts the carrying out of works and the erection or placing on land of any structures for the purpose of minerals prospecting or for the purpose of searching for petroleum, provided an appropriate licence has been granted by the Minister for Transport, Energy and Communications under the Minerals Development Acts 1940 to 1979 and the Petroleum and Other Minerals Development Act 1960 respectively.[129]

5.7.2 Agricultural structures

The following structures attract exemptions under Classes 6 to 8 are (subject to certain conditions and limitations):

> CLASS 6 – Works consisting of the provision of a roof to the structure for the housing of pigs, cattle, sheep, goats, poultry, donkeys, horses, deer or rabbits, having a floor area not exceeding 300 square metres (whether or not by extension of an existing structure) and any ancillary provision for effluent storage.
>
> CLASS 7 – Works consisting of the provision of roofless cubicles, open loose yards, self-feed silo or silage areas, feeding aprons, assembly yards, milking parlours, sheep dipping units, effluent storage facilities or structures for the making or storage of silage or any other structures of a similar character or description, having an aggregate floor area not exceeding 300 square metres, and any ancillary provision for effluent storage.
>
> CLASS 8 – Works consisting of the provision of any store, barn, shed, glasshouse or other structure, not being of a type specified in Class 6 or 7 of this Part of this Schedule, and having a floor area not exceeding 300 square metres.

Condition 1 attached to Classes 6 and 7 stipulates that the structures be used for agricultural purposes only.[130] Class 8 structures may be used for agricultural or forestry purposes, but not for the housing of animals or the storage of effluent. Conditions relating to effluent storage have been tightened up for classes 6 and 7. In each case, condition 6 stipulates that:

---

[129] The restoration condition attached to the former exemption for mining under Sched. 3, Pt. III, Class 6 is no longer in evidence.

[130] Use for agricultural purposes under Classes 6 and 7 does not include use of the structures as stables for horses used for show jumping and other recreational activities where this is the dominant purpose for which they are kept: see *Sykes v. Secretary of State for the Environment* [1981] 1 W.L.R. 1092 and para. 5.2.2, above. See also An Bord Pleanála section 5 Ref. No. 27/RF/680.

"No such structure shall be situated, and no effluent from such structure shall be stored, within 100 metres of any dwellinghouse (other than the dwellinghouse of the person providing the structure) or other residential building or school, hospital, church or building used for public assembly, save with the consent in writing of the owner and, as may be appropriate, the occupier or person in charge thereof."

It should be noted also that the second condition attaching to Classes 6, 7 and 8 specifies a threshold area for structures of a particular class beyond which planning permission must be obtained. Condition 2 provides:

"The total area of such structure, together with any other such structure situate within the same farmyard complex or within 100 metres of that complex, shall not exceed 450 (for classes 6 and 7) or 900 (for class 8) square metres floor area in aggregate."

5.7.2.1 Land Reclamation

Class 9 relates to certain work carried out works for the purpose of agriculture or forestry:

"Development consisting of the carrying out, on land which is used only for the purpose of agriculture or forestry, of any of the following works –

(a) field drainage,
(b) land reclamation,
(c) the removal of fences,
(d) the improvement of existing fences,
(e) the improvement of hill grazing, or
(f) the reclamation of estuarine marsh land or of callows, where the preservation of such land or callows is not an objective of a development plan for the area."

While class 9 is headed *"Land Reclamation"*, this heading is not a guide to the interpretation of the class.[131] Only paragraphs (b) and (f) are necessarily related to land reclamation.[132] While the pre-existing exemption for land reclamation under section 4(1)(i) of the 1963 Act was held, in *Tralee U.D.C. v. Stack*,[133] to be applicable only to development carried out by the Minister for Agriculture, there is no restriction on the identity of the agency to whom the exemption under Class 9 is available. In other words, it can be relied on equally by developers in the public and private sectors.

---

[131] Interpretation Act 1937, s.11(g).
[132] It is not possible to claim an exemption under para. (b) for development which falls within the scope of para. (f) as to construe the Regulations in this manner would nullify the protection of the environment and the ecology of estuarine marshland which para. (f) was designed to achieve: *Irish Wildbird Conservancy and the Commissioners of Public Works v. Clonakilty Golf and Country Club*, unreported, High Court, Costello P., July 23 1996 (under appeal).
[133] Unreported, High Court, January 13, 1984.

The restrictions under article 10 apply to this category of exempted development, but the restriction most likely to be of relevance is that referred to at
paragraph (vi), which provides that development which interferes with a view or
prospect of special amenity value or special interest the preservation of which is
an objective of a development plan, or draft thereof, or draft variation thereof,
will not amount to exempted development.

The first internal restriction in Class 9 itself is that the a development must be
"on land which is used only for the purpose of agriculture or forestry." As the
exemption applies under paragraphs (b) and (f) to the reclamation of land, this
would be a physical impossibility if the wording of the class were to be
interpreted literally because it implies that the land to be reclaimed must *simultaneously* "be used" for agriculture or forestry . The expression "land" would,
therefore, appear to refer to the generality of the land immediately surrounding
the intended development, but it is by no means clear as to how far it extends. It
could be argued that the land referred to can only apply to land within the
occupational unit upon which the development is to take place. This would
normally coincide with the "planning unit".[134]

It may be that the reference to agricultural purposes was intended to refer to
the purposes of the works, but if this is so, then it was most unhappily phrased.
Because of the uncertainty surrounding the wording of Class 9, it is difficult to
anticipate with confidence the way in which it would be applied by the court.

In determining whether works constitute land reclamation so as to gain the
benefit of the exemption the "primary object" of the works should be examined.
In *Lennon v. Kingdom Plant Hire*,[135] Morris J. held that the primary object of
extensive excavation of rock was not to improve the land but to gather boulders
to enable the respondents to fulfil their contract to provide boulders for the
County Council's coastal protection systems.[136] He described the factors to be
taken into acount in determining whether what is at issue is land reclamation:

> "Every case must be considered on its own merits. Matters which should be taken
> into account would include the primary object in carrying out the work, the depth
> and area of any excavation which *bona fide* land reclamation requires, the area in
> which it is proposed to carry out the work and the type of terrain on which the
> work is to be done."

The exemption under paragraph (f) is quite a significant provision in the context of
nature and wildlife conservation. It refers to *preservation* rather than *protection*, a
distinction which may be of importance in that, in the slightly different context of
listed buildings, a distinction is normally maintained in development plans between

---

[134] See *Burdle v. Secretary of State for the Environment* [1972] All E.R. 240, approved by the High
Court in *Rehabilitation Institute v. Dublin Corporation*, unreported, High Court, Barron J.,
January 14, 1988.
[135] Unreported, High Court, December 13, 1991.
[136] This case was concerned with the application of the exemption for land reclamation under s.4(1)(i)
but the principle should apply with equal force to land reclamation under Class 9 of Pt. III.

those buildings which are listed for preservation and those which are merely listed for protection. While there is obviously a large degree of overlap between the two words, preservation would appear to entail something more in the nature of "keeping in the same condition". On the other hand, some level of interference might be consistent with an objective for the protection of the site.

However, it can be argued strongly that any ambiguity in the wording of class 9, paragraph (f) should be resolved in a manner which would facilitate the implementation of the provisions of any E.U. Directive to which it was designed to give effect.[137] It can be further argued that this particular provision was intended to give effect to Council Directive 79/409/EEC (the "Birds Directive") and Council Directive 92/43/EEC (the "Habitats Directive").

5.7.3 Structures for keeping horses, ponies and greyhounds

Classes 10 to 12 of Part II are also new and relate to structures used for the purpose of housing and keeping horses, ponies or greyhounds. Such animals are normally kept for sporting or recreational purposes rather than "agricultural" purposes.[138]

5.8 SECOND SCHEDULE, PART IV – USE CLASSES

5.8.1 Use Classes

Part IV of the Second Schedule describes 11 classes of use. Article 11(1) provides that a change of use within any one of these classes amounts to exempted development unless it would contravene a condition of a planning permission or would be inconsistent with any use specified or included in such a permission. The purpose of the use classes is to exempt changes of use within each class: it is not to be assumed, therefore, that a change of use from one use class into another use class *ipso facto* amounts to a material change of use, although in practice this will usually be the case.[139] The use classes are not in any way intended to be comprehensive and, indeed, many uses are properly regarded as *sui generis*. In addition, certain uses are expressly excluded from the ambit of the use classes by article 11(4)(b). These relate to any use:

- as an amusement arcade,
- as a motor service station,
- for the sale or leasing, or display for sale or leasing, of motor vehicles,
- for taxi business or for the hire of motor vehicles,
- as a scrap yard, or a yard for the breaking of motor vehicles,
- for the storage or distribution of minerals.

---

[137] *Murphy v. Bord Telecom* [1988] I.L.R.M. 53.
[138] See para. 5.2.2.1, above.
[139] The fact that the legislature has divided uses into different classes suggests that similar planning impacts apply within each class and that therefore different planning impacts apply as between use classes.

The benefit of an exemption under the use classes may only be claimed where the change of use is from one lawful use to another. Thus, for example, where a premises changes its use from an electrical shop to a grocery shop, the change will not amount to exempted development as being within Class 1, *i.e.* "use as a shop for any purposes", if the first use as an electrical shop is itself an unauthorised use. Similarly, if the change of use to an electrical shop was authorised by a particular planning permission which also contains a condition restricting the user to use as an electrical shop, the change of use will not receive the benefit of the exemption. It has also been held that token implementation of a use to bring it within a particular use class may not be sufficient for that purpose.[140]

In order to determine whether a particular use falls within one of the use classes, the definitions in article 8 must be consulted. The restrictions contained in article 10 do not, however, apply to Part IV of the Second Schedule. Uses which are ordinarily incidental to any use specified under Part IV partake of the character of that use and are not excluded from being incidental to that use because they are specified under the use classes as a separate use.[141] It would appear that such a use must be incidental to the class as a whole. It has also been held that any intensification of use occurring within a particular use class constitutes exempted development.[142]

Under the 1994 regulations, the number of use classes has been reduced from 16 to 11, principally by removing class 4 – "use as a general industrial building for any purpose" – and classes 5, 6, 7 and 8 which related to uses for special industrial processes. The former classes 15 and 16 have been amalgamated with one minor amendment, *i.e.* the addition of "a bingo hall". A number of other significant changes have taken place and these are considered below.

5.8.1.1 CLASS 1: use as a shop

The definition of a "shop" under the 1977 Regulations was extremely open-ended as it included a structure used "for any other purpose appropriate to a shopping area". This catch-all phrase has been dropped in the new definition, and restaurants have also been expressly excluded.[143] The former definition of a shop was as follows:

> "'Shop' means a structural use for the carrying on of any retail trade or retail business wherein the primary purpose is the selling of goods by retail and includes a structural use for the purposes of a hairdresser, undertaker or ticket agency or for the reception of goods to be washed, cleaned or repaired, or for any other purpose appropriate to a shopping area, but does not include a structural use as a funfair, garage, petrol filling station, office, or hotel or premises (other than a restaurant) licensed for the sale of intoxicating liquor for consumption on the premises."

---

[140] *Kwik Save Discount Group v. Secretary of State for Wales* (1981) P. & C.R. 166.
[141] 1994 Regulations, art. 11(3).
[142] *Brooks & Burton Ltd v. Secretary of State for the Environment* [1977] 1 W.L.R. 1294.
[143] Restaurants were included in the 1977 definition of a shop, although take-away uses were excluded by the description of Class I of Pt. IV of Sched. 3. Restaurants can give rise to traffic and parking problems and other disamenities associated with late night activity, particularly in residential areas.

The new definition provides:

> "'Shop' means a structure used for all or any of the following purposes, where the sale, display or service is principally to visiting members of the public[144] –
>
> (a) for the retail sale of goods,
> (b) as a post office,
> (c) for the sale of tickets or as a travel agency,
> (d) for the sale of sandwiches or other cold food for consumption off the premises,
> (e) for hairdressing,
> (f) for the display of goods for sale,
> (g) for the hiring out of domestic or personal goods or articles,
> (h) as a launderette or dry cleaners,
> (i) for the reception of goods to be washed, cleaned or repaired,
>
> but does not include use for the direction of funerals or as a funeral home or as a hotel, a restaurant or a public house, or for the sale of hot food for consumption off the premises, or any use to which Class 2 or 3 of Part IV of the Second Schedule applies."

It can be seen that funeral homes are specifically excluded from the definition as these may have significant traffic impacts and inherently conflict with the use patterns of a lively shopping precinct.[145] Take-aways, *i.e.* uses "for the sale of hot for consumption off the premises", are also expressly excluded from the definition. Article 11(b) also excludes any premises used for the sale or leasing, or display for sale or leasing, of motor vehicles.

While there are certain disamenities in planning terms associated with those uses excluded from Class 1, changes from these uses to use as a shop are positively encouraged by the first four exemptions granted under Class 13 of Part I of the Second Schedule which refers to the following categories of changes of use:

> "(a) from use for the sale of hot food for consumption off the premises, or for the sale or leasing, or display for sale or leasing of motor vehicles, to use as a shop,
> (b) from use as a public house to use as a shop,
> (c) from use for the direction of funerals, as a funeral home, as an amusement arcade or restaurant, to use as a shop,
> (d) from use to which Class 2 of Part IV of this Schedule applies to use as a shop."

Intensification of retailing activity cannot take a particular use for any of the purposes referred to in the definition of "shop" outside Class 1 itself.[146] Nor can the sub-division of a shop take the change of use involved outside the use class.[147]

---

[144] See *R. v. Thurrock Borough Council, ex p., Tesco Stores Ltd* [1994] J.P.L. 328, in which it was held that if there was a restriction on the persons who were permitted access to the premises, it could not be said to be used for the sale of goods to "visiting members of the public", within the meaning of Part A, Class A1 of the U.K. Town and Country Planning (Use Classes) Order, 1987. Class 1, above, is worded in a very smiliar fashion but includes the word "principally", which is omitted from its U.K. equivalent.

[145] See further *Grist* above, n.85, *op. cit.*, p.52.

[146] See *Royal Borough of Kensington v. Mia Carla* [1981] J.P.L. 50.

[147] See Interpretation Act 1937, s.11(a). See An Bord Pleanála section 5 Ref. No. 62/RF/713, included at (1995) IPELJ 100.

In deciding whether a use is "ordinarily incidental" to use as a shop, it is not appropriate to take into account the peculiarities of particular areas or particular customers.[148] It would appear that a use can only be regarded as "ordinarily incidental" to Class 1 where the particular use involved is of a particular type which is "ordinarily incidental" to use as a shop in the generic sense, as distinct from being incidental to any of the specific types of shop included under Class 1.

It is a question of fact and degree as to whether a use is ancillary to the use as a shop or is sufficiently independent to acquire the character of a separate use. In *SJD Properties Limited v. Secretary of State for the Environment*,[149] Woolf J. upheld the conclusion of the Secretary of State that the showing of films in coin operated booths on the first floor of a "sex-shop" was not ancillary or incidental to its shop use, although the films were available for sale on the ground floor.[150] It had been argued by the appellants that the film booths were essential to allow prospective purchasers to see what it was they were being offered for sale; a comparison was made with the provision of listening facilities in shops selling records, and of changing rooms in dress shops. Woolf J. refused to accept this argument, saying:

> "There is clearly a real distinction between allowing a person to view a film for the purposes of seeing whether he wished to purchase the film and allowing a person to view a film at a charge in such circumstances that, if he wanted to do so, he could purchase the film thereafter and get a refund of the charge . . . There (is) a clear distinction between what happens in a record shop where you (are) allowed to try out the record without charge from what was happening in these premises."

A retail use may itself be ancillary or "ordinarily incidental" to some other primary use, so that the appropriate planning unit must first be defined.[151]

5.8.1.2 CLASS 2: Use for the provision of:

(a) financial services
(b) professional services (other than health or medical services)
(c) any other services (including use as a betting office)where the services are provided principally to visiting members of the public:

The growth of activity in services dealing directly with members of the public has led to the creation of this new use class which differentiates between services which attract retail-type activity and offices which generate little activity: it was

---

[148] *Hussain v. Secretary of State for the Environment* (1967) 23 P. & C.R. 330.
[149] [1981] J.P.L. 673.
[150] It has been humorously suggested that the exclusion of "hot food shops" from the definition of "shop" could be extended to "hot" products (see [1981] J.P.L. 677). Manchester records in an article entitled, "Much Ado About the Location of Sex Shops" (1982) J.P.L. 89 that – "When the House of Hamburger delicatessen in Brewer Street, Soho, closed in January 1989 and was replaced by a sex shop, this became the one hundred and sixty-fourth sex establishment in an area of less than one square mile. . ."
[151] See, *e.g. Williams v. Minister of Housing and Local Environment* (1967) 65 L.G.R. 495.

held in an English decision that use as a solicitor's office did not fall within the equivalent class under the U.K. Town and Country Planning (Use Classes) Order 1987, Class A2. In *Kalra v. Secretary of State for the Environment*,[152] David Widdicombe Q.C., sitting as a Deputy Judge, stated that to qualify the financial or professional service must principally provide an over-the-counter service like a shop to members of the public who come in off the street.[153] Building societies and mortgage advice centres would appear to fall within Class 2 because their services are provided directly to the public.

In a recent reference to An Bord Pleanála under section 5 of the 1963 Act it was determined that a change of use of the ground floor of a building from use as an employment bureau to use as a building society branch office fell within the scope of Class 2.[154]

5.8.1.3 CLASS 3: Use as an office, other than a use to which class 2 of this Part of this Schedule applies

There is no definition for "office" in the 1994 Regulations, but it would appear that it does not now include a bank, as was the case under the 1977 Regulations. In *Cusack and McKenna v. Minister for Local Government and Dublin Corporation*, it was argued by the applicants that as a considerable part of the work in a dentist's practice related to office duties, the use of the premises by such fell within the expression "use as an office for any purpose" in the former Class 2 under the 1977 Regulations, now repealed. McWilliam J. rejected this argument as the essential part of a dentist's premises was the surgery, used together with any other rooms required for the use of dental equipment and the preparation of dental materials.

In *Rehabilitation Institute v. Dublin Corporation*,[155] Barron J. equated the use of a building for administrative purposes with "use as an office for any purpose". However, in *London Residuary Body v. Secretary of State for the Environment*,[156] it was held that the characterisation of the overall use as an administrative use does not lead to the inevitable conclusion that there is an office use. Simon Brown J. concluded that the use of a building for the exercise of local governmental functions was in fact a use *sui generis*.[157] The determination of the Secretary of State that a change from this use to an office use would amount to a material change of use was upheld as not being unreasonable. Simon Brown J. also observed that the use of a site should be judged "*not* by reference to the subjective purpose of the activities being pursued on it rather than, as was clearly the correct approach, by reference to an objective determination of the real character of the activities

---

[152] [1995] J.P.L. B14.
[153] See also *R. v. Thurrock Borough Council*, above, n.144, as the meaning of "visiting members of the public".
[154] See Bord Pleanála section 5 Ref. No. 29a/RF/685.
[155] Unreported, High Court, Barron J., January 14, 1988.
[156] [1990] 1 W.L.R. 744.
[157] *Shephard v. Buckinghamshire County Council* (1966) 18 P. & C.R. 419, distinguished.

themselves." This decision was followed in *Inner London Educational Authority v. Secretary of State for the Environment*, Slade L.J. expressing the view that the amount of floor space given over to a particular use is a relevant, but not conclusive factor in determining the primary use of a complex of buildings.

5.8.1.4 CLASS 4: Use as a light industrial building

A "light industrial building" is defined as:

> "an industrial building in which the processes carried on or the plant or machinery installed are such as could be carried on or installed in any residential area without detriment to the amenity of that area by reason of noise, vibration, smell, fumes, smoke, soot, ash, dust or grit."

The meaning of "light industrial building" is further restricted by article 8 to take into account the nuisance effects of plant or machinery as well as "industrial processes", which were already referred to in the 1977 definition. The definition implied requires a hypothetical assessment of the effect of the industrial processes carried on within the building on "any residential area" as distinct from the area which happens to be contiguous with the building, whether this be residential or not.[158]

"Industrial building" is defined as:

> "a structure (not being a shop, or a structure in or adjacent to or belonging to a quarry or mine) used for the carrying on of any industrial process".

This definition, in turn, requires further clarification as to the meaning of "industrial process" which is defined as:

> "Any process which is carried on in the course of trade or business other than agriculture and which is for or incidental to the making of any article or part of an article (including a vehicle, aircraft, ship or vessel, or a film, video or sound recording), or the altering, repairing, ornamenting, finishing, cleaning, washing, packing, canning, adapting for sale, breaking up or demolition of any article, including the gutting, dressing or treatment of minerals."[159]

The importance of the requirement that the process be carried out in the course of a "trade or business" was examined in *Rael-Brook B. Limited v. Minister for Housing and Local Government*.[160] In considering whether an activity can be described as "business", the receipt of payment is a material factor, but the making of profit is not essential.[161]

---

[158] *W.T. Lamb Properties Limited v. Secretary of State for the Environment*; the building in that case was situated quite close to Gatwick Airport. The case highlights the technical difficulty in assessing noise levels where ambient noise levels outside the building are very high. Evidence relating to the measurement of levels within the building was accepted as being reasonable in the circumstances.

[159] Art. 8.

[160] [1987] 2 Q.B. 65. It was held that a cooking centre for school meals run by a local authority was "an industrial building". However, in *Tessier v. Secretary of State for the Environment* (1975) 31 P. & C.R. 161, it was held that the use of premises by a sculptor did not amount to an industrial use.

[161] See *Rolls v. Miller* (1884) 27 Ch.D. 71, (CA) a breach of covenant case which concerned the use of a charitable institution, called the "House for Working Girls".

5.8.1.5 CLASS 5: Use as a wholesale warehouse or as a repository

Class 5 refers to situations where the primary use is as a wholesale warehouse or repository. "Wholesale warehouse" is defined as:

> " A structure where business, principally of a wholesale nature, is transacted and goods are stored and displayed, but only incidentally to the transaction of that business."

"Repository" is defined as:

> "A structure (excluding any land occupied therewith) where storage is the principal use and where no business is transacted other than business incidental to such storage."

In its ordinary meaning, a warehouse is a place where goods are stored preparatory to their being taken elsewhere and sold rather than a building where retail sales are actually carried out.[162] In *Hooper v. Slater*,[163] a Divisional Court observed that a "warehouse" implied covered storage and so did not apply to the storage of caravans in the open.

5.8.1.6 CLASS 6: Use as a residential club, a guesthouse or a hostel (other than a hostel where care is provided)

This class is a modification of Class 10 under the 1977 Regulations which also included "a hotel providing sleeping accommodation". The uses described in class 6 are not defined in the 1994 Regulations or under section 2 of the 1963 Act. The common element in the uses comprising Class 6 is the transience of occupancy associated with them. A hostel where care is provided is expressly excluded from Class 6 but would appear to be included under Class 9.

In *Hammersmith v. Secretary of State for the Environment*,[164] the court observed that a "guesthouse" implied "something a little more delicate in the way of accommodation and conditions" than 16 students living in four bedrooms.

5.8.1.7 CLASS 7 – Use as:

(a) for public worship or religious instruction;
(b) for the social or recreational activities of a religious body;
(c) as a monastery or convent.

5.8.1.8 CLASS 8 – Use as:

(a) as a health centre or *clinic* for the provision of any medical or health services (but not for the use of the dwellinghouse of a consultant or

---

162 *Monomart (Warehouses) Ltd v. Secretary of State for the Environment* (1977) 34 P. & C.R. 305 *per* Lord Widgery C.J.; where it was held that the description "builders' merchant's warehouse" used in a planning permission did not apply to a do-it-yourself supermarket.

163 [1978] J.P.L. 252.

164 (1975) 30 P. & C.R. 19.

practitioner, or any building attached to the dwellinghouse or within the curtilage thereof for that purpose);

(b) as a *creche*;

(c) as a day nursery;

(d) as a day centre.

5.8.1.9 CLASS 9 – *Use as:*

(a) for the provision of residential accommodation and care to people in need of care (but not the use of a dwellinghouse for that purpose);

(b) as a hospital or nursing home;

(c) as a residential school, residential college or residential training centre.

This class expressly excludes the use of a dwellinghouse for the provision of residential accommodation and care. Class 13 of Part I of the Second Schedule exempts such a use where the number of persons with an intellectual or physical disability living in any such residence does not exceed six and the number of resident carers does not exceed two.[165]

5.8.1.10 CLASS 10 – *Use as:*

(a) an art gallery (but not for the sale or hire of works of art);

(b) a museum;

(c) a public library or public reading room;

(d) a public hall;

(e) an exhibition hall;

(f) a social centre, community centre or non-residential club; but not as a dance hall or concert hall.

5.8.1.11 CLASS 11 – *Use as:*

(a) a theatre;

(b) a cinema;

(c) a concert hall;

(d) a bingo hall;

(e) a skating rink or gymnasium or for other indoor sports or recreation not involving the use of motorised vehicles or firearms.

---

[165] It is interesting to note that Classes 8 and 9 have deliberately separated health centres and clinics from residential care institutions. Planning reasons for this separation are suggested in Grist, above, n.86, *op. cit.*, pp.55–56.

Chapter 6

APPLICATION FOR
PLANNING PERMISSION

The principle regulations governing the procedure for the making of planning applications and their content are contained in Part IV of the Local Government (Planning and Development) Regulations 1994.[1] These regulations effectively amend and consolidate the repealed provisions of the Local Government (Planning and Development) Regulations 1977 to 1993. While the Local Government (Planning and Development) Regulations 1990, which deal with the incorporation of environmental impact assessment into the application procedure have been revoked the European Communities (Environmental Impact Assessment) Regulations 1989 remain in force.

6.1.1 Obligation to obtain planning permission

Section 24(1) of the 1963 Act provides that planning permission is required:

> (a) for any development of land, which is not exempted development, or development commenced before the appointed day; and
> (b) for the retention of unauthorised structures which existed immediately before the appointed day.

Any person who carries out any development in breach of the obligation to obtain planning permission under the Act is guilty of an offence.[2] The owner or occupant of any unauthorised structure also has a positive incentive to obtain planning permission. Rule 2(b) of the First Schedule (Rules for determination of the amount of compensation) of the Local Government (Planning and Development) Act 1990 provides:

> "(b) no account shall be taken of. . .
> — (v) any value attributable to any unauthorised structure or unauthorised use".

An "unauthorised structure" is defined as follows:

> "(A) in relation to a structure in an area in relation to which a resolution under Section 26 of the Act of 1934 was passed, a structure other than —

---

[1]   S.I. No. 86 of 1994. Minor amendments were introduced by the Local Government (Planning and Development) Regulations 1995 (S.I. No. 69 of 1995).

[2]   1963 Act, s.24(2).

    (i) a structure in existence when that resolution was passed;

    (ii) a structure for which there was a general or special permission under that Act, being a permission which has not been revoked;

    (iii) a structure for the construction, erection, or making of which was the subject of a permission for development granted under Section 26 of this Act, being a permission which has not been revoked, or which exists as a result of the carrying out on or after the appointed day of exempted development;

    (iv) a structure for the retention of which a permission was granted under Section 27 of this Act, being a permission which has not been revoked;

    (v) a structure which, immediately before the appointed day, had the protection afforded by Section 15 of the Act of 1934; or

  (B) in relation to a structure in any other area, a structure other than —

    (i) a structure in existence on the commencement of the appointed day; or

    (ii) a structure the construction, the erection or making of which was the subject of a permission for development granted under Section 26 of this Act, being a permission which has not been revoked, or which exists as a result on or after the appointed day of exempted development."[3]

6.1.2 Types of application

A person seeking to develop land can apply for a "full" permission or for a permission in principle, referred to as an "outline" permission. The latter is a "permission for development subject to the subsequent approval of the planning authority".[4] An outline application need only be accompanied by "such plans and particulars as are necessary to identify the land to which the application relates and to enable the planning authority to determine the siting, layout or other proposals for development in respect of which a decision is sought".[5] Development cannot be commenced on foot of an outline permission until any necessary approval has been obtained.

There are two types of approval – "an approval consequent on an outline permission" or "an approval which is required to be obtained under a condition subject to which a permission or an approval is granted".[6]

Where unauthorised works have already been carried out or an unauthorised use has commenced it may be advisable to apply for permission for the retention of the structure or the continuance of the use.[7] These permissions take effect from the date when the unauthorised works were carried out or from the date when the unauthorised use commenced.[8] Permission may be sought for the retention of a structure or to continue a use where a temporary permission has

---

[3]   1963 Act, s.2(1).

[4]   1994 Regulations, art. 3.

[5]   *ibid.*, art. 20.

[6]   *ibid.*, art. 3.

[7]   1963 Act, s.28. Applications for the retention of structures which existed immediately before the appointed day and which were unauthorised structures on October 1, 1964, the commencement date of the Act, are dealt with under s.27.

[8]   1963 Act, s.28(2).

expired or where the applicant wishes to be released from a condition subject to which a previous permission was granted.[9]

6.1.3 Compliance with Permission Regulations

A decision of a planning authority may be set aside as having been made without jurisdiction where the applicant has failed to comply with the requirements of the permission regulations as compliance with these regulations is a pre-condition of the exercise of a planning authority's discretion to grant or refuse permission. Section 26(1) of the 1963 Act provides:

> "(1) Where —
>> (a) application is made to a planning authority in accordance with permission regulations for the permission for the development of land or for any approval required for such regulations; and
>> (b) any requirements relating to the application of or made under such regulations are complied with;
>> The authority may decide . . ."

It would be unduly harsh on a developer if a grant of planning permission could be invalidated for some minor infraction of the regulations, such as the omission of a north point on a plan, especially as a the planning authority is empowered to request further information to remedy any deficit in the content of an application. Despite the use of the word "shall" in the regulations, the courts have decided that certain regulations may be described as "directory" so that non-compliance does not render a decision invalid, while others are mandatory in nature. However, the courts have, on occasion, emphasised that a dispensation from the requirements of the regulations will only be granted for minor breaches. In *Monaghan U.D.C. v. Alf-A-Bet Promotions Limited*,[10] Henchy J. said in the course of his judgment:

> "I do, however, feel it pertinent to express the opinion that when the 1963 Act prescribed certain procedures as necessary to be observed for the purpose of getting a development permission, which may affect radically the rights or amenities of others and may substantially benefit or enrich the grantee of the permission, compliance with the prescribed procedures should be treated as a condition precedent to the issue of the permission. In such circumstances, what the Legislature has, either immediately in the Act or mediately in the regulations, nominated as being obligatory may not be depreciated to the level of a mere direction except on the application of the de minimis rule. In other words, what the Legislature has prescribed, or allowed to be prescribed, in such circumstances as necessary should be treated by the Courts as nothing short of necessary, and any deviation from the requirements must, before it can be overlooked, be shown by the person seeking to have it excused, to be so trivial, or so technical, or so peripheral, or otherwise so insubstantial that, on the principle that it is the spirit rather than the letter of the law that matters, the prescribed obligation has been substantially, and therefore adequately, complied with."[11]

---

[9]   1963 Act, s.28(4).
[10] [1980] I.L.R.M. 64.
[11] At p.68.

In *Mc Cabe v. Harding Investments Ltd*,[12] O'Higgins C.J. differentiated between those articles which concern what has to be done by an applicant prior to submitting his application to the planning authority, and those articles which govern the plans and particulars which have to accompany an application. The former "cater for and deal with the interests of the general public in an intended development" and consequently, are usually mandatory in nature, while the requirements contained in the latter regulations may not always be essential.

A person seeking to challenge the validity of a planning decision on the grounds of non-compliance with the regulations need not show that he or she has been directly affected by the decision. The permission is invalid "not by reason of the prejudice or disadvantage suffered by the person challenging it, but by reason of want of power and jurisdiction in the planning authority to exercise their right of granting or refusing permission pursuant to section 26 of the Act of 1963".[13] In *ESB v. Gormley*, the Defendant succeeded in having a decision by the planning authority to grant permission for an ESB supply line set aside on the basis of non-compliance with permission regulations even though, at the time of the publication of the notice, she was not in occupation of any lands through which the supply line was intended to run.

The permission regulations as a whole may be divided into four parts, as follows:

— Pre-application Publicity Requirements
— Particulars to accompany Planning Applications
— Procedure and Receipt of Applications
— Notification of Decisions

6.2 PRE-APPLICATION PUBLICITY REQUIREMENTS

6.2.1 Public participation in the planning process

The thread of public participation interpolates the provisions of the planning code, most notably those relating to the development plan, planning application and appeals procedure, and enforcement under section 27 of the 1976 Act. It has been emphasised by the courts on a number of occasions that the planning code involves three main parties: the applicant, the planning authority and the public as a whole. Under the 1994 Regulations, members of the public now enjoy an express statutory entitlement to make an observation in writing to a proposed development, although formerly the existence of such a right had been implied.[14] The purpose of the notification requirements is to afford to interested members

---

12   [1984] I.L.R.M. 105.
13   *ESB v. Gormley* [1985] I.R. 129.
14   1994 Regulations, art. 34 ; *State (Stanford) v. Dun Laoghaire Corporation* [1981] I.L.R.M. 87. By implication, any person who has made an observation is entitled to have it considered by the planning authority.

of the public an opportunity to make representations which must be taken into consideration in the determination of planning applications.

6.2.2 Who may apply?

Neither the Acts nor Regulations expressly limit the class of persons who may apply for planning permission. On the other hand, the content of several provisions indicates that the legislature intended to restrict the class to the owner or occupier of the land or someone acting with their authority. If any person were permitted to apply for planning permission this could interfere with the development potential of land to such an extent as to amount to an unconstitutional intrusion of individual property rights. In *Frescati Estates Limited v. Marie Walker*,[15] Henchy J. laid down the following rule:

> ". . . I consider that an application for development permission, to be valid must be made either by or with the approval of a person who is able to assert sufficient legal estate to enable him to carry out the proposed development or so much as the proposed development as relates to the property in question. There will thus be sufficient privity between the applicant (if he is not a person entitled) and the person entitled to enable the applicant to be treated, for all practical purposes, as a person entitled."

In *Schwestermann v. An Bord Pleanála*,[16] a permission was granted to Glenmoy Limited, who were described as applicants in the planning application and were also referred to in the application as "freehold owner", although the freehold owner at all relevant times was a company called Glenmoy Developments Limited. In fact, one James Hoare, who signed the application on behalf of the first company, was the owner of the controlling interest in both companies. Glenmoy Limited had been incorporated for the purposes of managing the property and it was contended on behalf of both companies, as notice parties in the proceedings, that it was only through inadvertence that Glenmoy Limited were named as applicant and as freehold owner in the notice of application.

O'Hanlon J., relying in particular on the judgment of Henchy J. in *Frescati Estates*, and on a passage from the judgment of Mr Justice Murphy in *Re Grange Developments Limited v. Dublin County Council (No. 1)*[17] upheld the planning decision. He said:

> " In my opinion, the application should be regarded as one made on behalf of, and with the knowledge and approval of, the freehold owner of the lands, and in any event I would also consider that on the facts of the present case, any one of three parties concerned – Glenmoy Limited, Glenmoy Developments Limited and James Hoare – had a sufficient interest in and connection with the lands concerned and the proposed development thereof, to sustain an application for

---

[15]   [1975] I.R. 177.
[16]   [1995] 1 I.L.R.M. 269.
[17]   [1986] I.R. 246.

planning permission made in the name of any one of the said parties. The question of knowledge and approval can hardly present any difficulty when Mr and Mrs Hoare were the only shareholders in, and directors of, both companies, at all relevant times."[18]

The sufficiency of the interest of a mineral developer who obtains the consent of the Minister for Transport, Energy and Communications to make an application in respect of lands in which he has no other interest was considered by the Supreme Court, on an application for leave for judicial review, in *Scott and Others v. An Bord Pleanála (Respondent) and Arcon Mines Limited, Kilkenny County Council and Others (Notice Parties).*[19] The Minister for Energy had formally consented to the making of the planning application by the company.

Section 12 of the Minerals Development Act 1979 provides as follows:

> "The exclusive right of working minerals is hereby vested in the minister, except as provided in this Part."

The applicant/appellant, Elizabeth Scott, was the owner of lands adjoining the lands under which a small portion of the total ore body to be worked pursuant to the permission was located.[20] It was argued on her behalf that as her consent had not been obtained to the making of the application, and as the mining company had no legal estate or interest in her lands or minerals, it was not entitled to make the application.

Egan J. held, once again following *Frescati*, that the mining company had sufficient interest to make the application as it had the approval of a person (*i.e.* the Minister) who was able to assert sufficient legal estate or interest to enable him to carry out the proposed development.[21]

6.2.3 Newspaper notice

An applicant for planning permission must publish a notice of his intention to make an application within the two weeks preceding the lodging of the application, in a newspaper circulating in the district in which the proposed development is located.[22] The High Court has expressed the view that a challenge to the validity of a planning permission may not be time-barred where the newspaper in which the notice of the application was published is not

---

18   O'Hanlon J. also indicated that the planning authority had power to make an appropriate correction on the planning register under s.8 of the Local Government (Planning and Development) Act 1963.

19   [1995] 1 I.L.R.M. 424 (Hamilton C.J., Egan and Blayney JJ. *nem diss*) November 11, 1994. On an application for leave for judicial review the applicant merely has to establish that there are substantial grounds for judicial review, see para. 10.1.5, below.

20   The permission for the operation of a lead/zinc mine near Galmoy, County Kilkenny was granted to the developers, Arcon Mines Limited, after an oral hearing lasting two weeks.

21   The appellants also contended that the consent of adjoining landowners was necessary before a planning application could be made because the development adversely affected water sources on the lands adjacent to the application site.

22   1994 Regulations, art. 14.

circulating in the vicinity of the proposed development.[23] In such circumstances, it might be argued that a strict operation of the statutory two month time limit constituted an infringement of the constitutional right of access to the courts of a person who was not otherwise made aware of the decision.

Article 15 provides that the newspaper notice "shall" contain as a heading the name of the planning authority to which the planning application will be made. It is no longer necessary to use as a heading the name of the city, town or county in which the development is proposed, as was required under the former regulations.[24] The newspaper notice must also state:

— the name of the applicant,
— whether the application is for a permission, an outline permission or an approval,
— the location of the land or the address of the structure,
— the nature and extent of the development,
— the number of any dwellings to be provided,
— in the case of an application for the retention of a structure, the nature of the proposed use of the structure and, where appropriate, the period for which retention is sought,
— in the case of an application for the continuance of any use, the nature of the intended use and the previous use,
— in the case of an application which requires an Environmental Impact Statement (EIS), that an EIS will be submitted with the application and that it will be available for inspection at the offices of the planning authority, together with any further information concerning the proposed development which may be furnished to the planning authority while the application is under consideration,
— where applicable, that the application is related to an activity for which an Integrated Pollution Control (IPC) licence is required.

A further newspaper notice will be required if the planning authority requests the applicant to submit an EIS after the application has been lodged.[25] This may arise where the application should initially have been accompanied by an EIS, or where the planning authority consider that the proposed development will be likely to have significant effects on the environment.[26] This newspaper notice should also be published in a newspaper circulating in the area of the proposed development and should contain the same headings. In addition, it should state:

---

[23] *per* Costello J. in *Brady v. Donegal County Council* [1989] I.L.R.M. 282. His decision was appealed to the Supreme Court which remitted the matter to the High Court on the grounds that there was insufficient evidence relating to the circulation of the newspaper to enable the court to decide the point: the case settled before the fresh hearing.
[24] 1977 Regulations, art. 15.
[25] 1994 Regulations, art. 17(1).
[26] See arts. 25(1) and 26(1).

— the name of the applicant,
— the date on which the planning application was made and its reference number in the planning register,
— the location of the land or the address of the structure,
— that an EIS will be submitted to the planning authority in connection with the planning application,
— that the EIS and any further information concerning the proposed development which may be furnished to the planning authority while the application is under consideration will be available for inspection at the offices of the planning authority,
— where applicable, that the proposed development is related to an activity for which an IPC licence is required.

An applicant may be required to publish a further newspaper notice in certain circumstances after the application has been lodged.[27]

6.2.4 Site notice

Article 14 also provides that, before lodging a planning application, an applicant must erect or fix a site notice on the land or structure concerned.[28] The regulations stipulate that this should be done not later than the making of the application it must be maintained in position for a period of at least one month after the making of the planning application and must be renewed or replaced if it is removed or becomes defaced or illegible within that period.[29] Article 16 provides that the site notice must be "painted or inscribed, or printed and affixed" on a durable material. It must be securely erected or affixed in a conspicuous position, either on or near the main entrance to the land or structure, or on any other part of the land or structure adjoining a public road, as long as it can be read by those using the public road. If the land or structure to which the application relates does not adjoin a public road, the site notice should be erected or fixed in a conspicuous position on the land or structure so as to be easily visible and legible from a position outside the land or structure. The position of the site notice must be shown on a plan accompanying the planning application.

Article 16 also sets out the information which must be contained in a site notice. For obvious reasons, the location of the proposed development need not be stated. In addition, there is no requirement, presumably because of limitations of space, to

---

27 Art. 17(2). See para. 6.6.6, below.
28 Under the 1977 Regulations, an applicant could elect to publish notice of his intention to make an application either in a newspaper notice or on a site notice, but under the 1994 Regulations both are mandatory.
   The requirement for a site notice does not apply to overhead transmission or distribution lines for conducting electricity which are erected by an electricity undertaking, or to overhead telecommunications lines which are erected by Bord Telecom Eireann or by any person to whom a licence under s.111 of the Postal and Telecommunications Services Act 1983 (No. 24) has been granted: art. 14(2).
29 Art. 16(5).

make reference in the notice to the submission of an EIS or to the fact that the proposed development relates to an activity for which an IPC licence is required. A planning authority may request an applicant to give further notice on site where:

— the site notice does not comply with the requirements of Article 16, referred to above,
— it is misleading or inadequate,
— it has not been maintained in position for a period of one month after the making of the planning application,
— it has been defaced or become illegible and has not been renewed or replaced.[30]

The applicant will be obliged to furnish such evidence of compliance with the request by the planning authority for further notice as the authority may seek.

6.2.5 Name of applicant

"It is inherent in the planning code that the planning authority and the public shall have an opportunity of vetting the planning application in the light of, amongst other matters, the identity of a named and legally existing applicant."[31] On the other hand, the courts are reluctant to set aside a planning decision where they can be satisfied that (a) the application was made by a real person with an interest in the land; (b) that the misstatement was not deliberate; and (c) that neither the planning authority nor the public were misled. Where the intention behind the misstatement of the applicants's name is to mislead the public this is likely to result in the permission being set aside if challenged.[32]

In *State (Alf-A-Bet Promotions Ltd) v. Bundoran U.D.C.*,[33] a notice in the window of the premises intended to be developed as an amusement arcade indicated that an application was to be made to the Urban District Council by a company called Alf-A-Bet Ltd. The company never subsequently came into existence. However, one of the persons on whose behalf the property had been bought in trust was named in the application as the secretary of the company. The application was also made by architects who were well known to the Council. McWilliam J. was satisfied that the application was genuine and that the clients had a sufficient interest to support the application. He said:

---

[30] 1994 Regulations, art. 17(2). Note that art. 17(2)(c) was substituted by the 1995 Regulations, art. 4. Some practical problems associated with the requirements in relation to site notices are discussed by McCrossan in (1994) IPELJ at 117.

[31] *State (Finglas Industrial Estates Ltd) v. Dublin County Council*, unreported, Supreme Court, February 17, 1983, *per* Henchy J.

[32] See *State (N.C.E.) v. Dublin County Council*, unreported, Supreme Court, May 14, 1980, in which the application was made in the name of an associate company of the real applicant.

[33] (1978) 112 I.L.T.R. 9. See also *Inver Resources Ltd v. Limerick Corporation* [1987] I.R. 159, although the point arose *obiter* as Barron J. held that the application – for judicial review was statute-barred.

> "It does not appear to me that, apart from circumstances so very unusual as in *Frescati Estates Limited v. Walker* where the application was not genuine, the actual identity of the applicant is material. Accordingly, provided that the application was made by a person with an interest in the matter, the mere fact that a company name which had not been formed or was inaccurately or incorrectly named would not of itself be sufficient to render the application invalid . . .".

Similarly, the court was not prepared to penalise a developer in *State (Toft) v. Galway Corporation*,[34] for what could have been characterised as a slight case of dyslexia. An application was made in the name of a company called Spirits Rum Ltd, although the real applicant was Rum Spirits Ltd. The prosecutor sought to have the decision of the corporation set aside on the grounds that the applicant's name was incorrectly given and because particulars of the applicant's interest in the land had not been furnished. O'Higgins C.J. refused to grant such an order, as the applicant was fully aware of the true identity of the applicants. He quoted with an approval an excerpt from Costello J.'s judgment in the High Court as follows:

> "I concluded that the Corporation had jurisdiction to make the impugned order. The Regulations provide that an 'applicant' is required to publish notice of his intention to make the application (Regulation 14 and Regulation 15), and that the planning application is to be accompanied by the name and address of the 'applicant' (Regulation 17) but the mistake made in the applicant's name in the notices and in the application did not, in my opinion, deprive the Corporation of jurisdiction in relation to the application. Rum Spirits Ltd. had authorised the making of an application under the Act of 1963 and the Corporation had before it an application on which it was required to adjudicate. It is true that the application was brought in the name of a non-existent company, but it was not a non-existent application. It is possible that certain errors in applications might be such as to vitiate the entire proceedings under the Section and deprive the planning authority of jurisdiction but it seems to me that the mistake made in the present case did not do either. The Corporation had before it an application which it was empowered to consider and upon which it could adjudicate. The Corporation had power to correct the error by amending its order so as to show the company's correct name, and s.8 of the Act of 1963 acknowledged the right of the Corporation to make corrections in its planning register."

In *Dunne (Frank) Ltd v. Dublin County Council*,[35] the name furnished in the newspaper notice was "F. Dunne" while the letter of application was expressed to have been made "on behalf of Frank Dunne Ltd". The application had in fact been submitted by Mr Frank Dunne on behalf of the company, as principal. Pringle J. held that there had been sufficient compliance with the terms of the regulation.[36]

---

[34] [1981] I.L.R.M. 439.

[35] [1974] I.R. 45.

[36] The ommission of the word "limited" from the description of the applicant company in the newspaper notice was held not to be fatal to the validity of the planning application in *Blessington & District Community Council Ltd v. Wicklow County Council*, unreported, High Court, Kelly J., July 19, 1996.

6.2.6 Location of land

In *Crodaun Homes Ltd v. Kildare County Council*,[37] Griffin J. stated:

> "In my view, to satisfy the requirement of stating 'the location of the land', both the letter and the spirit of the regulations require that in the case of land, and in particular land which is not in an urban area, the site on which it is proposed that the development should take place must be correctly and accurately so described in relation to the district in which the land is situate – for example by the estate of which it forms part, or the townland, or the neighbouring village – as to be readily and reasonably identifiable."

The statement of the address or location of the proposed development should be capable of being understood by persons who do not live in the vicinity of the lands, as well as inhabitants of the area. In *Crodaun Homes*, a newspaper notice describing the location of a proposed development according to its local nomenclature as "Leixlip Gate, County Kildare", was held to be inadequate to comply with the regulations although the local postman and doctor and other inhabitants of the locality gave evidence that they knew where "Leixlip Gate" was.

By contrast, Murphy J. in *O'Donoghue v. An Bord Pleanála*[38] held that a description of land by reference to its site number was adequate and not misleading, as none of the people living in the neighbourhood of the proposed development would have had difficulty in identifying the site, which was the only remaining undeveloped site on a small estate of 32 houses. He also considered it relevant that nobody had "come forward" to say that they were in fact misled by the advertisement and continued:

> "Whilst ordinarily one does not know if members of the public have been misled by an advertisement, in the present case where a concerned neighbour has carried his challenge to the planning permission to the High Court one would expect that he would have ascertained from local residents their reaction to the proposed development and most particularly whether they were misled by any advertisement which they read with regard to it. However, apart from any inference which might be drawn from the absence of that evidence I am satisfied that the description of the location is adequate and in no way misleading."

In *ESB v. Gormley*, the proposed development consisted of a transmission line which the ESB intended to lay for a distance of over 40 miles across County Wexford. Only the townland where the line entered and the townland where it left County Wexford were indicated in the newspaper notice. Finlay C.J., giving the judgment of the Supreme Court, said:

> "It does not seem to me that the form of advertisement would even notify an owner or occupier of lands that the townlands in which he resided might be affected, let alone inform him that his actual property might be affected, except

---

[37] [1983] I.L.R.M. 1.
[38] [1991] I.L.R.M. 750.

insofar as may have applied to the limited number of persons living in either of the two nominated townlands."

In the later case of *Dooley v. Galway County Council*,[39] Denham J. set aside a decision of the planning authority where there were 18 townlands of the same name as that referred to in the newspaper notice in the County of Galway, as the site of the proposed development was not "readily and reasonably identifiable".

6.2.7 Nature and extent of development

Before the judicial review of planning decisions became established, developers often used euphemistic descriptions of development proposals in the hope of evading public scrutiny. The courts have since been vigilant in ensuring that members of the public are not misled by newspaper notices as to the nature and extent of development. The planning authority is entitled to require the applicant to publish a further notice if it appears that the original notice is in breach of the regulations, is misleading or not sufficiently informative to members of the public. Considerable delay and expense may be caused to a developer by such a request, as a decision to grant or refuse permission may not issue for two months from the date of the publication of the further notice.[40]

In *Monaghan U.D.C. v. Alf-A-Bet Promotions Ltd*,[41] the appellants published in the local newspaper, the Northern Standard, notice of their intention to apply for planning permission for "extensions and improvements to a premises at The Diamond, Monaghan". In fact, the intention was to use the premises as an amusement arcade. Subsequently, a few days after the application was received, a second newspaper notice was published at the request of the planning authority. The respondent council refused planning permission, but the appellants claimed to be entitled to a decision to grant permission as the council had not made a decision within two months of receiving the application.[42] The council replied by submitting that the application was invalid because it had not been made in accordance with the requirements contained in the regulations, in that, (a) the first newspaper did not contain, as a heading, the name of the town of Monaghan[43]; and (b) did not state the nature and extent of the development.

---

39   [1992] 2 I.R. 136.
40   1963 Act, s. 26(4)(b).
41   [1980] I.L.R.M. 64.
42   s.26(4) of the 1963 Act provides that a decision to grant permission or approval is deemed to have been made where the planning authority fail to give notice to the applicant of its decision within the "appropriate period". However, compliance with the permission regulations is a pre-condition to this entitlement.
43   Art. 15 of the 1977 Regulations required that the notice "contain, as a heading, the name of the city, town or county in which the land or structure is situate ...". Under the 1994 Regulations, the heading should refer to the name of the relevant planning authority. See para. 6.2.3, above.

The Supreme Court held that the appellants were in breach of both of these requirements which were mandatory in nature, and not directory, and it followed that a decision to grant permission by default could not result.[44]

It is a matter of judgment as to what level of detail a proposed developmnent must be described in the notice. Access to a development is often a critical element as planning permission can often be refused because its location would give rise to a traffic hazard. In *Keleghan v. Corby and Dublin Corporation*,[45] it was held that a newspaper notice of an application for permission to erect three temporary pre-fabricated classrooms at a secondary school, which omitted any reference to a new access road to the school through an existing cul-de-sac, did not comply with the requirement that the "nature and extent" of the development be properly disclosed. But in many cases, the public may be deemed to have notice that an access would necessarily form part of the proposed development. Murphy J. pointed out in *O'Donoghue v. An Bord Pleanála* that it would be wrong to infer from the decision in *Keleghan*:

> "a general proposition to the effect that notice of a proposal to erect buildings is entirely separate from and does not include intention to create access to the buildings so erected."

In that case, the newspaper notice was in the following terms:

> "Dublin County Council Revised Plan for bungalow on site at Old Rectory Park, Taney Road, Dundrum for Tallon Properties Ltd."

The applicant contended that the notice was deficient because, *inter alia*, it failed to indicate that the access to the proposed bungalow would be from Old Rectory Park and not through an imposing entrance already in existence on Taney Road. Murphy J. held that the absence of any reference to the access was not fatal to the validity of the application. Distinguishing the *Keleghan* case, he analysed the situation in a pragmatic way in the following passage:

> "In the *Keleghan* case the Court drew attention to the fact that the permission related to three temporary pre-fabricated classrooms in grounds which were in excess of six acres, so that there was nothing in the notice which alerted the residents in the cul de sac to the fact that the development might possibly include a roadway giving access to the school through the cul de sac. As McMahon J. pointed out (at p.145):
>
> > 'Such an access is not necessarily or normally incidental to the erection of pre-fabricated buildings and, as far as the evidence goes, it was not provided for the service of these classrooms but for a separate reason altogether. Therefore, it appears, that the public did not get proper notice of the application.'

---

[44] It has been commented that the courts are likely to take a rather unsympathetic view of the applicant's failure to comply with permission regulations where the applicant is seeking to avail of a default decision to grant permission. See O'Sullivan and Shepherd. It is probably also true to say that in recent years the courts have been reluctant to accept challenges from third parties to the grant of planning permission on the grounds of non-compliance with application and pre-application procedures, where no more substantive ground subsists.

[45] 111 I.L.T.R. 144, (HC).

In the present case, the site is not measured in acres but in metres: at most 618 square metres. Once a building – of whatever size or configuration – is erected on the site there must be access to it and every member of the public reading the advertisement would have been conscious of the fact. The argument in the present case is simply that the granite piers on Taney Road which, as I have speculated, probably formed the entrance to the rectory itself, would be adapted as the means of access to the new bungalow. What is said is that the public, or more particularly, the residents in the Old Rectory Park may have been lulled into a false sense of security in assuming that there would be no access from the estate itself which might cause a traffic hazard. Again it seems to me unreasonable to draw any such inference or to impose upon an applicant for planning permission the duty to act on the assumption that concerned parties would proceed on such a basis. Indeed, if anything the description of the location as being both a site and as being located in the Old Rectory Park would alert neighbours to the fact that the proposed development was within the mouth of the estate rather than out on Taney Road."

In the absence of anybody being actually misled, the court will be reluctant to be set aside a permission because of the ommission of some detail in the notice, as, for example, where the fact that a building to be demolished is a "habitable house" is not disclosed.[46]

The words "nature and extent" are intended to refer to the physical aspects of the development and do not impose a duty on the applicant to indicate its "possible or even probable consequences". A newspaper notice was held not to be defective because it failed to put the public on notice of the potential dangers associated with a proposed liquid petroleum gas storage tank.[47] It also appears that it may be sufficient compliance with the regulations to describe a use as "existing" despite the fact that it is unauthorised; the alternative being, reference to an earlier unauthorised use, would be more misleading.[48]

6.3 PARTICULARS TO ACCOMPANY PLANNING APPLICATION

6.3.1 Plans and particulars to accompany planning applications generally

The 1994 Regulations introduced considerable changes in the content of planning applications generally. The definitions section of the Regulations indicates that the expression "planning application" is intended to include an outline application, an application for an approval, an application for permission for the retention of a structure, and an application for permission for the continuance of any use of any structure or other land. "Permission" as defined under the regulations includes outline permission.[49] As used in the documents issued by

---

46 See *Blessington*, above, n.36 and *Cunningham v. An Bord Pleanála* unreported, High Court, May 3, 1990.
47 *Calor Teoranta v. Sligo County Council* [1991] I.R. 267.
48 See *Blessington*, above, n.36.
49 Art. 3.

the planning authority, "permission" usually refers to "full permission", although occasionally conditions may be imposed requiring the further approval in the sense of agreement of the planning authority for certain matters. Articles 18, 19 and 23 relate to the contents of applications generally, but Article 20 provides that a less exacting standard of compliance with Article 18 is required for outline applications.[50] All planning applications must contain the following information:

— the name, address and telephone number, if any, of the applicant and of any person acting on his behalf,
— the address to which any correspondence should be sent,
— whether the application is for a permission, an outline permission or an approval,
— particulars of the land or structure concerned, including its location or address,
— particulars of the interest in the land or structure held by the applicant,
— if the applicant is not the owner, the name and address of the owner,
— two copies of the relevant page of the newspaper in which notice of the application appeared,
— the text of the site notice,
— four copies of a location map, to a scale of not less than 1:10, 560 (which should be indicated on the map) and marked or coloured so as to identify clearly the application site,
— the area of the land to which the application relates,
— the number of any dwellings to be provided,
— the gross floor space[51] of any buildings, except in the case of an application for a single dwellinghouse or a number of such houses,
— where applicable, that the development consists of or comprises an industrial activity or isolated storage to which Regulations 12 to 18 of the European Communities (Major Accident Hazards of Certain Industrial Activities) Regulations 1986,[52] as amended by the European Communities (Major Accident Hazards of Certain Industrial Activities) (Amendment) Regulations 1989[53] and the European Communities (Major Accident Hazards of Certain Industrial Activities) (Amendment) Regulations 1992[54] apply,

---

[50] Note that special provision for the erection by an electricity undertaking of overhead transmission or distribution lines were introduced by the Local Government (Planning and Development) Regulations 1995, art. 5.

[51] "Gross floor space" is defined under art. 18(2) as "the area ascertained by the internal measurement of the floor space on each floor of a building or buildings (including internal walls and partitions), disregarding any floor space provided for the parking of vehicles by persons occupying or using the building or buildings where such floor space is incidental to development to which the application primarily relates". It should not be assumed that this is necessarily the same definition as that used under the relevant development plan.

[52] S.I. No. 292 of 1986.

[53] S.I. No. 194 of 1989.

[54] S.I. No. 21 of 1992.

— where applicable, that the proposed development is related to an activity for which an IPC licence is required.

— four copies of a site or layout plan drawn to a scale of not less than 1:500 (which should be indicated on the plan).

6.3.2 Plans and particulars to accompany applications other than outline

The following plans and particulars should accompany all applications other than outline applications[55]:

— four copies of a location map, to a scale of not less than 1:10, 560 (which should be marked on the map) and marked or coloured so as to identify clearly the application site and its boundaries,

— four copies of a site or layout plan, to a scale of not less than 1:500,

— four copies of drawings of floor plans,to a scale of not less than 1:100

— four copies of elevations, to a scale of not less than 1:100,

— four copies of sections, to a scale of not less than 1:100,

— such other particulars as necessary to describe the works or structure to which the application relates,

— where the application is principally for a material change of use or for the continuance of any use, a statement of the existing use and of the use proposed or, where appropriate, of the former use and the use proposed to be continued, together with particulars of the nature and extent of any such proposed use,

— where applicable, an EIS.

In the case of more complex developments, considerable savings in time may be made through prior consultation with the planning authority as to the extent of information which they require.[56] However, it is often difficult to foresee or forestall any request for further information which the planning authority might consider it appropriate to make, as a result of which the period for the consideration of the application is extended.

6.3.3 Description of interest

A technical description of the applicants's interest is not necessary as the planning authority have power to require the applicant to submit further infomation as to his estate or interest or right over the land.[57] The expression "owner" has been held to be a sufficient description of an applicant's interest.[58]

---

[55] See 1994 Regulations, art. 23 in relation to the details to be included in plans and drawings.

[56] See further, McHugh, "Negotiating with Planning Authorities" (1994) IPELJ 1.

[57] 1994 Regulations, art. 33 (1).

[58] *Burke v. Drogheda Corporation* [1981] I.L.R.M. 439, dealing with the similar provision under art. 3 (a) of the 1964 Regulations. McWilliam J. held that the plaintiff was entitled to a default decision.

6.3.4 Fees for planning applications

Fees are payable for all planning applications.[59] In addition, a fee is payable for an application for an extension or further extension to the life of a planning permission.[60] An application cannot be determined by the planning authority unless it has received the fee required.[61] Fees differ according to the type of application being made and according to the nature and extent of the development for which permission is sought. There is provision for exemptions for certain applications relating to development to be carried out by or on behalf of voluntary organisations. Reduced fees are payable in certain circumstances and refunds may be granted for repeat applications.[62]

6.4 OUTLINE AND APPROVAL APPLICATIONS

6.4.1 Applications for outline permission

An "outline permission" indicates that a proposed development is acceptable in principle. It is defined as "permission for development subject to the subsequent approval of the planning authority".[63] An outline application need only be accompanied by "such plans and particulars as are necessary to identify the land to which the application relates and to enable the planning authority to determine the siting, layout or other proposals for development in respect of which a decision is sought".[64] Thus, the omission from a site plan of the north point and location of buildings in the vicinity of the proposed structure (which were both included in a second plan), and the absence of drawings of elevations and dimensions of a petrol station canopy were held not to invalidate an application for outline permission.[65]

6.4.2 When an outline application cannot be made

An application for outline permission cannot be made for the retention of structures or to continue any use of land which is unauthorised.[66] Nor can an outline application be made where an EIS is required under Article 24 of the European Communities (Environmental Impact Assessment) Regulations 1989.[67] The obvious rationale for this rule is that neither the planning authority nor An

---

[59] Art. 88.

[60] Art. 107.

[61] 1982 Act, s.10(2) (a). A "default" decision to grant permission cannot be deemed to have been made until at least two months after the prescribed fee has been received: 1982 Act, s. 10(2)(b). See also *Maher v. An Bord Pleanála* [1993] 1 I.R. 439.

[62] Fees are dealt with under Pt. VII of the Regulations and Sched. 6 thereto.

[63] Art. 3.

[64] Art. 20.

[65] *Molloy and Walsh v. Dublin County Council* [1990] I.R. 90; [1990] I.L.R.M. 633.

[66] Art. 20(2)(a).

[67] Art. 20(2)(b)(i).

Bord Pleanála would be able to properly assess the environmental impacts of a proposed development due to the lack of detail furnished. Similarly, an outline application may not be made for any development which concerns an activity for which an IPC licence is required, if the proposed development is of the same nature as a category of development specified under Article 24, though it falls short of the threshold indicated for that category.[68] Finally, where the planning authority receive an outline application for a development of the same type as a category of development specified under Article 24, but which falls short of the threshold indicated for that category, it must notify the applicant that an outline application is not acceptable if it forms the view that the proposal is likely to have significant effects on the environment.[69]

6.4.3 Effect of outline permission

An outline permission does not authorise the carrying out of any development until an approval consequent on that outline permission has been granted for the whole or part of the site the subject matter of the outline permission.[70] A condition attached to an approval granted on foot of an outline permission may also require a further approval to be obtained relating to details of the proposed development, before development can commence.

6.4.4 Matters to be dealt with at outline stage

The planning code does not distinguish between those matters which must be determined at the outline stage and those matters which may be reserved for the approval of the planning authority. In practice, an outline permission will often indicate those matters which should be dealt with in an application for approval. Some guidance is provided by the Department of Environment Advice and Guidelines (1982) which recommends that any major restrictions should be determined by way of condition at that stage.[71] In particular, the guidelines recommend that an application for approval should not be refused for reasons relating to basic land-use considerations, the unsuitability of a particular site for the proposed development, the inadequacy of services, or the effect on the site of a road reservation. It is also suggested that stringent or onerous conditions should be attached at outline stage, *e.g.* conditions relating to the reduction in height, scale or bulk of structures, requirements to reserve parts of the site free of development, financial contributions and security conditions. Developers are cautioned not to expect planning authorities "to write a blank cheque" at outline stage:

---

[68] Art. 20(2)(b)(ii).
[69] Art. 20(3).
[70] Art. 21.
[71] See para. 10.615 of "DOE Advice and Guidelines".

"It follows that the plans and particulars submitted with an outline application should be sufficient to provide a clear picture of what is intended and to enable the planning authority to determine the intensity or quantity of use proposed, at least in general terms. For example, an outline application which is expressed to relate only to "residential and ancillary development" on a large site and which is accompanied by little more than a site plan, will be difficult to process properly and, if granted, could give rise to serious difficulties at approval stage; in such a case, it would not be unreasonable (and would be consistent with the regulations) to require the developer to specify whether houses or flats were intended, the number of units involved, the nature and extent of the ancillary development, and so on." (Paragraph 10.702)

The writer has noticed a trend for some planning authorities to grant permission for an unspecified number of homes and apartments at outline stage. The legality of this practice must be in some doubt having regard to the requirement for the developer to state the nature and extent of the development. Furthermore, it does not appear to be consistent with the above guidelines.

6.4.5 Applications for approval

The word "approval" has two meanings under the Regulations: it can mean either "an approval consequent on an outline permission" or "an approval which is required to be obtained under a condition subject to which a permission or an approval is granted".[72] The grant of an outline permission does not authorise the carrying out of any development until an approval of the former type has been granted or until an approval of the latter type has been granted where the terms of an approval granted consequent on an outline application requires such further approval.[73]

An application for approval may be made for a specified part of a development for which outline permission was granted. Separate applications may be made for other parts of the same development from time to time.[74] It is essential that the application for approval in such cases relates to the same planning unit as that to which the original application for outline permission related. In *Silverhill Development Company Limited v. An Bord Pleanála*,[75] a developer applied for outline planning permission for a proposed development consisting of a 40 bedroom hotel, 34 chalets and a recreation building. Permission was granted subject to the condition that the chalets and recreation room be omitted from the development. Subsequently, the owner sold off a back part of the site on which the chalets and recreation buildings would have been located. An Bord Pleanála refused to grant planning approval for the erection of the hotel on the remaining land on the grounds that there was no correspondence between the site shown in

---

[72] Art. 3.
[73] Art. 21.
[74] Art. 22(1)(b).
[75] Unreported, High Court, O'Hanlon J., March 16, 1984.

the application for approval and the site which was the subject of the outline application. O'Hanlon J. refused to grant orders of certiorari or mandamus to direct the Board to issue an approval in accordance with the terms of the application. He stated as follows:

> "It appears to me that the area of the planning unit – the lands on which the development is to take place – must always be a material consideration for the planning authority in reaching a decision whether to grant or refuse permission. If an applicant, having obtained outline planning permission to develop land of a certain area, comes forward at a later stage with a proposal to develop land of a different area this may radically alter the attitude a planning authority should take to the application in the interests of the proper planning and development of the area over which they exercise jurisdiction. It seems to me to be contrary to the spirit and intention of the Act that they should, in such circumstances, find their hands tied by an outline permission previously granted by them when an application was made for permission to develop a larger area of land. If the applicant is no longer in a position to make an application for development approval in respect of the original planning unit, he should, in my opinion, be obliged to submit a fresh application for permission in respect of such part of the original lands as he now wishes to develop."

The *Silverhill* decision is essentially an application of the principle that where there are two mutually inconsistent permissions for the same site, the implementation of one renders the other incapable of implementation.[76]

6.4.6 Parameters of outline permission are binding except were change in circumstances

As the outline permission upon which it is based indicates the acceptability of the proposed development in principle, an application for approval consequent on an outline permission should not normally be refused for reasons of principle.[77] Outline applications are designed to reduce the planning costs to a developer. The "whole procedure would be defeated, if at the approval stage, the planning authority were to re-open the question of whether the development is acceptable in principle".[78]

An application for planning approval consequent on an outline permission must, therefore, be considered within the parameters of the outline permission. An exceptional situation may be distinguished where the background planning circumstances, against which the decision to grant outline permission was made have changed so that different considerations apply at the time that application for planning approval is made.[79]

---

[76] *Pilkington v. Secretary of State for the Environment* [1973] 1 W.L.R. 1527.
[77] *State (Pine Valley Developments Ltd) v. Dublin County Council* [1982] I.L.R.M. 169.
[78] *ibid., per* Barrington J.
[79] See *Irish Asphalt Ltd v. An Bord Pleanála*, unreported, Supreme Court, May 22, 1996.

6.4.7 Contents of approval application

An application for an approval consequent on an outline permission must be accompanied by such further plans and particulars as would be required for a "full" permission under article 19.[80] On the other hand, an application for an approval which is required to be obtained under a condition subject to which a planning permission or approval was granted need only be accompanied by such plans and particulars as are necessary to enable the planning authority to make a decision on the matter for which the approval is sought.[81]

6.5 ENVIRONMENTAL IMPACT STATEMENTS

This topic is considered in greater detail in Chapter 7, but an outline is provided below.

6.5.1 Applications to be acompanied by EIS

Planning applications for certain projects require the preparation by the applicant of an environmental impact statement (EIS) to enable interested persons and the planning authority to assess the significant effects of the project on the environment. Where the proposed development concerns an activity for which an integrated pollution control (IPC) licence is also required, the planning authority are prohibited from taking into account matters relating to the risk of environmental pollution from the activity.[82] These matters are taken into consideration by the Environmental Protection Agency in the context of an application for an IPC licence.

An EIS must be submitted with a planning application for permission for any development which is "specified development" under Article 24 of the European Communities (Environmental Impact Assessment) Regulations 1989.[83] The 1994 Regulations have extended the requirement for an EIS to proposals which would constitute "specified development" but for the fact that they fall short of the thresholds under the First Schedule to the 1989 Regulations where the development involves an activity for which an IPC licence under the Environmental Protection Agency Act 1992 will be required.[84] In both of these cases the project concerned loses its exempted development status under the planning code.[85]

In addition, planning authorities must request an EIS to be submitted where the development proposed would have been specified development were it not for the

---

[80]   Art. 22(1)(a).
[81]   Art. 22(2).
[82]   See the inspector's report on the Masonite planning appeal.
[83]   1994 Regulations, art. 24 provides that all types of development listed under Pts. I and II of Sched. 1 are specified for the purposes of the regulations. See art. 24 of the 1989 Regulations.
[84]   1994 Regulations, art. 24(10)(b).
[85]   *ibid.*, art. 10(1)(c).

fact that it falls short of the threshold laid down for that type of development, if the authority is of the opinion that the development "would be likely to have significant effects on the environment".[86] The Board may also request an EIS where the planning authority has not requested one, if it considers that the development proposed is likely to have significant effects on the environment.

If an applicant, despite being under no obligation to do so, decides to submit an EIS for a development which falls short of the threshold indicated but would otherwise amount to "specified development", the planning authority are obliged to deal with the application as if the EIS had been submitted in accordance with Article 24(1).[87]

Where the planning authority receive a planning application for which an EIS is mandatory but which is not accompanied by an EIS, the applicant must be notified in writing to inform him of this fact and to require him to submit an EIS.[88] Such a notice is not served where an exemption from the requirement of an EIS has been granted.[89]

6.5.2 Exemptions from EIS requirement

The Minister may grant an exemption from the requirement for the submission of an EIS and, in such circumstances, may apply other requirements.[90] The planning authority must give notice in writing to the applicant "as soon as may be" after receipt of notice of the grant of the exemption, requiring the applicant to comply with the Minister's requirements.[91] The applicant does not have to comply with any requirements relating to the risk of environmental pollution where the proposed development concerns an activity which will require an IPC licence. On the other hand, if no IPC licence will be required to carry out the proposed development, the applicant must comply with each of the requirements laid down by the Minister. In the event that the applicant does not comply with the requirements of the Minister, the planning authority are obliged to serve a notice on the applicant requiring compliance.[92]

The planning authority are obliged to require the applicant to submit an EIS for a proposed development which falls short of a particular threshold specified in the First Schedule to the 1989 Regulations, where the development would

---

[86] Such a notice will cease to have effect where an exemption is granted by the Minister from the date of the receipt by the planning authority of notice of the grant of the exemption.

[87] 1994 Regulations, art. 27(1).

[88] *ibid.*, art. 25(1).

[89] *ibid.*, art. 25(20)(a). Any such notice which has already been served ceases to have effect from the date of receipt by the planning authority of a notice of a grant of exemption by the Minister: art. 25(3)(a).

[90] *ibid.*, art. 25(2)(b).

[91] s.25(3) of the 1963 Act, as inserted by art. 7 of the 1989 Regulations. However, the Guidance Notes on the 1994 Regulations issued by the Department of the Environment indicate that exemptions will only be granted in "wholly exceptional circumstances".

[92] 1994 Regulations, art. 24(3)(b).

otherwise amount to "specified development" if they consider that it would be likely to have significant effects on the environment. Such a notice will cease to have effect where an exemption is granted by the Minister from the date of the receipt by the planning authority of notice of the grant of the exemption.

6.5.3 Outline applications

Outline applications may not be made for proposed development which requires an EIS under Article 24 of the 1989 Regulations. The rationale for this rule is that neither the planning authority nor An Bord Pleanála would be able to properly assess the environmental impacts of a proposed development due to the lack of detail furnished. Similarly, an outline application may not be made for any development which concerns an activity for which an IPC licence is required, if the proposed development is of the same nature as a category of development specified under Article 24, though it falls short of the threshold indicated for that category.[93] Finally, where the planning authority receive an out-line application for a development of the same type as a category of development specified under Article 24, but which falls short of the threshold indicated for that category, it must notify the applicant that an outline application cannot be submitted if it forms the view that the proposal is likely to have significant effects on the environment.[94]

6.5.4 Content of Environmental Impact Statements

An Environmental Impact Statement must contain the information referred to in paragraph 2 of the Second Schedule to the 1989 Regulations and may also contain the information in paragraph 3 of that Schedule.[95] On receipt of an EIS, the planning authority must assess the compliance of the EIS with those infor-mation requirements, but where the proposed development relates to an activity for which an IPC licence is required, the planning authority must exclude from this assessment of compliance any matters relating to the risk of environmental pollution from the activity.[96] Within these parameters, if an EIS is found to be inadequate, the planning authority are obliged to inform the applicant in writing and to require him to submit such further information or particulars as may be necessary to ensure compliance.[97]

---

[93] Art. 20(2).
[94] Art. 20(3).
[95] E.C. (Environmental Impact Assessment) Regulations 1989, art. 25.
[96] 1994 Regulations, art. 28(2)(a).
[97] *ibid.*, art. 28(2)(b).

6.6 PROCEDURE AFTER RECEIPT OF APPLICATION

6.6.1 Procedure on receipt

On receipt of a planning application, the planning authority stamp documents with the date of their receipt and, if satisfied that the application complies with the requirements of the permission regulations, send to the applicant or the person acting on his behalf an acknowledgement stating the date of receipt of the application.[98] If the planning authority consider that the planning application does not comply with the relevant regulations, they may inform the applicant that the application is invalid and cannot be considered by the planning authority, or, alternatively, may require the applicant to furnish further particulars, plans, drawings or maps to ensure compliance with the regulations. If the planning authority take the view that the application is invalid, they must return to the applicant all documentation which accompanied the application.

The applicant must also be required to submit an EIS where he has not complied with the mandatory requirement for the EIS to be submitted.[99]

6.6.2 Weekly list of applications

Lists of applications giving details of proposed developments are published by the planning authority on a weekly basis.[100] The list should indicate those planning applications for which an Environmental Impact Statement has been submitted, or which concern an activity for which an IPC licence is required. It should indicate any planning application in which an EIS has been received by the planning authority after the date of receipt of the application. It should indicate if any notice has been served on the applicant informing him that the application is invalid, or of any notice requiring the applicant to furnish further documentation to secure compliance with the requirements of the regulations. The list should also alert interested members of the public as to the submission of further documentation in response to a request for further information by the planning authority or an invitation to modify the proposed development.

Weekly lists must be displayed for a period of not less than two months at the offices of the planning authority for public inspection during office hours. They must also be displayed for public inspection in each public library located in the functional area of the planning authority and in each mobile public library operating in that area. Weekly lists may also be displayed in any other place which the planning authority selects, and may be made available for publication, or published, in a newspaper circulating in the area of the planning authority. The

---

[98] 1994 Regulations, art. 29.
[99] 1989 Regulations, art. 25(1). See para. 6.5.1, above.
[100] *ibid.*, art. 30.

planning authority also has a discretion to make the lists available by other means. The members of the planning authority may, by resolution, direct that weekly lists be made available to them. Copies of weekly lists are available for purchase at the offices of the planning authority during office hours at a reasonable cost. Any person or body is entitled to have copies of the weekly list sent to them by post for a fee, not exceeding the reasonable cost of making the copy, and the cost of postage. Weekly lists of decisions and planning applications must also be published and displayed by the planning authority on a similar basis.

6.6.3 Persons and bodies to be notified of planning applications

The planning authority are also required to notify certain bodies of planning applications received by them, depending on the nature and effects of the application received. These bodies are listed under article 32(1) – the Arts Council, Bord Failte, An Taisce, the Commissioners of Public Works, any relevant local authority (where any existing or proposed development of that authority would be obstructed or reduced in value or where an issue as to a financial contribution for services by the local authority under section 26(7) of the 1963 Act is raised), the National Authority for Occupational Safety and Health, Irish Aviation Authority, the National Roads Authority, and the Environmental Protection Agency (where an integrated pollution control (IPC) licence is required). Certain additional bodies must be notified of the receipt of an EIS.[101]

The planning authority is obliged to notify the Minister of any planning application with which an Environmental Impact Statement has been submitted, or where the planning authority intend to require the submission of an Environmental Impact Statement if the proposed development is likely to have significant effects on the environment in another member state of the European Community.[102] This notice gives brief details of the application and, in particular, should indicate whether the development relates to an activity for which an IPC licence is required. The planning authority are also obliged to furnish the Minister with a copy of any Environmental Impact Statement received in connection with a planning application for which the notice was served. The Minister may require the planning authority to furnish particulars, information or documents concerning the application if he considers that the development is likely to have significant effects on the environment in another member state of the European Community.

6.6.4 Requests for further information by planning authority

The planning authority are entitled to request further information concerning a planning application. Article 33(1) provides as follows:

---

[101]   1994 Regulations, art. 32(4).
[102]   *ibid.*, art. 31.

"33 (1) Where a planning authority receives a planning application, they may, by notice in writing, require the applicant —

(a) to submit any further information (including any plans, maps or drawings or any information as to any estate or interest in or right over land) which they consider necessary to enable them to deal with the application,

(b) to produce any evidence which they may reasonably require to verify any particulars or information given in or in relation to the application.

(2) A planning authority shall not require an applicant who has complied with a requirement under sub-article (1) to submit any further information, particulars or evidence save as may be reasonably necessary to clarify the matters dealt with in the applicant's response to the said requirement or to enable them to be considered or assessed. (2A) Where further information is received by a planning authority pursuant to a requirement under sub-article (1) or (2) and the planning authority consider that such information contains significant additional data in relation to the effects on the environment of the development to which the planning application was given in accordance with article 32.[102]

(3) Where there is a failure or refusal to comply with a requirement under any of the foregoing sub-articles within one month of such requirement, the planning authority may, if they think fit, determine the application in the absence of the information or evidence specified in the requirements."[103]

A request for further information has the effect of extending "the appropriate period" for the making of a decision on an application by a further two months from the date of receipt of the information required. It has been held that a request for additional copies of plans does not constitute a request for "further information" so as to extend this period.[104] Article 33(2) also makes clear that a planning authority is not entitled to require an applicant who has complied with a requirement under sub-article (1) to submit any further information, particulars or evidence unless this is necessary to clarify the matters dealt with in the applicant's response or to enable them to be considered or assessed. Where an applicant fails or refuses to comply with any requirement under article 33 or with any reasonable request to clarify the matters dealt with within one month of the requirement being made, the planning authority may determine the application in the absence of the information or evidence sought. An Bord Pleanála also has power to declare that an application is to be regarded as having been withdrawn.[105]

---

[102] 1994 Regulations, art. 33(2A) as inserted by Local Government (Planning and Development) Regulations 1995, art. 6.

[103] The words "any of the foregoing sub-articles" substituted for "sub-articles (1) or (2)" by 1995 Regulations, art. 6(b)

[104] *Herringdale Developments Ltd v. Naas U.D.C.*, unreported, High Court, Finlay P., November 17, 1977, referred to in Walsh, *op.cit.*, p.40.

[105] See 1992 Act, s.16.

6.6.5 Modifications to proposed development

Article 35 enables a planning authority to invite an applicant to submit modifications to proposed development where they are disposed to granting a permission or approval. It may request the applicant to submit revised plans or other drawings or particulars indicating the nature of the modification, and may decide to grant a permission or an approval on the basis of such plans, drawings or particulars.

This provision would appear to enable an applicant to test a number of different possible modifications. Where the revised plans indicate an alteration as distinct from a modification of the original proposals, a decision to grant permission for such alterations may be invalid on the grounds that the public have been excluded from making representations concerning the altered proposal.[106] Inviting a modification of plans does not "stop the clock" in the same way as a request for further information and in practice the planning authority will usually seek the consent of the applicant to extending the time for the consideration of the application.[107]

6.6.6 Further notice of application

The publication of a further newspaper notice may be required by the planning authority under article 17(2) in the following circumstances:

 (a) if the newspaper in which it has been published does not have a sufficiently large circulation in the district in which the land or structure to which the planning application relates is situate, or

 (b) does not state whether the application is for a permission, an outline permission or an approval, or

 (c) if the notice does not state the location of the land or the address of the structure to which the application relates (as may be appropriate), or

 (d) if the original notice is misleading or inadequate for the information of the public, whether because of its content or for any other reason, or

 (e) where a period of more than two weeks has elapsed between the publication of the original notice and the making of the planning application.

A further newspaper notice will also be required if the planning authority requests the submission of an EIS after the application is lodged.[108]

The planning authority may require a fresh site notice where the original notice has not been published in the manner prescribed in article 16, or where the notice is misleading or inadequate. A further site notice may also be required where the

---

[106] See *State (Abenglen Properties Ltd) v. Dublin Corporation* [1984] I.R. 381. See also para. 8.2.3.1, below.

[107] See para. 8.4, below.

[108] See para. 6.2.3, above.

original notice has not been maintained in position for a period of one month after the making of the planning application or where it has been defaced or become illegible and has not been renewed or replaced. In the case of both newspaper notices and site notices, the applicant is obliged to republish the notice in the manner and in the terms prescribed by the planning authority and will usually be required to submit evidence of compliance to the planning authority.[109]

A planning authority may also require an applicant to give such further notice as they may specify where plans, drawings or other particulars are submitted to the planning authority by an applicant in response to an invitation by the planning authority to submit modifications of the proposed development. This power may also be exercised where further information is received from an applicant more than three months after a request for further information is made by a planning authority.

6.6.7 Planning file

Any person may inspect the planning file for a particular planning application at the office of the planning authority during office hours. Each application has an individual file which is cross-referenced according to the planning register reference number to location maps which are also available for inspection. A number of different reference numbers may exist for the same site, depending on the number of applications which have been made, and often the planning authority will maintain separate maps for different periods of years.

Significant improvements were made in the access to documentation received by the planning authority in the context of a planning application under the 1992 Act. The inclusion of the technical reports of the planning authorities on the planning file enables an interested person to ascertain the rationale behind a particular decision. In certain cases, the technical reports may indicate the dis- sension of a particular division of the planning authority, *e.g.* roads, from the decision ultimately made. This information may be of considerable benefit in the preparation of an appeal against the decision of the planning authority. The planning authority are initially required under article 36 to make the following documentation available for inspection by members of the public during office hours at the offices of the authority from "as soon as may be" from receipt of the document until the application is withdrawn or the decision of the authority on the application is given:

> (a) a copy of the planning application and of any drawings, maps, parti- culars, evidence, environmental impact statement, other written study

---

[109] There may be difficulties in practice with the application of the requirements for site notices. The regulations do not explain, for example, during what period a site notice must be displayed if it is removed or becomes defaced within the period of one month after the making of the planning application. (see further McCrossan, (1994) IPELJ 117).

or further information received or obtained by the planning authority from the applicant in accordance with the regulations;

(b) any submissions or observations in writing on the planning application which are received by the planning authority;

(c) a copy of any report prepared by or on behalf of the planning authority on the planning application, *e.g.* the planning or traffic engineer reports;

(d) a copy of the decision of the planning authority and a copy of the notification of the decision given to the applicant.

These documents should remain available for inspection for a period of one month from the date that the planning authority gives its decision or, where there are one or more appeals until each of the appeals is withdrawn, determined or dismissed or, in the case of an appeal against the condition or conditions only, until a direction is given to the planning authority by the Board. The planning authority are also required to furnish the same documentation to the Board within 14 days of a copy of an appeal being sent to them by the Board. Copies of any appeal lodged are made available for public inspection at the offices of the planning authority, although there is no express statutory requirement for the authority to do so.

Copies of any EIS or extracts from such statement may be purchased during office hours at the offices of the planning authority for a reasonable fee. Unfortunately, there are no statutory provisions empowering the planning authority to furnish copies of any of the other documentation on the planning file and it is the practice of the majority of planning authorities not to provide copies to ordinary members of the public. Indeed, the facilities afforded for public inspection generally are totally inadequate and undermine public participation in the planning process.

In the event of a grant of permission or approval by the planning authority or An Bord Pleanála, the documents referred to must be made available for public inspection during the "life" of the permission (including any additional period for which the duration of the permission is extended), or in the case of temporary permissions or permissions which are subject to conditions of the type described in section 26(2)(j) or 27(2)(f) of the 1963 Act, for a period of five years from the date of grant.[110]

6.6.8 Submissions or observations on planning applications

Prior to the introduction of the 1994 Regulations, the right of members of the public to object to a proposed development at the application stage was derived by implication from a requirement of the regulations that any person or body who had submitted submissions or observations in writing to the planning to be notified of the decision of the planning authority. The 1994 Regulations confer an

---

[110] 1994 Regulations, art. 36(2)(a). As to the availability for inspection of documents relating to an appeal or reference at the offices of the Board, see para. 9.2.5, below.

express right. Article 34 provides that any person or body may make submissions or observations in writing to a planning authority on a particular planning application. Submissions or observations should not be made concerning the risk of environmental pollution from any activity to which the proposed development relates where the activity is also subject to the licensing procedure of the Environmental Protection Agency.

6.6.9 Minimum period for determination of planning applications

Article 39 prohibits the planning authority is prohibited from making a decision on an application for which no EIS is required before the expiration of a period of 14 days from the receipt of the application or, where the applicant has been required to publish a further notice of the application, from the date on which that notice was published. The purpose of this provision is to afford interested members of the public an opportunity to make an observation on the application. This minimum period is extended to 28 days where an EIS is submitted with the application, running from the date on which the application is received or, where the planning require the submission of a fresh notice, from the date on which such notice is given. In the event that an EIS is requested by the planning authority after the application has been submitted, the 28 day period runs from the date of receipt of the EIS or, where the planning authority require a further notice, from the date that the notice is given.

6.6.10 Withdrawal of planning application

A planning application may be withdrawn, by notice in writing, at any time before the giving of the decision of the planning authority.[111] An Bord Pleanála also has power to declare that an application is to be regarded as having been withdrawn.[112]

6.7 NOTIFICATION OF DECISIONS

6.7.1 Weekly list of planning decisions

A list of decisions given by the planning authority during the preceding week should be made available in a similar manner to the weekly lists of applications and proposed determinations, referred to at para. 6.5.2, above.[113]

---

[111]   1994 Regulations, art. 40.
[112]   See 1992 Act, s.16.
[113]   Art. 42.

6.7.2 Persons or bodies to be notified of decision on planning application

The planning authority has a duty to notify a number of persons and bodies specified under article 32 of their decision on an application.[114] They are also obliged to notify any person or body who has made submissions or observations in writing to the planning authority unless the planning authority have published its weekly list of decisions in a newspaper circulating in the area of the proposed development.[115] Such notification must be given within three working days of the giving of the decision. The planning authority are also obliged to publish notice of any decision on an application for which an EIS was submitted in a newspaper circulating in the area in which the proposed development is located, unless they have published a weekly list in the newspaper referring to that decision. The planning authority may choose to publish a newspaper notice concerning their decision on any planning application in connection with which an EIS was not submitted. Finally, where the Minister has been notified of a decision concerning a proposed development which is likely to have significant effects on the environment of member states of the European Communities, the planning authority must send a notice of the decision to him within three working days of giving their decision.

6.7.3 Form of notification of decision

The planning authority do not have to inform persons or bodies other than the applicant of the details of their decision. Article 41 provides for the form of notification of the decision to the applicant.

The notice must contain certain minimum information concerning the application, including reference to the fact, where appropriate, that the proposed development relates to an activity which is licensable under the Environmental Protection Agency Act 1992.

---

[114] See para. 6.6.3, above.
[115] 1994 Regulations, art 43. See also *Nolan v. Dublin Corporation* (JR No. 124, 1989) referred to in O'Sullivan and Shepherd at 4.101.

Chapter 7

ENVIRONMENTAL IMPACT ASSESSMENT

In February 1990 environmental impact assessment (EIA) was introduced into Ireland as a legal requirement for certain types of development which affect the environment to a significant extent. The European Community (Environmental Impact Assessment) Regulations 1989 together with the Local Government (Planning and Development) Regulations 1990 provided for the incorporation of EIA into the system of development control. Both measures were necessitated by Council Directive 85/337/EEC on the assessment of the effects of certain public and private projects on the environment.[1] A previous attempt to implement the directive by way of ministerial directive was declared ineffective by the High Court in July 1988 in a case taken against An Bord Pleanála by four farmers objecting to the proposed Merell Dow Pharamaceutical Plant in Killeagh, County Cork.[2] The 1990 regulations have since been repealed by the Local Government (Planning and Development) Regulations 1994, which provide for the incorporation of EIA into the planning application and appeals procedures.[3] The requirement of EIA places an additional burden on the developer, but where it is introduced at an appropriate stage of project development, it may be a useful and ultimately cost-saving instrument in the planning negotiation process.

7.1.1 Definition of terms

Environmental assessment is the term used in the Directive, but as implemented in Ireland this has become "environmental impact assessment" (EIA) which has been defined as:

" a process for anticipating the effects on the environment caused by a development."[4]

---

[1]   [1985] O.J. L175/40.
[2]   *Browne v. An Bord Pleanala* [1989] I.L.R.M. 865.
[3]   EIA is also relevant to a number of other consent procedures apart from planning control under various acts: the Foreshore Acts 1933–92 (foreshore leases and licences), Arterial Drainage Act (drainage schemes), Fisheries (Consolidation) Act 1959 (salmonid breeding), Petroleum and Other Minerals Development Act 1960 (petroleum leases), Gas Act 1976 (gas pipelines), Environmental Protection Agency Act 1992 (integrated pollution control licences) and the Roads Act 1993 (motorways, busways and other road development). See further Scannell, *Environmental and Planning Law* (1995) pp.304–308
[4]   *Environmental Protection Agency, Draft Guidelines on the Information to be Contained in Environmental Impact Statements* (1995), p.11.

The aim of the Directive is "prevention at source" and to this end assessment must take place before development consents are granted. The implementing regulations therefore require that applications for such consents be accompanied by an EIS, which provides the information on the basis of which the assessment is made. It is defined as:

> "a statement of the effects, if any, which the proposed development, if carried out, would have on the environment."[5]

It involves:

> "a systematic analysis of the proposed development in relation to the existing environment, at a stage in the design process where changes can still be made to avoid adverse impacts."[6]

7.1.2 The 1985 Directive

The main aim of the Directive is the prevention of pollution at source, a principle which has become a cornerstone of E.U. environmental policy. The Preamble to the Directive refers to "the need to take effects on the environment into account at the earliest possible stage in all the planning and decision-making processes." However, the EIA process envisaged by the Directive is essentially concerned with the communication of information: it is not a "green" procedure in so far as it does not predicate a good decision in environmental terms.[7]

Under the directive, EIA is mandatory for projects listed under Annex I. Projects under Annex II may be subject to EIA "where member states consider that their characteristics so require". Member states may specify certain types of Annex II projects as being subject to assessment or may establish criteria and/or thresholds for the determination as to which projects of the classes listed in Annex II are to be subject to EIA. A large number of Annex II projects are included in the First Schedule to the 1989 Regulations which lists the classes of development for which EIA is mandatory.[8]

---

[5] E.C. (Environmental Impact Assessment) Regulations 1989, art. 5; 1994 Regulations, art. 3.

[6] *Environmental Protection Agency, Draft Guidelines*, see p.11.

[7] Ironically, as implemented under the planning code, the EIA procedure as it applies to local authority development is not neutral in that it requires that the Minister certify that the proposed development will not have significant adverse effects or that it will embody the best practicable means to prevent or limit such effects. On the other hand, the procedure as applied to private sector development is not guaranteed to provide a "green,' solution to the environmental problems posed by the proposed development. A planning authority can grant permission for a project which will have very serious environmental effects, which have not been mitigated in its design, on the grounds that it will bring great economic benefits to an area. See Scannell and Stevenson, "Environmental Impact Assessment: New European Obligations", (1986) 4 *Irish Journal of Environmental Science* 22.

[8] See Pt. II thereof. The Economic and Social Committee (ESC) has issued its opinion on the proposal for a directive to amend the 1985 Directive which would, *inter alia*, extend the projects to which EIA applies. See [1992] O.J. C-196/1 (ESC Opinion) and [1994] O.J. C-130/8 (proposed directive) and (1994) IPELJ 90 and (1995) IPELJ 80.

Article 1.4 provides that projects serving national defence purposes are not covered by the Directive. Neither does the Directive apply to projects the details of which are adopted by a specific act of national legislation.[9] Member States may also, in exceptional circumstances, exempt a specific project in whole or in part from EIA requirements.[10]

The Regulations follows the pattern of the directive which sets out the minimum information requirements at Article 5.2 and, in Annex III, the information which member states "may consider relevant to a given stage of the consent procedure". It is intended by the directive that developers would only be required to supply the information contained in Annex III to the standards of current knowledge and methods of assessment.[11] In addition, there is an exclusion envisaged for confidential information. The competent authorities are entitled to have regard to "limitations imposed by national regulations and administrative provisions and accepted legal practices with respect to industrial and commercial secrecy and safeguarding of the public interest".[12]

Article 6 of the Directive leaves it open to Member States to "determine the manner in which the public is consulted". Article 6(2) requires that the public be "given an opportunity to express an opinion before the project is initiated". There is therefore no positive requirement under Irish or E.U. law that the public be consulted at the scoping stage or at any other time prior to the publication of the EIS. "Good practice" would nonetheless seem to require such consultation.

The directive is of importance because of the doctrine of direct effect and the canon of interpretation under European Union law, accepted by the Irish courts, that implementing legislation must be interpreted purposively so as to give effect to the directive where the words used by the legislation are ambiguous.[13] The doctrine of direct effect received a body-blow in the case of *Browne v. An Bord Pleanála*, where Barron J. held that An Bord Pleanála was not an "emanation of state", responsible for the implementation of the directive as an "emanation" or "arm" of state with the consequence that individual citizens were not entitled to rely on the provisions of the Directive as establishing rights enforceable against the Board.[14] This decision has been put in doubt by the Court of Appeal in England in *Foster v. British Gas*,[15] and the subsequent decision of the European Court in the same case.[16] The question is whether the provisions of the directive are unconditional and sufficiently clear and precise to confer rights on individuals. It is submitted that the provisions of the EIA Directive have direct effect to the extent that they relate to projects for which EIA is

---

9   Art. 1.5.
10   Art. 2.3.
11   1985 Directive, Art. 5.1.
12   *ibid.*, Art. 10.
13   *Murphy v. An Bord Telecom* (1988) I.L.R.M. 53.
14   See above, n.2. See Scannell, "EIA: Browne v. An Bord Pleanála" (1990) 2 J.P.E.L. 209.
15   (1988) 2 C.M.L.R. 697.
16   Case 188/89; see also, *Fratelli Constanzo v. Commune Di Milano*, Case 103/88.

mandatory, *i.e.* projects under Annex I, but not where member states have a discretion to impose EIA requirements, *i.e.* in the case of projects under Annex II.

7.1.3 Projects subject to EIS requirement

An environmental impact statement must be submitted with a planning application for permission for any development which is "specified development" under Article 24 of the 1989 Regulations.[17] The 1994 Regulations have extended the requirement for an EIS to proposals which would constitute "specified development" but for the fact that they fall short of the thresholds under the First Schedule to the 1989 Regulations in cases where the development involves an activity for which an IPC licence under the Environmental Protection Agency Act 1992 is required.[18] The categories of exempted development under article 9 of the 1994 Regulations do not apply in either of these situations where the obligation to submit an EIS applies at the initial operation stage.

In addition, planning authorities must require an EIS to be submitted where the development proposed would have been specified development were it not for the fact that it falls short of the threshold laid down for that type of development, if the authority is of the opinion that the development "would be likely to have significant effects on the environment".[19] The Board may also request an EIS where the planning authority has not requested one, if it considers that the development proposed is likely to have significant effects on the environment. If an applicant decides himself to submit an EIS for a development which falls short of the threshold indicated but would otherwise amount to "specified development", the planning authority are obliged to deal with the application as if the EIS had been submitted in accordance with Article 24(1).[20]

It has been established that where an EIS is required under the 1989 regulations, compliance with this requirement is a pre-condition to the exercise of the jurisdiction of the planning authority and An Bord Pleanála under section 26 of the Local Government (Planning and Development) Act 1963 to decide on a planning application. Failure to comply can result in the grant of permission being set aside in judicial review proceedings. In *Shannon Regional Fisheries Board v. An Bord Pleanála*[21] the applicant sought an order of certiorari quashing

---

[17] Art. 24 provides that all types of development listed under Sched. 1, Pts. 1 and II are specified for the purposes of the regulations. Sched. 1 is set out in full at pp.179–185, below.

[18] 1994 Regulations, art. 24(10)(b). See the inspector's report on the Masonite planning appeal. Where the proposed development concerns an activity for which an integrated pollution control (IPC) licence is also required, the planning authority are prohibited from taking into account matters relating to the risk of environmental pollution from the activity. These matters are taken into consideration by the Environmental Protection Agency in the context of an application for an IPC licence.

[19] The notice of such a requirement will cease to have effect where an exemption is granted by the Minister from the date of the receipt by the planning authority of notice of the grant of the exemption.

[20] 1994 Regulations, art. 27(1).

[21] Unreported, High Court, Barr J., November 17, 1994.

the decision of An Bord Pleanála to grant permission for a large piggery at Kilnaleck, Co. Cavan, which is in the Lough Sheelin catchment area. The permission was granted in the absence of an EIS, and the applicant, who had already obtained leave to apply for judicial review, claimed that An Bord Pleanála had no jurisdiction to determine the appeal in the absence of an EIS which was required under Article 24.

Paragraph 1(e) of Part II of the First Schedule to the 1989 Regulations refers to:

> "Pig-rearing installations where the capacity would exceed 1,000 units on gley soil or 3,000 units on other soils and where units have the following equivalent:
> 1 pig = 1 unit,
> 1 sow = 10 units."

The planning application was for the retention of a pig unit incorporating not more than 400 gilts and 20 boars. It was contended on behalf of An Bord Pleanála that a gilt is a female pig which does not become a sow until she has proved herself by having her first litter. On the basis of that definition, the development did not exceed the scale for which an EIS is required since the number of units permissible on foot of the permission would be less than 1,000.[22]

The Board also argued that the court ought not to interfere with the adoption of the former definition by the planning authority unless it was satisfied that it was wholly irrational.

Barr J. rejected this latter submission, holding that it was a matter for the court to interpret the regulation in view of the fact that the meaning of "sow" was not free from doubt. Adopting a purposive approach to the interpretation of the regulation, he stated:

> "The regulation recognises and deals with this situation by providing a formula for measuring the size and scale of production of a piggery by allocating points per animal based on maximum occupancy and differentiating between sows on the one hand, which are allocated 10 units, and all other pigs, which are allocated one unit each. The logic of this formula is perfectly clear. Pregnant pigs, all of which have a potential for generating through their expected offspring a substantially greater amount of slurry than single pigs, are allocated a greater number of units to reflect that situation. When one has regard to the object of the regulation as I have outlined, it follows that there is no practical distinction between a pregnant pig which is a gilt awaiting her first litter and a pregnant pig which already has had one or more litters . . . I have no doubt that under the regulation all pregnant pigs should be similarly assessed for the allocation of units and I would define a pregnant gilt as being a 'sow' in that context."

He granted the relief sought by the applicant, including an order of certiorari quashing the decision of An Bord Pleanála.[23]

---

[22] An 1886 definition which derived from the southwest Lincolnshire and Gloucestershire area and which was referred to in the *Oxford English Dictionary*, (2nd ed.) referred to a gilt as "a female pig, called by this name until it has had a second litter".

[23] The case also emphasises that it is the capacity of the structures for which permission is sought and not their intended use by the applicant which is the relevant criterion for determining

In *Max Developments Limited v. An Bord Pleanála*,[24] Flood J. had to consider whether the development proposed was a project of the type specified under paragraph 10(b) of Part II of the First Schedule to the 1989 Regulations, which refers to:

> "Urban development projects which would involve an area greater than 50 hectares in the case of projects for new or extended urban areas, and an area greater than 2 hectares within existing urban areas."

Flood J. held that it was within the jurisdiction of the Board to decide the mixed question of fact and law as to whether the proposed development was in "an existing urban area" or "a new and extended urban area". He decided that if the Board had erred in law in not requiring an EIS, it had erred within jurisdiction and, consequently, no substantial grounds existed on the basis of which leave could be granted.[25]

Max Developments was decided before the commencement of the 1994 Regulations. Article 56(1) of the 1994 Regulations now provides:

> "Where an appeal is against a decision of a planning authority on a planning application which relates to development which, in the opinion of the Board, is development –
>
> (a) of a class for the time being specified under Article 24 of the Environmental Impact Assessment Regulations (or under any provision amending or replacing the said Article 24), ...
>
> and an environmental impact statement was not submitted to the planning authority in respect of the planning application, the Board shall require the applicant to submit to the Board an environmental impact statement."

In *RGDATA v. An Bord Pleanála*,[26] Barron J. had to determine whether he should grant leave to the applicants to challenge the validity of a decision of the Board on a planning application for which, the applicants argued, an environmental impact statement (EIS) was required, but with which none had been submitted.

The notice parties, *Newbay Properties*, had been granted permission for a shopping centre development in Monaghan town which the applicants said was over 2 hectares in area and was situated within an urban area within the terms of paragraph 10(b) quoted above. The respondents did not deny that the proposed development was situate in an urban area. The grounds of appeal against the

---

whether the requirement of EIS is applicable. Nor would the imposition of a condition restricting the number of livestock or other units of production, it is suggested, cure an application which should have been accompanied by an EIS.

Practical problems may arise in determining the capacity of structures shown in plans accompanying a planning application but it can be presumed that the courts will not generally be willing to interfere with any factual determination of a planning authority or An Bord Pleanála.

24 [1994] 2 I.R. 121.
25 See also *RGDATA v. An Bord Pleanála*, unreported, Barron J. See commentary on case at (1996) IPELJ 99.
26 Unreported, High Court, April 30, 1996.

decision of the planning authority submitted by the applicant's pointed out that the area of the site had not been set out in any of the documentation furnished by *Newbay Properties*, but did not specifically allege that it was over two hectares. *Newbay Properties* were subsequently permitted to adduce evidence as to the area of the site which they maintained was less than 2 hectares. The applicants also submitted their measurement of the site which was slightly more than two hectares. The Board accepted the evidence as to area of *Newbay Properties* and granted permission. In a short judgment, Barron J. refused leave for judicial review, stating:

> "In the present case, the main question is whether the Respondent was entitled to act as a matter of opinion on the evidence as adduced on behalf of Newbay properties...
>
> In my view, there is no evidence of a substantial remediable error by the Respondent on either of the headings submitted. Neither submission constitutes a substantial ground. Accordingly, relief will be refused."

Whilst it is not explicit in his judgment, it would appear that Barron J. refused leave in this case because any error made by the Board (if such there was) was made within jurisdiction. Article 56(1) enables the Board to form an opinion as to whether an EIS is required and it would seem that such an opinion cannot be challenged unless it is an opinion which no reasonable planning appeals board could have held.[27]

The position may be different where a decision of the planning authority is challenged. If no EIS has been submitted with an application for which one is required, this non-compliance with permission regulations would appear to go to the jurisdiction of the planning authority to adjudicate on a planning application under section 26(1) of the 1963 Act. The "catch-22" is that if the planning authority's decision is challenged, an applicant may be met with the objection that the decision should first of all have been appealed to An Bord Pleanála, particularly in view of the Board's power to request an EIS under Article 56(1). It is submitted that the planning authority's decision should be subject to judicial review where the issue goes to its jurisdiction but the decisions as to whether the existence of an appeal acts as a bar to judicial review in such cases are not uniform.[28]

7.1.4 Exemptions from EIS requirement

The Minister may grant an exemption from the requirement for the submission of an EIS and, in such circumstances, may apply other requirements.[29] The applicant is only obliged to comply with these requirements in so far as they

---

[27] *O'Keeffe v. An Bord Pleanála* [1993] I.R. 39.

[28] See *Tennyson v. Dun Laoghaire Corporation* [1991] 2 I.R. 527, *Healy v. Dublin County Council*, unreported, High Court, Barron J., April 29, 1993.

[29] 1963 Act, s.25(3), as inserted by art.7 of the 1989 Regulations.

relate to matters other than the risk of environmental pollution. On the other hand, if no IPC licence will be required to carry out the proposed development, the applicant must comply with each of the requirements laid down by the Minister. In the event that the applicant does not comply with the requirements of the Minister, the planning authority are obliged to serve a notice on the applicant requiring compliance.[30]

7.1.5 Significant environmental effects

The decision as to whether a development is "likely to have significant effects" is one for the planning authority or the Board, as the case may be, and their decision cannot be set aside unless it is totally unreasonable.[31] It would appear that such a decision may not be set aside by the Courts unless it "flies in the face of fundamental reason and common sense".[32]

It is not clear how a planning authority decides that a development which does not reach the relevant thresholds would be likely to have significant effects on the environment thus meriting the making of an EIS.[33] There is a danger than planning authorities may take a minimalist view as to the circumstances in which an EIS should be required. Article 2 of the Directive refers to the "nature, size or location" of the project as the determinant, but the wording of the preamble also suggests that there is a presumption that EIA will be required for Annex II projects. The relevant portion reads as follows:

> "Whereas projects of other types may not have significant effects on the environment in every case and whereas these projects should be assessed where the member states consider that their characteristics so require."

It is also worth noting that the wording of the regulations makes it mandatory on the planning authority and the Board to request an EIS.

Since the concept of EIA derives from the U.S. National Environmental Protection Act 1969, it is possible that some of the tests for discovering whether a project has significant environmental effects will be applied here. In the case of *Hanly v. Kliendrenst*,[34] the degree of change from current land use and the absolute quantity of the impact were considered to be the major factors.[35]

---

[30] Art. 25(2) of the 1989 Regulations.

[31] See *R. v. Swale Borough Council, ex p. Royal Society for the Protection of Birds* [1991] J.P.L. 39.

[32] See *State (Keegan) v. Stardust Compensation Tribunal* [1986] I.R. 642; approved in *O'Keeffe*, above, n.27.

[33] It is advisable to approach the planning authority at an early stage in order to find out whether a request is likely to made and Simon Brown J. observed that a proposed development should not be considered in isolation if it is inevitably likely to form part of a larger development at the same location as otherwise the requirement of an EIS could be evaded by piecemeal development. But it should be borne in mind that the view expressed by the planning authority at this stage will not be binding.

[34] 417F. to d.283 (2nd. Cir. 1972).

[35] Cited in Scannell, above, n.3, *op. cit.*, p.296.

7.1.6 Content of environmental impact statements

An EIS must contain the information referred to in paragraph 2 of the Second Schedule to the 1989 Regulations and may include the information in paragraph 3 of that Schedule.[36] On receipt of an EIS, the planning authority must assess the compliance of the EIS with those information requirements, but where the proposed development relates to an activity for which an IPC licence is required, the planning authority must exclude from this assessment of compliance any matters relating to the risk of environmental pollution from the activity. Within these parameters, if an EIS is found to be inadequate, the planning authority are obliged to inform the applicant in writing and to require him to submit such further information or particulars as may be necessary to ensure compliance.

The Second Schedule provides as follows:

1. An Environmental Impact Statement shall contain the information specified in Paragraph 2 (referred to in this Schedule as "the specified information").
2. The specified information is:
   (a) a description of the development proposed, comprising information about the site and the design and size or scale of the development;
   (b) the data necessary to identify and assess the main effects which that development is likely to have on the environment;
   (c) a description of the likely significant effects, direct and indirect, on the environment of the development, explained by reference to its possible impact on –
   * Human Beings
   * Flora
   * Fauna
   * Soil
   * Water
   * Air
   * Climate
   * The Landscape
   The interaction between any of the foregoing:
   * Material Assets
   * The Cultural Heritage
   (d) where significant adverse effects are identified with respect to any of the foregoing, a description of the measures envisaged in order to avoid, reduce or remedy those effects; and
   (e) a summary in non-technical language of the information specified above.

---

[36] E.C. (Environmental Impact Assessment) Regulations, 1989, art. 25.

3. An environmental impact statement may include, by way of explanation or amplification of any specified information, further or any of the following matters –

   (a) the physical characteristics of the proposed development, and the land-use requirements during the construction and operational phases;

   (b) the main characteristics of the production processes proposed, including the nature and quantity of the materials to be used;

   (c) the estimated type and quantity of expected residues and emissions (including pollutants of surface water and ground water, air, soil and substrata, noise,vibration, light, heat and radiation) resulting from the proposed development when in operation;

   (d) (in outline) the main alternative (if any) studied by the applicant, appellant or authority and an indication of the main reasons for choosing the development proposed, taking into account the environmental effects;[37]

   (e) the likely significant direct and indirect effects on the environment of the development proposed which may result from –

   (i) the use of natural resources,

   (ii) the emission of pollutants, the creation of nuisances, and the elimination of waste;

   (f) the forecasting methods used to assess any effects on the environment about which information is given under sub-paragraph (e); and

   (g) any difficulties, such as technical deficiencies or lack of knowledge, encountered in compiling any specified information.

   In paragraph (e), "effects" includes secondary, cumulative, short, medium and long-term, permanent, temporary, positive and negative effects.

4. Where further information is included in an environmental impact statement pursuant to paragraph 3, a non-technical summary of that information shall also be provided.

Even this brief outline of the information to be included in an EIS indicates that a considerable degree of technical detail will often be required. Planning authorities regularly employ outside consultants to monitor and advise on the sufficiency of information contained in an EIS and to assess the impacts of the underlying project.

In certain situations, a study of alternatives is required by the 1989 Regulations. Although Article 25 of the Regulations provides that an EIS "may" also contain the information specified in Paragraph 3 of the Second Schedule

---

[37] Note that a study of alternatives is a mandatory requirement for an EIS in relation to proposed road development under the Roads Act 1993, s.51.

thereto (which refers to '(d) (in outline the main alternatives (if any) studied by the applicant, appellant or authority and an indication of the main reasons for choosing the development proposed, taking into account the environmental effects'), Article 25 must be interpreted in a manner which is consonant with the provisions of the 1985 Directive to which it was designed to give effect.

Article 5 of the Directive requires in mandatory terms:

> ". . . Member States *shall* (emphasis added) adopt the necessary measures to ensure that the developer supplies in an appropriate form the information specified in Annex III inasmuch as:
>
> > (a) The Member States consider that the information is relevant to a given stage of the consent procedure and to the specific characteristics of a particular project or type of project and of the environmental features likely to be affected: . . . "

Included in the information specified in Annex III is:

> "2. – Where appropriate, an outline of the main alternatives studied by the developer and an indication of the main reasons for his choice, taking into account the environmental effects."

In *Browne v. An Bord Pleanála*,[38] Barron J. held that "it was solely for the authority to determine upon the sufficiency of an environmental impact study". It is nonetheless conceivable that a decision of the planning authority or the Board could be set aside by the courts where minimum informational requirements were not adhered to by the applicant.[39]

7.1.7 EPA draft guidelines

Section 72 of the Environmental Protection Agency Act 1992 provided for the preparation by the Agency, in consultation with the appropriate Minister, of guidelines on the information to be contained in EISs. Developers as well as planning authorities will be obliged have regard to these guidelines. The guidelines have been published in draft form to allow a gestation period within which amendments may be made in response to comment from practitioners involved in this growth area. It may also be necessary to make further changes to the current document when a proposed new E.U. Directive on environmental assessment in the member states is adopted.[40] The document itself indicates June 1997 as the approximate date for the implementation of the guidelines in final form.

While the current document has no legal status, there is no doubt that it will be employed by planning authorities and other agencies involved in environmental decision-making in the evaluation of EISs for project permits and licences.

---

[38]   [1991] 2 I.R. 209.
[39]   See 1963 Act, s.26. See *Rehabilitation Institute v. An Bord Pleanála*, unreported, High Court, July 29, 1991, referred to in Scannell, *op. cit.*, p.291.
[40]   See n.8, above.

7.1.8 EIA in the determination of planning applications

In considering an application for permission, the planning authority and An Bord Pleanála must have regard to any environmental impact assessment submitted by the applicant, any supplementary information which was requested and any observations on the EIS made by third parties.[41] Where other Member States of the European Union have expressed views as to the effects of the proposed development on the environment, these must also be taken into account. As a "public authority" within the meaning of section 3 of the Environmental Protection Agency Act, the Board is obliged to take into account any environmental quality objectives published by the Agency provided that the proposed development is not related to an activity which will require an integrated pollution control (IPC) licence.[42] However, neither the planning authority nor the Board are entitled to have regard to matters concerning the risk of environmental pollution posed by a development which will require an IPC licence before the activity to which it relates can commence.'[43]

7.2 DEVELOPMENT BY LOCAL AUTHORITIES

An EIS must be prepared by or on behalf of a local authority for any development to which Part IX of the 1994 Regulations applies and which is "specified development" under Article 24 of the 1989 Regulations.[44] Local authority development outside its own functional area (which, apart from road development, is generally not exempted) is subject to the same EIA procedure as applies to the private sector. The categories of exempted develoment under Article 9 of the 1994 Regulations do not apply in either of these situations where the obligation to submit an EIS with a planning application arises at the initial stage.[45] In addition, the Minister must request an EIS to be submitted where the development proposed would have been specified development were it not for the fact that it falls short of the threshold laid down for that type of development under the First Schedule to the 1989 Regulations, if the Minister is of the opinion that the development would be likely to have significant effects on the environment".[46]

Part IX does not apply to development outside the area of the local authority as this will generally require planning permission. However, any works required for the construction of a new road or the improvement of a road which is not a

---

[41] 1963 Act, s.26(1)(A), (inserted by the E.C. (Environmental Impact Assessment) Regulations, 1989, art. 8); 1963 Act, s.26(5), as substituted by 1992 Act, s.3(a). Note that s.26(5A) was also repealed by 1992 Act, s.22.

[42] See EPA Act 1992, s.75.

[43] Section 26(1A)(b). See also Environmental Protection Agency Act 1992, s.98, discussed at para. 8.1.4, below.

[44] See *O'Keeffe* above, n.27.

[45] Art. 24 provides that all types of development listed under Pts. I an II of Sched. 1 to the 1989 Regulations are "specified development" for which an EIS is mandatory.

[46] 1994 Regulations, art. 10(1)(c).

proposed road development within the meaning of the Roads Act 1993 will be subject to the procedure under Part IX.

The EIS must be made available for inspection and for purchase for a period of at least one month from the date of publication of a newspaper notice of the application.[47] The local auhority must apply to the Minister for certification, enclosing three copies of the EIS, "as soon as may be" after it has published the newspaper notice of the application and notified certain specified bodies.[48] Further information may be sought by the Minister as to the effects on the environment of the proposed development. The additional information received may necessitate the publication by the local authority of a fresh newspaper notice and further notification of the relevant bodies to which notice was given, where the Minister so requires.[49] There is provision for consultation with another E.U. Member State where the Minister considers that the proposed development would have significant effects on its environment or where that State is likely to be so affected and so requests.[50] The Minister is obliged to have regard to the EIS prepared by the local authority (including any additional information furnished at his request) and to any submissions made to him by interested persons or bodies, or member states which have been consulted.[51]

Development for which an EIS is required may not be undertaken unless the Minister has certified:

> (i)   that the proposed development (or the proposed development as varied or modified by him) will not, in his opinion have significant and adverse effects on the environment; or
>
> (ii) that it will embody the best practicable means to prevent or limit such effects.

7.2.1 Development by State authorities

Development by State authorities, *i.e.* a government minister or the Commissioners of Public Works, requires the preparation of an EIS for:

> –   specified development listed under the First Schedule to the European Communities (Environmental Impact Assessment) Regulations 1989, or

---

[47]   1994 Regulations, art. 117.

[48]   *ibid.*, art. 120. A notice must be sent to the following bodies where certain of their interests are affected: the Arts Council, Bord Failte, An Taisce, the Commissioners of Public Works, the National Monuments Advisory Council, other local authorities whose functional areas would be affected, the Irish Aviation Authority, the appropriate Regional Fisheries Board or Health Board, or Shannon Free Airport Development Company Limited.

[49]   1994 Regulations, art. 124.

[50]   *ibid.*, art. 125.

[51]   *ibid.*, art. 126.

– development which is of the same type but falls short of the threshold for that category under the Schedule, and in respect of which the state authority considers that it would be likely to have significant effects on the environment.[52]

The EIA procedure for development by State authorities which requires permission is identical to that for private sector development generally. Where a proposed development by a state authority is exempted from the requirement to obtain planning permission, the state authority must have regard to the EIS and to any submissions made in relation to the EIS by members of the public, or, where provided for, submissions made by Member States, before it undertakes any development.[53] Curiously, a state authority may, all be it in "exceptional circumstances" and after consultation with the Minister for the Environment, exempt itself from the requirement of an EIS and apply other requirements in its place.[54]

7.2.2 First Schedule, Part 1: Development for the purposes of these Regulations

1.–A crude-oil refinery (excluding an undertaking manufacturing only lubricants from crude oil) or an instalation for the gasification and liquefaction of 500 tonnes or more of coal or bituminous shale per day.

2.–A thermal power station or other combustion installation with a heat output of 300 megawatts or more, or a nuclear power station or other nuclear reactor (except a research installation for the production and conversion of fissionable and fertile materials, whose maximum power does not exceed 1 kilowatt continuous thermal load).

3.–An installation designed solely for the permanent storage or final disposal of radioactive waste.

4.–An integrated works for the initial melting of cast-iron and steel.

5.–An installation for the extraction of asbestos or for the processing and transformation of asbestos or products containing asbestos:-

(a) where the installation produces asbestos-cement products, with an annual production of more than 20,000 tonnes of finished products; or

(b) where the installation produces friction material, with an annual production of more than 50 tonnes of finished products; or

(c) in other cases, where the installation would utilise more than 200 tonnes of asbestos per year.

6.–An integrated chemical installation.

---

52   E.C. (Environmental Impact Assessment) Regulations 1989, art. 23.
53   Exemptions for State authorities are considered under Chap. 5 at paras. 5.3 and 5.5.11. Provision was also made for the making of regulations by the Minister concerning environmental impact assessment of exempted development to be carried out by State authorities, but no such regulations have yet been made. See Local Government (Planning and Development) Act 1993, s.2(1)(b).
54   Above, n.52, art. 23(2).

7.–A line for long-distance railway traffic, or an aerodrome with a basic runway length of 2,100 metres or more.

8.–A trading port, or an inland waterway which permits the passage of vessels of over 1,350 tonnes or a port for inland waterway traffic capable of handling such vessels.

9.–A waste disposal installation for the incineration or chemical treatment of hazardous waste, or the filling of land with such waste.

Part II: Agriculture

1.–*(a)* The use of uncultivated land or semi-natural areas for intensive agricultural purposes, where the area involved would be greater than 100 hectares.

(b) Water-management projects for agriculture, where the catchment area involved would be greater than 1000 hectares or where more than 50 hectares of wetlands would be affected.[55]

(c) (i) Initial afforestation, where the area involved, either on its own or taken together with any adjacent area planted by or on behalf of the applicant within the previous three years, would result in a total area planted exceeding 70 hectares and for the purposes of this sub-paragraph an area, other than an area planted before the 1st day of October, 1996, shall be deemed to be adjacent if its nearest point lies within 500 metres of any part of the area involved.[56]

   (ii) Land reclamation for the purposes of conversion to another type of land use, where the area involved would be greater than 100 hectares.

(d) Poultry-rearing installations, where the capacity would exceed 100,000 units and where units have the following equivalents:
   1 broiler = 1 unit
   1 layer, turkey or other fowl = 2 units.

(e) Pig-rearing installations, where the capacity would exceed 1000 units on gley soils or 3000 units on other soils and where units have the following equivalents:
   1 pig 1 unit
   1 sow 10 units.

(f) Seawater salmonid breeding installations with an output which would exceed 100 tonnes per annum; all salmonid breeding installations consisting of cage rearing in lakes; all salmonid breeding installations

---

55   See *Irish Wildbird Conservancy and the Commissioners of Public Works v. Clonakilty Golf and Country Club Ltd*, unreported, July 23, 1996 (under-appeal) in which Costello P. did not find it necessary to deal with the applicants' argument that the excavation of drains amounted to a "water management project".

56   Substituted E.C. (Environmental Impact Assessment) Regulations, 1996.

upstream of drinking water intakes; other freshwater salmonid breeding installations which would exceed 1 million smolts and with less than 1 cubic metre per second per 1 million smolts low flow diluting water.

(g) Reclamation of land from the sea, where the area of reclaimed land would be greater than 20 hectares.

Extractive Industry

2.–*(a)* Peat extraction which would involve a new or extended area of 50 hectares.

(b) All geothermal drilling and drilling for the storage of nuclear waste material; drilling for water supplies where the expected supply would exceed 5,000 cubic metres per day.

(c) All extractions of minerals within the meaning of the Minerals Development Acts, 1940 to 1979.

(d) Extraction of stone, gravel, sand or clay, where the area involved would be greater than 5 hectares.

(e) All extraction of petroleum (excluding natural gas). All onshore extraction of natural gas; offshore extraction of natural gas where the extraction would take place within 10 kilometres of the shoreline.

(g) All surface industrial installations for the extraction of coal, petroleum (excluding natural gas), natural gas, ores, or bituminous shale.

(h) All coke ovens (dry coal distillation).

(i) All installations for the manufacture of cement.

Energy industry

3.–*(a)* Industrial installations for the production of electricity, steam and hot water (other than installations comprehended by Part I of this Schedule) with a heat output of 300 megawatts or more.

(b) Industrial installations for carrying gas, steam and hot water with a potential heat output of 300 megawatts or more; transmission of electrical energy by overhead cables where the voltage would be 200 kV or more.

(c) Installations for surface storage of natural gas, where the storage capacity would exceed 200 tonnes.

(d) Installations for underground storage of combustible gases, where the storage capacity would exceed 200 tonnes.

(e) Installations for surface storage of fossil fuels, where the storage capacity would exceed 100,000 tonnes.

(f) Installations for industrial briquetting of coal and lignite, where the production capacity would exceed 150 tonnes per day.

(g) All installations for the production or enrichment of nuclear fuels.

(h) All installations for the reprocessing of irradiated nuclear fuels.

(i)   All installations for the collection and processing of radioactive waste (other than installations comprehended by Part I of this Schedule).

(j)   Installations for hydroelectric energy production with an output of 20 megawatts or more, or where the new or extended superficial area of water impounded would be 30 hectares or more, or where there would be a 30 per cent. change in the maximim, minimum or mean flows in the main river channel.

Processing of metals

4.–(*a*) Iron and steelworks, including foundries with a batch capacity of 5 tonnes or more, and forges, drawing plants and rolling mills where the production area would be greater than 500 square metres (other than installations comprehended by Part I of this Schedule).

(b)   Installations for the production (including smelting, refining, drawing and rolling) of non-ferrous metals excluding precious metals, where the melting capacity would exceed 0.5 tonnes or where the production area would be greater than 500 square metres.

(c)   Installations for pressing, drawing and stamping of large castings, where the production area would be greater than 500 square metres.

(d)   Installations for surface treatment and coating of metals, where the production area would be greater than 100 square metres.

(e)   Installations for boilermaking, manufacture of reservoirs, tanks and other sheet-metal containers, where the production area would be greater than 500 square metres.

(f)   All installations for manufacture and assembly of motor vehicles and manufacture of motor-vehicle engines.

(g)   Shipyards, where the area would be 5 hectares or more, or with capacity for vessels of 10,000 tonnes or more (deadweight).

(h)   All installations for the construction of aircraft with a seating capacity exceeding 10 passengers.

(i)   Manufacture of railway equipment, where the production area would be greater than 3000 square metres.

(j)   Swaging by explosives, where the floor area involved would be greater than 100 square metres.

(k)   All installations for the roasting and sintering of metallic ores.

Manufacture of glass

5.–Installations for the manufacture of glass, where the production capacity would exceed 5,000 tonnes per annum.

Chemical industry

6.–*(a)* All installations for treatment of intermediate products and production of chemicals (other than installations comprehended by Part I of this Schedule).
- *(b)* All installations for production of pesticides and pharmaceutical products, paint and varnishes, elastomers and peroxides.
- *(c)* (i) Storage facilities for petroleum, where the storage capacity would exceed 50,000 tonnes,
  - (ii) Storage facilities for petrochemical and chemical products, where such facilities are isolated storage to which the provisions of Regulations 12 to 18 of the European Communities (Major Accident Hazards of Certain Industrial Activities) Regulations, 1986 (Statutory Instrument Number 292 of 1986) apply.

Food industry

7.–*(a)* Installations for manufacture of vegetable and animal oils and fats, where the capacity for processing raw materials would exceed 40 tonnes per day.
- *(b)* Installations for packing and canning of animal and vegetable products, where the capacity for processing raw materials would exceed 100 tonnes per day.
- *(c)* Installations for manufacture of dairy products, where the processing capacity would exceed 50 million gallons of milk equivalent per annum.
- *(d)* All installations for commercial brewing and distilling; installations for malting, where the production capacity would exceed 100,000 tonnes per annum.
- *(e)* Installations for confectionary and syrup manufacture, where the production capacity would exceed 50,000 tonnes per annum. Installations for the slaughter of animals, where the daily capacity would exceed 1,500 units and where units have the following equivalents:
  1 sheep = 1 unit
  1 pig = 2 units
  1 head of cattle = 5 units.
- *(g)* All industrial starch manufacturing installations.
- *(h)* All fish-meal and fish-oil factories.
- *(i)* All sugar factories.

Textile, leather, wood and paper industries

8.–*(a)* All wool scouring, degreasing or bleaching factories.
- *(b)* All installations for manufacture of fibre board, particle board or plywood.
- *(c)* All installations for manufacture of pulp, paper or board.
- *(d)* Fibre-dyeing factories, where the dyeing capacity would exceed 1 tonne per day of fibre or yarn.

(e) Cellulose-producing and production installations, where the production capacity would exceed 10,000 tonnes per annum.

(f) Tannery, leather-dressing or fell-mongering factories, where the capacity would exceed 100 skins per day.

Rubber industry

9.–Installations for manufacture and treatment of elastomer-based products, where the production capacity would exceed 10,000 tonnes per annum.

Infrastructure projects

10.–*(a)* Industrial-estate development projects, where the area would exceed 15 hectares.

(b) Urban-development projects which would involve an area greater than 50 hectares in the case of projects for new or extended urban areas, and an area greater than 2 hectares within existing urban areas.

(c) Ski-lifts and cable-cars, where the length would exceed 500 metres.

(d) (i) Construction of a new road (other than a motorway comprehended by the European Communities (Environmental Impact Assessment) (Motorways) Regulations, 1988 (Statutory Instrument Number 221 of 1988)) of four or more lanes, or the realignment or widening of an existing road so as to provide four or more lanes, where such new, realigned or widened road would be eight kilometres or more in length in a rural area, or 500 metres or more in length in an urban area.

(ii) construction of a new bridge which would be 100 metres or more in length.

(iii) new or extended harbours (other than a trading port comprehended by Part I of this Schedule), where the area, or additional area, of water enclosed would be 20 hectares or more, or which would involve the reclamation of 5 hectares or more of land, or which would involve the construction of additional quays exceeding 500 metres in length.

(iv) all aerodromes (other than aerodromes comprehended by Part I of this Schedule) with paved runways exceeding 800 metres in length.

(e) Canalisation and flood-relief works, where the catchment area involved would be greater than 5000 hectares.

(f) Dams and other installations designed to hold water or to store it on a long-term basis, where the new or extended area of water impounded would be 30 hectares or more.

(g) All tramways, elevated and underground railways, suspended lines or similar lines of a particular type, used exclusively or mainly for passenger transport.

(h) Oil and gas pipelines exceeding 80 kilometres in length.

(i) Installation of overground aqueducts with a diameter of 1000 millimetres or more and a length of 500 metres or more.

(j) Sea water marinas where the number of berths would exceed 300 and fresh water marinas where the number of berths would exceed 100.

Other projects

11.–(a) Holiday villages involving more than 100 holiday homes, stationary caravans or trailers; hotel complexes having an area of 20 hectares or more or an accommodation capacity exceeding 400 beds.

(b) All permanent racing and test tracks for cars and motor cycles.

(c) Installations for the disposal of industrial and domestic waste with an annual intake greater than 25,000 tonnes (other than installations comprehended by Part I of this Schedule).

(d) Waste water treatment plants with a capacity greater than 10,000 population equivalent.

(e) Sludge-deposition sites where the expected annual deposition is 5,000 tonnes of sludge (wet).

(f) Storage of scrap iron, where the site area would be greater than 5 hectares.

(g) Test benches for engines, turbines or reactors, where the floor area would exceed 500 square metres.

(h) All installations for manufacture of artificial mineral fibres.

(i) All installations for manufacture, packing, loading or placing in cartridges of gunpowder and explosives.

(j) All knackers' yards in built-up areas.

12.–(a) All modifications of developments of a class mentioned in paragraph 3 or paragraph 9 of Part I of this Schedule; all modifications of nuclear power stations or other nuclear reactors (except research installations for the production and conversion of fissionable and fertile materials, whose maximum power does not exceed one kilowatt continuous thermal load).

(b) Modifications of developments of a class mentioned in paragraphs 1, 2 (other than nuclear installations), 4, 5 or 6 of Part I of this Schedule which would increase the productive capacity of the development concerned by 20 per cent. or more.

(c) (i) Any extension of the runways of an aerodrome of a class mentioned in paragraph 7 of Part I of this Schedule which would increase the runway length by 30 per cent. or more.

(ii) Any modification of a port, inland waterway or inland waterway port of a class mentioned in paragraph 8 of Part I of this Schedule which would increase its traffic handling capacity by 20 per cent. or more.

Chapter 8

DETERMINATION OF PLANNING APPLICATIONS

The determination of planning applications or "development control" is an important function of the planning authority as the quality of its decision making affects the quality of the built environment. This decision making function is generally exercised in line with the strategic policies expressed in the development plan and any special amenity area order for the area in question. In addition, planning authorities will normally apply development control standards relating to density, car space provision, site coverage, plot ratio, height restrictions and other design standards contained in the development plan. More recently, the role of government policy has become an increasingly important factor in influencing planning decisions.

8.1 THE DECISION-MAKING POWER

Section 26 of the Local Government (Planning and Development) Act 1963 is perhaps the most important provision in the planning code as it delimits the decision making powers of the planning authority and An Bord Pleanála. Both the planning authority and the Board have a duty to act judicially and may not "fetter" their discretion under section 26.[1] It can be seen also that compliance with the application procedure under Part IV of the 1994 Regulations is a precondition to the exercise of the planning authority's discretion to grant or refuse permission with or without conditions.[2] Section 26(1) provides:

"Where –

    (a) application is made to a planning authority in accordance with permission regulations for permission for the development of land or for an approval required for such regulations; and

    (b) any requirements relating to the application of or made under such regulations are complied with;

---

[1] See *Athlone Woollen Mills Co. Ltd v. Athlone UDC* [1950] I.R. 1; *Sharpe (P. & F.) Ltd v. Dublin City and County Manager and Dublin County Council* [1989] I.L.R.M. 565. The duty to act judicially is considered further below at para. 8.5.6, below as it applies to the elected members in the context of s.4 resolutions.

[2] This is discussed in Chap. 6, above. Note that the regulations governing EIS and the procedure for their submission form part of the permission regulations with which an application must comply.

the authority may decide to grant the permission or approval subject to or without conditions or to refuse it; and in dealing with any such application the planning authority shall be restricted to considering the proper planning and development of the area of the authority (including the preservation of the improvement of the amenities thereof), regard being had to the provisions of the development plan, the provisions of any special amenity area order in relation to the said area and the matters referred to in sub-section 2 of this section."

8.1.1 Relevant considerations

In determining a planning application, the planning authority is restricted to considering the proper planning and development of their functional area. It "has a duty to disregard any irrelevant or illegitimate factor that might be advanced".[3] In general, the planning authority is not entitled to take into account the personal circumstances of a particular applicant although this principle may not operate strictly in practice.[4] Nor is it entitled to take into account its liability to pay compensation to a developer as a consequence of a refusal of permission or the attachment of an onerous condition, even though the development plan purports to make it a relevant consideration.[5] It has been held also that the fact that the grant of planning permission may facilitate future breaches of the planning code is not a relevant consideration.[6]

Many of the planning considerations to be taken into account are the subject of specific conditions under section 26(2) and the authority is obliged to have regard to the matters to which these conditions refer. The planning authority is also obliged to "have regard" to the provisions of the development plan and any relevant special amenity area order (SAAO) but it has been held that it may not take into account the provisions of a draft plan.[7]

It has been held in the context of a similar provision to section 26 of the 1963 Act under English town and country planning legislation that to have regard to

---

3   *Sharpe (P&F) Ltd*, above, n.1.

4   Lord Scarman in *Great Portland Estates plc v. Westminster City Council* [1984] 3 All E.R. 744 observed that it "would be inhuman pedantry to exclude from the control of our environment the human factor". Development plans often allow for a relaxation of their policies against ribbon development and housing in rural areas on the basis of "need", which may in turn be equated with the personal circumstances of the particular applicant or members of his family.

5   *Grange Developments Ltd v. Dublin County Council* [1989] I.R. 296, 315; *Eighty Five Developments v. Dublin County Council*.

6   Unreported, High Court, Flood J., November 19, 1993. See the commentary in "Kelly v. An Bord Pleanála", (1994) IPELJ 96.

7   *Chawke Caravans Ltd v. Limerick County Council*, unreported, High Court, Flood J., February 1991: See 1963 Act, s.2(7). However, it appears that the planning authority is entitled to take into account the provisions of a 'development plan which has been adopted after a planning application has been submitted but before it has been adjudicated upon: *State (Abenglen Properties Ltd) v. Dublin Corporation* [1984] I.R. 383. It has been suggested that the decision in *Chawke* was *obiter*, and that the planning authority can have regard to the provisions of a draft plan where an issue as to material contravention of the plan does not arise. See further Scannell, *Environmental and Planning Law* (1995), p.195–96. See also para. 2.2.6, above.

the development plan does not connote "slavish adherence".[8] Greater weight has to be accorded to the development plan under the Irish planning code, as planning authorities are obliged to "take such steps as may be necessary for securing the objectives which are contained in the provisions of the development plan".[9] This general duty is applicable to the decision making function under section 26. Furthermore, the extent of the obligation to "have regard to" government policy under section 7(1) of the Local Government Act 1991 was considered by the High Court in *Glencar Explorations Plc. v. Mayo County Council*,[10] in which Blayney J. stated that the County Council could not be said to have had regard to government mining policy where it adopted as part of its development plan a policy which was diametrically opposed to that policy.

Public participation in the decision-making process is guaranteed by a number of provisions under the 1994 Regulations. The entitlement of any member of the public to make submissions in relation to a planning application, formerly derived by implication from the duty of the planning authority to notify objectors, is now expressly enshrined in the planning code.[11] Planning authorities are also obliged to consult with certain prescribed bodies depending on the nature and effects of the proposed development on the interests of the body concerned.[12]

Any environmental impact assessment which has been submitted by the applicant must also be considered by the authority together with any relevant submissions concerning it made by third parties.[13] Where other Member States of the European Union have expressed views as to the effects of the proposed development on the environment, these must also be taken into account. Information, advice or recommendations may be given to planning authorities by the Environmental Protection Agency to which they are obliged to have regard and they must also consider any environmental quality objectives published by the Agency under section 75 of the Environmental Protection Agency Act 1992. However, neither the planning authority nor the Board are entitled to have regard to matters concerning the risk of environmental pollution posed by a development which will require an integrated pollution control (IPC) licence before the activity to which it relates can commence.[14] Both the planning authority and An Bord Pleanála are required, where appropriate, to have regard to:

---

8   *Enfield London Borough Council v. Secretary of State for the Environment* [1975] J.P.L. 155; see Nowlan, p.42.
9   1963 Act, s.22.
10   [1993] 2 I.R. 237.
11   Art. 34. As to the former position, see *State (Stanford) v. Dun Laoghaire Corporation* [1981] I.L.R.M. 97 (recorded judgment).
12   See para. 6.6.3, above.
13   1963 Act, s.26(1)(A), inserted by the European Communities (Environmental Impact Assessment) Regulations, 1994, Art. 6. Note that both developer and planning authority must have regard to guidelines prepared by the Environmental Protection Agency on the information to be contained in an EIS: see EPA Act 1992, s.72(2). See para. 7.1.7, above.
14   s.26(1A)(b) and art. 34(2). See also Environmental Protection Agency Act 1992, s.98, discussed at para. 8.1.4, below.

    (a) the probable effect which a particular decision by it on the matter would have on any place which is not within, or on any area which is outside, the area of the relevant planning authority, and

    (b) any other consideration relating to development outside the area of that authority.

In evaluating any proposal, the planning authority or An Bord Pleanála are entitled to consider the common good, including any humanitarian purpose which it is claimed it will achieve.[15]

Planning authorities must also take into account any general policy directives on planning which have been issued by the Minister.[16] Only two such directives have been issued at the time of writing. Another relevant consideration is government policy, to which the planning authority are obliged to have regard.[17] Similarly, An Bord Pleanála is obliged to keep itself informed of the policies and objectives of the Minister for the Environment, planning authorities and any other "public authority" (including Government Ministers and the Commissioners of Public Works) referred to under section 5 of the 1976 Act or prescribed by regulation.[18] It has also been held that An Bord Pleanála are entitled to have regard to the fact that a particular scheme has its origin in an international agreement to which Ireland is a party.[19]

8.1.2 Permission for retention of structures and continuance of use

Permission may be obtained for the retention of unauthorised structures or for the continuance of an unauthorised use.[20] The provisions of Part IV of the Act apply in the same way as to the other permissions discussed and consequently the application procedure and the power of the planning authority and An Bord Pleanála to determine applications is identical. In particular, the planning authority and An Bord Pleanála are restricted to considering proper planning and development. It has been held that this means that the planning authority is not entitled to take into account the extent to which the development for which retention permission is sought deviates from a permission granted as this is "a matter which the statute has excluded from the range of its consideration".[21]

---

[15] See *Keane v. An Bord Pleanála and the Commissioners of Irish Lights*, unreported, High Court, Murphy J., June 20, 1995.

[16] 1982 Act, s.5.

[17] Local Government Act 1991, s.7. See *Glencar Explorations plc. v. Mayo County Council* case, above.

[18] The full list of "public authorities" is referred to below at para. 6.6.3. See also *State (Coras Iompar Éireann) v. An Bord Pleanála*, unreported, Supreme Court, December 12, 1984.

[19] See *Keane*, above n.15.

[20] 1963 Act, s.28(1). Where the structures were in existence prior to October 1, 1964, the governing provision is s.27 of the 1963 Act. Scannell, *op. cit.*, at p. 187, refers to a decision where it was held that retention permission cannot be obtained for the unauthorised demolition of buildings: *In the matter of a reference under s.82(3) of the Local Government (Planning and Development) Act 1963, and DGS Ltd and An Bord Pleanála*, unreported, High Court, April 10, 1992.

[21] *State (Fitzgerald) v. An Bord Pleanála* [1985] I.L.R.M. 117.

The permission operates to retrospectively validate the unauthorised structure or use from the date on which the structure was erected or the unauthorised use commenced.[22] Permission may be sought to permit the retention of a structure or the continuance of a use without having to comply with any condition subject to which permission for the structure or use was granted.[23]

8.1.3 Material contravention of the development plan

A planning authority may not grant planning permission in material contravention of the development plan unless the statutory procedure prescribed under section 26(3) is followed.[24] This involves the publication of a notice of intention to grant planning permission in a newspaper circulating in the area of the proposed development and the passing of a resolution by three-quarters of the elected members of the planning authority requiring that a decision to grant permission be made. Failure to adopt the material contravention procedure where it is required may result in the decision being declared invalid in subsequent judicial review proceedings.[25]

An Bord Pleanála, on the other hand, may, at its discretion, grant planning permission for development which would materially contravene the provisions of the development plan.[26] While the Board is obliged to have regard to the provisions of the development plan, it is not under any statutory duty to give effect to its objectives.

8.1.4 The interface between planning control and IPC licensing control

The respective roles of the planning authority and the Environmental Protection Agency (EPA) in the authorisation of development to which the requirement for integrated pollution control (IPC) licensing applies has been the cause of considerable controversy since the Environmental Protection Agency Act 1992 was first published as a bill. Planning authorities and An Bord Pleanála have traditionally been involved in environmental protection in their decision making which arose naturally from their land use and amenity planning functions. Pollution considerations are explicitly recognised as planning concerns in the non-compensatable reasons for refusal and conditions under the Local Government (Planning and Development) Act 1990.[27] Paragraph 7 of the Third Schedule relates to the refusal of permission where:

> "The proposed development would cause serious air pollution, water pollution, noise pollution or vibration or pollution connected with the disposal of waste."

Paragraphs 22 and 25 of the Fourth Schedule relate to non-compensatable conditions which are designed to prevent or reduce pollution:

---

[22] 1963 Act, s.28(2).
[23] *ibid.*, s.28(4).
[24] This procedure is considered in more detail below at para. 8.5.
[25] See *Tennyson v. Dun Laoghaire Corporation* [1991] 2 I.R. 527, discussed at para. 10.2.7, below.
[26] 1976 Act, s.14 (8).
[27] See also 1963 Act, s.26(2)(bb), inserted by s.39(c) of the 1976 Act.

"22. Any condition prohibiting, regulating or controlling the deposit or disposal of waste materials and refuse, the disposal of sewage and the pollution of rivers, lakes, ponds and gullies and the seashore.

. . .

25. Any condition relating to measures to reduce or prevent the emission or the intrusion of noise or vibration."

The Air Pollution Act 1987 made the licence for atmospheric emissions dominant by providing that any condition attached to a planning permission would cease to have effect when a licence under the Act was granted.[28] However, the Environmental Protection Agency Act 1992 was to create a much greater chasm between planning and environmental controls. Section 98 of the EPA Act 1992 effectively removes the jurisdiction of the planning authority and the Board in pollution matters where the development for which permission is sought relates to an activity for which a licence has been granted or will be required. Section 98(1) provides:

"Notwithstanding, section 26 of the Act of 1963, or any other provisions of the Local Government (Planning and Development) Acts 1963 to 1991, where a licence or revised licence under this Part has been granted or is or will be required in relation to an activity, a planning authority or An Bord Pleanála shall not, in respect of any development comprising or for the purposes of the activity–

(a) decide to refuse permission or an approval under Part IV of the Act of 1963 for the reason that the development would cause environmental pollution, or

(b) decide to grant such permission subject to conditions which are for the purposes of the prevention, limitation, elimination, abatement or reduction of environmental pollution from the activity,

and, accordingly–

(i) a planning authority in dealing with an application for a permission or for an approval for any such development shall not consider any matters relating to the risk of environmental pollution from the activity;

(ii) An Bord Pleanála shall not consider any appeal made to it against a decision of a planning authority in respect of such an application, or any submissions or observations made to it in relation to any such appeal, so far as the appeal, or the submissions or observations, as the case may be, relates or relate to the risk of environmental pollution from the activity."

The effect of this provision is that neither the planning authority nor the Board can give any weight to considerations relating to the risk of environmental pollution where an IPC licence is or will be required.[29] The extent of this prohibition can only be assessed when the definition of "environmental pollution" is considered.[30] It is defined under section 4(2) of the EPA Act as:

---

[28] Air Pollution Act 1987, s.56.

[29] The EPA would appear to have formed the view that it is not a licensing authority for the construction phase which precedes the establishment of an activity which will require an IPC licence: see Inspector's Report on the Masonite appeal dated October 20, 1995 (Ref. 12.096064).

[30] There is no definition for "environmental pollution" under the planning code. However, it is reasonable to assume that it is coterminous with its expression under the EPA Act, given the context in which it arises.

"(a) "air pollution" for the purposes of the Air Pollution Act, 1987.
(b) the condition of waters after the entry of polluting matter within the meaning of the Local Government (Water Pollution) Act 1977.
(c) the disposal of waste in a manner which would endanger human health or harm the environment and, in particular
  (i)   create a risk to waters, the atmosphere, land, soil, plants or animals,
  (ii) causing nuisance through noise or odours, *or*
  (iii) adversely affect the countryside or places of special interest, *or*
(d) noise which is a nuisance, or would endanger human health or damage property or harm the environment."

Thus, the definition of environmental pollution deals with the forms of pollution controlled under pre-existing pollution legislation. The extent of the encroachment of the EPA Act on land use concerns traditionally the preserve of planners can be seen from the definition of "polluting matter" referred to in section 4(2)(b) which is found under section 1 of the Local Government (Water Pollution) Act 1977. The second limb of this definition relates to the uses to which the waters are put. "Polluting matter" is defined as including:

"any poisonous or noxious matter, and any substance (including any explosive, liquid or gas) the entry or discharge of which into any waters is liable to render those or any other waters poisonous or injurious to fish, spawning grounds or the food of any fish, or to injure fish in their value as human food, or to impair the usefulness of the bed and soil of any waters as spawning ground or their capacity to produce the food of any fish or to render such waters harmful or detrimental to public health or to domestic, commercial, industrial, agricultural or recreational uses".

"Air pollution" is defined as:

"a condition of the atmosphere in which a pollutant is present in such a quantity as to be liable to—

  (i)   be injurious to public health, or
  (ii) have a deleterious effect on flora and fauna or damage property, or
  (iii) impair or interfere with amenities or with the environment."

"Emission" in this context, means an emission of a pollutant into the atmosphere. A "pollutant" is defined as:

"any substance specified in the First Schedule or any other substance or energy which, when emitted into the atmosphere, either by itself or in combination with any other substance, may cause air pollution".

The recent report of the Inspector assigned to the Masonite appeal, while not intended as a critique of the structures created by the legislation, gives an insight into the problems engendered by the division of functions between the EPA and the planning authority.[31] The Inspector concluded that it results in "two separate

---

[31] See Brassill, "The Interface Between Planning and IPC after Masonite" (1996) IPELJ 20. The Board's senior inspector on this appeal was Mr Padraig Thornton.

balancing acts in which the benefits of the development are weighed against separate sets of drawbacks or disadvantages". He suggests that these two separate balancing acts "might give a different result from one such exercise taking all advantages, benefits, drawbacks and disadvantages into account".[32]

While the Board itself did not follow its Inspector's recommendation on the Masonite appeal, it would appear to have accepted his views as a definitive statement of the manner in which the uneasy juxtaposition of planning and environmental controls is to operate in practice. It appears also from the Inspector's report that the EPA has formed the view that its licensing functions do not extend to the construction phase which precedes the establishment of an activity licensed under the 1992 Act. The Inspector remarked on the irony of a situation where the planning control system was being used to control environmental pollution at the construction phase when the planning authority was being excluded from considering environmental pollution aspects in a long term land use context. The division of functions between the planning authority is not conducive to an integrated approach to environmental protection.[33]

8.1.5 Motorway, busway and protected road schemes

Neither a planning authority nor An Bord Pleanála can decide to grant permission, nor can a "default" decision to grant permission be deemed to have been made for any development of land:

(a) which would involve access to or from a motorway or a busway or which would conravene the provisions of an protected road scheme approved by the Minister,

(b) which it is proposed to be compulsorily acquired under a scheme,

(c) where such development would affect rights proposed to be compulsorily acquired under the scheme, *or*

(d) which would contravene the provisions of a scheme.[34]

8.2 PLANNING CONDITIONS

8.2.1 The power to impose conditions

A general power to attach conditions to a grant of planning permission exists by virtue of sub-section (1) of section 26(1) of the 1963 Act. Section 26(2) also

---

[32] This in turn raises question as to whether current legislative structures are calculated to achieve the E.U. policy objective of sustainable development.

[33] Note that art. 9A of the 1994 Regulations exempts works which are required to be carried out under a condition attached to an IPC licence.

[34] Roads Act 1993, s.46(1). These restrictions may be removed or modified depending on whether the Minister refuses to approve a scheme or approves it subject to modifications. As to circumstances in which a "default permission" may arise, see s.26(4) of the Local Government (Planning and Development) Act 1963, para. 8.5.3, below. See also *Nolan v. Minister for the Environment* [1991] 2 I.R. 548, (SC).

enables planning authorities to impose a number of specific conditions, which is "without prejudice to the generality" of sub-section (1).

The criteria for the validity of conditions suggested by *Pyx Granite* and *Newbury* is loosely followed below. These criteria apply both to conditions imposed pursuant to the general power and those specified under sub-section (2). The general power to impose a condition must be exercised within the limitations imposed by section 26.[35] Where an application is made which complies with permission regulations, the authority:

> "may decide to grant the permission or approval subject to or without conditions or to refuse it. . .".

In *Pyx Granite Company Limited v. Minister of Housing and Local Government*,[36] Lord Denning stated in the context of a similarly wide power to impose conditions under English legislation:

> "Although the planning authorities are given very wide powers to impose such conditions as they think fit, nevertheless, the law says that those conditions, to be valid, must fairly and reasonably relate to the permitted development. The planning authority are not at liberty to use their powers for an ulterior object, however desirable that object may seem to them to be in the public interest."

In *Newbury District Council v. Secretary of State for the Environment*,[37] Viscount Dilhorne said:

> "That the conditions imposed must be for a planning purpose and not for any ulterior one, and that they must fairly and reasonably relate to the development permitted. Also they must not be so unreasonable that no reasonable planning authority could have imposed them."

8.2.2 Conditions must be imposed in accordance with their statutory purpose

8.2.2.1 Conditions must not be imposed for an ulterior purpose

The principle that conditions should be imposed for a planning purpose and not for an ulterior one means that conditions should not be attached where the same result could be achieved under more specific legislation. In *Dunne Limited v. Dublin County Council*,[38] Pringle J. expressed the opinion that a condition

---

[35] Walsh J. in *State (Abenglen Properties Ltd) v. Dublin Corporation* [1984] I.R. 381 at 396 goes so far as to suggest that conditions imposed pursuant to the general power under s.26(i) "must be of the same nature indicated in the particulars set out in sub-section 2". See *Killiney and Ballybrack Development Association Limited v. The Minister for Local Government and Templefinn Estates*, Supreme Court, *per* Henchy J., April 24, 1978, Note that the words "such conditions as they think fit" do not appear in s.26.

[36] [1958] 1 Q.B. 554.

[37] [1981] A.C. 578.

[38] [1974] I.R. 45.

attached to a planning permission requiring that houses be constructed so as to provide sound insulation against aircraft noise was *ultra vires*, because the matter could have been more appropriately dealt with by building regulations which the Minister had power to make under section 86 of the 1963 Act.[39] This ruling resulted in the insertion of section 26(2)(bb) to allow for the imposition of conditions to deal with the effect of noise.[40]

In *R v. Hillingdon London Borough Council, ex parte Royco Homes Limited*[41] the conditions in question provided that the first occupiers of the residential development in question should be drawn from persons on the Council's housing waiting list and that for a period of 10 years from the date of first occupation the occupiers of the dwelling should have security of tenure under rent legislation. The Divisional Court held that the conditions were *ultra vires* as they in effect required the applicant to implement the functions of the Council *qua* housing authority.

Development Control – Advice and Guidelines, a lengthy circular issued to planning authorities by the Department of the Environment in 1982, suggested that in determining whether the use of a planning condition is appropriate, there may be circumstances where it may be necessary to impose planning conditions to control negative impacts of a proposed development despite the availability of a more specific regulatory code, particularly where "there is good reason to believe that they cannot be dealt with effectively by other means". The ability of the other system of control to achieve the desired result would appear to be the most important factor.[42] The Guidelines nonetheless conclude:

> "At best the imposition of conditions in relation to matters which are the subject of other controls is an undesirable duplication. In practice, such an approach can give rise to conflict and confusion if the effect of a condition on a development is different from that of a specific control provision."[43]

8.2.2.2 *Conditions restricting the occupation of buildings*

It is legitimate to restrict the occupation of buildings to a particular class of persons where the restriction serves a planning purpose. Section 28(6) of the 1963 Act provides, *inter alia*, that:

> ". . . permission may also be granted subject to a condition specifying that the use as a dwelling shall be restricted to persons of a particular class or description and that provision to that effect shall be embodied in an agreement pursuant to section 38 of this Act. . ."

Planning authorities have been advised not to restrict the occupation of property to a named individual or to the applicant or his family as it is likely that such a

---

[39] Building Regulations are now made under the Building Control Act 1990.
[40] This paragraph was added by the 1976 Act, s.39(c).
[41] [1974] Q.B. 720.
[42] *Ladbroke (Rentals) Ltd v. Secretary of State for the Environment* [1981] J.P.L. 427.
[43] At para. 10.622.

restriction would not fall within the terms of section 28(6).[44] In *Fawcett Properties Limited v. Buckingham County Council*,[45] planning permission was granted for two cottages subject to a condition providing that occupation of the cottages was to be limited to persons employed in agriculture or forestry. The House of Lords held that the condition was reasonably related to planning purposes – in particular, the furtherance of the planning authority's green belt policy – and did not place an unreasonable restriction of the use of the cottages.

It would appear that the duration of the restriction should not be longer than the remaining life of the current development plan.

8.2.2.3 *Conditions must not abdicate the jurisdiction of the planning authority or the Board*

Planning authorities and the Board frequently make the more detailed aspects of development the subject of negotiated agreement between the planning authority and the developer by means of attaching planning conditions to this effect. The legality of the practice has never been free from doubt. The main objection to the practice is that it precludes a right of appeal in relation to the matters dealt with by the condition.[46]

The validity of a condition which stipulated that details of an access to a proposed development was to be submitted for agreement to the planning authority was considered, *obiter*, by McMahon J. in *Keleghan and Others v. Corby and Dublin Corporation.*,[47] McMahon J. said:

> "A planning authority is entitled to grant permission subject to conditions requiring work to be done, but when that is done, the planning permission must specify the work to be done and any person who thinks he is prejudiced by it, can appeal because he has before him details of the work to be done, but in this case what was granted was permission for access subject to details to be submitted for agreement. The public would have no knowledge what details were in fact being agreed and no way of appealing against the details agreed on between the applicants and the planning authority. It might be that the houses in the cul-de-sac were of a particular architectural style and agreement was reached with the planning authority for the erection of a gate in complete disharmony with the buildings in the cul-de-sac. The public in the cul-de-sac ought to have a right of appeal against this."

---

44 See *Development Control-Advice and Guidelines* (DOE, 1982). Typically, single houses may be permitted in rural areas under development plan policy only on the basis of need' which usually amounts to family or employment connection with the land. Such permissions frequently have occupancy conditions of one type or another. One possible justification for such conditions is that they are in ease of the applicant as a strict application of development plan policies against ribbon development would dictate a refusal of permission. See also *Peak Park Joint Planning Board v. Secretary of State for the Environment* [1991] J.P.L. 744.

45 [1961] A.C. 636.

46 But note that the decision by the planning authority to approve plans on foot of such condition may be judicially reviewed. See *Gregory v. Dun Laoghaire Rathdown County Council*, unreported, High Court, Geoghegan J., July 16, 1996.

47 III I.L.T.R. 144.

A number of conditions leaving matters of detail to be agreed between the applicant and the planning authority at a later stage were challenged in *Boland v. An Bord Pleanála*.[48] The case concerned a challenge to the validity of a decision of An Bord Pleanála to grant permission to the Minister for the Marine for the extension and refurbishment of the existing ferry terminal at St Michael's Wharf, Dun Laoghaire Harbour, which was intended to accommodate a new high speed ferry service. In particular, the applicants questioned the validity of certain conditions attached to the permission which left certain matters relating to traffic to be agreed between the Minister for the Marine and the planning authority. The applicant contended that the use of these conditions constituted an abdication by the Board of its responsibility to determine the application for permission, particularly when traffic was the central issue in the appeal.

Keane J. (then in the High Court), had refused the applicants relief but had been prepared to certify that a point of law of exceptional public importance was involved and the applicant was enabled to appeal the decision to the Supreme Court.

Section 14 (4) of the Local Government (Planning and Development) Act 1976 provides as follows:

> "In case there is attached to a permission or approval granted under section 26 of the Principal Act a condition which provides that a contribution or other matter is to be agree between the planning authority and the person to whom the permission or approval is granted and that in default of agreement the contribution or other matter is to be determine by the Minister, the condition shall be construed as providing that in default of agreement the contribution of other matter is to be determined by the Board."

Hamilton C.J. (with whose judgment Barrington J. agreed) rejected the applicant's contention that traffic matters were the central issue in the appeal as there had been a number of other important factors in the Board's decision. He upheld the validity of the Board' decision and, in an important passage, set out the principles on the basis of which the Board were entitled to impose condition requiring matters to be agreed:

1. The Board is entitled to grant permission subject to conditions.
2. The Board is entitled, in certain circumstances, to impose a condition on the grant of a planning permission in regard to a contribution or other matter and to provide that such contribution or other matter be agreed between the planning authority and the person to whom the permission or approval is granted.
3. Whether or not the imposition of such a provision in a condition imposed by the Board is an abdication of the decision-making powers of the Board depends on the nature of the "other matter', which is to be the subject matter of the agreement between the developer and the planning authority.

---

[48] Unreported, High Court, Keane, J., December 9, 1994.

4. The "matter" which is permitted to be the subject matter of agreement between the developer and the planning authority must be resolved having regard to the nature and the circumstances of each particular application and development.

5. In imposing a condition, that a matter be left to be agreed between the developer and the planning authority the Board is entitled to have regard to

   (a) the desirability for leaving to a developer who is hoping to engage in a complex enterprise a certain limited degree of flexibility having regard to the nature of the enterprise;

   (b) the desirability of leaving technical matters or matters of detail to be agreed between the developer and the planning authority, particularly when such matters or such details are within the responsibility of the planning authority and may require re-design in the light of practical experience;

   (c) the impracticability of imposing detailed conditions having regard to the nature of the development;

   (d) the functions and responsibilities of the planning authority;

   (e) whether the matters essentially are concerned wit off-site problems and do not affect the subject lands;

   (f) whether the enforcement of such conditions require monitoring or supervision.

6. In imposing conditions of this nature, the Board is obliged to set forth the purpose of such details, the overall detail to be achieved by the matters which have been left for such agreement; to state clearly the reasons therefor and to lay down criteria by which the developer and the planning authority can reach agreement.

Blayney J. (with whose judgment Barrington J. also agreed) held that, in considering whether the conditions were *ultra vires* the Board, their relevance in the context of the overall planning application had to be examined. In the instant case, he considered that they were "very peripheral". Blayney J. added a further criterion to the guidelines of the Chief Justice relating to the exercise of the Board's discretion to grant such conditions:

> "Could any member of the public have reasonable grounds for objecting to the work to be carried out pursuant to the condition, having regard to the precise nature of the instructions in regard to it laid down by the board, and having regard to the fact that the details of the work have to be agreed by the planning authority?
>
> I am satisfied having regard to the nature of the work to be done and having regard to the very detailed instructions set out in the conditions, and the purpose for which they were imposed, no member of the public could reasonably have objected to them and so the Board in imposing the conditions in this form was not interfering with or prejudicing any right of the public."

In *McNamara v. An Bord Pleanála*,[49] an application for judicial review of the decision of An Bord Pleanála to refuse permission for a huge municipal dump for baled waste of 64 hectares at Arthurstown, County Kildare ("the Kill Dump") was heard before Barr J.[50]

The Learned Judge had to consider a challenge to a number of conditions attached to the permission on the grounds that they represented an unlawful application of the Board's power to determine the planning application. Relying on the decision of the Supreme Court in *Boland*, Barr J. held that those conditions which left a number of technical matters to be agreed between the developer and the planning authority fell within the acceptable limits of delegation set down by Hamilton C.J. In the case of two of the conditions, Barr J. noted that the Board had reserved to itself the power to decide the matters in default of agreement between the developer and the planning authority.[51]

Condition 22 provided for the regulation of traffic to and from the landfill facility and stipulated that an agreement should be entered into between the developer and Kildare County Council to regulate the route to be used by traffic associated with the development. It was contended by the applicant that this condition was invalid because the Board had no power to regulate traffic on public roads and on the grounds that the proposed agreement between Kildare County Council and the developer regulating the route to be used was an unlawful delegation of the Board's obligations.

While the Learned Judge accepted that the Board had no power to regulate the generality of traffic using the public highway for a particular purpose, he held that the Board was not seeking to impose route restrictions on the public at large in relation to the dump, but only restrictions on the developer and its agents as to the routes which heavy vehicles had to avoid or adopt in connection with user of the dump. In his view, this was within the powers of the Board.

The Learned Judge held that it was appropriate for the Board to delegate its functions to Kildare County Council, as the traffic authority concerned, so as to provide that it should regulate the route to be taken by the developer's heavy vehicles serving the dump. In so holding, he referred explicitly to the criteria laid down by the Chief Justice in *Boland* which recognised the Board was entitled to have regard to whether the matters to be agreed were essentially concerned with off-site problems which did not effect the subject lands. Furthermore, Barr J. did not accept that members of the public would be excluded from making submissions on the matters to be agreed or that Kildare County Council would refuse to co-operate in that regard.

---

[49] Unreported, May 10, 1996.
[50] Leave to apply for judicial review had previously been granted by Carroll J., unreported, January 24, 1995.
[51] See 1976 Act, s.14(4).

While it appears that certain matters of detail may be made the subject of an agreement between the developer and the planning authority, such a condition may be invalid where the planning authority is given too wide a discretion as to a critical element of the development. The necessity for the conditions attached to a decision of the Board to establish parameters for agreement between the developer and the planning authority was emphasised in the earlier case of *Houlihan v. An Bord Pleanála*,[52] in which a developer was granted planning permission by An Bord Pleanála for the erection of 22 holiday homes, a reception block and the diversion of a road at Ballyferriter, Co. Kerry. A number of the conditions attached to the permission made certain matters the subject of further agreement between the planning authority and the developer. The first condition required agreement between the planning authority and the developer as to the revision of a layout plan to accommodate the re-siting of the northern boundary of the property. The third condition required agreement to be reached on the manner in which an effluent discharge main was to be re-routed in an easterly direction. Another condition required agreement with the planning authority on a number of technical matters. Yet another condition stipulated that a public access road along the western boundary of the site should be constructed to the requirements of the planning authority.

In judicial review proceedings to quash the decision of An Bord Pleanála, in which the developer was a notice party, the applicant argued that there were so many matters (12 in all) to be agreed between the developer and Kerry County Council that their resolution could result in a totally different development from that originally applied for. Furthermore, he argued that he was deprived of his statutory right of appeal as far as the matters to be agreed were concerned.

Murphy J. held that the nature and extent of the matters which could be left for agreement was largely a matter of degree. He held that the Board was justified in stipulating that the new access road should be completed in accordance with the requirements of the planning authority. He also took the view that a number of technical matters could properly be left to be agreed between the planning authority and the developer. He held, however, that the condition concerning the effluent discharge delegated too wide a discretion to the planning authority, indicating that he would have had no difficulty in upholding the condition imposed by An Bord Pleanála if it had prescribed that the main should be re-routed along a wide but defined pathway on a particular line to be selected by the developer with the approval of the planning authority.

He granted an order of certiorari quashing the decision and referred the matter back to An Bord Pleanála so that the Board could identify with greater particularity the line to be followed by the re-routed effluent discharge main and to enable it to clarify what was involved in the alteration of the northern boundary of the site.

---

[52]   Unreported, High Court, Murphy J., October 4, 1993.

8.2.3 Conditions must be fairly and reasonably related to the development permitted

The rationale for this principle is that the planning authority should only concern itself with the nature and extent of the application submitted for its consideration. The operation of the principle very often arises in the case of a condition imposed under section 26(2)(a).[53]

In *Newbury District Council v. Secretary of State for the Environment*, planning permission had been granted for the use of two existing hangers on a disused airfield as warehouses. The permission was subject to a condition requiring the removal of the buildings 10 years later. The House of Lords held that the condition had been imposed for a planning purpose, as the hangar was detrimental to amenity in the area. However, it was found that on the evidence, the Secretary of State was entitled to conclude that the condition requiring the removal of the hangars was not fairly and reasonably related to the permission which involved a temporary change in their use. The condition was *ultra vires* for this reason.

8.2.3.1 Conditions altering the nature of the development proposed

The main objection to this type of condition is that the effect of its imposition is to deprive members of the public of an opportunity of objecting to the alteration involved. Curiously, no reference was made to this objection in the leading Irish case of *State (Abenglen) v. Dublin Corporation*.[54] The facts were that an application for outline planning permission was lodged for "office development, four storeys over open floor and three storey residential development". A condition attached to the outline permission reduced the height of the block for office use to three storeys in overall height (*i.e.* two storeys lower) and reduced the overall office content to a maximum of 40 per cent.

Henchy J., in the majority of the Supreme Court, held that although the permission granted differed substantially from that applied for and, in fact, could be described as a "radical alteration", the permission was valid, as it was effected by the imposition of conditions which the planning authority were authorised to impose under section 26 of the 1963 Act. He pointed out that the planning authority were not obliged to invite modifications or revised plans in accordance with the procedure prescribed under the regulations when they decided to grant permission for a modified development.[55]

Walsh J. dissenting, considered it doubtful that modifications could be imposed by way of conditions, and expressed the view that conditions imposed under section 26(1) had to be of the same type as those specified under subsection (2). It followed that a condition substantially altering the nature of the

---

[53] *State (F.P.H. Properties SA) v. An Bord Pleanála* [1987] I.R. 698, 706 (HC, SC) and *British Airports Authority v. Secretary of State,* 1979 S.L.T. 197. See para. 8.3, below.
[54] [1984] I.R. 381. See also *Thomas McDonagh and Sons Ltd v. Galway Corporation* [1995] 1 I.R. 191.
[55] See 1994 Regulations, art. 35.

proposed development could not be validly imposed. Walsh J. also found that the condition concerned altered the essential nature of the application and that the planning authority should, therefore, have refused the application for the reasons which led them to require the alteration.[56]

In the writer's view, the judgment of Henchy J. goes too far, but Walsh J.'s interpretation of section 26 is too restrictive. The best statement of principle would appear to lie somewhere in between and has been developed in a number of U.K. decisions. These cases emphasise that it is the opportunity of the public to object to the proposed amendment to the application which is the principle factor to be considered.[57] This reasoning applies with equal, if not greater force, under the Irish planning code in the light of the express right of all members of the public to object to new development.[58]

In *Wheatcroft (Bernard) v. Secretary of State for the Environment,*[59] Forbes J. put forward the following test:

> "The true test is, I feel sure, that accepted by both Counsel: is the effect of the conditional planning permission to allow development that is in substance not that which was applied for? Of course, in deciding whether or not there is a substantial difference, the local planning authority or the Secetary of State would be exercising a judgment, and a judgment in which the courts would not ordinarily interfere unless it is manifestly unreasonably exercised. The main, but not the only criterion on which that judgment should be exercisied is whether the development is so changed that to grant it would be to deprive those who should have been consulted on the change of development of the opportunity of such consultation . . ."

Forbes J. pointed out that where there had been "root and branch" opposition to development of any extent, it should not be necessary to go through the process of consultation about the lesser development. In *Wheatcroft* the alteration to the initial application consisted of the reduction of the number of dwellings for which permission was sought from 420 to 280, with a corresponding reduction in area from 35 acres to 25 acres.

It is likely that the courts in this jurisdiction would, on the basis of the more recent Supreme Court decision in *O'Keeffe v. An Bord Pleanála,*[60] allow the planning authority or An Bord Pleanála, as the case may be, considerable latitude in deciding whether an amendment to the proposed development amounted to such

---

56   At p.396 of report.
57   Most of the decisions have concerned the *reduction* in the area and the extent of the proposed development: see *Kent County Council v. Secretary of State for the Environment* (1976) 33 P. & C.R. 70; *Wheatcroft (Bernard) Ltd v. Secretary of State for the Environment* (1982) 42 P. & C.R. 223; and *Wessex Regional Health Authority v. Salisbury District Council* [1984] J.P.L. 344.
58   See 1994 Regulations, art. 34. On the question as to what constitutes a material alteration as distinct from a mere modification of the application, see *State (Abenglen)* above, n.35. See also *R. v. St Edmundsbury Borough Council* [1985] 1 W.L.R. 1168.
59   (1982) 42 P. & C.R. 233.
60   [1993] 1 I.R. 39. In other words, the planning authority or Board's decision on this matter would have to be so totally unreasonable that no reasonable tribunal could have reached that decision.

a substantial alteration as to preclude a proper adjudication on the application. In *Wessex v. Regional Health Authority v. Salisbury District Council*,[61] Glidewell refused to set aside a decision of the Secretary of State which reduced the scale of the development for which permission had been sought from 48 houses on eight acres to 37 on the same site, as it was not "manifestly unreasonable". On the other hand, in *Breckland District Council v. Secretary of State for the Environment*,[62] Mr David Whitticombe Q.C. was prepared to hold that a decision by the Secretary of State to permit an increase in the area of a gypsy caravan site from 1 acre to 1.5 acres was "perverse" and it was set aside.

8.2.3.1 *Conditions imposing restrictions on existing use rights may be ultra vires*

In *State (O'Hara and McGuinness) v. An Bord Pleanála*,[63] Barron J. accepted the proposition that "where a right already exists, the land owner cannot be deprived of it by oblique means, but only by the means laid down by the statute". On the other hand, a condition may abrogate existing use rights if the condition is reasonably related to the proposed development *i.e.* if the need for the condition arises as a result of the planning impacts of the new proposal.[64]

A condition which prohibits a change of use from one use to another within the same use class under Part IV of the Second Schedule to the 1994 Regulations is valid. Such a condition is contemplated by Article 11(1) of the 1994 Regulations.[65]

8.2.4 Conditions must not be unreasonable

A condition attached to a grant of permission may be held by the courts to be void for "unreasonableness" where it is one which no reasonable authority would have attached.[66] The question is whether the decision "flies in the face of fundamental reason and common sense".[67]

8.2.4.1 *Factors beyond the control of the applicant*

It is not reasonable for a planning authority to impose a condition requiring an applicant to do something which is outside his control. In *British Airports Authority v. Secretary of State for Scotland*,[68] the Scottish Court of Sessions held that a condition attached to a planning permission which required the British Airports Authority to control the direction of take off and landing of aircraft at

---

61 [1984] J.P.L. 344.
62 (1992) 65 P. & C.R. 34.
63 Unreported, High Court, May 8, 1986.
64 See *Kingston-upon-Thames Royal London Borough Council v. Secretary of State for the Environment* [1973] 1 W.L.R. 1549.
65 See *City of London Corporation v. Secretary of State for the Environment* (1971) 71 L.G.R. 28.
66 *Westminster Bank Limited v. Minister of Housing and Local Government* [1971] A.C. 508. See *O'Keeffe*, above, n.60 [1993] I.R.39.
67 *State (Keegan) v. Stardust Compensation Tribunal* [1986] I.R. 642; *O'Keeffe*, above, n.60.
68 Above, n.53.

Aberdeen airport was *ultra vires* as the Civil Aviation Authority exercised control over these matters. However, a condition which prohibits the commencement of development until the happening of some event which is outside the applicant's control (*e.g.* the creation of an access through neighbouring land) may be valid.[69]

8.2.4.2 Condtions must not be uncertain

"A planning condition is only void for uncertainty if it can be given no meaning or no sensible or ascertainable meaning and not merely because it is ambiguous or leads to perverse results. It is the daily task of the Courts to resolve ambiguities of language and to choose between them; and to construe words so as to avoid ambiguities or to put up with them".[70] A condition which contains an option will not necessarily be invalid for that reason.[71] An owner of land who has been put upon enquiry as to the effect of a condition may not be able to rely upon its uncertain effect in enforcement proceedings.[72]

8.2.4.3 Conditions must be necessary

A condition which achieves no useful purpose may be invalid, for example, where the matter has already been dealt with under another planning permission which has been implemented.[73]

8.2.4.4 The reason stated for the imposition of the condition must be sufficient to support the imposed condition.

The reason for the imposition of a condition is part of the decision so that if it does not properly justify its imposition the condition my be invalid.[74] In *Killiney and Ballybrack Residents Association v. Minister for Local Government (No. 2)*[75] it was argued that one of the conditions attached to the grant of permission was invalid as the reason was insufficient to support the imposed conditions. The condition was as follows:

> "No house shall be constructed on the part of the site to the south of the culverted stream before the expiration of three years from the date of this order."

---

[69] See *Grampian Regional Council v. City of Aberdeen District Council* (1983) 47 P. & C.R. 633. See further below at para. 8.3 .

[70] *per* Lord Denning in *Fawcett Properties Ltd v. Buckingham County Council* [1958] All E.R. 521. This decision was followed by the High Court in *Irish Asphalt Ltd v. An Bord Pleanála*, unreported, Costello P., July 28, 1995. The Supreme Court subsequently held that no appeal lay against Costello P.'s refusal of leave to appeal; unreported judgment, May 23, 1996. See also *Alderson v. Secretary of State for the Environment* [1984] J.P.L. 429 (condition restricting occupation to persons employed "locally" in agriculture); *Mixnam's Properties Ltd v. Chertsey U.D.C.* [1964] 2 W.L.R. 1210. Also, *Dun Laoghaire Corporation v. Frescati Estates Ltd* [1982] I.L.R.M. 469.

[71] *State (F.P.H. Properties SA)* above, n.53.

[72] *Donegal County Council v. O'Donnell,* unreported, High Court, June 25, 1982.

[73] *British Airports Authority*, above, n.53.

[74] 1963 Act, s.26(8). The reason, therefore, appears on the face of the record. See also *State (Sweeney) v. Minister for the Environment and Limerick County Council* [1979] I.L.R.M. 35.

[75] [1978] I.L.R.M. 78.

The reasons stated in the permission was:

> "To control and regulate the development so as to ensure that sewage disposal facilities are satisfactory in relation to residential development on the site".

The reason given for the condition implied by its terms that sewage facilities were inadequate at the time of the grant of planning permission. The plaintiffs argued that if the applicants complied with what was required by the condition, this would not necessarily result in adequate sewage facilities for the proposed development.

In the Supreme Court, Henchy J., with whom the other judges agreed, left open the question as to whether the condition was invalid from the beginning for having been given for a bad reason, as he held that the condition had been spent since the date that proceedings were issued, with the result that it was no longer possible to challenge the validity of the permission for this reason. The learned judge did, however, deliver the following important statement of law in relation to the justification of conditions:

> "It would seem, therefore, that the power to impose a condition in a development permission must be exercised within the limitations imposed by Section 26. In deciding whether the grantor of the permission has kept within those limitations, it is necessary to look at the reason which the section requires to be given in support of it. If the reason given cannot fairly and reasonably be held to be capable of justifying the condition, then the condition cannot be said to be a valid exercise of the statutory powers. For instance, if the reason given is the attainment of an objective, and compliance with the condition could not possibly attain that objective, the condition will be held bad because it was given for an unreasonable reason."

8.3 SPECIFIC CONDITIONS UNDER SECTION 26(2)

Section 26(2) enables planning authorities to impose a number of specific conditions, which is "without prejudice to the generality" of sub-section (1). The requirements of relevance and reasonableness discussed above apply equally to these specific conditions which are set out below:

   (a) Conditions for regulating the development or use of any land which adjoins, abuts or is adjacent to the land to be developed and which is under the control of the applicant, so far as appears to the planning authority to be expedient for the purposes of or in connection with the development authorised by the permission.

Section 26(2)(a) expressly empowers the planning authority or An Bord Pleanála to attach a condition relating to an area outside the application site provided that the land in question is under the control of the applicant and provided that it "adjoins, abuts or is adjacent to" the application site. It is not necessary to have an estate or interest in land to have the necessary "control" provided that the applicant has such right over the land as is required to implement the condition.[76] The other main criterion which must be met before such a condition can be imposed is that the condition be "expedient for the purposes of or in connection with the development". This would appear to be another version of the requirement that the condition be "fairly and reasonably related" to the proposed development.

In *State (FPH Properties SA) v. An Bord Pleanála*,[77] Lynch J. had to consider conditions imposed by the Board on the grant of permission for residential development related to the retention and restoration of a house known as Furry Park House, which was situated on land adjacent to the application site and owned by the prosecutor. Adopting a purposive interpretation, Lynch J. looked at the general power to make a decision on a planning application. One of the matters which the authority had to consider was "the preservation and improvement of amenities". Lynch J. observed that there was a relationship between the restoration of Furry Park House and the proposed development "in that it would improve the visual attractiveness of the whole area and in that it would also preserve for low density residential purposes the house itself and its site which immediately adjoins the area to be developed". He concluded that the preservation of Furry Park House was "expedient for the purposes of and in connection with the development authorised".[78]

His decision was reversed by the Supreme Court, McCarthy J. holding that a condition to restore a house situated on land which was not within the application site could not be imposed in the absence of an express statutory power to do so. McCarthy J. accepted the argument of the developer's counsel that section 26(2)(a) represented an encroachment on property rights and consequently had to be strictly construed. He said that while he "had no doubt it appears to the planning authority to be highly expedient to require the developer to spend a significant sum of money in preserving Furry Park House . . . that does not make it expedient for the purposes of or in connection with the proposed development".

Another way of looking at the *Furry Park* case would have been in terms of the causal relationship between the development and the mischief which the condition was designed to suppress *viz.* the injury to the amenity and open character of the area surrounding Furry Park House. If this relationship is not sufficiently close, then a condition is likely to be invalid. This was the conceptual approach adopted by the Court of Sessions in the important Scottish case of *British Airport Authority v. Secretary of State.*[79]

The appellants had obtained outline planning permission for the construction at Aberdeen Airport of a new aircraft apron, a new terminal building with associated carpark, improved runway approach lighting, and improvements to existing

---

[76]   See *George Wimpey & Company Limited v. New Forest District Council* [1979] J.P.L. 314. But see also *Atkinson v. Secretary of State for the Environment* [1983] J.P.L. 599.
[77]   Above, n.53.
[78]   See also *Pyx Granite Co. Ltd v. Minister of Housing* [1960] A.C. 260.
[79]   See Purdue, Young, Rowan-Robinson, *Planning Law and Procedure* (1989) at p.233.

taxi-ways. The redevelopment of the airport was intended to accommodate an expected increase in traffic volumes. The planning authority imposed conditions which purported to restrict operational hours at the airport and to control the direction of take off and landing. In dealing with the respondent's argument that the conditions did not "fairly and reasonably relate to the permitted development", the Court held that the Secretary of State was entitled to find that there was:

> "a close relationship between the permitted development and future noise levels and that the conditions designed to control the mischief of aircraft noise associated with the use of the runway were fairly and reasonably related to that development."

In the event, the court held that the conditions were invalid for other reasons but it is useful to compare the facts of this case with those of *British Airway Helicopters Limited v. Secretary of State* which was heard at the same time. In that case the appellants obtained planning permission for a one storey building to provide an office for their flight operations headquarters for their United Kingdom operations as a whole, and accommodation for ground training of flying personnel. One of the conditions attached to the grant of permission restricted the operational hours at the terminal. Once again, the appellants argued that this condition was not "fairly and reasonably related to the permitted development". In this case, it was held that the permitted development had no connection whatever with the helicopter operations of the appellants at the airport and the condition was consequently invalid.

A condition which requires works to be done or an access to be provided on land outside the applicant's control which is not included in the application site is not enforceable by an applicant for planning permission. However, if the same requirement is expressed as a condition precedent to the commencement of development it may be valid. In *Grampian Regional Council v. City of Aberdeen District Council*,[80] the House of Lords held that a condition which prevented development from going ahead until a road closure had taken place was valid, desite the fact that it was not in the developer's power to secure compliance with the conditions. Subsequently, the Court of Appeal in *Jones v. Secretary of State for Wales*[81] upheld the power to impose a condition requiring that the proposed development should not be carried out until some obstacle to it proceeding, such as the need to obtain a land owner's consent to vehicular access to the development, had been overcome. But the court also held that if there was no reasonable prospect of the consent being granted, this would invalidate the condition. *Jones* was subsequently overruled by the House of Lords in *British Railways Board v. Secretay of State for the Environment*,[82] in which it was held that the

---

[80] (1983) 47 P. & C.R. 633.
[81] (1990) 88 L.G.R. 942.
[82] [1994] J.P.L. 32. Subsequently, this decision was overruled in practical terms by the Secretary of State who issued a policy statement that Grampian type conditions should not be imposed unless there was a reasonable prospect of their being fulfilled.

fact that the owner of land adjacent to the application site is not prepared to grant access to the proposed development is not a good reason for refusing permission as planning decisions must be made in the public interest and not on the basis of an individual landowner's opposition to development.

(b) Conditions for requiring the carrying out of works (including the provision of car parks) which the planning authority consider are required for the purposes of the development authorised by the permission.

(bb) Conditions for requiring the taking of measures to reduce or prevent –

(i) the emission of any noise or vibration from any structure comprised in the development authorised by the permission which might give reasonable cause for annoyance either to persons in any premises in the neighbourhood of the development or to persons lawfully using any public place in that neighbourhood, or

(ii) the intrusion of any noise or vibration which might give reasonable cause for annoyance to any person lawfully occupying any such structure.[83]

(c) Conditions for requiring provision of open spaces.

(d) Conditions for requiring the planting of trees, shrubs or other plants or the landscaping of structures or other land.

(e) Conditions for requiring the giving of security for satisfactory completion of the proposed development (including maintenance until taken in charge by the local authority concerned of roads, open spaces, car parks, sewers, watermains or drains).

The DOE guidelines state that the amount of the security and the terms on which it is required to be given, should enable the planning authority, without cost to themselves, to complete the necessary services (including roads, footpaths, watermains, sewers, lighting and open space) to a satisfactory standard in the event of default by the developer.

(f) Conditions for requiring roads, open spaces, car parks, sewers, watermains or drains in excess of the immediate needs of the proposed development: see s.26(7).

In *Thomas McDonagh & Sons Limited and McDonagh Fertilisers Limited v. Galway Corporation*,[84] a planning condition required a developer to provide a multi-storey car park which was in excess of the immediate needs of the proposed development, which included a hotel and a number of retail units. The Supreme Court held that the condition was justifiable even though the developer would not be able to recover a

---

[83] This amendment to s.26(2) was introduced as a result of the decision in *Dunne (Frank) Limited v. Dublin County Council*. [1974] I.R. 45.

[84] Above, n.54.

contribution from the planning authority for its provision because it remained within his responsibility. Given that a successful applicant or subsequent owner has no obligation to take up a particular planning permission, the logical extension of this decision is that a local authority would be able to effectively prevent a permission from being implemented in full unless a private car park were built, at least where the provision of a car park at the application site was indicated as a specific objective under the development plan. The question of unreasonableness and consequent invalidity may nonetheless arise where what is required to be provided under section 26(2)(f) is not self-financing, *e.g.* open spaces.[85]

(g) Conditions for requiring contribution (either in one sum or by instalments) towards any expenditure (including expenditure on the acquisition of land and expenditure consisting of a payment under sub-section (7) of this section) that was incurred by any local authority in respect of works (including the provision of open spaces) which have facilitated the proposed development, being works commenced neither earlier than the 1st. day of August, 1962, nor earlier than seven years before the grant permission for the development.

(h) Conditions for requiring contribution (either in one sum or by instalments towards any expenditure, including expenditure on the acquisition of land) that is proposed to be incurred by any local authority in respect of works (including the provision of open spaces facilitating the proposed development), subject to stipulations providing for: –

(i) where the proposed works are, within a specified period, not commenced, the return of the contribution or the instalments, thereof paid during that period (as may be appropriate);

(ii) where the proposed works are within the said period, carried out in part only or in such manner as to facilitate the proposed development to a lesser extent, the return of a proportionate part of the contribution or the instalments thereof paid during that period as may be appropriate); and

(iii) payment of interest on the contribution of any instalments thereof that have been paid (as may be appropriate) so long and in so far as it is or they are retained unexpended by the local authority.

These last two paragraphs enable the planning authority to impose conditions requiring contributions in relation to works facilitating the proposed development which have already been carried out or are going to be carried out in the future.[86] Such conditions can only be imposed in accordance with the limitations laid down

---

[85] See further *per* Finlay C.J. at [1995] 1 I.R. 202 and *Bord na Mona v. An Bord Pleanála and Galway County Council* [1985] I.R. 205. See also Simons, "Planning Conditions & Planning Gain" (1994) IPELJ 12.

[86] For case studies of a number of appeal decisions on financial contributions, see Phillips, "Select Review of Planning Decisions" (1995) IPELJ 51.

in these two paragraphs. The condition may provide that in default of agreement the contribution is to be determined by the Board.[87]

In *Bord na Mona v. An Bord Pleanála and Galway County Council*[88], a condition required developers to make a "contribution" of £300,000 towards the reconstruction of a county and regional road serving the proposed development. The developers had appealed against the condition only, and An Bord Pleanála had directed the planning authority to attach the condition to the grant of permission. The full amount was to be paid in three annual instalments commencing from the date of the grant.

The validity of the condition was challenged on three grounds. First of all, that the imposition of a time limit for the payment of a contribution in the circumstances defeated the intention of the legislature, as evinced in section 2 of the 1982 Act, to allow a person to whom planning permission had been granted, five years from the date of grant to carry out the proposed development. This argument was accepted by Keane J. who said that:

> "the public interest is ensuring that the developer makes an appropriate contribution to the cost of works which will facilitate the development, is adequately met by a condition requiring the developer to make the contribution within a specified period of his commencing his development."

The second ground on which the condition was challenged was that the requirement of a contribution was unconfined by the limitations laid down by Section 26(2)(h) of the 1963 Act with respect to the return of all or part of the contribution, and the repayment of interest accruing which remained unexpended by the local authorities. Keane J. held that, as the condition was concerned with works facilitating the proposed development, it could be regarded as having been imposed within the limitations of section 26(2)(h).

The third ground on which the plaintiff relied was that the contribution of £300,000 amounted to the total cost of the works, although only part of the works were necessary to service the applicant's site and the planning authority only had power to seek a contribution for a proportion of that cost. Keane J. found that section 26(2)(h) did not prevent the planning authority from claiming the entire cost. This ruling may also be criticised on the grounds that the phrase "contribution" in paragraph (9) implied that some element of proportionality to the benefit accruing to the development from the works undertaken.[89]

The decision in *State (Finglas Industrial Estate Limited) v. Dublin County Council*[90] concerned a condition required a financial contribution to be made towards the provision of a public water supply and piped sewerage facilities in the area of a proposed development subject to agreement between the developers

---

[87] 1976 Act, s.14(4).
[88] Above, n.85.
[89] See Scannell, "Bord na Mona v. An Bord Pleanála" (1986) 8 DULJ 96–101.
[90] Unreported, Supreme Court, February 17, 1983.

and the planning authority concerning the amount, time and method of payments, or, in default of agreement, in accordance with the determination of the Minister for Local Government. The council had no foul sewer system within three miles of the lands and the only existing one in the Finglas area was overloaded. It was held by the Supreme Court that the condition should be construed as referring to a contribution towards the cost of providing a public water or piped sewerage facilities in the area only if the relevant planning authority were either willing or legally bound to make such provision.

- (i) Conditions for requiring compliance in respect of the land with any rules made by the planning authority under sub-section (6) of this section.[91]
- (j) Conditions for requiring the removal of any structure authorised by the permission, or the discontinuance of any use of the land so authorised at the expiration of a specified period and the carrying out of any works required for the reinstatement of land at the expiration of that period.[92]

8.4 SEVERANCE OF CONDITIONS

8.4.1 Severability of conditions

The rule as to the severability of conditions was stated by McCarthy J., giving the judgment of the Supreme Court in *State (F.P.H. Properties SA) v. An Bord Pleanála*,[93] as follows:

> "Unless it can be demonstrated that the respondents would have granted the relevant permissions subject only to other conditions, if it had been advised that the impugned condition was invalid, in my view the impugned condition is not severable from the remainder of the permission."

The court held that conditions which required developers to carry out restoration works on a house of architectural significance which was adjacent to the site for which permission had been obtained for an apartment development, although invalid, were not severable from the permission as a whole. However, he refused to remit the decision to the Board for its reconsideration.

In *Bord na Mona v. An Bord Pleanála and Galway County Council*,[94] Keane J. said:

> "In principle, it seems wrong that a planning permission should be treated as of no effect simply because a condition attached to it, which is nothing to do with planning considerations is found to be *ultra vires*. Again, if a condition of a

---

[91] The rules relate to advertisement structures but no such rules have been made.
[92] Conditions requiring the re-instatement of land are frequently attached to permissions for mining development and tipping of waste.
[93] [1987] I.R. 698.
[94] Above, n.85.

> peripheral or insignificant nature attached to a permission is found to be *ultra vires*, it seems wrong that the entire permission should have to fall as a consequence. But where the condition relates to planning considerations and is an essential feature of the permission granted, it would seem equally wrong that the permission should be treated as still effective although shorn of an essential planning condition."

In that case, a condition which required the developer to make a contribution to the improvement of the road network in the vicinity of the proposed development was found to be invalid. On the question of severance, Keane J. said:

> ". . . to treat the permission as authorising the Plaintiffs to carry out a major development without making any contribution whatever to the improvement of the road network which would be necessitated by their development would be to treat them as having been granted a permission which it was never the intention to the legislature that they should have. It seems to me that, in these circumstances, it is not possible to sever the offending condition from the permission and, accordingly, the decision to grant permission must be treated as a nullity in its entirety."

8.5 DECISION-MAKING PROCEDURE

8.5.1 Material contravention procedure

A planning authority may not grant planning permission in material contravention of the development plan unless the statutory procedure prescribed under section 26(3) is followed.[95] Failure to adopt the material contravention procedure where it is required may result in the decision being declared invalid in subsequent judicial review proceedings.[96] The procedure requires the planning authority to publish notice of its intention to grant planning permission in at least one daily newspaper circulating in the area of the proposed development.[97] The planning authority must consider any representations which are received by them within 21 days of the publication of the notice. Finally, a resolution requiring the Manager to decide to grant permission must be passed by three quarters of the elected members of the planning authority.[98]

8.5.2 Time within which planning authority must determine planning application

A decision on an application for which no EIS is required may not be made before a period of 14 days has elapsed since the receipt of the application or,

---

[95] *State (Pine Valley Developments Ltd) v. Dublin County Council* [1982] I.L.R.M. 196; 1963 Act, s.22.

[96] See *Tennyson*, above, n.25, discussed at para. 10.2.7, below. But see *Healy v. Dublin County Council*, unreported, High Court, October 4, 1993.

[97] Copies of the notice must be given to the applicant and to any person who has made submissions on the planning application.

[98] The voting requirement was changed by the Local Government Act 1991, s.45.

where the applicant has been required to publish a further notice of the application, since the date on which that notice was published. The purpose of this provision is to allow members of the public an opportunity to make submissions on the application.[99] This minimum period is extended to 28 days where an EIS is submitted with the application, running from the date on which the application is received or, where the planning require the submission of a fresh notice, from the date on which such notice is given. In the event that an EIS is requested by the planning authority after the application has been submitted, the 28 day period runs from the date of receipt of the EIS or, where the planning authority require a further notice, from the date that the notice is given.

The maximum period for the determination of planning applications depends on the procedure adopted by the planning authority. Assuming that no request for further information or for the publication of a fresh notice is made by the planning authority, the period will be two months from the date on which the application was made. If a request for further information is made by the planning authority, or the applicant is required to publish a fresh notice of his application, the period is extended by a period of two months from the date of compliance with the notice. The period for making a decision may also be extended by the planning authority obtaining the written consent of the applicant to an extension of the appropriate period, provided that such consent is obtained before the expiration of the period.[100] Where the material contravention procedure under section 26(3) of the 1963 Act is invoked the appropriate period is the period of two months beginning on the day on which the notice of intention to grant planning permission in material contravention of the development plan or any special amenity area order is published.

The word "month" means calendar month.[101] Section 11(h) of the Interpretation Act 1937 also provides that:

> "where a period of time is expressed to begin on or be reckoned from a particular day, that day shall, unless the contrary intention appears, cannot be deemed to be included in such period."

It is often not possible for the planning authority to administratively process and adjudicate upon large applications within a period of two months so that a request for further information may sometimes be used as a means of "buying time". A request issued for this reason may not be effective to stop the period of two months from running.[102] A request for additional copies of plans does not constitute a request for "further information" for the purposes of the default procedure.[103] Similarly, a letter requesting an applicant to "clarify" his modification

---

[99] 1994 Regulations, art. 39.
[100] See 1963 Act, s.26(4A), as inserted by the 1976 Act, s.39(f).
[101] See Sched., para. 19 to the Interpretation Act of 1937; *Tiernan Homes v. Fagan*, unreported, Supreme Court, July 23, 1981.
[102] See Walsh *Planning and Development L aw* (2nd ed., Keane ed.), p.40; 1994 Regulations, art. 33(2).
[103] *Herringdale Developments Ltd v. Naas Urban District Council*, unreported, High Court, November 17, 1977, referred to in Nowlan at p.261. See also Walsh *loc. cit.*

to a proposed development cannot be regarded as a proper request for further information.[104] Nor can a notice seeking the submissions of alternative proposals for an element of the proposed development which is unnacceptable to the planning authority.[105]

8.5.3 Default decision

Planning permission or approval may be obtained by default where the planning authority fail to give notice to an applicant of their decision on an application which complies with permission regulations within "the appropriate period" *i.e.* the period within which the planning authority are required to determine a planning application.[106] In such circumstances, the decision by the planning authority to grant the permission or approval is regarded as having been given on the last day of that period. The planning authority have no power to grant permission where an application has not complied with mandatory requirements under permission regulations and a decision to default will not be deemed to have been granted in such circumstances.[107] An applicant for permission is not entitled to benefit from the mistake of the planning authority where he himself has been "less than meticulous" in the observance of the planning code.[108] Furthermore, once a planning application has lapsed, a default decision cannot be claimed.[109]

The default procedure results in a decision to grant planning permission or approval only where the planning authority do not give notice to the applicant of their decision within the "appropriate period".[110] The date of the "giving" of the notice is therefore critical. It was held in *Freaney v. Bray Urban District Council*[111] that the date on which the applicant actually receives notification of the decision by the planning authority is the relevant date. It has also been held that when the date of receipt cannot be clearly established, service is deemed to be effected at the time on which the notice would be delivered in the ordinary course of post.[112] A person who furnishes information on behalf of the applicant

---

[104] *State (Conlon Construction Ltd) v. Cork County Council,* unreported, High Court, July 21, 1975, followed in *State (N.C.E.) v. Dublin County Council* [1979] I.L.R.M. 249.

[105] *O'Connor's Downtown Properties Ltd v. Nenagh U.D.C.* [1993] 1 I.R. 1.

[106] 1963 Act, s.26(4). In *Burke v. Drogheda Corporation* [1981] I.L.R.M. 439, McWilliam J. held that the plaintiff was entitled to a grant of outline permission only, as the details submitted were sufficient only for outline and the application itself was not clear as to whether full or outline permission was being sought.

[107] See para. 6.1 *et seq.*

[108] See *Creedon v. Dublin Corporation* [1983] I.L.R.M. 39; *Dublin County Council v. Marren* [1985] I.L.R.M. 593.

[109] *Murray v. Wicklow County Council,* unreported, High Court, March 12, 1996.

[110] In *Child v. Wicklow County Council,* unreported, High Court, Costello P., January 20, 1995, a claim that the applicant's were entitled to a permission by default failed as the county council records showed that two notifications of their decision to refuse permission were sent by registered post and were not returned. This evidence had not been refuted by any evidence of the applicants.

[111] [1970] I.R. 253.

[112] See Interpretation Act 1937, s.18; *contra, State (Murphy) v. Dublin County Council,* where O'Keeffe P. held that the relevant date was the date of posting by the planning authority.

in response to a request for further information by the planning authority does not necessarily have any general authority to act on behalf of the applicant, so that notification to that person may not suffice to prevent the operation of the default provisions where the applicant is not also notified.[113]

A "default decision" may be appealed to An Bord Pleanála in the same manner as a decision to grant planning permission or approval made within the appropriate period. The default procedure cannot operate to produce a decision which is in material contravention of the development plan, as an order of mandamus "cannot issue to compel the planning authority . . . to consider an application to do something which would be illegal if done."[114] Similarly, a default permission cannot issue where the planning authority do not have sufficient information to determine whether a proposal is in material contravention of the development plan or not. This was established in *Calor Teoranta v. Sligo County Council.*[115]

The facts were that on the June 30, 1989, the applicants lodged a planning application for the development of a Bulk LPG Depot, but failed to give particulars of the thermal insulation of the LPG tank. Sligo County Development Plan provided that "no new developments will be permitted which do not structurally meet the requirements of the Fire Services Act". Subsequently, by letter dated September 8, 1989, they furnished the requisite details of the thermal insulation. On the November 10, 1989, a decision to refuse planning permission was made by the County Council. It was accepted that this decision had been given within two months of the receipt of the respondent of the details concerning the thermal insulation of the tank. The applicants claimed to be entitled to a permission by default on August 31, 1989, which was two months from the date of the application. Barron J. refused an application for a declaration that a default permission had issued, stating:

> "The objection of the Fire Officer to the plans as originally presented was based upon the absence of any protection of the tank in the event of fire, which would delay the onset of explosion. If the thermal insulation intended had been indicated, he would have made no objection to this ground. It is clear from this, that in his view, the tank without such insulation was a definite danger and, that he would not have been entitled to recommend that permission for such a development should be granted, as it would have constituted a material contravention of the Development Plan. Since the applicants could not therefore have obtained a valid permission from the respondent, they equally cannot obtain a valid default permission."

---

[113] *Molloy v. Dublin County Council* [1990] 1 I.R. 90.
[114] *per* Walsh J. in *State (Pine Valley Developments) v. Dublin County Council* [1982] I.L.R.M. 196. See also *Murray* above, n.109 and *Sharpe (P. & F.) Ltd v. Dublin City and County Manager* [1989] I.R. 701.
[115] [1991] 2 I.R. 267.

8.5.4 Mandamus where default decision

The default procedure results in a "decision to grant" planning permission or approval, so that an order of mandamus compelling the planning authority to issue a grant of planning permission has to be obtained before development can be commenced. Delay or the deliberate abandonment of a claim may disentitle an applicant to relief by way of mandamus. A developer who chooses to pursue other applications for planning permission may be considered to have abandoned his claim to a permission by default.[116]

In *State (Abenglen Properties Ltd) v. Dublin Corporation*, both Henchy J. and Walsh J. rejected the argument that if a decision was quashed as being *ultra vires* by the planning authority, the applicant was entitled to a default permission. Walsh J. expressed the opinion that the decision of the planning authority was *ultra vires*, but "nonetheless a decision for the purposes of the default provisions". The prosecutors had conceded that their only purpose in seeking to have the decision quashed was to obtain a default permission. O'Higgins C.J. held that the default procedure could not be used in this way to obtain a benefit never intended by the legislation and as the remedy of certiorari, which the applicants were seeking, as a remedy, was a discretionary one, he concluded that it should not be granted.

Both O'Higgins C.J. and Henchy J. in *Abenglen* considered that the availability of an alternative remedy *viz.* the appeal to An Bord Pleanála was a further reason why the court should exercise its discretion to refuse an order of certiorari. On the other hand, an appeal to An Bord Pleanála is not a remedy equally beneficial, convenient or effective as an order of mandamus.[117] In *Molloy and Walsh v. Dublin County Council*,[118] Blayney J. rejected the Corporation's submission that the plaintiffs ought to have availed of their right of appeal to the Board as there was no reason for them to appeal because under section 26(4) they were deemed to have a decision in their favour by operation of law.[119]

8.5.5 Damages for delayed grant

A developer who has suffered financial loss due to the delay of the planning authority in making a grant of planning permission, may be entitled to damages for breach of statutory duty.[120]

---

[116] *State (Conlon Construction Ltd)* above, n.104. But the making of an appeal does not constitute the abandonment of a claim for relief by way of mandamus where the applicant was not aware of his entitlement to a grant at the time of the making of the appeal: *State (N.C.E. Ltd) v. Dublin County Council*, above, n.104.

[117] See *State (N.C.E)* per McMahon J., above n.104. The applicant was granted an order of mandamus in circumstances where he was not aware of his entitlement to a decision by default at the time his appeal was lodged.

[118] Above, n.113.

[119] He distinguished *Creedon*, above, n.108, on the grounds that the planning authority had in that case a made decision to refuse permission, though an invalid one, within two months of the application being made.

[120] *O'Neill v. Clare County Council* [1983] I.L.R.M. 141.

8.5.6 Section 4 resolutions

The determination of planning applications is an executive function of the planning authority. However, section 4 of the City and County (Amendment) Act 1955, enables the elected representatives of a local authority, by resolution, to require a manager of a local authority to do anything which it is within the executive power of the local authority or manager to do. The manager to whom such a direction has been given does not have a right or duty to exercise a discretion in a judicial manner as to whether or not he will obey the direction unless the resolution is itself invalid.[121] The obligation to act in a judicial manner in adjudicating on a planning application is by virtue of the service of notice of intention to propose a resolution under section 4 of the 1955 Act, transferred from the Manager to the elected members of the authority.

In *Sharpe (P. & F.) Ltd v. Dublin County Council*,[122] the Supreme Court held that the requirements contained in section 26(3)(c), that the material contravention procedure be invoked where a section 4 resolution was being used to obtain a grant of planning permission, indicated that section 4 was intended to apply to planning decisions in general.[123] However, the practicability of employing section 4 to compel the manager to grant permission was put in considerable doubt by a number of subsequent judicial decisions.

The obligation of the elected members to act in a judicial manner presents practical difficulties. In *Sharpe*, Finlay C.J. noted that if the councillors in that case had proceeded to consider the resolution under the material contravention procedure "it would have been necessary to ensure that all persons with a potential interest in the result of their deliberations should be given a fair and ample opportunity to be heard and their point of view properly and adequately considered".[124] The planning authority must restrict themselves to considering the proper planning and development of the area.[125] A decision which takes into account the personal circumstances of a particular applicant may be invalid.[126] The members also have to consider the application for permission having regard to the parameters laid down in the development plan and any SAAO for the area. In *Flanagan v. Galway City and County Manager and Galway County Council*,[127] the council minutes disclosed that the proposer of a section 4 resolution to direct the manager to grant permission for the retention of a commercial store, had stated that

---

[121] See *Child v. Wicklow County Council*, above, n.110 in which Costello P. held that the county manager was entitled to ignore a s.4 resolution which was illegal without the necessity of obtaining a court order to this effect.

[122] Above, n.105.

[123] Finlay P. also observed, *obiter* that it was implicit from the wording of s.26(3)(c), that a s.4 resolution was equally applicable to planning decisions which were not in material contravention of the plan.

[124] At p. 580.

[125] 1963 Act, s.26(1).

[126] But see *Stringer v. Minister of Housing and Local Government* [1971] 1 All E.R. 65; *Great Portland Estates plc v. Westminister City Council* [1985] A.C. 661.

[127] [1990] 2 I.R. 66.

the applicant would have to emigrate if his application for the retention of a commercial store was refused. The seconder said that the applicant employed five people who would otherwise be a "burden on the State". Six members of the council had visited the plaintiff's premises in the two weeks preceding the council meeting and on the morning of the meeting he was met by all of the council members, some of whom questioned him on the proposed development.

Blayney J., referred to Finlay C.J.'s *dictum* in *Sharpe*, to the effect that the planning authority had a duty "to disregard any irrelevant or illegitimate factor that might be advanced". He held that, in considering the personal circumstance of the applicant and his employees, the councillors had not restricted themselves to considering the proper planning and development of their area. The resolution was, therefore, invalid.

In many cases, section 4 resolutions have been passed requiring the manager to set in motion the material contravention procedure despite strong advice to the contrary from technical and planning officers. If there is no evidence in the minutes of the council meeting at which the resolution was considered to indicate that the proposal was in accordance with the proper planning and development of the area it may be set aside as a decision which no reasonable authority would have made.[128]

In *Sharpe* an application was made for access to the dual carriage way at Palmerstown from a large housing development. It had been refused by the planning authority and the Board on a number of occasions. The elected members of Dublin County Council gave notice of their intention to consider a proposal for a direction pursuant to section 4 of the City and County (Amendment) Act 1955 directing the county manager to grant planning permission for the application. A number of reports from the county manager incorporating the reports of the county engineer and head of the road section all recommended refusal on the grounds of road safety. The councillors passed the resolution by a substantial majority. The county manager having taken legal advice, refused to comply with the direction and instead purported to issue notification of a decision to refuse planning permission. On the facts of the case the council members had not given any public notice of their intention to consider the resolution so that the resolution passed pursuant to section 4 of the 1955 Act was a nullity. However, it was stated, *obiter*, by Finlay C.J., giving the judgment of the Supreme Court, that if the only matters which had been before the planning authority were reports of the county manager and his engineering staff, that the resolution would have been so unreasonable as to be invalid, and the county manager would not have been obliged to obey the direction.

In the more recent case of *Child v. Wicklow County Council*,[129] Costello P. refused to grant a declaration that the decision of the Wicklow county manager to

---

128   *Keogh v. Galway Borough Corporation (No. 2)* [1995] 2 I.L.R.M. 312.

129   Above, n.110.

ignore a section 4 resolution was invalid, as the councillors had no basis for refusing to accept the advice contained in the reports of the County Manager and county medical officer who were opposed to the development proposed. There was no evidence in the very full minutes of the council meeting on which their decision was based.[130] Consequently, the president held that the councillors had not taken into account the proper planning and development of the area and had acted unreasonably in not accepting the advice of their officials. He further held that if the county manager was correct in his view that the section 4 resolution was invalid, he was entitled to ignore it without applying to court to have it quashed.

The biggest difficulty in the application of section 4 resolutions to planning matters is that the elected members are obliged to consider whether they should attach conditions to any grant of permission which they are minded to give, and, if so, what conditions are appropriate. In *Kenny Homes v. Galway City and County Manager and Galway Corporation*,[131] the councillors did not have the choice given the form of the resolution; they could simply grant or refuse permission for the development in question. The terms of the resolution did not refer to conditions as the councillors were under the misapprehension that the manager had a discretion to attach suitable conditions. Blayney J., was not satisfied that the duty to act judicially had been discharged. He said:

> "The relevant part of the resolution under section 4 was that it required the City and County Manager to grant outline planning permission to Kenny Homes. The resolution had to be passed in that form or rejected. It is doubtful if it could have been amended but in any event there was no attempt to amend it. But in the form as proposed it was not open to the City Council to consider whether this permission, if they decided to grant it, should be subject to conditions. The sole option open to them was to grant the permission or refuse it. They could not consider the option of granting outline permission subject to conditions as the form of the resolution did not allow for this. They were precluded accordingly from complying with the provisions of the section in reaching their decision and in my opinion it follows that they could not have made a valid decision under section 26 since they were prevented from making a determination on one of the fundamental matters in the section, namely, whether the permission, if they granted it, should be subject to or without conditions."

Even if the councillors in *Kenny Homes* had framed a resolution which referred to a form of permission with conditions attached, this would have fettered their discretion to grant permission without conditions or to attach other conditions. There does not appear to be any form of procedure which could have been adopted to ensure that the duty of the members to act judicially was discharged. Blayney J., remarked in the course of his judgement;

---

[130]   There was a history of refusal of planning permission for the site.
[131]   [1995] 1 I.R. 178.

"Since the members of the local authority have to consider an application for planning permission under section 26 in a judicial manner, they must be free to observe and comply with all of the provisions of the section in considering what is the right decision to come to. It may be to refuse permission; to grant permission without conditions; or to grant it subject to conditions, setting out what the conditions are to be. For the decision to be reached in a judicial manner, it seems to me that all these options must be open for consideration by the local authority. If this is correct, it is very difficult to see what form the resolution could take which would leave the local authority free to consider all the options possible under the section and at the same time require a "particular act, matter or thing specifically mention in the resolution . . . to be done or effected. . ." In my opinion Section 4 is much more suited to executive functions which do not have to be exercised in a judicial manner".

Clearly it would be extremely difficult if not impossible for a large body of councillors to consider in a judicial manner what type of conditions might be attached to a permission. It would be necessary, at the very least to vote on individual conditions. Once again this procedure might be open to the objection that the discretion of the councillors was fettered on the grounds that they were limited to considering particular conditions.

Blayney J., concluded in *Kenny Homes*:

"while it is clear from the decision of the Supreme Court in *Sharpe* that a direction to grant permission may be the subject of a section 4 resolution, in my opinion that section is not an appropriate instrument for such a direction".

While the intention of the legislature to apply section 4 of the City and County (Amendment) Act 1955 to planning decisions was confirmed in *Sharpe*, it may be that in practice the provision is inoperable, because of the impossibility of obtaining a decision from the elected members of the planning authority which may be said to have been reached in a judicial manner, taking into account all relevant considerations. One exit from the morass has been suggested by Mr Justice Keane, all be it for different reasons:

"while the legislature are presumed to know the law, it is always open to a Court to say that a particular enactment has proceeded on an erroneous view of the law and has accordingly misfired".[132]

8.6 EFFECT OF GRANT OF PLANNING PERMISSION

8.6.1 Obligation to make a grant

The planning authority are obliged to issue a grant where they decide to grant a permission or approval and

---

[132] Walsh, *Planning and Development Law* (2nd ed., Keane ed.) at para. 6.19.

- no appeal is lodged during the appeal period,
- an appeal is lodged but is subsequently withdrawn or dismissed by the Board,
- the Board, having considered an appeal against the planning authority's decision to grant, direct the authority to attach, amend or remove any condition or conditions.

In each case, the planning authority must issue a grant "as soon as may be" after the occurrence of the event in question. Similarly, the Board obliged to make the grant "as soon as may be" after its decision to grant.[133]

The grant of planning permission or approval does not entitle a person to carry out any development which requires other licences or permits or is otherwise unlawful.[134]

8.6.2 Reasons for decision

Both the planning authority and An Bord Pleanála are obliged to state their reasons for refusing planning permission or approval or for the imposition of conditions attaching to a grant of permission or approval.[135] The planning authority, unlike the Board, need not state its reasons for granting permission. The reasons given should be "sufficient first to enable the courts to review it and secondly to satisfy persons having recourse to the tribunal that it has directed its mind adequately to the issue before it".[136] In *State (Sweeney) v. Minister for the Environment and Limerick County Council*,[137] Finlay P. stated that the purpose of the requirement for reasons was:

> "to give to the applicant such information as may be necessary and appropriate for him, firstly, to consider whether he has got a reasonable chance of succeeding in appealing against the decision of the planning authority and, secondly, to enable him to arm himself for the hearing of such an appeal."

It is not clear whether the planning authority has a duty to give all its reasons for the refusal of permission. It has been held that they may extend the reasons for refusal on a second similar application.[138] The doctine of *res judicata* only applies to decisions on identical applications.

But even in the case of an identical application, a change in the planning context or an alteration of the development plan will provide a basis for the

---

[133] 1963 Act, s.26(9).
[134] 1963 Act, s.26(11). See Costello P.'s judgment in *Howard v. Commissioners of Public Works* [1994] 1 I.R. 101, for a discussion as to whether a planning authority can grant planning permission for a development which is unlawful.
[135] 1963 Act, s.28(6).
[136] *O'Donoghue v. An Bord Pleanala* [1991] I.L.R.M. 750.
[137] [1979] I.L.R.M. 35.
[138] *State (Aprile) v. Naas U.D.C.* [1985] I.L.R.M. 510; and see Scannell, above, n.7, *op. cit.*, p.209.

planning authority to depart from an earlier decision.[139] Nonetheless, the precedents set by previous decisions of the planning authority or An Bord Pleanála often provide powerful arguments in favour of and against development in the context of planning appeals because of the need for consistency in planning decisions.[140]

8.6.3 Planning permission enures for the benefit of the land

A grant of planning permisssion is not personal to the applicant but runs with the land. Section 28(5) of the 1963 Act provides as follows:

> "Where permission to develop land or for the retention of a structure is granted under this Part of this Act, then, except as may be otherwise provided by the permission, the grant of permission shall enure for the benefit of the land or structure and of all persons for the time being interested therein, but without prejudice to the provisions of the Part of this Act with respect to the revocation and modification of permissions granted thereunder".[141]

As a general rule, planning permission enures for the benefit of the land until the operation of the statutory provisions relating to the duration of planning permission bring it to an end.[142] One important exception is that where a condition under section 26(2)(e) requiring the giving of security for the satisfactory completion of a proposed development, or a condition under section 26(2)(g) or (h) for requiring contribution towards any expenditure by any local authority in respect of works facilitating the proposed development is imposed, the permission or approval has no effect until the condition or conditions have been complied with. If the condition requires payment by instalment, the permission will remain operative so long as payments are made on time, but will cease to have effect if there is a default in paying an instalment.[143]

The benefit of a planning permission for a change of use which has been implemented may be lost where a new use is implemented whether this is the subject of a planning permission or not, and even where the owner always intended to resume the former use.[144] In *Cynon Valley Borough Council v. Secretary of State for Wales and Oi Mee Lam*, planning permission was granted in 1958 for the use of premises as fish and chip shop. In 1978 Mrs Oi Mee Lam purchased the premises a going concern. She intended to continue the business but through ill health was unable to do so. Instead she let the premises on a short term basis

---

[139] See *State (Kenny and Hussey) v. An Bord Pleanála,* unreported Supreme Court, December 20, 1994. See also *Irish Asphalt Ltd v. An Bord Pleanála,* unreported, Supreme Court, July 28, 1995.

[140] See *North Wiltshire District Council v. Secretary of State for the Environment* (1992) 65 P. & C.R. 137.

[141] Nowlan, *op. cit.,* at p.49 suggests that the right to use architect's plans may follow from the attachment of planning permission to the land.

[142] See *State (Kenny and Hussey),* above, n.139. See also *Camden London Borough Council v. McDonald's Restaurants Ltd* (1992) 65 P. & C.R. 423.

[143] 1963 Act, s.26(10)(b).

[144] *Cynon Valley Borough Council v. Secretary of State for Wales and Oi Mee Lam,* 53 P. & C.R. 68. See also *Grillo v. Minister of Housing and Local Government* (1968) 208 E.G. 1201.

to a Mr and Mrs Evans who used the premises as an antique shop. Mrs Lam, who had intended to resume the use of the premises as a fish and chip shop when she recovered her health, eventually regained possession of the premises in 1983. She was informed that fresh planning permission was needed for the proposed resumption of her business. Balcombe L.J. held that the original planning application for use as a fish and chip shop was "spent" when it was implemented in 1958, so that permission was now required for the change of use from use as an antique shop to use as a fish and chip shop. The planning permission authorised a material *change* of use, not the use itself.

A somewhat thornier question is whether a use rendered lawful by planning permission can be lost as a result of non-use in the same manner as a pre-1964 use can be abandoned, so that the resumption of the former use constitutes a material change of use. The Court of Appeal in *Slough Estates Ltd v. Slough Borough Council (No. 2)*[145] held that a planning permission could be abandoned at the election of the person entitled to its benefit. But this decision was disapproved by the House of Lords in *Pioneer Aggregates Ltd v. Secretary of State for the Environment.*[146] A mining company had obtained planning permission to work limestone from a quarry subject to conditions, *inter alia*, in relation to the restoration of the site on completion of quarrying. Sixteen years later the company wrote to the planning authority giving notice that they would cease quarrying at the end of that year. The planning authority informed them that they were satisfied that the restoration conditions had been complied with. Ten years later, again the new owner wished to resume quarrying. The main issue was whether the original planning permission had been abandoned.

The House of Lords held that the doctrine of abandonment did not apply because of the express statutory provision that planning permission enured for the benefit of the land. The new owner of the site was entitled to resume quarrying under the terms of the original permission. Lord Scarman observed that to apply the concept of abandonment to a use where planning permission existed would lead to uncertainty and confusion in the law. The Town and Country Planning Act 1971[147] was a comprehensive code into which equitable concepts should not be imported unless they were absolutely necessary:

> "Planning control is the creature of statute. It is an impositon in the public interest of restrictions upon private rights of ownership of land. The public character of the law relating to planning control has been recognised by the House in *Newbury District Council v. Secretary of State for the Environment*[148] It is a field of law in which the courts should not introduce principles or rules derived from private law unless it be expressly authorised by Parliament or necessary to give effect to the purpose of the legislation. Planning law, though a comprehensive code imposed in

---

145 [1969] 2 Ch. 305.
146 [1985] A.C. 132.
147 This has since been replaced by the Town and Country Planning Act 1990.
148 [1981] A.C. 578.

the public interest, is, of course based on the land law. Where the code is silent or ambiguous, resort to the principles of private law (especially property and contract law) may be necessary so that the courts may resolve difficulties by the application of common law or equitable principles. But such cases will be exceptional. And, if the statute law covers the situation, it will be an impermissible exercise for the judicial function to go beyond the statutory provision by applying principles merely because they may appear to achieve a fairer solution to the problems being considered. As ever in the field of statute law it is the duty of the courts to give effect to the intention of Parliament as evinced by the statute, or statutory code, considered as a whole."

The decision of the House of Lords was impliedly approved by McCarthy in the Supreme Court in *State (Kenny and Hussey) v. An Bord Pleanála*,[149] but that was in the context of operational development. While it may be accepted that the introduction of the doctrine of abandonment may cause uncertainty in situations where a discontinued use was contemplated by a particular planning permission, the view put forward by Lord Scarman produces uncertainty of a different sort – "the unexploded bomb effect" referred to by Balcombe L.J. in *Cynon Valley*. In other words, if the planning permission was not regarded as "spent" where a use had been effectively abandoned, an old use could come back to life under the terms of an even more ancient permission, thereby creating problems for overall development control.[150] A still more cogent reason for introducing the concept of abandonment is that the planning permission which enures for the benefit of the land under section 28(5) of the 1963 Act, enures only for the purposes of authorising the *change* of use referred to in the permission, not the use itself. This was the main argument accepted by Balcombe L.J. in *Cynon Valley*:

". . . where the development for which planning permission is required is a material change of use, the permission is to change from Use A to Use B, and is not merely a permission to use the property for Use B for the indefinite future."[151]

The lack of clarity in the law in this area does not make the conveyancer's life any easier. Legislative intervention would appear to be needed to flesh out the implications of section 28(5).

8.6.4 Interpretation of planning permission

A grant of planning permission should be interpreted in its ordinary meaning. In *XJS Investments Ltd v. Dun Laoghaire Corporation*,[152] McCarthy J. stated in the Supreme Court:

---

[149] Above, n.139. McCarthy J. based his conclusion in this regard on the provisions relating to the life of a permission: see 1982 Act, s.2.
[150] One authoritative commentator holds the view that the concept of abandonment applies equally to implemented planning permissions. See Alder, "The Loss of Existing Use Rights" (1989) J.P.L. 814.
[151] Above, n.144 at 76.
[152] [1987] I.L.R.M. 659.

"Certain principles may be stated in relation to the true construction of planning documents:

(a) To state the obvious, they are not Acts of the Oireachtas or subordinate legislation emanating from skilled draftsmen and inviting the accepted canons of construction applicable to such material.

(b) They are to be construed in their ordinary meaning as it would be understood by members of the public without legal training as well as by developers and their agents, unless such documents, read as a whole, necessarily indicates some other meaning . . ."

A general rule became established that a planning permission which makes no reference to any material accompanying the application or any other documentation should be construed as a self-contained document.[153] However, it is common practice for planning authorities to attach a condition to a planning permission or approval requiring the development to be carried out in accordance with the application together with any accompanying plans and particulars.[154] A planning permission which incorporates a reference to the application for permission together with the plans lodged must be construed by reference not only to its direct contents but also to the application and the plans lodged.[155] It has recently been held in England that the mere recital of the application number in the top of a permission is not sufficient to incorporate the particulars of the application into the planning permission but the correctness of this decision has been doubted by at least one commentator.[156]

Even where a planning permission does not incorporate a specific reference to the application, there may be grounds for interpreting the permission in the light of the application and accompanying documents, at least where the permission itself is ambiguous, as these will be contained on the planning register which is available for inspection by the public.[157] But the permission may not be interpreted by reference to pre-application discussions between the developer and planning authority. "Members of the public, entitled to rely on a public document,

---

153 See *Slough Estates Ltd v. Slough Borough Council (No. 2)* [1971] A.C. 958; *Miller-Mead v. Minister of Housing and Local Government* [1963] 2 Q.B. 196. Note that the U.K. cases before 1971 have to be approached with some caution as prior to the Town and Country Planning Act 1971 there was no requirement that a local planning authority had to keep a register of planning applications.

154 Such a condition was attached in *Readymix*, discussed below.

155 *Readymix (Eire) v. Dublin County Council and Minister for Local Government*, unreported, Supreme Court, July 30, 1974. See also *Wilson v. West Sussex County Council* [1963] 2 Q.B. 764, in which Willmer L.J. warned at p.777 against "a very unfortunate practice on the part of a planning authority, when granting a planning permission, to incorporate by reference correspondence which may well not be accessible to subsequent purchasers of the propery concerned.'

156 *R. v. Secretary of State for the Environment* [1995] J.P.L. 135; [1995] EGCS 95 (CA). See also [1995] J.P.L. 139 for comment on Schiemann J.'s decision at first instance, in which the commentator observes that "already . . . it is good conveyancing practice, in investigating title to look at both the application and the grant in establishing the planning rights of a property".

157 See Comment appended to *Wivenhoe Port Ltd v. Colchester Borough Council* at [1985] J.P.L. 396; see also Purdue, Young, Rowan-Robinson *op. cit.*, at p.271.

surely ought not to be subject to the risk of its apparent meaning being altered by the introduction of such evidence."[158] In *Readymix (Eire) v. Dublin County Council and Minister for Local Government*,[159] the Supreme Court declined to have regard to any understanding which existed between the planning authority and the developer as to the nature of the development for which permission was sought. Henchy J. said:

> "Since the permission notified to an applicant and entered into the register is a public document, it must be construed objectively as such and not in the light of subjective considerations special to the applicant or those responsible for the grant of the permission. Because the permission is an appendage to the title to the property, it may possibly not arise for interpretation until the property has passed into the hands of those who have no knowledge of any special circumstances in which it was granted."

Despite this statement of the law by Henchy J., the courts have been willing to have regard to the pre-application negotiations between a developer and the planning authority where there was an ambiguity in the terms of the permission.[160] Lord Reid in *Slough Estates* also accepted that extrinsic evidence might be required "to identify a thing or place referred to".[161] Furthermore, it appears that extrinsic evidence may be referred to in the context of "renewal aplications".[162]

The context in which developer's aspirations are expressed in an application is not always clear. For example, material may be enclosed with an outline application showing the proposed development as it is intended to be completed on receipt of approval. If a developer wishes not to risk being bound by such documentation at outline stage, it should clearly be labelled "for illustrative purposes only".[163]

A grant of permission may specify the purposes for which a structure erected under the terms of that permission may or may not be used, but where no purpose is specified, the permission is to be construed as including permission to use the structure for the purpose for which it is designed.[164] In *McMahon v. Dublin Corporation*,[165] Barron J. held that the purpose had to be determined objectively from the documentation lodged with the application. On the facts of the case he

---

[158] *per* Lord Reid in *Slough Estates Ltd* above, n.153 at p.962, referring to the admissibility of extrinsic evidence; quoted with approval by Henchy J. in *Readymix*.

[159] Unreported, Supreme Court, July 30, 1974.

[160] *Jack Barrett (Builders) Ltd v. Dublin County Council*, unreported, Supreme Court, July 28, 1983, which concerned the responsibility of the developer for the construction of a service road indicated in the plans; *Dun Laoghaire Corporation v. Frescati Estates Ltd*, [1982] I.L.R.M 469.

[161] [1971] A.C. 958. Lord Reid observed in *Slough*: "The interpretation of the purported planning permission remains wrapped in mystery, and days of argument have not shown what it means."

[162] See *Manning v. Secretary of State for the Environment* [1976] J.P.L. 634. See Moore, *A Practical Approach to Planning Law* (5th ed.) p.233.

[163] But see *Dun Laoghaire Corporation v. Frescati Estates Ltd*, above, n.160.

[164] 1963 Act, s.28(6).

[165] Unreported, High Court, June 19, 1996.

held that the use of 10 town houses at Landsdowne Village, Sandymount, Dublin 4, for commercial lettings was a use not authorised by the permission for their erection, to which was attached a condition which excluded non-residential uses. In *Wilson v. West Sussex County Council*,[166] Diplock L.J. said that:

> ". . . 'designed' in the context of an outline permission must mean intended to be used. It cannot mean an architectural design 'for a particular use' for, at the time of the permission, there may not be any architectural designs for the cottage at all and designed in the subsection cannot have different meanings according to whether the permission is an outline permission granted before the architectural designs are in existence or a final permission granted after architectural designs have been completed."

On the other hand the view was expressed by Lord Parker in *Belmont Farm Ltd v. Minister of Housing and Local Government*,[167] that the phrase meant:

> "designed . . . in the sense of its physical appearance and layout . . . it cannot merely mean for the purpose for which it was intended by the proposed erector."

In *Readymix*, Pringle J. in the High Court preferred this latter interpretation. Henchy J. stated that he found it unnecessary to decide which was the correct statement of the law, as on either view the development of a Readymix plant was within the scope of the permission granted. On balance, the views of Barron J. in the *Landsdowne Village* case and of Lord Parker in *Belmont* would appear to be preferable as it is undesirable that a successor in title to an applicant for planning permission should be bound by the applicant's intentions of which he may not be aware.

In interpreting the terms and conditions of a planning permission, the words should be given their ordinary meaning. It has been held that a permission which is granted by reference to plans and specifications lodged with the application may have a term implied that the developer will "use reasonable care and skill and provide proper and adequate materials for the purpose of the building works unless the specifications lodged by him qualify this obligation in some way and are accepted in such qualified form by the planning authority".[168] An apparently contradictory conclusion was nonetheless reached by a Divisional Court in *Sutton London Borough Council v. Secretary of State for the Environment*.[169] In that case the local planning authority had attached a condition that the type and treatment of the materials to be used on the exterior of the building should be approved by the authority prior to the develpment being carried out. Lord Widgery C.J. observed:

> "I do not regard planning in general as being concerned with the quality of work which is done. Approaching this case with that in mind I can see no reason

---

[166] [1963] 2 W.L.R 669.
[167] 60 L.G.R. 319.
[168] *Coffey v. Hebron Homes Ltd, Nore Properties Ltd and others*, unreported, High Court, July 27, 1984.
[169] (1975) 119 S.J. 321.

whatever why one should imply in this condition an unusual requirement, namely, that the work shall be done to any particular standard, be it of good workmanlike standard or otherwise. A condition of this kind must be construed according to the ordinary use of language. . .".

The conclusion which may be drawn from the at times conflicting cases on the construction of planning permission is that:

". . . an adviser cannot expect to advise a client on the planning position on a site without consideration of not only all relevant permissions but also all relevant documents and plans. Whether or not one should go to the painful extreme of examining all application correspondence on the planning file is a matter of judgment, but one should be aware that all such evidence is admissible."[170]

8.6.5 Effect of appeal documents on interpretation of permission

If a planning permission can be interpreted by reference to an underlying planning application which is incorporated in the terms of the permission, what is the status of appeal documents in the construction of decisions by the Board?

The point arose in *MCD Management Services Limited v. Kildare County Council.*[171] Outline planning permission had been granted for a racing circuit in 1967, and this was followed by an approval in the same year. On May 18, 1994, Kildare County Council granted permission for the retention of further development of the site consisting *inter alia* of stores, hospitality buildings and a new grandstand. Condition 1 attached to the said permission stipulated that the proposed development should be carried out in accordance with the documents, drawings and particulars submitted to the planning authority except where these were altered or amended by conditions in the permission. The third condition attached to the said permission read as follows:

"The overall development shall be used solely for the operation of motor vehicles racing. Any alternative uses, including concerts, and any retail sales or markets or any kind, shall be the subject of prior planning application in each case."

The reason for attaching the condition was stated as follows:

"To limit the use of the overall complex to the uses for which planning permission already exists, and to prevent unauthorised development".

Condition 3 and one other condition were appealed to An Bord Pleanála by Mondello Park Sports Limited. In its letter of appeal, the appellant's architect submitted that condition 3 was unduly restrictive and indicated that it was the wish of the appellants to develop the venue for other uses, to include concerts, subject to certain restrictions, including the frequency and times at which such concerts would be held.

---

[170] See Graham, "The Interpretation of Planning Permissions and a Matter of Principle" (1991) J.P.L. 104, at p.112.

[171] [1995] 2 I.L.R.M. 532.

The Board decided to address itself only to the conditions appealed against rather than to treat the appeal as if the application had been made to it in the first instance.[172] By order dated the October 11, 1994, the Board directed the planning authority to remove conditions 3 and 11 from the planning permission.

A company involved in concert promotion, MCD Management Systems Limited, decided to hold "Feile 1995" at Mondello Park over the three days from the August 4 to 6, 1995 inclusive. In judicial review proceedings to challenge a warning notice served on the company, the nett issue to be determined in the proceedings was whether the holding of Feile 1995 at Mondello Park was permitted by the decision of An Bord Pleanála.

The company contended that the letter of appeal submitted to An Bord Pleanála formed part of the application which was considered by the Board and that the removal by the Board of condition 3 indicated the Board's intention that the holding of concerts at Mondello Park be permitted. Reliance was placed on section 26(5)(b) of the 1963 Act, as amended by section 3 of the 1992 Act, which requires the Board to determine an application "as if it had been made to the Board in the first instance", which was interpreted by Costello J. (as he then was) in *O'Keeffe v. An Bord Pleanála*,[173] as meaning:

> "that it is determining the matter *de novo* and without regard to anything that had transpired before the Planning Authority."

Laffoy J. refused to accept this argument as the appeal was an appeal against conditions only, and one in which the Board had decided that the determination of the application as if it had been made to it in the first instance would not be warranted. In these circumstances, the decision of the planning authority continued to subsist subject to such variation of the conditions as the Board directed and, consequently, the letter of appeal could not be used as an aid to the construction of the decision emanating from the Board.

The judgement of Laffoy J. does not address the issue as to the role of an appeal document in interpreting a permission granted by An Bord Pleanála after a "full" appeal.[174] In *MCD*, the appeal was one against conditions only and the application was not considered *de novo* by the Board.

8.6.6 Duration of planning permission

Although a planning permission "enures for the benefit of the land", its life may be spent due to the expiration of limits on its duration imposed by statute or under the terms of the permission itself. Section 2 of the 1982 Act imposes limits on the duration of planning permission which vary according to the date on

---

[172] The Board has this discretion under s.15(1) of the Local Government (Planning and Development) Act 1992

[173] [1993] 1 I.R. 39 at 52.

[174] In the context of a full appeal, the Board are required to determine the application "as if it had been made to the Board in the first instance": see 1963 Act, s.26(5)(b), as amended.

which the planning permission was granted. These time limits do not relieve developers of the obligation to comply with planning conditions or to complete the services and open space requirements for the development permitted. Nor do they affect any permission which under the terms or conditions of the permission is granted for a longer or shorter period than the statutory period. Section 2 (2) provides that the time limits imposed do not affect:

(a) any permission for the retention of any structure;

(b) any permission granted for a limited period;

(c) any permission which is subject to a condition requiring the removal of any structures or the discontinuance of any use of the land authorised by the permission at the expiration of a specified period and the carrying out of any works required for the re-instatement of the land at the end of that period;

(d) any permission which is of a class or description specified in regulations made by the Minister for the purposes of the section;

(e) in the case of a house, shop, office or other building which itself has been completed, the provision of any structure or works included in the relevant permission and which are either necessary for or ancillary or incidental to the use of the building in accordance with that permission;

(f) in the case of a development comprising a number of buildings of which only some have been completed, the provision of roads, services and open spaces included in the relevant permission and which are necessary for or ancillary to such buildings;

(g) the continuance of any use, in accordance with a permission, of land;

(h) where a development has been completed (whether to an extent described in paragraph (a) of subsection 2 otherwise), the obligation of any person to comply with any condition attached to the relevant permission whereby something is required either to be done or not to be done.

The planning authority or the Board may decide to grant planning permission of more than five years duration i.e. the time limit which currently applies. Longer periods are often allowed for large scale development which are to be phased over time. Equally, temporary permissions for less than five years may be granted. Unless a longer or shorter period is specified in the planning permission, the "appropriate period" or "life" of a planning permission is calculated as follows:

(a) A permission granted before the first day of November 1976 expired on October 31, 1983.

(b) A permission granted not earlier than the November 1, 1976 and not later than October 31, 1982, expired either seven years after the date of the grant or October 31, 1987 whichever date was the earlier.

(c) A permission granted on or after the November 1, 1982 expires five years after the date of the grant.

8.6.7 Extension of duration of permission.

An application may be made to the planning authority to extend the "appropriate period" or "life" of a permission to enable development authorised by a permission which has expired to be completed. Such an application may not be made earlier than one year before the period is due to expire.[175] Section 4(1) of the Local Government (Planning and Development) Act 1982 provides:

"On an application being made to them in that behalf, a planning authority shall, as regards a particular permission, extend the appropriate period, by such additional period as the authority consider requisite to enable the development to which the permission relates to be completed, if, and only if, each of the following requirements is complied with:

(a) the application is in accordance with such regulations under this Act as apply to it,

(b) any requirements of, or made under, such regulations are complied with as regards the application, and

(c) the authority is satisfied in relation to the permission that –

   (i)   the development to which such permission relates commenced before the expiration of the appropriate period sought to be extended, and

   (ii) substantial works were carried out pursuant to such permission during such period, and

   (iii) the development will be completed within a reasonable time."

If the conditions referred to under section 4(1) are fulfilled the planning authority must grant an extension. The planning authority is entitled to confine its reasons for the refusal of an extension to a recital of the particular condition on which it relies, although it is entitled to elaborate on its reasons if it considers it appropriate.[176] In *State (McCoy) v. Dun Laoghaire Corporation*,[177] a developer challenged the validity of the planning authority's refusal to extend the life of a permission for the stated reason that the particular permission for which the extension was sought had been rendered incapable of implementation as development had already been carried out under two other permissions which was inconsistent with that permission. Gannon J. held that where the requirements set out in the section have been fulfilled the planning authority have no residual discretion and are obliged to extend the duration of the planning permission. He found that the reason given for the refusal to grant the extension supported a negative finding under section 4(1)(c), *i.e.* that the development would not be

---

[175] 1994 Regulations, art. 80. The particulars to be contained in these applications are set out under art. 81.

[176] *Frenchurch Properties Ltd v. Wexford County Council* [1992] 2 I.R. 268.

[177] [1985] I.L.R.M. 533.

completed within a reasonable time and that the reason given was consequently a material consideration.

The word "works" in section 4(1)(c)(ii) is not to be equated with the definition of "works" under section 2 of the 1963 Act, so that pre-fabricated structures manufactured off-site which are exclusively designed for the proposed development can be included in any calculation as to whether "substantial works" have been carried out.[178] But how much works have to be carried out to meet the requirement of "substantial works" under the section? In *Frenchurch Properties Ltd. v. Wexford County Council*,[179] Lynch J., rejecting the notion of any rule of thumb, stated:

> "Perhaps in a small development "substantial works" would require a substantial proportion of the development and even 40% to 50% to be carried out if an extension to the life of the permission were to be granted. On the other hand it may well be in a very large development "substantial works" might have been carried out even though a much lesser proportion than 40% to 50% of the development might have been completed before the expiration of the permission. It is a matter for the planning authority *bona fide* using its own expertise to decide whether or not substantial works were carried out pursuant to the permission."

The power to extend is given "as regards a particular permission" and "to enable the development to which the permission relates to be completed". It was held by the Supreme Court in *Garden Village Construction Co. Limited v. Wicklow County Council*,[180] that the planning authority are only entitled to consider the "particular permission" which they are being asked to extend. The Supreme Court reversed the decision of Geoghegan J. to quash the refusal of the county manager to extend the duration of a planning permission for the development of 287 houses at the Garden Village, Newtownmountkennedy, Co. Wicklow. The county manager had refused to extend the period of the permission as he was not satisfied that "substantial works" had been carried out pursuant to the permission. It was accepted by both parties that no works had been carried out on the application site. Geoghegan J. held, notwithstanding, that certain infrastructural works had been carried out on adjoining lands which were for the benefit of the relevant plot as well as those lands and that these works might be considered to have been carried out "pursuant to" the planning permission for the application site. Accordingly, he held that the county manager should have taken these works into account in deciding whether "substantial works" had been carried out.

At the time of the application for an extension only 125 houses had been built in the overall development, but a large proportion of the roads and surfaces had already been installed. The developers' principal contention was that the planning

---

[178] See *Frenchurch Properties Ltd*, above, n.176. Lynch J. found that pre-fabricated floor slabs and steel work were "unique to this development and incapable of being used on any other building project or development".

[179] Above, n.176.

[180] [1994] 3 I.R. 413.

permission should not be looked at on its own but in the context of the planning permissions for the adjoining lands. They argued that a large part of the infrastructural works was surplus to the needs of the particular place where they were constructed and were required to service the relevant plot.

In its judgment, which was delivered by Blayney J., the Supreme Court held that the infrastructural works referred to constituted "development" within the meaning of section 3 of the 1963 Act. It further held that the infrastructural works were lawfully carried out "under and in accordance with" the planning permission obtained in respect of the lands on which they were located; it was equally correct to say that they were carried out "pursuant to" such planning permission. The court held that it was not possible to say that the infrastructural works were also carried out "pursuant to" the planning permission relating to the relevant plot. Whether such development benefited the relevant plot was immaterial for the purposes of section 4(1)(c)(ii). The Supreme Court accepted the planning authority's view that they were only entitled to consider the "particular permission" which they were asked to extend. The power to extend was given "as regards a particular permission" and "to enable the development to which the permission relates to be completed".[181]

It is noteworthy that the Supreme Court made no reference to one of the grounds on which Geoghegan J. relied for his decision, *viz.* that there was a condition attached to the planning permission which required the development to be carried out in accordance with the documents and details lodged with the application. These related to the entire planned development which included the roads and services covered by the earlier permission. For this reason, Geoghegan J. held that the infrastructure could be regarded as having been carried out "pursuant to" the permission for which the extension was sought. On the basis of Gannon J.'s judgment in *McCoy*, this condition requiring compliance with the plans and particulars lodged formed part of the "particular permission". Furthermore, the planning authority has power to attach a condition which regulates the development of land which adjoins, abuts or is adjacent to the application site when this is under the control of an applicant.[182] Therefore, the works might have been regarded as carried out pursuant to the planning permission relating to the permission for which the extension was sought.[183]

The decision to extend the appropriate period may be obtained by default where the planning authority fail to give notice of their decision to the applicant

---

[181] *State (McCoy) v. Dun Laoghaire Corporation* [1985] I.L.R.M. 533, followed; *Frenchurch Properties*, above, n.176 distinguished; *O'Keeffe*, above n.173 at 67, referred to.

[182] See s.26(2)(a) of the 1963 Act; see also *Thomas McDonagh & Sons Limited and McDonagh Fertilisers Limited v. Galway Corporation* [1995] 1 I.R. 191 where the planning authority imposed a condition on a permission for a hotel development that a five storey car park be constructed even though this had been the subject of an entirely separate application (see further [1994] IPELJ 42).

[183] On the other hand, it would be artificial to regard works as having been carried out pursuant to a "particular planning permission" when they have already been carried out before that permission was granted, but this would appear not to have been the case on the facts of the *Garden Village* case.

on an application which complies with the regulations, within a period of two months beginning on the day of receipt by the planning authority of the application, or the date when any requirements of the planning authority under the regulations have been complied with, whichever is the later.[184] An application may be made for a further extension to the appropriate period where an extension has already been granted by default or otherwise.[185] The planning authority are precluded from granting a further extension unless they are satisfied that the development has not been completed due to circumstances beyond the control of the developer.[186]

Sections 2 to 4 of the 1982 Act have important implications for conveyancing practice. Where development has been or is being carried out on foot of an outline permission and approval the life of a permission runs from the date of the grant of outline permission and not the grant of approval. If an outline permission has expired before approval has been obtained, an application should be made to extend the appropriate period to enable an application for approval to be made. An application for retention permission may have to be made to cover any works originally authorised by planning permission which has been carried out after the expiration of that permission.

8.6.7 Multiple permissions

A developer may apply for any number of permissions for the same land. Where two permissions are mutually inconsistent the implementation of one renders the other incapable of implementation.[187] It is not possible to seek to establish a composite planning permission by implementing the most attractive elements out of several permissions and omitting others.

In *Dublin County Council v. Loughran*,[188] the respondent built a house with an access onto the Castleknock Road. The access was authorised under the terms of a 1956 permission but, the general house type was taken from other permissions and the particular house type was authorised under a retention permission from An Bord Pleanála. Murphy J. held that the development was unauthorised as no single permission authorised the whole.

If the developer of such an estate wishes to alter aspects of the overall development before it has been completed, the appropriate procedure is to apply for planning permission for a variation to the original plans on foot of which the

---

184 1982 Act, s.4(2). See *Lee and Flynn v. Wicklow County Council*, unreported, High Court, Flood J., December 1, 1995 where there was a dispute as to whether both of the named applicants had been notified within the "appropriate period".

185 1982 Act, s.4(3).

186 The particulars which must accompany such an application are dealt with under 1994 Regulations, art. 82. The applicant must furnish particulars of the circumstances which are beyond his control.

187 *Dwyer-Nolan Developments Ltd v. Dublin County Council*, Unreported, High Court, April 21, 1986; and *Pilkington v. Secretary of State for the Environment* [1974] 1 A E.R. 283. *F. Lucas & Sons Ltd v. Dorking Borough Council* 62 L.G.R. 111.

188 [1985] I.L.R.M. 166.

earlier permission was granted. The application for a variation should incorporate the partial development which has occurred as otherwise any further development may be unauthorised.

8.6.8 Severable permissions

As a general rule, a planning permission must be implemented in its entirety but in certain cases the permission may be regarded as severable so that individual plot owners may have a defence to enforcement proceedings. A planning permission for a residential development consisting of houses on their own sites may be regarded as severable to the extent that enforcement proceedings may not be taken against individual purchasers of sites where a developer has not completed the estate in accordance with the terms of a planning permission for the development of the estate as a whole.[189] However, a purchaser should satisfy himself or herself that the conditions have been complied with as of the date of purchase.

8.6.9 Liability of planning authority arising from grant

The liability of the planning authority in negligence and more unusually, in public nuisance, has been considered in two important decisions of the Supreme Court.

In *Sunderland v. McGreavey, Rogers and Louth County Council*,[190] the plaintiffs claimed that the council were negligent in permitting the erection of a dwellinghouse on a site liable to serious flooding and in permitting the construction of a septic tank on the same site. The dwellinghouse had been built on a different part of the site to that for which permission had been granted. The council had stated in a letter to the plaintiffs that "in general the conditions of the planning permission have been complied with". In the Supreme Court, McCarthy J. considered that the Council *qua* planning authority owed no duty of care to the plaintiffs. He held that they were not liable for damage resulting from the lack of proper services provision arising from non-compliance with the terms of the planning permission.

In *Convery v. Dublin County Council*,[191] the applicants sought a mandatory injunction directing the respondent council to abate a nuisance caused by vehicular traffic using three roads in the Springfield Estate as an access route to Tallaght Town Square and other destinations. The roads had become a "rat run" as a result of a temporary access arrangement which had continued for a number of years. Evidence was given that the excessive weight and volume of vehicles was causing one of the roads to break up and that cracks were appearing in houses. It was claimed that the noise level was unbearable and that windows had to be kept closed due to the stench of fumes; children were in danger and there had been a number of fatal accidents.

---

[189] *Dwyer-Nolan Developments Ltd*, above, n.137.
[190] Unreported, High Court, October 13, 1995.
[191] [1990] I.L.R.M. 658.

In deciding whether the Council could be compelled to abate the nuisance, Carroll J. took a number of factors into account. The Council *qua* planning authority had imposed a particular road design on the developer without ensuring that the road infrastructure was adequate or would be within a reasonable time. They had not sought a contribution towards infrastructure which was needed for the development. The elected members of the Council had, according to Carroll J., "bowed to the number of objectors (representing voters) who have become used to inflicting themselves on the residents of the three roads." Following *Kelly v. Dublin County Council*,[192] Carroll J. concluded that "the failure of the Council to take any concrete steps to alleviate the problem amounts to negligence".

The judgment of the Supreme Court was delivered by Keane J. (O'Flaherty and Barrington JJ. concurring), who dismissed the Plaintiff's claim in nuisance in the following passage:

> "As to the claim founded on nuisance, the traffic did not originate in any premises owned or occupied by the County Council and was not generated as a result of any activities carried out by them. The fact that the traffic had reached a volume which caused significant inconvenience and discomfort for the residents was the result of a combination of factors: the development of large scale residential and commercial projects by private interests, the decisions of thousands of individual drivers to use this particular route, and the failure of central government to allocate funds for the provision of the necessary roads infrastructure, to mention the most obvious. The decisions of the County Council to which objection is taken is only one of a number of factors which has resulted in the present position. To treat the County Council, in these circumstances, as being the legal author of a public nuisance would be entirely contrary to principle and wholly unsupported by authority."

Keane J. held that the planning authority or An Bord Pleanala on appeal could not be said to have authorised the commission of any unlawful act as section 26(11) of the 1963 Act provided that –

> "A person shall not be entitled solely by reason of a permission or approval under this section to carry out development."

Following *Sunderland and McGreavey* which he held to have reversed, *sub silientio*, the earlier decision of the Supreme Court in *Weir v. Dun Laoghaire Corporation*, Keane J. dismissed the claim in negligence on the basis that the duty of the local authority was owed to the public in general and that the Plaintiffs were not affected in a sufficiently proximate manner by the performance of its duties as to enable them to affix liability on the local authority either as road authority or planning authority.

A developer who has suffered financial loss due to the delay of the planning authority in making a grant of planning permission may be entitled to damages for breach of statutory duty.[193]

---

[192] Unreported, High Court, O'Hanlon J., February 21, 1986.
[193] *O'Neill v. Clare County Council* [1983] I.L.R.M. 141. See also *State (Pine Valley Developments Ltd) v. Minister for the Environment* [1982] I.L.R.M. 169.

Chapter 9

PLANNING APPEALS

The changes in the procedure for planning appeals introduced by the Local Government (Planning and Development) Act 1992 bore the imprint of the intensive lobbying from the construction industry which preceded its introduction as a bill. Delays in planning appeals and the ensuing financing costs had been jeopardising many development projects. The underlying cause of these delays was the failure to impose effective time limits on the making of submissions by parties to an appeal.

The 1992 Act introduced a "one shot", appeal system under which all grounds of appeal had to be submitted within a period of one month of the planning authority giving its decision. Prior to the 1992 Act, members of the public and practitioners involved in the preparation of appeals had enjoyed the luxury of submitting initial grounds of appeal which could be elaborated upon at a later stage. The addition of further time limits for submissions to be made on other appeals brought to an end the ongoing exchange of documentation which frequently took place under the old system of appeals. To ensure that these improvements resulted in a greater efficiency in the output of decisions, a four month "deadline" was placed on the determination of appeals by the Board. This "deadline" was expressed in the Act as an "objective" in recognition of the fact that more complex appeals might require a greater period of consideration.

An Bord Pleanála handled 2,330 appeals in 1994 according to its annual report. Of these appeals, 98.5 per cent were determined within four months, compared with 78 per cent in 1993 and 34 per cent in 1992.

9.1 COMPOSITION AND FUNCTIONS OF AN BORD PLEANÁLA

9.1.1 Composition of Board

An Bord Pleanála was established under the Local Government (Planning and Development) Act 1976.[1] It is a body corporate composed of a chairperson, a deputy chairperson and five ordinary members.[2] The Chairman is appointed by the Government from three or less candidates selected by an independent committee consisting of

---

[1] 1976 Act, s.2.
[2] 1983 Act, s.3.

- the President of the High Court
- the Chairman of the County Councils General Council,
- the Chief Engineering Adviser of the Department of the Environment,
- the Chairman of An Taisce
- the President of the Construction Industry Federation, and
- the President of the Executive Council of the Irish Congress of Trade Unions.[3]

The office of Chairman is a wholetime appointment and is held for a term of seven years which may be renewed by the Government for a second term.[4] The ordinary members of the Board are appointed by the Minister the Environment but must include four members drawn from the nominees of four types of organisation which are in his opinion

- representative of persons whose professions or occupations relate to physical planning and development,
- representative of persons concerned with the protection and preservation of the environment,
- concerned with the promotion of economic or other development or are representative of property developers or the construction industry,
- concerned with the promotion of community interests.[5]

The Minister has prescribed a number of organisations in each of these categories.[6] The fifth ordinary member is an established civil servant appointed by the Minister from his Department.[7]

The quorum for a meeting of the Board is three. It is unlawful to communicate with the Chairman or with an ordinary member of the Board for the purpose of influencing his or her consideration of an appeal reference or other matter.[8]

9.1.2 Functions of the Board

The most important function of the Board under the planning code is to hear appeals from decisions of the planning authority on planning applications.[9] In addition, the Board has the following functions:

- the determination of references under section 5 of the 1963 Act,
- the determination of financial contributions in default of agreement between the applicant and the planning authority,[10]

---

[3]   1983 Act, s.5(2).
[4]   *ibid.*, ss.5(11) and (12).
[5]   *ibid.*, s.7(1)
[6]   1994 Regulations, arts. 45–48.
[7]   1983 Act, s.7(2)(e).
[8]   *ibid.*, s.14.
[9]   The Board also deals with appeals under air and water pollution legislation and under the building control code.
[10]   See 1976 Act, s.14(4).

- the confirmation of a purchase notice under section 29 of 1963 Act or the making of such other decision under the section
- the determination of appeals against a notice under section 30 of the 1963 Act revoking or modifying permission,
- the determination of appeals against a notice under section 37 of the 1963 Act requiring the discontinuance of any use of land or imposing conditions on the continuance of such use,
- the determination of appeals from a notice under section 44 of the 1963 Act requiring the removal or alteration of a hedge,
- the determination of appeals against a tree preservation order under section 45 of the 1963 Act,
- the determination of appeals against a conservation order under section 46 of the 1963 Act,
- the determination of appeals against an order under section 48 of the 1963 Act creating a public right of way,
- the determination of appeals under section 85 of the 1963 Act against refusal of consent,
- the determination of appeals against the grant, refusal, withdrawal or continuance of, or against the conditions attached to, a licence under section 89 of the 1963 Act to erect, construct, place or maintain petrol pumps and other specified types of appliances and structures on public roads,
- the determination of appeals against an acquisition notice (relating to open space) under section 25 of the 1976 Act,
- the determination of a dispute under section 15 of the 1990 Act as to whether a new structure would or does substantially replace a demolished or destroyed structure.

9.2 PROCEDURE FOR MAKING APPEAL

9.2.1 Contents of appeal

The 1992 Act introduces a "one-shot appeal" system. Section 4(1) sets out the requirements for an appeal:

"An appeal shall –
(a) be made in writing;
(b) state the name and address of the appellant;[11]
(c) state the subject matter of the appeal;
(d) state in full the grounds of appeal and the reasons, considerations and arguments on which they are based;
and

---

[11] The name of the appellant together with the address of the agent will not suffice. See Phillips, "Select Review of Recent An Bord Pleanála Planning Appeal Decisions and Changes in Procedures" (1995) IPELJ 103.

    (e) be accompanied by such fee (if any) as may be payable in respect of such appeal in accordance with regulations under Section 10 of the Act of 1982."

An appeal which does not comply with any of these requirements is invalid.[12] The appellant must state the grounds of appeal and arguments on which they are based in full, whether or not he has requested, or intends to request, an oral hearing of the appeal. An appellant is not entitled to elaborate or make further submissions on his initial grounds of appeal or to submit further grounds of appeal unless the Board considers it appropriate to request further submissions "in the interests of justice".[13] Any unsolicited additional submissions or grounds of appeal received by the Board cannot be considered by it.[14] Similarly, only documents, particulars or other information which accompany an appeal can be considered by the Board, subject to the discretion of the Board to require the submission of further documents which are necessary to enable it to determine an appeal.[15]

9.2.2 Time limit and service

An appeal against a decision on a planning application must be made within a period of one month beginning on the day of the giving of the decision of the planning authority.[16] Any appeal received outside the time limit is invalid.[17] There is some confusion as to whether "the day of the giving of the decision" refers to the day on which the decision is made by the planning authority or on which notification of the decision is received. In practice, the Board treats the day the decision is made as the date from which the appeal period runs.[18] The day on which the decision is given is counted as part of the appeal period.[19] For example, if a decision is made by the planning authority on November 11, the time for the making of an appeal will expire on December 10.

    There is no extension of the appeal period for appeals made by post, as formerly existed.[20] However, where the last day of the period of one month falls

---

12   Where a prescribed fee is paid by cheque, the fee is received by the Respondent on the day the cheque is delivered to it, provided that the cheque is subsequently honoured in the normal way: *Maher v. An Bord Pleanála* [1993] 1 I.R. 439.

13   The power of the Board to request further submissions in the interests of justice is conferred by s.9 of the 1992 Act.

14   1992 Act, s.7. See *Mulhall v. An Bord Pleanála*, unreported, High Court, McCracken J., March 21, 1996.

15   *ibid.*, s.10 deals with the power of the Board to require the submission of documents.

16   1963 Act, s.26(5)(f) as inserted by s.3(a) of the 1992 Act.

17   1992 Act, s.17(1)(a).

18   The better view would appear to be that the planning authoriity does not "give " its decision until. the applicant receives it: See *Freeney v. Bray U.D.C.* [1982] I.L.R.M. 29, although O'Keeffe P. in *State (Murphy) v. Dublin County Council* [1970] I.R. 253, held that the decision was given on the day it was posted: See 1963 Act, s.7. Having regard to the practice of the Board it is essential to regard the appeal period as running from the day that the decision is made.

19   See Interpretation Act 1937, s.11(h).

20   Section 22 of the 1976 Act was repealed by s.22 of the 1992 Act. Although an appeal can be made by sending it by pre-paid post, it must still be received within the appeal period: 1992 Act, s.17(1)(a). Delivery by hand is preferable having regard to the vagaries of the postal system.

on a Saturday, Sunday, a public holiday or any other day on which the offices of the Board are closed, an appeal will be treated as being on time if it is received either by hand or in the post on the next day on which the offices of the Board are open.[21] Late appeals, whether they are received by post or otherwise, are deemed to be invalid and the Board has no discretion to consider them.[22]

Section 4(5) indicates the manner in which an appeal must be lodged:

> " An appeal shall be made –
>
> (a) by sending the appeal by pre-paid post to the Board;
> or
> (b) by leaving the appeal with an employee of the Board at the offices of the Board during office hours[23]; or
> (c) by such other means as may be prescribed."

9.2.3 To appeal or not to appeal?

Any person may appeal to the Board against a decision of the planning authority to grant or refuse planning permission or approval for proposed development, or for the retention of or for the continuance of any use.[24] The first question which an applicant who has been refused permission or who has been granted permission subject to onerous conditions has to consider is as to whether he has an entitlement to compensation on foot of the planning authority's decision.[25] An applicant may lose his entitlement to compensation if the form of decision granted on appeal excludes liability to pay compensation under the 1990 Act.

A developer also has to assess whether a revised planning application might enjoy greater success than an appeal.[26] The planning authority are automatically parties to any appeal and obviously their views as to the proper planning and development of their functional area carry considerable weight with the Board. In many cases, it may be more productive to consult with the relevant officers of the planning authority with a view to making a fresh application when an unfavourable decision has been obtained so that the planning authority's objections to the original proposal may be accomodated.[27] In other cases, the views of the planning authority may be so entrenched that an appeal is the only realistic option.

---

[21] See 1992 Act, s.17(1)(b) and also art. 49(6)(ii) which is in similar terms.

[22] 1992 Act, s.17(1)(a).

[23] No definition of "office hours" is provided by the Acts or regulations or under the Interpretation Act 1937.

[24] 1963 Act, s.26(5), as substituted by the 1992 Act, s.3. "Approval" is defined as "an approval consequent on an outline permission or an approval which is required to be obtained under a condition subject to which a permission or an approval is granted under the Act".

[25] A claim for compensation may be made where none of the reasons stated in a refusal of permission by the planning authority are referred to in Sched. 3 to the 1990 Act, or, in the case of a grant of permission, where conditions other than those listed in Sched. 4 have been attached. See Chap. 12 .

[26] In 1994, permission was granted in 29 per cent of appeals against refusal. See the An Bord Pleanála, *Report and Accounts 1994*, p.18.

[27] In practice, many planning authorities are reluctant to discuss an application which is the subject of an appeal.

It is quite common for developers to lodge an appeal against the planning authority's decision at the eleventh hour so that a third party who is slow to react may find himself excluded due to the operation of the statutory time limit. Where a developer is certain to appeal it may be prudent for a third party to appeal a decision by the planning authority with which he or she is in accord so that they are not excluded from being a party to the appeal.[28]

An alternative approach is for the third party to wait until an appeal is lodged by the developer and then submit an observation. The disadvantage with this approach is that as an observer he is not entitled to request an oral hearing and in other respects may not be allowed to participate as fully in the appeal as a party. In practice, however, where a request for an oral hearing is granted to some other person who is a party to the appeal, observers will usually be allowed to take an active part in the hearing but may, at the discretion of the inspector, be precluded from cross-examining relevant witnesses.

One possible solution to the dilemma created by the statutory time limit is for the third party to lodge a brief summary of his grounds of appeal accompanied by a request for an oral hearing. If the applicant subsequently appeals, an observation can then be submitted by another third party containing a more detailed rebuttal of the grounds advanced in favour of the proposed development. Both parties can then be jointly represented at any oral hearing and will in practice enjoy the status of full parties to the appeal. It is clearly not satisfactory that such devices have to be resorted to and it is evident that the statutory procedure is not totally in harmony with the principles of natural justice.[29]

9.2.4 Appeal against conditions only

Another tactical decision which a developer has to make concerns a situation where a broadly favourable decision is obtained from the planning authority but to which one or more onerous conditions is attached. While the Act allows for the making of an appeal against one or more conditions in isolation, such an appeal can put the entire proposal at risk as the Board has a discretion to determine the application in its entirety as if it had been made to it in the first instance.[30]

---

[28] If a third party appeals against a refusal in this situation he should indicate in his grounds of appeal that he is seeking to have the decision of the planning authority confirmed, but for reasons additional to those given by the planning authority. Note that there does not appear to be any position under the planning code enabling an appellant to withdraw an appeal. However, the Board has power to declare applications or appeals to have been withdrawn under s.16 of the 1992 Act. The operation of the provisions for the making of an appeal would appear to be most unsatisfactory from the point of view of third parties.

[29] In 1994, third-party appeals resulted in a refusal of permission in 25 per cent of cases and permission was granted with revised conditions in 63 per cent of such appeals. See An Bord Pleanála, *Report and Accounts 1994*, p.18.

[30] In 1994, the statistics for such appeals show that planning permission was granted with the same conditions in 11 per cent of cases and permission refused in 5 per cent of such appeals. See An Bord Pleanála, *Report and Accounts 1994*, p.18. For an analysis of select appeal decisions concerning financial contribution, see Phillips, above, n.11. *loc. cit.*

Section 15(1) of the Local Government (Planning and Development) Act 1992 provides as follows:

"15–(1) Where –
> (a) an appeal is brought from a decision of a planning authority to grant a permission or approval and
> (b) the appeal relates only to a condition or conditions that the said decision provides that the permission or approval shall be subject to, and
> (c) the Board is satisfied, having regard to the nature of the condition or conditions, that the determination by the Board of the relevant application *as if it had been made to it in the first instance would not be warranted*,

then, subject to compliance by the Board with *sub-section (2)*, the Board may, in its absolute discretion, give the relevant planning authority such directions as it considers appropriate relating to the attachment, amendment or removal by that authority either of the condition or conditions to which the appeal relates or of other conditions".

In deciding whether to treat the appeal as one against conditions only the Board is restricted under section 15(2) of the 1992 Act to considering the following factors:–

- the conditions appealed
- any previous permission or approval considered relevant
- the proper planning and development of the area (including the preservation of amenities)
- the development plan
- any applicable special amenity area order

9.2.5 Availability of documents relating to planning applications and appeals

Any person can inspect the planning authority file on a particular application. When a decision is made on a planning application,[31] section 5 of the 1992 Act requires the planning authority to make the following documents available for inspection by the public during office hours at the offices of the planning authority:

> (a) A copy of the planning application and of any drawings, maps, particulars, evidence, environmental impact statement, other written study or further information received from the applicant;[32]
> (b) A copy of any report prepared by or on behalf of the planning authority on the planning application;
> (c) A copy of the decision of the planning authority and a copy of the notification of the decision given to the applicant.

---

[31] "Planning application" under s.5 of the 1992 Act includes applications for the retention of an unauthorised structure and for approvals required under a condition subject to which a permission or approval is granted. See definition of "approval" under 1994 Regulations, art. 3.

[32] Copies of an EIS received by the Board should also be made available for inspection or purchase for a reasonable fee at the offices of the Board: 1994 Regulations, art. 59.

These documents should remain available for inspection for a period of one month from the date that the planning authority gives its decision, or, where there are one or more appeals, until each of the appeals is withdrawn, determined or dismissed, or, in the case of an appeal against a condition or conditions only, until a direction is given to the planning authority by the Board.[33] The planning authority are also required to furnish the same documentation to the Board within 14 days of a copy of the appeal being sent to them by the Board.[34] Copies of any appeal lodged are also made available for public inspection at the offices of the planning authority.[35]

The documents relating to an appeal or other matter received by the Board after April 10, 1996 must also be made available for inspection at the offices of the Board.[36] These documents will, when the appeal has been determined, include the inspector's report and recommendation' on the appeal which provides an insight into the factors which may have weighed with the Board, although in some major appeals the inspector's recommendation has been rejected. Copies of any of these documents, excluding any plans or other drawings or photographs, or of extracts from documents may be obtained at the Board's offices. Any EIS submitted in connection with an application must be made available for inspection and for the purchase of extracts or the complete document.[37] The documents must be made available for a period of five years from the date on which the appeal or other matter is determined or dismissed or from the date on which the Board gave a direction to the planning authority in relation to an appeal against conditions.

9.2.6 Replying submissions by parties to the appeal

Each party to an appeal is entitled to be furnished with a copy of every other appeal as soon as it has been received by the Board, and to make submissions or observations on its contents within one month of the date of receipt.[38] Any submissions or observations received by the Board outside this period cannot be considered by the Board unless they have been specifically requested by it "in the interests of justice". If no submissions are received by the Board from a party to the appeal within the time allowed, the Board may determine the appeal without further notice.

---

[33] 1992 Act, s.5.

[34] *ibid.*, s.6. Note that there is no requirement for submissions by third parties on a planning application to be forwarded to An Bord Pleanála.

[35] 1994 Regulations, art. 64. The planning authority receives a copy of the appeal from the Board: See 1992 Act, s.7(1).

[36] 1994 Regulations, art. 72A, as inserted by Local Government (Planning and Development) Regulations 1995, (S.I. No. 75 of 1995), art.2. This does not apply to appeals or other matters which have been withdrawn.

[37] 1994 Regulations, arts. 59(1) and 59(2).

[38] *ibid.*, s.7.

9.2.7 Observations by non-parties

Any person who is not a party to an appeal may make submissions or observations in writing to the Board. within one month of the appeal being received by
the Board, or, where notice of receipt of an environmental impact statement is
published, within one month of its publication. Any submissions or further
documents which are received outside that period cannot be considered by the
Board, unless they have been specifically requested by the Board "in the interests
of justice".[39] But these time limits do not apply to submissions made by another
Member State arising from consultation about the environmental effects of a
particular development for which an environmental impact statement was
furnished. An observation must be accompanied by the prescribed fee or it will
be deemed invalid and will not be considered by the Board. Request for further
submissions or documents.

Section 9 provides that the Board can exercise a discretion, where it
considers it appropriate "in the interests of justice", to request any party or any
other person who has made submissions to the Board on an appeal, to make
further submissions on any matter which has arisen in the appeal. In such a case
the Board may serve a notice requesting the person concerned to make their
submissions within a period of not less than 14 days and not more than 28 days
from the date of service of the notice. Similarly, section 10 vests in the Board a
power to serve a notice requiring any party to submit a document, particulars or
other information within 14 days of the date of service, where the Board considers it "necessary for the purpose of enabling it to determine an appeal."
Having considered any response to either of these two notices, the Board may
dismiss or otherwise determine the appeal without further notice when the period
specified has expired.

9.2.8 Natural justice

The principle of *audi alterem partem* may impose a duty on the Board in certain
circumstances to exercise its discretion to request further submissions or
documents to ensure that a decision made by the Board is not flawed on natural
justice grounds. The Board has a duty to act judicially in relation to any submissions or observations made by parties to the appeal or non-parties who have
made an observation on an appeal, although the duty owed to observers is not as
extensive to the latter. In *State (Haverty) v. An Bord Pleanála*, the court was
concerned with the entitlements of those with observer status under the old
appeals procedure. In this case, the prosecutrix had requested from the Board and
was supplied with a copy of the grounds of appeal lodged by the applicant for
planning permission against a refusal by the planning authority. A detailed
response was made on her behalf to the Board. Some time later, additional

---

[39]   See 1992 Act, ss.9 and 10.

submissions on the original grounds of appeal were lodged by the developers. The prosecutrix did not receive these additional submissions. A conditional order of certiorari was initially granted on the grounds that the Board had acted in breach of the rules of natural justice as it had purported to adjudicate on the application without furnishing all submissions made on behalf of the applicant/developer to the prosecutrix so as to enable her to make submissions on them.

At the subsequent hearing to have the order made absolute, Murphy J. held that the prosecutrix was not entitled to be notified of the additional submissions or to be afforded an opportunity to reply to them. He said that the right of a member of the public to object to the decision of a planning authority to grant or refuse permission was "based on public interest or community spirit" and was not a right of property. He stated *obiter*, however, that if an applicant/developer

> "extended the original submission so radically as to constitute a different or additional case, in that event natural justice might well require An Bord Pleanála to postpone its decision until it had afforded interested parties an opportunity of commenting upon the revised submission."[40]

In *McGoldrick v. An Bord Pleanála*,[41] the applicant sought to have quashed a decision of the respondent on a reference submitted to it under section 5 of the Local Government (Planning and Development) Act 1963 that certain works to an annexe to the rear of a house sub-divided into flats did not constitute exempted development. The works in question had also been the subject of a retention application and refusal by the Board, the application having been made in response to a warning notice from the Board. The same inspector adjudicated on the appeal and on the reference.[42]

The applicant had submitted to the Board that the works were exempted under section 4(1)(g) as they did not materially affect the external appearance of the house. He had also stated that the entire building had been let in flats prior to the commencement of the 1963 Act and tendered as evidence letters from neighbouring residents which tended to show that the annexe pre-dated the Act. Letters to the contrary effect from a local residents' association, who were opposed to the development, were also considered by the Board. The applicant had offered to furnish additional evidence if what was tendered by him was deemed to be inadequate. The inspector, in his report, concluded on the evidence before him that the annexe was an unauthorised extension of recent origin.

Barron J. considered that the implication of the inspector's finding was that both the applicant and his architect were guilty of deception although they were

---

[40]   The putting forward of an "additional case" would appear to be precluded by the 1992 Act, s.4(3), subject to the discretion of the Board under s.9.

[41]   Unreported, High Court, Barron J., May 26, 1995.

[42]   No objection was taken to the fact that the same inspector determined the appeal and the section 5 reference. Barron J. commented that he could see no reason why the evidence used on the appeal should not have been used on the reference.

not given an adequate opportunity to meet the case which was being made against them. He found that the applicant had never been informed that the matter was being determined upon the basis that the averments of fact made on his behalf were not being accepted or that the real issue was the extent of the annexe and the date at which it had been constructed to that extent. The applicant was granted the relief sought.[43]

Barron J. dismissed the respondent's argument that relief should be refused on the ground that an appeal to the High Court from the Board's decision on the reference had been lodged and that this constituted an adequate remedy. He held that the applicant was entitled to have the particular issues of fact upon which his applications had been refused determined by the Board.

In *Mulhall v. An Bord Pleanála*,[44] the basis of the applicant's appeal against the granting of permission by the Board to the developers had been that the proposed development would give rise to a traffic hazard in so far as the use by the applicant of two entrances to his farmyard which were opposite the Georgian Inn was concerned. The applicant had also submitted certain photographs to the Board showing the use of the said entrances by his farm machinery in order to establish the existence of the alleged traffic hazard but the Board had refused to consider them as the applicant had, at that stage, already submitted his grounds of appeal. The applicant sought to argue on the application for leave that the Board should have requested them under section 9 of the 1992 Act.[45] McCracken J. held that if the Board had requested the photographs, they would have had an obligation to consider them, but they were unable to do this because of section 4(3) of the 1992 Act which provides:

> "without prejudice to section 9, an appellant should not be entitled to elaborate in writing upon, or make further submissions in writing in relation to, the grounds of appeal stated in the appeal or to submit further grounds of appeal and any such elaboration, submissions or further grounds of appeal that is or are received by the Board shall not be considered by it."

9.2.9 Matters other than those raised by the parties

The Board may take into account matters other than those raised by the parties or by any person who has made submissions or observations to the Board on the appeal, if they are considerations to which the Board are entitled to have regard under section 26(5).[46] Notice in writing must be given to each of the parties or

---

[43] See also *Nova Colour Graphic Supplies Limited v. The Employment Appeals Tribunal* [1987] I.R. 426.

[44] Unreported, High Court, March 21, 1996.

[45] In *Mulhall*, above, n.14 the background circumstances which allegedly gave rise to the need for further submissions were that certain road markings had been made on the roadway outside the applicant's farmyard entrances after his grounds of appeal had been lodged. Photographs intending to illustrate the impact of the road markings on the use of the entrances were then submitted by the applicant but were rejected by the Board.

[46] *i.e.* 1963 Act, s.26(5) as inserted by 1992 Act, 3(a)

"observers" of the matters which the Board proposes to take into account. In the event that an oral hearing is about to be held, or where an oral hearing of the appeal has already concluded and the Board considers it expedient to reopen the hearing, the notice should state that submissions on the relevant matters may be made to the person conducting the hearing. If the Board does not propose to hold an oral hearing, or to reopen a hearing which has already been concluded, the notice should state that submissions or observations may be made to the Board in writing within a specified period of not less than 14 or more than 28 days from the date of service of the notice. The usual prohibition on the elaboration of such submissions or the making of further submissions applies.[47]

9.2.10 Oral hearings

A party to an appeal may request an oral hearing, but the Board has an absolute discretion as to whether or not to grant it.[48] The Board will normally only grant an oral hearing for more complex appeals, in cases in which there is wide public or neighbourhood interest, or where the Board considers that written procedures may not be adequate to ensure proper treatment of the appeal. In a small number of cases the Board has granted an oral hearing in the absence of a request being made.[49]

A request for an oral hearing of an appeal must be made in writing to the Board and must be accompanied by the prescribed fee. A request for an oral hearing made by the appellant must be made within one month of the giving of the decision by the planning authority. Any other party to the appeal may make such a request within one month of the day on which a copy of the appeal is sent to that party by the Board. A request which is received after the expiration of these time limits, or is not accompanied by the appropriate fee, cannot be considered by the Board. Where the Board decides to determine the reference or appeal without an oral hearing, it must serve notice of its decision on the person requesting the hearing.

At least seven days notice must be given by the Board to all parties and observers of the time and place of the opening of the oral hearing, unless all of them are willing to accept shorter notice.[50] A request for an oral hearing may be withdrawn at anytime and parties and observers must be informed accordingly.

---

[47] See *Killiney and Ballybrack Development Association v. Minister for Local* (1974) 112 I.L.T.R. 69 and *Law v. Minister for Local Government*, unreported, High Court, Deale J., May 7, 1974, considered at para. 10.2.3, below.

[48] 1992 Act, s.12. An observer is not entitled to request an oral hearing.

[49] In 1994, requests for oral hearings were made to the Board in 89 cases, representing four per cent of all appeals. The Board directed that oral hearings be held in 28 cases, *i.e.* almost one third of the requests were granted. The Board also directed that oral hearings be held in nine cases in which requests for hearings had not been made by any of the parties but where the Board considered them to be were justified. See An Bord Pleanála, *Report and Accounts 1994*, p.10.

[50] 1994 Regulations, art. 74(2).The time or place of the hearing may be altered by the Board at any time before it is opened subject to the same provisions as to notice.

9.2.11 Procedure at oral hearing

An oral hearing may be conducted either by the Board or by a person appointed by the Board.[51] In practice, oral hearings are generally heard by an inspector appointed by the Board. The Inspector has discretion as to the procedure for the hearing which must be conducted "without undue formality". He decides the order of appearance of the parties. The inspector may allow any party to appear in person or to have representation. A person who is not a party to an appeal or reference or an observer may be heard at the discretion of the inspector where it is considered to be in the interests of justice.[52]

The inspector has a discretion as to the manner in which he conducts oral hearings. The "guillotining" of cross-examination does not necessarily result in a breach of the rules of natural justice. In *Keane v. An Bord Pleanála*,[53] observers were allowed to cross-examine certain witnesses but were stopped on at least two occasions by the inspector. Murphy J. did not accept that any breach of natural justice had been shown by the applicants to have occurred. He observed:

> "To evaluate the inspector's decision properly and confidently, it. would be necessary to have attended throughout the entire proceedings and indeed to undersand the issues raised therein or, at least, to have a complete transcript of the proceedings."

Where there is a conflict between the evidence put forward by a third-party appellant and the first-party appellant which is critical to the determination of an appeal or reference, the Board will, in certain circumstances, be obliged to give all parties an adequate opportunity to adduce further evidence before it accepts the evidence of either side.[54]

The *nemo iudex* principle has rarely been invoked in planning appeals. On the application for leave in *Keane v. Bord Pleanála*,[55] Murphy J. rejected as unstateable an argument that the inspector had acted in breach of natural justice by allowing a former chairman of An Bord Pleanála, since practising as a planning consultant, to give evidence on behalf of the first-party appellant.

The inspector may adjourn a hearing *sine die* or until a specific date. If the hearing is adjourned indefinitely, at least seven days notice of the time and place of the reopening of the oral hearing must be given to each of the parties to the appeal or reference, unless all of the parties agree to accept shorter notice. A hearing which has been closed may be reopened by the inspector but unless the Board considers it expedient to do so, an oral hearing will not usually be reopened

---

[51] 1994 Regulations, art. 74(5).

[52] *ibid.*, art. 75.

[53] Unreported, High Court, June 20 1995. See also, *McNally v. Martin* [1995] I.L.R.M. 351, *per* Flaherty J., quoted with approval by Murphy J. in *Keane*.

[54] *McGoldrick* n.41, above. See para. 9.2.8, above. But see *RGDATA v. An Bord Pleanála*, High Court, Barron J., April 30, 1996. See para 10.2.2, below.

[55] Unreported, High Court, June 20, 1995. See also *R. v. Hendon U.D.C., ex p. Chorley* [1933] 2 K.B.

after the inspector's report on the hearing has been submitted to the Board.[56]

If, for any reason, an inspector is unable or fails to carry out his functions in conducting an oral hearing or of making a report on that hearing, the Board may appoint another person to replace him.[57]

9.2.12 Powers of inspector at an oral hearing

An inspector at an oral hearing has the following powers:

(i) He may require any officer of the planning authority to furnish him with any information relating to the reference or appeal which he reasonably requires;

(ii) He may visit and inspect any land to which the reference or appeal relates.[58]

(iii) He may take evidence on oath and may administer oaths. (The same immunities and privileges are available to a person giving evidence before an oral hearing of a planning appeal as may be claimed by a witness before the High Court);[59]

(iv) He may, by notice in writing, require the attendance of any person at the hearing, either to give evidence or to produce any books, deeds, contracts, accounts, vouchers, maps, plans or other documents in his possession, custody or control which are relevant to the hearing.[60] Provision is also made for the recovery of reasonable and necessary expenses by a person required to attend. An offence is committed where a person required to attend refuses or wilfully neglects to attend, wilfully alters, conceals or destroys any document to which the notice relates, or refuses or wilfully fails to produce any document to which the notice relates.

The Board may engage consultants or advisors.[61] It may also refer any questions of law on any reference, appeal or section 76 hearing to the High Court for a decision.[62] When an oral hearing has been closed, the inspector, having considered the evidence tendered, makes a report to the Board which includes a recommendation as to the form of decision which he considers appropriate. The Board makes its decision on the appeal having considered the report and the inspector's recommendation.[63]

---

[56] 1994 Regulations art. 76.
[57] *ibid.*, art. 77.
[58] 1963 Act, s.82(5)(a). Any person who obstructs him in the excercise of this power is guilty of an offence. Further powers to enter onto land are referred to under s.83 of the 1963 Act, see above.
[59] 1963 Act, s.82(6).
[60] *ibid.*, s.82(7).
[61] 1976 Act, s.13
[62] 1963 Act, s.82(3)
[63] 1976 Act, s.23

9.2.13 Power to dismiss appeals

The Board has power to dismiss appeals where it considers them to be "vexatious, frivolous or without substance or foundation".[64] Section 14 provides:

> "Subject to sub-section (2), the Board shall in the following circumstances have an absolute discretion to dismiss an appeal –
>
> (a) where, having considered the grounds of appeal, the Board is of the opinion that the appeal is vexatious, frivolous or without substance or foundation; or
> (b) where, having regard to –
> (i) the nature of the appeal (including any question which in the Board's opinion is raised by the appeal), and
> (ii) any previous permission or approval which in its opinion is relevant;
> the Board is satisfied that in the particular circumstances the appeal should not be further considered by it."

The Board also has power to dispose of appeals where it is of the opinion that the appeal or any application for planning permission or approval to which the appeal relates should be regarded as having been withdrawn.[65]

9.3 DETERMINATION OF APPEALS

9.3.1 Jurisdiction of the Board

The Board may grant permission or approval even if the proposed development is in material contravention of the development plan or special amenity area order for the area of the authority in which the proposed development is located. The Board determines the application as if it had been made to it in the first instance.[66] This phrase has been interpreted to mean that the Board are not concerned with any lack of jurisdiction in the planning authority when it made its decision. In *O'Keeffe v. An Bord Pleanála*,[67] Costello J. said that the Board:

> ". . . should not have any regard to what had happened before the planning authority . . . no defect in the proceedings before the planning authority should have any bearing, or impose legal constraints on the proceedings before the Board."

On the other hand, the Board have power to deal with errors of law which were not made in excess of jurisdiction.[68] In that case Henchy J. observed that:

> ". . . the Acts envisage the operation of a self-contained administrative code with resort to the Courts only in exceptional circumstances."[69]

---

[64] 1992 Act, s.16.
[65] *ibid.*, s.16.
[66] 1963 Act, s.26 (5)(b), as substituted by 1992 Act, s.3.
[67] [1993] 1 I.R. 39.
[68] See *State (Abenglen Properties Ltd) v. Dublin Corporation*, [1984] I.R. 381 *per* Henchy J.
[69] [1984] I.R. at 405.

The Board had power to refer of law which arises in any appeal or on any reference to the High Court for its determination.[70]

9.3.2 Relevant considerations

The determination of an appeal is made by the Board itself having considered the report of the inspector assigned to the appeal including his or her recommendation. The practice generally followed by the Board, at least when an oral hearing has been granted, is to delegate on of its members to consider the entire file of documents and evidence, in addition to the inspector's report, when the hearing and all submissions are closed. The member in question will then make a presentation of the entire case to a meeting of the members of the Board.[71] It is not unusual for the Board not to follow the recommendation of its inspector.[72]

The Board is restricted to considering the proper planning and development of the area of the planning authority within which the proposed development is situate, including the preservation and improvement of the amenities of that area. It is obliged to have regard to the following matters:

(a) The provisions of the development plan.[73]

(b) The provisions of any special amenity area relating to the area of the planning authority to whose decision the appeal relates. material contravention.[74]

(c) Any matters relating to the conditions which may be attached to a planning permission or approval under section 26(2) of the 1963 Act.

(d) Any general policy directives as to planning and development issued by the Minister.[75]

(e) Any EIS submitted including any supplemental information requested by the Board, together with any observations on the EIS by third parties.[76]

(f) Any environmental quality objectives published by the Agency provided that the proposed development is not related to an activity for which an IPC licence is required.[77]

(g) All relevant grounds of appeal and submissions by third parties, with the exception that where the proposed development relates to an

---

[70]   1963 Act, s.82(3). See *Max Developments Ltd v. An Bord Pleanála* [1994] I.R. 121.

[71]   See *Simonovich v. An Bord Pleanála*, unreported, High Court, Lardner J., July 24, 1988.

[72]   At the time of writing the inspector's recommendation was not followed in a number of significant appeals, including the appeal against a landfill at Arthurstown, County Kildare and the appeal against the Masonite plant in County Leitrim.

[73]   The Board may decide to grant planning permission or approval even if the proposed development is in material contravention of the development plan:1976 Act, s.14(8).

[74]   However, the Board may decide to grant planning permission or approval even if the proposed development is in material contravention of the special amenity area order: 1976 Act, s.14(8).

[75]   1982 Act, s.7.

[76]   1963 Act, s.26(5)(d), as substituted by 1992 Act, s.39(a).

[77]   See Environmental Protection Agency Act 1992, s.75.

activity for which an IPC licence is required, any matter relating to the risk of environmental pollution from the activity must be excluded from its consideration.[78]

In addition, the Board may, at its discretion, have regard to:

(i) Where the Board considers it appropriate, the probable effect which a particular decision by it would have on any area which is outside the area of the planning authority to whom the application was made and any other consideration relating to development outside the area of that authority.

(ii) Where the Board are deciding whether to specify a period of more than five years during which a planning permission under Section 26 of the 1963 Act is to have effect, it may have regard to "the nature and extent of the relevant development and any other material considerations".[79]

(iii) Where the Board is exercising its discretion to treat an appeal as one against a condition or conditions only, it may also take into account the terms of any previous permission or approval considered by the Board to be relevant.[80]

The Board has a duty "so far as may in the opinion of the Board be necessary for the performance of its functions, to keep itself informed of the policies and objectives for the time being of the Minister, planning authorities and any other body which is a public authority whose functions have or may have a bearing on the proper planning and development. . .".[81]

"Public Authority" is defined as –

- any Minister of State other than the Minister for the Environment,
- the Commissioners of Public Works in Ireland,
- the Irish Land Commission,
- a Harbour Authority within the meaning of section 2 of the Harbours Act, 1946 and
- any other statutory body which is for the time being declared to be a public authority for the purposes of the section.

Article 164 extends the definition to the following bodies:

- Bord Failte Éireann
- Bord Telecom Éireann
- An Chomhairle Éalaion
- Coras Iompair Éireann

---

[78]   *ibid.*, s.98(1). See further para. 8.1.4, above.
[79]   1982 Act, s.3. The exercise or refusal to exercise this power is regarded as forming part of the relevant decision of the planning authority.
[80]   1992 Act, s.15(2).
[81]   1976 Act, s.5; see *State (CIE) v. An Bord Pleanála*, Unreported, Supreme Court, December 12, 1984.

- the Electricity Supply Board
- Forfas
- the National Monuments Advisory Council
- An Post
- the Shannon Free Airport Development Company Limited
- Udaras na Gaeltachta

9.3.3 Irrelevant considerations: risk of environmental pollution

The risk of environmental pollution is no longer a relevant planning consideration when a planning authority or An Bord Pleanála come to determine a planning application, if the proposed development constitutes or is being carried out for the purposes of an activity for which an IPC licence has been granted or will be required. Neither a planning authority no An Bord Pleanála can refuse permission or an approval for the reason that the development would cause environmental pollution nor can they attach conditions for the prevention, limitation, elimination, abatement or reduction of environmental pollution from the activity.[82]

9.3.4 Powers of entry on land and ancillary powers

A member of the Board or an authorised person may, subject to the provisions of section 83 of the 1963 Act, enter on any land at all reasonable hours between the hours of 9 a.m. and 6 p.m. for any purpose connected with an appeal or reference.[83] He may do anything which is reasonably necessary for the purpose for which the entry is made, and is specifically entitled to survey, make plans, take levels, make excavations, and examine the depth and nature of the sub-soil. The consent of the occupier, or the owner, as appropriate, must be obtained or the member of the Board or authorised person must give not less than 14 days notice in writing of his intention to make the entry. Such entry can only be prevented in the latter case by the owner or occupier seeking an order prohibiting entry from the District Court.[84]

9.3.5 Modification of applications

Article 63 of the 1994 Regulations enables the Board to invite an applicant to submit modifications to proposed development, but unlike Article 35, which prescribes the equivalent procedure for planning authorities, it is not restricted to situations where the Board are disposed to granting a permission or approval. The Board may invite the applicant to submit to the Board, in duplicate, revised plans or other drawings, modifying, or other particulars providing for the

---

[82] See further discussion at para. 8.1.4, above.
[83] An "authorised person" is defined as a "person who is appointed by the planning authority, the Minister or the Board to be an authorised person for the purposes of the section.
[84] 1963 Act, s.83(4).

modification of the development to which the appeal relates. Where the revised plans constitute an alteration rather than a modification to the proposal, this may raise the question as to whether members of the public have had an adequate opportunity to make representations concerning the altered proposal.[85]

9.3.6 Costs

The Board may direct the planning authority to pay costs to the appellant or to the Board irrespective of the result of the appeal.[86] Costs may also be awarded to the planning authority, to any of the other parties to the appeal or to the Board against the appellant where the decision of the planning authority is confirmed on appeal, or where the decision of the planning authority is varied, but the Board does not accede in substance to the appellant's grounds of appeal. In practice, and award of costs is not usually made by the Board.

9.3.7 Notification of decision

Article 65 of the 1994 Regulations stipulate those matters which must be included in a notification given by the Board of a decision on an appeal. The date and effect of the decision is entered on the planning register within a period of seven days.

---

[85] See para. 8.2.3.1, above.
[86] 1963 Act, s.18; 1976 Act, s.19. Note that s.19(2) of the 1976 Act which placed a monetary limit of £200 on the sum which could be recovered has been repealed by the 1992 Act, s.22.

Chapter 10

JUDICIAL REVIEW

10.1.1 Introduction

The courts have a very significant role in the development control process despite their concern to distance themselves from planning functions. Unlike their U.K. counterparts, the Irish judges have been instrumental in determining the scope of development control by defining what is meant by "development". Similarly, the supervisory jurisdiction of the courts has been invoked to review the decisions of planning authorities and An Bord Pleanála. However, in reviewing their decisions, the courts have sought to emphasise that it is not their function to adjudicate on the merits of particular proposals.

Originally, the former prerogative writs of certiorari, mandamus and prohibition existed only to challenge the decisions of inferior courts, but their scope was extended to include the review of decisions of bodies which were under a "duty to act judicially".[1] The principle of *ultra vires* upon which the judicial review of administrative decisions is based requires that an administrative body must not act in excess of its authority under law. The principle may itself be split up into a number of sub-principles: the tribunal or body must act in accordance with the rules of natural or constitutional justice, with any procedural requirements specified under statute, must not fetter its discretion but exercise it in a reasonable manner; and so on.

In *R. v. Hillingdon Borough Council, ex parte Royco Homes Ltd*,[2] Widgery C.J. said that since the decision of the House of Lords in *Ridge v. Baldwin*, there was "no reason for this Court holding otherwise than that there is power in appropriate cases for the use of the prerogative orders to control the activity of a local planning authority".[3] In reviewing the exercise of planning authorities of their powers under planning legislation, the courts have restricted themselves to considering matters of law as distinct from the merits or otherwise of the decision by the planning authority or the Board. The decision has perhaps been best stated by Lord Brightman in *Chief Constable of the North Wales Police v. Evans*:

---

[1]   "Judicial Acts" have been described as "not necessarily the acts of a judge or legal tribunal . . . but . . . (acts) done by a competent authority on consideration of facts and circumstances and imposing liabilities or affecting the rights of others".

[2]   [1974] Q.B. 720.

[3]   [1964] A.C. 40.

"Judicial review is concerned, not with the decision but with the decision-making process. Unless that restriction on the power of the Courts is observed, the Courts will in my view, under the guise of preventing the abuse of power, be itself guilty of usurping power. . . . Judicial review, as the words imply, is not an appeal from a decision, but a review of the manner in which the decision was made."[4]

10.1.2 Judicial review procedure

Reducing delays in the planning system was, as has been seen already, the main purpose behind the Local Government (Planning and Develoment) Act 1992. In *KSK Enterprises v. An Bord Pleanála*,[5] Finlay C.J. stated as follows:

"From these provisions, it is clear that the intention of the legislature was greatly to confine the opportunity of persons to impugn by way of judicial review decisions made by the planning authorities, and in particular one may assume that it was intended that a person who has obtained a planning permission should at a very short interval after the date of such decision, in the absence of a substantial review, be entirely legally protected against subsequent challenge to the decision that was made and therefore presumably left in a position to act with safety on the basis for that decision."[6]

Section 19(3) of the 1992 Act is the vehicle for amendments to the procedure for challenging planning decisions, substituting a new section 82 (3A) and (3B) for section 82 (3A) of the 1963 Act[7]:

"(3A)   A person shall not question the validity of —
   (a)   a decision of the planing authority on an application for a permission or approval under Part IV of this Act, or
   (b)   a decision of the Board on any appeal or on any reference, otherwise than by way of an aplication for judicial review under Order 84 of the Rules of the Superior courts (S.I. No. 15 of 1986) (hereafter in this section referred to as 'the Order')
(3B) (a)   An application for leave to apply for judicial review under the Order in respect of a decision referred to in subsection (3A) of this section shall —
   (i)   be made within the period of two months commencing on the date on which the decision is given, and
   (ii)   be made by motion on notice grounded in the manner specified in the Order in respect of an ex parte motion for leave) to
      (I)   if the application relates to a decision referred to in subsection (3A)(a) of this section, the planning authority concerned and,

---

4   [1982] 1 W.L.R. 1155 at 1160. Quoted with approval by Finlay C.J. in *O'Keefe v. An Bord Pleanála* [1993] 1 I.R. 39 at 71.
5   [1994] 2 I.R. 128.
6   See dicta to similar effect from Costello J. (as he was then) concerning the two month time limit in *Cavern Systems Dublin Ltd v. Clontarf Residents Association and Dublin Corporation* [1984] I.L.R.M. 29. See also Benson, Matheson Ormsby Prentice, Ove Arup, "The Impact of Planning, Licensing and Environmental Issues on Industrial Development", a report to the Industrial Policy Review Group (1992).
7   s.82(3A) was inserted by the 1976 Act, s.42(a).

where the applicant for leave is not the applicant for the permission or approval under Part IV of this Act, the applicant for such permission or approval,

(II) if the application relates to a decision referred to in subsection 3(A)(b) of this section, the board and each party or each other party, as the case may be, to the appeal or reference,

(III) any other person specified for that purpose by order of the High Court,

and such leave shall not be granted unless the High Court is satisfied that there are substantial grounds for contending that the decision is invalid or ought to be quashed.

(b) (i) The determination of the High Court of an application for leave to apply for judicial review as aforesaid or of an application for such judicial review shall be final and no appeal shall lie from the decision of the High Court to the Supreme Copurtin either case save with the leave of the High Court which leave shall only be granted where the High Court certifies that its decision involves a point of law of exceptional public importance and that it is desirable in the public interest that an appeal should be taken to the Supreme court.

(ii) This paragraph shall not aply to a determination of the HIgh Court in so far as it involves a question as to the validity of any law having regard to the provisions of the Constitution . . ."

10.1.3 Procedure for challenge

The new section 82(3A) limits the form of proceedings which can be used to challenge a planning decision. An application for judicial review is only available under Order 84 of the Rules of the Superior Courts.[8] The application for leave to apply for judicial review is made by motion on notice, as distinct from the normal procedure under Order 84 where the initial application was made *ex-parte*. The application for leave has, as a result, become a much more critical stage of the procedure in the control of the judicial review of planning decisions and may represent "the end of the road" in a greater number of cases.

The applicant is required to serve a notice of motion together with grounding affidavit and a statement of grounds within two months of the date of the giving of the decision or reference impugned.[9] The statement of grounds specifies the relief required and the grounds on which that relief is sought.[10] These documents must be served on each of the parties required by the section. In the case of a

---

[8] Prior to the passing of the Act, proceedings to challenge the validity of a planning decision could be commenced either by way of plenary summons or by way of an application for leave for judicial review. But while an application for an order of certiorari, for example, was by way of motion and, therefore, a reasonably expeditious form of relief, the action by way of plenary summons was a lengthier process. Furthermore, the plenary summons had to be issued but not necessarily served within the two month time limit.

[9] 1963 Act, s.82(3B). In *Inver Resources Limited v. Limerick Corporation* [1978] 1 I.R. 289., Barron J. suggested that the time limit operated to prohibit further legal challenge even in circumstances where the application was not properly advertised.

[10] Forms are contained under Appendix O of the Rules of the Superior Courts.

third party challenge to a decision of the planning authority, the applicant for permission must be served as well as the planning authority. Where the challenge is to a decision or reference of the Board, both the planning authority and the applicant, in addition to any other party to the appeal or reference on which the decision was made, must be joined as notice parties and served with the proceedings. Failure to serve any party on whom service is required by the section within the two month time limit will invalidate the application. The court may also direct that some other person be served. It is not necessary that the application should be opened in court within the two month period; once the proceedings are served on all of the mandatory parties, the application is regarded as having been "made" as the section requires.[11]

To add any new ground whether by amendment of the statement of grounds or by the introduction of new affidavit evidence after the expiration of the two month period is impermissible. It is not possible to circumvent the difficulties posed by the time limit by drafting a "catch all" plea to be honed into a more specific ground at a later date. For example, it is not possible to rely on a general contention that the environmental impact statement accompanying an application is defective and to specify these defects after the time limit has elapsed.[12] Where irrationality is relied upon as a ground, the species of irrationality must be pleaded. Further affidavit evidence may be adduced outside the time limit provided that such evidence does not add to the grounds relied upon. Additional evidence may not be adduced for the purposes of verifying grounds where these have not already been verified.

Order 84, Rule 22 requires a respondent who intends to oppose the application for judicial review to file a statement of opposition together with a grounding affidavit on all parties within seven days of the service of the notice of motion or such other period as the court may direct. It is not clear precisely how this requirement applies to the judicial review of planing decisions as the procedure is *sui generis* to the extent that the initial application for leave is on notice whereas all other applications for leave to apply for judicial review are *ex parte*. A literal interpretation of the rule would suggest that the statement of opposition should be filed and served by the respondent prior to the hearing of the application for leave and this construction would also appear to be the reading most consistent with natural justice principles.

Discovery of all relevant material on which the decision is based should be sought prior to the application for leave. However, an affidavit of discovery will not necessarily disclose all of the material on which the decision was based. If a

---

[11] *KSK Enterprises,* above, n.5.
[12] *McNamara v. An Bord Pleanála*, High Court, unreported, May 10, 1996, in which Barr J. followed the *ex tempore* judgment of Murphy J. in the High Court in *Keane v. An Bord Pleanála and the Commissioners of Irish Lights*, delivered on May 23, 1995. In the latter case Murphy J. referred to the "extraordinarily brief time limit" under s.82(3B), raising doubts as to its constitutionality.

full minute or list of the relevant material is not contained in the discovered documents, it is necessary for the applicant, by motion or otherwise, to seek the delivery of such a list as the onus is on the applicant to establish the extent of the material which was before the decision-making authority.[13]

At the hearing of the application for leave the applicant must establish that he or she has "a sufficient interest" in the planning decision and that he or she has "substantial grounds" for contending that the decision is invalid. At the determination of the hearing the court may refuse leave or allow the application to go forward on some or all of the grounds relied upon in the statement of grounds.

10.1.4 Meaning of "decision"

A decision by Dublin County Council to refuse a developer's cheque in purported discharge of a condition which required the developer to pay a financial contribution for services to Dublin County Council and/or Dublin Corporation, was held not to be a "decision" caught by the time limit under section 82(3A). The Supreme Court held in *State (Finglas Industrial Estates Ltd) v. Dublin County Council*,[14] that the condition was *ultra vires* and as the planning authority could only attach a condition which required a contribution to be agreed between *the planning authority to whom the application was made* and the person making the application. It was also held that mandamus could not issue to compel a planning authority to accept money where there was no public duty to accept it.

The approval of revised plans by a planning authority on foot of a condition granted by An Bord Pleanála is a decision capable of being judicially reviewed.[15]

10.1.5 Substantial grounds

"Substantial grounds" must be shown before an applicant can obtain leave to apply for judicial review.[16] The most helpful statement as to what constitutes "substantial grounds" was furnished by Carroll J. In *McNamara v. An Bord Pleanála*,[17] The applicant, acting as chairman and representative of the Kill Residents Group, was seeking to quash a decision of An Bord Pleanála to grant planning permission to Dublin County Council (as it then was) for a landfill site at Kill, County Kildare.[18] Carroll J. stated:

> "What I have to consider is whether any of the grounds advanced by the appellant are substantial grounds for contending that the Board's decision was invalid. In order for a ground to be substantial it must be reasonable, it must be arguable, it must be weighty. It must not be trivial or tenuous. However, I am not concerned in

13 *per* Finlay C.J. in *O'Keefe*, above, n.4.
14 Unreported, February 17, 1983.
15 *Gregory v. Dun Laoghaire Rathdown County Council*, unreported, Geoghegan J., July 16, 1996.
16 1963 Act, s.82(38)(a), as inserted by the 1992 Act, s.19(3).
17 Unreported, High Court, January 24, 1995.
18 The oral hearing of the appeal from the refusal of Kildare County Council to grant permission lasted five weeks.

trying to ascertain what the eventual result would be. I believe I should go no further than satisfying myself that the grounds are 'substantial'. A ground that does not stand any chance of being sustained (for example, where the point has already been decided in another case) could not be said to be substantial. I draw a distinction between the grounds and the various arguments put forward in support of those grounds. I do not think I should evaluate each argument and say whether I consider it is sound or not. If I consider a ground, as such, to be substantial, I do not also have to say that the applicant is confined in this argument at the next stage to those which I believe may have some merit."

The applicant contended in his first ground that the Environmental Impact Statement (EIS) submitted with the planning application was defective in that it did not contain any reference to the excavation of saturated sand and gravel to below the water line (to a depth of four metres), which was stipulated by Condition 10 of the planning permission. He claimed that such extensive excavation required an EIS in itself as it consisted of the "extraction of stone, gravel, sand or clay where the area involved would be greater than five hectares".[19] This ground was held to be substantial.

In his second ground, the applicant claimed that the newspaper notice published prior to the planning application was inadequate in that it did not refer to the additional development required by Condition 10. Carroll J. held that this was also a substantial ground.

The learned judge then went on to consider whether there were substantial grounds for challenging the validity of a number of conditions which left certain matters to be agreed between the planning authority and the applicant. In doing so, she referred to *Boland v. An Bord Pleanála*, in which Keane J. had granted a certificate to the applicants to appeal to the Supreme Court against his decision to uphold the validity of similar conditions requiring matters to be agreed. Carroll J. held, in effect, that the certification of a point of law of exceptional public importance in such similar circumstances bound her to hold that the grounds in the case before her were substantial also.

Finally, Carroll J. granted leave on other grounds relating to the validity of planning conditions concerning traffic and road improvements which the applicant claimed would be impossible to enforce because Kildare County Council would be unwilling to do so.[20]

Consideration of an application for leave should not involve a detailed examination of the grounds on which relief is sought. In *Scott and Others v. An Bord Pleanála (Respondent) and Arcon Mines Limited, Kilkenny County Council*

---

[19]   Para. (2)(d) of Sched. 1 to the European Communities (Environmental Impact Assessment) Regulations 1989.

[20]   Carroll J. deferred any consideration as to the extent to which the applicant was limited by the formal grounds relied upon in his notice of motion until the substantive hearing. Barr J. subsequently refused leave, having excluded a number of grounds which had been added by the applicants after the expiration of the two month time limit under s.82(3B) of the 1963 Act, as inserted by s.19(3) of the 1992 Act.

and Others (Notice Parties), the applicants argued that Costello J. had treated the application for leave as if it was a judicial review hearing rather than restricting himself to a consideration as to whether the grounds were substantial or not, but this argument was rejected by the Supreme Court.[21] Egan J., giving the judgment of the court, said that the words "substantial grounds" in effect required that the grounds must be "reasonable" as the court was concerned with legal grounds rather than factual argument. On this basis, the court upheld Costello J.'s view that the question as to whether the applicant had a sufficient legal interest to apply for planning permission was a substantial one.

10.1.6 Appeals to the Supreme Court

The new statutory provisions for judicial review of planning decisions have also made it much more difficult to appeal from a decision of the High Court. Appeals to the Supreme Court from a decision of the High Court on an application for leave or on the application for judicial review itself will be allowed only where leave of the High Court judge is obtained unless the constitutionality of a law is at issue.[22] Such leave may only be granted where the High Court certifies:

> ". . . that its decision involves a point of law of exceptional public importance and that it is desirable in the public interest that an appeal should be taken to the Supreme Court."

It is not essential for the trial judge to specify the precise point of law involved.[23] The decision of the High Court judge to refuse a certificate is not appealable.[24]

10.2 GROUNDS FOR JUDICIAL REVIEW

The decision-making powers of planning authorities must be exercised in accordance with the statutory provisions under which they are conferred. The

---

[21] Unreported Supreme Court, (Hamilton C.J., Egan and Blayney JJ., *Nem Diss*) November 11, 1994. Although Order 84 of the Rules of the Superior Court 1986 offers no real guidance on the point, the practice generally followed is that a statement of opposition from the respondent is not required at the leave stage. This means that the respondent in judicial review proceedings does not have to give notice of the legal arguments on which his opposition is based, while the other side will have already shown its hand.

[22] It has been commented that a High Court judge is, in these circumstances, acting as a judge in his own cause and that this restriction of the constitutional right of appeal to the Supreme Court offends against principles of natural justice: O' Sullivan and Shepherd, para. 4.103. See also *Corrigan v. Irish Land Commission* [1977] I.R. 317.

In *Scott v. An Bord Pleanála*, Supreme Court, Hamilton, Egan, and Blayney JJ., *nem diss.*, November 29, 1994, the Supreme Court held, following the *People (at the suit of the Attorney General) v. Ronald Giles* [1974] I.R. 422, that it was not essential for the trial judge to specify the precise point of law involved.

[23] *Scott*, above, n.21, following *People (at the suit of the Attorney General) v. Ronald Giles*.

[24] *Irish Asphalt Ltd v. An Bord Pleanála,* unreported, Supreme Court, Hamilton C.J., Blayney and Denham JJ., in which the court followed the decision in *Minister for Justice v. Wang Zhu Jie* [1993] 1 I.R. 426.

planning authority must not fetter its discretion by committing itself to make its determination in a particular way.[25] Relevant considerations must be taken into account and irrelevant factors must be excluded. Fair procedures must be followed in arriving at its determination and, in particular, the maxim *audi alterem partem* must be observed. A planning authority's decision may also be set aside on grounds of unreasonableness but only where it can be established that no reasonable planning authority would have made the decision challenged. These are the basic principles which apply to all administrative decisions which affect the rights of individuals.[26] The application of these principles to planning decisions has in part been considered elsewhere so that the classification below should not be considered to be comprehensive.

10.2.1 Unreasonableness

A decision of the planning authority or the Board can only be set aside on this ground where the decision is "so unreasonable that no reasonable authority would ever have come to it"[27] or where it flies in the face of fundamental reason and common sense.[28] The boundaries of irrationality are set by the reluctance of the courts to interfere with the jurisdiction of the planning authority and the Board in planning matters, and is perhaps best expressed in the judgment of Finlay C.J. in *O'Keefe v. An Bord Pleanála*,[29] where he stated:

> "The court cannot interfere with the decion of an adminisrative decision-making authority merely on grounds that:
> (a) it is satisfied that on the facts as found it would have raised differnt inferences and conclusions, or
> (b) it is satisfied that the case against the decision made by the authority was much stronger than the case for it. . .
> I am satisfied that in order for an applicant for judicial review to satisfy a court that the decision-making authority has acted irrationally . . . it is necessary that the applicant should establish to the satisfaction of the court that the decision-making authority had before it no relevant material which would support its decision."

The onus of establishing that there was no material on which the decision could have been based is on the applicant.[30] It is therefore advisable for an applicant to seek disclosure of all material relevant to the decision prior to the application for leave to apply for judicial review.[31] In *O'Keefe v. An Bord Pleanála*, the Supreme

---

[25] For example, the authority should not fetter its discretion because of a general policy which bears upon the decision before them but to which they are not bound by statute to have regard: see *Stringer v. Minister of Housing and Local Government* [1971] 1 All E.R. 65.

[26] See further, Alder, *Development Control* (2nd ed.) pp.26–153.

[27] *per* Lord Greene M.R. in *Associated Provincial Picture Houses v. Wednesbury Corporation* [1948] 1 K.B. 223, at p. 230. See *Gregory v. Dun Laoghaire Rathdown County Council*, unreported, Geoghegan J., July 16, 1996.

[28] *The State (Keegan) v. The Stardust Compensation Tribunal* [1986] I.R. 642.

[29] Above, n.4.

[30] *Sharpe (P. & F.) Ltd v. Dublin City Manager* [1989] I.R. 701.

[31] *per* McCarthy J. in *O'Keefe*, above, n.4.

Court held that there was sufficient material in the recitals of evidence heard before the inspector and contained in his report to enable the Board to have come to a different conclusion to that of its inspector and, indeed, the opinion formed by its assessor on the proposed erection by Radio Tara of a long-wave transmitting station at Clarkestown in County Meath.[32]

The question of unreasonableness in decision-making cannot be determined where there is no record of the decision challenged and in this situation the trial judge is entitled to consider the matter *de novo*.[33]

10.2.2 Error on the face of the record

In *State (Abenglen Properties Ltd) v. Dublin Corporation*[34] Henchy J. emphasised that the remedy of certiorari is only available where there is an error on the face of the record or a breach of natural justice:

> "Where an inferior Court or a Tribunal errs within jurisdiction without recording that error on the face of the record, certiorari does not lie. It is only when in such cases there is the extra flaw that the Court or Tribunal acted in disregard of the requirements of natural justice that certiorari will issue. In the present case, there is no suggestion that the Corporation, in dealing with this application, acted in disregard of any of the regulations of natural justice. They went wrong in law, if at all, in answering legal questions within their jurisdiction, and they did not reproduce any such legal error on the face of the record of their decision. Consequently, in my view, they did not leave themselves open to certiorari in respect of their decision."[35]

Walsh J. stated:

> "However, a Court ought never to exercise its discretion by refusing to quash a bad order when its continued existence is capable of producing damaging legal effects".[36]

In *Cunningham v. An Bord Pleanála*,[37] the applicant sought to have a decision of An Bord Pleanála set aside on the grounds first, that the newspaper notice concerning the planning application did not refer to the fact that the buildings which it was intended to demolish were "habitable dwellings", and secondly, that the Board in adjudicating on the application, had failed to have regard to the fact that these buildings were in fact "habitable dwellings". The application form which

---

[32]   A condition attached to a planning permission may be set aside on the grounds of unreasonableness, for example where the extent of a financial contribution bears no reasonable relation to the size or needs of the development for which permission is sought. See *Bord na Mona v. An Bord Pleanála* [1985] I.R. 205. See para. 8.3, above.

[33]   *Keogh v. Galway Corporation (No. 2)* [1995] 2 I.L.R.M. 312. See para. 2.1.3, above.

[34]   [1984] I.R. 381.

[35]   Henchy J. stressed that the primary reason for his decision to refuse certiorari was that any error of law was not made in excess of jurisdiction and did not appear on the face of the records.

[36]   Above, n.34.

[37]   Unreported, High Court, May 3, 1990.

had been completed on behalf of the developer, gave the response "not to the best of our knowledge" to the question on the application form as to whether the proposal involved demolition or partial demolition or change of use of any habitable house. Dealing with the point on the newspaper notice, Lavan J. stated that he had "formed a clear view that the notice ought to have included those two words 'habitable house'" and that he could not overlook their absence as being "trivial, technical, peripheral, or unsubstantial". On the response contained in the application form, he found as a fact that An Bord Pleanála had not been misled by the "lack of frankness" on behalf of the developer. On the third point raised by the applicant, namely, that An Bord Pleanála had failed to consider the desirability or otherwise of demolishing a habitable house, he held that in the words of Henchy J. in the *State (Abenglen Properties Ltd) v. Dublin Coportion*[38] that if they had erred, they had erred within jurisdiction and any error that they may have made did not appear in the face of the record.[39]

In *Max Developments Limited v. An Bord Pleanála*,[40] Flood J. held that it was within the jurisdiction of the Board to decide the mixed question of fact and law as to whether the proposed development was in an existing urban area or a new and extended urban area, an issue which determined the appropriate threshold for the requirement that an EIS be submitted with a planning application for an "urban development project".[41] He said that if the Board erred in law, it had erred within jurisdiction and, consequently, no substantial grounds existed on the basis of which leave could be granted.

10.2.3 Failure to observe the rules of natural justice

A decision which has been made in breach of basic principles of natural justice is deemed to be *ultra vires* and void.[42] The two fundamental rules are *audi alterem partem* ("hear the other side") and *nemo iudex in sua causa* ("no man shall be a judge in his own cause").[43] The *maxim audi alterem partem*, while remaining a general rule, has been given more detailed and specific expression in the context

---

[38] Above, n.33.

[39] A similar ground failed in *Blessington & District Community Council Ltd v. Wicklow County Council*, unreported, High Court, Kelly J., July 19, 1996.

[40] [1994] 2 I.R. 121.

[41] European Communities (Enviromental Impact Assessment) Regulations, 1989, Sched. 1, Pt. II, para. 10(b). See also *RGDATA v. An Bord Pleanála*, unreported, High Court, Barron J., April 30, 1996.

[42] The principles of natural justice amount to basic rules of fairness of procedure which gain an additional significance in view of the guarantee by the State under Art. 40.3.1 of the Constitution "to defend and vindicate the personal rights of the citizen": see *Re Haughey* [1971] I.R. 217.

[43] For an example of a breach of the *nemo iudex* principle, see *R. v. Hendon U.D.C., ex p.* Chorley [1933] 2 K.B. 696. On the application for leave in *Keane v. Bord Pleanála*, Unreported, High Court, June 20, 1995, Murphy J. rejected as unstateable the contention that the inspector had acted in breach of natural justice by allowing a former chairman of An Bord Pleanála, to give evidence on behalf of the Commissioners for Irish Lights to whom permission had been granted by the Board.

of the planning code and in particular, in the regulations governing the procedure for the making of observations and appeals, and in the context of the publicity requirements associated with the publication of the draft development plan and the making of a planning application. However, it has a sphere of operation beyond the express provisions of the Acts and regulations.[44]

In *Killiney and Ballybrack Development Association v. Minister for Local Government and Templefinn Estates Ltd*,[45] an inspector included in his report details of a site inspection carried out by him after the conclusion of the oral hearing on a planning appeal. The court set aside the decision of the Minister as it was "shown to be based on materials other than those disclosed at the public hearing".[46]

In *Law v. Minister for Local Government*,[47] the second named defendants applied for, but were refused, planning permission to erect 34 houses by Dublin County Council. The plaintiff was one of a number of local residents who had objected to the planning application. The second named defendants then appealed to the Minister against the refusal, and an oral hearing of the appeal was held. While not an appellant, the plaintiff was present at the hearing as an objector to the proposed development. In particular, he and a number of other local residents objected to the provision of septic tanks on the site for the disposal of sewage, as these would constitute a danger to the public. In his written report to the Minister, the inspector who had conducted the hearing, recommended that before any decision was made concerning drainage arrangements, trial holes in the ground should be opened and the soil tested for soakage by Dublin County Council, with a view to considering alternative proposals for drainage put forward by the second named defendant. The inspector recommended that if the tests proved satisfactory, permission should be granted for not more than 13 houses. The tests were carried out by the second named defendant in the presence of a representative of Dublin County Council. They showed that the soil conditions were suitable for septic tanks. Consequently, acting on the inspector's report and the engineering opinion on the tests, the Minister granted outline planning permission for the construction of 27 houses. Neither the plaintiff nor any of the other local residents were informed of the proposed tests, nor were the results of the tests communicated to them. The plaintiff consequently brought proceedings claiming that:

---

[44] See, for example, *State (Stanford) v. Dun Laoghaire Corporation* [1981] I.L.R.M. 97 (the "Torca Cottage" case), which involved the late Professor of Classics, of Trinity College, Dublin, W.B. Stanford. See also *State (Haverty) v. An Bord Pleanála* [1987] I.R. 485 and *McGoldrick v. An Bord Pleanála*, unreported, High Court, Barron J., May 26, 1995. See also para. 9.2.8, above.

[45] (1974) 112 I.L.T.R. 69.

[46] See also *Murphy v. Dublin Corporation* [1972] I.R. 215; *Geraghty v. Minister of Local Government* [1976] I.R. 153; *State (Genport) Ltd v. An Bord Pleanála* [1983] I.L.R.M. 12. See 1992 Act, s.13.

[47] Unreported, High Court, May 7, 1974.

(1) the permission was granted upon evidence not contained in the report, *i.e.* the soakage test evidence;

(2) the tests had been carried out in violation of the plaintiff's rights as an objector, either to be present at the said tests or, alternatively, to have been furnished with the results of the tests so that he could have carried out his own tests or have been in a position to evaluate and, if warranted, impugn the results of the tests.

He claimed that the Minister's order was *ultra vires* as it had been made in disregard of judicial principles and of the principles of constitutional and natural justice. Deale J. acceded to the arguments and set aside the decision of the Minister.

10.2.4 Failure to take into account relevant considerations and failure to exclude irrelevant considerations

These are essentially separate grounds of judicial review and are considered elsewhere.[48]

10.2.5 Indequacy of record of decision

Both the planning authority and An Bord Pleanála are obliged to state the reasons for refusing planning permission and for the imposition of the conditions. The Board must also furnish its reasons for granting permission.[49] In addition, both the planning authority and An Bord Pleanála have a duty to ensure that an adequate note is taken of their deliberations to permit their procedure to be reviewed by a court and to inform the parties participating in the administrative process, at least in general terms, of the reason for its decision.[50] There may be cases where the absence of a record could result in the quashing of a decision, but only in conjunction with other circumstances which indicated that the decision was unreasonable. In *O'Donoghue v. An Bord Pleanála*,[51] Murphy J. stated:

> "it is possible to imagine cases where the absence of any adequate records of the decision-making process will force a Court to the conclusion that the decision arrived at was wholly unreasonable. It is less clear why the absence of appropriate records would have itself, and independently of any want of justification for the decision of the Tribunal, invalidate its conclusion."

---

[48] See in particular paras., 8.1.1, 8.2.4, 8.4.5, and 9.3.1, above.

[49] 1963 Act, s.26(8). The Board may be entitled to rely on general reasons for its decision to grant permission where the reasons incorporate reference to the conditions attached to the permission, although such a practice would appear to be open to criticism. See *O'Keeffe*, above, n.4.

[50] *Sharpe (P. & F.) Ltd v. Dublin City and County Manager, per* Finlay C.J. However, it would appear that the dicta of the Chief Justice were meant only for the guidance of administrative bodies and did not form the basis of the decision to quash the resolution of the councillors in that case.

[51] [1991] I.L.R.M. 750 at 759.

In *O'Donoghue*, the Board rejected its inspector's conclusion that a proposed development would lead to over development of the application site. Murphy J. found that there was "an extraordinary paucity of information in the form of written record as to the process by which the Board reached its decision and in particular the justification for rejecting the expert advice tendered to them". Nonetheless, he held that there was sufficient information available to the Board in a layout plan accompanying the planning application to enable it to reach a conclusion which conflicted with that of its inspector.[52]

As has already been seen, the question of unreasonableness in decision-making cannot be determined where there is no record of the decision challenged and in this situation the trial judge is entitled to consider the matter *de novo*.[53]

10.2.6 Non-compliance with pemission regulations

This ground of judicial review has been addressed in Chapter 6.

10.2.7 Material contravention procedure not followed

There are two conflicting decisions on the subject as to whether a failure by a planning authority to follow the material contravention procedure prescribed under section 26(3) of the 1963 Act is a matter which can be dealt with by An Bord Pleanála or is exclusively a matter for the courts.

In *Tennyson v. Dun Laoghaire Corporation*,[54] Barr J. held that the Corporation had misinterpreted the density provisions of the Dun Laoghaire Development Plan of 1984 and had consequently granted planning permission for a residential development which was in breach of density standards and in material contravention of the Development Plan. Barr J. distinguished between the respective roles of An Bord Pleanála and the courts in the following terms:

> "The Oireachtas has provided in the planning code a forum for the adjudication of appeals from decisions of planning authorities within the first category, i.e. those relating to planning matters *per se*. Such appeals are heard and determined by An Bord Pleanála which is a tribunal having the benefit of special expertise in that area. The Court is not an appropriate body to adjudicate in such matters and, in my view, ought not to interfere in disputes relating to purely planning matters. However, where the dispute raises an issue regarding a matter of law such as the interpretation of the wording of the development plan in the light of relevant statutory provisions and the primary objective of the document, then these are

---

52 Murphy J. did not think it necessary for the Board to make any positive finding as to the area of the site or the proposed buildings. He also suggested in *O'Donoghue* that it is necessary for An Bord Pleanála to address in its reasons for refusal the substantive issues which led the planning authority to conclude that the proposed development would be contrary to the proper planning development of their area.

53 *Keogh v. Galway Corporation (No.2)*, unreported, High Court, Morris J., March 3, 1995. See para. 2.1.4, above.

54 [1991] 2 I.R. 527. See Macken, "The Legal Status of the Development Plan – Environmental Contract or Development Guidelines" (1995) IPELJ 11 at 15–16.

matters over which the Court has exclusive jurisdiction. An Bord Pleanála has no authority to resolve disputes on matters of law."[55]

In dealing with the argument of the planning authority that the applicants had an adequate alternative remedy as they had already lodged a notice of appeal to An Bord Pleanála, he simply stated:

> "That submission was specifically rejected by the Supreme Court in *Sharpe (P&F) Ltd v. Dublin City and County Manager*[56]"

Subsequently, in *Healy v. Dublin County Council*,[57] Barron J. was not prepared to hold that planning permission had been granted in material contravention of the Development Plan where four per cent of the proposed development site was to be used for a non-permitted use, and a further 30 per cent of the site was to be put to commercial use, although the zoning under the then current Development Plan was "to protect and/or improve residential amenities. The planning authortiy were proposing to replace this zoning objective under the Dublin County Draft Development Plan 1991 by a new objective "to protect and enhance the special, physical and social character of town and village centres", which was applied to the site under the Dublin County Draft Development Plan, 1991.

In the instant case, Barron J. accepted the evidence of the senior planner for the respondents who was of the opinion that the proposed development would not involve a material contravention of the 1980 Development Plan. He proceeded to determine that the question as to whether or not a proposed development was in material contravention of the Development Plan was "primarily a matter to be determined in accordance with the provisions of the planning code itself", and therefore a matter for An Bord Pleanála.[58] He held that even though in the instant case, the appeals had been lodged by parties other than the applicants, An Bord Pleanála had jurisdiction to determine the appeal although the planning authority had no jurisdiction to grant the permission in the first instance.[59] In support of this proposition, he referred to *O'Keeffe v. An Bord Pleanála*,[60] where Costello J. held, following the *State (Abenglen Properties Ltd) v. Dublin Corporation*,[61] that an *ultra vires* decision was nontheless a "decision" so that it could trigger an appeal to An Bord Pleanála. He held that the right of appeal which had not in fact been brought by the applicant (it was brought by other third parties), should first have been exhausted.[62] However, it is interesting to note that Costello J. in the course of

---

[55] See *per* O'Higgins C.J. in the *State (Abenglen Properties Ltd) v. Dublin Corporation* [1984] I.R. 381.
[56] [1989] I.R. 701.
[57] Unreported, High Court, April 29, 1993. See Galligan, "Judicial Review of Planning Decisions – Howth House Revisited" (1994) IPELJ 119.
[58] But see *Calor Teoranta v. Sligo County Council* [1991] 2 I.R. 267
[59] The appeals were lodged by parties other than the applicants.
[60] Above, n.4.
[61] Above, n.55.
[62] [1980] A.C. 574.

his judgment referred to the decision of the Privy Council in *Calvin v. Carr*, where it was held that "a decision of an administrative tribunal reached in breach of natural justice was void (rather than voidable) but until declared to be void by a competent Court it was capable of having some effect or existence in law and could not be considered as being legally non-existent.

It would appear, therefore, that An Bord Pleanála may be deprived of its jurisdiction to entertain an appeal where the decision of a planning authority has subsequently been declared void by a court. However, *Healy v. Dublin County Council* appears to suggest that where there is in existence an appeal against the decision of a planning authority, its decision cannot be challenged before the courts. Such a result does not appear to be contemplated by section 82(3B), which refers specifically to the questioning of the validity of a decision of a planning authority.

10.2.8 Decision to grant permission in default

A decision to grant permission may be deemed to be made where the planning authority do not make a decision on a planning application within the "appropriate period".[63] A similar procedure operates for applications for extensions to the duration of planning permission.[64] The appropriate remedy in both of these situations is mandamus to compel the planning authority to make a grant on the foot of the said decision made by operation of law.[65]

10.3 BARS TO RELIEF

10.3.1 Time limit

The applicant is required to file and serve the proceedings within two months of the date of the giving of the decision or reference impugned.[66] Failure to serve any of the mandatory parties within the two month time limit will invalidate the application. The application need not be opened in court within the two month period; once the necessary documentation has been filed and served on all of the mandatory parties, the application has been "made".[67]

Doubts about the constitutionality of the two month time limit have been raised by the Courts on a number of occasions. In *Brady v. Donegal County Council*,[68] the second named defendant had published in a newspaper called the *Derry Journal* notice of her intention to apply to the County Council for permission to use her field at Kill, Dunfanaghy, in County Donegal, as a caravan

---

63 1963 Act, s.26(4). See paras. 8.5.3 and 8.5.4, above.
64 1982 Act, s.4.
65 The application for mandamus should be preceded by a letter to the planning authority requesting them to make the grant.
66 1963 Act, s.82(3B) as inserted by 1992 Act, s.19(3).
67 *KSK Enterprises Ltd* above, n.5. See para. 10.1.3, above.
68 [1989] I.L.R.M. 282.

park for the siting of 10 caravans. Planning permission was granted but the plaintiffs brought proceedings in which they claimed a declaration that the decision was invalid as the *Derry Journal* was not a newspaper circulating in the area of the proposed development. It was submitted by the second named defendant that the proceedings were statute barred as they had not been brought within the two month time limit. The plaintiffs alleged that they were not aware of their cause of action prior to the expiration of the statutory period as they had not seen the newspaper notice, and that if the time limit were to operate in this way, their constitutional rights of access to the courts would be infringed. Costello J. granted a declaration that section 82(3A) was unconstitutional.[69] It was never established whether the newspaper notice requirements had actually been infringed in the circumstances of the case. The case was appealed to the Supreme Court and remitted to the High Court for this reason, but was ultimately settled.[70]

It is not certain whether the two month time limit applies to mandamus proceedings in which an applicant is seeking a "default permisssion".[71] In the *State (Pine Valley Developments Ltd) v. Dublin County Council*, Barrington J., in the High Court, was of the opinion that it did not. It had been argued by the applicant that the only purpose of an application for mandamus was to direct the planning authority to provide evidence of a decision which had come into existence by operation of law. Barrington J.'s observations in this regard would appear to be *obiter*, however, as the Minister's decision was made before section 82 (3A) as inserted by the 1976 Act, section 42(a), had been brought into force.

An application for leave to apply for mandamus should normally be preceded by a letter to the planning authority requesting it to make the grant of permission sought.

10.3.2 Locus standi

Order 84, Rule 20(4) of the Rules of the Superior Courts requires an applicant for leave to apply for judicial review to have "a sufficient interest in the matter to which the application relates". The question of whether or not a person has sufficient interest is a mixed question of law and fact, but the factual circumstances are usually more important.[72]

Although it is not possible to form any generally applicable rule, it would appear that a person who has made an observation to An Bord Pleanála or who is a member of an association of perons which is itself an appellant will have

---

[69] s.82(3A), as inserted by the 1976 Act, s.42(a) has since been replaced by ss.83(3A) and (3B) as substituted by the 1992 Act, s.19(3).

[70] In *Inver Resources Ltd* above, n.9, Barron J. suggested that the time limit operated to prohibit further legal challenge even in circumstances where the application was not properly advertised. At any rate, an applicant must be able to show that he has been damnified by the absence of a saver clause. See *Blessington & District Community Council Ltd v. Wicklow County Council*.

[71] Above, n.33.

[72] *State (Lynch) v. Cooney* [1982] I.R. 337, applied by Egan J. in the Supreme Court in *Chambers v. An Bord Pleanála* [1992] 1 I.R. 134.

sufficient locus standi to meet with the requirements of Order 84, Rule 20(4).[73] The impact of the decision on the applicant's personal situation and the degree of his involvement in opposing the planning application are relevant factors in establishing the necessary *locus standi*.[74] However, such *locus standi* may be lost where an applicant fails to make submissions to An Bord Pleanála on the issues which he later intends to raise in judicial review proceedings.

In *Law v. Minister for Local Government*,[75] the applicant did not enjoy any standing at the oral hearing under the express provisions of the 1964 regulations which were then the operative regulations governing appeals.[76] Notwithstanding this, Deale J. did not consider that the applicant should be disqualified from challenging the decision of the Board merely by virtue of his not being a "party" to the appeal. The inspector had "a duty as well as a discretion to hear those whose interests require[d] that they should be heard as a matter of natural justice. . .". The plaintiff had played an active role in opposing the planning application and had a sufficient interest in the outcome of the decision to invest him with *locus standi* to challenge the Minister's decision.[77]

In *Chambers v. An Bord Pleanála*,[78] the applicants had objected to the application by the second named defendant to Cork County Council for planning permission for the erection of a pharmaceutical manufacturing facility at Ringsakiddy, Co. Cork. Their home was approximately 1.7 miles from the proposed site. A decision to grant planning permission subject to 36 conditions was made by Cork County Council, and decisions to grant licences under water and air pollution legislation were also made. Seventeen separate notices of appeal were lodged, including one by "Responsible Industry for Cork Harbour (R.I.C.H.)" which had formed an association with a number of other appellants known as the Cork Evironmental Alliance. The plaintiffs were members of R.I.C.H. but were not otherwise appellants and had not made any independent observation during the course of the appeal.

In the High Court, Lavan J. found as a fact that the plaintiffs had delayed in prosecuting their action and had failed to offer a bona fide explanation for their failure to exercise their statutory rights. He held that their conduct precluded them from instituting court proceedings to set aside the decision of An Bord Pleanála. His decision was reversed in the Supreme Court, McCarthy J. stating

---

[73] *Law v. Minister for Local Government*, Unreported, High Court, Deale J., May 9, 1974; *Chambers*, above, n.72.
[74] See *Chambers*, above, n.72.
[75] See above, n.72.
[76] Local Government (Planning and Development) Act 1963 (Appeals and References) Regulations 1964 (S.I. No. 216 of 1964).
[77] Deale J. stated: "I am of the opinion and hold that Mr. Law's participation in the events already set out, and his interest as a resident in preventing septic tanks from being used near his house, give him the legal right to have that interest protected in a Court of Chancery and he is therefore entitled to maintain this action . . ."
[78] Above, n.72.

that the plaintiffs "clearly have locus standi in the action", with Egan J. taking a more benign interpretation of the plaintiff's involvement at the appeal hearing:

> "The Learned Trial Judge was correct in finding that the Plaintiffs were not named objectors in the application before Cork County Council but they were certainly involved with a body known as R.I.C.H. ("Responsible Industry for Cork Harbour") who were objectors and who subsequently appealed to the first Defendant. The Plaintiff stated that they left it to R.I.C.H. to deal with the appeal and their attitude in this regard can readily be understood, particularly as there were nineteen appellants in all."

In deciding whether *locus standi* exists, the court may have regard to the fact that a person other than the applicant may in reality be driving the proceedings. The point arose in *Cunningham v. An Bord Pleanála*,[79] in which Lavan J. held that the applicant was correct in his contentions that a developer, in omitting to refer to the intended demolition of a habitable dwelling in the newspaper notice preceding the planning application, had failed to comply with the requirement that the notice must specify the nature and extent of the proposed development. Lavan J. nonetheless held that his failure to raise this issue as or by way of objection to the planning authority, or during the appeal before An Bord Pleanála, had effectively disqualified him from raising it in a challenge by way of judicial review. He also considered it relevant that the named applicant did not appear to be the real applicant.

> "During the application process and the appeal process, none of these parties made objection to the proper planning authorities as to the issues they have before me. The applicant is not likely to be a person of sufficient financial substance. He is most certainly acting on behalf of other unidentified persons who thereby carry no legal liability. He, and those unnamed persons, caused or permitted the respondents to believe that they had dealt with or defeated all of the objections which were likely to be put in their path. Most importantly, he and his friends knew or ought to have known that the respondents would retain a building contractor and would suffer at this stage likely unascertainable financial loss due to ordering their contractor to cease his building activities. To grant the applicant his release would be unfair, unjust and inequitable. I reiterate what I said earlier, namely that the code, as laid down by the 1963 Act, the 1976 Act and the regulations made thereunder, envisage the operation of a self-contained administrative code, with resort to the Courts only in exceptional circumstances.
>
> For the reasons stated, including my finding that the applicant is, in essence, a conduit for unnamed persons who had ample opportunity to, and who did make their objections in the course of the planning process . . . I find that the matter of objection upon which the applicant has succeeded is not such an exceptional circumstance as to permit me to grant him a declaration."

10.3.3 Adequacy of an appeal to An Bord Pleanála

The judgment of O'Higgins C.J. in *State (Abenglen Properties Ltd) v. Dublin Corporation* suggests that the availability of an appeal to An Bord Pleanála does

---

[79] Unreported, High Court, May 3, 1990.

not bar relief where the complaint is that the decision of the planning authority is made without jurisdiction or in breach of natural justice. However, while it is not stated in terms, it is clear that O'Higgins C.J. regarded an appeal to An Bord Pleanála as an effective remedy in the circumstances of *Abenglen* as he regarded the question as to whether or not a proposed development was in material contravention of the development plan as "primarily a matter to be determined in accordance with the planning code itself" and, consequently, a matter for An Bord Pleanála. However, where an issue arises as to whether the decision of the planning authority was made in material contravention of the development plan, questions of natural justice may arise as the material contravention procedure envisages public participation to the extent that it involves a decision by the members of the planning authority who are elected to represent their views.[80]

In *Molloy and Walsh v. Dublin County Council*,[81] Blayney J. rejected the Corporation's submission that the plaintiffs ought to have availed of their right of appeal to the Board as there was no reason for them to appeal because under section 26(4) they were deemed to have a decision in their favour by operation of law.[82]

The making of an appeal against a late decision may preclude a subsequent application for mandamus to compel a planning authority to grant a default permission on the grounds that the making of an appeal is not consistent with a contention that the decision made outside the "appropriate period" is invalid.[83] However, in *The State (N.C.E. Limited) v. Dublin County Council*,[84] McMahon J. was prepared to grant such an order where a developer was not aware of his entitlement to mandamus at the time that his appeal was lodged.

The continuation with a planning appeal may be a bar to subsequent relief in judicial review proceedings where an inspector offers a party to the appeal an opportunity to go to court while the appeal is still at hearing but that party declines to accept the invitation. In *Max Developments Ltd v. An Bord Pleanála*[85] the applicants had made an observation to An Bord Pleanála on an appeal in which they contended that the proposed development required the submission of an environmental impact statement, and that An Bord Pleanála was precluded from dealing with the planning application as an EIS had not been submitted. At the oral hearing of the appeal, counsel for the applicants made submissions to like effect. The inspector advised counsel for the applicants that he did not accept that an EIS was required but that he would adjourn the oral hearing to permit the applicants to make

---

80 See para. 10.2.7, above.

81 [1990] I.R. 90.

82 He distinguished *Creedon v. Dublin Corporation* [1983] I.L.R.M. 339 on the grounds that the planning authority had in that case made a decision to refuse permission within two months of the application being made.

83 The *State (Conlon Construction Limited) v. Cork County Council*, unreported, High Court, July 31, 1975.

84 [1979] I.L.R.M. 249.

85 [1994] I.R. 121.

application to the High Court for such relief as counsel might advise concerning the appeal. Following an adjournment, counsel for the first-named applicant confirmed to the inspector that the applicants did not propose to proceed with an application to the High Court at that juncture and the oral hearing was proceeded with on the following days. An Bord Pleanála subsequently granted planning permission for the proposed development.

On an application for leave to apply for judicial review of the Board's decision, Flood J. held that because the applicants had been given an opportunity to take proceedings, either by way of case stated or such other proceedings as they might have considered appropriate, they were precluded from making an application at that stage.[86]

10.3.4 Section 5 procedure more appropriate

If the only issue in judicial review proceedings to quash an enforcement notice is as to whether or not the development specified in the notice is exempted development, the court in the exercise of its discretion should refuse an order of certiorari.[87] In this context, the procedure under section 5 of the 1963 Act for the determination of this issue is more appropriate. On the other hand, if an applicant is able to show that the decision to serve an enforcement notice is one which no reasonable authority would have taken, he may be entitled to relief.

10.3.5 Other discretionary considerations

The court has a discretion as to whether relief should be granted in any judicial review proceedings. It may consider such factors as the conduct of the parties and any other factors peculiar to the case such as the reasons for which relief is sought.[88] Delay or laches is unlikely to be a significant factor in the exercise of the court's discretion given the two month time limit for the bringing of proceedings.

---

[86] He also refused relief as the particular question at issue, *i.e.* whether the proposed development was located in a "new or extended urban area" or "an existing urban area", was a mixed question of fact and law primarily for the Board to determine. If An Bord Pleanála had erred in law, they had erred within jurisdiction.

[87] *O'Connor v. Kerry County Council* [1988] I.L.R.M. 660.

[88] See *State (Abenglen) v. Dublin Corporation* [1984] I.R. 381.

Chapter 11

ENFORCEMENT OF PLANNING CONTROL

11.1 THE PLANNING INJUNCTION

One of the main achievements of the Local Government (Planning and Development) Act 1976 was to make available to the individual citizen a swift and convenient remedy to enforce planning control. Section 27 of that Act provided for such a remedy so that on application to the High Court, the planning authority or "any person" could obtain an order prohibiting unauthorised development or requiring compliance with the terms of an existing planning permission. However, the remedy as originally framed proved to be inadequate for a number of reasons.

The wording of the section only provided for mandatory orders for the renewal or demolition of part of an unauthorised structure where a developer was in breach of a permission or a condition attached to it. Thus, ironically, a person who had at least applied for planning permission but was in breach of that permission was in a worse position than a developer who had chosen to turn a blind eye to the development control process.[1]

The remedy could formerly only be obtained in the High Court, thus decreasing its overall effectiveness of the remedy as a means of policing the environment. Mr Justice Keane had remarked extra-judicially as far back as 1983:[2]

> ". . . it might seem somewhat unreasonable that witnesses should have to travel from Donegal for a hearing in Dublin, when the matter could be readily dealt with by the Circuit Court. Consideration should be given to amending the legislation so as to enable the Circuit Court, in defined circumstances, to deal with applications under the Section."

A further difficulty associated with the former section 27, now replaced under the Local Government (Planning and Development) Act 1992, was that there was no time limit to the bringing of proceedings under the section. The effect of this, taken together with the absence of a time limit for the service of an enforcement notice under section 35 of the 1963 Act was that conveyancers had to investigate the planning status of property right back to October 1, 1964 to satisfy themselves that the current use of land was immune from enforcement.

---

[1]   See *Morris v. Garvey* [1983] I.R. 319; *Dublin County Council v. Kirby* [1985] I.L.R.M. 325.
[2]   "The 1963 Planning Act – Twenty Years On" (1983) 3 DULJ 92.

The 1992 Act corrected these deficiences by substituting a "new and improved" section 27.[3] Because the remedy remains substantially the same, the case law which previously applied, continues to be relevant to the interpretation of the courts' powers under the new section.

11.1.1 Scope of remedy

It is worth setting out the first three sub-sections in full as they define the scope of the remedy and the nature of the relief which may be obtained:

27(1) Where –

(a) development of land, being development for which a permission is required under Part IV of the Principal Act, has been carried out, or is being carried out, without such permission; or

(b) an unauthorised use is being made of land –
the High Court or the Circuit Court may, on the application of a planning authority or any other person, whether or not the person has an interest in the land, by order require any person to do or not to do, or to cease to do, as the case may be, anything that the Court considers necessary and specifies in the order to ensure, as appropriate –

   (i) that the development or unauthorised use is not continued,

   (ii) in so far as is practicable, that the land is restored to its condition prior to the commencement of the development or unauthorised use.

(2) Where any development authorised by a permission granted under Part IV of the Principal Act has been commenced but has not been, or is not being, carried out in conformity with the permission because of non-compliance with the requirements of a condition attached to the permission or for any other reason, the High Court or the Circuit Court may, on the application of a planning authority or any other person, whether or not that person has an interest in the land, by order require any person specified in the order to do or not to do, or to cease to do, as the case may be, anything which the Court considers necessary to ensure that the development is carried out in conformity with the permission and specifies in the order.

(3) An application to the High Court or the Circuit Court for an order under this section shall be by motion and the Court, when considering the matter, may make such interim or interlocutory order (if any) as it considers appropriate. The order by which an application under this

---

[3] See 1992 Act, s.19(4)(g), which came into force on the October 19, 1992 except for the provisions regarding time limits which came into operation on the January 1, 1994: see S.I. No. 221 of 1992.

section is determined may contain such terms and conditions (if any) as to the payment of costs as the Court considers appropriate.

An application under section 27 may be brought by any person to the High Court or the Circuit Court "whether or not the person has an interest in the land". A person bringing an application under section 27 does not have to prove any damage peculiar to himself although, in practice, the remedy is often used to protect the property or commercial interests of an individual or company.

The section requires proof of development which is unauthorised. Consequently, where the respondent can show that there is no development or that any development which has occurred commenced before October 1, 1964 or is exempted development, he will have a satisfactory defence to the application.

Section 27(1) applies only to development or unauthorised uses for which no permission has been granted. "Development" in paragraph (a) may be taken as referring to "works" only, as "use" is referred to in paragraph (b)[4]. It applies where development "has been carried out" after the October 19, 1992 as well as to ongoing development so that unauthorised development which has been completed without planning permission can now be addressed.[5] Sub-section (1) is no longer "merely prohibitory"[6] as mandatory orders can be granted. The court may order "any person to do or not to do, or to cease to do, as the case may be, anything that the court considers necessary".[7] In case any doubt existed as to the nature of the mandatory orders that can be made, sub-section (1) specifically provides for the making of orders to ensure "in so far as practicable, that the land is restored to its condition prior to the commencement of the development or unauthorised use".[8] Orders restraining further development or the continuance of an unauthorised use may be made under section 27(1).

---

4   s.3(1) of the 1963 Act provides that:
        "Development" in this Act means, save where the context otherwise requires, the carrying out of any works on, in or under land, or the making of any material change in the use of any structure or other land.

5   s.27, as amended, does not apply to works carried out prior to the commencement of sub-section (6)(a), *i.e.* October 19, 1992: See Local Government (Planning and Development) Act, 1992 Commencement Order 1992 (S.I. No. 221 of 1992), art. 3(3).
    Section 27 (1) (a) would appear to be a situation "where the context otherwise requires" for the purposes of the definition under s.3 of the 1963 Act. See n.4, above.

6   See *Morris v. Garvey* [1983] I.R. 319, *per* Henchy J. referring to s.27(1) before the changes introduced by the 1992 Act.

7   As this wording mirrors that in sub-section (2) it may be be presumed that the same range of orders as were formerly available under that subsection are open to the court, *mutatis mutandis*, under the first sub-section, and that the same limitations apply, see below.

8   In *Seery v. Gannon*, Blayney J. (*ex tempore*, March 9, 1992) refused an order under the former section 27(1) which would have compelled the respondents to remove meat which had been dumped without planning permission in a disused quarry after a fire at the Ballaghadereen meat plant, as the dumping had ceased and he had no power to make a mandatory order (see reference at pp.9–10 of unreported judgement of O'Hanlon J. in the subsequent proceedings under s.11 of the Local Government (Water Pollution) Act 1977 as amended by s.8 of the Local Government (Water Pollution)(Amended) Act 1990).

Section 27(2) applies to development for which permission was granted but which is not being carried out in compliance with the terms and conditions of that permission. "Development" in the context of section 27(2), includes both the "carrying out of works" and the making of any "material change of use". It refers both to works which have been completed and works which are being carried out. The court may order any person specified in the order "to do or not to do, or to cease to do, as the case may be, anything which the court considers necessary to ensure that the development is carried out in conformity with the permission and specifies in the Order". The order can only compel compliance with the terms and conditions of the planning permission and the court is not empowered to substitute alternative terms; nor can the court seek to secure a partial compliance with the planning permission after the development to which it relates has been completed.[9] In *Dublin Corporation v. McGowan*,[10] Keane J. refused to grant an order to secure compliance with a condition attached to a planning permission for the erection of a mews house at the rear of an existing house, which required that the existing house should be maintained in a maximum of three residential units. The respondent had purchased the house several years after the development had been completed but as he was not aware of this condition, had continued to use the premises as seven residential units. Keane J. stated:

> "In this case the development was completed a number of years ago. There is no suggestion that the building of the mews house to the rear of the premises was not completed to the entire satisfaction of the planning authority. Therefore, this section is entirely inappropriate, particularly when it is borne in mind that the condition attached to the planning permission did not require the developer to do anything; he was simply required not to interfere with an existing state of affairs. Planning permission was granted on the assumption of three units, not the division into seven units which the present owner has been required to change to three units. The condition attached to the planning permission envisaged an existing building in three units and Section 27(2) is therefore wholly inappropriate to this situation. In any event, I would respectfully adopt the approach of Gannon J. in *Dublin County Council v. Browne and Others*, that this section was not intended to enable the planning authority to secure a partial completion of a development. It is intended to ensure that a development is completed in accordance with the planning permission and does not apply to the present situation".

Although very wide in its terms, section 27(2) (and, by extension, section 27(2)) is not intended to include a claim in damages, for example, where a purchaser of property wishes to sue the vendor for damages arising after the sale caused by the vendor's failure to comply with conditions contained in the planning permission for the development of the property.[11] Nor was section 27(2) intended to allow

---

[9]   *Dublin County Council v. Browne*, unreported, High Court, October 6, 1987.
[10] [1993] 1 I.R. 405. See para. 11.2.7.
[11] *Drogheda Corporation v. Gantley*, unreported, High Court, July 28, 1983.

the court to construe and enforce private contractual arrangements between other parties which are entirely collateral or merely ancillary to the permitted development. In *Drogheda Corporation v. Gantley*,[12] Gannon J. refused to order payment of a fine under a bond made between an insurance company, the applicant and the respondent.

The court has power under section 27(1) to grant an order directing that the land be restored to its condition prior to the commencement of the development or unauthorised use provided that this is practicable. In *Dublin County Council (now Fingal County Council) v. Macken*,[13] a section 27 application was brought to restrain the intensification of quarrying operations. O'Hanlon J. granted a mandatory order directing the respondents to carry out such remedial works as might be necessary to rectify environmental damage which had been caused on, and in the vicinity of, the lands of the first-named respondent, and on various roads which had taken "heavy" punishment from the traffic generated by the intensification of use.

While the order made by O'Hanlon J. may be welcomed as a "green" approach by the courts to enforcement, his jurisdiction to make the order is by no means clear. It would appear that the original small-scale quarrying activity, although unauthorised, was not the subject of any planning permission, so that the proceedings were brought under the first limb of section 27. On a literal interpretation of the subsection, the "land" to be restored relates to the land on which the unauthorised use or development was taking place.

Section 27(4) enabled Rules of Court to be made which facilitate the granting of an order against "a person whose identity is unknown".[14]

11.1.2 Time Limits

The time limits (which are also set out in the table at the end of this chapter) within which proceedings may be brought within section 27 are set out under sub-section (6) and are as follows:

(I) For works which are being carried out or have been carried out without permission: Five years from the day on which the development was substantially completed.[15] This time limit does not apply to development carried out without permission prior to October 19, 1992.[16]

(II) For an unauthorised use of land (whether commenced before or after October 19, 1992): Five years from the day on which the use first commenced.

---

12 Unreported, High Court, July 28, 1993.
13 Unreported, High Court, May 13, 1994.
14 See the Rules of the Superior Courts (No. 1) 1996 (S.I. No. 5 of 1996) and the Circuit Court Rules (No. 1) 1995 (S.I. No. 215 of 1995) set out at paras. 11.3.1 and 11.3.3, below.
15 As to the meaning of "substantially completed", see *Frenchchurch Properties Ltd v. Wexford County Council* [1992] 2 I.R. 268. See also para. 8.5.7 above.
16 1976 Act, s.27(b)(a)(i), as inserted by 1992 Act, s.19(4)(g); S.I. No. 221 of 1992 (commencement order).

(III) For the development carried out otherwise than in accordance with the terms and conditions of an existing permission: (i.e. from the date of the expiration of the "appropriate period" under section 2 of the 1982 Act, or, where this period has been extended, from the expiration of the extended period).[17]

In *South Dublin County Council v. Myles Balfe and others*,[18] the respondent raised the time limit under sub-section (6)(b)(i) as a defence. Costello P. held that as the use sought to be restrained had been discontinued and other uses had intervened, a new wrongful act had occurred when the use was recommenced and it was from that date that the time limit began to run in respect of the existing use of the land.

11.1.3 Companies as respondents

Where an order under section 27 is sought against a company, it may be appropriate to join the directors of the company to ensure that the company carries out its obligations. Different considerations apply where the directors are no longer in control of the company, for example, where a company sells off houses on an estate of which it is the registered owner but goes into liquidation before the estate has been completed to the satisfaction of the planning authority in accordance with the terms of a planning permission. In the absence of any evidence of impropriety on the part of the directors the Court will not normally make the directors personally responsible for the default of the company. In *Ellis v. Nolan and others*[19] it was held that the Court was not jusified in making an order against the director of a company in liquidation in respect of a house which had not been built by the company in accordance with the plans lodged with the application for planning permission, merely because the director had made the application in his own name.

Summary proceedings under section 27 are not the appropriate forum for investigating allegations of fraud surrounding a particular development, and the courts will usually decline to exercise jurisdiction for this purpose[20]. Such allegations are best dealt with in plenary proceedings or in the context of an investigation by a liquidator into the affairs of a company. Murphy J. explained the position thus in *Dublin County Council v. O'Riordan*[21]:

> "Section 27 of the 1976 Act is a valuable summary remedy available to a wide range of interested parties to ensure compliance with the terms under which planning permissions are granted. This is a very desirable goal but just as certainly

---

[17] This time limit applies whether the development in question was carried out before or after October 19, 1992.

[18] Unreported, Costello P., November 3, 1995.

[19] Unreported, High Court, McWilliam J., May 6, 1983.

[20] *ibid.*

[21] [1986] I.L.R.M. 104. *Ellis* and *O'Riordan* were followed by Hamilton P. in *Dun Laoghaire Corporation v. Parkhill Developments Ltd*, where he could find "no evidence of impropriety" on the part of the second named respondent who was a director of the respondent company which was insolvent.

requires that if and in so far it is to be alleged that the party against whom such an order is sought has been guilty of fraud or the misapplication of monies that some form of plenary proceedings should be instituted in which the party charged with such misconduct would have the opportunities which the legal system provides for knowing the full extent of the case being made against him and to have a proper opportunity to defend himself against it. Similarly, where the application turns upon the relationship between a director or shareholder in a company in which he is interested, I would anticipate that in most cases it will be necessary that the relationship should be investigated in the first instance by a liquidator in accordance with the procedure provided in the Companies Act for that purpose rather than seeking to establish all of the relevant facts from proceedings designed to be heard on affidavit."

11.1.4 Onus of proof in section 27 proceedings

The authorities as to where the onus of proof in Section 27 proceedings lies are not uniform. In *Lambert v. Lewis*,[22] Gannon J. held that the onus of proof was on the respondent to establish that he was entitled to the benefit of an exemption under the use classes contained in the 1977 Regulations, since repealed. This decision was approved by Finlay P. (as he then was) in *Dublin Corporation v. Sullivan*.[23] The Supreme Court subsequently held in *Dillon v. Irish Cement*[24] that the exempted development provisions:

". . . should be strictly construed in the sense that for a developer to put himself within them he must be clearly within them in regard to what he proposes to do."

The rationale behind this approach is that the provisions of the exempted development regulations:

". . . put certain users or proposed developers of land into a special and privileged category. They permit the person who has that in mind to do so without being in the same position as everyone else who seeks to develop his lands, namely, subject to the opposition of views or interests of adjoining owners or persons concerned with the amenity and development of the countryside."

On the other hand, the Supreme Court has previously observed that the provisions of the planning code must be construed strictly so that any ambiguity should be resolved in favour of the protection of the pre-existing property rights of the developer.[25]

---

22 Unreported, High Court, November 24, 1982.
23 Unreported, High Court, December 21, 1984: see also *Dublin County Council v. Browne*, above, n.9. In *Lennon v. Kingdom Plant Hire*, which concerned exemptions for land reclamation conferred by s.4(1)(i) of the 1963 Act and art. 6 of the 1984 Regulations, it was accepted by the respondent in s.27 proceedings that the onus of establishing that they fell within the scope of the exemptions rested on them.
24 Unreported, Supreme Court, November 26, 1986.
25 See *Dublin Corporation v. Moore* [1984] I.L.R.M. 339 (parking of ice cream van in the driveway of a private house). The issue in that case, however, was whether a material change of use had occurred; it was not argued that the use of the driveway was exempted as a "use within the curtilage of a dwellinghouse" under section 4(1)(h) of the 1963 Act.

However, in *Dublin Corporation v. Regan Advertising*[26] Blayney J., having referred to the definition of unauthorised use, under section 2 of the 1963 Act, held that the onus of proof lay with the applicant to show that the use of which it complained fell within that definition. In other words, the definition of unauthorised use:

> "a use commenced on or after the appointed day, the change in use being a material change and being a development other than development the subject of a permission granted or exempted development"

– required the proof of a negative, *i.e.* that the development was not exempted. Similarly, in *Carroll and Colley v. Brushfield Ltd* (the *Clarence Hotel* case), Lynch J. held that the onus was on the applicants to prove that the development against which the orders were sought was not exempted development.

Notwithstanding *Regan Advertising* and the *Clarence Hotel* case, the balance of authority is in favour of a rule which would require the respondent to prove that he enjoys the benefit of an exemption. Although this represents a departure from the general principle that a plaintiff must prove his case, the rationale offered by the court in *Dillon* appears reasonable. Even if a respondent were to argue successfully that the onus of negativing the existence of the exemption lay with the applicant, it is still possible that this onus could be displaced due to the existence of circumstances, including the planning history of the site, which tended to show that the exemption could not be relied upon.[27] Finally, while most of the relevant authorities concern an unauthorised use of land, there does not appear to be any basis for differentiating the application of the rule to unauthorised works carried out without permission, although the applicant has to establish the occurrence of development "being development for which a permission is required".[28]

11.1.5 Res Judicata

Because of the lower standard of proof required in civil proceedings, a finding of not guilty in criminal proceedings under the planning code will not act as a bar to the bringing of an application under section 27 against the same person. In *Meath County Council v. Martin Daly*,[29] it was held that a finding of not guilty in a District Court prosecution for failure to comply with a warning notice did not preclude section 27 proceedings. Similarly, in *Dublin County Council v. Taylor*, Blayney J. held that a District Court Judges's finding, on a prosecution for failure to comply with a warning notice, that the respondent was entitled to a "default" decision, did not estop the planning authority from instituting proceedings under the section, nor was it relevant to those proceedings.[30]

---

[26]   [1989] I.R. 61.
[27]   See *Dublin County Council v. Browne*, above, n.9.
[28]   1976 Act, as amended, s.27(1)(a).
[29]   [1987] I.R. 391.
[30]   See 1963 Act, s.26(4).

11.2 PRINCIPLES UPON WHICH THE COURT EXERCISES ITS DISCRETION

11.2.1 Remedy analogous to an injunction

The word "may" used in each of the three sub-sections in section 27 imports a discretion which may be exercised by the High Court in deciding whether to grant or refuse an order. There are four principle guidelines as to how this discretion will be exercised.

First, the High Court has said in *Avenue Properties Ltd v. Farrell Homes Ltd*[31] that the order is analogous to the ordinary equitable injunction. This analogy is reinforced by the reference to "interim" and "interlocutory" orders under sub-section (3). It follows from this that many of the principles on which courts of equity have exercised their discretion will also be relevant on an application for an order under section 27. Their application in the context of planning law, which is essentially a branch of public law, may sometimes contrast with their operation in private law situations. For example, the public convenience may be a relevant consideration in section 27 proceedings, although this factor may be excluded from consideration or be given less weight under the law of nuisance.[32]

Second, in the context of equitable injunctions generally, it has been held that the court's discretion must be exercised "in accordance with settled legal principles".[33] This has been echoed by Barrington J. where he observed that "the powers conferred on the High Court are not arbitrary powers but must be exercised in accordance with principles which are judicially acceptable".

The third indication as to how the court will exercise its discretion in the future is the manner in which it has exercised its discretion on previous occasions. From an examination of the case law, a number of factors may be discerned which are considered individually below.

Finally, particular attention should be paid to two judicial *dicta*. In *Dublin County Council v. Matra Investments Ltd*[34] Finlay P. (as he was then) said in the context of an application under section 27(2):

> "In my view, the Order should be made if I am satisfied there is an unauthorised use of the land, unless exceptional reasons are shown by the respondents."

In the Supreme Court, Henchy J. said:

> "It should require exceptional circumstances . . . before the Court should refrain from making whatever order . . . as is necessary to ensure that the development is carried out in conformity with the permission".

---

[31] [1982] I.L.R.M. 21.
[32] See *Bellow v. Cement Ltd* [1948] I.R. 62. But see *Gleason v. Syntex, Irish Times,* September 29, 1982, referred to in Scannell, *op. cit.*, p.44.
[33] *Beddow v. Beddow* (1878) 9 Ch.D. 89.
[34] 114 I.L.T.R. 306.

11.2.2 Delay

The maxim "delay defeats equities" has long influenced the exercise by the courts of their discretion to grant or refuse an injunction. The doctrines of laches and acquiescence evolved to address the situation where a person had failed or neglected to assert his rights and the respondent had been prejudiced by the delay. An applicant under section 27 may also be disentitled to relief for this reason.[35] Delay remains a potential bar to relief despite the introduction of time limits for the bringing of an application under the section.

11.2.3 Lapse of time

Lapse of time should be considered as a factor separate from delay although it is not clear what the effect of the creation of the new time limits will be on this ground for the refusal of an order. It is possible that where an applicant has not been guilty of an unreasonable delay, the court might nevertheless hold that to issue an order under section 27 would be an undue hardship to the respondent.

In *Dublin Corporation v. Mulligan*,[36] the respondent had been using part of his premises for a solicitor's practice for a number of years before the planning authority became aware that it was unauthorised. Finlay P. (as he then was) refused to grant an order restraining the use of this part of the premises due to the lapse of time since the commencement of the use, but granted an order in relation to another portion of the premises which had been converted to office use at a much later date when the respondent was well aware of the attitude of the planning authority to the unauthorised use.[37] The learned judge pointed out that the refusal of an order in relation to the portion of the premises used for his professional practice did not mean that any successors in title to that portion would be immune from enforcement: the use remained an illegal one despite the refusal of the order. It is significant to note that in this case the "vested interest" which was upheld by the court was acquired over the period of six years before the proceedings were commenced, *i.e.* a period extending beyond the new five year time limit.

A letting for profit can not be the subject of a vested interest in the context in which that term was used in *Mulligan*. In *Dublin Corporation v. Kevans*,[38] the respondent had converted residential premises into offices for his own personal use without obtaining planning permission but subsequently let the offices as an investment. A gap of two years intervened between the conversion to office use

---

[35] See *Dublin Corporation v. Mulligan*, unreported, High Court, May 6, 1980, *Dublin County Council v. Matra Investments Ltd*, above. The question as to whether or not a significant delay between the commencement of an unauthorised user and an application to the court under s.27 is a ground for refusing an order depends upon the facts of each particular case: *Dublin Corporation v. Kevans and Others*, unreported, High Court, July 14, 1980, *per* Finlay P. (as he then was).

[36] Above, n.35.

[37] He was prepared to grant a stay of only three months on this order.

[38] Above, n.35.

and its subsequent discovery by the planning authority. Finlay P. held that no vested interest had been acquired by virtue of the lapse of time and granted an order restraining the unauthorised use.[39]

11.2.4 Technicality of the breach

An order may be refused at the discretion of the court where the infringement of planning control is merely technical or trivial, provided that there has been no deliberate or conscious violation of the Planning Acts and no serious detriment to public amenities. In these circumstances, the court will normally take into account the potential impact of an order on a respondent in proportion to the benefit to be gained. In *Avenue Properties Ltd v. Farrell Homes Ltd*,[40] Barrington J. refused an order where the respondents had departed from the terms of a planning permission for an office block in three minor respects only: the line of the building had been moved a few feet in the direction of an adjacent residential building, projections had been omitted and could not be added subsequently, and the basement had also been ommitted.

In *Marry v. Connaughton*,[41] proceedings under section 27 were adjourned to allow time for the consideration by An Bord Pleanála of an application for the retention of a number of houses by the respondent. The Board granted permission, but the applicants argued on a re-hearing of the section 27 application that the exact location of the houses had been wrongly described in the plans lodged with the application for retention. O'Hanlon J. held that as the inspector had inspected the houses *in situ* before making his report the retention permission was intended to relate to the houses as they had been actually erected. The retention permission consequently removed any taint of illegality from the development the location for which did not deviate substantially from that indicated in the plans.

In *White v. McInerney Construction Limited*,[42] the appellant/applicant brought three appeals against orders made by Lardner J. concerning a residential development of 66 houses at Middle Glanmire Road, Cork. Although Lardner J. had held that, construction works had commenced without prior agreement with the planning authority concerning screening details (as required by one of the planning conditions), he held that the planning authority were probably acting reasonably in allowing the development to proceed notwithstanding the absence of such agreement. The applicant had also relied on the non-compliance of the respondent with two further conditions which ought to have been complied with before development commenced – a contribution to drainage work to be carried out by the local authority, and the entering into of a bond. The planning authority

---

[39] A stay of 12 months on the execution of the order was granted to permit the respondent to re-adjust his financial position.
[40] Above, n.21.
[41] Unreported, High Court, January 25, 1984.
[42] Unreported, Supreme Court, Hamilton C.J., O'Flaherty and Blayney JJ., *nem diss*, November 29, 1994.

had agreed that the obligation could be discharged on a phased basis. Although there had not been a literal compliance with the conditions, Lardner J. had refused relief as it would have been unreasonable to bring the development to a halt when the planning authority had agreed to its proceeding.[43] His decision on both counts was upheld by the Supreme Court on the basis of the wide discretion granted under the section.[44]

11.2.5 Public convenience

The court is entitled to take into account the public convenience when deciding whether to grant or refuse an order under section 27. It is not clear how much weight will be given to this factor. In *Stafford v. Roadstone Ltd*,[45] Barrington J. stated as follows:

> "In the normal case a Court of equity, in deciding whether or not to issue an injunction, would be primarily concerned with the position that exists between the parties to the litigation. But it appears to me that if a private citizen comes forward under Section 27 as a watchdog of the public that the Court, in exercising its discretion, is entitled to look not only at the convenience of the parties but at the convenience of the public. Again, it appears to me that the Oireachtas could hardly have intended that the High Court would be obliged on the application of a private citizen with no interest in the lands automatically to close down, e.g. an important factory, because of some technical breach of the planning law irrespective of the inconvenience to workers and the public generally."

In *Stafford* and in *Dublin County Council v. Sellwood Quarries Ltd*,[46] the court, while not prepared to grant an order because of the loss of employment which would result, was equally not prepared to approve an unauthorised development. In *Stafford*, Barrington J., being satisfied that there had not been "any deliberate or conscious violation of the Planning Acts", refused the order but required the respondents to apply to the planning authority for permission. An order was also refused in *Sellwood Quarries* by Gannon J., but he indicated that he was prepared to grant an order in the parallel nuisance action to restrain the operations to some degree "unless some alternative course can be devised consistent with the proper implementation of the requirements of the Planning Acts on the part of both parties".

By contrast, Hederman J. in the Supreme Court in *Dublin County Council v. Tallaght Block Co. Ltd*[47] made no reference to the public convenience or to employment considerations in granting orders under the section.

---

[43] See also *Blainroe Estate Management Co. Ltd v. IGR Blainroe Ltd*, unreported, High Court, March 18, 1994; in which Geoghegan J. took into account the fact that Wicklow County Council had effectively given an extension of time for complying with a condition against the sub-division of a site by serving a warning notice. He also considered it relevant that the planning authority had not seen fit to attach the same condition to a subsequent permission.

[44] It was also noted by Blayney J. that the development had in fact been completed since the orders were made by the High Court.

[45] Unreported, January 17, 1980.

[46] [1981] I.L.R.M. 23.

[47] [1982] I.L.R.M. 469, (HC); [1985] I.L.R.M. 512, (SC).

It is submitted that the *Tallaght Block* case can be distinguished from *Stafford* and *Sellwood Quarries* on two possible grounds. Firstly, the Supreme Court may have taken the view that the respondent in *Tallaght Block* was acting in "deliberate and conscious violation" of the planning code. Secondly, what was involved in *Tallaght Block* was the resumption of an abandoned use at a greater scale rather than an intensification of use as in *Stafford* and *Sellwood Quarries*. *Tallaght Block* and the two earlier cases are not, therefore, *in pari materia*.

11.2.6 Planning considerations

The fact that an unauthorised development may actually improve the amenities of an area is not a consideration in favour of allowing the developent to stand unless the breach of planning control is technical only. In *Dublin Corporation v. Maiden Poster Sites*,[48] Murphy J. granted an order restraining the use for the exhibition of advertisements of the outer wall of premises which had become badly dilapidated, although he apparently accepted the respondent's submission that its appearance had in fact been improved in the process. He took the view that the respondents "knew or ought to have known" of the need to obtain planning permission and was reluctant "to facilitate the respondents in continuing to derive a substantial income from an unauthorised development".

11.2.7 Other equitable considerations

The reasonableness of the conduct of both parties prior to the institution of proceedings and afterwards may be relevant. In *Stafford v. Roadstone Ltd*,[49] Barrington J. observed:

> "Traditionally, courts of equity have always retained a wide discretion in themselves as to whether they should or should not issue an injunction. They have always retained the right to refuse an injunction to a plaintiff who has not come into the court with clean hands or to accept an undertaking, in lieu of an injunction, in an appropriate case."

In *Leech v. Reilly*,[50] O' Hanlon J. refused an order where the applicant had not facilitated the respondents genuine attempts to comply with the conditions attached to a retention permission and had refused to allow the defendant access to his property which was necessary to complete the works specified under the permission. Both applicant and respondent have a duty to disclose any facts relevant to the exercise of the court's discretion.

In *O'Connor and Spollen Concrete Group Ltd v. Frank Harrington Ltd*[51] one of the respondents was carrying out quarrying activities near Coney Island,

---

48 [1983] I.L.R.M. 48.
49 See above, n.46.
50 Unreported, High Court, May 28, 1987.
51 Unreported, High Court, April 26, 1983.

County Sligo where the applicant kept livestock on approximately 200 acres. On a number of occasions when the applicant was going to move his cattle from the island, he found his way obstructed for a short period on the narrow road to the beach at Coney Island due to blasting. A resolution of the dispute between the parties might have been achieved as the applicant usually needed to move his cattle at low tide.

The application was originally brought by the first named applicant, who from the date of the first application to court was in receipt of financial backing from the second named applicant, who was also a competitor of the last named respondents. This fact was never disclosed to the court. The respondents, had endeavoured to ascertain the attitude of the planning authority to the intensification of activities on the quarry site, and were satisfied that it was not unduly concerned. Barr J. refused the order on the grounds that the applicants had not come to the court with clean hands, while the respondents had acted in good faith. He said:

> "It is well settled since time immemorial that for a party to seek equitable relief by way of injunction the Court in exercising its discretion takes into consideration the conduct of that party and relief will be refused if the Plaintiff does not come to the Court with clean hands. I am satisfied that this principle applies with equal force to applications made under Section 27 of the 1976 Act. In seeking such relief an applicant should put before the Court fairly and with candour all facts known to him which are relevant to the exercise of the Court's discretion and he should satisfy it about his bona fides and the true purpose of his application."

The court may be lenient to a respondent who was not aware of circumstances which made the development unauthorised. In *Dublin Corporation v. McGowan*,[52] the respondent was under the mistaken belief that there was no planning permission in existence which restricted the use of premises to not more than those residential units. A planning search failed to disclose the existence of a planning permission which had been granted in 1969 for the erection of a mews house at the rear of the premises at Leinster Road, Rathmines. One of the conditions of the planning permission provided that the existing house on the site which was the subject of the section 27 proceedings, should be maintained in a maximum of three residential units as existing. In refusing an order under section 27 to restrain the user of the home for more than three residential units, Keane J. took into account the fact that the breach of the planning permission was not deliberate:

> "Apart from these considerations, I would consider it unjust and inequitable that an order should be made in circumstances such as the present where, if anybody is to blame, it is the person who misled the planning authority at the stage of the application for planning permission or who thereafter simply converted the house into seven units in defiance of the planning permission. It is not necessary to express any view as to what happened in relation to that matter as I have no evidence in relation to it. In any event, the then owner of the premises and the

---

[52] [1993] 1 I.R. 405.

applicant for planning permission is not a party to these proceedings. It would be manifestly unjust to have the draconian machinery of the section brought into force against a person who behaved in good faith throughout."[53]

The court is also concerned to prevent unjust enrichment resulting from breaches of the planning code.[54]

11.2.8 Section 5 references

The jurisdiction of the High Court pursuant to section 27 is not ousted by the institution of proceedings under section 5 of the Local Government (Planning and Development) Act 1963. Section 5(1) provides:

> "If any question arises as to what, in any particular case, is or is not development or exempted development, the question shall be referred to and decided by An Bord Pleanála."

Costello J. in *Patterson v. Murphy and Trading Services Ltd*[55] held that a reference under section 5 was mandatory only in the context of the procedures established under the Act of 1963. The court has a wide discretion under section 27, and may adjourn the section 27 application so that an application under section 5 can be brought, or may alternatively decide the issue itself. As most section 27 applications are likely to be urgent, the court will normally decide the question of development or exempted development without referring the matter to An Bord Pleanála. In *Cork Corporation v. O'Connell*[56] Griffin J. said:

> "Because of the likely urgency of any such matter, an application to the High Court under the Section (i.e. Section 27) is made by way of motion, without the necessity of instituting proceedings in the normal way. It would indeed be curious if by merely alleging that development was exempted development, however, unmeritorious that allegation might be, the teeth provided by the important section could be entirely removed."[57]

11.2.9 Balancing all factors

The weight which the court will attach to any particular factor will vary with the circumstances of each individual case. By and large, the court is engaged in a balancing process, considering in turn the rights of each of the three parties: the developer, the planning authority, and members of the public. In spite of the foregoing attempt to set out guidelines on which the court will exercise its discretion, it must be remembered that only in exceptional cases will the court refuse an order under the section where an unauthorised development has taken place.

---

53   Keane J. also observed that subsequent purchasers of the premises would not be protected by reason of the refusal of an order in those proceedings. See *Mulligan v. Dublin Corporation*, unrepoted, High Court, May 6, 1980. See para. 11.2.3, above.

54   *Dublin Corporation v. Maiden Poster Sites*, above, n.48.

55   [1978] I.L.R.M. 85.

56   *ibid.*

57   See also *Dublin Corporation v. Regan Advertising Ltd* [1986] I.R. 171, *per* Griffin J., *nem diss.*

11.3 PRACTICE AND PROCEDURE

11.3.1 Applications to the High Court: Order 103 of the Rules of the Superior Courts

The practice and procedure governing applications to the High Court under section 27 is contained in Order 103 of the Rules of the Superior Courts 1986, as amended.[58]

1. In this order "the Act" means the Local Government (Planning and Development) Act, 1976.
2. An application for an Order under Section 27 of "the Act" shall be by motion on notice to the person against whom relief is sought.
3. The notice of motion shall be entitled in the matter of "the Local Government (Planning and Development) Act, 1963–1984, on the application of the person bringing the application; shall state the relief sought; describe the land or development sought to be affected; shall state the name and place of residence or address for service of the person seeking relief; the date upon which it is proposed to apply to the Court for relief; and shall be filed in the Central Office.
4. Notice of the motion shall be given to the person against whom the relief is sought (the respondent); but if it shall appear to the Court that any person to whom notice has not been given ought to have or ought to have had such notice, the Court may either dismiss the application, or adjourn the hearing thereof, in order that such notice may be given, upon such terms (if any) as the Court may think fit to impose.
5. There must be at least 10 days between the service of the notice and the day therein for the hearing of the motion.
6. (a) Subject to the right of the Court to give such directions in that behalf as it considers appropriate or convenient, evidence at the hearing of a motion under Rule 2 shall be by affidavit.
   (b) Any affidavit to be used in support of the motion shall be filed in the Central Office and a copy of any such affidavit shall be served with the notice. Any affidavit to be used in opposition to the application shall be filed in the Central Office by the respondent within seven days of the service on him by the applicant's affidavit, and the respondent must within such period serve a copy of any affidavit intended to be used by him on the applicant.
7. Pending the determination of an application under Section 27 of "the Act", the Court on the application of the applicant or the respondent, by interlocutory Order, (or if satisfied that delay might entail irreparable or

---

[58] Rule 8 of Ord. 103 was added by the Rules of the Superior Courts (No. 1) 1996 (S.I. No. 5 of 1996) to provide for orders to be made against persons unknown. See 1976 Act, s.27(4), as amended.

serious mischief, by interim order on application *ex parte*); may make any Order in the nature of an injunction; and for the detention, preservation or inspection of any property or thing; and for all or any of the purposes aforesaid may authorise any person to enter upon or into any land or building; and for all or any of the purposes aforesaid may authorise any sample to be taken or any observations to be made or experiment to be tried, which it may consider appropriate, necessary or expedient.

8. (1) Notwithstanding anything previously contained in this Order, in any case in which the identity of the person or persons alleged to be carrying on an unauthorised development is unknown to the applicant, the court may, if satisfied that the applicant has made sufficient and reasonable enquiries in all the circumstances and that the order (whether interim, interlocutory or otherwise) is otherwise justified, make the order sought and shall give such directions in accordance with this rule as to service of the order as appears reasonable and practicable in the circumstances.

(2) (1) Unless for special reason which the Court shall specify, the Court shall direct that notification of the making of the order be affixed to the site on which the unauthorised development is taking place together with a copy of the order of the Court.

(2) Such notification shall include:

(a) the title and record number of the proceedings;

(b) the name and address of the applicant;

(c) the name and address of the applicant's solicitors (if any);

(d) a statement of the nature of the unauthorised development;

(e) a summary of the order of the Court including when the said order was made.

(3) Such notification and copy order shall be in a transparent weather proof enclosure and shall be securely affixed to the site in question at or adjacent to any entrance to or any exit of any kind from the site and in any event in a prominent and visible position and capable of being read.

(3) Any proceedings taken under this rule shall be taken against "a person or persons unknown", as the case may be.

(4) Any person, not already a party to the proceedings, claiming to be affected by the making of any order under this rule may apply to the Court by motion on notice to be joined as a party and the Court may make such order therein as appears just and proper.

(5) The Court may, in addition to making an order under subrule (2)(1) above, also direct service of and or notification of the order on any person and in such a manner as may be specified.

(6) The provisions of this rule are without prejudice to the power of the Court to make an order under Order 10 or Order 11, either in addition to or in lieu of making an order under this rule.

(7) In any proceeding under this Order where there are a number of respondents and where the identity of at least one of the respondents is unknown the Court may, in addition to or in lieu of making an order providing for service and/or notification of such order be made on some or all of the known parties on behalf of the person or persons unknown.

11.3.2 Applications to the Circuit Court: Order 67A of the Circuit Court Rules

Applications to the Circuit Court are made to the Circuit judge for the land in which the subject of the application is situate.[59] Order 67A of the Circuit Court Rules 1950 sets out the procedure governing applications to the Circuit Court under section 27[60]:

1. In this Order
"the 1992 Act" means the Local Government (Planning and Development) Act, 1992;
"the 1976 Act" means the Local Government (Planning and Development) Act, 1976.

2. All applications made or proceedings taken before these Rules shall have come into operation but which are in accordance with the existing Rules and practice of the Court shall have the same validity as applications made or proceedings taken in accordance with these Rules.

3. An application under this Order shall be brought in the county in which the respondent, or any one of the respondents, ordinarily resides or carries on any profession, business or occupation or where the land or development sought to be affected or any part thereof is situate.

4. (a) An application for an order under Section 27 of the 1976 Act, as amended by Section 19(4)(g) of the 1992 Act, shall be by motion on notice to the person against whom relief is sought, subject to the provisions of Rule 4(b) hereof.

(b) An order under Section 27 of the 1976 Act, as amended by Section 19(4)(g) of the 1992 Act, against a person whose identity is unknown to the applicant; shall be referred to as "an order under Rule 4(b)", and the person against whom it is granted or sought shall be referred to as "the respondent".

(c) An applicant for an order under Rule 4(b) shall, instead of complying with Rule 4(a), describe the respondent by reference to -
(i) a photograph, or

---

[59]   s.27(5), as amended.
[60]   Ord. 67A was inserted by the Circuit Court Rules (No. 1) 1995 (S.I. No. 215 of 1995).

(ii) any other means whereby the Respondent can be identified, with sufficient particularity to enable service to be effected; and the form of the notice of motion shall be modified accordingly.

(d) An applicant for an order under Rule 4(b) shall, in addition to the requirements of Rules 5 and 8 of this Order, include in the affidavit grounding the application and filed in accordance with the provisions of Rule 8 hereof, or shall file a separate affidavit containing, the following averments:

(i) verifying that he was unable to ascertain, within the time reasonably available to him, the respondent's identity;

(ii) setting out the action taken to ascertain the respondent's identity and

(iii) verifying the means by which the respondent has been described in the originating application and that the description is the best that the applicant is able to provide.

(e) Rule 4(c) hereof is without prejudice to the power of the Court to make an order for substituted service.

5. The notice of motion shall be entitled in the matter of the Act on the application of the person bringing the application: shall state the relief sought: describe the land or development sought to be affected: shall state the name and place of residence or address for service of the person seeking relief: the date upon which it is proposed to apply to the court for relief: and shall be filed in the Office of the Court for the County in which the application is being brought in accordance with Rule 3 hereof (hereinafter referred to as "the appropriate Office").

6. Subject to the provisions of Rule 4 hereof and without prejudice to the power of the Court to make an order for substituted service, notice of the motion shall be given to the person against whom the relief is sought (the respondent): but if it shall appear to the Court that any person to whom notice has not been given ought to have or ought to have had such notice, the Court may adjourn the hearing thereof, in order that such notice may be given, upon such terms (if any) as the Court may think fit to impose or may dismiss the application.

7. There must be at least ten days between the service of the notice and the day named therein for the hearing of the motion.

8. (a) Subect to the right of the Court to give such directions in that behalf as it considers appropriate or convenient, evidence at the hearing of the motion under Rule 4 shall be by affidavit.

(b) Any affidavit to be used in support of the motion shall be filed in the appropriate Office and a copy of any such affidavit shall be served with the notice. Any affidavit to be used in opposition to the application shall be filed in the appropriate Office by the respondent within seven days of the service on him of the applicant's affidavit, and the respondent must within such period serve a copy of any affidavit intended to be used by him on the applicant.

9. Pending the determination of an application under Section 27 of the 1976 Act, as amended by Section 19(4)(g) of the 1992 Act, the Court on the application of the applicant or the respondent, by interlocutory order, (or if satisfied that delay might entail irreparable or serious mischief, by interim order on application *ex parte*) may make any order in the nature of an injunction: and for the detention, preservation or inspection of any property or thing: and for all or any of the purposes aforesaid may authorise any person to enter upon or into any land or building; and for all or any of the purposes aforesaid may authorise any sample to be taken or any observations to be made or experiment to be tried, which it may consider appropriate necessary or expedient.

11.3.3 Application by motion

Application is brought by way of motion, grounded upon affidavit, thus ensuring an effective and speedy method of obtaining relief. Interim or interlocutory orders are available under the section.[61] In cases of extreme urgency, an application for an interim order may be brought *ex parte*, whereupon the court may grant or refuse the order or alternatively, grant liberty to serve short service of the notice of motion. Where an *ex parte* or interim order is granted, this enures until a fuller hearing of the application on notice. The court may at this stage make an interlocutory or final order, which may contain such terms and conditions (if any) as to the payment of costs as the court considers appropriate, or may adjourn the application for further hearing. It is open to the court not to deal with the issues at the interlocutory stage but to defer a decision until after a plenary hearing. The decision as to whether the court should make an order at the interlocutory stage pending a fuller hearing is influenced by the principles applicable to interlocutory relief generally. But in *Johnson and Staunton Ltd v. Esso Ireland Ltd*, Costello J. indicated that the public interest which section 27 was designed to protect demanded that "illegal development should be halted until the court has had an opportunity to examine all the circumstances of the case to see whether there are any reasons why it should not permanently stop the development".

11.3.4 Joinder of parties

It would appear that, in certain circumstances at least, an application may be brought to have another party joined as an applicant in proceedings which have already been commenced. In *Irish Wildbird Conservancy and the Commissioners of Public Works in Ireland v. Clonakilty Colf and Country Club Limited*, an *ex parte* order under section 27 was initially obtained by the first named applicant to restrain further acts of development at Cloheen Intake, Clonakilty, County Cork which was perceived to be an important habitat for certain species of wild birds. The respondents had been

---

[61]   1976 Act, s.27(3) , as inserted by 1992 Act, s.19(4)(g).

refused permission by An Bord Pleanála for the development of a links golf course and claimed that the acts complained of amounted to drainage works which were exempted. The Commissioners of Public Works had taken an active part as parties to the oral hearing which preceded the refusal of permission by the Board and had also been involved in the practical implementation of the 1979 Birds Directive and the 1992 Habitats directive. Furthermore, they were a statutory consultee in relation to the site in question. Carney J. made an order allowing them to be joined as co-applicants in the proceedings.

11.3.5 Evidence to be heard

Evidence is usually heard by way of affidavit. Where there is a conflict of fact on the affidavits, the court may grant liberty to either side to cross-examine the deponents or to allow the case to made on oral evidence, and may make such orders as to discovery of documents as are deemed necessary. A respondent will not in general be entitled to raise at the hearing of the motion a point by way of defence which was not raised in the affidavits.[62] If an applicant considers that it would be advantageous to have his application heard on oral evidence, an application should be made at the interlocutory stage of the proceedings.[63] Hearsay evidence may be allowed at the interim or interlocutory stage, but is not admissible on the hearing of an application for a final order under the section.[64] An exception to the hearsay rule is recognised where declarations as to user are made against interest either by one of the parties to the action or by a predecessor in title to a party to the action.[65] The court may also make an order "for the destruction, preservation or inspection of any property".[66] A final order may be made under section 27 upon a determination only of the issues put before the court on affidavit unless the court makes an order that the evidence is to be heard orally.

11.3.6 Adjournments and liberty to apply

Adjournments may be granted to allow the respondent to apply for planning permission for the retention of unauthorised development which it is sought to enforce. The court has a supervisory role under section 27 and may direct that the application be listed again for re-hearing in order to monitor compliance with the terms of any order which it has made or with the terms and conditions of any relevant planning permission. As a matter of practice, both sides have liberty to apply to the court. However, the purpose of this procedure is not to allow revisionary orders where a final order has already been made under the section. In *Drogheda Corporation v. Gantley and Brothers*,[67] Gannon J. said:

---

62 *South Dublin County Council v. Balfe*, unreported, High Court, November 3, 1995.
63 *White v. McInerney Construction Limited* [1995] I.L.R.M. 374.
64 *Dublin Corporation v. McGowan* [1993] I.R. 405.
65 *South Dublin County Council v. Balfe*, above n.62.
66 R.S.C. 1986, Ord. 103, r. 7.
67 Unreported, High Court, July 28, 1983.

"The addition to an order of the expression "liberty to apply" is made in practice to enable further application to be made to the Court for the implementation of its order by way of enforcement or variation or suspension. I do not think this formula may be used for the purpose of requiring the Court to revise its decision or to entertain and resolve further to (sic) other matters in dispute which the parties had omitted to submit to the Court. It is not in my view a formula which permits a party found in default to resort to a type of third party procedure for the purpose of obtaining contribution or of casting on some third party the burden of compliance with the order made upon the claim."

11.4 ENFORCEMENT NOTICES

The enforcement notice procedure may be availed of by planning authorities to secure compliance with planning controls where development has been carried out without permission or where the owner or occupier of a structure or lands is not complying with the terms or conditions of a permission which has been implemented.

The Local Government (Planning Development) Act 1963 provdies three types of enforcement notice:

- Section 31 Notices
- Section 32 Notices
- Section 35 Notices

Particulars of the service of an enforcement notice or its withdrawal must be entered on the planning register. There is no appeal against an enforcement notice. Non-compliance with its terms may result in either prosecution or direct action by the planning authority to remedy the breach of planning control. Notices may also be served by the planning authority requiring the removal or alteration of structures or the discontinuance of uses which are perfectly lawful under the planning code if such measures need to be taken in the interests of proper planning and development. These notices are appealable.

11.4.1 The decision by the planning authority to take enforcement action

Enforcement action may not be taken under the provisions just referred to, unless the planning authority consider it "expedient" to do so. In deciding whether it is expedient, the planning authority are restricted to considering –

(a) the proper planning and development of the area of the authority (including the preservation and improvement of its amenities).
(b) the development plan.
(c) any special amenity area amentiy order for the area.
(d) the probable effect which a particular decision might have on any place which is not within, or is outside their area;
(e) any relevant Ministerial policy directives.
(f) the terms of any condition attached to an existing permission for the development, unless the development has been carried out without permission.

The planning authority may be directed by the Minister to serve an enforcement notice under section 31 or section 35, but not under section 32.[68] An enforcement notice may be withdrawn by the planning authority by notice in writing.[69] The fact that an enforcement notice has been withdrawn must be recorded on the planning register.

On an application for judicial review, it has been held that the decision to serve an enforcement notice cannot be challenged on the grounds that the development sought to be enforced against is exempted, unless it can be shown that the conclusion of the planning authority that it was exempted was totally unreasonable.[70] In *O'Connor v. Kerry County Council*,[71] Costello J. expressed the view that the appropriate procedure would be to have the issue determined by An Bord Pleanála under section 5 of the 1963 Act. He also held that the planning authority is not obliged to communicate its intention of serving an enforcement notice in advance of actually doing so. Nor was it under any obligation to recite the particular grounds for its decision to serve an enforcement notice; resort to the statutory wording was sufficient.

11.4.2 Service of enforcement notices

In the case of each of the three types of enforcement notices the planning authority is required to serve the notice on both the owner and occupier of the land. "Owner" is defined as –

> "a person, other than a mortgagee not in possession, who, whether in his own right or as trustee or agent for any other person, is entitled to receive the rack rent of the land or, where the land is not let at a rack rent, would be so entitled if it were so let".

Thus, a lessor or sub-lessee of the land who takes in a rack rent must be served. Curiously, it has been held that a freeholder who lets at less than a rack rent is not an owner within this definition, but in these circumstances the lessee would be, as he is in a position to sub-let at a rack rent, *i.e.* market rent at the time when the lease was granted.[72] It has been held that an occupier may include a licensee.[73] If the name of the owner of occupier cannot be ascertained by reasonable enquiry, the notice may be addressed to "the owner" or "the occupier", without naming him.[74]

The modes of service are prescribed by section 7(1) of the 1963 Act which provides –

---

68   *i.e.,* a notice seeking compliance with a condition for the retention of a structure.
69   1976 Act, s.28.
70   *O'Connor v. Kerry County Council* [1988] I.L.R.M. 660.
71   *ibid.*
72   See *London Corporation v. Cusack-Smith* [1955] A.C. 337; *Borthwick-Norton v. Collier* [1950] 2 K.B. 594, (CA).
73   *Stevens v. London Borough of Bromley* [1972] 1 All E.R. 712, noted in Keane, *Local Government in the Republic of Ireland*, p.211. But see *James v. Minister of Housing and Local Government* [1965] 3 All E.R. 602.
74   1963 Act, s.7 (2).

(1) Where a notice or copy of an order is required or authorised by this Act or any order or regulation made thereunder to be served on or given to a person, it shall be addressed to him and shall be served on or given to him in some one of the following ways:

(a) where it is addressed to him by name, by delivering it to him;

(b) by leaving it at the address at which he ordinarily resides,[75] or in a case in which an address for service has been furnished, at that address;

(c) by sending it by post in a prepaid registered letter addressed to him at the address at which he ordinarily resides, or, in a case in which an address for service has been furnished, at that address;

(d) where the address at which he ordinarily resides cannot be ascertained by reasonable enquiry and the notice or copy is so required or authorised to be given or served in respect of any land or premises, by delivering it to some person over 16 years of age resident or employed on such land or premises or by affixing it in a conspicuous position on or near such land or premises.[76]

Where a notice or copy of an order must be served on or given to the owner or occupier of land and the name of the owner or occupier cannot be ascertained by reasonable enquiry, it may be addressed to "the owner" or "the occupier", without naming him.[77]

11.4.3 Obligation to give information to planning authority

A planning authority may serve a notice on the occupier of any structure or land, or any person receiving rent from the land, (whether on his own behalf or for some other person), requiring him to give details of his interest in the land and the name and address of every person who has an interest in the lands.[78] The information must be furnished to the planning authority within the period specified in the notice which should allow not less than 14 days. Failure to comply with the notice or the making of a statement in writing which is false or misleading in a material respect to the knowledge of the person served, constitutes an offence.

---

[75] A company registered under the Companies Acts is deemed to be ordinarily resident at its registered office. Other bodies corporate and unincorporated bodies are deemed to be ordinarily resident at their principal office or place of business: s.7(3).

[76] A copy of any such notice affixed on land or on premises must be published within a period of two weeks in at least one newspaper circulating in the area in which the person is last known to have resided. It is an offence for any person to remove, damage or deface such a notice without lawful authority during the period of three months after it has been affixed. There is provision also for the Minister to dispense with service of a notice or a copy order on the grounds that injury or wrong would result.

[77] 1963 Act, s.7(2).

[78] *ibid.*, s.9.

11.4.4 Section 31 notice

A notice under section 31 may be served where development has been carried out without planning permission or in breach of a condition of planning permission. This notice is not appropriate to situations where development is on-going, or where a person has failed to comply with the terms, as distinct from the conditions, of a planning permission.[79]

Where the development was carried out without planning permission the notice must be served within a period of five years from the date that the development was carried out. In the case of non-compliance with a condition, the time limit is five years from the date specified in the condition, or, if no date is specified, from the date specified in a "latest date notice" served by the planning authority.[80] A "latest date notice" cannot be served five years or more after the "life" of the permission has been spent.[81] In the case of a permission for the retention of a structure, the five year time limit runs from the date on which the permission was granted.[82] An enforcement notice under section 31 may be served, whether or not there has been a prosecution for non-compliance with the terms of a warning notice.[83]

The section 31 Notice must specify:

(1) the development which is alleged to have been carried out without permission, or, the extent to which any condition has not been complied with;

(2) the steps to be taken to restore the land to its condition before the development took place, or for securing compliance with the condition;

(3) the period within which these steps must be taken.

The notice may require the removal or alteration of any structures, the carrying out of works or the discontinuance of any use. It takes effect at the expiration of the period specified in the notice which must be not less than one month from its service.[84] Any expenses incurred by the owner or occupier in complying with an enforcement notice under this section are deemed to be incurred for the use and at the request of the person who carried out the unlawful development, and are consequently recoverable against him.[85] Section 31 (8) provides for the circumstances in which an offence may be committed where a notice is not complied with:

---

[79] See *Dublin County Council v. Hill* [1994] 1 I.R. 86.

[80] A purchaser should ascertain whether a latest date notice was served.

[81] 1963 Act, s.31(c)(i) as inserted by s.19(1)(a) of the 1992 Act. Any permission which was granted after November 1, 1982 has a "life" of five years, unless a longer period has been specified in the permission or an extension to its duration has been granted by the planning authority, see 1982 Act, ss.3 and 4.

[82] 1963 Act, s.31(c)(ii) as inserted by s.19(1)(a) of the 1992 Act.

[83] 1976 Act, s.26(6).

[84] 1963 Act, s.31(4).

[85] *ibid.*, s.31(6).

"(8) Where, by virtue of an enforcement notice, any use of land is required to be continued, or any condition is required to be complied with in respect of any use of land or in respect of the carrying out of any works thereon, then, if any person, without the grant of permission in that behalf under this Part of this Act, uses the land or causes or permits the land to be used, or carries out or causes or permits to be carried out those works in contravention of the notice, he shall be guilty of an offence . . ."[86]

No planning permission is required for reverting to the use which immediately preceded the unauthorised use to which the enforcement notice is addressed, provided the former use was lawful.[87] If the immediately preceding use was unlawful, planning permission must be obtained for any new use of the land.

11.4.5 Section 32 notice

This type of notice applies to situations where planning permission for the retention of a structure has been granted but the owner or occupier has not complied with a condition attached to that permission. It may be served within five years from the date specified in the condition for compliance, or, where the condition omits to specify a date, within five years of the date specified in a "latest date notice" served by the planning authority. A latest date notice may not be served after the expiration of five years from the date on which the permission was granted.[88] An enforcement notice under section 32 may be served, whether or not there has been a prosecution for non-compliance with the terms of a warning notice.[89]

It should be served on the owner (the definition of which is the same as under section 31 of the 1963 Act) and the occupier of the premises and should specify:

(a) The extent to which it is alleged that the relevant condition has not been complied with.

(b) The period within which any steps to ensure compliance with the condition must be taken.

It may require –

(a) the removal of the structure;

(b) the alteration of the structure;

(c) the carrying out of works (including the provision of car parks) which the planning authority consider are required if the retention of the structure is to be permitted;

(d) the provision of space around the structure;

(e) the planting of trees, shrubs or other plants or the landscaping of the structure or other land.

---

[86] An offence may also be committed under s.34: see below.

[87] 1963 Act, s.31(9). See *Young v. Secretary of State for the Environment* [1983] 2 All E.R. 1105, cited with apparent approval in *Rehabilitation Institute v. Dublin Corporation*, unreported, High Court, Barron J., January 14, 1988. No permission is required for compliance with any notice served under ss.31, 32, 33, 35 or 36 of the 1963 Act: See 1963 Act, s.40(c).

[88] 1963 Act, s.32(1)(c), as inserted by s.19(1)(b) of the 1992 Act.

[89] 1976 Act, s.26(6).

11.4.6 Section 35 notice

This notice may be served where development which is the subject of a planning permission has not been, or is not currently being, carried out in conformity with the *terms* of that permission. It has been held by the Supreme Court in *Dublin County Council v. Hill*,[90] that a section 35 notice may not be served to secure compliance with a condition, as section 31 expressly addresses itself to non-compliance with a *condition*, and section 35 must be interpreted narrowly having regard to its criminal consequences. Section 35 applies to ongoing development and development which has been carried out in breach of the terms of a planning permission, but does not apply to development undertaken without planning permission. There is a time limit of five years from the date of expiration of the "life" of the planning permission in respect of which compliance is sought.[91] An enforcement notice under Section 35 may be served, whether or not there has been a prosecution for non-compliance with the terms of a warning notice.[92]
The notice must specify:

(1) The steps to be taken to secure the carrying out of the development in conformity with the permission; and

(2) The period within which such steps are to be taken.

11.4.7 Direct action by the planning authority

Each of the enforcement notice provisions enable the planning authority to take direct action where the terms of a notice have not been complied with. It is given powers of entry onto the land to take the necessary steps and may recover any reasonable expenses against the owner of the land. However, the planning authority is not entitled to enter land on foot of a section 31 notice to secure the discontinuance of any use of the land.[93] This restriction is not expressly applied to the other two forms of enforcement notice.

11.4.8 Prosecution for non-compliance with enforcement notices

There are three types of prosecutions for non-compliance with enforcement notices:

- Prosecution under section 31 for non-compliance with a section 31 notice.
- Prosecution under section 34 for non-compliance with a section 31 or Section 32 notice.
- Prosecution under section 35 for non-compliance with a section 35 notice.

---

[90] Above, n.79.
[91] *i.e.* the "appropriate period" under s.2 of the 1982 Act, or, in cases where an extension of the "appropriate period" has been granted, from the end of that period.
[92] 1976 Act, s.26(6).
[93] 1963 Act, s.31(5).

Liability to prosecution under section 31(8) extends to any person who "causes or permits" land to be used or "causes or permits" works to be carried out in contravention of the notice. A prosecution may also be taken under this sub-section for failure to take steps required by the terms of a notice to discontinue a use.

An offence is committed under section 34 where the "owner" of land fails to comply with the terms of a section 31 or a section 34 notice within the time specified in the notice or within such extended period as the planning authority may allow.[94] A prosecution may not be taken under this section where the failure to comply relates to the discontinuance of the use of any land. A defence exists where the original owner served can show –

> (a) that he has ceased to be the owner of the land in question before the end of the period specified for compliance (or of such extended period as the planning authority may allow); and
> (b) that the failure to take the steps specified in the notice was attributable in whole or in part to the default of the person who succeeded him as "owner"; and
> (c) That he took all reasonable steps to ensure compliance with the notice.

If this defence is to be availed of, the original defendant is obliged to make a complaint as against his successor in title, and must give the prosecution not less than three clear days notice of his intention to have him brought before the court in the proceedings. If the original defendant can establish (a) and (b) above, his successor in title may be convicted. A person who receives the rent of the land as agent for another person is not regarded as an "owner" in this context. Any person who obstructs an owner who is endeavouring to comply with the terms of a notice is guilty of a separate offence under the section, but an occupier is entitled to fourteen days notice of the owner's intention to take the relevant steps before a prosecution of this offence may be brought.

The three offences for non-compliance with enforcement notices may only be prosecuted summarily and are punishable on conviction by a maximum fine of £1,000.[95] Where a defendant is being tried for a continuing offence, issue estoppel may not be relied upon to relieve the prosecution of proof of the essential elements of the offence, including service of the enforcement notice. In *Dublin Corporation v. Flynn*, the Supreme Court held that the defendant was entitled to a dismiss because the prosecution failed to adduce evidence of the making and service of the enforcement notice on the trial of a continuing offence under section 34(5). Henchy J. said:

---

[94] *ibid.*, s.34(1).
[95] 1992 Act, s.20(1). Continuing offences are punishable by a maximum fine of £200 for each day on which the offence continues: 1992 Act, s.20(5)(a), amending the relevant provisions of the 1963 Act.

"It is of the essence of a criminal trial that it be unitary and self-contained, to the extent that proof of the ingredients of the offence may not be established as a result of a dispersal of the issues between the Court of Trial and another tribunal. Evidence of a previous conviction, whether given as an ingredient of or as an element in the charge, or given pursuant to a special statutory permission, does no more than provide conclusive proof of that conviction. As to the issues that were decided against the accused in the earlier trial, the conviction does not operate to foreclose those issues in the subsequent trial."

11.4.9 Prosecutions for breach of the obligation to obtain planning permission

Section 24 of the 1963 Act imposed a general obligation to obtain planning permission for development commenced after the October 1, 1964, which is not exempted development, and for the retention of any structure which was at that date an unauthorised structure. Any person who carries out development without such permission is guilty of an offence and is liable on conviction on indictment to a fine not exceeding £1 million or to imprisonment for two years, or both. A continuing offence is punishable by a fine not exceeding £10,000 for each day on which the offence is continued, or by imprisonment for a term of two years, or by both fine and imprisonment. The offence is also triable summarily and a person convicted is liable to a maximum fine of £1000 or to imprisonment for up to six months.[96] For continuing offences, the maximum fine on summary conviction is £200 for each day during which the offence is continued (not to exceed £800 in total) or imprisonment of up to six months with or without fine.[97]

Summary proceedings may be commenced –

(a) Within six months from the date on which the offence was committed; or

(b) Within three months from the date on which evidence sufficient, in the opinion of the person by whom the proceedings are instituted, to justify proceedings, comes to such person's knowledge; whichever is the later.[98]

Such proceedings cannot be instituted later than five years from the date on which the offence was committed.[99] The presumption is that the development is neither exempted development nor development commenced before October 1, 1964 until the contrary is shown by the defendant, and this applies to the prosecution of any continuing offence as well.[100] The onus of proving the existence of any planning permission for the development in relation to which the proceedings are taken is on the defendant: it is not for the prosecution to negative the existence of such

---

[96] See 1982 Act, s.9(1), as amended by s.20(7) of the 1992 Act.
[97] 1982 Act, s.9(1), as amended by s.20(7) of the 1992 Act.
[98] 1976 Act, s.30(1).
[99] *ibid.*, s.30(2).
[100] 1963 Act, s.24(4).

permission.[101] The taking of proceedings under section 24 does not preclude a prosecution for non-compliance with the terms of an enforcement notice served under section 31 of the Act.[102]

11.4.10 Warning notices

Section 26 of the 1976 Act provides for the service of warning notices where a breach of planning control is likely to take place or is taking place on an ongoing basis.[103] It does not apply to works which have already been carried out. Section 26(1) provides:

"(1) Where it appears to a planning authority that –
    (a) land is being or is likely to be developed in contravention of Section 24 of the Principal Act; or
    (b) any unauthorised use is being or is likely to be made of land;[104] or
    (c) any tree or other feature (whether structural or natural) or any other thing the preservation of which is required by a condition subject to which a permission for the development of any land was granted, may be removed or damaged;
the planning authority may serve on the owner of the land a notice (in this section subsequently referred to as a warning notice) and may give a copy of the said notice to any other person who in their opinion may be concerned with the matters to which the notice relates."

The warning notice should contain the following elements:

- A description of the land concerned;
- in relation to land likely to be developed in contravention of section 24, a requirement that it should not be commenced;
- in relation to land which is being developed in contravention of section 24, a requirement that it be discontinued forthwith;
- in relation to any unauthorised use of land being or likely to be made of land, a requirement that the use be discontinued forthwith or that it shall not be commenced;
- in relation to a condition requiring the preservation of any tree, other feature or thing, a requirement that the tree, other feature or thing be neither removed nor damaged and that any reasonable steps necessary for its preservation be taken by the owner of the land;
- a requirement that the owner of the land take adequate steps to ensure compliance with the notice;
- a warning that proceedings may be taken under section 26 of the 1976 Act by the planning authority against the owner and any other person who fails to comply with the requirements of the notice or

---

[101] 1976 Act, s.36.
[102] 1963 Act, s.31(7).
[103] Note that s.26 was amended by the 1992 Act, s.19(4).
[104] The words "or is likely to be" were inserted by 1992 Act, s.19(4)(e).

who assists or permits any development or use of land or the doing of any other thing in contravention of the notice.

Any person who "knowingly" fails to comply with the requirements of a warning notice may be prosecuted on indictment.[105] Liability extends also to any person who "knowingly assists or permits" in the doing of any thing in contravention of the notice.[106] It is not necessary for the prosecution to show, and it is assumed until the contrary is shown by the defendant, that the development, if any, was neither exempted development nor development commenced before the appointed day.[107] Nor do the prosecution have to negative by evidence the existence of any permission, and the onus of proving such permission is on the defendant.[108]

The offence is punishable on indictment by a maximum fine of £1 million, or, a term of imprisonment of up to two years, or by both imprisonment and fine; on summary conviction, by a maximum fine of £1000 or a term of imprisonment of up to six months, or by both imprisonment and fine.[109] An enforcement notice under sections 31, 32 or 35 of the 1963 Act may be served, whether or not there has been a prosecution for non-compliance with the terms of a warning notice.

Particulars of any warning notice served must be entered on the planning register. Warning notices may not be withdrawn at any stage by the planning authority.

11.4.10.1 *Warning notices for the preservation of trees and other features*

Where a warning notice relates to a condition requiring the preservation of a tree, other feature or thing, anything done with the consent in writing of the planning authority who served the notice does not constitute an offence.[110] Where it is the owner that is being prosecuted, the fact that the tree, or other feature or thing was removed or damaged need only be proved. A defence exists where an owner can show that he has taken or caused to be taken reasonable steps to secure compliance with the requirements of a warning notice for the preservation of any tree, other feature or thing, and that he acted at all times in good faith in relation to the notice.[111] The objective of this provision would appear to be to prevent liability attaching to an owner where the damage has been inflicted by some other person. In the prosecution of persons other than the owner of the land, it appears that a presumption that the defendant acted "knowingly" is intended to operate but section 26(7)(b) which creates this presumption is by no means

---

[105] 1976 Act, s.26(4).
[106] *ibid.*, as amended by the 1992 Act, s.19(4).
[107] 1976 Act, s.26(8). This applies to continuing offences also: See 1992 Act, s.20(4).
[108] 1976 Act, s.36.
[109] 1982 Act, s.9(1), as amended by s.20(7) of the 1992 Act. Continuing offences are punishable on conviction on indictment by a fine not exceeding £10,000 or to two years imprisonment, or by both: 1992 Act, s.20(3).
[110] 1976 Act, s.26(3).
[111] *ibid.*, s.26(7)(a).

clearly expressed. A tree will be regarded as being removed if it is cut down or otherwise wilfully destroyed.[112]

The time limits for the summary prosecution of offences under section 26 of the 1976 Act are the same as those which apply to summary prosecutions under section 24(2) of the 1963 Act.[113]

11.4.11 Notices requiring the removal or alteration of structures

Notices requiring the removal or alteration of a structure which is not unauthorised, may be served by the planning authority under section 36 of the 1963 Act on the owner and occupier and on any other person who, in the opinion of the planning authority, may be affected by the notice. Any replacement appearing to the planning authority to be suitable may be ordered. A similar notice may also be served where the structure concerned is unauthorised and an enforcement notice cannot be served because of the relevant time limits. This provision would at first appear to defeat the purpose of the time limits introduced by the 1992 Act, but the entitlement of the owner or occupier to compensation would appear to have made the section unpopular with planning authorities to the extent that such notices rarely issue. The decision to serve a section 36 notice is subject to the same restrictions as apply to enforcement notices.

An appeal may be brought against the notice to An Bord Pleanála by any person at any time before the date specified in the notice. An Bord Pleanála may confirm the notice with or without modification or annul it, and is restricted to considering the same matters as those governing the planning authority. The notice takes effect when the time for the taking of an appeal has passed without an appeal being lodged, or from the date an appeal has been withdrawn or determined.

The planning authority has power where a notice has not been complied with to enter on the structure to effect the removal, alteration or replacement of the structure as may be specified in the notice. Where a person complies with the notice he is entitled to recover reasonable expenses incurred by him in carrying out the removal or alteration and any replacement specified by the notice, less the value of any salvageable material. Any person having an interest in the structure may be entitled to compensation from the planning authority where he can show that the value of his interest in the structure existing at the time of the notice has been reduced, or that he had suffered damage by being disturbed in his enjoyment of the structure. Alternatively, a person whose interest has been affected may serve a purchase notice on the planning authority requiring them to purchase the land on which the structure is or had been situated.[114]

An offence is committed where a person uses the land or "causes or permits" the land to be used in contravention of the terms and conditions of the notice.

---

[112] 1976 Act, s.26(9).
[113] *ibid.*, s.30(5).
[114] See 1963 Act, s.29. The Board has power to cancel the notice: See 1963 Act, s.36(9).

11.4.12 Notices requiring the discontinuance of a use

A notice requiring the discontinuance of any use of land or imposing conditions on its future use may be served under section 37 of the 1963 Act by the planning authority on the owner or occupier of land and on any other person who in the opinion of the planning authority will be affected by the notice.[115] A section 37 notice may only be served five years after the unauthorised use commenced.

The provisions as to the considerations to be taken into account before a decision to serve a notice is made, appeals, the taking effect of the notice and the application of section 29 purchase notices are the same, *mutatis mutandis,* as those for section 36 notices.[116] Compensation is also payable on the same principles as apply to section 36 notices except that no compensation is payable for damage resulting from the imposition of conditions imposed in order to avoid or reduce serious water pollution or the danger of such pollution. Liability to pay compensation is also excluded where land has been used for advertising for more than five years, whether such use was continuous or intermittent or whether or not the advertising was exhibited on the same place on the land. Where the planning authority are under a duty to acquire an interest in land under the purchase notice procedure, compensation is not payable under the 1990 Act.

An offence is committed where a person uses the land or "causes or permits" the land to be use in contravention of the terms or conditions of the notice.

11.4.13 Enforcement of open spaces

Section 25 of the 1976 Act vests planning authorities with powers to compulsorily acquire open space required to be provided under terms or conditions of a planning permission. These have been considered already at para 3.1.14, above.

11.5 SUMMARY OF ENFORCEMENT TIME LIMITS

TYPE OF ENFORCEMENT	WHEN AVAILABLE	TIME LIMIT
PROSECUTION– s 24/1963 Act	Unauthorised development	5 years from the date on which unauthorised development occurred.
ENFORCEMENT NOTICE s.31/1963 Act	(1) Development carried out without planning permission	(1) 5 years from the date on which development carried out without permission.
	(2) Development in breach of conditions (as distinct from terms) of ordinary permission.	(2) 5 years from the expiration of the "life" of the permission plus any extended period, or, five years after date specified in condition or "latest date notice" whichever occurs earlier.

---

[115] Particulars of a s.37 notice must be entered on the planning register: s.37(9).

[116] It seems likely that the section was intended to correct the mistakes of previous planning decisions or non-enforcement by the planning authority and that consequently an entitlement to compensation is granted.

		(see note 6 below).
	(3) Breach of condition of permission for retention of structure.	(3) 5 years from the date of grant of permissiom
ENFORCEMENT NOTICE– s.32/1963 Act	Breach of condition of permission for retention of structure.	5 years from the date of grant of permission
ENFORCEMENT NOTICE– s.35/1963 Act	Ongoing development or development which has been carried out in breach of terms (as distinct from conditions) of permission	5 years from expiration of 'life" of permission plus any period for which permission extended.
WARNING NOTICE– s.26/1976 Act	(1) Ongoing works or works likely to be carried out without permission or in breach of permission.	(1) Not applicable.
	(2) Unauthorised use likely to be made, or already being made, of land.	(2) 5 years from thc datc on which unauthorised use first commenced.
	(3) Tree or feature to be preserved under condition may be removed or damaged.	(3) Not applicable.
PLANNING INJUNCTION– s.27/1976 Act.	(1) Ongoing works or works works carried out without planning permission.	(1) 5 years from the date on which development substantially completed.
	(2) Unauthorised use.	(2) 5 years from the date on which use commenced.
	(3) Development which is not being carried out in conformity with planning permission.	(3) 5 years from expiration of "life" of permission *plus* any period for which permission extended.

Notes on table:

1. All of these time limits are now operational since January 1, 1994: see Local Government (Planning and Development) Act 1992, (Commencement) Order, 1992 (S.I. No. 221 of 1992.

2. They apply to developments before and after the commencement of the Act.

3. Summary proceedings under section 27 cannot be instituted later than five years from the date on which the offence was committed: see section 30 of the 1976 Act. The date of commission of an unauthorised use runs from the date of commencement of the unauthorised use. While it is technically possible for proceedings on indictment to be taken, this is an unlikely event given that such proceedings would have to be instituted by the Director of Public Prosecutions who, it may be expected, would be extremely reluctant to institute proceedings after 5 years or more.

4. Time limits run from the expiration of the "life" of full permission or outline permission, not approval.

5. Any permission which was granted after the November 1, 1982 has a "life" of five years, unless a longer period has been specified in the permission, or an extension has been granted by the planning authority: see 1982 Act, sections 3 and 4.

6. Section 31(1) of the 1963 Act prevents the planning authority from serving an enforcement notice under this section five years or more after the date for compliance specified in the condition, or the date specified in a "latest date notice" served by the planning authority, when no such date is specified. A purchaser must therefore ascertain whether a latest date notice has been served or not.

7. While time limits may render unauthorised development immune from enforcement, this does not make it lawful. see restrictions contained in new 1994 Regulations.

11.6 PLANNING AND LICENSING

The precise relevance of planning objections to licensing applications has not yet clearly been defined by the courts. While it has been established that breaches of the planning code for which the applicant or licensee was responsible affect his "character" for licensing purposes, the extent to which planning permission is necessary before a new licence can be granted has not yet been determined.[117] It has been held by the Supreme Court that planning permission is not an essential prerequisite to the granting of a declaration under section 15 of the Intoxicating Liquor Act 1960.[118] In *Re Tivoli Cinema*,[119] Lynch J stated:

> "The planning code and the licensing code are separate and distinct codes of law and the fact that the area to be licensed may exceed that authorised for use as a bar by planning permission does not prevent the licence from being granted for a greater area. However, a use of part of the premises other than the bar for supplying and or intoxicating liquor would involve an unauthorised use of such other part of the premises which could be restrained under the planning code and might then be used as a ground for objection to renewal of the licence . . .

It has been argued that the decision in *Tivoli* should be restricted to its own facts, *i.e.* where the premises were already licensed in part.[120] Indeed, it is difficult to

---

117 As to the effect of planning breaches on the character of the applicant, see *Re Application of Kenneth McGovern* (application for gaming certificate). See objections to the renewal of a liquor licence under s.4(7) of the Courts (No.2) Act 1986 and objections to the granting of a dancehall licence under s.2(2) of the Public Dance Halls (Ireland) Act 1935.
118 *Re Application of Thomas Kitterick* 105 I.L.T.R. 105.
119 Unreported, High Court, January 24, 1994.
120 McDonald, *Hotel, Restaurant and Public House Law*, pp.99–100.

see how a court can determine the "fitness" or "convenience" of premises so as to consider an objection to the grant of a new licence certificate under section 4 of the Licensing (Ireland) Act 1833, in, circumstances where the physical structure of the premises proposed to be licensed may be substantially modified due to the necessity to comply with conditions attached to the grant of any planning permission which is required. In practice, therefore, an applicant for a new licence is wise to regard planning permission for the subject premises as an essential proof.[121] Similar reasoning would apply to applications for a public dance licence under section 2 of the Public Dancehalls Act 1935 where the District Judge is required to determine the "suitability" of premises. From a practical point of view, it is useful for the court to have the benefit of the views of the planning authority and perhaps, An Bord Pleanála, on the land use considerations involved in the change of use of the premises proposed to be licensed and on their fitness for such purposes. In *Donnelly v. Regency Hotel*,[122] Carswell J. stated:

> "I do not think that the court ought to absolve itself of its own statutory task of deciding upon the suitability by placing complete reliance upon the determination of a statutory agency, however skilled and experienced in a technical field the latter may be. It may, however, legitimately take the view that it will be slow to reach a conclusion which is at variance with the considered decision of a competent agency such as a planning authority."

The necessity for the applicant for a new licence to show that he has planning permission for the premises proposed to be licensed becomes even stronger where he has previously been guilty of breaches of the planning code. In *Re the Application of Thomas Kitterick*,[123] Walsh J. stated in the Supreme Court:

> "The Intoxicating Liquor Act of 1960 requires that the Court be the authority which is to be satisfied for the purpose of that Act. It quite clearly cannot delegate its functions to the planning authority. At the same time it must acknowledge that it would be quite contrary to the policy of the courts in the administration of law that any court order should form the basis of an illegal act."

Previous infringements of the planning code will not necessarily disqualify a licensee and the attitude of the planning authority to such infringements is a factor which may be taken into consideration as a matter for the discretion of the judge. Finlay P. stated as follows in *Re Comhaltas Ceoitoiri Éireann*[124]:

---

[121] Different considerations may arise where a question of intensification of use is raised. In an application for a dancing licence under s.2 of The Public Dancehalls Act 1935 heard at the end of July 1996, the President of the District Court decided that it was not appropriate for the licensing court to determine the question as to whether planning permission was required for the use of part of a hotel for dancing: *Re O'Dwyer Brothers*.

[122] [1985] N.I. 144, 151. See further, McDonald, *op. cit.*, pp.252–253.

[123] Above, n.118.

[124] Unreported, High Court, Finlay P., December 14, 1972.

"It is however proper that I should add my view that where what is before the learned District Justice by way of objection is an allegation of a breach of the Planning Acts that subject to his discretion as to the strength and validity of such an objection it would certainly be open to him to have regard in the one case to the absence of any proceedings instituted by the Planning Authority and in the other case to the absence of any proceedings or conviction. It would be open to a District Justice in his discretion to take the view that the body charged with the enforcement of planning permission and conditions attached to it being the same body as imposed those conditions is the person whom he might expect to act most vigilantly in relation to any breach."

Chapter 12

COMPENSATION

12.1 INTRODUCTION

The right to develop land is an element of the "bundle of rights" attaching to land which can be delimited "in accordance with principles of social justice" where the interests of the common good require.[1] In *Central Dublin Development Association v. The Attorney General*[2] Kenny J. stated that:

> ". . . town and regional planning is an attempt to reconcile the exercise of property rights with the demands of the common good and Part IV defends and vindicates as far as practicable the rights of the citizens from an unjust attack on their property rights."

In its 1988 Report, the Irish Planning Institute Sub-Committee on Planning and Compensation referred to the aim of the compensation provisions under the planning code as attempting "to provide a balance between the need to plan for the benefit of the community, particularly as identified in the development plan and the rights of an individual who has suffered loss as a result of a planning decision". Under the legislation which in fact ensued, the Local Government (Planning and Development) Act 1990, the odds were heavily stacked against the recovery of compensation by the individual who found his development aambitions frustrated by a decision of the planning authority.

The scheme of Part VI of the 1963 Act which formerly contained the compensation provisions was that a prima facie entitlement to compensation arose where a refusal of planning permission or a grant subject to conditions resulted in a reduction in the value of the land. This prima facie entitlement could be removed in a number of different circumstances, which included a situation where the planning authority or An Bord Pleanála furnished as one of its reasons for refusal a reason in respect of which the Act expressly provided that compensation was not payable. One of the major reasons for the high incidence of claims was that the payment of compensation was not excluded where one of the reasons for refusal was that the proposed development would materally contravene the provisions of the development plan.

The 1963 Act also provided that in order to prevent a claim arising as a result of an adverse planning decision the planning authority could give a statutory undertaking that planning permission would be granted for a particular type of

---

[1]   Art. 43.2 of the Constitution; see *Dreher v. Irish Land Commission* [1994] I.L.R.M. 94.
[2]   (1975) 109 I.L.T.R. 69.

development in the event of an application being made.[3] This provision was intended to ensure that a developer could only claim for the actual loss resulting from the restriction of his development rights by taking into account the possibility of alternative development in the future. Unfortunately, the whole undertaking procedure was misconceived and ultimately misfired. In *Grange Developments v. Dublin County Council*,[4] the Supreme Court held that the decision of a planning authority to give an undertaking was "a step entirely equivalent to the consideration by a planning authority as to whether to grant or refuse an application for permission". In determining a planning application, the planning authority were consequently restricted to considering the proper planning and development of their area and were not entitled to have regard to their liability to pay compensation or to the form of planning permission which might, if granted or undertaken to be granted, avoid such liability. The quasi-contractual nature of the undertaking which effectively bound the planning authority to exercise their discretion to grant or refuse planning permission conflicted with the rights of third party objectors and appellants to have their representations considered. As a result, the undertaking procedure did not survive the introduction of the Local Government (Planning and Development) Act 1990 which introduced a new comprehensive code for the determination and assessment of compensation claims.

The 1990 Act amended and consolidated the law relating to compensation for the refusal of planning permission and the imposition of conditions. It extended the reasons for which a planning authority may refuse planning permission or attach conditions to a planning permission without incurring a liability to pay compensation. In particular, it provided that no compensation was to be payable where the reason given for a refusal related to the material contravention of a land use zoning objective under the development plan. It also enabled the planning authority to refuse permission without liability to compensation where the reason for the refusal was that the capacity of existing or prospective water supplies or sewerage facilities was required for prospective development for which a grant of permission was already in existence, or where the development would be premature by reference to any order of priority for development indicated in a development plan.

It introduced a new notice procedure which replaced the undertaking procedure. This allows a planning authority to preclude a compensation claim from arising by serving a notice stating that, in their opinion, an alternative development ought to attract planning permission. The notice only ceases to be effective in this regard if planning permission is subsequently refused or a condition imposed which attracts compensation under the Act.

The Act also amended certain provisions of the sanitary services code in removing the right of an occupier of premises to connect to a public sewer and this is now subject to the consent of the sanitary authority concerned.

---

3   1963 Act, s.57.
4   Unreported, High Court, December 2, 1988.

12.2 ENTITLEMENT TO COMPENSATION FOR DECISIONS ON PLANNING APPLICATIONS

Section 11 confers a prima facie entitlement to compensation where the value of land is reduced as a result of a decision by the planning authority or An Bord Pleanála to refuse permission or to grant permission subject to conditions or where a planning permission is revoked or modified. The claim is made to the planning authority even where the entitlement arises as a result of a decision of An Bord Pleanála. The *prima facie* entitlement is, in the words of the explanatory memorandum which accompanied the Bill, "heavily qualified" by section 12 which provides that no compensation will be payable where

— the proposed development is of a kind described in the Second Schedule,[5]

— the reasons for refusal of permission including a reason specified in the Third Schedule,[6]

— the conditions for which compensation is sought is of a type specified in the Fourth Schedule,[7]

— the refusal of permission or the attachment of conditions relates to the retention of an unauthorised structure,

— the planning authority are obliged to acquire an interest in land arising out of the service of a purchase notice.

The non-compensatable circumstances set out in the Second, Third and Fourth Schedules were intended to be provided "by reference to specified considerations of community interest" but have in practical terms been effective in removing any entitlement to compensation in all but a few cases. While a claimant must have an interest in the lands for which compensation is sought at the time of the decision to refuse planning permission, it is not necessary for him to retain that legal interest up to the time that his compensation is assessed.[8] In *Dublin Corporation v. Smithwick* Finlay P. (as he then was) stated:

"It seems to me in general that there would be considerable injustice in forcing upon a person who is the owner of land, who has applied for permission and has had it refused and is then entitled to apply for compensation, the additional burden that he is prevented in order to acquire his compensation from disposing of his land if that is the most immediate best way of saving his loss."

---

5   See para. 12.3, below.
6   See para. 12.4, below.
7   See para. 12.5, below.
8   *Dublin Corporation v. Smithwick* [1976–77] I.L.R.M. 280.

12.2.1 Prohibition against double compensation

Section 7 prohibits double compensation where a claimant has an entitlement under another statute and provides that a claimant is not entitled to any greater amount of compensation under the 1990 Act than the amount to which he would be entitled arising out of the same matter under the other enactment.

12.2.2 Determination of claims for compensation

A claim for compensation must be made within six months of notification of the decision of the planning authority or An Bord Pleanála.[9] The planning authority may agree the amount of compensation to be paid, but in default of agreement, it is determined by arbitration under the Acquisition of Land (Assessment of Compensation) Act 1919. The arbitrator has a jurisdiction to make a nil award. The reduction in the value of any interest in land is calculated by reference to the rules for the assessment of compensation under the First Schedule to the 1990 Act.[10]

12.2.3 Form of claims

Part VIII of the Local Government (Planning and Development) Regulations 1994 makes provisions for the form in which compensation claims are to be made and the provision of evidence in support of such claims.[11] A compensation claim must be made to the planning authority in writing and must include the following information:

— the name and address of the claimant,
— his interest in the lands,
— the decision in respect of which the claim is made,
— the provision of the 1990 Act under which the claim is made,
— the amount of the claim.
— the basis on which the amount of compensation sought has been calculated,
— the names and addresses of all other persons (so far as they are known to the claimant, having an interest in the land to which the claim relates,
— where the claimant does not know of any other persons having an interest in the land, a statement to the this effect should be made.[12]

If a compensation claim does not comply with any of these requirements, the planning authority must serve a notice requiring the claimant to comply with that

---

9   There is no provision for an extension of this period under the 1994 Regulations.
10   See para. 12.5, below.
11   The 1994 Regulations repealed the Local Government (Planning and Development) (Compensation) Regulations 1990.
12   1994 Regulations, art. 109(1).

requirement and may defer consideration of the claim until then. The planning authority is obliged to notify in writing every person, other than the claimant, appearing to them to have an interest in the land to which the claim relates, within one month of the receipt of a claim or, where the claim does not initially comply with the requirements of the regulations, within one month of compliance with the requirements of the planning authority in this regard.[13] The notice should indicate the time remaining for the making of a claim for compensation.

Article 111 enables the planning authority to serve a notice on the claimant requiring him to provide evidence in support of his claim or evidence as to his interest in the land to which the claim relates, and the planning authority may suspend further consideration of the claim until the claimant has complied with the notice.

12.2.4 Registration of compensation

A planning authority must enter in the planning register the details of any compensation payment which has been made or which has become payable as a result of a decision to grant or refuse planning permission or to revoke or modify planning permission where the amount of the payment exceeds £100.[14]

12.2.5 Recovery of compensation by planning authority

Section 10 prohibits any person from carrying out development on land to which a compensation statement relates until the amount of compensation recoverable by the planning authority under this section has been paid or secured to their satisfaction. If the compensation payment was made in relation to a condition attached to a decision to grant permission, this does not preclude development in accordance with the terms and conditions of that permission. The prohibition applies to development "of a residential, commercial or industrial character, consisting wholly or mainly of the construction of houses, flats, shops or office premises, hotels, garages and petrol filling stations, theatres or structures for the purposes of entertainment, or industrial building, (including warehouses), or any combination thereof". This would appear to exclude almost all forms of profitable development until compensation has been repaid.

The obligation to repay compensation does not apply to:

— exempted development,
— development permitted by any permission for which a statement has been registered (where compensation has been paid for the attachment of a condition),
— development on foot of any permission to which conditions are attached which do not exclude the payment of compensation, where

---

[13] *ibid.*, art. 110.
[14] 1990 Act, s.9. The entry must be made within a period of 14 days from the date of preparation of the statement: see s.9(2)(b).

the development is of a type specified in a section 13 notice which has been served by the planning authority in connection with the same land.

The amount of compensation repayable to the planning authority will depend on whether the development which it is proposed to carry out includes all or only part of the site for which compensation has been paid. If the intended development occupies only part of the original site, the planning authority must, but only if it is practicable to do so, carry out an apportionment of the amount of compensation repayable according to the extent to which the part and the remainder of the original site appear to be affected by the decision which gave rise to the claim. If no apportionment has been made, the amount of compensation is treated as having been distributed rateably according to area.

Where part of a compensation payment is attributed to part of the land under an apportionment, the apportioned amount is treated as rateable within that part of the land according to area. This means that no further apportionment is necessary where a developer only decides to proceed with part of the proposed development. The planning authority are not entitled to recover compensation twice where further development is carried out on land in relation to which a compensation statement has been registered if the planning authority have already recovered compensation for that land. If any person disputes an apportionment made by a planning authority, the dispute is submitted to a property arbitrator.

A planning authority may direct that the compensation be repaid as a single capital payment or by instalment.[15] Interest is only payable where payment is made by way of instalments. To have provided otherwise would have encouraged the sterilisation of land.

The obligation to repay compensation applies to the successors in title of the person to whom the compensation payment was made, so that the existence of a compensation statement must be taken into account in establishing the contract price on the sale of land. It is advisable for a purchaser to enquire at the time of purchase as to whether a claim for compensation has been made by the vendor or any previous owner, particularly in circumstances where an inspection of the planning register discloses a refusal of permission. In such circumstances, the purchaser may find himself in a position where he is obliged to repay any compensation subsequently assessed by an arbitrator before he is entitled to carry out any development on foot of a subsequent permission.

12.2.6 Notice preventing compensation

Section 13 provides that compensation is not payable where a notice is served by a planning authority on a person by whom a claim has been made, stating that the land for which planning permission has been refused or for which permission

---

[15]   1990 Act, s.10(6).

is being granted subject to conditions, is in their opinion, capable of other development for which planning permission ought to be granted. Article ll3 of the Local Government (Planning and Development) Regulations 1994, which prescribes the form of notice under section 13, provides that it must contain a statement in outline of the nature and extent of the alternative development of which the land is capable. The alternative development must be of a type specified in section 13(2) namely – "development of a residential, commercial or industrial character, consisting wholly or mainly of the construction of houses, flats, shops or office premises, hotels, garages and petrol filling stations, theatres or structures for the purpose of entertainment or industrial buildings, (including warehouses), or any combination thereof". The notice must be served not less than three months after a claim for compensation has been received.

The notice remains in force for five years unless it is withdrawn within that period or planning permission is granted for a development in accordance with the section 13 notice, subject to no conditions or to conditions for which compensation is payable. The notice may also be annulled by the refusal of planning permission for development in a manner consistent with a notice or where planning permission is granted subject to compensatable conditions. In these circumstances, the original compensation claim is revived. Once the notice has expired, a claimant is not entitled to compensation where an application for planning permission has not been made within the "life" of the notice.

A notice which expresses the planning authority's opinion that the land is capable of other development, which is in fact in material contravention of the development plan will be deemed to be invalid for this reason, even where the notice makes it a condition that a resolution be passed by the members of the planning authority to make any necessary variations in the development plan.[16]

12.2.7 Power of Minister to order payment of compensation

Section 14 was inserted "to give a constitutional balance" to the provisions of the Act which exclude the payment of compensation. It provides that the payment of compensation will not be excluded due to the operation of section 12 where planning permission is refused or is granted subject to any condition of a type specified in paragraph 8 or 9 of the Fourth Schedule where the Minister makes an order declaring that he is satisfied that it would be just and reasonable that compensation would not be paid. In the event that such an order is made, any claim must be made to the planning authority in the normal manner, the Minister has no role in the assessment of the quantum of compensation, only in the entitlement to claim. The Minister may make such an order only where

---

[16] *Browne v. Cashel U.D.C.*, unreported, High Court, March 26, 1993. See also s.22 of the 1963 Act which imposes a duty on the planning authority to give effect to the objectives contained in its development plan.

an application has been made within two months of the notification of the decision by An Bord Pleanála, unless the Minister allows a longer period.[17] The requirements for an application are set out under article 112.

The Minister may not make an order under the section in the following circumstances:

- where there has been a refusal of permission for the erection of any advertisement structure or for the use of any land for the exhibition of any advertisement,
- where there has been a refusal of permission for development including any structure or any addition to or extension of a structure where the reason or one of the reasons for the refusal is that the structure, addition or extension
  (i) would infringe an existing building line, or where none exists, a building line determined by the planning authority or by the Board;
  (ii) would be under a public road;
  (iii) would endanger the health or safety of persons occupying or employed on the structure or any adjoining structures; or
  (iv) would be prejudicial to public health,
  or where a section 13 notice has been served.

The Minister, may, however, make an order where a section 13 notice has been served if planning permission has been granted for development of a type specified in the notice where any condition of a kind specified in paragraph 8 or 9 of the Fourth Schedule has been attached to the permission.

12.2.8 Structures substantially replacing structures demolished or destroyed by fire

Section 15 provides that compensation is not excluded by section 12 where permission is refused for the erection of a new structure which substantially replaces a structure demolished or destroyed by fire in the two years preceding the application. Similarly, liability to pay compensation cannot be excluded by section 12 where a condition is attached to a decision to grant permission for such a structure which prevents the structure being used for the purpose for which it was last used or which requires the structure to be set back or forward. Disputes on questions as to whether a new structure "substantially" replaces a demolished or destroyed structure are determined by An Bord Pleanála.

---

[17] There is no time limit for the making of a decision by the Minister under s.14, nor can a time limit be implied: *Dublin Corporation v. Smithwick*, above, n.8.

12.2.9 Prohibition on assignment of compensation

A person is not entitled to assign to any other person an entitlement to compensation or any part of any prospective compensation under section 11, and any purported assignment is deemed to be void.[18]

12.3 DEVELOPMENT IN RESPECT OF WHICH A REFUSAL OF PERMISSION WILL NOT ATTRACT COMPENSATION

12.3.1 Second Schedule to the 1990 Act

The second schedule to the 1990 Act lists a number of types of development in relation to which a refusal of permission will not attract the payment of compensation:

1. "Any development that consists of or includes the making of any material change in the use of any structures or other land".

The refusal of permission for "any development that consists of or includes the making of any material change in the use of any structures or other land" does not attract compensation. In *Viscount Securities Limited v. Dublin County Council*,[19] the High Court had to consider whether the equivalent provision under section 56(1)(a) of the 1963 Act excluded the compensation for the erection of a large number of houses in an area of County Dublin zoned for agricultural purposes. Relying on the judgement of Kenny J. in the *Central Dublin Development Association Limited and others v. The Attorney General*,[20] Finlay P. (as he then was) held that the development comprised "works" and could not, therefore, also constitute a material change of use, having regard to the definition of "use" under section 2 of the 1963 Act, which "does not include the use of the land by the carrying out of any works thereon".

2. "The demolition of a habitable house.[21]
3. The demolition of a building of artistic, architectural or historical interest which it is a development objective of the development plan to preserve.
4. The erection of any advertisement structure.
5. The use of land for the exhibition of any advertisement.[22]
6. Development in an area to which a special amenity area order relates.

---

[18]   1990 Act, s.16. This affects decisions under Pt. IV of the 1963 Act only, *i.e.* decisions on planning applications or decisions to revoke or modify a planning permission.
[19]   (1976) 62 I.L.T. 17.
[20]   109 I.L.T.R. 69.
[21]   For the definition of "habitable house", see 1994 Regulations, art. 8.
[22]   Both "advertisement" and "advertisement structure" are defined under the 1963 Act, s.2.

7. Any development of land with respect to which there is available (notwithstanding the refusal of permission) a grant of permission under Part IV of the Principal Act for any development of a residential, commercial or industrial character, if the development consists wholly or mainly of the construction of houses, flats, shops or office premises, hotels, garages and petrol filling stations, theatres or structures for the purpose of entertainment, or industrial buildings, (including warehouses), or any combination thereof, subject to no conditions other than conditions of the kind referred to in the Fourth Schedule.

8. Any development on land with respect to which compensation has already been paid under section 11, or under section 55 of the Principal Act, by reference to a previous decision under Part IV of that Act involving a refusal of permission".

12.3.2 Road development

A person is not entitled to direct access from any land adjoining a motorway to the motorway or from the motorway to such land; and planning authorities are precluded from granting permission for any development providing such access.[23] Neither a planning authority nor An Bord Pleanála can decide to grant permission, nor can a "default" decision to grant permission be deemed to have been made for any development of land:

(a) which would involve access to or from a motorway or a busway or which would conravene the provisions of an protected road scheme approved by the Minister,
(b) which it is proposed to be compulsorily acquired under a scheme,
(c) where such development would affect rights proposed to be compulsorily acquired under the scheme,
(d) which would contravene the provisions of a scheme.[24]

Compensation is not payable for any refusal of permission for such development. Nor is compensation payable for any condition relating to:

– the prohibition of direct access to or from a motorway or busway;
– the prohibition, closure, stopping up, removal, alteration, diversion or restriction of direct access to or from a protected road.[25]

---

[23] Roads Act 1993, s.43(2).
[24] *ibid.*, s.46(1). These restrictions may be removed or modified depending on whether the Minister refuses to approve a scheme or approves it subject to modifications. As to the circumstances in which a "default permission" may arise, see s.26(4) of the Local Government (Planning and Development) Act 1963, paras. 8.5.3 and 8.5.4, above.
[25] Roads Act 1993, s.46(3).

12.4 NON-COMPENSATABLE REASONS FOR REFUSAL FOR DECISIONS UNDER PART IV OF THE 1963 ACT

The non-compensatable reasons for the refusal of permission which would exclude compensation are set out in the Third Schedule. The extensive list of non-compensatable grounds for the refusal of planning permission which subsequently appeared in the Third Schedule to the 1990 Act reflects the increased importance of the development plan as a basis for the restriction of property rights.

It is not necessary for the planning authority or An Bord Pleanála to employ the precise wording of the provision on which reliance is placed in order to defeat a claim for compensation.[26] It is sufficient that the reason given falls clearly within the meaning of the paragraph relied upon. In *XJS*, McCarthy J. observed that planning documents —

> "are not acts of the Oireachtas or subordinate legislation emanating from skilled draughtsmen and inviting the accepted canons of construction applicable to such material . . . they are to be construed in their ordinary meaning as it would be understood by members of the public, without legal training, as well as by developers and their agents, unless such documents, read as a whole, necessarily indicate some other meaning.

12.4.1 Third Schedule: non-compensatable reasons for refusal

Section 12 of the 1990 Act provides that the following reasons for refusal are non-compensatable.

1. Development of the kind proposed on the land would be premature by reference to any one or combination of the following constraints and the period within which the constraints involved may reasonably be expected to cease —
    (a) any existing deficiency in the provision of water supplies or sewerage facilities,
    (b) the capacity of existing or prospective water supplies or sewerage facilities being required for prospective development as regards which a grant of a permission under Part IV of the Principal Act, an undertaking under Part VI of that Act or a notice under section 13 exists.
    (c) the capacity of existing or prospective water supplies or sewerage facilities being required for the prospective development of another part of the functional area of the planning authority, as indicated in the development plan,

---

[26]   *Dublin County Council v. Eighty Five Developments Ltd (No. 2)* [1992] 2 I.R. 392.

(d) the capacity of existing or prospective water or sewerage facilities being required for any other prospective development or for any development objective, as indicated in the development plan.

(e) any existing deficiency in the road network serving the area of the proposed development, including considerations of capacity, width alignment, or the surface or structural condition of the pavement, which would render that network, or any part of it, unsuitable to carry the increased road traffic likely to result from the development.

(f) any prospective deficiency (including the considerations specified in subparagraph (e) in the road network serving the area of the proposed development which —

(i) would arise because of the increased road traffic likely to result from that development and from prospective development as regards which a grant of permission under Part VI of that Act or a notice under section 13 exists, or

(ii) would arise because of the increased road traffic likely to result from that development and from any other prospective development or from any development objective, as indicated in the development plan, and

(iii) would render that road network, or any part of it, unsuitable to carry the increased road traffic likely to result from the proposed development".

Prior to the 1990 Act, planning authorities were liable to the payment of compensation where the stated reason for refusal was that the spare capacity in the public sewer was required for future development on other lands.[27] Section 23 of the Public Health (Ireland) Act 1878 conferred an absolute right on the occupier of premises to connect to the public sewer.

Section 25 of the 1990 Act now makes it necessary for the owner or occupier of premises to obtain the consent of the sanitary authority, which may attach appropriate conditions. Paragraph 1 of the Third Schedule lists a number of non-compensatable reasons relating to the prematurity of proposed development because of a deficiency in the provision of water supplies, sewerage facilities or the road network serving the area of the proposed development.[28] It extends the reasons for refusal to situations where water supplies, sewerage facilities or the road network is required for prospective development for which a grant of planning permission is already in existence or where an undertaking to grant planning permission or a section 13 notice remains in force.

---

[27]   *Shortt v. Dublin County Council* [1983] I.L.R.M. 377 (SC); [1982] I.L.R.M. 117 (HC).

[28]   The right to a supply of water for domestic purposes under s.23 of the Waterworks Clauses Act 1847 does not now apply to a dwellinghouse which is an unauthorised structure or the use of which constitutes an unauthorised use: see section 26 of the 1990 Act.

In assessing the adequacy of the road network, a planning authority is entitled to take into account the capacity, width, alignment, or the surface or structural condition of the pavement, which would render the network, or any part of it, unsuitable to carry the increased road traffic likely to result from the development. To exclude the payment of compensation on the basis of any prospective deficiency in the road network, a planning authority must consider that the deficiency "would render that road network, or any part of it, unsuitable to carry the increased road traffic likely to result from the proposed development".

2. Development of the kind proposed would be premature pending the determination by the planning authority or the road authority of a road layout for the area or any part thereof.

3. Development of the kind proposed would be premature by reference to the order of priority, if any, for development indicated in the development plan.

If there is no development indicated for the area in which the site for an application for proposed development is located, the planning authority are not entitled to refuse permission by reference to the order of priority for the development indicated in the development plan, and any such reason attached to a permission may be declared *ultra vires* and invalid. So, in *Hoburn Homes Limited v. An Bord Pleanála*[29] it was held by the High Court that a vaguely worded policy in the Cork County Development Plan, "to slow down the growth in the west harbour area", did not indicate a priority for the development of that area so as to render paragraph 3 of the Third Schedule a relevant consideration.

4. The proposed development would endanger public safety by reason of traffic hazard or obstruction of road users or otherwise.

In *Dublin County Council v. Eighty Five Developments Limited (No. 2)*,[30] the Supreme Court had to consider whether a reason for refusal which made reference to the fact that the proposed development would give rise to a "traffic hazard" but did not go so far as to state that it would endanger public safety for that reason, fell within the meaning of section 56(1)(e) of the 1963 Act.[31] The reason stated that "the proposed development, located on the main Donabate road which is sub-standard in width and alignment, would give rise to traffic hazard by reason of the additional turning movements which it would generate." Finlay C.J. analysed the reason in the following fashion:

"(1) It states that the proposed development would generate additional movements of traffic.

(2) It states that those turning movements would occur on the main Donabate road, which is sub-standard in width and alignment.

---

29 [1993] I.L.R.M. 368.
30 See above, n.26.
31 This reason is now incorporated in para. 4 of Sched. 3 to the 1990 Act.

(3) It states that those turning movements on that road would give rise to traffic hazards.

It seems to me that it is an inevitable conclusion from that analysis that what the refusal of planning permission based on those reasons is intended to do is to protect the safety of the public using the road. To put the matter in another way, the hazard referred to in that reason can only, having regard to the other factors stated in the reason, be a hazard or danger to public safety.

The decision of this court in the *XJS* case was not, as has been contended, a decision to the effect that a reason for the refusal of planning permission could only be non-compensatory, within the provisions of section 56, if it following the precise wording of one of the sub-sections or sub-clauses of that section."

Egan J., dissenting from the majority judgment, found that the onus of proof which lay on the planning authority to establish that the wording of their refusal fell within the meaning of the statutory provision had not been discharged. While allowing that the omission of the words "endanger public safety" was not necessarily fatal from the planning authority's point of view, he was of the view that "traffic hazard" was not synonymous with "public safety", even with the benefit of the additional words used in the reason for refusal.

References in a reason for refusal furnished by An Bord Pleanála to "a number of shortcomings" in the proposed development, and to the "awkward alignment and restricted sightlines of the access road" were not sufficient to bring the proposal within the rubric of development which would "endanger public safety by reason of traffic hazards".[32]

"5. The proposed development, by itself or by the precedent which the grant of permission for it would set for other relevant development, would adversely affect the use of a national road or other major road by traffic.

6. The proposed development would interfere with a view or prospect of special amenity value or special interest which it is necessary to preserve".

In *J. Wood & Company Limited v. Wicklow County Council*,[33] Costello J. held that the reference to the "visually sensitive location" of the proposed development, could not be construed as meaning that permission was refused because of the necessity of preserving a view or prospect of special amenity value. On the other hand, in *XJS Investments Limited v. Dun Laoghaire Corporation*,[34] McCarthy J. observed, *obiter,* that a reason for refusal given by the planning authority which did not specifically refer to "a view or prospect of special amenity value or special interest" appeared to fall within section 56(1)(g) of the 1963 Act (*i.e.* the equivalent provision to paragraph 6) because the stated reason conveyed a similar sense and meaning.

32 *J. Wood & Company Ltd v. Wicklow County Council* [1995] 1 I.L.R.M. 51.
33 *ibid.*
34 [1987] I.L.R.M. 659.

"7. The proposed development would cause serious air pollution, water pollution, noise pollution or vibration or pollution connected with the disposal of waste".

The widespread influence of the "polluter pays principle" in environmental legislation is reflected in this paragraph. This type of reason for refusal may not be given where the proposed development is related to an activity for which an IPC licence is or will be required.[35]

"8. 'In the case of development including[36] any structure or any addition to or extension of a structure, the structure, addition or extension would –
  (i)   infringe an existing building line or, where none exists, a building line determined by the planning authority or by the Board,
  (ii) be under a public road,
  (iii) seriously injure the amenities,[37] or depreciate the value, of property in the vicinity,
  (iv) tend to create any serious traffic congestion,
  (v)   endanger or interfere with the safety of aircraft or the safe and efficient navigation thereof,
  (vi) endanger the health or safety of persons occupying or employed in the structure or any adjoining structure, or
  (vii) be prejudicial to public health.
9. The development would contravene materially a condition attached to an existing permission for the development.
10. The proposed development would injure or interfere with a historic monument which stands registered in the Register of Historic Monuments under section 5 of the National Monuments (Amendment) Act, 1987, or which is situated in an archaeological area so registered".

In *J. Wood & Company Limited v. Wicklow County Council*, (see above) Costello J. held that the reason given by An Bord Pleanála for the refusal of planning permission for a housing development which referred to an "inadequate setting provided for St Crispin's Cell which is a national monument", and which also referred to the "shortcomings" of the development, was not equivalent to stating that the proposed development would "injure" or "interfere with" the national monument. He also considered it relevant that in a subsequent refusal for permission, An Bord Pleanála had relied on the actual language used in paragraph 6.[38]

---

35 Environmental Protection Agency Act 1992, s.98.
36 The word "including" appears in an extensive sense, so that the paragraph is applicable to a development involving a multiplicity of structures: see *Dunbar Limited v. Wicklow County Council*, unreported, High Court, July 6, 1989, in which Murphy J. interpreted the words "development comprising any structure or any addition to or extension of a structure" as incorporating the plural as well as the singular. See also *XJS Investments Limited*, above, n.34, *per* Murphy J. in the High Court and *per* McCarthy J. in the Supreme Court.
37 In the claim of *XJS Investments Limited*, above, n.34, McCarthy J. refused to equate the expression "overall character" with "amenities" under the corresponding provision to para. 8(iii) of Sched. 3 to the 1990 Act (*i.e.* s.56(1)(i)(iii) of the 1963 Act).
38 A similar approach was taken by McCarthy J. in the *XJS* case, above, n.34.

"11. The development would contravene materially a development objective indicated in the development plan for the use solely or primarily (as may be indicated in the development plan) of particular areas for particular purposes (whether residential, commercial, industrial, agricultural or otherwise)."

A refusal of planning permission on the grounds that the development will materially contravene the zoning provisions of the development plan does not attract compensation. The wording of any such reason for refusal must fall clearly within the meaning of paragraph 11 of the Third Schedule. Although a specific objective, *e.g.* for the provision of a hospital, amounts to a "reservation for a particular purpose" within the meaning of Rule 2(1)(iv) of the Third Schedule,[39] it has been held in *O'Connor v. Clare County Council*[40] that this does not prevent it from also being a "development objective" for the purposes of paragraph 11.

In that case, an application was made for the construction of a shop and storage unit to be located in a small area at the Cliffs of Moher in County Clare which was shown for development on a map contained in the relevant development plan. It was the stated policy of the County Council under the development plan "to provide or permit the provision of an integrated visitor facility contained within a single building" in the area shown for development. Planning permission was refused for the shop and storage unit although it was located within the development area, for the reason that it would constitute a material contravention of the policy contained in the development plan that the visitor facility should be provided within a single building. Murphy J. said:

"The limited area designated for development could hardly be described as being 'zoned' in the sense in which that is ordinarily understood. That term is generally used to describe a wider area where activities or developments having some measure of uniformity may be undertaken by a considerable number of owners or occupiers. However, there does not appear to be anything in Reason 11 aforesaid which would prevent a planning authority from indicating a specific development objective in relation to a limited area with a view to or as a consequence of formulating a development objective in relation to an adjoining larger area. As clearly as words and plans can provide, the Clare County Council have indicated their development objective that the area specified is one for "development" is to be used for the particular purposes of an integrated visitor facility which is described in detail in the 1991 Plan. It seems to me that any other development or use of that site or any part, as a shop and storage unit or otherwise than in the context of an integrated visitor facility would contravene materially this development objective".

Murphy J. concluded that the payment of compensation was precluded by the reason referred to, which fell within paragraph 11 of the Third Schedule.

"12. Paragraph 11 shall, subject to paragraph 13, not apply in a case where a development objective for the use specified in paragraph 11 applied to the land at any time within the five years immediately prior to the date on which the relevant application was made for permission under Part IV of the

---

[39] See *Shortt*, above, n.27, and *Meenaghan v. Dublin County Council* [1984] I.L.R.M. 616.
[40] Unreported, High Court, February 11, 1994. See 1994 Regulations, art. 11.

Principal Act to develop the land, and the development would not have contravened materially that development objective.

13. Paragraph 12 shall not apply in a case where a person acquired his interest in the land —
    (a) after the development objective referred to in paragraph 11 has come into operation, or
    (b) after notice has been published
        (i) in accordance with section 21 of the Principal Act, of a proposed new development plan or of proposed variations of a development plan, or
        (ii) in accordance with section 21A of the Principal Act, of a material alteration of the draft concerned, indicating in draft the development objective referred to in paragraph 11".

Paragraphs 12 and 13 of the Third Schedule to the 1990 Act specifically envisaged that "down-zoning" may occur in the variation of a development plan or in the adoption of a new plan. These paragraphs ensure that liability to pay compensation is not excluded by a refusal for zoning reasons where down-zoning has taken place, provided that the conditions under paragraphs 12 and 13 are met.[41] In particular, liability to compensate may be excluded where the person claiming compensation acquired his interest after the lands had been re-zoned or after notice of the proposed changes of zoning were published in the manner set out in paragraph 13.

"14. For the purposes of paragraph 13, the onus shall be on a person to prove all relevant facts relating to his interest in the land to the satisfaction of the planning authority.

15. In this Schedule, each of the terms 'road authority' and 'national road' has the meaning assigned to it under the Roads Act 1993."

12.5 NON-COMPENSATABLE CONDITIONS FOURTH SCHEDULE: CONDITIONS WHICH MAY BE IMPOSED WITHOUT COMPENSATION

Section 12 provides that the attachment of the following conditions will not attract the payment of compensation:

1. A condition, under section 26(2)(*e*) of the Principal Act, requiring the giving of security for satisfactory completion of the proposed development (including maintenance until taken in charge by the local authority concerned of roads, open spaces, car-parks, sewers, watermains or drains.

2. A condition, under section 26(2)(*g*) of the Principal Act, requiring a contribution towards expenditure incurred by any local authority in respect of works (including the provision of open spaces) which have facilitated the proposed development.

---

[41] A challenge to the constitutionality of "zoning" under the development plan was repelled in *Central Dublin Development Association Limited*, above, n.20.

3. A condition, under section 26(2)(*h*) of the Principal Act, requiring a contribution towards expenditure on the acquisition of land) that is proposed to be incurred by any local authority in respect of works facilitating the proposed development.

4. A condition, under section 26(2)(*j*) of the Principal Act, requiring the removal of an advertisement structure.

5. Any condition under section 26(2)(*j*) of the Principal Act in a case in which the relevant application for permission relates to a temporary structure.

6. Any condition relating to all or any of the following matters —
   (*a*) the size, height, floor area and character of structures;
   (*b*) building lines, site coverage and the space about dwellings and other structures;
   (*c*) the extent of parking places required in, on or under structures of a particular class or size or services or facilities for the parking, loading, unloading or fuelling of vehicles;
   (*d*) the objects which may be affixed to structure;
   (*e*) the purposes for and the manner in which structures may be used or occupied, including, in the case of dwellings, the letting thereof in separate tenements.

7. Any condition relating to the design, colour and materials of structures.

8. Any conditions reserving or allocating specified land for structures of a specified class or classes, or prohibiting or restricting either permanently or temporarily, the erection, construction or making of any particular class of structures on any specified land.

9. Any condition limiting the number of structures of a particular class which may be constructed , erected or made, on, in or under any specified land.

10. Any conditions relating to —
    (*a*) the disposition or layout of structures or structures of any specified class (including the reservation of reasonable open space in relation to the number, class and character of structures in any particular development proposal);
    (*b*) the manner in which any land is to be laid out for the purpose of development, including requirements as to road layout, landscaping, planting;
    (*c*) the provision of water supplies, sewers, drains and public lighting;
    (*d*) the provision of service roads and the location and design of means of access to roads;
    (*e*) the provision of facilities for parking, unloading, loading and fuelling of vehicles on any land.

11. Any condition relating to the alteration or removal of unauthorised structures.

12. Any condition relating to the layout of the proposed development, including density, spacing, grouping and orientation of structures in relation to roads, open spaces, and other structures.

13. Any condition relating to the provision and siting of sanitary services and recreational facilities.
14. Any condition reserving, as a public park, public garden or public recreation space, land normally used as such.
15. Any condition relating to the preservation of buildings of artistic, architectural or historical interest.
16. Any condition relating to the preservation of plaster work, staircases, woodwork or other fixtures or features of artistic, architectural or historical interest and forming part of the interior of structures.
17. Any condition relating to the preservation of caves, sites, features and other objects of archaeological, geological or historical interest.
18. Any condition relating to the preservation of views and prospects and of amenities of places and features of natural beauty or interest.
19. Any condition relating to the preservation and protection of trees, shrubs, plants and flowers.
20. Any condition prohibiting, restricting or controlling, either generally or within a specified distance of the centre line of any specified road, the erection of all or any particular forms of advertisement structure or the exhibition of all or any particular forms of advertisement.
21. Any condition preventing, remedying or removing injury to amenities arising from the ruinous or neglected condition of any structure, or from the objectionable or neglected condition of any land attached to a structure or abutting on a public road or situate in a residential area.
22. Any condition prohibiting, regulating or controlling the deposit or disposal or waste materials and refuse, the disposal of sewage and the pollution of rivers, ponds, gullies and the seashore.
23. Any condition for preserving any existing public right of way access to seashore, mountain, lakeshore, riverbank, or other place of natural beauty or recreational utility.
24. Any condition relating to a matter in respect of which a requirement could have been imposed under any other Act, or under any order, regulation, rule or bye-law made under any other Act, without liability for compensation.
25. Any condition relating to measures to reduce or prevent the emission or the intrusion of noise or vibration.
26. Any condition prohibiting the demolition of a habitable house.
27. Any condition relating to the filling of land.
28. Any condition in the interest of ensuring the safety of aircraft or the safe and efficient navigation thereof.
29. Any condition determining the sequence in which works shall be carried out or specifying a period within which works shall be completed.
30. Any condition restricting the occupation of any structure included in a development until the completion of other works included in the development or until any other specified condition is complied with or until the planning authority consent to such occupation.

12.5.1 Non-compensatable conditions under the Roads Act 1993

- the prohibition of direct access to or from a motorway or busway;
- the prohibition, closure, stopping up, removal, alteration, diversion or restriction of direct access to or from a protected road.[42]

12.6 OTHER CIRCUMSTANCES IN WHICH COMPENSATION PAYABLE

Compensation may be payable under the 1990 Act where the value of land is reduced as the result of a decision to refuse planning permission or to grant permission subject to onerous conditions. However, compensation may also be payable where the value of any interest in land is reduced or where any person having an interest in the land has suffered damage by being disturbed in his enjoyment of the land, as a consequence of certain other actions of the planning authority or An Bord Pleanála. In each case, the action of the planning authority which triggers the reduction in value is treated as the "decision" so as to entitle an owner or occupier to recover compensation under section 11 of the Act.[43] The other circumstances in which compensation may be payable are:

- the revocation or modification of permission.[44]
- the service of a notice requiring the removal of structures or the discontinuance of any use.[45]
- the removal or alteration of any hedge no foot of a notice under section 44 of the 1963 Act.[46]
- the refusal of a felling consent under a tree preservation order made pursuant to section 45 of the 1963 Act.[47]
- where a public right of way is created compulsorily under section 48 of the 1963 Act.[48]
- where damage is caused due to an authorised entry on land under section 83 of the 1963 Act.[49]
- where cables, wires or pipelines are placed, renewed or removed under section 85 of the 1963 Act.[50]

---

[42] Roads Act, 1993, s.46(3).
[43] 1990 Act, s.6. Tree preservation orders are considered at para. 3.1.3, above.
[44] *ibid.*, s.17.
[45] *ibid.*, ss.18 and 19.
[46] *ibid.*, s.20.
[47] *ibid.*, s.21.
[48] *ibid.*, s.22.
[49] *ibid.*, s.23.
[50] *ibid.*, s.24.

12.6.1.1 *The revocation or modification of permission*

A claim for compensation made be made to the planning authority by any person having an interest in land for expenditure reasonably incurred in carrying out works rendered abortive by the revocation or modification of planning permission.[51] The provisions of the Act apply to a revocation notice or modification notice in the same way as they apply to refusals of planning permission or decisions to grant permission subject to conditions. The time of the service of the notice is treated as the time of a decision for the purposes of applying time limits under the Act. No compensation is payable for any works carried out before the grant of the permission which is revoked or modified, or for any other loss or damage arising out of anything done or omitted to be done before the grant of that permission.

12.6.1.2 *Service of a notice requiring the removal of structures or the discontinuance of an authorised use*

A compensation claim may be made where notices under section 36 or 37 of the 1963 Act requiring the removal of structures or the discontinuance of an authorised use or the compliance with conditions on the continuance of any use of land are served.[52] Compensation is not payable for the reduction in the value of any interest arising out of compliance with notices where a purchase notice has been served and, consequently, the planning authority are obliged to acquire the interest.[53]

12.6.1.3 *The refusal of felling consent*

Where a planning authority or An Bord Pleanála decide to refuse a felling consent under an order under section 45 of the 1963 Act, or to grant any such consent subject to conditions, compensation is payable for the reduction in the value of the land to which the decision relates.[54] Compensation is also payable to any person who had an interest in the land at the time of the decision and whose enjoyment of the land was disturbed as a result. Compensation is not payable for the refusal of a felling consent required under a tree preservation order in the following circumstances:

- where the order declares that any tree, trees or group of trees affected which are not comprised in woodlands, are of special amenity value or special interest,
- where a condition attached to a felling consent requires replanting of any trees comprised in woodlands and the order declares that it is essential for the condition to be attached in the interests of amenity,

---

[51]   1990 Act, s.17. Any expenditure reasonably incurred in the preparation of plans or items of a similar nature in connection with the works which have to be aborted can be recovered by way of compensation.

[52]   1990 Act, ss.18 and 19. See paras. 11.4.11 and 11.4.12, above.

[53]   See 1963 Act, ss.36(9) and 37(8).

[54]   1990 Act, s.21.

- where a condition is attached to a decision to grant a felling consent which requires a specified proportion of trees comprised in woodlands (but not more than 20 per cent of such trees) to be preserved and the order declares that it is essential that the condition be attached because of the special amenity value or special interest of the trees concerned,
- where a condition is attached to a decision to grant a felling consent requiring the felling of extraction of trees comprised in woodlands to be phased over a period of up to 20 years in the manner specified in the order, and where the order declares that such a condition is an essential condition because of the special amenity value or special interest of the trees concerned.

12.7 RULES FOR THE DETERMINATION OF THE AMOUNT OF COMPENSATION

The rules applicable to the assessment of the amount of compensation are contained in the First Schedule to the 1990 Act[55]:

1. The reduction in value shall, subject to the provisions of this Schedule, be determined by reference to the difference between the antecedent and subsequent values of the land, where —

   (a) the antecedent value of the land is the amount which the land, if sold in the open market by a willing seller immediately prior to the relevant decision under Part IV of the Principal Act (and assuming that the relevant application for permission had not been made), might have been expected to realise, and

   (b) the subsequent value of the land is the amount which the land, if sold in the open market by a willing seller immediately after the said decision, might be expected to realise.

2. In determining the antecedent value and subsequent value of the land for the purposes of *Rule 1* —

   (a) regard shall De had to —
      (i) any contribution which a planning authority might have required or might require as a condition precedent to development of the land,
      (ii) any restriction on the development of the land which, without conferring a right to compensation, could have been or could be imposed under any Act or under any order, regulations, rule or bye-law made under any Act.

---

[55] A more detailed consideration of the case law interpreting the rules below may be found in McDermott and Woulfe, "Compulsory Purchase and Compensation in Ireland: Law and Practice" (1992), Chap. 10.

(iii) the fact that exempted development might have been or may be carried out on the land, and

(iv) the open market value of comparable land, if any, in the vicinity of the land whose values are being determined;

(b) no account shall be taken of —

(i) any part of the value of the land attributable to subsidies or grants available from public moneys, or to any tax or rating allowances in respect of development, from which development of the land might benefit,

(ii) the special suitability or adaptability of the land for any purpose if that purpose is a purpose to which it could be applied only in pursuance of statutory powers, or for which there is no market apart from the special needs of a particular purchaser or the requirements of any statutory body as defined in *Rule 5*; provided that any *bona fide* offer for the purchase of the land which may be brought to the notice of the arbitrator shall be taken into consideration,

(iii) any increase in the value of land attributable to the use thereof or of any structure thereon in a manner which could be restrained by any court, or is contrary to law, or detrimental to the health of the inmates of the structure or to public health or safety or to the environment,

(iv) any depreciation or increase in value attributable to the land, or any land in the vicinity, being reserved for a particular purpose in a development plan, . . ."

The meaning of the phrase "land . . . being reserved for a particular purpose in a development plan" in paragraph 2(iv) of the First Schedule to the 1990 Act was examined in *Dublin County Council v. Shortt*.[56] The Supreme Court upheld the decision of McMahon J. in which he distinguished the use of the phrase "particular purpose" under section 19 of the 1963 Act (where it was used to mean purposes which are residential, commercial, industrial, agricultural or otherwise), from its use in Rule 11. The larger proportion of land which had been compulsorily acquired was designated "Q" under the County Dublin Development Plan of 1972 which indicated an objective "to preserve an area of high amenity". A small proportion of the land was designated "T" for which the objective was "to provide for recreational open space and ancillary structures". The land was an open undeveloped space in an area in which there had been extensive residential development. McMahon J. found that the land was reserved for a particular purpose within the meaning of Rule 11 and that the arbitrator was therefore entitled to ignore the particular purpose and to assess the value on the basis that there was no reservation. He stated:

---

56   [1983] I.L.R.M. 377. The Supreme Court were considering the equivalent provision under the 1963 Act, Sched. 4, r.11. See also *Holiday Motor Inns Ltd v. Dublin County Council*, unreported, High Court, McWilliam J., December 20, 1977 and *Dublin Corporation v. McGinley and Shackleton* [1976–77] I.L.R.M. 343, discussed in McDermott and Woulfe, *op.cit.*, pp. 224–25.

"In the context of Rule 11, the word 'reserved' means set apart and 'particular purpose' means a purpose distinct from the purpose for which the other land in the area is zoned. Rule 11 therefore refers to land which is set apart from the other land in the area and zoned for a particular purpose and in valuing such land the arbitrator is to disregard the setting apart and value the land at the value it would have had if it had not been so reserved, that is the value having regard to the purposes for which the land generally in the area is zoned. The intention of the rule is to protect the owner from the detrimental effect on the value of his land of the reservation of the land for the particular purpose for the benefit of the community and to ensure that the owners of other land do not profit from it."

This decision was followed in a similar situation in *Meenaghan v. Dublin County Council*.[57]

The rationale of the rule is that the proprietary rights of an individual owner of land should not be sacrificed for the benefit of the community at large. However, it is difficult to demarcate a line beyond which land is not merely reserved or "set apart" for a particular purpose but becomes the subject of a "development objective" within the meaning of section 19(2) of the 1963 Act. In *Monastra Developments Limited v. Dublin County Council*,[58] Carroll J. decided that the Leopardstown racecourse was too large an area to be considered as "land set apart from other land in the area" in the development plan.

"(v) any value attributable to any unauthorised structure or unauthorised use,
(vi) (I) the existence of proposals for development of the land or any other land by a statutory body, or
    (II) the possibility or probability of the land or other land becoming subject to a scheme of development undertaken by such statutory body,and
    (c) all returns and assessments of capital value for taxation made or acquiesced in by the claimant may be considered.
3.—(1) In assessing the possibilities, if any, for developing the land, for the purposes of determining its antecedent value, regard shall be had only to such reasonable possibilities as, having regard to all material considerations, could be judged to have existed immediately prior to the relevant decision under Part IV of the Principal Act.
(2) Material considerations for the purposes of the foregoing sub-rule shall, without prejudice to the generality thereof, include –
    (a) the nature and location of the land,
    (b) the likelihood or unlikelihood, as the case may be of obtaining permission, or further permission, to develop the land in the light of the provisions of the development plan,
    (c) the assumption that, if any permission to develop the land were to be granted, any conditions which might reasonably be imposed in relation to matters referred to in the *Fourth Schedule* (but no other consideration) would be imposed, and
    (d) any permission to develop the land, not being permission for development of a kind specified in *section 13 (2)*, already existing at the time of the relevant decision under Part IV of the Principal Act.

---

57   [1984] I.L.R.M. 616.
58   Unreported, High Court, January 31, 1992.

4.—(1) In determining the subsequent value of the land in a case in which there has been a refusal of permission –

> (a) it shall be assumed, subject to *sub-rule (2)*, that, after the refusal, permission under Part IV of the Principal Act would not be granted for any development of a kind specified in *section 13 (2)*, . . ."

This provision would appear to be in ease of the claimant as it in effect provides that no allowance may be made for any possible alternative future development of a worthwhile nature. In calculating the value of a claimant's interest after the refusal, it is to be assumed that planning permission will not be granted for any development of a kind specified in section 13(2).[59]

> "(b) regard shall be had to any conditions in relation to matters referred to in the *Fourth Schedule* (but no other conditions) which might reasonably be imposed in the granting of permission to develop the land.
>
> (2) In a case in which there has been a refusal of permission in relation to land in respect of which there is in force an undertaking under Part VI of the Principal Act, it shall be assumed in determining the subsequent value of the land that, after the refusal, permission under Part IV of the Principal Act would not be granted for any development other than development to which the said undertaking relates.
>
> 5.—(1) In *Rule 2*, "statutory body" means:
>
> (a) a Minister of the Government,
> (b) the Commissioners of Public Works in Ireland,
> (c) a local authority within the meaning of the Local Government Act, 1941,
> (d) a harbour authority within the meaning of the Harbours Act, 1946,
> (e) a health board established under the Health Act, 1970,
> (f) a vocational education committee within the meaning of the Vocational Education Act, 1930,
> (g) a board or other body established by or under statute,
> (h) a company in which all the shares are held by, or on behalf of, or by directors appointed by, a Minister of the Government, or
> (i) a company in which all the shares are held by a board, company, or other body referred to in *paragraph (g) or (h)*.
>
> (2) In *sub-rule* (1) (h) and (i), "company " means a company within the meaning of section 2 of the Companies Act, ..."

12.8 THE PURCHASE NOTICE[60]

Where An Bord Pleanála refuses planning permission or grants planning permission subject to conditions, then, if the owner of the land claims –

(a) that the land has become incapable of reasonably beneficial use in its existing state,

---

[59] s.10 prohibits any person from carrying out development on land in respect of which compensation has been paid until the amount of that compensation has been repaid to the planning authority, although certain limited development may be carried out: see para. 12.2.5, above.

[60] This topic is dealt with in greater detail in McDermott and Wolfe, *op. cit.,* pp. 306–310.

    (b) that the land cannot be rendered capable of reasonably beneficial use by the carrying out of any other development for which permission has been granted, or for which the planning authority have undertaken to grant permission (the undertaking procedure has been abolished by the 1990 Act), and

    (c) in a case where permission to develop the land was granted subject to conditions, that the land cannot be rendered capable of reasonably beneficial use by the carrying out of the permitted development in accordance with those conditions,

he may, at any time within the period of six months after the decision (or such longer period as the Minister may allow) serve on the planning authority a notice requiring the planning authority to purchase his interest in the land.[61]

The planning authority is obliged to serve on the owner by whom the purchase notice was served within three months of the date of the service of the purchase notice, a notice stating either:

    (a) that the authority are willing to comply with the purchase notice or,

    (b) that for reasons specified in the notice, the authority are not willing to comply with the purchase notice or,

    (c) that for reasons specified in the notice served on the owner, the authority are not willing to comply with the purchase notice and that they have transmitted a copy of the purchase notice together with a copy of the notice served on the owner to the Minister.

The entitlement to serve a purchase notice is dependent on whether, as a matter of fact and degree, the land in its existing state (taking account of any existing permissions and any undertaking to grant permission) is incapable of reasonably beneficial use. It is not sufficient that the land is of less use or value to it in its present state than it would have been if it had been able to develop the land and realise its development potential.[62] The relevant factors in considering whether the land is capable of a reasonably beneficial use would appear to be the physical state of the land, its size, shape and surroundings, and the general pattern of land-use in the vicinity of the land.

The purchase notice must relate to the whole of the land which was the subject of the planning decision. However, if part of the land is capable of reasonably beneficial use the planning authority are not obliged to purchase the land. The owner of the land has to show that the whole of the land which was the subject of the planning decision is incapable of reasonably beneficial use.[63] In

---

[61]   In *State (Thomas McInerney and Co. Ltd) v. Dublin County Council* [1985] I.R. 1, the court refused to lift the corporate veil where the purchase notice was served by a company which was a member of the same group of companies as the owner of the land.

[62]   See Purdue, Young, Rowan-Robinson, *Planning Law and Procedure*, p.390.

[63]   *Wain v. Secretary of State for the Environment* (1981) 44 P. & C.R. 289.

such circumstances, it would appear that the only option for a landowner is to apply for planning permission to develop that part of the land which is incapable of reasonably beneficial use and then serve a purchase notice in the event of an adverse decision.

There are no Irish decisions on the question as to what constitutes a reasonably beneficial use. "Reasonableness" is always a matter of degree. A use of relatively low value may be reasonably beneficial by being used in conjunction with neighbouring or adjoining land.[64] Some U.K. ministerial decisions, while not in any way binding are persuasive in this jurisdiction, suggest that in appropriate circumstances use as a garden may be a reasonably beneficial use (whether independently or in conjunction with adjoining land).[65]

The planning authority are not entitled to have regard to purely theoretical possibilities: there must be a real possibility of a potential purchaser of the lands.[66] It is submitted that the person serving the notice is entitled to copies of any submissions made by the planning authority to An Bord Pleanála in the event of their refusing to comply with the purchase notice, and to respond to such submissions. The planning authority also have a duty to furnish reasons for their unwillingness to comply with the purchase notice.

---

[64] See U.K. Circular 13/83 interpreting the equivalent statutory provision under the Town and Country Planning Act 1971.

[65] The *Encyclopedia of Planning Law and Practice* analyses some of the U.K. ministerial decisions on agricultural use at P.137.10.

[66] See *Adams & Wade Limited v. Minister for Housing and Local Government* (1965) 18 P. & C.R. 60.

Chapter 13

PLANNING AND CONVEYANCING: GUIDELINES FOR PRACTITIONERS

by Patrick Sweetman

13.1 THE LAW SOCIETY OF IRELAND GENERAL CONDITIONS OF SALE[1]

13.1.1 The planning warranty: general condition 36

General Condition 36 of the Law Society Conditions of Sale is entitled "Development" and deals with the question of planning permission, building bye law approval and building control. It reads as follows:

36. (a) Unless the Special Conditions contain a provision to the contrary, the Vendor warrants:

(1) either

(i) that there has been no development (which term includes material change of use) of, or execution of works on or to, the subject property since the 1st day of October, 1964, for which Planning Permission or Building Bye-Law Approval was required by law

or

(ii) that all Planning Permissions and Building Bye-Law Approvals required by law for the development of, or the execution of works on or to, the subject property as at the date of sale, or for any change in the use thereof at that date were obtained (save in respect of matters of trifling materiality), and that, where implemented, the conditions thereof and the conditions expressly notified with said Permissions by any Competent Authority in relation to and specifically addressed to such development or works were complied with substantially

and

(2) that no claim for compensation has ever been made under Part 111, Local Government (Planning & Development) Act, 1990

---

[1]   1995 Edition.

provided however that the foregoing warranty shall not extend to (and the Vendor shall not be required to establish) the obtaining of Approvals under the Building Bye-Laws or compliance with such Bye-Laws in respect of development or works executed prior to the 1st day of October, 1964.

(b) The Vendor shall, with the copy documents to be delivered or sent in accordance with Condition 7, furnish to the Purchaser copies of all such Permissions and Approvals as are referred to in Condition 36(a) other than in the proviso thereto, and (where relevant) copies of all Fire Safety Certificates and (if available) Commencement Notices issued under Regulations made pursuant to the Building Control Act, 1990 and referable to the subject property.

(c) The Vendor shall, on or prior to completion of the sale, furnish to the Purchaser

    (i) written confirmation from the Local Authority of compliance with all conditions involving financial contributions or the furnishing of bonds in any such Permission or Approval (other than those referred to in the said proviso) or alternatively formal confirmation from the Local Authority that the roads and other services abutting on the subject property have been taken in charge by it without requirement for payment of moneys in respect of the same.

    (ii) A Certificate or Opinion by an Architect or an Engineer (or other professionally qualified person competent so to certify or opine) confirming that, in relation to any such Permission or Approval (other than those referred to in the proviso aforesaid) the same relates to the subject property; that the development of the subject property has been carried out in substantial compliance therewith and that all conditions (other than financial conditions) thereof and all conditions expressly notified with said Permission by any Competent Authority and specifically directed to and materially affecting the subject property or any part of the same have been complied with substantially (and, in the event of the subject property forming part of a larger development, so far as was reasonably possible in the context of such development).

(d) Unless the Special Conditions contain a stipulation to the contrary, the Vendor warrants in all cases where the provisions of the Building Control Act, 1990 or of any Regulations from time to time made thereunder apply to the design or development of the subject property or any part of the same or any activities in connection therewith, that there has been substantial compliance with the said provisions in so far as they shall have pertained to such design development or activities and the Vendor shall, on or prior to completion of the sale, furnish to the Purchaser a Certificate or Opinion by an Architect or an Engineer (or other professionally qualified person competent so to certify or opine) confirming such substantial compliance as aforesaid.

"Development" is defined in the general conditions as having the same meaning as that conferred on it by the Local Government (Planning & Development) Act 1963 so that the statement at 36(a)(1)(i) that it includes a material change of use is purely to highlight that fact.

"Competent Authority" is defined as including "the State, any Minister thereof, Government Department, State Authority, Local Authority, Planning Authority, Sanitary Authority, Building Control Authority, Fire Authority, Statutory Undertaker or any Department, Body or person by statutory provision or order for the time being in force authorised directly or indirectly to control, regulate, modify or restrict the development, use or servicing of land or buildings, or empowered to acquire land by compulsory process.

Where General Condition 36(a) is left intact, a vendor warrants that the planning position in relation to the property is fully in order, in that either there has been no development whatsoever since October 1, 1964 which required Planning Permission, Building Bye-Law Approval or compliance with the Building Regulations, or that all necessary Planning Permissions and Building Bye-Law Approvals have been obtained and that they and the Building Control Act 1990 and the regulations thereunder have been complied with.

The warranty at 36(a)(1)(ii) has been extended by the 1995 edition of the Conditions of Sale. It warrants that if a planning permission has been implemented, the conditions expressly notified with any such permission by any competent authority in relation to and specifically addressed to any development or works were complied with substantially.

Thus for example, where the engineering department of the local authority issue requirements which are notified with a planning permission, the vendor is warranting that the development complies with these requirements, even where they are not specifically incorporated in the permission.

Where existing property is being sold a vendor who gives this warranty must be satisfied that no competent authority issued conditions with any planning permission which were not incorporated therein. It may be very difficult to establish the position, and unless vendors can do so, they should remove this element of the warranty by an appropriate special condition.

Section 22(7) of the Building Control Act 1990 provides that no enforcement action will be taken and building bye laws approval will be deemed to have been granted in respect of all works carried out prior to December 13, 1989 unless the local authority served a notice before December 1, 1992 stating that the works constituted a danger to public health or safety. Therefore it is not necessary for a purchaser to concern him or herself with building bye laws in respect of works carried out prior to December 13, 1989 unless such a notice was served. However, appropriate evidence to show that the works were carried out prior to December 13, 1989 would be required.

Many house extensions and garage conversions are exempted developments. Previously, if the property was in an area where building bye laws applied, the works lost their exempt status by reason of article 11(1)(a)(iv) of the Local Government (Planning & Development) Regulations 1977 (S.I. No. 65 of 1977) if no building bye laws approval was obtained or the works did not comply with a bye laws approval. However, those regulations have been revoked and replaced by the Local Government (Planning & Development) Regulations 1994 (S.I. No. 86 of 1994) so that, provided the works are exempted under the 1994 Regulations, such previously unauthorised development will now enjoy exempt status.

The full significance of condition 36(a) must be appreciated by a prospective vendor who must disclose any planning irregularity in the special conditions. Failure to do so will leave the vendor open to an action for breach of warranty, apart from the fact that it may be extremely difficult to compel the purchaser to complete the sale. Where the vendor is simply unaware of the planning history of the property, the warranty in general condition 36 should be restricted to cover only the period in respect of which the vendor has the appropriate knowledge. The importance of this condition is highlighted by a marginal note in the printed General Conditions of Sale which reads "In cases where property is affected by an unauthorised development or a breach of Condition/Conditions in a Permission/ Approval amounting to a non-conforming development or where the Bye-Law Amnesty covered by section 22(7), Building Control Act 1990 is relevant, it is recommended that same be dealt with expressly by Special Condition"

Condition 36(a)(2) was first introduced in the 1995 edition of the Conditions of Sale. Any claim for compensation must be registered on the planning register maintained pursuant to section 8 of the Local Government (Planning & Development) Act 1963 by virtue of condition 9 of the Local Government (Planning & Development) Act 1990 (provided that the amount of compensation payable exceeds £100.00). It has always been good conveyancing practice for the vendor's solicitor to carry out a planning search prior to drafting a contract for sale. This provision makes such a search all the more important.

36(b) requires production of all permissions and approvals, fire safety certificates and if available commencement notices under the Building Regulations. The words "if available" are inserted in the light of the Law Society recommendation that a solicitor should not insist on production of a commencement notice if it is not readily available.[2]

36(c)(i) requires a vendor to furnish evidence of compliance with financial conditions. In the alternative the vendor can provide formal confirmation from the local

---

[2]   See Conveyancing Committee notes on Building Control Act 1990 and Regulations issued with the *Law Society Gazette* November 1994, see para. B.12, below.

authority that the roads and other services abutting on the subject property have been taken in charge by it without any requirement for the payment of moneys in respect of the same. This is an extension of a Law Society recommendation[3] in relation to second hand houses in housing estates. However, the proviso that in order to avail of such alternative, the roads must be taken in charge "without requirement for payment of moneys in respect of the same" introduces a complication. The parties to the contract will not necessarily know whether the local authority required payment of moneys in respect of the taking in charge. As a matter of practice, if the local authority issues a letter confirming that the roads and services have been taken in charge, and that letter makes no mention of payment of moneys, then such a letter will usually be accepted as satisfactory evidence of compliance with financial conditions.

It is common for a local authority to agree to accept payment of financial contributions from a builder/developer by way of staged payments. If a property is purchased in the early stages of a larger development, then the only evidence of compliance with the financial condition may be a letter from the Local Authority confirming that the stage payments have been discharged to date. If that property is sold five years later, a purchaser may seek evidence that the entire financial contribution has been paid.

Again, the Conveyancing Committee of the Law Society have considered this question and have issued recommendations.[4] It is recommended that it is only necessary to produce letters confirming compliance with financial conditions up to the date of first purchase of the dwellinghouse. However, a vendor relying on this recommendation must insert the appropriate special condition in the contract. This recommendation only applies to houses in estates and not to one off houses on individual sites.

36(c)(ii) requires the production of a certificate or opinion of compliance with planning and bye law requirements from an architect or an engineer or other professionally qualified person competent so to certify or opine. The Conveyancing Committee of the Law Society have set out recommended criteria in relation to the qualifications of persons offering certificates or opinions of compliance.[4] However, the general conditions of sale do not define "architect" or specify who is competent to certify or opine, and accordingly the identity and qualifications of the person who will prove compliance with planning and building control requirements should be established by the purchaser before contracts are exchanged.

36(c)(ii) also provides that the certificate or opinion to be furnished must confirm that all conditions expressly notified with a permission by a Competent Authority and specifically directed to and materially affecting the property or any part of it have been complied with substantially. Neither the RIAI forms of opinion nor the Law Society specimen certificates of compliance cover such conditions (other than where incorporated in the permission by a condition

---

3   Issued with *Newsletter*, May 1987, see para. B.3, below.
4   *The Law Society News*, October 26, 1994, see para. B.2, below.

therein), so that conveyancers dealing with second hand property must delete this condition by an appropriate special condition unless they can obtain a supplemental certificate from an architect or engineer covering the point. If a vendor is agreeing to give a certificate containing this provision then he should first check that his architect or engineer will be in a position to do so.

In relation to dwellinghouses built before January 1, 1975 the Law Society have recommended that as it was not the practice at the time to furnish an architect's certificates of compliance, a purchaser's solicitor should not insist on one.[5] However two points should be noted. First, if a vendor seeks to rely on this recommendation he or she must restrict the warranty contained in general condition 36(a) by inserting the appropriate special condition. Secondly, the recommendation relates to second hand houses built prior to July 1, 1975 only. It does not relate to any other type of property.

36(d) warrants that the provisions of the Building Control Act 1990 and the regulations thereunder have been complied with. The warranty is to the effect that where the provisions of the Building Control Act or the regulations thereunder apply to the design or development of the property, or any activities in connection therewith, that there has been substantial compliance with the Act and regulations. The vendor is required to produce a certificate or opinion by an architect or engineer, or other professionally qualified person competent to certify compliance, confirming such substantial compliance.

If such warranty is excluded in the general conditions of sale, a purchaser should satisfy him or herself by way of pre-contract inquiries as to compliance with the regulations prior to the exchange of contracts by way of pre-contract enquiries. The Law Society have issued a standard set of requisitions.[6]

General Condition 36 should be read in conjunction with General Condition 48 which provides that all obligations under the contract which are not implemented by deed of assurance and which are capable of continuing or taking effect after completion shall enure and remain in full force and effect. Accordingly, a purchaser would have a remedy against the vendor even if the planning difficulty only came to light after the sale had been completed.

13.2 TIME LIMITS ON ENFORCEMENT

13.2.1 Practical considerations

Condition 36 of the Law Society General Conditions of Sale (1995 Edition) provides a purchaser with a warranty by the vendor that all developments on or to the property since October 1, 1964 comply with the requirements of the Planning Acts, and where applicable, Building Bye-Laws and the Building

---

[5] Practice Note, *Gazette*, February 1993, see para. A.2, below.
[6] See para. 13.10, below.

Control Act 1990. In the light of the new time limits on enforcement introduced by the Local Government (Planning & Development) Act 1992 ("the 1992 Act"),[7] conveyancing practice is moving away from that warranty.

It is unrealistic to expect a vendor to stand over a planning warranty relating to developments over a period of 30 years. Most vendors will not have owned the property for that period and will not have the necessary knowledge to give such a warranty. Accordingly, vendor's solicitors frequently seek to limit the warranty or to delete it entirely. In the light of the 1992 Act a purchaser should be more readily persuaded to accept such limitations, or even deletion.

The current trend is towards an investigation by the purchaser's advisors of the planning position before contracts are entered into. Where there are any unauthorised works or uses, a purchaser will have to consider their significance as, unfortunately, the 1992 Act does not render the unauthorised development lawful or authorised. It simply prevents enforcement action being taken after a specified period.

Different considerations will apply to different situations, which can broadly be divided into five categories.

13.2.2 Buildings erected without permission

When a building is five years old or more and has been erected without permission, no order for its demolition can be made under the planning code. However, it is still an unauthorised structure, giving rise to the following considerations:

- (a) Works which would otherwise be exempt under the Local Government (Planning & Development) Regulations 1994 ("the 1994 regulations") are not exempt if they consist of the extension, alteration, repair or renewal of an unauthorised structure, by virtue of article 10(1)(a)(viii) of the 1994 Regulations.
- (b) The planning authority may be reluctant to grant permission for alterations, additions or a change of use of an unauthorised structure, or may impose onerous conditions.
- (c) The owners right to compensation in the event of compulsory acquisition will be affected in that the value of the unauthorised structure must be disregarded.
- (d) If the building is destroyed by fire or otherwise, the planning authority could prevent re-construction by refusing planning permission, and would not be required to pay compensation under the Planning Acts if a non-compensatable reason is furnished for its decision.
- (e) The possibility that the local authority might invoke the provisions of section 36 or 37 of the Local Government (Planning & Development) Act 1963, requiring the removal or alteration of a structure, or discon-

---

[7]   See the table on p.308, above.

tinuance of a use, should be considered. A claim for compensation may be made where such notices are severed.[8]

13.2.3 Alterations without permission to an existing authorised building

As a result of the 1992 Act, a purchaser can take a much more practical view of alterations or extensions completed over five years previously. Although the provisions of article 10(1)(a)(viii) of the 1994 regulations will apply to the unauthorised development, the other considerations in category 1 above are likely to be of lesser significance unless substantial works have been carried out.[9] A purchaser will need to consider the requirements of his bank or other financial institution and will have to qualify any certificate of title sought by the lender. The lender should only be concerned as to the effect that the unauthorised development might have on the value or saleability of the property, which in the majority of cases will be negligible.

13.2.4 Works carried out in breach of the conditions or terms of a permission

This category includes the initial construction of a building as well as subsequent alterations or extensions. If the breach is minor, it can safely be ignored as having little practical significance once the period for enforcement has expired. However, where compliance with a condition is fundamental to the grant of permission so that its breach renders the development something different in character to that for which permission was granted, the position would deserve close scrutiny and each case would require consideration on its own merits. Development carried out in breach of a fundamental condition attached to planning permission would amount to unauthorised development which would attract the consequences referred to under category 1 above.

It should be noted also that where a building is constructed in breach of a condition, the time limit for enforcement may be considerably longer than five years.[10]

13.2.5 Unauthorised uses

In many cases of unauthorised user, the value of the property will have been enhanced by the passing of the 1992 Act, although the provisions of article 10(1)(a)(viii) of the 1994 regulations will still apply to any extension, alteration, repair or renewal (*i.e.* they will not enjoy exempt status under the 1994 Regulations), and it may be difficult, if not impossible, to obtain planning

---

[8]   1990 Act, ss.18 and 19.
[9]   As to the effect of an unauthorised extension on the structure as a whole, see *Dublin Corporation v. Langan*, unreported, High Court, May 14, 1982, and para. 5.2.5, above.
[10]   See the table on p.308, above.

permission for works while an unauthorised use continues. In addition, any enhanced value of the building attributable to the unauthorised use would be disregarded in assessing compensation, either on compulsory acquisition, or where permission to rebuild is refused following destruction by fire.

It may be open to the Director of Public Prosecutions under section 24(3) of the Local Government (Planning & Development) Act 1963, as amended, to prosecute anybody carrying on an unauthorised use. There is an argument that the offence recurs each day it continues, so that no time limit applies. It will take a decision of the courts to clarify the matter beyond doubt.

A purchaser will need to consider the possibility of action being taken outside the planning code e.g. by the Fire Officer under the Fire Services Act 1981, by the sanitary services division of the local authority, or by Health and Safety Officers under the Public Health Acts and the Safety Health and Welfare at Work Act 1989. In addition, any future alterations may involve onerous requirements under the Building Control Act 1990.

13.2.6 Licensed premises

One of the considerations in an application for a new liquor licence, the revival of an existing licence, or in connection with the extension of an existing licensed premises, is that the premises complies with planning requirements. Any unauthorised development could cause serious difficulties and may put licences in jeopardy.

13.3 CONTRACT FOR SALE CONDITIONAL ON PLANNING PERMISSION

The essential ingredients for a "subject to planning" special condition are:

(a) That the contract be conditional upon a grant of permission issuing.
(b) That the nature of the permission sought be described.
(c) The period within which the application for permission is to be lodged should be specified.
(d) A provision whereby the contract comes to an end where permission is refused, either by the local authority, or by Bord Pleanála on appeal.
(e) A closing date.
(f) A cut-off date by which the necessary permission must be obtained.

Some additional elements often included are:

(g) A mechanism whereby the parties (or either of them) can rescind in the event of unacceptable conditions being imposed.
(h) Provision prohibiting the lodgement of any objection.
(i) Provision allowing or prohibiting the appeal by either party either against the decision of the local authority or any conditions thereof.

(j) Provision for payment of the costs of the application and legal costs incurred in the event of an unsuccessful application.

(k) Delegation of responsibility for compliance with any conditions which may be imposed, and production of appropriate evidence of compliance.

(l) Provision whereby the proposed application and/or any appeal must be approved by the vendor prior to lodgement.

(m) Provision whereby copies of all correspondence between the planning authority and the purchaser must be sent to the vendor.

(n) Provision dealing with copyright in the plans and specifications.

(o) A covenant by the purchaser to deal expeditiously with any requirements of the planning authority on foot of any request for further information.

(p) A dispute resolution mechanism.

The purchaser will wish to ensure that the condition describes in as much detail as possible the nature of the proposed development. The vendor will usually wish to describe the proposed development in general terms. The vendor runs the risk that if the permission is refused the value of the property may be reduced.

A purchaser will seek the right in his or her absolute discretion to reject a planning permission if dissatisfied with the conditions imposed. The vendor will wish to ensure that the purchaser cannot use this as a pretext upon which to walk away and will therefore attempt to specify the criteria which would be deemed unacceptable. A common example arises on an application for planning permission for a housing estate. The contract might provide that if permission is not granted for a minimum number of houses the purchaser can rescind. Alternatively there may be a scale by which the consideration payable will reduce or increase according to the number of houses for which permission is granted.

In addition the purchaser will require a mechanism whereby he can walk away if the conditions imposed make development unviable – such as onerous financial conditions. The vendor may seek to specify what level of financial obligations would entitle the purchaser to rescind.

Where the vendor is making the application, particularly in the case of a retention permission, he or she should insert a clause providing that the purchaser will not appeal or procure that an appeal is lodged against any decision to grant permission.

13.3.1 Cut-off date

The cut-off date is important. Without it the parties might be bound indefinitely into the transaction while the planning application proceeded to An Bord Pleanála and possibly from there to the High Court and ultimately the Supreme Court. This provision should be drafted so as to give either or both parties the option to terminate after a certain date rather than providing for automatic termination.

When agreeing a cut-off date, the possibility that the local authority may make a request for further information (and thus extending the date by which it must give its decision) should be considered.

The condition should provide that in the event of termination the deposit will be refunded, less any deductions as may be agreed.

13.4 SPECIMEN CONDITIONS

Set out below are these specimen conditions making a contract conditional on the issue of planning permission. Obviously each case will give rise to different considerations, and the specimen condition will require adaption to meet the particular requirements of a given situation.

13.4.1 Special condition making the contract subject to issue of planning permission for a house.

This condition gives the purchaser absolute discretion in deciding which conditions are to be acceptable.

(a) This contract is subject to the issue of planning permission for the construction of a dwellinghouse on the subject property upon terms acceptable to the purchaser. The purchaser shall apply for such planning permission immediately following the exchange of this contract. The application shall be lodged on foot of plans and specifications agreed between the parties prior to the date hereof and the purchaser shall use all reasonable endeavours to ensure that planning permission is obtained as soon as possible.

(b) The closing date shall be the date seven days after the date of issue of the grant of permission.

(c) In the event that:

    (i) the planning authority issue a decision to refuse such permission and no appeal against such decision is made within the statutory appeals period

    (ii) the planning authority grants such permission subject to conditions which the purchaser notifies the vendor in writing within seven days from the date of notification of such permission are unacceptable to the purchaser

    (iii) An Bord Pleanála decides to refuse such permission

or

    (iv) An Bord Pleanála decides to grant such permission subject to conditions which the purchaser notifies the vendor in writing within seven days from the date of notification of such decision are unacceptable to the purchaser

this contract shall be at an end.

(d) In the event that no grant of permission has issued within nine months from the date hereof then either party may at any time thereafter by service of notice in writing terminate this contract.

(e) In the event of the termination of this contract pursuant to clause (c) or (d) hereof, the purchaser shall be refunded his/her deposit without deduction and without interest, costs or compensation.

(f) In the event that:

    (i)   The planning authority issues a decision to refuse such permission
    or

    (ii) The planning authority issues a decision to grant such permission subject to a condition or conditions which the purchaser notifies the vendor in writing within seven days from the date of such decision are unacceptable to the purchaser

then the purchaser may (but shall be under no obligation to) appeal to An Bord Pleanála against such decision to refuse permission or against such condition or conditions as are unacceptable to the purchaser, as the case may be.

13.4.2 Special condition making contract subject to issue of retention planning permission

In this instance the vendor reserves the right to rescind if unacceptable conditions are imposed. This is because he/she is contracting to give a certificate of compliance and will accordingly be responsible to deal with any conditions attaching. The time scale is such that no appeal to An Bord Pleanála is envisaged.

(a) Application for retention planning permission has been made to the planning authority in respect of: (specify the unauthorised development)

(b) The closing date herein shall be seven days after the date of issue of the grant of retention permission.

(c) In the event that the planning authority issues a decision to refuse such permission or to issue it subject to conditions which the vendor advises the purchaser within 10 days from the date of such decision are unacceptable to the vendor then this contract shall be at an end.

(d) In the event that such retention permission does not issue within three months from the date hereof then either party may at any time thereafter by service of notice on the other party in writing terminate this contract.

(e) In the event of the termination of this contract pursuant to condition (c) or (d) hereof the purchaser shall be refunded his/her deposit without deduction and without interest costs or compensation.

(f) The purchaser hereby covenants with the vendor that the purchaser shall not appeal or procure an appeal against the decision of the planning authority to grant such retention permission.

(g) On completion the vendor will furnish to the purchaser the grant of retention permission together with the certificate of an architect, engineer or other person competent to so certify, confirming substantial compliance therewith and any conditions attaching thereto.

(h) General Condition 36 of the within general conditions is varied accordingly.

13.4.3 Special condition making the contract subject to planning permission

This is a specimen condition weighted in favour of a vendor, who requires to monitor the application at every stage and satisfy him/herself that the purchaser is making every effort to obtain permission. The purchaser is not entitled to terminate the contract if planning permission issues within the specified period, even if he/she does not like the conditions attaching.

(a) This contract is subject to the issue of planning permission for the construction of *[specify the nature of the proposed development]* on the subject property. The purchaser shall apply for such planning permission within *[seven]* days following the exchange of this contract and time shall be of the essence in that regard. The application shall be lodged on foot of plans and specifications agreed between the parties prior to the exchange hereof.

(b) The purchaser shall use all reasonable endeavours to ensure that the application for planning permission is successful and that planning permission is obtained as soon as possible.

(c) (i) The purchaser shall furnish to the vendor without delay copies of all notices and correspondence received from or sent by it to the planning authority and/or An Bord Pleanála

    (ii) Any submission or observation made by the purchaser to the planning authority or An Bord Pleanála whether on foot of a request for further information or otherwise shall first be approved in writing by the vendor which approval shall not be unreasonably withheld.

(d) In the event that:

    (i) the planning authority issue a decision to refuse such permission and no appeal against such decision is made within the statutory appeals period

or

    (ii) An Bord Pleanála decides to refuse such permission
this contract shall be at an end.

(e) (i) In the event that the planning authority issues a decision to refuse such permission the purchaser may (but shall be under no obligation to) appeal to An Bord Pleanála. Any such appeal shall

   first be approved in writing by the vendor which approval shall not
   be unreasonably withheld or delayed.

  (ii) The purchaser shall furnish the appeal to the vendor for approval
    not less than five days prior to the last date for lodgement thereof.

(f) The purchaser shall not appeal any decision of the planning authority
 to grant permission, or any condition attaching to any such decision.

(g) In the event that no grant of permission has issued within nine months
 from the date hereof (time being of the essence) then either party may at
 any time thereafter by service of notice in writing terminate this contract.

(h) In the event of the termination of this contract pursuant to clause (d)
 or (g) hereof, the purchaser shall be refunded its deposit without
 deduction and without interest, costs or compensation.

(i) The closing date shall be the date seven days after the date of issue of
 the grant of permission.

13.5 PURCHASING WITH THE BENEFIT OF PLANNING PERMISSION

A planning permission attaches to the property so that a subsequent owner can
develop on foot of it. It is not necessary in a sale to transfer or assign the benefit
of any existing permissions. However, it is crucial that the site being acquired is
identical to the site shown on the plans on foot of which the planning permission
has been granted. Thus, where planning permission was obtained for a house on
a two acre holding, a purchaser who only buys portion of the two acre site does
not have the benefit of the planning permission and cannot develop on foot if it.
A purchaser must therefore carefully check the plans lodged on foot of which the
planning permission was obtained to ensure that the plans show an identical site
to that being acquired.

  Different considerations apply where a developer is selling off a number of
sites in a larger development. Where the one planning permission covers the
whole development the parties will agree as to who will be responsible for
compliance with the different conditions attaching. The vendor may construct the
roads and services. The purchaser may be responsible for the erection of
structures on the sites and compliance with financial conditions. The vendor may
require a covenant by the purchaser to comply with the terms of the planning
permission in so far as it relates to the sold land so that the future development of
the retained lands is not prejudiced.

  Where one is buying with the benefit of an outline permission, one must be
aware of the possibility that a grant of approval may be refused even though it is
on all fours with the outline permission. This would only arise in exceptional
cases, where there has been a material change in the circumstances from the
point of view of proper planning and development of the area between the date
of the grant of outline permission and the time of the application for approval.

McCarthy J. accepted this proposition in *State (Kenny and Hussey) v. An Bord Pleanála*[11] and Barron J. followed it in *State (Tern Houses (Brennanstown) Ltd) v. Bord Pleanála*.[12] Barron J. stated "If there was a conflict between the immediate implementation of an outline permission and the proper planning and development of the area, it is the latter which must prevail".[13]

One also needs to consider the life of the planning permission. A planning permission usually has a life of five years from the date of the grant of permission.[14] The life of a permission consisting of an outline permission and an approval runs from the date of the grant of the outline permission. Accordingly a purchaser buying with the benefit of an outline permission will need to ensure that he or she has sufficient time to obtain a grant of approval (taking into account the possibility of an appeal) and then to substantially complete the development within the five year period.

A planning authority does have power to extend the life of the planning permission.[15] It must do so if satisfied that substantial works have been carried out pursuant to the permission during its initial life and that the development will be completed within a reasonable time.

13.6 CERTIFICATES OF COMPLIANCE

13.6.1 Planning and building control

Following the introduction of the building regulations and the building control regulations the Royal Institute of Architects in Ireland (RIAI) issued a set of five standard forms of opinion on compliance for use by its own members. The Law Society of Ireland have recommended that the March 1993 edition of these forms is acceptable.

Forms 1, 2 and 3 deal with the building regulations while forms 4 and 5 deal with planning permission and building bye-laws approvals.

The Law Society have produced its own forms of certificates of compliance, dated May 7, 1993. There are two forms dealing with compliance with planning and building bye-laws (one for a full service and the other for a part only service) and two dealing with compliance with planning and building regulations (again full service and part only service). The Law Society have issued detailed notes in relation to its forms and those of the RIAI.[16]

The RIAI recommends to its members that they use its standard forms. The other certifying professions generally follow the Law Society version.

---

[11]   Unreported, Supreme Court, Carroll J., December 20, 1984.
[12]   [1985] I.R. 725.
[13]   See also, more recently, the Supreme Court decision in *Irish Asphalt Ltd v. An Bord Pleanála*.
[14]   Local Government (Planning and Development) Act 1982, s.2.
[15]   *ibid.*, s.4.
[16]   See Practice Notes, *Law Society News*, November 1993 at A.8, below.

The RIAI suggests that persons accepting forms from its members should check that the persons completing the forms are in fact members of that Institute and that the forms carry the RIAI membership stamp. It also recommends that the original printed form be used rather than photocopies as this makes it very much easier to check that no amendments or alterations have been made to the standard wording.

Frequently certificates of compliance are offered which are neither in the RIAI format or in the Law Society format. The RIAI form is often adapted without incorporating the definitions contained in the original version, rendering the document unintelligible. Care should be exercised when one is offered a form which is not in the RIAI or Law Society format, to ensure that it contains all the salient elements.

Building bye-laws can still apply to a development, even after June 1, 1992, where application for building bye-laws approval was made prior to that date. The form of architect's certificate certifying compliance with planning and building bye-laws in relation to a house in a housing estate, as set out in the November 1978 *Law Society Gazette* as amended in the June 1982 *Gazette*[17] may be furnished in such cases and is acceptable.

A purchaser should agree the format of the architect's certificate to be produced on completion, and the qualifications of the person who will give that certificate before signing the contract.

A separate form of certificate is in preparation by the RIAI for use in the sale of apartments. It is anticipated that this will cover not only the apartment but also the building in which it is situate and the development of which it forms part. This certificate has not yet been published at the time of writing.

13.6.2 Check list

The following is a check list of the requirements for a certificate of compliance. It should:

- specify the qualifications of the person who will give the certificate.
- specify the means of knowledge to give the certificate, *i.e.* details of inspections and knowledge of the plans, drawings and other particulars on foot of which the planning permission and fire safety certificate issued.
- confirm that the planning permission and fire safety certificate are those relating to the development.
- confirm that the design of the development is in substantial conformity with the building regulations.
- confirm that the development is in substantial compliance with the planning permission.

---

[17] See para. A.6, below.

- where the planning permission covers a larger development of which the works being certified form part, and that larger development has not yet been completed, confirm that the general conditions of the planning permission have been substantially complied with in so far as is reasonably possible up to the date of the certificate.
- confirm that the development is in substantial compliance with the building regulations.
- not contain any qualifications or exceptions other than ones which are generally acceptable in practice, such as those set out in the RIAI forms. Where necessary, independent evidence of compliance with matters excluded from the terms of the certificate should be obtained.
- be dated.
- be signed

It is fundamental, in certifying compliance with the building regulations, that the issue of the design of the works be dealt with. Where the certifying person did not design the works, a further certificate should be obtained from the appropriate person certifying compliance with the design elements.

Where the certificate refers to "Confirmations" (as in RIAI Form 5,) copies of such confirmations should be obtained.

13.6.3 Qualifications of persons giving certificates of compliance

There has been considerable debate in recent years as to the requisite qualifications of persons offering certificates or opinions of compliance with planning and building bye laws, and more recently, compliance under the Building Control Act. The November 1994 edition of the Law Society Gazette deals with this issue. The Conveyancing Committee of the Law Society recommends that it is reasonable for solicitors to accept certificates or opinions of compliance from:

(i) persons with a degree or a diploma of degree standard in architecture;
(ii) persons who have been in practice as architects on their own account for 10 years;
(iii) chartered engineers;
(iv) persons with a degree in civil engineering;
(v) persons who have been in practice on their own account as engineers in the construction industry for 10 years;
(vi) qualified building surveyors;
(vii) persons from another jurisdiction in the European Union whose qualification is entitled to recognition in Ireland under the Architect's Directive.[18]

---

[18] E.C. Directive 85/384/EEC (Council Directive, June 10, 1985).

A proposal has been submitted to the E.C. Commission to amend the Directive to include persons whom the Minister for the Environment certifies have, over a period of at least five years immediately prior to the date of coming into force of the Directive, pursued architectural activities, the nature and importance of which in the opinion of the Minister gives that person an established right to pursue those activities. A list of those persons with requisite experience is being prepared by the Department of the Environment. Any person on that list or for whom a certificate has issued under the proposed amendment would also come within category (ii) above.

13.7 CONDITIONS ATTACHING TO A PLANNING PERMISSION

Section 26(2) of the Local Government (Planning & Development) Act 1963 sets out various types of conditions which a local authority may include in a planning permission. A local authority is not restricted to those conditions and can impose any conditions it considers appropriate, in the context of the proper planning and development of its area provided they are reasonably related to the application made.

From the conveyancing perspective it is useful to divide planning conditions into five categories.

13.7.1 Conditions regulating development works

The planning permission can give a prospective purchaser considerable information about proposed developments in the immediate area of the property being purchased. For example, it might designate open spaces or provide reservations for roads or halting sites. Whereas such information is no substitute for carrying out a comprehensive planning search there is an onus on professionals advising purchasers to fully inform their clients of all matters appearing in the planning documentation. In addition, such conditions may require the developer to obtain wayleaves of adjoining owners for the passage of services, putting a conveyancer on notice that such wayleaves are required.

Often in the context of housing estates, a condition will provide that certain houses not be built. The planning site number and the subsequent house number as built are not always the same and it is not unheard of for a developer to erect houses which the planning permission required to be omitted.

A condition can be imposed requiring that part of a larger development be ceded to the local authority and a conveyancer, on notice of this requirement, should ensure that it has been complied with.

13.7.2 Conditions precedent

These are conditions which must be complied with before a development is to commence. Very often certain matters must be agreed with the Health Officer,

Fire Officer or Engineering Department. Typically, conditions will be imposed requiring that steps be taken to protect trees and to preserve open spaces prior to the commencement of development.

In town house developments in urban areas, the local authority may not take the development in charge and instead may require that a management company be set up to manage the common areas within the estate. In these circumstances, the local authority often requires that the structure of such management company be agreed with them prior to the commencement of development.

Where one is on notice that a condition precedent has not been complied with it is not sufficient to rely on the production of an architects opinion on compliance and a conveyancer will have to examine each situation on its merits.

13.7.3 Financial conditions

There are two main types of financial conditions. The local authority will often require a developer to make a contribution towards the provision of services for the development. In large scale developments the financial condition may be expressed as a certain sum per house or industrial unit as the case may be, and often will be index linked because the development may be not be commenced immediately upon the grant of planning permission.

The second type of condition relates to a bond for the satisfactory completion of the common areas within the development, prior to the local authority taking them in charge. This security condition can be in the form of an indemnity bond, a cash lodgement or a guarantee from a body approved by the local authority. Bonds are often arranged in stages so that a bond may be obtained covering only a portion of the development. Provided a developer furnishes evidence that the financial conditions have been complied with for the particular property to be acquired, a purchaser can safely proceed.[19]

13.7.4 Conditions restricting future development

Such conditions are increasingly common and are popular particularly in urban areas where the size of the gardens being sold with dwelling units is limited. They also arise in the context of commercial property, particularly in relation to advertising signs and shop fronts in sensitive areas.

It is crucial for a professional adviser to alert his or her client to the existence of such a condition, as article 10(1)(a)(i) of the Local Government (Planning & Development) Regulations 1994 provides that any development referred to in the Second Schedule will not be exempt if it contravenes a condition attaching to a condition or is inconsistent with a use specified in a permission.

Sometimes such conditions prohibit any further development without planning permission. Other conditions are worded so as to prevent the erection of additional

---

[19] See p.329, above.

structures and this is clearly preferable. Planning conditions of this type will be of less significance to residential property in the future in the light of the new exemptions for extensions to dwellinghouses contained in the 1994 Regulations, exemptions for and in particular the requirement that any such extension must not reduce the area of private open space of a dwellinghouse to the rear thereof to less than 25 square meters.[20]

When considering whether development is exempted development, it is important to obtain a copy of any planning permission relating to the site, to ensure that there is no condition restricting development, and that the development being considered is consistent with a use specified in the permission.

A further type of condition, popular in Leinster Counties, restricts the use of the property to members of the family of the applicant. This occurs in cases where a farmer wishes to develop a site on part of his farm and the local authority does not wish to encourage linear development. In the past, by reason of the absolute wording of the condition, problems arose because no lending institution would lend on the security of the property. This gave rise to problems in financing the construction of the dwelling. In addition, such a condition makes it impossible to sell the house. Where such a condition is encountered, application should be made in an appropriate case for a new planning permission to free the property of this condition.

The local authority have recognised the difficulties that such a condition has caused and now provide that the house when constructed on the site must first be occupied by the applicant or a member of his or her family.

13.7.5 Conditions which incorporate previous permissions

Where an alteration to or revision of an existing permission has been obtained, the revised planning permission often incorporates the terms of the earlier permission. In such a case, a copy of the earlier permission should be obtained and its terms considered.

13.8 BUILDING CONTROL

Relevant legislation:

The Building Control Act 1990[21]
The Building Control Regulations 1991[22]
The Building Regulations 1991[23]
The Building Control (Amendment) Regulations 1994[24]
The Building Regulations (Amendment) Regulations 1994[25]

---

[20] Local Government (Planning and Development) Regulations 1994.
[21] (No. 3 of 1990)
[22] (S.I. No. 305 of 1991)
[23] (S.I. No. 306 of 1991)
[24] (S.I. No. 153 of 1994)
[25] (S.I. No. 154 of 1994)

The Building Control Act 1990 and the regulations made under it ("the regulations") constitute a system for regulating building works and lay down minimum standards for design, construction, workmanship, materials etc. Different standards apply depending on the use of the building.

Unlike the building bye-laws which they replace the regulations apply throughout the country.

The regulations are divided into 12 sections:

A STRUCTURE
B FIRE
C SITE PREPARATION AND RESISTANCE TO MOISTURE
D MATERIALS AND WORKMANSHIP
E SOUND
F VENTILATION
G HYGIENE
H DRAINAGE AND WASTE DISPOSAL
J HEAT PRODUCING APPLIANCES
K STAIRWAYS, RAMPS AND GUARDS
L CONSERVATION OF FUEL AND ENERGY
M ACCESS FOR DISABLED PEOPLE

The Department of the Environment has issued Technical Guidance Documents in relation to each section. It is not obligatory to follow the Technical Guidance Documents but doing so constitutes prima facie evidence of compliance with the regulations.

The regulations themselves are expressed in extremely general terms with generous use of phrases such as "adequate" and "reasonable" so that they leave considerable room for interpretation.

The main provisions came into force on June 1, 1992. From that date all works for the erection of buildings or the alteration or extension of existing buildings must comply with the regulations unless the works are covered by any of the exemptions specified below.

In addition certain refurbishment works and fitting out works will be affected and must comply with the regulations.

The regulations apply to a change of use of a building from a single dwelling to multi-residential use. They also apply where a change of use occurs which, if the building had been originally designed for the new use would require a higher standard of performance to comply with the regulations than the existing use (a "material change of use").

13.8.1 Exemptions

The principal exemptions from the requirement to comply with the regulations are:

(a) Works commenced before June 1, 1992.

(b) Works carried out on foot of a building bye laws approval application for which was made prior to June 1, 1992.

(c) Alterations to buildings which do not affect the structural or fire safety aspects of the building.

(d) Detached domestic garages with a floor area not exceeding 25 square metres and a height of not more than 3 metres, or in the case of a pitched roof, 4 metres.

(e) Single storied detached buildings in the grounds of a dwellinghouse with a floor area not exceeding 23 square metres, a height of not more than 3 metres or in the case of a pitched roof, 4 metres, and used exclusively for recreational or storage purposes as opposed to use for trade or business or human habitation.

(f) Single storey extensions to existing dwellings ancillary to a dwelling and consisting of a conservatory, porch, carport or covered area with a floor area not exceeding 25 square metres (or 2 square metres in the case of a porch) and a height less than 3 metres, or if a pitched roof, 4 metres.

(g) Certain temporary structures.

(h) Certain farm buildings.

13.8.2 Commencement notices

Not less than seven, and not more than 21 days notice in writing of the commencement of works, or the making of a material change of use must be given to the Building Control Authority ("the Authority"). This requirement to serve a commencement notice came into effect on June 1, 1992.

The notice must contain the following information:

1. The address of the building and its use or proposed use.
2. A description of the proposed works or change of use.
3. The name and address of:
   (a) The owner
   (b) Any other person who is carrying out the works (*e.g.* the builder).
   (c) The person from whom the plans for the works can be obtained. (*e.g.* the architect)
   (d) The person from whom notification of the pouring of foundations and of the covering up of any drainage system can be obtained (*e.g.* the builder).

13.8.3 A commencement notice is not required in respect of:

1. Works exempt from the requirement to comply with the regulations
2. Works carried out by a building control authority in its own area.
3. Garda Stations, military barracks, court houses and certain other buildings for officers of the State, and certain works carried out for security or national security reasons.
4. The provision of services fittings and equipment to a building not involving a material alteration.
5. Exempt development under the Planning Acts except
   (a) where a fire safety certificate is required or
   (b) for material alterations (other than minor works) in a shop or industrial building

13.8.3.1 Definitions

A "material alteration" is an alteration where the works, or any part of the work, carried out by itself would be subject to a requirement of the regulations concerning structure or fire safety.

"minor works" means works consisting of the installation, alteration, or removal of a fixture or fitting, or works of a decorative nature.

"shop" is defined in the Building Control (Amendment) Regulations 1994 as including a building used for retail or wholesale trade or business (including retail sales by auction, self-selection and over-the-counter wholesale trading, the business of lending books or periodicals for gain and the business of a barber or hairdresser) and premises to which the public is invited to deliver or to collect goods in connection with their hire, repair or other treatment, or where they themselves may carry out such repairs or other treatments.

"office" is defined as including premises used for the purpose of administrative or clerical work (including writing, book keeping, sorting papers, filing, typing, duplicating, machine calculating, drawing and the editorial preparation of matter for publication, handling money (including banking and building society work) or telephone system operation.

"industrial building" is defined as including a factory or other premises used for manufacturing, altering, repairing, cleaning, washing, breaking-up, adapting or processing any article, generating power or slaughtering livestock.

It will be noted that the definitions differ from those in the exempt development regulations.

13.8.4 Fire Safety Certificates:

A Fire Safety Certificate is required for:-

    (a) the erection of a building;
    (b) a material alteration in
       (i) a building containing a flat,
       (ii) a hotel, hostel or guest house,
       (iii) an institutional building,
       (iv) a place of assembly, or
       (v) a shopping centre,

    other than a material alteration consisting solely of minor works

    (c) a material alteration in a shop, office or industrial building where
       (i) additional floor space is being provided within the existing building, or
       (ii) the building is being sub-divided into a number of units for separate occupancy,
    (d) the extension of a building by more than 25 square metres;
    (e) a material change of use of a building;

to which Part B of the first schedule to the 1991 Regulations (being the fire regulations) apply.

An "institutional building" includes a hospital, nursing home, home for old people or for children, school or other similar establishment used as living accommodation or for the treatment, care or maintenance of persons suffering from illness or mental or physical disability or handicap, where such persons sleep on the premises.

A "place of assembly" includes (i) a theatre, public library, hall or other building of public resort used for social or recreational purposes, (ii) a non-residential school or other educational establishment (iii) a place of public worship (iv) a public house, restaurant or similar premises used for the sale to members of the public of food or drink for consumption on the premises, but no building shall be treated as a place of assembly solely because it is a building to which members of the public are occasionally admitted;

"Shopping centre" includes a building which comprises a number of individually occupied premises to which common access is provided principally for the benefit of shoppers.

The definition of "flat" was amended in the 1994 regulations and now refers to separate and self-contained premises constructed or adapted for residential use and forming part of a building from some other part of which it is divided horizontally. Duplex apartments are clearly flats under this definition.

The application for a fire safety certificate must be in the prescribed form and be accompanied by a detailed plan showing compliance with the fire regulations and particulars of the proposed use. Any application which does not contain the necessary information is invalid. The certificate is issued by the Authority.

The authority has two months within which to issue the certificate, with or without conditions, or to refuse it. If it fails to issue a decision within that time a default procedure, akin to that applicable to a planning application, applies, whereby the certificate must automatically issue to the applicant.

There is a procedure whereby the applicant can appeal to An Bord Pleanála against the decision of the Authority, either in part or in its entirety.

The authority is required to maintain a register of all applications for Fire Safety Certificates with details of the decision of the authority or of An Bord Pleanála on appeal. This register is available for public inspection.

It is an offence to carry out works or make a material change of use without first obtaining a fire safety certificate.

13.8.5 A fire safety certificate is not required in respect of:

1. Works exempt from the requirement to comply with the regulations.
2. Works commenced or a material change of use made before August 1, 1992.
3. A building (other than a flat) the proposed use of which is as a dwelling
4. Works carried out by a building control authority in its own area.
5. The provision of services, fittings and equipment to a building not involving a material alteration.
6. A material alteration, consisting only of minor works, in a building containing a flat, a hotel, hostel or guesthouse, an institutional building, place of assembly or shopping centre.
7. A material alteration in a shop, office or industrial building unless additional floor space is being provided within an existing building or the building is being sub-divided into a number of units for separate occupancy.
8. Works carried out to a building in compliance with a notice served under section 20 of the Fire Services Act 1981.
9. Certain single storey buildings used solely for agriculture.

The definition of "agriculture" is identical to that contained in the Local Government (Planning & Development) Act 1963.

13.8.6 Alteration or Extension of Existing Buildings

The regulations apply to all material alterations (not being repair or renewal) or extensions of existing buildings, in that all works done must comply with the regulations. In addition, the alteration or extension cannot result in a new or greater contravention of the regulations.

13.8.7 Services fittings and equipment

The regulations apply to all works in connection with the provision of services fittings and equipment (whether new or by way of replacement) which are subject to the requirements of the Hygiene, Drainage and Waste Disposal, and the Heat Producing Appliances regulations. There is no requirement to serve a Commencement Notice or obtain a Fire Safety Certificate for such works unless the works involve a material alteration.[26]

13.8.8 Dispensations/relaxations

One can apply to the Building Control Authority for dispensations or relaxations of building regulations. If no decision is made by the Authority within two months, the dispensation or relaxation is deemed to have been granted.

There is an appeal procedure if an applicant is dissatisfied with the Authority's decision, the appeal again lying to An Bord Pleanála.

The Minister for the Environment also has power to dispense with, or relax, any regulations in respect of any particular class of building operation, works or materials, subject to such conditions as he deems appropriate.

13.8.9 Liability, penalties and enforcement

Failure to comply with any requirement of the Building Control Act or the regulations is an offence. Fines of up to £10,000.00, and/or a term of imprisonment not exceeding two years can be imposed for failure to comply with the regulations, or failure to comply with an enforcement notice. If the offence is committed by a company with the consent or connivance of, or is attributable to any neglect on the part of any director, manager or secretary of that company, that person shall also be guilty of the offence.

Enforcement notices may be served by the Authority on the owner of the building or any other person involved in the works. It can set out the works required to ensure compliance with the regulations, and may prohibit the use of a building or part of it until these works are done.

The Authority has power to enter a building and carry out the remedial works if the enforcement notice is not complied with, and can recover the cost from the owner or the person who carried out works in breach of the regulations, as a simple contract debt.

The Authority also has power to enter buildings to inspect them and any plans or documents relating to the works, and to take samples of materials being used.

There is a limitation period of five years from completion of the works or change of use, after which no enforcement notice can be served.

---

[26] See p.363, above.

The Act also provides for a procedure similar to the "planning injunction" under section 27 of the Planning Act 1976[27] (as amended by the 1992 Act),[28] whereby the Authority can seek a High Court Order requiring alterations, the making safe of any structure, the discontinuance of works or prohibiting the use of the building where the Authority considers that there is a substantial risk to health or safety. There is no time limit on this action.

13.8.10 Building bye-laws

The Building Control Act 1990 replaces building bye-laws made under section 41 of the Public Health (Ireland) Act 1878, section 23 of the Public Health Ireland (Amendment) Act 1890 and section 33 of the Dublin Corporation Act 1890. Bye Laws had been made in the following areas:

> Bray U.D.C.
> Dublin Corporation
> Dublin County Council
> Dun Laoghaire Corporation
> Cork Corporation
> Galway Corporation
> Limerick Corporation
> Naas U.D.C.

In areas where local authorities had made building bye-laws, it was necessary to obtain a building bye laws approval before carrying out structural works or other works involving drainage, sewerage disposal and the like. Such an approval could not be obtained retrospectively. Therefore technically the absence of a building bye laws approval was a defect which could not be cured other than by demolishing the structure. Accordingly in such a situation it became established practice to accept the certificate of an architect confirming that the works complied with the building bye laws as at the date the works were carried out, and that in the opinion of the architect, bye-laws approval would have been granted if it had been applied for.[29]

However, section 22 (7) of the Building Control Act 1990 provides that all works carried out prior to December 13, 1989 are deemed to comply with building bye-laws unless a notice was served by the Authority before December 1, 1992 stating that the works constituted a danger to public health or safety.

Building bye-laws remain relevant in relation to works carried out between December 13, 1989 and June 1, 1992, and works carried out pursuant to building bye-law approvals applied for prior to June 1, 1992.

---

27 Local Government (Planning and Development) Act 1976.
28 Local Government (Planning and Development) Act 1992.
29 See Practice Note, *Law Society Gazette*, May 1986. See p. 370, below.

13.8.11 Multi-Storey buildings

The Local Government (Multi-Storey) Act 1988 does not apply to buildings commenced after June 1, 1992 save where built on foot of a building bye laws approval applied for on or before that date.

The 1988 Act does still apply to multi-storey buildings constructed between January 1, 1950 and June 1, 1992.

13.8.12 Fire Services Act 1981

The Fire Services Act is unaffected by the Building Control Act and all of the enforcement powers of the fire officer under the Fire Services Act remain.

13.9 REPLYING TO PLANNING REQUISITIONS ON TITLE[30]

The current edition of the Law Society of Ireland requisitions on title is the 1996 edition. Requisition 27 relates to planning and is reproduced below in bold

27. PLANNING

Local Government (Planning & Development) Acts 1963 ("the Planning Acts")

There is a provision at the beginning of the requisitions whereby any reference to any Act shall include any extension amendment modification or re-enactment thereof and any regulation order or instrument made thereunder and for the time being in force. Consequently, the full citation of the Planning Acts is not used.

1   Has there been in relation to the property any development (including change of use or exempted development) within the meaning of the Planning Acts on or after the 1st October 1964.

In the majority of cases there will have been development since 1964, given the wide meaning of the word "Development" in the Planning Acts. It will normally be clear from the title documents furnished whether a building was constructed prior to October 1, 1964. It may be that the building was erected on foot of the Town & Regional Planning Acts 1934–39 which preceded the current planning code. In such a situation the planning documentation should be retained with the title deeds, but no evidence of compliance by way of Architects Certificate is generally sought and none is required under condition 36 of the *Law Society General Conditions of Sale*.[31]

In many situations, such as sales by liquidators or personal representatives who have no personal knowledge of the property, this requisition will be

---

[30]   1996 Edition
[31]   See condition 36(c)(ii) at p.344, above.

precluded by contract. Alternatively, the contract may provide that the planning warranty will only extend over a specified period.

2 In respect of all such developments furnish now (where applicable):

a Grant of Planning Permission

A vendor is required by the General Conditions of Sale[32] to furnish copies of all relevant Planning Permissions obtained since October 1, 1964 unless the special conditions of the contract provide to the contrary. A purchaser must ensure that he/she receives a copy of the Grant of Permission and not merely the Decision to Grant, which may subsequently have been appealed.

or

b Outline Planning Permission and Grant of Approval.

Where a grant of approval has issued on foot of an outline planning permission, it is necessary to obtain a copy of both the outline permission and the grant of approval. The outline permission may contain conditions which were not carried through in the grant of approval, but which nevertheless apply and must be complied with. In addition, the life of the planning permission is calculated from the date of the grant of outline permission, not from the date of the grant of approval.[33]

c Building Bye-Law Approval (if applicable).

Building bye-laws are no longer relevant for works completed before December 13, 1989 provided the local authority did not serve a notice in relation to any such works before December 1, 1992.[34] If no copy of the building bye-law approval is available, a purchaser should be prepared to accept a statutory declaration confirming that the works were carried out before December 13, 1989 and as such are deemed to comply with building bye-laws by virtue of section 22(7) of the Building Control Act 1990. Note, however, that special condition 36(b) of the General Conditions of Sale does require the vendor to furnish a copy of such bye-law approval so that if it is not available, the position will have to be covered by the vendor in the special conditions to the contract.

d Evidence of Compliance with financial conditions by way of letter/receipt from the Local Authority.

The usual means of establishing compliance with financial conditions is by the production of a letter from the local authority confirming that the sum required has been paid or that the appropriate bond is in place. However, under the 1995

---

[32] See condition 36(b) at p.343, above.
[33] See p.353, above.
[34] See p.366, above.

edition Law Society conditions of sale, a vendor can instead produce formal confirmation from the local authority that the roads and other services have been taken in charge.[35]

Where financial conditions fall due for payment on a phased basis a purchaser is only concerned to ensure that the payments have been paid up to the date when the house was first sold by the developer.[36]

e **Certificate/Opinion from an Architect/Engineer that the Permission/ Approval relates to the property and that the development has been carried out in conformity with the Permission/Approval and with the Building Bye-Law Approval (if applicable) and that all conditions, other than financial conditions, have been complied with.**

Unless the general conditions of the contract have been varied by special condition, the vendor will have contracted to give this certificate. The Law Society have approved the form of certificates of compliance.[37]

As the General Conditions of Sale do not define "Architect" or "Engineer", a purchaser should establish in an appropriate case by pre-contract enquiry the qualifications of the architect or engineer who will give the certificate, or should seek the inclusion of a condition in the contract that the certificate to be given will be made by a person whose qualifications are in accordance with Law Society recommendations[38] and that the architect's certificate will be in a form approved by the Law Society.

Where a vendor wishes to avail of the Law Society recommendation in relation to new houses built prior to 1975,[39] then a special condition must appear in the contract.

f **In respect of exempted developments in each case the grounds upon which it is claimed that the development is an exempt development and furnish a certificate/opinion from an Architect/Engineer in support of such claim.**

This requisition was first introduced in the 1996 edition of the Law Society requisitions on title, although the practice of requiring the production of a certificate to confirm that a development was exempt is long established. A prudent purchaser will seek such a certificate even if it appears at first sight that the works are exempt. For example, it may be clear that the area of an extension to a dwelling is less than 23 square metres. However, are the height restrictions set out in the 1994 Regulations[40] (as amended by the 1995 Regulations[41])

---

35   See p.343, above.
36   See pp.344 and 358, above.
37   See p.354, above.
38   See p.356, above.
39   Practice Note, *Gazette*, February 1993, see p.379 below. See p.345, above.
40   Local Government (Planning and Development) Regulations 1994 (S.I. No. 86 of 1994).
41   Local Government (Planning and Development) Regulations 1995 (S.I. No. 69 of 1995).

infringed ? Is the area of open space in the rear garden reduced below 25 square metres ? Do any of the restrictions in article 10 of the 1994 Regulations apply?

On the other hand, a change of use from one retail use to another, within class 1 of the second schedule part IV of the 1994 Regulations is exempted development provided that the use comes within the definition of "shop" in article 8. No architects certificate to confirm the position would normally be required.

3 In respect of developments completed after the 1st November 1976 furnish now evidence by way of Statutory Declaration of a competent person that each development was completed prior to expiration of the Permission/Approval.

The provisions of section 2(5) of the Local Government (Planning & Development) Act 1982, set down time limits within which the development must be substantially completed. This requisition seeks confirmation that the development was completed within the life of the planning permission. Very often this can be established from the title documents, *e.g.* if there is a lease or conveyance with a building covenant and a certificate of compliance endorsed. In addition the architect's certificate of compliance should be dated and will have been given upon completion of the property.

Where the planning permission has expired (and no extension has been obtained under section 4 of the 1982 Act), but it is not clear from the title documents when the development was substantially completed, then the purchaser should seek a statutory declaration to confirm that the development was completed within the life of the permission.

4 Is the property subject to:

a Any Special Amenity Area, Preservation, Conservation or any other Order under the Planning Acts which affect the property or any part thereof.

Under the Planning Acts, where such orders are made, the local authority is required to enter them in the planning register established under section 8 of the Local Government (Planning & Development) Act 1963. A purchaser should ascertain whether there are any such orders in existence by inspection of the planning register. Under condition 35(b) of the General Conditions of Sale a vendor is not required to furnish details of the contents of the development plan other than an actual or proposed designation for compulsory acquisition. The onus is on a purchaser to carry out a planning office search before entering into the contract. Accordingly, frequently the answer to this requisition will be: "this is a matter for purchaser".

However, where a notice under the Planning Acts has been served on the vendor or is otherwise known by the vendor to be in existence, (not being a notice in relation to the contents of the development plan), the vendor is obliged to furnish details.

b Any actual or proposed designation of all or any of the property whereby it would become liable to compulsory purchase or acquisition for any purpose under the Planning Acts.

If a Compulsory Purchase Order has been made, then the vendor is obliged to put the purchaser on notice of it by reason of General Condition 35. A prudent purchaser will, in any event, make his/her own searches prior to contract to confirm whether any such Compulsory Purchase Order has been made or is being considered.

5 Is there any unauthorised development as defined in the Planning Acts.

"Unauthorised structure" is defined in section 2 of the 1963 Act. That definition is difficult and includes reference to permissions granted under the Town & Regional Planning Act 1934. For practical conveyancing purposes an "unauthorised structure" can be taken as being any structure erected after October 1, 1964 which was built other than in accordance with a planning permission obtained under the current planning code, and which is not exempt development.

6 If there is any such unauthorised development furnish prior to closing:

a A retention permission for such development

If there is an unauthorised structure, and the special conditions to the contract do not qualify the planning warranty, then the vendor is in breach of that warranty and is exposed to an action for breach of contract. It is likely to prove extremely difficult to complete the sale of the property until such time as the problem of the breach is resolved. The purchaser may be prepared to agree that the vendor make an application for retention permission, but if that permission issues subject to conditions which adversely affect the value of the property, then the purchaser would be entitled to seek compensation from the vendor (or to rescind).The purchaser is under no obligation to wait until such time as a retention permission issues and could serve a notice under condition 40 of the General Conditions of Sale, thereby rescinding the Contract, and might subsequently pursue an action against the vendor for breach of contractual warranty.

and

b Satisfactory evidence of compliance from an Architect/Engineer with the conditions in the said permission

Where a retention permission has been obtained in respect of an unauthorised structure, the purchaser will require an architect's certificate confirming compliance with any conditions attached to such retention permission.

and

c If applicable, satisfactory evidence from an Architect/ Engineer that the development substantially complies with the Bye-Laws or with the Regulations made under the Building Control Act 1990.

Building bye-laws will only be relevant in the areas where building bye-laws apply.[42] The opinion of compliance with the Building Regulations should be in the form approved by the Law Society.[43]

7 What is/are the present use/uses of the property.

This is a matter of fact in each case. However, a vendor's solicitor should ensure that he gets full instructions in relation to current uses, particularly where there is more than one. In a dwellinghouse, it may be that a part of the property was used as a doctor's surgery for example. In a commercial building where a number of uses co-exist, the purchaser should require the vendor to identify the primary use or uses of the building and any uses which are ancillary to that use or uses.[44]

8 Has the property been used for each of the uses aforesaid without material change continuously since the 1st day of October 1964.

If the answer to this requisition is "no" then there has been a development within the meaning of the Planning Acts and the purchaser will be required to produce the appropriate planning permission. If no planning permission has been obtained, then the same comments as at requisition 27.6a above apply.[45] The only means of rectifying the position is to discontinue the unauthorised use or obtain permission for continuance of such use.

Regard should be had to the principals of intensification of use and abandonment of use.[46]

Where there has been a change of use one needs to consider whether it is a material change.[47]

9 Give particulars of any application for permission and/or approval under the Planning Acts and the Building Bye-laws and state the result thereof.

Whereas this requisition is drafted so widely that it would cover the permissions referred to at 27.2 above, its real purpose is to obtain details of any applications for planning permission where no decision to grant permission has issued or a permission granted has not been acted upon. The purchaser seeks information in relation to any such application or permission.

Where a purchaser is acquiring property for the purposes of carrying out a development on foot of an existing permission, he will have checked out in detail the planning permission and the plans lodged on foot of which it was obtained. He will be concerned not only to establish the precise detail of the structure

---

[42] See p.366, above and notes on requisition 27.2c at p.368, above.
[43] See *Law Society Gazette*, March 1986, See para. A.10, below.
[44] See para. 4.3.3, above.
[45] See p.371, above.
[46] See para. 4.3.10, above.
[47] See para. 4.2, above.

which the permission allows, but also the time scale within which it must be completed.[48]

As building bye-laws have been replaced by the Building Control Act 1990 and the regulations thereunder, they are only relevant in this context in relation to applications for building bye-laws lodged with the local authority prior to June 1, 1992 and any approvals which may have issued on foot of such applications. There is no time limit within which works must be completed on foot of a building bye-law approval.

10 a Has any agreement been entered into with the Planning Authority pursuant to section 38 of the 1963 Act restricting or regulating the development or use of the property.

b If so furnish now copy of same.

Section 38 of the 1963 Act provides for the making of agreements with the planning authority whereby the development or use of land is restricted. This normally arises in a situation where the planning authority is prepared to grant permission for the development of one part of a land owner's holding on condition that another portion of his holding is sterilized so that there will be no development of that other portion in the future. Clearly, it is of crucial importance to a purchaser to know whether the plot of ground he is buying has been sterilised in such a manner. Details of any such section 38 agreement must be registered on the planning register so that a purchaser who has carried out his planning searches will be aware of the situation .

11 a Has there been any application for or award of compensation under the Planning Acts.

b If so, furnish now copy of same.

A purchaser is concerned to know whether any compensation has been paid by the planning authority by reason of a refusal to grant permission or the attachment of an onerous condition. The Local Government (Planning & Development) Act 1990 provides that where any such compensation is paid, subject to certain limited exceptions, no development can be carried out on the land in question until such time as the compensation is refunded to the local authority. The obligation to repay compensation does not apply to:

— exempted development.
— development permitted by any permission for which a statement has been registered (where compensation has been paid for the attachment of a condition)

---

[48] See para. A.5, above.

— development on foot of any permission to which conditions are attached which do not exclude the payment of compensation where the development is of a type specified in a notice under section 13 of the 1990 Act which has been served by the planning authority in connection with the same land.

c Has a statement of compensation been registered on the Planning Register under section 9 of the 1990 Planning Act prohibiting development of the property under section 10 of the said Act.

Where compensation is paid, the local authority is required to enter the details on the planning register so that a purchaser who has carried out his planning search will be aware of the position before contracts are exchanged.

12 a If any development was carried out prior to the 13th of December 1989 and Building Bye-Law Approval was either not obtained or not complied with furnish now Declaration that the development was completed prior to the 13th of December 1989 and that no Notice under Section 22 of the Building Control Act 1990 was served by the Building Control Authority between the 1st June 1992 and the 1st of December 1992.

The requisition is drafted widely enough to capture all works requiring building bye-law approval whether or not they are exempted development. See the notes on requisition 27.2 c.[49]

The building control authority can only serve a notice under section 22 of the Building Control Act 1990 where they consider that the works constitute a danger to public health or safety. Unfortunately there is no public register which can be inspected to see whether any such notice was served.

b Has there been any development carried out since the 13th of December 1989 with the benefit of Building Bye-Law Approval. If so, furnish now copy of same and draft Engineer's/Architect's Opinion of Compliance.

A purchaser will require production of a building bye-laws approval where the works have been carried out in a building bye-law area[50] between December 13, 1989 and June 1, 1992, or on foot of a bye-laws approval applied for prior to June 1, 1992, and will require an architects certificate of compliance with such building bye-laws approval.[51]

Where no building bye-law approval has been obtained, a purchaser will require the certificate of an architect to the effect that the works have been carried out in substantial compliance with building bye-laws in force at the date of construction and that had building bye-law approval been applied for, in the

---

[49] See p.368, above.
[50] See p.366, above.
[51] See RIAI Form 5 and Law Society forms 3 and 4.

view of the architect, it would have been granted.[52] Under the Law Society General Conditions of Sale a purchaser is not required to accept such a certificate unless the special conditions so provide, although the practice of accepting such certificates is well established.

13 Furnish now Statutory Declaration by a competent person evidencing user of the property from the 1st October 1964 to date.

In many cases, the vendor will decline to give such a declaration on the basis that, for example, the property consists of a residence and is being sold as such. However, where a purchaser is seeking to rely on an established use dating pre-1964, for example where a house has been divided into a number of residential units, he/she will insist upon appropriate evidence confirming such established use.

Where a property has been built on foot of a planning permission issued subsequent to October 1, 1964 and the user has not changed since the date of grant of that permission, then normally no such declaration would be required.

13.10 REPLYING TO BUILDING CONTROL REQUISITIONS[53]

28. Building Control Act 1990 and any regulations, orders or instruments thereunder (referred to collectively as "the Regulations")

1. Is the Property, or any part thereof affected by any of the provisions of the Regulations?

If any works have been carried out since June 1, 1992 other than on foot of a Building Bye-Law Approval application for which was made prior to that date, then the answer here is yes, unless one of the exemptions applies.[54]

2. If it is claimed that the Property is not affected by the Regulations state why. Evidence by way of a Statutory Declaration of a competent person may be required to verify the reply.

In most cases the answer will be that no works have been carried out since June 1, 1992 so that the Building Regulations do not apply.

Where there is doubt as to when the works were completed, a statutory declaration confirming that the works were completed prior to that date may be sought. Where it is claimed that the works are exempt from any requirement to comply with the regulations then the position may need to be confirmed by way of declaration or certificate of an appropriate person.

---

[52] See *Law Society Gazette*, March 1986. See also p.393, below.
[53] *Law Society Requisitions on Title*, 1996 Edition.
[54] See p.361, above.

3 If the property is affected by the Regulations furnish now a Certificate/ Opinion of Compliance by a competent person confirming that all necessary requirements of the Regulations have been met.

The certificate should be in a form acceptable to the Law Society, *i.e.* in either the Law Society format or the RIAI March 1993 edition.[55]

4 a Has a Commencement Notice been given to the Building Control Authority in respect of the property.

b If so, furnish now a copy of the same.

Where no copy of the Commencement Notice is available, a purchaser need not be unduly concerned. Failure to obtain a Commencement Notice is an offence under the Building Control Act. However, a subsequent owner of the property do not expose him of herself to criminal liability and the local authority has no power to take action against the property arising out of the failure to obtain such a commencement notice.

It is nonetheless considered good practice to obtain a copy of the Commencement Notice where it is available.

5 If the property is such that a Fire Safety Certificate is one of the requirements of the Regulations:

a A copy of the Fire Safety Certificate must be attached to and referred to in the Certificate of Compliance which should confirm that the works to the property have been carried out in accordance with the drawings and other particulars on foot of which the Fire Safety Certificate was obtained and with any conditions of the Fire Safety Certificate.

Neither the standard format of the Law Society certificate or the RIAI form specifically refers to the conditions attached to the fire safety certificate, but instead certify that the works have been carried out in substantial compliance with the Building Regulations. As compliance with fire safety certificate conditions forms part of the Building Regulations, the Law Society and RIAI certificates of compliance incorporate compliance with any requirements of the fire safety certificate. Where a purchaser is furnished with either the standard Law Society format of certificate or the RIAI version,[56] then he/she can accept the position.

b Confirm that no appeal was made by the Applicant for such Certificate against any of the conditions imposed by the Building Control Authority in such Fire Safety Certificate.

---

55 See p.354, above.
56 *ibid.*

Only the applicant can appeal a decision to issue a fire safety certificate or any conditions attached. If any appeal was lodged it would appear on the register of fire safety certificates maintained by the local authority pursuant to article 19 of the Building Control Regulations 1991.

6 a Has any Enforcement Notice under Section 8 of the Building Control Act been served.

b If so furnish now a copy of the Notice and a Certificate of Compliance made by a competent person.

Such an enforcement notice may be served by the Building Control Authority where works have not been designed or have not been constructed in conformity with the Building Regulations. Such a notice must be served within the period of five years commencing on the date of completion of the works or of any material change in the purpose for which the building is used.

Where no works have been carried out and there has been no change of use since June 1, 1992 no such notice can have been served.

7 If any application has been made to the District Court under section 9 of Building Control Act, 1990 furnish details of the result of such application.

Unless works have been carried out since 1st June 1992, no such application can have been made. Such an application is made by a person on whom an Enforcement Notice is served, and is an application to annul, modify or alter such a notice.

8 a Has any application been made to the High Court under Section 12 of Building Control Act 1990.

b If so furnish a copy of any Order made by the Court and evidence of any necessary compliance with such order by a Certificate of a competent person.

This is a procedure similar to the "planning injunction" procedure under section 27 of the Local Government (Planning & Development) Act 1976.[57] It allows a Building Control Authority to apply to the High Court for an Order requiring the removal, alteration or making safe of any structure, service, fitting or equipment, or the discontinuance of any works, or restricting or prohibiting use of a building until the removal, alteration or making safe of any structure, service, fitting or equipments, or the discontinuance of any work, as the case may be, has been effected. There is no time limit within which such action must be taken.

---

[57]   As amended by the Local Government (Planning and Development) Act 1992.

Appendix A

PRACTICE NOTES

A.1 CERTIFICATES OF COMPLIANCE WITH PLANNING PERMISSION[1]

It is at present the universal practice for Builders and Vendors of new houses to furnish evidence of compliance with the conditions of the Planning Permission for the erection thereof. The normal evidence furnished is as follows:

(1) Compliance with conditions requiring financial contributions is normally proved by furnishing copy letters from the Planning Authority confirming compliance. In passing, it should be said that this is not always as simple as it might seem on a large estate with a variety of different Planning Permissions.

(2) Compliance with the other conditions is proved by furnishing a Certificate from an Architect or Engineer, confirming that the Planning Permission (and usually also the Building Bye Laws Approval) relates to the house in question and that the house was completed in at least substantial compliance with the conditions thereof. The Law Society have agreed a form of Certificate with the Royal Institute of Architects and the Solicitors for the main Lending Institutions (Gazette – November 1978).

Many solicitors have enquired as to correct requirements of a purchaser's solicitor or a mortgagee's solicitor dealing with the sale of a second-hand house built since 1st October 1964.

The Conveyancing Committee feel that it is unreasonable for solicitors to insist now on being furnished with documentation which it was not the practice to furnish at the time. They have caused enquiries to be made as to when the practice of getting these Certificates of Compliance became general conveyancing practice and have been advised that it became so in 1970. The Committee accordingly advise members of the Society that in their opinion, the solicitors should only insist on such Certificates on second-hand houses built since 1970.

In considering the matter, the Committee discussed the frequently stated belief that Solicitors need not concern themselves with any of these matters if the house had been built for over five years. The Committee were of the opinion that this theory does not have any basis in law.

---

[1] *Law Society Gazette*, December 1979.

A.1.1 From what date must they be obtained?[2]

In December 1979 the Conveyancing Committee recommended that solicitors should only insist on Certificates of Compliance with Planning Permission in relation to second-hand houses built since 1st January 1970. The Committee has received many queries in connection with this matter and it seems clear that the practice of getting Certificates of Compliance with Planning Permission in relation to all new houses was not as widespread as the Committee was led to believe when it made its original recommendation. Representations have been made to the Committee that in view of the fact that the date chosen is almost 19 years ago that some adjustment be made in the date and also that some steps should be taken to lobby for some statutory limit in relation to planning.

Having considered the matter very carefully the Committee has decided that:—

1. It is now revising its recommendation to only insist on Certificates of Compliance with Planning Permission in relation to houses built since 1st January 1975. Consequential changes to the Contract and to the Requisitions will be made at the next reprint. It is not intended that this date would be reviewed regularly. The Committee has chosen a date at which it is satisfied it either was or should have been universal practice in relation to the purchase of new houses to obtain Certificates of Compliance.

2. The Society made representations several years ago to the Department of the Environment seeking the imposition of some statutory limit in relation to planning breaches. It is also understood that the topic may be dealt with in a forthcoming Report by the Law Reform Commission.

A.2 PRIVATE RESIDENTIAL PROPERTY[3] AND CLAUSE 36 OF THE CONTRACT FOR SALE

When preparing the 1988 Edition of the Contract for Sale, the Conveyancing Committee decided to change clause 36 by providing that where planning permission had been granted since 1 January, 1970 a certificate of compliance with planning permission was to be handed over on closing. When drafting this clause it had been intended to apply only to private residential property. In all other transactions special conditions should have been inserted in the contract but in practice this was rarely done.

When re-examining the contract the Conveyancing Committee decided that it would be preferable for the general conditions to provide that 1 October, 1964 would be the operative date in relation to all planning matters.

When the 1991 Edition of the standard Contract for Sale was produced a practice note was issued (June, 1991 *Gazette*) which recommended that special

---

2   *Law Society Gazette*, August 1989.
3   *Law Society Gazette*, February, 1993.

conditions should be utilised to implement the recommendations of the Conveyancing Committee or of other Law Society Committees.

The recommendation of the Conveyancing Committee is that where private residential property is a subject matter of a contract for sale it is reasonable for a vendor's solicitor to insert a special condition in the contract providing that no certificate of compliance with planning permission will be handed over in respect of the erection of, or alteration to, a private residential property where the work was completed prior to 31 December, 1975 (the appropriate planning permission must still be furnished).

Conveyancing Committee

A.3 COMPLIANCE WITH PLANNING CONDITIONS WHEN ESTATE IN CHARGE[4]

The Conveyancing Committee and the Joint Committee with the Building Societies have been considering for some time the question of conveyancing practice in relation to evidence of compliance with conditions of Planning Permissions. A particular problem area is in relation to the sale of second hand houses where there is no evidence of compliance with financial or other conditions. It had been suggested that solicitors should not concern themselves about compliance with conditions where it was established that the roads and services had been taken in charge by the Planning Authority. The Committees have had discussions with representatives of the County and City Managers Association and Dublin County Council and accordingly made the following recommendations:

(1) Conveyancers dealing with the second or later purchase of residential houses where the roads and services are in charge of the Local Authority should not concern themselves with enquiries as to compliance with financial conditions in a Planning Permission unless he is on notice of some problem.

(2) This recommendation applies only to houses forming part of a building estate and built at the same time as the main development. It does not apply to once-off houses or to infill development.

(3) There have been instances where houses forming part of a building estate have been built without Planning Permission so this recommendation is not to change the obligation on a purchaser's solicitor to see that there is, in fact, Planning Permission for the house and where appropriate under other recommendations to seek a certificate from an Architect or Engineer that the house has been built in accordance with same.

---

[4] *Law Society Newsletter*, May 1987.

(4) The Committees wish to draw the attention of practitioners to their long standing recommendation that it is unreasonable for solicitors to insist now on being furnished with documentation which it was not the practice to furnish at the time. In particular, where payment of financial contributions and/or levies are being paid by instalments, solicitors should only be concerned with the payment of contributions up to the date of the first purchase of any house.

A.4 EVIDENCE THAT ROADS AND SERVICES ARE IN CHARGE OF THE LOCAL AUTHORITY[5]

The Conveyancing Committee consider that it is quite acceptance for a solicitor to certify either from his own personal knowledge or from an inspection of the Local Authority records that Road and Services are in charge of the Local Authority. Such Certificate where forthcoming, should be accepted by a Purchaser in lieu of a letter from the Local Authority itself.

A.5 WHO SHOULD CERTIFY COMPLIANCE?[6]

The Conveyancing Committee has investigated the guidelines to be adopted by solicitors in advising clients on the qualification of persons offering Certificates of Compliance with planning permission and, where appropriate, building by-laws and building regulations.

The Committee is satisfied that the current practice is to accept Certificates of Compliance from chartered or civil engineers, persons with a degree in architecture, or persons (calling themselves architects or engineers) in professional practice on their own account either solely or in partnership for a period of at least 10 years.

The Committee has recently decided that it is reasonable for solicitors to accept Certificates of Compliance from qualified building surveyors. This is a professional qualification at degree level.

The Committee has also considered whether Certificates of Compliance should continue in the old form of a "certificate" or whether they should accept "Certificates of Opinion" as to *substantial* compliance, which some of the main architectural bodies feel is more appropriate. Having obtained the opinion of Senior Counsel the Committee has decided that the nomenclature is not materially significant and that it is reasonable for solicitors to accept either "Certificates" or "Certificates of Opinion".

The E.C. Directive 85/384/EEC (Council Directive of June 10, 1985) which is sometimes hereunder referred to as "the Architect's Directive" deals with the

---

5   *Law Society Gazette*, February 1989.
6   *The Law Society News*, October 26, 1994.

mutual recognition of diplomas, certificates and qualifications in architecture. it is important to understand that this Directive was not intended to regulate the practice of architecture in Member States, but rather to facilitate the free movement of architects between them. The Irish qualifications recognised in the Directive are set out below.

The Minister for the Environment, Mr. Smith, was asked in the Dail on 6th of April, 1993 when he intended to establish a review system for architects whose work had traditionally been accepted in this country, but who were not covered by the E.C. Architects' Directive; what form the review would take; and whether he would ensure that such architects would be admitted to the list of architects being prepared by him.

The Minister said in reply:

> "A proposal has been submitted to the EC Commission to amend the Architects Directive in order to bring under its protection persons whose established right to practice, and consequently their right to the protection of the Directive was overlooked when the Directive was being negotiated. The proposed amendment would allow for the issue of a certificate by the Minister for the Environment that the person concerned had over a period of at least five years immediately prior to the date of coming into force of the Directive pursued architectural activities, the nature and importance of which in the opinion of the Minister gave that person an established right to pursue those activities. The number of persons involved would be relatively small".

> "Pending amendment of the Directive, and in order to protect their position in the meantime, a list will now be prepared of those persons who would have the requisite experience to qualify for certification under the proposed amendment. To this end, I have already decided that persons with the requisite length of experience who, on the date of coming into force of the Directive, were members of the Irish Architects Society or were corporate architect members of the irish Branch of the Architects and Surveyors Institute or of the Irish Branch of the Incorporated Association of Architects and Surveyors would, by virtue of such membership have been included in the Directive had their position not been overlooked and that these would, accordingly, qualify for certification. The claims of others to have the necessary experience to qualify for certification under the amended Directive will be reviewed on an individual basis. Details of the review procedure have not yet been finalised".

The following is the text of the proposed Amendment to the Architects' Directive:

To add the following additional qualification to Article 11(f) of the Directive.

> "a certificate issued by the competent authorities to the effect that a person, who, on the date of entry into force of this Directive, had, over a period of at least five years immediately prior to that date, pursued architectural activities the nature and importance of which in the opinion of the competent authorities give that person an established right to pursue those activities".

The Committee understands that the Department of the Environment is preparing a list of those persons who would qualify for protection under the Directive, should the amendment be accepted. In the meantime, the Department has advised financial institutions and local authorities that architects whose work has traditionally been accepted should not be prevented from continuing to practice by any form of discriminatory action. The Department has given similar advice to the Law Society and this seems reasonable to the Committee.

The qualifications recognised in Ireland by the Architects' Directive are a Degree of Bachelor of Architecture awarded by the National University of Ireland (B. Arch.)(NUI), the Diploma of Degree standard in Architecture awarded by the College of Technology, Bolton Street, Dublin. (Dip. Arch.), the Certificate of Associateship of the Royal Institute of Architects of Ireland (ARIAI) and the Certificate of Membership of the Royal Institute of the Architects of Ireland (MRIAI).

It has been suggested by various professional bodies that Solicitors be advised automatically to accept certificates from their members on the sole basis of such membership. Some of these bodies have student members and technician members, and the Committee feels that relying solely on membership can only lead to confusion. This suggestion was accordingly rejected.

In future the Committee feels that it is reasonable for solicitors to accept Certificates of Compliance or Certificates of Opinion from:

(a) Persons with a degree or a diploma of degree standard in Architecture

(b) Persons who have been in practice as Architects on their own account for ten years. This would include persons certified by or included on a list prepared by the Minister for the Environment as persons who in the Minister's opinion are appropriately qualified as described supra.

(c) Chartered Engineers

(d) Persons with a degree in Civil Engineering

(e) Persons who have been in practice on their own account as Engineers in the construction industry for ten years

(f) Qualified Building Surveyors

(g) Persons from another jurisdiction in the European Union whose qualification is entitled to recognition in Ireland under the Architect's Directive.

The Committee has consistently advised solicitors to exercise caution in relation to the qualifications of persons from whom they will recommend acceptance of Certificates of Compliance. The reason for this is obvious. The Committee takes the view that if a solicitor advises a client to accept a Certificate of Compliance in relation to a development (such as a house or a house extension) from a person who is not adequately qualified, and a problem arises, the solicitor will almost certainly be sued for negligence on the basis that he or she should not have accepted the Certificate from a person who was not adequately qualified.

When advising a client in a house purchase transaction regarding any material point such as whether a Certificate of Compliance relative to a house or extension is in an acceptable form, or is given by a person with an acceptable qualification, solicitors usually apply a three-fold test:

1. In the solicitor's own opinion, is the particular matter in order and in accordance with good conveyancing practice?
2. Will it be acceptable under the rules or guidelines of the Bank or Building Society from whom the client is borrowing? and,
3. Will it be acceptable to most other solicitors if the property were to be put up for sale again in the near future?

If the answer to any of these questions is in the negative the solicitor will normally advise his or her client not to accept the situation and advise the client not to proceed with the transaction unless the difficulty is resolved.

If a query arises over the qualification of a person giving a Certificate the solicitor should take care to make it clear that he or she is not making the decision but is advising the purchaser, and that the final decision as to whether or not to proceed with the purchase is the client's responsibility. Most purchasers, particularly those borrowing, will tend to be cautious and accept their solicitor's advice, but some will take a commercial judgment and proceed despite what the solicitor perceives as a problem. Obviously, if a client decides to proceed despite the solicitor's concerns, it is good practice for the solicitor to confirm the advice in writing. Solicitors should also bear in mind that while the Law Society will assist and advise its members in regard to best practice, none of this can absolve the individual solicitor from his or her responsibility to the client. Each solicitor must look at each individual case on its own merits.

The Committee recognises that there may be exceptional cases involving persons practising as architects whose competence is recognised in their own locality and whose certificates may be generally acceptable in that locality, even though their qualifications or experience fail to meet one or some of the criteria mentioned above. Having said that, solicitors are cautioned that in a resale it may be difficult to persuade potential purchasers to accept any departure from the foregoing guidelines.

A.6 ARCHITECTS' CERTIFICATES[7]

Recommendation of the Joint Committee of Building Societies' Solicitors and the Law Society.

In 1978 the Law Society agreed with the Legal Institute of Architects of Ireland on a form of Certificate of Compliance with Planning Permission for use in speculative Housing Developments, where the Architect does not supervise the building on a regular basis. The text of this Certificate was published in the Gazette in November 1978. The Institute of Architects circulated the form of Certificate to their members.

---

[7]   *Law Society Gazette*, June 1982.

In November, 1980, arising out of certain difficulties in practice that arose in the Dublin area, the Joint Committee recommended a variation in this Certificate by the addition of a new paragraph.

Members of the Institute of Architects declined to issue Certificates containing the proposed new paragraph until the variation had been agreed by their own Council.

Discussions took place between representatives of the Joint Committee and representatives of the Architects. A revised form of Certificate has now been agreed with the Institute and the text of this is set out below.

The Joint Committee is satisfied that this Certificate is a reasonable one for a solicitor for a purchaser or a Leading Institution to accept. The Committee became aware, in the course of their discussions with the Institute of Architects, that Architects were under the impression that their Certificates also certified compliance with conditions for payment of financial contributions or entering into bonds for security for satisfactory completion or cash deposits in lieu thereof. The Joint Committee's representatives were of the opinion that Solicitors had, as a matter of practice always sought verification from the Planning Authority in respect of conditions for financial contribution or security deposit, and that it was not reasonable to expect Architects to accept responsibility for such matters. Practitioners will note that the current Certificate specifically excludes responsibility for compliance with conditions for payment of financial contributions or the giving of security for satisfactory completion.

I am an Architect retained by:

And I certify that:

1. I visited the office of the Planning Authority and there inspected the house plans, estate layout plan, specification and other drawings and documents which were represented by the Planning Authority as those on foot of which the Permission/Approval mentioned at Paragraph 2 & 3 hereunder were granted.

2. The Notification of Grant of Permission/Approval
   Decision Order No. and Date:...
   Register Reference No:..
   Planning Control No:..
   Dated:..
   related to the erection of houses on inter-alia sites.....................
   .... (both inclusive) as detailed on the said estate layout plan.

3. The Building Bye-Laws Approval Notice:
   Register No:..
   Order No:..
   Planning Control No:..

relates to inter-alia sites on the said estate layout plan (both inclusive as detailed).

I Further Certify that I have inspected the house that has been built on the site and that, in my opinion, this house has been erected in substantial compliance with the Notification of Grant of Permission mentioned at Paragraph 2 above and the Building Bye-Laws Approval Notice mentioned at Paragraph 3 above and that the position of the house and site is in substantial compliance with the estate layout plan mentioned at paragraph 1 above in so far as the estate has been completed.

I Also Certify that the general conditions on the Planning Permission relating to the estate of which this house forms part (excluding any conditions for payment of financial contributions or the giving of Security for satisfactory completion) have been substantially complied with in so far as is reasonably possible at this state of the development.

I am of the Opinion that if the house and site have not been built and or laid out exactly in accordance with the Planning Permission and Bye Law Approval, the differences are unlikely to affect the planning and development of the area as envisaged by the Planning Authority and expressed through the above mentioned approvals.

It Should Be Noted that I did not supervise the erection of this house in the course of its construction. Thus the inspection was a superficial one only and could take no account of work covered up. The comparison of the site layout with the estate layout plan was visual only.

SIGNED ....

....

A.7   RE: PLANNING/BUILDING REGULATIONS[8]

The Conveyancing Committee has been working for a considerable period on the preparation of new forms of Certificates of Compliance to replace the form of certificate of compliance with Planning and Building Bye-Laws originally published by the Law Society in the Gazette in November 1978.

Four new forms of certificate of compliance and a memorandum explaining their important features are attached.

The RIAI have published a set of five Architects Opinion on Compliance and the RIAI have very kindly agreed to send a full set of these five specimen forms to each firm of Solicitors in the Country. With this Newsletter is a memorandum explaining their important features as far as the Law Society are concerned.

The Committee would prefer Solicitors to get certificates of compliance on the Law Society forms and Solicitors should try to negotiate that its forms will be used where possible.

It is suggested that Solicitors should insert the RIAI forms and the attached documentation in their copy of the Conveyancing Handbook. As soon as all the

---

[8]   *The Law Society News*, November 1993.

guidelines are issued the Committee will be revising Chapter 7 of the Handbook which deals with planning.

The Committee is aware that Solicitors have tended to exercise caution in relation to the qualifications of persons from whom they will accept certificates of compliance. The reason for this is obvious. If a Solicitor advises a client to accept a Certificate of compliance in relation to a development such as a house or a house extension from a person who is not adequately qualified and a problem arises the Solicitor will almost certainly be liable in negligence on the basis that he should not have accepted or recommended acceptance of the certificate from a person who was not adequately qualified.

When advising a client in a house purchase transaction regarding any material point such as whether a Certificate of Compliance relative to a house or extensions is in an acceptable form or given by a person with an acceptable qualification Solicitors usually apply a three-fold test:

1. In the Solicitor's own opinion is the particular matter in order and in accordance with good conveyancing practice;
2. Will it be acceptable under the rules or guidelines of the Bank or Building Society from whom the client is borrowing; and,
3. Will it be acceptable to most other Solicitors if the property were to be put up for sale again in the near future.

If the answer to any of these questions is in the negative the Solicitor will normally advise his or her client not to accept the situation and to advise the Client not to proceed with the transaction unless the particular difficulty is resolved. Solicitors apply somewhat similar tests in relation to commercial property but obviously the requirements are more variable and more stringent in relation to the same.

If a query arises over the qualification of a certifier the Solicitor should take care to make it clear that he or she is not making the decision but is advising the purchaser and that the final decision in the matter of whether to proceed with the purchase or not is the clients. Most purchasers, particularly those borrowing, will tend to be cautious and accept their Solicitor's advice but come will take a commercial judgment and proceed despite what the Solicitor perceives as a problem. Obviously if a client decides to proceed despite the Solicitor's concerns, it is good practice for the Solicitor to confirm the advice in writing. Solicitors should also bear in mind that while the Law Society will assist and advise its members in regard to best practice none of this can absolve the individual solicitor from his responsibility to the client. Each solicitor must look at each individual case on its own merits.

The Committee is carrying out a review of this whole area and will issue further guidelines when the practice in relation to the use of the various certificates has settled down. The Society intends to hold several seminars to explain the certificates and to assist practitioners in dealing with the complicated issues that arise in relation to this increasingly complex area.

The Conveyancing Committee is preparing draft requisitions pending revision of the printed forms and these will be issued as soon as possible.

A.8   LAW SOCIETY FORMS OF CERTIFICATE OF COMPLIANCE FOR CONVEYANCING PURPOSES[9]

The Society has prepared four forms of certificate of compliance.
These are:—

1. A certificate of compliance with planning permission and building regulations, full service.
2. A certificate of compliance with planning permission and building regulations, part service.
3. A certificate of compliance with planning permission and building bye-laws, full service.
4. A certificate of compliance with planning permission and building bye-laws, part service.

Part Service means that the certifier designs the house, obtains planning permission therefore but does not make periodic inspections in the course of construction and gives a certificate based on one inspection when the house is practically completed.

Full service means a case where the certifier designs the house, obtains planning permission therefore and makes periodic inspections while the building is being constructed.

Normally a certifier would give a full service in connection with larger developments and part service would only arise in connection with speculative developments.

These forms had been agreed with the following professional bodies and will be used when appropriate by their Architects and Building Surveyors. Enquiries regarding membership can be made to the contact points listed below where a register is kept.

1. The Irish Architects Society. It has its registered offices at 35, Fitzwilliam Place, Dublin 2. Phone Number 6688685. The Honorary Secretary is John C. O'Grady, 67, Grosvenor Rd, Dublin 6. Phone Number 4979990 and 4979620. Fax Number 4976777
2. The Incorporated Association of Architects and Surveyors, Irish Branch. It has its office at Hogan House, Hogan Place, Dublin 2. Phone Number (01) 661 3022, Fax (01) 661 3130.
3. The Architects and Surveyors Institute. Its Secretary is Arthur Dunne who can be contacted at 7 Woodbine Park, Blackrock, County Dublin

---

9   *The Law Society News*, November 1993, pp.9–24.

– Phone Number 269 4462. Its memberships officer's name is Des Holmes. Phone Number 286 2369

4. The Society of Chartered Surveyors, 5, Wilton Place, Dublin 2, Phone No. 676 5500, 676 3276. The General Secretary is Tony Smyth.

The following points should be noted:

1. There are notes at the end of each form intended to assist those filling them in.
2. The forms are not sacrosanct and should be adopted to meet the circumstances of any particular case.
3. Compliance of the design with building regulations is just as important as compliance of the construction and therefore the form of certificate of compliance based on the original agreed form of certificate of compliance originally published in 1978, which did not separate design and construction, would not be appropriate in relation to certification of compliance with building regulations.
4. The Building Control Act and the Regulations thereunder provide for a notice called a Commencement Notice to be given to the Building Control Authority by relevant parties. While Building Control Authorities keep a register for their own use neither the Act nor any of the Regulations give the public a right of access to it and after a lapse of time, there will be extreme difficulty and indeed it may often prove impossible to establish whether a Commencement Notice was or was not served in relation to any particular development. It is clearly very important for the maintenance of good standards of building that Building Control Authorities monitor building standards. The service of Commencement Notices in every case will be an important ingredient in this process. The maintenance of such standards however and taking a though line with persons who fail to serve Commencement Notices or breach the Act or Regulations is a matter for the Building Control Authorities. It hardly seems reasonable however that the failure to serve a Commencement notice should make a particular property unsaleable. The effect of not serving the Commencement Notice in any case is that the person or persons carrying out the development commits an offence but this should not impact on a subsequent owner. In most cases, therefore, it seems reasonable for Solicitors for subsequent owners not to concern themselves unduly about whether a commencement Notice was served or not. The Committee sees no point in insisting on the production of a copy of the Commencement Notice if such copy is not readily available.
5. The Building Control Act and the Regulations thereunder also impose an obligation on the relevant parties to apply for a Fire Safety Certificate in relation to all new structures other than single dwellings, (not being

flats) and in relation to any material developments by way of extension alteration or change of use. The Building Control Regulations
provide for an official register to be kept of all applications for Fire
Safety Certificates and the decision in relation thereto and whether an
appeal was made against the decision. This Register will be available
to the public. It is clear that Fire Safety Certificates and their
complaints are going to be of vital important for Conveyances. The
tenor of the Act and the relevant Regulations obviously intend that
Fire Safety Certificate would be obtained before the development
commences. Indeed where a FSC is required in relation to the erection
of any building or the material extension or alteration of any building
it is an offence to start work without first getting the Fire Safety
Certificate. It is already clear that this is not always going to happen,
particularly in relation to fitting out buildings where retailers are in a
hurry to get a shop open. The Fire Safety Certificate procedure is a
paper exercise only. Plans, specification and various particulars are
submitted and in due course the Building Control Authority, assuming
the submissions are in order, issues the Fire Safety Certificate either
subject to conditions or not which in effect says that provided that the
development is carried out in accordance with the details submitted,
and presumably any conditions thereof, that it complies with the Fire
Section of the Building Regulations. Solicitors are already being
asked to accept situations where the development is carried out first
and the Fire Safety Certificate is obtained later. There does not seem
to be any serious problem for a subsequent owner in accepting such a
situation because any offence is committed by the party or parties
obliged to obtain the Fire Safety Certificate or carrying out the work.
Solicitors should take care that the Certificate of Compliance they get
deals fully with the situation. It would be particularly important to
have clear confirmation in such a case that any conditions of a Fire
Safety Certificate had been complied with.

6. The Committee has been advised that it would be almost impossible for
an Architect or Engineer who was not involved in the design to certify
compliance of a structure or works with the Building Regulations or with
a Fire Safety Certificate. Even in the case of fitting out a building
therefore it would be extremely unwise for a person to have such work
commenced unless an appropriately qualified person whose certificate
was likely to be accepted by conveyancers was involved in the design of
the work and made sufficient inspections to be able to later issue a
certificate of compliance.

7. Most commercial and industrial buildings have Architects and Engineers
involved in the design and making inspections while the building work is
being carried out. Most large-scale housebuilding is designed by an

Architect or Engineer but is not inspected in the course of construction. The Architect or Engineer in due course gives a certificate of compliance based on a single visual inspection at completion. Most once-off houses do not have an Architect or Engineer involved and this and extensions and conversions to private houses is the sector where most problems are likely. Persons borrowing from a Building Society when building a new house are normally required to have an appropriately qualified person involved who will be able to certify that they designed and carried out inspections of the structure at certain specified stages of construction. It seems likely that there are going to be problems for some people who have houses built, converted or extended without professional guidance and indeed some houses are likely to be unsaleable as a result.

8. In relation to Building Bye Laws, Solicitors should note the provisions of Section 22(7) of the Building Control Act, 1990, where an amnesty is granted to work carried out prior to the 13th December 1989, and approval of such works under the Building Bye Laws is deemed to have been granted. Proceedings shall not be taken on the basis of non compliance with Building Bye Laws unless before 1st December 1992 the Local Authority served a notice on the owner stating the works constituted a danger to public health or safety.

9. The Committee has agreed to monitor the operation of the forms of certificate without Professional bodies mentioned above and to the review them in the light of experience. The use of the two certificates referring to Building Bye-Laws will gradually disappear over the next five years.

10. It has been decided not to advise Solicitors to ask for confirmation or verification of the existence and adequacy of certifiers Professional indemnity Insurance. The position in this respect will be kept under review.

A.9 RIAI FORM OF ARCHITECTS OPINION ON COMPLIANCE FOR CONVEYANCING PURPOSES

Most Architects in Ireland, are members of the Royal Institute of Architects of Ireland. This institute has offices at 8, Merrion Square, Dublin 2, phone number 6761703. Its General Secretary is John Graby.

The RIAI has recently published five forms of Architects opinion on compliance. Theses are:

Form 1. Architect's opinion on compliance with building regulations. This is a form for use where a professional Architectural service has been provided at the design and construction stage of the relevant building or works.

Form 2.   Architect's opinion on compliance with building regulations. This is a form for use for Buildings or works in connection with which a design only service has been provided and where a fire safety certificate is not required.

Form 3.   Architect's opinion on exemption from Building Regulations. This form is for use for Buildings or works exempt from any need for compliance with building regulations.

Form 4.   Architect's opinion on compliance with planning permission and/or exemption from planning control.

Form 5.   Architect's opinion on compliance with planning permission and/or exemption from planning control and/or bye-law approval.

The following points should be noted regarding these certificates:

1. Copies can be obtained at a cost of £3 each from the RIAI.

2. The RIAI forms refer at the commencement to its member being a registered member of the RIAI this being a Qualification listed in directive 384/85/EEC. (The Architect Directive) The Society feels that this is completely unnecessary and should not be included in certificates by Irish Architects in relation to domestic developments.

3. Form 4 of the RIAI forms deals only with compliance with planning and/or exemption from Planning control. The Society feels that this is a good idea and will probably adopt a similar practice when it revises its own forms.

4. All five forms have attached advice notes as to their completion. In the Society's opinion both the certificates and the advice notes are quite complicated and not very user friendly. Solicitors should check that any certificate they are asked to accept has been completed prima facia in accordance with the advice note. This is not to say that the advice notes should be followed slavishly merely that they should only be departed from for good reason. The Society would have preferred the certificates to be given on the certifiers notepaper as is envisaged in the Society's own forms. Also details such as the Architects membership number and the membership stamp are not something that the Society feels are necessary but if Solicitors are accepting an RIAI form of certificate it is probably better to get these details completed. The former will facilitate checking an Architects qualifications. The Society has never recommended that Solicitors advise clients to accept certificates of opinion based solely on the membership of any Institute and has not changed its view in this respect.

5. The original form of Architects certificate of compliance was drafted jointly by the Law Society and the RIAI and was published as an agreed form. The five new forms were prepared by the RIAI. A sub-committee of the Conveyancing Committee agreed on behalf of the Society to

recommend that Solicitors accept these forms in appropriate cases. This recommendation relates to the March, 1993 issue of the forms and subsequent forms. Earlier editions contained some printing errors.

6. Form 3; Architects Opinion on Exemption from Building Regulations deals with different situations where relevant buildings or works are exempted from the Building Regulations for one reason or another. One of the alternative suggested wording reads:

> "I am advised by the Employer that the Relevant Building or Works were commenced prior on 1 June 1992 and based on this information I am of the opinion that the Relevant Building or Works is exempt from any need for compliance with the Building Regulations."

The information given to the architect is of course heresay and any solicitor would seek corroboration of the facts from someone who was actually aware of his own knowledge that the work had in fact so commenced. This would normally be confirmed by statutory declaration.

A.10 JOINT COMMITTEE ON LAW SOCIETY & BUILDING SOCIETIE'S SOLICITORS"

A.10.1 House extension – failure to obtain building bye laws approval.[10]

Solicitors are increasingly coming across cases where house extensions have been erected or a conversion of a garage has taken place which development would be exempted development under the Planning Acts but the necessary Building Bye Laws Approval was not obtained. The attitude of the Local Authority, quite correctly, is that they are unable to issue Building Bye Laws Approval retrospectively as it involves approval of matters like foundations and other items which cannot later be inspected.

The Committee considers that a reasonable practice for a Solicitor for a Building Society is to accept a Declaration or a Certificate from a professionally qualified person on the general lines of the following:

> "I.. of..aged twenty-one years and upwards DO SOLEMNLY AND SINCERELY DECLARE as follows:
> 1. I have examined the extension constructed by....................................
> ....at his house number..
> 2. I am satisfied from the measurements of the said extension that it would have qualified as an exempt development as defined by the Local Government (Planning and Development Acts, 1963 to 1976) except for the failure to obtain Building Bye Laws Approval.
> 3. I am informed that Building Bye Laws Approval was not obtained for the development. It is impractical to inspect the foundations or work covered up subject thereto I have inspected the same in so far as I could reasonably do so

---

[10] *Law Society Newsletter*, March 1986.

and I am satisfied that the extension is built in substancial compliance with Building Bye Laws as at the date of construction.
4. I am qualified to make this Dec laration by virtue of being.
5. I make this solemn Declaration conscientiously believing the same to be / by true virtue of The Statutory Declarations Act 1938 and for the Satisfaction of the Purchaser of the said premises." *The Law Society Newsletter*, March 1986.

A.11 EXEMPTED DEVELOPMENT[11]

The Joint Committee of Building Societies' Solicitors and the Law Society has issued the following Practice Note, which is intended to replace in its entirety the note which appeared as practice Note (2) in the Recommendations of the Joint Committee issued as a supplement with the January *Gazette*, 1982.

By virtue of Regulations made in 1964 under the Local Government Planning & Development Act 1963 an extension (of up to 120 square feet in the case of a single-storey, or upto 180 square feet in the case of a two-storey) added to the rere of a dwellinghouse which complied with the other criteria was "exempted development".

Under the Local Government (Planning & Development) Regulations 1977 (S.I. No. 65 of 1977), which came into effect on 15th March 1977, the exempted area of an extension was extended to 18 square metres and the distinction in area between single and two-storey extensions was removed.

The 1977 Regulations also introduced as an exempted development the conversion of a garage attached to the rere to the side of a dwellinghouse.

Under the Local Government (Planing & Development) (Amendments) Regulations 1981, which came into effect on 1st May 1981, the area of exemption for an extension was extended to 23 square metres.

A great many conveyancing transactions involve houses which have been extended or the garage converted and it frequently arises that an extension would not have been an exempted development under the Regulations applicable at the time it was built (or, in the case of a garage, at the time of conversion(but, in fact, would be exempted development if carried out now.

The Committee has considered the position carefully and particularly the fact that it is the intention of the Minister of Environment that Planning Authorities should not be concerned with matters relating to extensions or conversions that come within the current guide lines. The Committee accordingly recommends that solicitors for purchasers and mortgages should not insist upon application being made for permission to retain the structure or conversion, provided that an appropriate Certificate is furnished to verify that the extension would be exempted development under current regulations.

It is almost inevitable in such a case that no Building Bye-Laws Approval would have been obtained (in are where they are applicable). It is important to

---

[11] *The Law Society Gazette*, April 1983.

note the compliance with Building Bye-Laws is a condition of the entitlement to the exemption and this should be carefully dealt with in any Architect's Certificate.

A.12 BUILDING CONTROL ACT AND BUILDING REGULATIONS[12]

The Conveyancing Committee has been considering the implications for Solicitors of the above Act and Regulations thereunder the main provisions of which come into effect on 1st June and 1st August next.

The May Gazette includes an Article on the topic by Joan Fagan and John Furlong of William Fry Solicitors. Rory O'Donnell, who is a member of the Committee has also prepared a paper on the subject of the Building Regulations and the Committee has decided to circulate a copy of this which covers the main provisions of the Act and Regulations.

We are aware Solicitors are anxious to know the Committee's views in relation to necessary changes in contracts and requisitions.

General Condition 36 of the Contract will required to be altered by adding in an additional warranty that all development to which the Building Regulations applied have been carried out in accordance with the terms of the Act and Regulations. The provisions about Building Bye-Laws will not be deleted yet because they will apply where appropriate to buildings started up to the 1st June 1992 and all buildings which are built on foot of the transitional arrangements. In the Committee's opinion a substantial percentage of the new buildings which will be constructed over the next year or so in the Building Bye-Law areas will be carried out on foot of the transitional arrangements which will apply for some years, and these development will not have to comply with the Building Regulations. For example of a developer applies for a planing permission and building bye-laws approval on 30th May 1992 it may receive Bye-Laws Approval in say three months time, Planning Permission in say six months time and be entitled to build availing of the transitional arrangements for the life of that planning permission, without having to concern itself with the new building regulations.[13]

Pending the revision of the printed contract this should be dealt with by Special Condition.

It seems to the Committee that the investigation of the position in relation to Fire Safety Certificate will be a matter which should be dealt with pre-contract. Rory O'Donnell's suggested pre-contract requisition is as follows:

Has there been in relation to the property any development (including change of use) to which the Building Control Act 1990 and any Regulations made thereunder apply?

---

[12] *The Law Society Newsletter*, May 1992.
[13] The 1995 edition of the Law Society Conditions of sale now incorporates a warranty in respect of the Building Control Act 1990. See also p.318, above.

In respect of any such development furnish (where applicable):

1. A copy of the commencement notice given
2. A copy of the entire application for the Fire Safety Certificates;
3. A copy of the Fire Safety Certificates issued; and
4. A Certificate of Opinion by an Architect or a suitably qualified person confirming that the works or change of use to which the Building Regulations apply have been carried out in substantial compliance with the Building Regulations.

NOTE: The reason for asking for a copy of the Application is that the Regulations made under the Building Control Act do not oblige the Building Control Authority to retain for inspection copies of the Application and it is anticipated that problems will arise in future due tot he inability of Architects and other professionals to get access to documentation upon which the Fire Safety Certificate was granted. Obviously a copy of the Application would not be essential if one received a satisfactory Certificate of Compliance.

The Committee has been advised that a new house costing £50,000 in Dublin would cost about £1,000 more to be built in compliance with the new standards. The regulations are unlikely to have any marked effect on the cost of construction of commercial or industrial buildings most of which have been built to an equal standard over the last five years or so.

A sub-Committee of the Conveying Committee has commenced discussions with the representatives of the Royal Institute of Architects of Ireland over the form of Certificate of Opinion that Architects will give in relation to compliance with Building Regulations. It will obviously be some time before the issues arising and any form of certificate will be resolved but in the meantime the Committee's preliminary view is that solicitors will want Certificates of Opinion of substancial compliance with Building Regulations in relation to new structures and buildings which have been materially altered or undergone a change of use in accordance with the usual form. Architects are concerned about the strict liability involved under the Act and the liabilities they may incur by giving certificates. They are happy to certify that the design of a building complies with the Building Regulations when they have actually designed it. There are obvious difficulties where part of the relevant design was carried out by a Structural or Mechanical and Electrical Engineer. Should the Architects get certificates from these other professional and include them in an overall certificate? Also if the building contains a lift the lift may be designed by the manufacturer. The greatest problem seems to be in relation to speculative developments. Normally the Architect designs the development and gets planning permission but then has no involvement at all until house are finished when the architect would carry out a superficial inspection for the purposes of planning and bye laws certification. The responsibility to build in accordance with the design and the Building Regulations is on the Builders. Some Architects feel that they could not certify compliance with the construction phase under the Building Regulation unless they or the Building Control Authority monitored compliance with construction. The Conveyancing Committee will do what it can to address these issues and will have the profession notified as soon as anything meaningful is resolved.

The Conveyancing Committee suggests the Solicitors should ensure that clients embarking on new building projects should get the whole issue of certification and the forms to be given sorted out at the time the Architects and other members of the design team are appointed.

A.13 NOTES EXTRACTED FROM PRE-CONTRACT REQUISITIONS ON THE BUILDING CONTROL ACT 1990 AND THE BUILDING REGULATIONS[14]

A.13.1 Note 1 and 2

Note 1. While Building Control Authorities keep a register for their own use the regulations do not give the public a right of access to it and after a lapse of time it may prove difficult and perhaps impossible to establish whether a Commencement Notice was or was not served in relation to a particular development. It is clearly very important for the maintenance of good standards of building that Building Control Authorities monitor building standards. The Purpose of the Commencement Notice is to put them on notice that a development is commencing so that they can monitor a development in such a manner as they see fit, There are two points that arise in relation to a development if no Commencement Notice was served.

(a) The first is whether there is any downside for a subsequent owner from a conveyancing point of view. Carrying out a development without serving a Commencement Notice is an offence and leaves the parties involved liable to prosecution. It will not impact otherwise on a subsequent owner. Solicitors should ask if a Commencement Notice was served and for a a copy thereof. We do not feel that Solicitors should insist on a copy if it is not readily available. The Conveyancing Committee has already that solicitors for subsequent owners should not concern themselves unduly whether a Commencement Notice was served or not or whether a copy of the Commencement Notice is available or not.

---

[14] Issued with the *Law Society Gazette*, November 1994.

(b) The second point arises from the non service of a Commencement Notice is that it may have been a deliberate omission. In most cases it will turn out to be a mere oversight and in some of those cases the Building Control Authority will have carried out the usual foundation inspections by arrangement with the contractor. There may be cases however, where a contractor or developer want sot carry out work and due to something about the manner in which it is proposed to carry it out, does not wish to have the Building Control Authority know about it and be in a position to see what is done and accordingly, does not serve a Commencement Notice. This scenario is unlikely to arise if there is an architect structural engineer involved in the development and if it arises at all is more likely to happen where a builder is operating without the assistance of professionals.

What is anything can a solicitor do? In any case, where you establish that a Commencement Notice has not been served the circumstances should be investigated. If it seems to have been a genuine oversight and this is confirmed by a reputable professional or if building control was aware of the development and carried out inspections no further action should arise. If there is any reason for disquiet as to whether the omission to serve a Commencement Notice was deliberate or not you should recommend to your client to seek the advice of an architect or structural engineer to consider whether any further surveys are necessary and possibly in an extreme case, to review the decision to proceed with the purchase at all.

Note 2. While conveyancing practice is to seek a certificate from a competent person of compliance with a Fire Safety Certificate it will be important also for a property owner to be able to know what precise work was the subject of the Fire Safety Certificate. This is not a conveyancing point and is really a commercial matter of the property owner.

In situations where the property being purchased is an apartment there should be no need for the individual apartment owners to have a copy of the application so long as the management company has it.

The same would normally apply to commercial developments such as a shopping center. Ordinarily, in relation to shopping centres there would be one significant difference which is that a developer will normally get a Fire Safety Certificate in relation to the centre as a whole and in particular its common areas. The individual purchases or lessees would normally take a shop unit in its unfinished state (called shell finish) and would have to apply for and get a Fire Safety Certificate for the fit out the same.

A.14 THE LAW SOCIETY'S STANDARD GENERAL CONDITIONS OF SALE[15]

Section 22 (7) of the Building Control Act, 1990, contains a most helpful amnesty with regard to works executed prior to 13 December, 1989 in contravention of bye-laws.

Section 19 of the Local Government Planning and Development) Act, 1992, introduced important alleviations in relation to enforcement procedures under the planning legislation. There are dealt with comprehensively in an article by *John Gore-Grimes* published at page 383 et seq of the *Gazette* for December, 1992. (Vol. 86 No. 10).

A vendor, anxious to avail of the foregoing amnesty and/or alleviations or any extension thereof and to rely on same, should disclose the non-conforming matter in his Special Conditions (possibly detailing appropriate dates and other relevant data by way of Statutory Declaration), and provide (likewise by Special Condition) for any required consequential relaxation in, or departure from, the application of General Condition 36.

Failure to cover a non-confirming issue as suggested or in some other appropriate manner will mean that the full vigour of General Condition 36 will continue to operate with resultant exposure on foot of the warranties therein specified.

It should be mentioned that the latest (1991) edition of the Society's General Conditions of Sale was published prior to the coming into operation of the Building Control Act, 1990, and its attendant regulations, and same are, therefore, not referred to therein. Accordingly, any party desiring to provide for evidence of compliance with such regulations should cater for same by way of Special Condition.

Conveyancing Committee

---

[15]   *Law Society Gazette*, September 1993.

SUBJECT INDEX

Note: references are to page numbers

abandonment of planning permission, 223–24
abandonment of use
  discontinuance of use, 77–79
  doctrine of abandonment, 77–80
  extinguishment, and, 80
  intention to abandon use, 78–79
  presumption of abandonment, 78
  resumption of abandoned use, 77–80
access to information, *see also*
  planning file; public inspection of planning documents
  functions of planning authority, 2–3
access to or from motorway or busway
  refusal of permission for development involving compensation, exclusion of, 322
access to public road
  formation, laying out, or material widening of, 109
accidents, *see* emergency situations
acquisition notices (section 25), 51–52, 308
  appeals, 51–52
  registration requirement, 5
acquisition of land, *see also* purchase notices
  powers of planning authority, 11
act judicially, duty to, *see* duty to act judicially
additional copies of plans
  requests for, 160
address of proposed development, 145–46
adjoining, abutting or adjacent land
  planning conditions relating to, 205–8

adjournment
  injunction hearing, 296–97
  oral hearing, 249
administrative use, 131
adverse planning decisions
  compensation, entitlement to, 315; *see further* compensation
advertisement structures, 110
  definition, 123
  exempted development provisions, 123
  planning conditions relating to, 211, 330
    exclusion of compensation, 331
  refusal of permission for erection of
    exclusion of compensation, 321
advertisements
  definition, 123
  exempted development provisions, 123
  exhibition of
    buildings of artistic, architectural or historic interest, 110
    refusal of permission for, 321
  planning conditions relating to
    exclusion of compensation, 331
  repair and tidying of
    powers of planning authorities, 46–47
advisors
  power of Board to engage, 250
aerodromes
  environmental impact statement, development requiring, 180, 184, 185
afforestation, 86, 180
  exempted development provisions
    removal of exempted development status, 87

agreement
    conditions stipulating matters to be
        left to, 196–200
    development or use of land,
        regulating, 38–39
        registration requirement, 4
    planting of trees, shrubs and other
        plants
        registration requirement, 5
    public right of way, preserving,
        45
agricultural planning unit, 89–90
agricultural structures
    exempted development provisions,
        124–25
        threshold area, 125
    farm buildings, 361
agricultural use
    agricultural processes, 90
    ancillary agricultural uses, 89
    definition of "agriculture", 88–89
    exempted development provisions,
        86, 87–90
    farm gate sales, 89–90
    housing of animals, 124
    intensive use, 87
    keeping and breeding of animals,
        88–89
    occasional killing of animals, 90
    storage use, change to, 64–65
agriculture, *see also* agricultural use
    definition, 88–89
    development works
        exempted development
            provisions, 125–27
    environmental impact statements,
        development requiring, 180–81
    fences, improvement or removal
        of, 125
    field drainage works, 125
    hill grazing, improvement of, 125
    intensive agriculture, 180
    land reclamation, 125, 180, 181
    pig-rearing installations, 180
    poultry-rearing installations, 180
    water-management projects, 180
air navigation, 327, 331

air pollution, 191
    definition, 192
    licences
        works necessary to comply
            with, 121
        refusal of permission on grounds
            of, 327
aircraft manufacturing installations,
    182
aircraft safety, 327, 331
airfields, 120
alteration of development plan
    material alteration, 25, 26–27
alteration of hedge
    notice requiring, 43–44
alteration of structure
    building regulations, 364
    carrying out of works for
        exempted development
            provisions, 86
    interior of structure, 92–93
    notices requiring
        section 31 notices, 300
        section 36 notices, 307
    unauthorised alterations, 347
alterations
    definition, 54
alterations to proposed development
    revised plans, drawings etc., 161
alternative development
    notice as to, 318–19
        duration of, 319
        specified development, 319
amenities, *see also* special amenity
        area orders
    development for amenity
        purposes
        exempted development
            provisions, 119
    preservation of, *see* preservation of
        amenity
    serious injury to
        refusal of permission on
            grounds of, 327
    views or prospects, *see* views or
        prospects of special amenity
            value

amusement arcades, 127
  change of use from, 117,
    129
ancillary use, 64, 65–66
  agricultural use, uses ancillary to,
    89
  composite or concurrent uses,
    67–68
  functional dependence,
    69–70
  intensification of use, 66
  material change of use, 66
  new ancillary uses, 65
  "ordinarily incidental", 66–67
  physical and functional separation,
    68–71
  primary use inactive, where, 71
  severance of link with primary
    use, 72
  shops, 130
  subordinate use, 65
animal and vegetable products
  packing and canning installations,
    183
animals
  breeding and keeping of, *see also*
    agricultural use
    food production, for, 88
    grazing purposes, for, 88–89
    horses, 88, 89, 124, 127
    livestock, 88
    pig-rearing installations, 180
  housing and keeping of
    exempted development
      provisions, 124, 127
    sporting or recreational
      purposes, for, 88–89, 127
  occasional killing of animals kept
    on a farm, 90
announcements (advertisements),
  123
antennae
  telecommunications antennae,
    118
  wireless and television antennae,
    114
apartment blocks, 64n

appeals
  Bord Pleanála, to, 239
    acquisition notices (section 25),
      51–52
    conservation orders, 44
    hedge removal or alteration
      notices, 43
    planning applications,
      determinations on, *see*
        planning appeals
    tree preservation orders, 42
  High Court, to
    section 5 references,
      determinations on, 85
    removal or alteration of structure,
      notice requiring (section 36),
        307
  Supreme Court, to
    judicial review applications,
      262
applicant
  judicial review applications
    locus standi, 272–73
  planning permission, for, *see*
    planning applicant
applications
  approval, for, 153–55
  leave to apply for judicial review,
    257–58, 258–59
  outline permission, for, *see* outline
    permission
  planning injunction (section 27
    proceedings), *see* planning
      injunctions
  planning permission, for, *see*
    planning applications
appropriate period, *see also* time
  limits
  determination of planning
    application, 212–14
  extension of period, 160
  life of planning permission,
    230
appropriate planning unit
  determination of, *see* planning unit
appropriation of land
  powers of planning authority, 11

approval
    applications for, 153–54
        contents, 155
        parameters of outline
            permission binding, 154
        specified part of development,
            153
    meaning, 153
    types of, 136
aqueducts, 14, 185
arbitration
    compensation claims, 316
archaeological, geological or
    historical interest
    caves, sites, features and other
        objects of
        conditions relating to
            preservation of, 331
        development objectives for
            preservation of, 50–51
        excavation of, 51, 122
architects' certificates, *see* certificates
    of compliance
architectural interest
    buildings and features of, *see*
        artistic, architectural or historic
        interest
army barracks
    exempted development provisions,
        104, 120
art galleries, 134
arterial drainage
    exempted development provisions,
        104, 120
artificial mineral fibre installations,
    185
artistic, architectural or historic
    interest
    buildings or structures of,
        109–10
        conditions relating to
            preservation of, 331
        demolition of, 321
        development plan providing for
            preservation of, 24, 50
        exhibition of advertisements,
            use for, 110

artistic, architectural or historic
    interest—*contd.*
    buildings or structures of—*contd.*
        listed buildings, 50
        painting of, 116
    fixtures or features of
        conditions relating to
            preservation of, 331
        development plan objectives,
            inclusion in, 50, 86–87
Arts Council, 159
asbestos extraction, 179
asbestos processing, 179
assessment of compensation
    rules for, 334–37
assignment of compensation
    prohibition on, 321
athletics
    laying out and use of lands for
        exempted development
        provisions, 119
atmospheric emissions, 191
Attorney General's office
    exempted development provisions,
        104
audi alteram partem, 245, 263, 266
authorised persons
    entry on land, powers of, 254

balloons (advertisement structure),
    123
banks, 131
barns, 124
bazaars, 122
beacons, 122
bed and breakfast accommodation
    conversion of private houses into,
        111
betting offices, 130–31
bingo halls, 134
bituminous shale, extraction of, 181
boats
    keeping or storage of, 115
Bord Fáilte Éireann, 25, 44, 159,
    253
Bord Gáis, An, 118
    "statutory undertaker", as, 92

Bord Pleanála, An, 25, 237
  Chairman, 237–38
  composition, 237–38
  duty to act judicially, 245
  powers and functions, 238–39
    appeals generally, 42, 43, 44,
      51–52, 239
    conditions, imposition of,
      197–200
    consultants or advisors,
      engagement of, 250
    disputes, determination of, 239
    financial contributions,
      determination of, 238
    modification to planning
      application, invitation to
      submit, 254–55
    planning appeals, 238, 251–52;
      see also determination of
      planning appeals;
      planning appeals
    planning applications,
      determination of, *see*
      determination of planning
      applications
    section 5 references,
      determination of, 85, 238
    vexatious or frivolous appeals,
      dismissal of, 251
    withdrawal of planning
      application, declaration as
      to, 160, 164
  quorum for meetings, 238
  unlawful communications with,
    238
Bord Telecom Éireann, 118, 253
  "statutory undertaker", as, 92
breaches of planning code, *see also*
  enforcement notices; enforcement
    of planning control; offences
  injunction applications (section
    27), *see* planning injunction
  penalties, *see* penalties for offences
  prosecution, *see* prosecution of
    offences
  section 31 notices, 300–301
  section 32 notices, 301

breaches of planning code—*contd.*
  section 35 notices, 302
  technical or trivial breaches, 286
  warning notices, 305–7
brewing industry, 183
bridge construction projects
  environmental impact statements,
    requiring, 184
  notification requirements, 14
bridge orders, 22
broadcast relay services
  connections to premises, 123
broadleaf forest
  replacement by conifer species, 87
building bye-laws, 360, 366
  vendor's warranty (General
    Conditions of Sale), 340–45
  works carried out prior to
    December 13, 1989, 342–43
building control, 359–67, *see also*
  building regulations
  building bye-laws, 360, 366
    vendor's warranty (General
      Conditions of Sale), 340–45
  fire safety certificates, 363–64
  legislation, 359–60
  practice notes, 395–98
  requisitions on title
    replying to, 375–77
building line
  development beyond, 109
  infringement of
    refusal of permission on
      grounds of, 327
building regulations, 360
  alteration or extension of existing
    buildings, 364
  application, 360, 364
  carrying out of works in
    compliance with exempted
    development provisions,
    107, 120n
  commencement notices, 361
    exemption from requirement,
      362
  definitions, 362
  dispensations/relaxations, 365

building regulations—*contd.*
  enforcement, 365
  exemptions, 361
  fire safety certificates, 363–64; *see
    also* fire safety certificates
  liability, 365
  penalties for offences, 365
  practice notes, 395–98
  sections, 360
  services fittings and equipment,
    365
  Technical Guidance Documents,
    360
  vendor's warranty of compliance
    with
    Law Society General
      Conditions of Sale, 341,
      345
building societies, 131
buildings, *see also* structures
  artistic, architectural or historic
    interest, of, *see* artistic,
    architectural or historic interest
  demolition, *see* demolition
  listed buildings, 50
  murals on, 116
  provision of
    powers of planning authority, 12
buoys, 122
Burdle principles, 63, 64, 67–71
burial grounds, 14, 122
busway schemes, 49, 193, 322

cables, wires, pipelines
  connections to premises, 123
  inspection, repair, renewal,
    removal or alteration
    exempted development
      provisions, 86, 91
  licences, 47–48
  overhead lines or cables
    construction of, 111
callows
  reclamation of, 125
canalisation projects
  environmental impact statements,
    development requiring, 184

car parking facilities
  curtilage of dwellinghouse, within,
    115
  planning conditions relating to,
    208, 330
  provision in excess of
    immediate needs, 208–9
caravans
  increase in number of, 77
  keeping or storage of
    curtilage of dwellinghouse,
      within, 115
  storage of, 133
casual trading area
  use of land for
    exempted development
      provisions, 86, 99
caves, sites, features
  archaeological, geological or
    historical interest, *see*
      archaeological, geological
      or historical interest
cellulose production installations,
  184
cement manufacture installations, 181
Central Fisheries Board, 25
central heating system
  provision for dwellinghouse, 113
certificates of compliance, 344–45,
  354–55
  building regulations, compliance
    with, 396–97, 398
  check list, 355–56
  date from which certificates must
    be obtained, 379
  forms of, 386–88
    Law Society forms, 354,
      388–91
    RIAI forms, 354, 355, 391–93
  Law Society General Conditions
    of Sale, 344–45
  planning conditions, compliance
    with
    when estate in charge, 380–81
  practice notes, 378–93
  private residential property,
    379–80

certificates of compliance—*contd.*
  qualification of persons offering
    certificates, 356–57
  practice notes, 381–84
  speculative housing developments
    architects' certificates, 384–86
certiorari, *see also* judicial review
  error on the face of the record,
    264–65
cessation of use, *see* abandonment;
  discontinuance of use
change of use, *see also* material
  change of use
  building regulations, application
    of, 360
  exempted development provisions,
    117
  changes within use classes,
    127–34; *see also* use classes
character of structure
  meaning of "character", 93
  works rendering appearance
    inconsistent with, 93
chemical industry
  environmental impact statements,
    development requiring, 180,
    183
Chief State Solicitor's office
  exempted development provisions,
    104
Chomhairle Ealaíon, an, 25, 253
churchyards, 122
CIE (Córas Iompair Éireann), 92,
  253
cinemas, 134
Circuit Court
  planning injunction applications,
    277–78
  practice and procedure (Order
    67A), 293–95
circuses, 122
clay, extraction of, 181
clinics
  medical services, provision of,
    133–34
clubs, 134
  residential, 133

coal
  extraction of, 181
  industrial briquetting, 181
coastal protection
  land reclamation works, 126
coke ovens, 181
commencement notices (building
  regulations), 361
  exemptions from requirement, 362
commercial brewing and distillation,
  183
Commissioners of Public Works in
  Ireland, 25, 100, 103, 159, 253,
  337
  arterial drainage schemes
    exempted development
      provisions, 104, 120
  development by, development by,
    13; *see also* State authorities
  nature reserves, 119
  pollution monitoring facilities
    exempted development
      provisions, 119–20
common good, interests of, 1, 91
  limitation of property rights, 313
community centres, 134
community structures or facilities
  maintenance of, 122
company, 337
  planning injunction sought against,
    281–82
compensation, 313 *et seq.*
  alternative development, notice as
    to (section 13), 318–19, 320
  assessment of, rules for, 316,
    334–37
  reduction in value of land,
    determination of, 316,
    334–37
  assignment of, prohibition on, 321
  consolidation of law, 314
  determination of claims, 316
    amount payable, assessment of,
      316, 334–37
    arbitration, 316
  double compensation, prohibition
    against, 316

compensation—*contd.*
  entitlement to, 30, 315
    discontinuance of use, notice
      requiring, 333
    felling consent, refusal of, 333
    other circumstances in which
      compensation payable, 332
    prima facie entitlement, 313,
      315
    removal of structure, notice
      requiring, 333
    revocation or modification or
      permission, 333
    section 36 notices, 307, 333
    section 37 notices, 308, 333
  evidence in support of claim,
    notice requesting, 317
  exclusions, 30, 315
    conditions not attracting
      compensation, 329–31
    material contravention of
      zoning objective, 314
    power of Minister to order
      payment, 319–20
    refusals not attracting
      compensation, 323–29
    road development, 322
    Roads Act 1993, under, 332
    Second Schedule, 321–22
    Third Schedule, 323–29
  form of claims, 316–17
    information to be included in
      claim, 316
  interest in land, 315
  Minister's power to order
    payment, 319–20
    restrictions on power, 320
    time for making applications,
      320
  new code (1990 Act), 314
  notice preventing, 318–19
  notification of claims, 317
  payment of
    function of planning authority, 3
    Minister's power to order,
      319–20
    registration requirement, 5, 317

compensation—*contd.*
  prima facie entitlement, 313,
    315
    qualifications, 315
  recovery by planning authority,
    317–18
    amount repayable, 318
    instalments, 318
    obligation to repay, 317–18
    successors in title, applicable
      to, 318
  reduction in value of land,
    determination of, 316, 334
  registration of payments in
    planning register, 317
  replacement of demolished or
    destroyed structures, 320
  time limit for bringing of claims,
    316
  vendor's warranty
    Law Society General
      Conditions of Sale, 340
compensation statements, 317–18
  registration requirement, 5
completion of development
  condition requiring security for,
    see security for satisfactory
      completion
composite or concurrent uses
  second rule in *Burdle*, 67–68
compulsory acquisition
  open spaces
    section 25 notices, 51–52, 308
  powers of planning authority, 11
  road development purposes
    refusal of permission excluding
      compensation, 322
concert halls, 134
concurrent uses, 67–68
conditions attached to planning
  permission, *see* planning
    conditions
confectionery and syrup manufacture,
  183
conifer forest
  broadleaf high forest, replacing,
    87

conservation orders, 40, 44
 offences, 44
 registration requirement, 5
Constitution of Ireland
 property rights, 139
  development plan and, 24,
   29–30
  limitation in interests of
   common good, 313
constitutional justice, *see* natural and
 constitutional justice
consultants
 power of Board to engage, 250
consultation with prescribed bodies,
 9, 188
continuance of unauthorised use
 applications for permission,
  136–37
 determination of, 189–90
contributions towards local authority
 expenditure
 planning conditions requiring, *see*
  financial contributions
convents, 133
conversions to dwellinghouse
 exempted development provisions,
  112–13
conveyancing
 building control
  building bye-laws, 366
  building regulations, 359–66
  fire safety certificates, 363–64
  Fire Services Act, 367
  multi-storey buildings, 367
  requisitions on title, replies to,
   375–77
 certificates of compliance, *see*
  certificates of compliance
 planning conditions, 357–59
 planning warranty (Law Society
  General Conditions of Sale),
  53, 340–45
 time limits on enforcement,
  345–48
 practice notes, *see* practice notes
 purchasing with benefit of
  planning permission, 353–54

conveyancing—*contd.*
 requisitions on title, replies to
  building control requisitions,
   375–77
  planning requisitions, 367–75
  "subject to planning" special
   conditions, 348–50
  specimen conditions, 350–53
Coras Iompair Éireann (CIE), 253
 "statutory undertaker", as, 92
corporation
 development by, *see also* local
  authority development
  exempted, 86
 planning authority, as, 1; *see also*
  planning authorities
costs
 planning appeals, 255
councillors, *see* elected members of
 local authority
county council
 development by, *see also* local
  authority development
  exempted, 86
 planning authority, as, 1; *see also*
  planning authorities
courthouses
 exempted development provisions,
  104, 120
courts, role of, 256
 supervisory jurisdiction, *see*
  judicial review
creches, 134
crop-growing, 88
crude-oil refineries, 179
cultural events, 122
curtilage of a dwellinghouse, *see also*
 dwellinghouse
 "curtilage", meaning of, 94–95
 development within
  exempted development
   provisions, 112–15
 "dwellinghouse", meaning of,
  95–96
 uses within
  exempted development
   provisions, 86, 94–99

Dáil Éireann
    office buildings or other
        premises
        exempted development
            provisions, 104
dairy farming, 88; *see also*
    agricultural use
damages
    breach of statutory duty
        delayed grant of planning
            permission, 216
dams, 14, 184
dance halls, 134
day centres, 134
day nurseries, 134
decision-making powers, 262–63
    abdication of jurisdiction
        conditions leaving matters to
            agreement, 196–200
    judicial review, *see* judicial review
decision-making procedure
    determination of planning
        applications, 212–20
decisions, *see* planning decisions
default decisions, 214–15
    extension of duration of planning
        permission, 233–34
    mandamus, 270
        time limit, applicability of,
            271
Defence Forces
    structures or facilities
        exempted development
            provisions, 104
definitions, *see* words and phrases
delay
    injunction applications, 285
demolition, 110
    artistic, architectural or historical
        interest, building of
        refusal of permission excluding
            compensation, 321
    exempted development provisions,
        121–22
    extension or conversion of
        dwellinghouse, ancillary to,
            113, 121–22

demolition—*contd.*
    habitable house, 121
        exclusion of compensation,
            321, 331
dental services, 131
Department of Defence
    exempted development provisions,
        104
Department of the Environment
    Advice and Guidelines (1982),
        152
    Technical Guidance Documents
        (building regulations), 360
Department of Foreign Affairs
    exempted development provisions,
        104
Department of Justice
    exempted development provisions,
        104
Department of the Taoiseach
    exempted development provisions,
        104
description of proposed development
    newspaper notices, information in,
        146–48
designation of areas for
    environmental protection, 49–50
determination of claims for
    compensation, 316
    arbitration, 316
    reduction in value of land,
        assessment of, 316
determination of planning appeals,
    251–55
    costs, award of, 255
    irrelevant considerations
        risk of environmental pollution,
            254
    jurisdiction of Board,
        251–52
    material contravention of
        development plan, 251
    modification of planning
        applications, 254–55
    notification of decision, 255
    powers of entry and ancillary
        powers, 254

determination of planning
appeals—*contd.*
relevant considerations,
252–54
area outside area of planning
authority, probable effects
on, 253
development plan, 252
environmental impact
statements, 252
environmental quality
objectives, 252
general policy directives, 252
grounds of appeal, 252–53
nature and extent of relevant
development, 253
planning conditions, 252
policies and objectives of
public authorities, 253–54
proper planning and
development, 252
special amenity area orders, 252
terms of previous permission or
approval, 253
third-party submissions, 252–53
determination of planning
applications, 6, 186
abdication of jurisdiction
planning conditions, through,
196–200
compensation provisions, 315; *see
also* compensation
conditions, imposition of,
193–212, *see also* planning
conditions
consultation with prescribed
bodies, 188
continuance of unauthorised use
permission for, 189–90
decision-making powers, 186–87,
262–63
abdication of, 196–200
decision-making procedure
material contravention
procedure, 212
time for determination,
212–14

determination of planning
applications—*contd.*
default decisions, 214–15
appeals, 215
damages for delayed grant,
216
mandamus, 216
duties of planning authority, 6
obligation to act judicially, 186,
217
environmental impact assessment,
177
executive function, 217
fair procedures, 263
IPC licensing control, and
interface between, 190–93
material contravention of
development plan, 190
statutory procedure, 212, 213
natural and constitutional justice,
263
public participation in
decision-making process, 188
reasons for decision, 221–22
relevant considerations, 187–89
Bord Pleanála, 189
common good, 189
development plan, 32–33,
187–88
environmental impact
assessment, 188
EU Member States, views of,
188
general policy directives, 189
government policy, 188, 189
pollution, 190–92
proper planning and
development, 6, 187, 189
special amenity area orders, 39,
187
retention of unauthorised structure
permission for, 189–90
section 4 resolutions, 7, 217–20
time limit, 212–14
default decisions, 214–15
maximum period, 213
minimum period, 164, 212–13

determination of planning
    applications—*contd.*
  time limit—*contd.*
    requests for further information
      and, 160
development, 53
  agreements regulating, 4, 38–39
  definitions, 53
    specific situations, 55–57
    sub-division of dwellings,
      56–57
    "works" and "use", 53–55
  disputes as to
    section 5 references, 85
  exempted from permission
    requirements, *see* exempted
      development
  intensification of use, 73–77
  local authority, by, *see* local
    authority development
  material change of use, 53, 54–71;
    see also material change of use
  obligation to obtain planning
    permission, 53, 135–36
    exemption from, *see* exempted
      development
    prosecution for breach, 304–5
  planning authorities, by, 3, *see*
    also local authority
    development
    exempted development
      provisions, 12–14
    powers of planning authority, 3,
      9, 10–14
    specific powers, 11–12
  planning unit
    determination of, 62–71; *see*
      also planning unit
  "specified development"
    environmental impact
      assessment regulations, 85,
      155, 169, 179–85
  State authorities, by, *see* State
    authorities, development by
development control, 186
  functions of planning authority,
    2

Development Control – Advice and
    Guidelines, 195
development objectives
  artistic, historic or architectural
    interest, features of, 86–87
  discretionary objectives, 22 •
  mandatory objectives, 21–22 ·
  written statement of, 22–23 ·
  zoning, 21, *see also* zoning
development plan, 20
  adoption, 27
    notification requirements, 27
  co-ordination of development
    plans, 28
  constitutionality of, 24, 29–30
  contents, 20–23
    maps, 22, 23
    written statement of objectives,
      22–23
  copies of, issue of, 27
  discretionary objectives, 22
  draft plan, 24
    material alteration, 25
    notification requirements, 24–25
    objections to, 24
    submissions, 24
  interpretation, 30–32
  local authority development, and,
    33–37
  mandatory objectives, 21–22
  material alteration, 26–27
  material change of use, relevance
    for, 61–62
  material contravention, *see also*
    material contravention of
      development plan
    grant of planning permission,
      33, 190, 212, 268–70
  Minister's powers in relation to,
    28–29
  notification requirements, 24–25
  objections, 24
  obsolete areas, designation of,
    29–30
  order of priority
    development premature on
      grounds of, 325

development plan—*contd.*
planning applications and, 32–33,
187–88
planning authority to "have regard
to", 32, 187–88
policy formulation, 22, 28
preparation of
obligation to make and review
plan, 20, 24
powers of Minister in relation
to, 28–29
reserved function, 20
review of, 20
road development and, 23
variation of, 26
power of Minister to request,
28
zoning, 21; *see also* zoning
down-zoning, 29–30
rezoning, 27–28
development works, *see* works
direct effect, doctrine of, 168–69
Director of Public Prosecutions,
office of
exempted development provisions,
104
directors of company
planning injunction sought against,
281–82
disabled persons
residence for, 117, 134
discontinuance of use
abandonment
doctrine of abandonment,
77–80
intention of abandonment,
78–79
presumption of abandonment,
78
resumption of abandoned use,
77–80
extinguished use, resumption of,
80–81
notices requiring
compensation, entitlement to,
333
registration requirement, 4

discontinuance of use—*contd.*
notices requiring—*contd.*
section 31 notices, 300
section 37 notices, 308, 333
planning conditions requiring, 211
discovery of documents
leave to apply for judicial review,
259–60
dismissal of planning appeal
vexatious or frivolous appeals,
251
display of goods for sale
structure used for, 129
distribution of minerals
use for, 127
docks, harbours, quays
development for industrial
purposes
exempted development
provisions, 117–18
documents, *see* planning documents
domestic waste disposal, 185
domestic water supply
exempted development provisions
(Class 40), 123
double compensation, prohibition
against, 316
down-zoning, 29–30, 329
drainage, *see also* arterial drainage
field drainage, 125
drains, 330
curtilage of dwellinghouse, within,
114
drilling
exploratory drilling or excavation,
123
geothermal, 181
minerals prospecting, 123
storage of nuclear waste material,
for, 181
dry cleaners, 129
Dublin
new administrative counties, 13, 91
Dublin County Council
Programme for the Settlement of
Travelling Peoples, 34
Dun Laoghaire-Rathdown, 13, 91

duration of planning permission, 222,
229–30, 310, 354
extension of, 231–34, 354
default, by, 233–34
duty to act judicially, 256
Bord Pleanála, 245
elected representatives
section 4 resolutions, 217,
219–20
planning authorities, 186,
217
dwelling
demolition of, 121
sub-division of, 56–57
dwellinghouse
bed and breakfast accommodation,
conversion to, 111–12
buildings for recreational or
storage purposes, 361
"curtilage", meaning of, 94–95
definition, 95–96
development within curtilage of
caravans and boats, 115
central heating system,
provision of, 113
exempted development
provisions, 112–15
extensions and conversions,
112–13, 121–22
garages, sheds and similar
structures, 113
gates, walls and fences, 114,
115
hard surfacing, 115
paths, drains, ponds and
landscaping works, 114
patio areas, 115
porches, 109, 115, 122
satellite dishes, 114
planning unit, 70
reconversion to single occupation,
117
single storey extensions, 361
uses within curtilage of
"curtilage", meaning of, 94–96
"dwellinghouse", meaning of,
95–96

dwellinghouse—*contd.*
uses within curtilage of—*contd.*
exempted development
provisions, 86, 94–99
garages used for living
purposes, 98–99
"incidental to the enjoyment of
the dwelling as such", 96–99
reasonableness, necessity for,
97–98

educational events, 122
effluent storage facilities, 124
EIS, *see* environmental impact
statement
elastomer-based products,
installations for, 184
elected members of local authority
re-zoning decisions, 27–28
reserved functions, 7, 9, 40, 48
section 4 resolutions, 7, 217–20
electricity installations, 181
Electricity Supply Board (ESB), 25,
254
"statutory undertaker", as, 92
electricity supply line
connections to premises, 123
electricity undertakings
exempted development provisions,
118
overhead lines or cables,
construction of, 111
emergency situations
development for dealing with, 15
State authorities, by, 106
employment considerations
injunction decision based on, 287
enclosure of land, 86, 110
energy industry
environmental impact statement,
development requiring, 181–82
enforcement notices, 297
building control, 365
decision to take enforcement action
relevant considerations, 297–98
direct action by planning
authority, 302

enforcement notices—*contd.*
  direction by Minister, 298
  discontinuance of use, requiring
      section 31 notices, 300
      section 37 notices, 308
  non-compliance with
      defences, 303
      penalties for offences, 303–4
      prosecution for, 302–4
  obligation to give information, 299
  registration requirement, 4, 297,
      298
  removal or alteration of structures,
      requiring
      section 31 notice, 300
      section 36 notices, 307
  section 31 notices, 300–301
      expenses, 300
      matters to be specified, 300
      time limits, 300, 310
  section 32 notices, 301
      matters to be specified, 301
      time limit, 301, 309
  section 35 notices, 302
      matters to be specified, 302
      time limit, 302, 309
  service of, 298
      modes of service, 298–99
      resumption of preceding use
          where, 82
  types of, 297
  warning notices, 305–7
  withdrawal of, 298
  works, requiring, 300
enforcement of building control, 365
  enforcement notices, 365
  entry on building, powers of, 365
  injunction procedure, 366
enforcement of planning control, 276
      et seq.
  discontinuance of use, notices
      requiring
      section 31 notices, 300
      section 37 notices, 308
  enforcement notices, *see*
      enforcement notices
  functions of planning authority, 2

enforcement of planning
      control—*contd.*
  injunctions (section 27 proceed-
      ings), *see* planning injunction
  open spaces
      acquisition notices, 308
  planning agreements, 39
  prosecution of offences
      breach of obligation to obtain
          planning permission, 304–5
      non-compliance with
          enforcement notices, 302–4
  removal or alteration of structure,
      notices requiring
      section 31 notices, 300
      section 36 notices, 307
  warning notices, 305–7
engine testing, 185
engineers' certificates, *see* certificates
      of compliance
entry on land
  powers of, 254
      building control, enforcement
          of, 365
      section 36 notices, 307
environmental assessment
  functions of planning authority, 3
environmental control
  planning control, and
      interface between, 190–93
environmental impact assessment
      (EIA), 166 *et seq.*, *see also*
          environmental impact
          statements
  definition of terms, 166–67
  EPA draft guidelines, 176
  EU Directive (1985), 166, 167–69
      aim of, 167
      application and scope, 167–68
      direct effect, 168–69
      minimum information
          requirements, 168
      public consultation, 168
  local authority development,
      18–19, 167n, 177–78
  planning applications,
      determination of, 177

environmental impact assessment
(EIA)—*contd.*
regulations, 166, 168
State authorities, development by,
178–79
environmental impact statements
(EIS)
content, 157, 174–76
EPA draft guidelines, 176
further information, 175
specified information, 174
study of alternatives, 175–76
technical detail, 175
definition, 167
development requiring, 108,
155–56, 169–72, 179–85
aerodromes, 180
agriculture, 180–81
artificial mineral fibres,
manufacture of, 185
asbestos extraction/processing,
179–80
cast-iron and steel melting
works, 179
chemical installations, 180,
183
crude-oil refineries, 179
energy industry, 181–82
engines, turbines or reactors,
test benches for, 185
exemptions from requirement,
156–57, 172–73
extractive industry, 181
food industry, 183
glass manufacture, 182
gunpowder and explosives,
manufacture of, 185
hazardous waste disposal
installations, 180
holiday villages, 185
infrastructure projects, 184–85
inland waterways, 180
knackers' yards in built-up
areas, 185
metal processing, 182
non-compliance with
requirement, 169–70

environmental impact statements
(EIS)—*contd.*
radioactive waste installations,
179
railway lines (long-distance),
180
rubber industry, 184
scrap iron storage, 185
significant environmental
effects, 173
sludge-deposition sites, 185
"specified development", 85,
155, 169, 179–85
textile, leather, wood and paper
industries, 183–84
thermal power stations, 179
trading ports, 180
waste disposal installations, 185
waste water treatment plants,
185
local authority development,
177–78
planning applications,
accompanying, 155–57
outline applications, 157
persons or bodies to be notified,
159
purchase of copies of, 163
registration requirement, 4, 5
specified development, 85, 155,
169, 179–85
State authorities, development by,
178–79
environmental pollution, *see*
pollution control
Environmental Protection Agency,
159
EIS draft guidelines, 176
IPC licensing control
planning control, interface with,
190–93
pollution monitoring facilities
exempted development
provisions (Class 42),
119–20
error on the face of the record,
264–65

ESB (Electricity Supply Board), 92,
254
estuarine marsh land
reclamation of, 125
EU Member States
submissions or observations on
planning appeal, 245
views of
planning authority to consider,
188
European Union law
direct effect, doctrine of, 168–69
environmental impact assessment
directive (1985), 167–69; *see
further* environmental impact
assessment
examination
powers of planning authority, 8
excavations
sites, features etc
archaeological, geological or
historical interest, of, 51, 123
executive functions, 7
determination of planning
applications, 217
exempted development, 84–85
advertisements, 123
agricultural purposes,
development for, 125–27
agricultural structures (Classes
6–8), 124–25
agricultural use, 86, 87–90
amenity or recreational purposes,
development for (Classes
30–32), 119
archaeological and other
excavations, 122
arterial drainage works (Class 46),
120
bed and breakfast accommodation
conversion of private house
into, 111–12
building regulations, works in
compliance with, 107, 120n
cables, wires, pipelines
inspection, repair, renewal,
removal or alteration, 86, 91

exempted development—*contd.*
casual trading area
use of land for, 86, 99
categories, 84
certain changes of use (Class 13),
117
community structures or facilities,
maintenance of, 122
conditions and limitations, 107
connections to premises (Class
44), 123
definitions, 107
demolition of building or structure
(Class 45), 121–22
disputes as to
section 5 references, 85
domestic water supply or group
water schemes (Class 40), 123
dwellinghouse, *see also*
dwellinghouse
development within curtilage
of, 112–15
uses within curtilage of, 86,
94–99
environmental impact assessment,
and, 85
exploratory drilling or excavation
(Class 41), 123
external works, 86, 93–94
fences, improvement or removal
of, 125
field drainage, 125
forestry purposes, development
for, 125–27
forestry use, 86, 87
gates, walls and fences, 116
general, 112–23
hill grazing, improvement of, 125
horses, ponies and greyhounds,
structures for, 127
industrial purposes, development
for, 117–18
internal works, 86, 92–93
land reclamation, 86, 99, 125–26
local authority development, 86,
91; *see also* local authority
development

exempted development—*contd.*
  local events, 122
  minerals and petroleum
    prospecting (Class 5), 124
  navigational aids, 122
  notices, development required by,
    82, 120–21
  painting of structures, 116
  planning condition, development
    required by, 82–83
  pollution control
    IPC licence condition,
      development in compliance
      with, 107
    monitoring facilities (Class 42),
      119–20
  practice notes, 394–95
  public agencies, development by,
    118, 119
    arterial drainage works (Class
      46), 120
    foreign visits, facilities for
      (Class 35), 119
    Garda Síochána security works
      (Class 48), 120
    national flags and emblems
      (Class 34), 119
    pollution monitoring facilities
      (Class 42), 119–20
    public buildings, works within
      curtilage of (Class 47), 120
  public sector development, 84
  recurrent uses, interchange of, 82
  regulations (1994), 106–12
    conditions and limitations
      (article 9), 107
    definitions, 107
    restrictions on *prima facie*
      exemptions (article 10),
      108–11
    specific exemptions under
      article 11, 111–12
    use classes, 111
  removal of exempted development
    status
    prescribed categories of
      development, 87

exempted development—*contd.*
  restrictions on exemptions, 108–11
  resumption of use
    enforcement notice served,
      where, 82
    expiration of temporary
      permission, on, 82
  road development, 86, 91
  rural development, 123–27
  seasonal uses, 68
  section 4 of 1963 Act, 86–99
  section 5 references, 85
  State authorities, certain
    development by, 103–6,
    119–20; *see also* State
    authorities
  statutory notices, licences or
    certificates
    works necessary to comply
      with, 82, 120–21
  statutory provisions, 84
  statutory undertakers,
    development by, 86, 91–92, 118
  telecommunications (Class 29),
    118
  temporary structures or uses, 117,
    122
    facilities for foreign visits
      (Class 35), 117
  "use", definition of, 85
  use classes, 111, 127–34
    specific exemptions, 111–12
exhibition halls, 134
exhibition of advertisements, *see*
  advertisements
existing use rights
  extinguishment of, 80
  resumption of extinguished use,
    80–81
  planning conditions restricting, 203
expenditure of local authority
  contributions to
    planning conditions requiring,
    see financial contributions
exploratory drilling or excavation
  exempted development provisions
    (Class 41), 123

extension of duration of planning
permission, 231–34
default, by, 233–34
"substantial works", 232
extensions to dwellinghouse
building bye-law approval, failure
to obtain
practice note, 393
exempted development provisions,
112–13
extinguished use
resumption of, 80–81
extractive industry
environmental impact statement,
development requiring,
181

fair procedures, 263
fairgrounds, 122
fairs, 122
farm buildings, *see* agricultural
structures
farm gate sales, 89–90
farm machinery and equipment
storage of, 89
farm produce
processing of, 90
sale from farmhouse, 89
farming, *see* agricultural use;
agriculture
fees
planning appeals, 240
planning applications, 151
felling consent
refusal of
compensation provisions,
333–34
fences
exempted development provisions,
116, 125
curtilage of dwellinghouse,
fences within, 114, 115
improvement or renewal of,
125
fencing of land, 86, 110
fibre-dyeing factories, 183

financial contributions
planning conditions requiring,
209–11, 222, 358
evidence of compliance with
[General Conditions of
Sale], 343–44
exclusion of compensation,
329–30
power of Board in relation to,
238
financial services, 130–31
fines, *see* penalties for offences
Fingal County Council, 13, 91
fire safety certificates, 363–64
exemptions from requirement, 364
pre-contract requisitions, 395–96,
398
register of applications, 364
works necessary to comply with
exempted development
provisions, 121
Fire Services Act 1981, 367
fire stations, 14
fish-farming, 88
salmonid breeding installations,
180–81
fish-meal and fish-oil factories, 183
fisheries
Regional Fisheries Boards,
development by, 120
flags
national flags and emblems
exempted development
provisions (Class 34), 119
flat
definition, 363
fire safety certificate provisions,
363
flood-relief works
environmental impact statements,
development requiring, 184
flora and fauna
conservation orders, 40, 44
flowers, *see* shrubs, plants, flowers
food industry
environmental impact statements,
development requiring, 183

food production
    creatures kept for
        "agriculture", as, 88; *see also*
            agricultural use
footpaths, *see* paths
foreign visits
    temporary structures and facilities
        exempted development
            provisions (Class 35), 119
forestry
    development works
        exempted development
            provisions, 125–27
    exempted development provisions,
        86, 87–90
        removal of exempted
            development status, 87
    fences, improvement or removal
        of, 125
    initial afforestation, 180
    land reclamation works, 125
    replacement of broadleaf high
        forest by conifer species, 87
Forfas, 25, 254
fossil fuels
    storage installations, 181
fraud
    planning injunction, applicability
        of, 281–82
frivolous appeals, 251
fruit growing, 88; *see also*
    agricultural use
"full" planning permission, *see*
    planning permission
    applications for, *see* planning
        applications
functional separation
    third rule in *Burdle*, 68–71
functions of planning authority, *see*
    also under planning authorities
    executive and reserved functions,
        7
funeral directors
    change of use from, 117, 129
funeral homes, 129
    change of use from, 117, 129
funfairs, 122

further information, requests for
    environmental impact statements,
        175
    planning applications, 158, 159–60
        effect of request, 160
further notices
    newspaper notices, 141–42, 146
    notice of planning application,
        161–62
further submissions or observations
    request for
        planning appeals, 245–47
future development
    planning conditions restricting,
        358–59

garages
    curtilage of dwellinghouse, within
        exempted development
            provisions, 113
    use for living purposes, 98–99
Garda Síochána
    security works
        exempted development
            provisions (Class 48), 120
    stations, premises, structures etc.
        exempted development
            provisions, 103, 104, 120
gas mains
    connections to premises, 123
gas pipelines
    environmental impact statements,
        development requiring, 184
gas undertakings
    exempted development provisions,
        118
gates
    exempted development provisions,
        116
        curtilage of dwellinghouse,
            gates within, 114
General Conditions of Sale, *see* Law
    Society General Conditions
        of Sale
general policy directives
    planning authority to have regard
        to, 189

geological interest
  caves, sites, features or other
      objects of, *see* archaeo-
          logical, geological or
          historical interest
geothermal drilling, 181
glass manufacture
  environmental impact statements,
      development requiring, 182
glasshouses, 113, 124
golf courses, 119
government buildings
  exempted development provisions,
      120
government departments
  exempted development provisions,
      104
government minister, 103, 253
  development by, *see* State
      authorities, development by
government policy
  planning authority to have regard
      to, 188, 189
grant of planning permission
  default decisions, 214–15, 270
      mandamus, 216
      time limit, applicability of,
          271
  delayed grant
      damages for, 216
  duration of, 229–30
      extension of, 231–34
      outline permission, 234
  effect of, 220
  enures for benefit of the land,
      222–24
      abandonment, doctrine of,
          223–24
  interpretation of, 224–28
      appeal documents, effect of,
          228–29
      extrinsic evidence, 226
      ordinary meaning, 227
      pre-application negotiations,
          consideration of, 226
  liability of planning authority
      arising from, 235–36

grant of planning permission—*contd.*
  material contravention of
      development plan
      statutory procedure, 33, 190,
          212, 268–70
  multiple permissions, 234–35
  obligation to make a grant,
      220–21
  section 4 resolutions, 217–20
  severable permissions, 235
  undertaking by planning authority,
      313–14
gravel, extraction of, 181
grazing land
  use of land as, 88; *see also*
      agricultural use
greenhouses, 113, 124
greyhounds
  housing and keeping of
      exempted development
          provisions, 127
group water schemes
  exempted development provisions
      (Class 40), 123
guesthouse
  use as, 133
gunpowder and explosives,
      manufacture of, 185
gymnasium, 134

habitable house
  definition, 121
  demolition, 121
      compensation, exclusion of,
          321
      conditions relating to, 331
hairdressers, 129
halting sites
  cases dealing with, 34–37
harbour authorities, 253, 337
  exempted development provisions,
      118
harbours
  environmental impact statements,
      development requiring, 184
  industrial undertaking, land used
      by, 117–18

hard surfacing
  curtilage of dwellinghouse, within,
    115
  industrial buildings, for, 117
hazardous waste, 180
health boards, 337
health centres, 133–34
hedges
  removal or alteration of
    notices requiring, 43–44
  trimming or cutting of
    notices requiring, 42n
helipads, 115
High Court
  appeals to
    section 5 references,
      determinations on, 85
  applications to
    injunctions (section 27
      proceedings), 277–78,
      292–93
    judicial review applications, *see*
      judicial review
hill grazing
  improvement of, 125
hire of domestic goods or personal
  articles
    structure used for, 129
hiring of motor vehicles, use for, 127
historic interest
  buildings, fixtures and
    features of
      generally, *see* artistic,
        architectural or historic
        interest
  caves, sites, features and other
    objects of, *see* archaeological,
      geological or historical
      interest
historic monuments
  protection of
    refusal of permission on
      grounds of, 327
hoardings, 116, 123
holiday villages, 185
home-grown produce
  sale from farmhouse, 89–90

horses
  breeding and keeping of
    exempted development
      provisions, 124, 127
  grazing purposes, for, 89
  showjumping purposes, for, 88
horticulture
  "agriculture", as, 88; *see also*
    agricultural use
hospitals, 134
hostel
  use as, 133
hotel complexes, 185
hotels, 129
houses, *see* dwellinghouse; habitable
  house; structures
hydroelectric energy production, 182

identity of planning applicant,
  143–44
illuminated signs, 123
implementation of planning
  permission, 92
improvement of structure
  carrying out of works for
    exempted development
      provisions, 86
incidental use, 65; *see also* ancillary
  use
indoor sports, use for, 134
industrial activities
  major accidental hazards, 111
industrial buildings
  changes of use, 118
  definition, 132
    building regulations, 362
  hard surface, provision of, 117
  light industrial building
    use as, 132
  storage within, 118
industrial-estate development
  projects, 184
industrial process
  definition, 132
industrial purposes, development for
  exempted development provisions,
    117–18

industrial waste disposal, 185
information
  access to
    duties of planning authority,
      2–3
    environmental impact statements,
      174–76
    further information, 175
    further information, requests for,
      158, 159–60
    interest in land, details of
      notice requiring, 8–9
    obligation to give, 299
    planning applications, on
      newspaper notices, 141
      planning file, 162–63
      site notices, 142–43
infrastructure projects
  environmental impact statements,
    development requiring,
      184–85
injunctions, *see* planning injunction
inland waterways
  development by statutory
    undertakers, 118, 119
  environmental impact assessment,
    180, 185
  ports
    environmental impact
      assessment, 180, 185
inspector
  planning appeals, 249
    powers and functions, 249, 250
  representation by, 6
integrated pollution control (IPC)
  licences, 85, 188
  development requiring, 108
  development works in compliance
    with, 107
  planning applications, 155
  planning control, and, 190–93
intellectual or physical disability,
  persons with
  residence for, 117, 134
intensification of use, 73–77
  ancillary use, 66
  composite or concurrent uses, 68

intensification of use—*contd.*
  material change of use, whether
    test to be applied (*Galway Co,
    Council v. Lackagh Rock*),
    74–76
  use class, within, 128
  shops, 129
intensive agriculture, 87, 180
interest in land
  applicant for planning permission,
    139–40, 150
  claimant for compensation, 315
  notice requiring information on,
    8–9
interim injunctions, 295
internal works
  exempted development provisions,
    86, 92–93
interpretation of development plan,
  30–32
interpretation of planning permission,
  224–28
  appeal documents, effect of,
    228–29
  pre-application negotiations,
    consideration of, 226
interpretative centres, 13
  Luggala and Mullaghmore
    decisions, 100–103
investigation
  powers of planning authority, 8
IPC licence, *see* integrated pollution
  control licence
Irish Aviation Authority, 159
Irish Land Commission, 100,
  253
Irish Planning Institute
  Sub-Committee on Planning and
    Compensation report (1988),
    313
iron and steel melting works, 179
iron foundries, 182

joinder of parties
  planning injunction applications,
    295

judicial approach
  material change of use
    differences between Irish and
      U.K. decisions, 57–60
judicial review, 256–57
  appeals to Supreme Court, 262
  application for leave to apply,
      257–58
    additional grounds, 259
    appeals to Supreme Court,
      262
    discovery, 259–60
    finality of decision of High
      Court, 258
    further affidavit evidence, 259
    grounding affidavit, 258
    interest of applicant, 260
    procedure, 258–59
    service of documentation,
      258–59
    statement of grounds, 258
    statement of opposition, 259
    "substantial grounds", 260–62
    time limit, 258–59
  bars to relief
    adequacy of appeal to Bord
      Pleanála, 273–75
    discretionary considerations,
      275
    locus standi, 272–73
    section 5 procedure more
      appropriate, 275
    time limits, 270–71
  decision-making process,
    concerned with, 257
  determination of High Court
    finality of decision, 258
  grounds for, 262–63
    default decisions, 270
    error on the face of the record,
      264–65
    failure to take account of
      relevant considerations, 267
    inadequacy of record of
      decision, 267–68
    irrelevant considerations,
      failure to exclude, 267

judicial review—*contd.*
  grounds for—*contd.*
    material contravention
      procedure not followed,
        268–70
    non-compliance with
      permission regulations, 268
    unreasonableness, 263–64
  meaning of "decision", 260
  procedure, 257–60
  time limits, 141, 270–71
  constitutionality, 271
"judicial zoning", 62

kites (advertisement structure), 123
knackers' yards, 185

land
  definition, 54
land filling, 331
land reclamation, 180
  exempted development provisions,
    86, 99, 125–26
    agricultural or forestry
      purposes, 125–26
    "primary object" of works, 99,
      126
  private individuals, by, 99
  sea, from, 181
land use zoning, *see* zoning
landscaping works
  curtilage of dwellinghouse, within,
    114
  planning condition requiring,
    208
lapse of time
  injunction applications and,
    285–86
launderette, 129
Law Society General Conditions of
    Sale
  building control, 359–67, *see also*
    building regulations
  requisitions on title, replying to,
    375–77
  works executed prior to 13
    December 1989, 399

Law Society General Conditions of
Sale—*contd.*
certificates of compliance, 344–45,
354–55
check list, 355–56
qualifications of persons giving
certificates, 356–57
RIAI standard forms, 354–55
planning conditions, 357
conditions precedent, 357–58
development works, regulating,
357
financial conditions, 358
future development, restricting,
358–59
previous permissions,
incorporating, 359
planning requisitions on title,
replying to, 367–75
planning warranty (General
Condition 36), 340–45
alterations without permission
to existing building, 347
building regulations, evidence
of compliance with, 341,
345
buildings erected without
permission, 346
certificates of compliance, 341,
344–45
"competent authority",
definition of, 342
development, meaning of,
53
financial conditions, evidence
of compliance with, 341,
343–44
licensed premises, 348
practical considerations,
345–46
production of documents, 341,
343
time limits on enforcement,
345–48
unauthorised uses, 347–48
works carried out in breach of
permission, 347

Law Society General Conditions of
Sale—*contd.*
practice notes, *see* practice notes
purchasing with the benefit of
planning permission, 353–54
"subject to planning" special
conditions, 348–49
cut-off date, 349–50
specimen conditions, 350–53
layout of development
planning conditions relating to, 330
leather industry
environmental impact statements,
development requiring, 183–84
libraries, 14, 134, 363
licences
IPC licences, *see* integrated
pollution control licences
petrol pumps etc, 47–48
works necessary to comply with
exempted development
provisions, 120–21
licensing applications
planning permission and, 310–12
previous infringements of
planning code, 311–12
life of planning permission, 229–31,
310, 354
extension of, 231–34
outline permission, 234, 354
light industrial building
definition, 132
use as
exempted development
provisions, 132
lighthouses, 122
listed buildings, 50, 126–27
painting of, 116
livestock
breeding and keeping of
"agriculture", as, 88; *see also*
agricultural use
grazing, for, 88–89
local authorities, 337, *see also*
planning authorities
development by, *see* local
authority development

local authorities—*contd.*
elected representatives, *see* elected
members of local authority
expenditure
planning conditions requiring
contributions to, *see*
financial contributions
powers and functions of, *see also*
powers and functions of
planning authority
ancillary powers, 10
compulsory acquisition, 11
executive and reserved
functions, 7, 9
general competence (Local
Government Act 1991), 9
performance of statutory
functions, 9–10
local authority development
development plan and, 33–37
material contravention of
development plan, 13, 33–37
environmental impact assessment,
15, 18–19, 167n, 177–78
exempted development provisions,
12–14, 86, 91
notification requirements, 15–17,
18–19
application of, 14
bodies to be notified, 16
categories to which
requirements do not apply,
15
decisions, notification of, 17–18
documents for public
inspection, 16–17
newspaper notices, 15–16, 18
pollution monitoring facilities
exempted development
provisions (Class 42),
119–20
report and decision of authority,
17–18
local events
use of land for
exempted development
provisions, 122

Local Government Act 1991
powers of planning authority
under, 9–10
location of land
statement of, in notice of planning
application, 145–46
locus standi
judicial review proceedings,
272–73
planning injunction, application
for, 278

maintenance of structure
carrying out of works for
exempted development
provisions, 86
manager of planning authority
executive functions, 7
section 4 resolutions and, 7,
217–20
mandamus
default decisions, 216, 270
time limit, applicability of, 271
manufacture
"industrial process", meaning of,
132
market gardens
use of land as, 88; *see also*
agricultural use
markets, 122
material alteration
development plan, 25, 26–27
fire safety certificate, requirement
of, 362
meaning of, 26, 362
material change of use, 53–55, 57
ancillary uses, 65–71
building regulations, application
of, 360
compensation, exclusion of, 321
composite or concurrent uses,
67–68
determination of materiality
development plan, relevance of,
61–62
judicial approach (U.K. and
Irish decisions), 57–60

material change of use—*contd.*
  determination of materiality—
      contd.
    "material for planning
      purposes", 60–61
    qualitative approach, 58–60,
      76
  intensification of use, 73–77
    test (*Galway County Council v.
      Lackagh Rock*), 74–76
  "judicial zoning", 62
  planning unit, *see also* planning
      unit
    determination of appropriate
      planning unit, 62–65
    new planning unit, creation of,
      69
    sub-division of, 72
  resumption of an abandoned use,
      77–80
  resumption of an extinguished use,
      80–81
  specific situations, 55–57
  sub-division of dwellings, 56–57
  sub-division of planning unit, 72
  vendor's warranty
    Law Society General
      Conditions of Sale, 340
material contravention of
    development plan
  local authority development, 13,
      33–37
  statutory procedure for grant of
      permission, 33, 190, 212,
      218
    failure to follow, 268–70
  zoning objective, contravention of
    refusal of permission on
      grounds of, 314, 328
material contravention of special
    amenity area orders, 39–40
meadow land
  use of land as, 88
medical services
  health centres or clinics, 133–34
mental illness, persons with
  residence for, 117

metals processing
  environmental impact statements,
      development requiring, 182
milking parlours, 124
minerals
  extraction, 181
  prospecting
    drilling for, 123
    exempted development
      provisions, 124
  storage or distribution, 127
mining, 40, 55
  preparatory works, 117
Minister for Agriculture, Food and
    Forestry, 25
Minister for Arts, Culture and the
    Gaeltacht, 25
Minister for Defence, 25
Minister for the Environment,
    25
  powers and functions of
    compensation, in relation to,
      319–20
    development plan, in relation
      to, 28–29
    environmental impact
      statements, 156
    special amenity area orders,
      confirmation of, 41
Minister for Transport, Energy and
    Communications, 25
Ministers of State, development by,
    103, 253; *see also* State
    authorities
minor works
  definition, 362
misleading notices, 161
modification of planning permission,
    see revocation or modification of
    permission
modifications to proposed
    development
  invitation to submit, 161
monasteries, 133
monuments, 122
mortgage advice centres, 131
motor service stations, 127

motor vehicles
    hiring of, use for, 127
    manufacture and assembly, 182
    sale or leasing of, use for, 127, 129
    yard for breaking of, 127
motorway schemes, 22, 49, 193, 322
multi-storey buildings, 367
multiple permissions, 234–35
murals on buildings or structures, 116
museums, 134

name of planning applicant, 143–44
National Authority for Occupational
    Safety and Health, 25, 159
national defence projects, 168
national flags and emblems
    exempted development provisions
        (Class 34), 119
national monuments
    excavations, 122
    protection of
        refusal of permission on
            grounds of, 327
National Monuments Advisory
    Council, 254
National Roads Authority, 23, 25, 43,
    159
    development plan, 22
    directions to road authority, 22
    contravention of special
        amenity order, 39–40
national security
    carrying out of works for
        exempted development
        provisions, 104
natural and constitutional justice,
    rules of
    audi alteram partem, 245, 263, 266
    breach of
        ground for judicial review, as,
            264, 266–67
    nemo iudex in sua causa, 249, 266
    oral hearings, 249
    planning appeals
        further submissions or
            observations, request for,
            245–47

natural gas
    extraction of, 181
    storage of, 181
nature and extent of development
    newspaper notices, information in,
        146–48
nature conservation, *see also* special
        amenity area orders
    reclamation of estuarine marsh
        land, 125, 126–27
nature reserves, 119
naval yards, 120
navigational aids, 122
neglected condition, land or
        structures in
    conditions relating to, 331
negligence
    planning authority, 235–36
nemo iudex in sua causa, 249, 266
newspaper notices
    acquisition notices, 51
    conservation orders, 44
    development plan
        adoption of, 27
        draft development plan, 24,
            25
    local authority development
        proposals, 15–16, 18
    material contravention of
        development plan, 33
    planning applications, 140–42
        circulating in the district,
            140–41
        contents, 141
        EIS requirement, where, 141–42
        further notice, 161–62
        further notices, 141–42, 146
        IPC licence requirement,
            where, 141
        location of land, 145–46
        misleading or inadequate
            notices, 161
        name of applicant, 143–45
        nature and extent of
            development, 146–48
        time limit, 140
    special amenity area orders, 39, 41

newspaper notices—*contd.*
State authorities, development by,
105
nil use, 77
abandonment, doctrine of, 77,
78
noise pollution
planning conditions relating to,
208, 331
refusal of permission on grounds
of, 327
non-parties
submissions or observations on
planning appeals, 245
non-residential clubs, 134
notice of planning application,
140
further notice, 161–62
newspaper notices, 140–42, 161,
see also newspaper notices
site notices, 142–43, 161, *see also*
site notices
notices, *see also* enforcement notices;
enforcement of planning control;
warning notices
acquisition notices – open spaces
(section 25), 308
advertisement notices, 123
compensation, preventing (section
13 notice), 318–19
development required by
exempted, 82, 120–21
discontinuance of use, requiring
section 31 notices, 300
section 37 notices, 308
evidence in support of
compensation claim,
requesting, 317
interest in land, requiring
information on, 8–9
newspapers, in, *see* newspaper
notices
oral hearings, 248
purchase notices, *see* purchase
notices
removal or alteration of hedge,
requiring, 43–44

notices—*contd.*
removal or alteration of structure,
requiring
section 31 notices, 300
section 36 notices, 307
revocation or modification of
permission, requiring, 4, 48–49,
333
service of, 8
site notices, 142–43; 161–162; *see
also* site notices
warning notices, 305–7
notification of planning decisions
appeal decisions, 255
failure to give notice within
appropriate period, 214
form of notification, 165
persons or bodies to be notified,
165
registration requirement, 4
time for, 165
weekly lists of decisions, 164
notification requirements
development plan, 24–25, 27
local authority development,
15–17, 18–19
planning applications, *see also*
notice of planning
application
persons and bodies to be
notified, 159
State authorities, development by,
105–6
nuclear fuels installations, 181
nuclear power stations
environmental impact statement,
development requiring, 179, 185
nuclear reactors
environmental impact statement,
development requiring, 179, 185
nuclear waste material
storage of
drilling for, 181
nuisance, abatement of
cutting down of trees, 42
nursery garden
sale of produce from, 89–90

nursery grounds, 88
nursing homes, 134

objects
  archaeological, geological or
    historical interest, of, *see*
    archaeological, geological or
    historical interest
observations, *see* submissions or
  observations
obsolete areas
  designation of, 29–30
occupation of structure
  planning conditions restricting,
    195–96, 358–59
    exclusion of compensation, 331
occupational unit, 63–65
occupier
  draft development plan,
    notification of, 24
  enforcement notice served on,
    298
  service of notice on, 8
offences
  breach of obligation to obtain
    planning permission, 135,
    304–5
  building regulations,
    non-compliance with, 365
  conservation orders, contravention
    of, 44
  enforcement notices,
    non-compliance with, 302–4
    section 31 notices, 300–301,
    303
  section 36 notice, contravention
    of, 307
  tree preservation orders,
    non-compliance with, 42–43
  warning notices, non-compliance
    with, 306
office
  change to shop use, 117
  definition
    building regulations, 362
    exempted development provisions,
    131–32

Office of Public Works, *see*
  Commissioners of Public Works in
  Ireland
offshore natural gas extraction, 181
oil pipelines
  environmental impact statements,
    development requiring, 184
oil refineries, 179
onus of proof
  section 27 proceedings, 282–83
open spaces
  acquisition notices (section 25), 5,
    51–52, 308
  planning condition requiring
    provision of, 208, 209
oral hearings, 248
  adjournment, 249
  conflict of evidence, 249
  discretion of Board to hold, 248
  inspector's report, 250
  natural justice
    "guillotining" of
      cross-examination, 249
    nemo iudex principle, 249
  notice of, 248
  powers and functions of inspector,
    249, 250
  procedure, 249–50
  public rights of way, 45
  reopening, 249–50
  requests for, 248
    time for making, 248
    withdrawal of, 248
"ordinarily incidental" use, 66–67
ores, extraction of, 181
ornamental garden
  laying out and use of land for,
    119
osier land, 88
outbuildings, 64–65
outdoor swimming pools, 119
outline applications, *see* outline
  permission
outline permission, 136
  applications for, 136, 151
    contents, 148–50, 151
    EIS requirement, where, 157

outline permission—*contd.*
  applications for—*contd.*
    matters to be dealt with at
      outline stage, 152–53
    plans and particulars, 148–50
    when application cannot be
      made, 151–52
  approval, 136
    applications for, 153–54
  definition, 136, 151
  effect of, 152
  expiry of permission before
    approval obtained, 234
  life of permission, 234, 310,
    354
  parameters binding, 154
owner
  draft development plan,
    notification of, 24
  hedge-trimming notice served on,
    42n
  meaning of, 298, 303
  service of notice on, 8; *see also*
    notices
    enforcement notices, 298, 303,
      306
    prosecution for non-compliance
      with, 303, 306
    tree preservation orders, 42
    warning notices, 306

painting of structures
  artistic, architectural or historical
    interest, structures of, 116
  exempted development provisions,
    116
  listed buildings, 116
paper industry
  environmental impact statements,
    development requiring, 183–84
parks
  laying out and use of land for, 119
particulars to accompany planning
  application
  description of interest, 150
  fees, 151
  plans and particulars, 148–50

paths
  exempted development provisions
    curtilage of dwellinghouse,
      paths within, 114
    private paths, 116
patio areas, 115
paving
  exempted development provisions,
    116
peat extraction, 181
penalties for offences
  breach of obligation to obtain
    planning permission, 304–5
  building regulations,
    non-compliance with, 365
  enforcement notices,
    non-compliance with,
      303–4
  warning notices, non-compliance
    with, 306
permission
  meaning of, 148–49
permission regulations, 135
  approval applications, 153–54
    contents of, 154
  compliance with, 137–38
  environmental impact statements,
    see also environmental impact
      statements
    applications to be accompanied
      by EIS, 155–56
    contents, 157
    exemptions from EIS
      requirement, 156–57
    further newspaper notice,
      141–42
    outline applications, 157
  mandatory or directory, whether,
    137–38
  minor infractions, 137
  non-compliance with, 137, 138,
    268
    failure to submit EIS, 169–72
  notification of decision, 164
    form of notification, 165
    persons or bodies to be notified,
      165

permission regulations—*contd.*
  notification of decision—*contd.*
    weekly list of planning
      decisions, 164
  outline applications, 151
    approval applications, 153–54,
      155
    effect of outline permission,
      152
    environmental impact
      statements, 157
    matters to be dealt with at
      outline stage, 152–53
    parameters of outline
      permission binding, 154
    when outline application cannot
      be made, 151–52
  particulars to accompany planning
    application
    description of interest, 150
    fees for planning applications,
      151
    plans and particulars, 148–50
  pre-application publicity
    requirements, 138
    location of land, 145–46
    name of applicant, 143–44
    nature and extent of
      development, 146–48
    newspaper notice, 140–42, *see
      also* newspaper notices
    public participation in planning
      process, 138–39
    site notice, 142–43
    who may apply, 139–40
  procedure after receipt of
    application, 158
    further notice of application,
      161–62
    minimum period for
      determination of
      applications, 164
    modifications to proposed
      development, 161
    persons and bodies to be
      notified, 159
    planning file, 162–63

permission regulations—*contd.*
  procedure after receipt of
    application—*contd.*
    requests for further
      information, 159–60
    submissions or observations,
      163–64
    weekly list of applications,
      158–59
    withdrawal of application, 164
petrol pumps
  licences, 47–48
petroleum extraction, 181
petroleum prospecting
  exempted development provisions
    (Class 5), 124
petroleum storage, 183
physical separation
  third rule in Burdle, 68–71
pig-rearing installations, 180
pipelines, *see* cables, wires, pipelines
pitch and putt courses, 119
place of assembly
  fire safety certificate, requirement
    of, 362
planning agreements, 4, 38–39
  enforcement, 39
planning appeals
  additional submissions, 240
  appeal documents
    effect of, on interpretation of
      permission, 228–29
  conditions only, appeals against,
    242–43
  consultants or advisors
    power of Board to engage, 250
  contents of appeal, 239–40
  costs, 255
  default decisions, 215
  determination of
    jurisdiction of Board, 251–52
    relevant considerations, 252–54
  documents
    availability for public
      inspection, 243–44
  entry on land, powers of, 254
  fees, 240

planning appeals—*contd.*
  grounds of appeal
    statement of, 240
  inspector's report, 250
  invalid, 240
  late appeals, 241
  natural justice, 245–47
  oral hearings, 248–51, *see further*
    oral hearings
    procedure, 249–50
  planning authority, role of, 2
  procedure, 239
    alternative approaches, 240–41
    contents of appeal, 239–40
    lodgment of appeal, 240
  public inspection of
    documentation, 163
  references to High Court, 250
  submissions or observations, 244
    EU Member States, 245
    further submissions, 245–47
    matters other than those raised
      by parties, 247–48
    natural justice, requirements of,
      245–47
    non-parties, by, 245
  time limit and service, 240–41
  vexatious or frivolous appeals
    power of Board to dismiss,
      251
planning applicants
  identity of, 143–44
  interest in land, 139–40, 150
  who may apply for planning
    permission, 139–40
planning applications, 135
  applicants, *see* planning applicants
  approval, applications for, 153–54
  contents
    generally, 148–50
    plans and particulars to
      accompany applications,
        drawings, maps, 148–50;
      see also plans
  decisions on, *see also* deter-
    mination of planning applica-
    tions; planning decisions

planning applications—*contd.*
  decisions on—*contd.*
    notification of, 164–65
    publication of, 165
  description of interest in land, 150
  description of proposed
    development, 146–48
  determination of, *see*
    determination of planning
    applications
  documents
    availability for public
      inspection, 243–44
  EIS requirement, where, 155–57,
    177
  fees, 151
  further information, requests for,
    158, 159–60
  further notice of application,
    161–62
  invalid applications
    procedure on receipt of, 158
  IPC licence requirement, where,
    155
  location of land, description of,
    145–46
  meaning of "planning
    application", 148
  modifications
    Board's power to invite
      applicant to submit,
        254–55
  modifications to proposed
    development, 161
  name of applicant, 143–44
  nature and extent of development,
    146–48
  notice of application
    further notice, 161–62
    newspaper notices, 140–42,
      161, *see also* newspaper
      notices
    site notices, 142–43, 161, *see
      also* site notices
  notification of decisions, 164–65;
    see also notification of
    planning decisions

planning applications—*contd.*
  notification requirements
    persons and bodies to be
      notified, 159
  obligation to obtain planning
    permission, 135–36
  outline applications, *see* outline
    permission
  permission regulations, 135,
    137–38, *see further* permission
    regulations
    compliance with, 137–38
    mandatory or directory,
      whether, 137–38
  planning file, 162–63
  plans and particulars
    additional copies of plans,
      requests for, 160
    all applications other than
      outline, 150
    further particulars, requests for,
      158, 159–60
    generally, 148–50
    revised plans, invitation to
      submit, 161
  pre-application publicity
    requirements, 138–48; *see also*
      notice of application (above)
  procedure on receipt, 158
    acknowledgement, 158
  public participation in planning
    process, 138–39
  registration requirement, 4
  regulations, 135; *see also*
    permission regulations
    compliance with, 137–38
  submissions or observations,
    163–64
    registration requirement, 4
  weekly list of applications,
    158–59
    display of, 158
    publication of, 158
  withdrawal of, 164
    power of Bord Pleanála to
      declare application
      withdrawn, 160, 164

planning authorities, 1
  ancillary powers, 8–9
  decision-making powers, 262–63
    judicial review, *see* judicial
      review
  definition, 1
  development by, 3, 9, 10–14,
    see also local authority
      development
    cables, wires and pipelines, 12
    exempted development
      provisions, application of,
      12–14
    material contravention of
      development plan, 33–37
    notification requirements,
      14–17
    powers, 10–12
  Dublin, 2
  duty of care, 235
  elected representatives, *see* elected
    members of local authority
  functions, *see* powers and func-
    tions of planning authorities
  executive and reserved
    functions, 7
  liability for grant of permission,
    235–36
  manager, 7
  negligence, 235–36
  official of
    representation by, 6–7
  policy directives and guidelines,
    duty to have regard to, 10
  powers and functions, *see* powers
    and functions of planning
    authorities
  reserved functions, 7, 9, 40, 48
  ultra vires doctrine, 5–7
  undertaking to grant planning
    permission, 313–14
    replacement of procedure, 314
planning conditions, 193
  adjoining, abutting or adjacent
    land, relating to, 205–8
  advertisement structures, relating
    to, 211, 330

planning conditions—*contd.*
  altering nature of proposed
    development, 201–3
  appeals against, 242–43
  building line, relating to, 330
  carrying out of works, requiring,
    208
  compensation
    entitlement to, 315
    non-compensatable conditions,
      329–32
  conditions precedent, 357–58
  contravention or non-compliance
    with, 108, 347
    planning injunction, 277, 279
    section 31 notices, 300–301
  conveyancing and, 357–59
  details to be agreed, conditions
    leaving, 196–200
  development works, regulating,
    357
  discontinuance of land, requiring,
    211
  existing use rights, restricting,
    203
  factors beyond control of
    applicant, 203–4
  fairly and reasonably related to the
    development, must be, 201–3
  financial contribution, requiring,
    209, 222, 329, 358
    evidence of compliance
      [General Conditions of
      Sale], 343–44
  future development, restricting,
    358–59
  imposition of
    abdication of jurisdiction,
      196–200
    compensation, entitlement to,
      315, *see also* compensation
    powers of, 193–94
    purchase notices arising from,
      337–39
    reasons to be given, 221–22
    ulterior purpose, for, 194–95
  landscaping, requiring, 208

planning conditions—*contd.*
  nature of development, altering,
    201–3
  necessary, must be, 204
  noise or vibration, relating to, 208
  occupation of buildings,
    restricting, 195–96
  open spaces, requiring provision
    of, 208, 209
  planting of trees, shrubs etc.,
    requiring, 208
  power to impose conditions,
    193–94
    criteria for validity, 194
  preservation of trees or other
    features, requiring
    warning notices for
      non-compliance with, 305,
      306–7
  purchase notice provisions, 337–39
  reasonable, must be, 203–5
  reasons for imposition, sufficiency
    of, 204–5
  relevant, must be, 201, 207
  removal of structure, requiring,
    211
  roads, open spaces, car parks etc.,
    in excess of immediate needs,
    208
  section 4 resolutions, 219–20
  security for satisfactory
    completion, requiring, 208,
    222, 329
  severability of, 211–12
  specific conditions under s. 26(2),
    205–11
  statutory purpose, accordance
    with, 194–200
  uncertainty, 204
  unnecessary conditions, 204
  unreasonable, 203
planning considerations
  injunction proceedings, 288
planning control
  environmental control and
    interface between, 190–93
  IPC licensing control and, 190–93

planning decisions, 186
   adverse decisions
      compensation, entitlement to,
         315; *see further*
         compensation
   appeals, decisions on
      registration requirement, 4
   challenge to validity of, *see*
      judicial review
   consistency, need for, 222
   decision-making power,
      186–87
      duty to act judicially, 186
   default decisions, 214–15
      appeals, 215
      mandamus, 216
   documents
      availability for public
         inspection, 243–44
   error on the face of the record,
      264–65
   failure to give notice within
      appropriate period, 214
   form of notification of decision,
      165
   judicial review, *see* judicial review
   natural justice, breach of, 266–67
   notification of, 164, 165, 214; *see*
      also notification of decisions
   persons or bodies to be notified of,
      165
   public participation in, 188
   publication of, 165
   record of
      inadequacy of, 267–68
   registration requirement, 4
   section 4 resolutions, 217–20
   unreasonable decisions, 263–64
   weekly lists of decisions, 164
planning documents
   interpretation of, 30–31, 225
      development plan, 30–32
   public inspection of, 2, 3, 162–63,
      243–44
planning file, 162–63
   documents to be made available,
      162–63

planning file—*contd.*
   public inspection, 3, 162
   technical reports, inclusion of, 162
planning injunction (section 27
      proceedings), 276–77
   companies as respondents, 281–82
   defence to application, 278
   discretion of court, exercise of
      balancing all factors, 290
      delay, 285
      employment considerations, 287
      equitable considerations,
         288–90
      lapse of time, 285
      planning considerations, 288
      principle guidelines, 284–90
      public convenience, 287–88
      reasonableness of conduct of
         parties, 288–90
      remedy analogous to an
         injunction, 284
      section 5 references, 290
      technicality of the breach,
         286–87
   fraud cases, 281–82
   locus standi, 278
   onus of proof, 282–83
   practice and procedure
      adjournments and liberty to
         apply, 296–97
      application by motion, 295
      applications to the Circuit
         Court (Order 67A of Circuit
         Court Rules), 293–95
      applications to the High Court
         (Order 103), 291–93
      evidence to be heard, 296
      interim orders, 295
      joinder of parties, 295–96
   res judicata, 283
   scope of remedy, 277–80
   time limits for bringing
      proceedings, 280–81, 309
planning official
   representation by
      not binding on planning
         authority, 6–7

planning permission
  applications for, *see* planning
    applications
  development carried out without
    permission, *see* unauthorised
    development
  development not in conformity
    with
    section 27 proceedings,
      277–97; *see also* planning
      injunction
    section 35 notices, 302
  duration of, *see* duration of
    planning permission
  "full" permission, 136
  interpretation of, 224–28
    effect of appeal documents,
      224–28
  licensing applications, and, 310–12
  multiple permissions, 234–35
  non-compliance with, 347
    enforcement notices, 297–308,
      see further enforcement
      notices
    injunction proceedings (section
      27), 277–97, *see also*
      planning injunction
  obligation to obtain, 53, 135–36
    breach of obligation, 135,
      304–5
    exemption from requirement,
      see exempted development
  outline permission, 136, *see also*
    outline permission
  purchasing with benefit of,
    353–54
  severable permissions, 235
  "subject to planning" special
    conditions, 348–50
  unauthorised use of land, *see*
    unauthorised use
planning register, 2, 3
  certified copies of entries, 3
  matters to be entered in, 4–5
planning requisitions on title
  replying to, 367–75
planning schemes, 20

planning unit, 62–63
  agricultural, 89–90
  determination of appropriate
    planning unit
    Burdle principles, 63, 64, 67–71
    composite or concurrent uses,
      67–68
    physical and functional
      separation, 68–71
  dwelling-house, 70
  intensification of use, 73–77
  occupational unit, 63–65
  primary and ancillary uses,
    65–66
    "ordinarily incidental",
      66–67
  resumption of abandoned use,
    77–80
  resumption of extinguished use,
    80–81
  seasonal uses, 68
  subdivision, 72
    material change of use, where,
      72
planning warranty
  Law Society General Conditions
    of Sale: General Condition
    36, 340–45; *see further* Law
    Society General Conditions
    of Sale
plans, maps, drawings etc.
  planning applications,
    accompanying, 150
    additional copies of plans,
      requests for, 160
    further information, requests
      for, 158, 159–60
    generally, 148–50
    revised plans, invitation to
      submit, 161
planting
  shrubs, *see* shrubs, plants,
    flowers
  trees, *see* trees
plants, *see* shrubs, plants, flowers
policy directives and guidelines, 10
political events, 122

pollution control, *see also* air
  pollution; noise pollution;
    water pollution
  "environmental pollution",
    meaning of, 191–92
  IPC licences, *see* integrated
    pollution control (IPC) licensing
  licences
    works necessary to comply
      with, 121
  monitoring facilities
    exempted development
      provisions, 119–20
  planning concern, as, 190–91
  planning conditions relating to
    exclusion of compensation, 331
  "polluter pays principle", 327
  "polluting matter"
    definition, 192
  refusal of permission on grounds of
    exclusion of compensation, 327
  risk of pollution, 254
ponds
  curtilage of dwellinghouse, within,
    114
ponies
  housing and keeping of, 127
porches
  curtilage of dwellinghouse, within,
    109, 115, 122
ports, 180
Post, An, 118, 254
post offices, 129
posters, 123
poultry-rearing installations, 180
powers and functions of Board, An,
  238–39; *see also* Bord Pleanála
powers and functions of planning
  authorities, 1, 2, 5
  access to information, provision
    of, 2
  acquisition notices (open spaces),
    51–52
  acquisition or appropriation of
    land, 11
  advertisements, repair and tidying
    of, 46–47

powers and functions of planning
  authorities—*contd.*
  ancillary powers, 8–9
  appeals process, in, 2
  archaeological, geological or
    historical interest, objects of,
    50–51
  compensation, payment of, 3
  compulsory acquisition, 11
  conservation orders, 44
  decision-making powers, 186–87,
    262–63
  designation of areas for
    environmental protection,
    49–50
  determination of planning
    applications, *see* determination
    of planning applications
  development control, 2
  development of land, 3, 9, 10–14,
    see also local authority
    development
    buildings, provision of, 12
    cables, wires and pipelines, 12
    exempted development
      provisions, 12–14
    notification requirements, 14–17
    sites, provision of, 11–12
    specific powers, 10–11
  enforcement of planning control, 2
  entry on land, *see* entry on land
  environmental assessment, 3
  executive and reserved functions, 7
  exercise of statutory powers, 6–7
    fettering of discretion, 6
  general competence, 9
  hedge removal or alteration
    notices, 43–44
  lease of land, 11
  licensing powers, 47–48
  listed buildings, in relation to, 50
  Local Government Act 1991,
    under, 9–10
  planning agreements, 38–39
  planning conditions, imposition of,
    193–94
  planning register, 3

powers and functions of planning
authorities—*contd.*
planting of trees, shrubs and other
plants, 43
policy directives and guidelines,
duty to have regard to, 10
preservation of amenities, 38–52;
see also preservation of amenity
public rights of way, 45–46
revocation or modification of
permission, 48–49
special amenity area orders, 39–41
statutory notices, issue of, *see*
notices
strategic planning and
development, 2
tree preservation orders, 41–43
trees, shrubs etc., planting of, 43
ultra vires doctrine, 5–7
powers of inspector
oral hearings, 249, 250
practice notes
Building Control Act and Building
Regulations, 395–97
pre-contract requisitions,
397–98
certificates of compliance, 378–79
architects' certificates, 384–86
compliance with planning
conditions when estate in
charge, 380–81
Law Society forms, 386–88,
388–91
private residential property,
379–80
qualifications of persons
certifying, 381–84
RIAI forms, 391–93
exempted development, 394–95
house extension
failure to obtain building bye
laws approval, 393–94
Law Society's standard General
Conditions of Sale, 399
roads and services in charge of
local authority, evidence of, 381
precedents, 222

premature development, refusal on
grounds of
exclusion of compensation, 314,
323–25
order of priority in development
plan, 325
road network, prospective
deficiency in, 324, 325
water supplies or sewerage
facilities, deficiency in
provision of, 323–24
prescribed bodies
conservation orders, for, 44
consultation with, 188
development plan notification
requirements, 25
preservation of amenity, 38
advertisements, repair and tidying
of, 46–47
archaeological, geological or
historical interest, objects of,
50–51
artistic, architectural or historic
interest
buildings of, 109–10
conservation orders, 40, 44
designation of areas for
environmental protection,
49–50
hedges, notices requiring removal
or alteration of, 43–44
licences
cables, wires and pipelines,
47–48
petrol pumps, 47–48
structures on public roads,
47–48
listed buildings, 50
open spaces, enforcement of,
51–52
planning agreements, 38–39
planning conditions relating to, 43,
331
warning notices for
non-compliance with, 305,
306–7
public rights of way, 45–46

preservation of amenity—*contd.*
  revocation or modification of
    permission, 48–49
  special amenity area orders,
    39–41
  tree preservation orders, 41–43
  trees, shrubs and other plants,
    planting of, 43
  views or prospects, *see* views or
    prospects of special amenity
    value
primary use, 64
  ancillary uses and, 65–66, *see also*
    ancillary use
  inactive primary use, where,
    71
  "ordinarily incidental", 66–67
  severance of link, 72
prisons
  exempted development provisions,
    104, 120
private open space
  laying out and use of land for,
    119
private roads, streets or ways
  exempted development provisions,
    116
professional services, 130–31
property rights, 139
  development plan and, 24
  limitation in interests of common
    good, 313
prosecution of offences
  breach of obligation to obtain
    planning permission, 304–5
  non-compliance with enforcement
    notices, 302–4
  time limits, 304, 307, 308–9
  warning notices, non-compliance
    with, 306–7
prospects of special amenity value,
  see views or prospects of special
    amenity value
protected road schemes, 23, 49, 193
public agencies, development by
  exempted development provisions,
    118, 119–20

public authorities
  definition, 253–54
  policies and objectives of
    Board to keep itself informed
      of, 253–54
public buildings
  works within curtilage of
    exempted development
      provisions (Class 47), 120
public convenience
  injunction decisions based on,
    287–88
public gardens, 331
public halls, 134
public health
  refusal of permission on grounds
    of, 327
public houses, 129, 363
  change of use, 117, 129
  licensing applications
    planning code and, 310–12
public inspection of planning
    documents
  appeals documentation, 4, 163,
    243–44
  applications documentation, 4,
    162–63, 243–44
  documents to be made available,
    162–63
    contents of planning register,
      4–5
  draft development plan, 24
  local authority development,
    proposals for, 16–17
    environmental impact
      statements, 18
  planning file, 3, 162–63
  State authorities, development by,
    105
  time for, 5
  weekly lists of applications,
    158
public libraries, 134, 363
public lighting
  planning conditions relating to,
    330
public parks, 331

public participation in planning
    process, 138–39
    decision-making process, 188
    planning file, inspection of, 162–63
    submissions or observations on
        planning applications, 163–64
public reading rooms, 134
public resort
    hall or other building of, 363
public rights of way, 45–46
    creation of, by planning authority,
        45
        registration requirement, 5
    obstruction of, 110
    planning conditions relating to, 331
    preservation of
        agreements for, 5, 45
        development plan objective, 24,
            45
public roads, *see also* road
    development
    carrying out of works under, 109
    means of access to
        formation, laying out, or
            material widening of, 109
        petrol pumps, cables, wires,
            pipelines etc, *on*
        licences for, 47–48
public safety
    refusal of permission on grounds of
        exclusion of compensation,
            325–26
public sector development, 84
public sewer, *see* sewers
public toilets, 14
public works, *see also* State
    authorities, development by
    interpretative centres
        Luggala and Mullaghmore
            decisions, 100–103
    structures incidental to use of, 119
public worship
    place of, 363
    use for, 133
publication of notices, *see* newspaper
    notices; site notices
pumping stations, 14

pumps or pumphouses
    domestic water supply or group
        water scheme, 123
purchase notices, 333, 337–39
    confirmation of, 239
    counter-notice, 338
    entitlement to serve, 338
    reasonably beneficial use, what
        constitutes, 339
    section 36 notices, following, 307
    section 37 notices, following, 307
    whole of the land, must relate to,
        338

quarries, 181
quarrying, 73

racing tracks, 185
radioactive waste installations, 179,
    182
railway equipment
    manufacture of, 182
railway lines, 180
railway undertakings
    exempted development provisions,
        118
railways, 184
reactors
    test benches, 185
reasons for decisions
    determination of planning
        applications, 221–22
    inadequacy of record of decision,
        267–68
reclamation of land, *see* land
    reclamation
recreational events, 122
recreational purposes
    animals kept for
        housing of, 127
    development for
        exempted development
            provisions, 119
    keeping of animals for, 88–89
recurrent uses, 68
    interchange of
        exempted development, 82

references to An Bord Pleanála
 section 5 references, 85
refusal of planning permission
 access to or from motorway or
  busway, development
  involving, 322
 compensation provisions, *see also*
  compensation
  circumstances in which
   compensation payable, 315,
   332–34
  development not attracting
   compensation, 321–22
  non-compensatable reasons for
   refusal, 323–29
 premature development, 314,
  323–24
 purchase notice provisions, 337–39
 reasons to be given, 221
 road development, on account of
  exclusion of compensation, 322
Regional Fisheries Boards, 25
 exempted development provisions,
  120
registration, *see* planning register
relevant considerations
 enforcement notices, 297–98
religious body
 social or recreational activities, use
  for, 133
religious events, 122, *see also* public
 worship
religious instruction, use for, 133
removal of advertisement structure
 planning condition requiring
  exclusion of compensation, 330
removal or alteration of hedge
 notice requiring, 43–44
  registration requirement, 4
removal or alteration of structure
 notice requiring
  compensation, entitlement to,
   333
  section 31 notices, 300
  section 36 notices, 307, 333
 planning conditions requiring, 211
  exclusion of compensation, 330

removal or damage of trees and other
 features
 planning conditions, contravention
  of
  warning notices, 305, 306–7
repayment of compensation
 amount repayable, 318
 apportionment, 318
 instalments, 318
 obligation to repay, 317–18
 successors in title, 318
replacement of structure demolished
  or destroyed by fire
 compensation for adverse
  decisions, 320
replacement of use, 79
reports
 local authority development
  proposals, on, 17
 registration requirement, 4
repository
 definition, 133
 use as, 133
requisitions on title, replies to
 building control requisitions,
  375–77
 planning, 367–75
res judicata, 221
 section 27 proceedings, 283
reserved functions, 7, 9
 development plan, making or
  variation of, 20
 revocation or modification of
  permission, notice requiring, 48
 special amenity area orders, 40
reservoir, construction of, 15
residential care institutions, 117, 134
residential club, 133
residential colleges, 134
residential schools, 134
residential training centres, 134
restaurants, 129, 363
 change of use from, 117, 129
resumption of use
 abandoned use
  abandonment, doctrine of,
   77–78

resumption of use—*contd.*
  abandoned use—*contd.*
    intention of abandonment,
      78–79
    material change of use,
      whether, 78
    presumption of abandonment,
      78
    enforcement notice, on service of,
      82
    extinguished use, 80–81
    replacement of use, distinguished
      from, 79
    temporary permission, expiration
      of
      resumption of "normal" use of
        land, 82
retail trade
  use as a shop
    exempted development
      provisions, 128–30
retention of unauthorised structure
  applications for permission,
    136–37
  determination of, 189–90
  non-compliance with permission
    section 32 notices, 301
revised planning permission, 359
revised plans, drawings etc.
  alterations to proposed
    development, 161
  modifications to proposed
    development, 161
revocation or modification of
  permission
  notice requiring, 48–49
    circumstances in which power
      may be exercised, 48–49
    compensation, entitlement to,
      49, 333
    registration requirement, 4
    reserved function, 48
    Roads Act 1993, under, 49
rezoning, 27–28
RIAI forms, 354–55, 391–93
rights of way, *see* public rights
  of way

road authorities
  directions to, 22, 39–40
road development, *see also* public
  roads
  development plan, and, 22
  environmental impact statements,
    184
  exempted development provisions,
    86, 91
  material contravention of
    development plan, 22
  motorway schemes, 22
  notification requirements, 14
  protected road schemes, 23, 49,
    193
  refusal of permission excluding
    compensation, 322
  revocation or modification of
    permission, 49
  special amenity area orders, and,
    39–40
  tree preservation orders and, 43
road network
  prospective deficiency in
    refusal of permission on
      grounds of, 324, 325
road users, obstruction of, 109
Roads Act 1993
  planning conditions excluding
    compensation, 332
  revocation or modification of
    permission, 49
roadside shrines, 119
Royal Institute of Architects in Ireland
  certificates of compliance
    standard forms, 354–55, 391–93
Royal Irish Academy, 44
rubber industry
  environmental impact statements,
    development requiring, 184
ruinous structures, 331
Rules of the Superior Courts
  planning injunction applications
    (Order 103), 291–93
rural development
  exempted development provisions,
    123–27

SAAOs, *see* special amenity area
orders
sale of produce
home-grown produce, 89–90
salmonid breeding installations,
180–81
sand, extraction of, 181
sanitary services
planning conditions relating to,
330, 331
public sewer, connection to, 314,
324
refusal of permission for
deficiency in, 324
satellite antennae, 110
satellite dishes, 114
satisfactory completion, security for,
see security for satisfactory
completion
scaffolds, 123
schools, 363
residential, 134
schoolyards, 122
scrap iron storage, 185
scrap yards, 127
sea water marinas, 185
Seanad Éireann
office buildings or other premises
exempted development
provisions, 104
seasonal uses, 68
seawater salmonid breeding
installations, 180
section 4 resolutions, 7, 217–20
obligation to act judicially, 217,
219–20
planning conditions, imposition of,
219–20
section 5 references, 85, 235, 275
appeals, 85
injunction applications and,
290
section 13 notices
compensation, preventing,
318–19, 320
section 25 notices
acquisition of open spaces, 308

section 27 proceedings, *see* planning
injunction
section 31 notices, 300–301, *see also*
enforcement notices
application, 300
expenses, 300
latest date notice, 300
matters to be specified in, 300
non-compliance with
offences, 300–301, 302, 303
prosecution for, 302–4
time limits, 300, 310
section 32 notices, 301, *see also*
enforcement notices
matters to be specified, 301
non-compliance with
prosecution for, 302–4
time limit, 301
section 35 notices, 302, *see also*
enforcement notices
application, 302
matters to be specified, 302
non-compliance with
prosecution for, 302–4
time limit, 302
section 36 notices
removal or alteration of structure,
requiring, 307
appeals, 307
compensation, 307
compensation provisions, 333
entry on land, powers of, 307
expenses, 307
offences, 307
purchase notices, 307
section 37 notices
discontinuance of use, requiring,
308
compensation, 308
compensation provisions, 333
purchase notices, 308
section 38 agreements
development or use of land,
regulating, 38–39
section 44 notices
hedge, removal or alteration of,
43–44

section 46 orders
 conservation orders, 43–44
security for satisfactory completion
 planning condition requiring, 208,
  222
  bonds, 358
  exclusion of compensation, 329
semi-natural areas
 intensive agricultural use, 87
sequence of works
 conditions determining, 331
service of notices, 8
 dispensation with requirement, 8
 enforcement notices, 298–99
service roads, 330
services, provision of
 exempted development provisions,
  130–31
 powers of planning authority, 12
services use
 change to shop use, 117
severability
 planning conditions, 211–12
 planning permissions, 235
sewage disposal
 conditions relating to
  exclusion of compensation, 331
sewerage facilities
 deficiency in provision of
  refusal of permission on
   grounds of, 323–24
 planning conditions relating to, 330
sewers
 connections to premises, 123, 314
 inspection, repair, renewal,
  removal or alteration
   exempted development
    provisions, 86
 laying of, 14
Shannon Free Airport Development
 Company Ltd, 25, 254
sheds
 agricultural structures, 124
 curtilage of dwellinghouse, within,
  113
sheep dipping units, 124
shipyards, 182

shop, *see also* shop use
 definition, 128–29
  building regulations, for, 362
shop use
 ancillary use, 130
 definition of "shop", 128–29
 exempted development provisions,
  128–30
 change of use to shop, 117, 129
 exclusions, 129
 intensification of use, 129
 "ordinarily incidental", 130
 sub-division of shop, 129
shopping centre
 definition, 362
 fire safety certificate, requirement
  of, 362
 pre-contract requisitions, 398
showgrounds, 122
shrubs, plants, flowers
 planting of
  planning conditions requiring,
   208
  powers of planning authorities,
   43
  registration of agreements for, 5
 preservation of
  planning conditions relating to,
   331
signs, 123
silage areas, 124
site notices
 planning applications, 142–43
  further notice, 143, 161–62
  information to be contained in
   notice, 142–43
  misleading or inadequate
   notices, 161–62
  regulations, 142
  time limit, 142
 State authorities, development by,
  105
sites, provision of
 powers of planning authority,
  11–12
skating rinks, 134
sludge-deposition sites, 185

social centres, 134
social events, 122
solicitor's office, 131
South Dublin County Council, 13, 91
special amenity area orders, 39–41
    exempted development provisions,
        restriction of, 110
    material contravention of,
        39–40
    notification requirements,
        39, 41
    objections, 41
    planning authority to "have regard
        to", 39, 187–88
    refusal of permission for
        development
        exclusion of compensation, 321
    reserved function, 40
    review, 41
special amenity value
    view or prospect of, *see* views or
        prospects of special amenity
        value
specified development
    (environmental impact state-
        ments), 155–56, 169, 179–85, *see
        also* environmental impact
        statements
sports
    animals kept for sporting purposes
        housing of, 127
    gymnasium, 134
    indoor sports, use for, 134
    laying out and use of lands for
        exempted development
        provisions, 119
    sporting events, 122
State authorities, development by, 13,
    100
    accident or emergency,
        development required by reason
        of, 106
    decision of State authority, 106
        notice of, 106n
    definition of "State authority", 100
    environmental impact assessment,
        178–79

State authorities, development
    by—*contd.*
    exemptions for certain
        development, 103–4
    foreign visits, facilities for
        (Class 35), 119
    Garda Síochána security works
        (Class 48), 120
    national flags and emblems
        (Class 34), 119
    pollution monitoring facilities
        (Class 42), 119
    public buildings, development
        within curtilage of (Class
        47), 120
    interpretative centres
        Luggala and Mullaghmore, 13,
            100–103
    notification requirements, 105–6
        documents to be made available
            for public inspection, 105–6
        newspaper notices, 105
        retrospective validation, 106
        submissions or observations, 105
            obligation of state authority to
                consider, 106
    statutory notices, licences or
        certificates, *see also* notices
        works necessary to comply with
            exempted development
            provisions, 82, 120–21
statutory undertakers, development by
    definition of "statutory
        undertaker", 92
    exempted development provisions,
        86, 91–92
    inland waters, 118, 119
statutory undertaking to grant
    permission, 313–14
steel foundries, 182
stone, extraction of, 181
storage
    curtilage of dwellinghouse, within
        buildings for storage purposes,
            361
    caravans, 115
    effluent storage facilities, 124

storage—*contd.*
  farm machinery and equipment, 89
  fossil fuels, 181
  minerals, 127
  natural gas, 181
  nuclear waste material
    drilling for, 181
  petroleum, 183
  repository, use as, 133
  scrap iron, 185
strategic planning and development
  functions of planning authority, 2
structures
  external works
    exempted development
      provisions, 93–94
  internal works
    exempted development
      provisions, 86, 92–93
  murals on, 116
  occupation of
    restriction to particular class of
      persons, 195–96, 331
  painting of, 116
  planning conditions relating to
    non-compensatable conditions,
      330
  public roads, on
    licensing, 47–48
  removal or alteration of
    notices requiring, 300, 307
    planning conditions requiring,
      211
  replacement of structure
    demolished or destroyed by fire
      compensation provisions, 320
  unauthorised, *see* unauthorised
    structures
sub-division
  dwellings, 56–57
  planning unit, 72
  shop, 129
"subject to planning" special
  conditions
  Law Society General Conditions
    of Sale, 348–50
    specimen conditions, 350–53

submissions or observations
  planning appeals
    EU Member States, 245
    further submissions, 245–47
    matters other than those raised
      by parties, 247–48
    non-parties, 245
    parties, made by, 244
  planning applications, 163–64, 188
    registration requirement, 4
substantial grounds
  leave to apply for judicial review,
    260
    meaning of "substantial
      grounds", 260–62
substantial works, 232
successors in title
  compensation, obligation to repay,
    318
sugar factories, 183
summary proceedings
  time limits, 308–10
    section 27 proceedings,
      280–81, 309
Supreme Court
  appeals to
    judicial review applications,
      262
survey
  powers of planning authority, 8
swimming pools, 14, 119

Taisce, An, 25, 44, 159
take-aways, 129
  change of use from, 117, 129
Tanaiste's office
  exempted development provisions,
    104
taxi business, 127
technical breach of planning control,
  286–87
technical reports, 162
telecommunications
  exempted development provisions,
    118
    antennae support structures,
      118

television antennae
exempted development provisions,
114
temporary permissions, 230
expiration of, 136–37
resumption of "normal" use of
land upon, 82
temporary structures or uses, 361
conditions attached to permission,
330
exempted development provisions,
117, 122
foreign visits, facilities for
(Class 35), 119
tents, 122
textile industry
environmental impact statements,
development requiring, 183–84
theatres, 134, 363
thermal power stations, 179
ticket agency, 129
time limits
compensation claims, 316
determination of planning
applications, 164, 212–14
default decisions, 214–15
development plan, review of, 20
duration of planning permission,
229–30, 310
extension of, 231–34
enforcement of planning control
planning injunctions, 280–81,
309
section 31 notices, 300, 308,
310
section 32 notices, 301, 309
section 35 notices, 302, 309
section 37 notices, 308
section 31 notices, 300, 308
section 32 notices, 301, 309
unauthorised development,
prosecution for, 304, 308
judicial review proceedings,
270–71
application for leave to apply,
257, 258–59
constitutionality, 271

time limits—*contd.*
Minister, applications to
compensation, payment of,
320
notification of decisions, 165
oral hearings, requests for, 248
planning appeals, making of,
240–41
submissions or observations on
planning appeals, 244
observations by non-parties,
245
summary prosecutions, 304,
307
warning notices, 309
Town and Regional Planning Acts
1934–39, 20
TPOs, *see* tree preservation orders
trading ports, 180
traffic congestion
refusal of permission on grounds
of, 327
traffic hazard, 109
refusal of permission on grounds of
exclusion of compensation,
325–26
tramways, 184
travel agency, 129
tree preservation orders (TPOs),
41–43
appeals, 42
notification requirements, 42
offences, 42–43
registration requirement, 4
revocation or variation, 42
trees, *see also* forestry; shrubs, plants
and flowers
felling consent
refusal or attachment of
conditions, 42, 333–34
planting of
planning conditions requiring,
208
powers of planning authorities,
43
registration of agreements for,
5

trees—*contd.*
preservation of
planning conditions relating to,
43, 305, 306–7, 331
tree preservation orders
(TPOs), 4, 41–43
warning notices, 43, 305, 306–7
removal or damage of
planning conditions,
contravening, 305, 306–7
trivial breach of planning control,
286–87
turbary
use of land for, 88
turbine testing, 185

Uachtarán na h-Éireann
office buildings or other premises
exempted development
provisions, 104
Údaras na Gaeltachta, 254
ultra vires doctrine, 5–7, 256
meaning of, 5–6
unauthorised development
enforcement of planning control
injunction proceedings (section
27), 277–97, *see also*
planning injunction
restoration of land, 280
section 31 notices, 300–301
retention of structure, application
for permission for; *see*
unauthorised structures
vendor's warranty
Law Society General
Conditions of Sale, 53,
340
warning notices, 305–7
unauthorised structures, 346–47
definition, 135–36
extension, alteration, repair or
renewal, 109
obligation to obtain planning
permission, 135
breach of, 304
removal or alteration
notices requiring, 307

unauthorised structures—*contd.*
retention permission
application for, 136–37
determination of applications,
189–90
non-compliance with
conditions, 301
unauthorised use, 347–48
application for permission for
continuance of, 136–37
determination of application,
189–90
date of commission of, 309
extension, alteration, repair or
renewal of structure, 109
injunction proceedings (section
27), 277–97, *see also* planning
injunction
notices requiring discontinuance of
section 31 notices, 300
section 37 notices, 308
restoration of land, 280
warning notices, 305–7
uncultivated land
intensive agricultural use, 87
underground railways, 184
undertaking to grant planning
permission, 313–14
replacement of procedure, 314
unjust enrichment, 290
unreasonableness of decision
judicial review, ground for, 263–64
urban-development projects
environmental impact statements,
requiring, 184
urban district council
development by, *see also* local
authority development
exempted, 86
planning authority, as, 1; *see also*
planning authorities
use, *see also* use classes
abandonment, *see* abandonment of
use
agreements regulating, 4, 38–39
agricultural, *see* agricultural use
ancillary, *see* ancillary use

use—*contd.*
 change of, *see* change of use;
  material change of use
 composite or concurrent uses,
  67–68
 definition, 54, 85
  exclusionary nature of, 54
 discontinuance, *see* discontinuance
  of use
 extinguished use, resumption of,
  80–81
 forestry use, *see* forestry
 intensification, *see* intensification
  of use
 "nil" use, 77, 78
 "ordinarily incidental", 66–67
 resumption, *see* resumption
  of use
 seasonal uses, 68
 shop, *see* shop use
use classes
 art galleries (Class 10), 134
 bingo halls (Class 11), 134
 changes within
  exclusions from exempted
   development provisions, 127
  exempted development
   provisions, 127–34
  intensification of use, 128
  restrictions, 128
 cinemas (Class 11), 134
 clinics (Class 8), 133–34
 community centres (Class 10), 134
 creches (Class 8), 134
 day centres (Class 8), 134
 day nurseries (Class 8), 134
 exempted development provisions,
  111
  specific exemptions (article
   11), 111–12
 exhibition halls (Class 10), 134
 financial services, provision of
  (Class 2), 130–31
 guesthouse (Class 6), 133
 gymnasium (Class 11), 134
 health centres (Class 8), 133–34
 hospitals (Class 9), 134

use classes—*contd.*
 hostel (Class 6), 133
 light industrial building (Class 4),
  132
 monasteries or convents (Class 7),
  133
 museums (Class 10), 134
 non-residential clubs (Class 10),
  134
 nursing homes (Class 9), 134
 offices (Class 3), 131–32
 professional services, provision of
  (Class 2), 130–31
 public halls (Class 10), 134
 public libraries (Class 10), 134
 purpose of, 127
 religious body
  social or recreational activities
   of (Class 7), 133
 religious instruction, use for (Class
  7), 133
 repository (Class 5), 133
 residential club (Class 6), 133
 residential colleges (Class 9), 134
 residential schools (Class 9), 134
 residential training centres (Class
  9), 134
 services, provision of (Class 2),
  130–31
 shop, use as (Class 1), 128–30
  definition of "shop", 128–29
 skating rinks (Class 11), 134
 social centres (Class 10), 134
 theatres (Class 11), 134
 wholesale warehouse (Class 5),
  133
use zoning, *see* zoning

validity of planning decisions
 challenge to, *see* judicial review
vans, 122
vexatious appeals, 251
vibration
 conditions relating to, 331
 planning conditions requiring
  measures to reduce or prevent,
  208

vibration—*contd.*
  refusal of permission on grounds
    of, 327
views or prospects of special amenity
  value
  interference with, 109
    refusal of permission on
      grounds of, 326
  preservation of
    planning conditions relating to,
      331
vocational education committees, 337

walls
  bounding roads, 116
  exempted development provisions,
    116
    curtilage of dwellinghouse,
      walls within, 114
warehouse
  meaning, 133
  wholesale warehouse, use as, 133
warning notices, 305–7
  contents, 305
  non-compliance with
    liability for, 306
    penalties for offences, 306
  preservation of trees or other
    features, 43, 306–7
  recording of particulars on
    planning register, 306
  registration requirement, 4, 306
  time limits, 309
waste disposal or deposit
  conditions relating to
    exclusion of compensation, 331
  use of land for
    notification requirements, 14
waste installations, 185
  hazardous waste, 180
  radioactive waste, 179, 182
water-management projects
  agriculture, for, 180
water pollution, 192
  licences
    works necessary to comply
      with, 121

water pollution—*contd.*
  monitoring facilities
    exempted development
      provisions, 119–20
  planning conditions relating to
    exclusion of compensation, 331
  refusal of permission on grounds
    of, 327
water supplies
  deficiency in provision of
    refusal of permission on
      grounds of, 323–24
  drilling for
    notification requirements, 14
  planning conditions relating to, 330
water treatment works
  construction or erection of
    notification requirements, 14
watermains
  connections to premises, 123
weekly lists
  planning applications, 158–59
    display of, 158
    publication of, 158–59
  planning decisions, 164
wells
  domestic water supply or group
    water scheme, 123
wholesale warehouse
  definition, 133
  use as, 133
wildlife conservation
  reclamation of estuarine marsh
    land, 125, 126–27
wired broadcast relay services
  connections to premises, 123
wireless antennae
  exempted development provisions,
    114
wires, *see* cables, wires, pipelines
withdrawal
  enforcement notices, 298
  planning applications, 160, 164
  requests for oral hearings, 248
wood industry
  environmental impact statements,
    development requiring, 183–84

woodlands, *see* trees
wool scouring, degreasing or
    bleaching, 183
words and phrases, 107
    advertisement, 123
    advertisement structure, 123
    agricultural, 88
    agriculture, 88–89
    air pollution, 192
    alterations, 54
    antecedent value of the land, 334
    approval, 153, 241n
    arm of state, 168
    as such, 96–99
    business, 132
    character, 93
    company, 337
    competent authority [Law Society
        General Conditions of Sale],
        342
    curtilage, 94–95
    the day of the giving of the
        decision, 240
    decision, 260
    development, 278, 279
    dwellinghouse, 95–96
    emanation of state, 168
    emission, 192
    environmental impact assessment,
        166–67
    environmental impact statement,
        167
    environmental pollution, 191–92
    flat, 363
    for the purposes of agriculture, 90
    further information, 160
    guesthouse, 133
    habitable house, 121
    have regard to, 187–88
    incidental, 65, 96, 97
    "incidental to the enjoyment of the
        dwelling as such", 96–99
    industrial building, 132, 362
    industrial process, 132
    institutional building, 363
    intensification, 73
    keeping of livestock, 88

words and phrases—*contd.*
    land, 54
    land being reserved for a particular
        purpose in a development
        plan", 335–36
    land set apart from other land in
        the area, 336
    light industrial building, 132
    material alteration, 362
    minor works, 362
    nature and extent, 148
    office, 362
    ordinarily incidental, 66–67,
        130
    outline permission, 136, 151
    owner, 150, 298, 303
    particular purpose, 335–36
    permission, 148–49
    place of assembly, 363
    planning application, 148
    planning authority, 1
    pollutant, 192
    polluting matter, 192
    public authority, 253–54
    public safety, 326
    pursuant to, 232, 233
    reasonableness, 339
    reasonably beneficial use, 339
    repository, 133
    reserved, 336
    shall, 137
    shop, 128–29, 362
    shopping centre, 363
    specified development, 155–56
    state authority, 100
    statutory body, 337
    statutory undertaker, 92
    subsequent value of the land,
        334
    substantial grounds, 260–62
    substantial works, 232
    traffic hazard, 326
    unauthorised structure, 135–36
    use, 54, 85, 321
    warehouse, 133
    wholesale warehouse, 133
    works, 54, 73, 232

works
  definition, 54, 73, 232
  development, as, 53–55
  planning condition requiring, 208
  temporary structures or uses, 117

zoning, 20, 21
  down-zoning, 29–30, 329

zoning—*contd.*
  "judicial zoning", 62
  material contravention of zoning
      objective
  refusal of permission on
      grounds of, 314, 328
  obsolete areas, 29–30
  rezoning, 27–28